# Journey from the North: A Memoir

## Storm Jameson

With an introduction by Vivian Gornick

PUSHKIN PRESS

Pushkin Press
Somerset House, Strand
London WC2R ILA

*Journey from the North* was first published in two volumes by the
Collins & Harvill Press in London, 1969 and 1970

First published by Pushkin Press in 2024

1 3 5 7 9 8 6 4 2

ISBN 13: 978-1-80533-044-8

Designed and typeset by Tetragon, London

Printed and bound in the United Kingdom by CPI Group (UK) Ltd, Croydon, CR0 4YY

*Written for my judges*
*the forgotten men and women who made me*

If a man has the temerity to write the story of his life, he should have a double aim: first, to show it and his little ego in relation to the time and place in which he lived his life, to the procession of historical events, even to the absurd metaphysics of the universe; secondly, to describe as simply and clearly as he can, his personal life, his relation, not to history and the universe, but to persons and himself, his record in the trivial, difficult, fascinating art of living from day to day, hour to hour, minute to minute.

LEONARD WOOLF: *Downhill All the Way*

# Contents

# 'If Only I Could Begin Again!'
## The mystery of a writer's métier

### Vivian Gornick

My mother, a high school graduate with no recourse to a critical vocabu-
lary, was a romantic reader, mainly of novels. Whenever I asked her how
she was liking the book in her hand, she'd narrow her eyes, look steadily at
me, and say, 'Powerful. Really powerful.' Or, conversely, 'Not powerful, not
at all powerful.' One day I gave her *Journey from the North*, a two-volume
autobiography written by Storm Jameson, a prolific English novelist at work
throughout the first half of the twentieth century. A week later I walked
into her apartment and there she was, lying on the couch, reading the first
volume. I said, 'How are you liking that book, Ma?' She sat up, swung her
legs over the side of the couch, and narrowed her eyes, as always, but this
time she said, 'I feel as though she's just in the room with me.' And then she
said, 'I'm going to be lonely when I finish this book.' I remember thinking,
What more could any writer ask of a reader?

Ten days after she had finished *Journey from the North*, I gave my mother
one of Jameson's many (forty-five, to be exact) novels to read. Her eyes lit up
and she accepted the book eagerly. But a week later, I saw that it had been
tucked into a small shelf above the telephone table and I had the distinct
impression that it had been laid aside. Yes, my mother confirmed, it had
been. 'I don't know why,' she said, 'but this book is nothing like that other
one.' And then she said, 'Not powerful, not at all powerful.'

I nodded my head at her. You're not alone, Ma, I thought. Over the years,
a few thousand other readers have been faced with the same discrepant
feelings about Jameson's autobiography on the one hand, and her fiction
on the other. For that matter, they have felt the same when puzzling over
other writers of fiction or poetry whose significant work turns out to reside
in a memoir. There is Edmund Gosse, for instance, a mediocre Victorian

poet who secured a place in English letters only with the publication, in late middle age, of his masterly memoir, *Father and Son*; then there is the colorful journalist Thomas De Quincey, whose fame rests entirely on the unforgettable *Confessions of an English Opium-Eater*; and, of course, our own James Baldwin, who wrote novels, plays, and poems but will be remembered chiefly for the sublime personal essays that are, in effect, his memoir.

I myself have something of a vested interest in this mysterious matter of a writer's natural métier. When I was young, everyone under the sun was writing a novel because the novel was the form of imaginative writing respected by high- and low-minded alike. Only through the novel, it was felt, could one achieve a work of literary art. So I, of course, like every other young person who dreamed of becoming a writer, labored intensively from earliest youth at writing one. By the time I was in my late twenties, I had to face the fact that while I was forever telling stories to friends, colleagues, relatives, nearly all of whom would crow at me, 'That's a novel, write it down!'—and here I was, writing it down, somehow, within the framework of a fiction—'it' refused to come to life.

It slowly dawned on me that I could tell stories effectively only when I was composing them in my own storytelling voice, out of my own lived experience, not in the voice of an invented narrator settled in a made-up situation. I was well into my thirties before I understood that I was born for the memoir. One can only wonder what Storm Jameson would have produced had she come earlier to the genre in which she wrote most naturally.

Margaret Ethel Jameson was born in 1891 in the northern English port town of Whitby. The family included a number of sea captains—one of whom was Margaret's father—and they had lived there for generations on both sides. They were a people of ingrown endurance, pragmatic to the bone, and possessed of the brusque, no-nonsense speech laced with sardonic irony for which Yorkshire men and women are still famous. In Jameson's time especially, a dread of emotional exposure seemed to haunt the entire population. To be seen caring about anyone or anything in Whitby was to put yourself at risk; you were made to feel vulnerable in a world that, once your guard was down, would show no mercy. Thus, an isolated, weather-beaten town carved into an irregularity on a rugged coast bred, as Jameson wrote in her autobiography, 'a crop of eccentrics, harmless fools, misers, house devils,

despots, male and some female, who behaved toward their families with a
severity' that the normally socialized rarely allowed themselves.

Childhood for the Jamesons was an extremity of delight (unearned) and
punishment (undeserved). On the delight side, there was Whitby itself and
the sea, a world of natural beauty in which to experience the sheer bliss of
being alive:

> Endless days on the shore in summer, from nine in the morning until
> six or seven at night... three children on the edge of an infinity of sand
> and water—enclosed in a boundless blue world, steeped in light, in a
> radiance of sun and salt.

On the punishment side, they had a father who was away at sea for months
at a time and very nearly mute when at home, and a hot-tempered mother,
a shockingly bored romantic who hated her husband, beat her children, and
lashed out regularly at the bitter disappointment of life. This mother—whose
thwarted spirit made Jameson's heart ache—became dramatically imprinted
on an impressionable young psyche, and was responsible for locking the girl
into a personality as angry, defensive, and yearning as her own. Not a single
person in Jameson's long, eventful life was ever to supplant her mother's
emotional influence; nor was any other place in the world to eclipse the
memory of Whitby's piercing loveliness as she experienced it in her youth.

In all probability, Jameson would have married a Whitby man, had half a
dozen children, and lived out her mother's life if, in 1908, she had not won a
scholarship to the newly created University of Leeds. The school, at that time,
was filled with the children of northern England's working class—people
like herself whose eyes were being opened to the excitement and promise
of a life they could not have previously imagined. It was there that Jameson
began to see herself as a woman with a literary gift and as a person stigma-
tized by a class system that placed her very close to the bottom. She found
both discoveries exhilarating; in no time she was writing stories and had
become a red-hot socialist determined on a political as well as a literary life.

The heady self-assurance that Jameson and her university friends felt
while still at school became both a shield and a sword. 'In those early years,'
she wrote,

I had no *consciousness* of being shabby, I thought I could go anywhere,
into any company... We emerged from our three starveling years with
a lighthearted confidence that we were conquerors.

But a few years out of school and the corrections of worldly judgment caused
a penetrating self-doubt to set in. At university, Jameson had been considered
a brain and a talent and nobody noticed what she wore. In London, she
learned that she was seen as an intellectual provincial and that she dressed
badly: 'It was only later that I began to covet an elegance I had discovered
I lacked.' There and then, the alternating influences of incredible brashness
and equally incredible insecurity stamped her personality for good and all.

The affliction of urban sophistication, however, was hardly Jameson's
first experience beyond student life to reveal itself as formative. While still
in school, she had fallen desperately in love with a ne'er-do-well, slept with
him, and in 1913, at the age of twenty-one, was forced to marry. Then, before
she knew where on earth she was, she had a baby—not *they* had a baby, *she*
had a baby—and that, as it was with most women, might have been that,
except that Margaret Jameson wasn't most women.

For a good five years, she and her husband, imagining themselves free
spirits in a new world, lived marginally, wandering from pillar to post, always
up north (Manchester, Liverpool, Leeds), vaguely seeking and finding jobs
that led nowhere. She didn't mind this gypsy existence, but as time wore on
she came to realize that she was unhappy with her husband, that she loved
the baby but hadn't bonded with him, and that she hated, hated, hated
domestic life. Within herself she began to drift and soon thought she would
die if she didn't get out of the house. It was only then,

at a time when I was tempted to knock my own head against the wall,
[that I understood] the fits of rage in which [my mother] jerked the
venetian blinds in her room up and down, up and down, for the relief
of hearing the crash.

She *had* to find a real job, she said; *had* to make a living, she said; had to
help save the marriage, she also said. So in 1918 she stashed the baby in
Whitby, said a 'temporary' goodbye to the husband, and fled to London,

where, with remarkable speed, she found work as a journalist by day and began writing a novel at night.

Two important things now happened: she adopted Storm Jameson as her professional name, and she established a style of life that came to resemble permanent vagabondage. From those first London years on, Jameson proved incapable of making a conventional home either for herself alone, or with the child she said she adored, or with the second husband (the historian Guy Chapman) whom she did indeed love dearly. For pretty much the rest of her life, she moved continually from one house or flat or squat to another, usually but not always in or around London, and later in life, when she had some money, found happiness only when wandering about in foreign places.

It was writing and political activism that grounded her. Throughout the *Sturm und Drang* produced by her lifelong compulsion to get up and go, Jameson wrote at least one novel a year, plus stories, essays, articles, and political journalism by the yard. At the same time—no matter where she was or what other responsibilities she had—she worked tirelessly as an activist, first campaigning for women's suffrage, then promoting social justice for the working class (otherwise known as naked hatred of capitalism), and then, in the Thirties and Forties, out of an impassioned opposition to fascism, becoming active in refugee rescue operations. By the beginning of the Second World War, she was president of the English branch of the writers' organization PEN (she served between 1938 and 1944) and in a position to work herself sick on behalf of the many European writers, artists, and intellectuals she helped escape the Nazis.

Jameson saw herself neither as a bohemian nor as an artist, only as an industrious scribbler driven by a restlessness whose origins she herself could not easily grasp. All she knew was that each time she pulled up stakes, she felt as though she was beginning anew; throughout her life she was hungry to begin anew. Whatever that concept meant to her, it inevitably included what she described as the 'forbidden' thrill of starting a novel. Within the first thirty pages of *Journey from the North*, she writes that in beginning a novel she always felt 'the indescribable excitement a woman is said to feel when her unborn child moves for the first time.' 'Forbidden' and 'said to feel': she could use these words descriptively but never insightfully; and at that, she used them only when she was close to eighty. Until then she spoke repeatedly—in her sardonic Yorkshire voice—of writing novels because they put food on the table and a roof over her head. This was the lifelong disclaimer with which she defended herself against the feared charge that, as she strongly suspected, she was only delivering a heap of middlebrow problem novels, easily consumed, easily forgotten. And she was right to fear this charge. If, at the age of seventy, Jameson had not sat down to write *Journey from the North*, she would surely have gone down into literary oblivion.

A reader's report on her first novel declares: 'It is loosely constructed; starts nowhere; ends nowhere; characters many and ill-defined. They do not live; they are vehicles for the author's theories and the expounding of his theme.' Nevertheless, the reader concludes (never imagining that Storm could be a woman's name), 'the man can write and is worth watching.'

Between the Twenties and the Sixties, Jameson achieved a more than respectable reputation as what, then as now, would be called a midlist writer of prodigious output. Her books sold well, she had many fans, publication was always assured, and in London she knew 'everyone.' Yet nearly all of Jameson's novels might well have come in for much the same assessment of that early reader's report—that they are primarily devoted to creating characters who are set in motion for the sake of exploring a social or political thesis: modern marriage seen from a woman's disadvantaged perspective, the postwar experience of an embittered generation in the Twenties, liberalism in crisis during the Thirties, fascism at home in the Forties, and, of course, tale after tale of murderously indifferent industrialists with a boot on the neck of disempowered workers, observed or interfered with by various progressive types.

The rise of fascism was especially compelling and, like many other writers on the left, Jameson justified the kind of writing she felt driven to produce in the run-up to the Second World War:

> The impulse that turned so many of us into pamphleteers and amateur politicians was neither mean nor trivial. I doubt whether any of us believed that books would be burned in England [or people] tortured and then killed in concentration camps. But all these things were happening abroad and intellectuals who refused to protest were in effect blacklegs. [That is, scabs.]

It wasn't that she couldn't write well—she could and did—but, forever in thrall to a thesis, her characters, in the main, not only fail to come alive on the page but hector the reader as well. In *Company Parade*—a novel based on the experience of the young Storm Jameson in interwar London—the protagonist, a self-styled socialist thrilled to have just published a popular novel, is chastised by another character, a full-blown radical: 'Don't you know you haven't any right to write novels unless you put in' the city's slums, capitalism's treachery, society's ruthless indifference? 'Whether you know it or not, you're being used... You're persuading [people] that all's for the best in the best of all possible worlds.' Imagine this kind of writing sprinkled through or even dominating the narrative of some thirty or forty novels!

Jameson knew her shortcomings. She understood very well what it meant to dig deep into the inner life of a character, and did not cry foul when, halfway through her career, a friend told her bluntly,

> You know far too much about human nature and too little about making what you know palatable. You don't give your imagination room to breathe, you dissect, and you write too many books too quickly.

However, here she stood and she could do no other.

But it hurt just the same. It hurt that she was refused literary recognition by the people who mattered: high-end modernists like the Bloomsberries. It hurt that they saw her only as a decent writer of the middle level; it hurt that, as a result of such ranking, she began, from the Fifties on, to grow morbidly insecure—'The fingers of one hand would be too many to count the times when I have looked forward to the publication of a novel, seeing too clearly the width of the gap between it and the great novels'—and became vulnerable to a 'profound sense of failure... that seizes me when I think about my novels... a tormenting sense of dryness, *accidie*, futility.' Late in life she felt compelled to destroy reviews, articles, and personal documents because, as she said, she wished she could 'sink without a trace,' as the trace she was leaving was of such inconsequence.

Once, deeply unhappy about the progress of the novel at hand, she came close to blaming the commands of commerce for her situation, even though she knew better. The following two paragraphs, here reprinted exactly as they appear in *Journey from the North*, tell that story:

> What is it that drives us to turn out our novel a year like articulate robots, to be praised or damned by critics as unfit as ourselves to talk about novels.
>     If only I could begin again!

And then, miraculously, she did.

Near the beginning of *Journey from the North*, Jameson announces her plan to concentrate for once on the inner life of her protagonist:

> How far can I hope to give a true account of an animal I know only from the inside? Nothing would have been easier for me than to write one of those charming poetic memoirs which offend no one and leave a pleasant impression of the author. I am trying to do something entirely different. Trying, in short, to eat away a double illusion: the face I show other people, and the illusion I have of myself—by which I live. Can I?

And with that announcement, some unexpected alchemy begins to exert its influence on the pages flying out of Jameson's typewriter (nearly eight hundred before she's done). The raw material of the memoir is remarkably similar to that of the novels—nearly all of which originated in Jameson's own experience—but the writer's *agenda* is not the same. It was the altered agenda that was responsible for one genre being abandoned in favor of another; and it was the changed genre that, quite magically, released an imprisoned imagination that betrayed a depth of understanding Jameson had never before felt free to let loose on her readers. Class, sex, social policies—all are to be relegated not to the background but to a supporting role in a developing point of view that is psychologically oriented from the start.

*Journey from the North* is a generous record of Jameson's life from earliest childhood up to the moment in advanced age at which she is writing—Whitby; early family life; university; marriage and motherhood; the London years in their various incarnations; every cause she was ever attached to; every town, city, or countryside she wandered about in; every person of note, talent, or fame she was ever thrown together with. What is important about this rather extraordinary recital is not the information it provides, but the impression it leaves that, beneath the surface of the somewhat overstuffed prose, a writerly concern is at work, directing the narrative and keeping it on track. The speaking voice, throughout the entire performance, has been described in reviews and biographical essays as ruthlessly honest; by which it is meant not that Jameson delivers a tell-all confessional, but rather that the reader can sense her grappling with something recalcitrant in the material that nonetheless draws her on. She realizes, just as we do, that there is much she does not know about this something. But we have no doubt that she is intent on telling us—*really* telling us—as much as she does know, and that intent is what counts.

Sartre once said that freedom is what you do with what's been done to you. *Journey from the North* is a glorious example of the gripping tale that can be fashioned out of the moment when a good writer feels compelled to examine that prophetic piece of wisdom.

In one of her novels, Jameson says of her fictional stand-in: 'Her mother was at the centre of her life. She rebelled against her... but she was bound to her by a love in which bitter and hurting things were drowned.' True and not true. Jameson's mother certainly was at the center of her life, and she did rebel against her but was yet bound to her by an emotion that, if one wishes, could be called love; however, no bitter and hurting thing ever drowned.

It's the mother who is the figure in Jameson's carpet; the mother—now brilliantly present, now dimly sighted, now putting in a surprise appearance—who embodies the pull of haunted memory threading itself through the memoir; the mother whose raw need seeps through Jameson's blood, mingling with her own, creating the kind of psychological embroilment that can not only shape the life of a child who identifies disastrously with a parent of the same sex, but endow it with mythic dimension.

Imagine a mother whose voice is daily filled with what Jameson in another novel describes as 'the shrewd, half-sneering, half-envious spite of the North'; a mother who, when a child says she has a headache, replies coldly, 'Nonsense, children don't have head-aches'; a mother who rages about the house when depressed and, out of pity for herself, inflicts the injustice of arbitrary beatings. Who could survive such acts of terror without first going numb and dumb inside, and then growing self-protective almost to the point of anomie? Jameson did both:

> Beginning young, I have had a great deal of practice not only in hiding my feelings but in hiding from them... Insincerity was one of the lessons I learned early and thoroughly, very early, very thoroughly.
>
> (Ah, how I came to love the rhetoric embedded in 'early and thoroughly, very early, very thoroughly'; here's another of its numerous iterations: 'It would not be true to say that the grief which tore its way through my body was for him [i.e., her first husband]; it was for the past, for what he had been to me; for the failure I, I, had made of our marriage.' That 'I, I'!)

The problem was that she could not leave her mother because she had become her mother. In the way of this kind of early damage, as Jameson could not leave behind that which had been done to her, she joined with it. Her mother's boredom became her boredom, as did the easy scorn, the blind resistance to authority, the deadly fear of emotional openness (a broken friendship is described as 'another failure of warmth'), beneath which lay her own ransomed life. The worst of it was her failure to take in the reality of her own child, just as her mother had failed to take in hers. ('Even now, I cannot explain why I was never at ease with the idea that I had a child who was my own, not simply handed to me to cherish and bring up.') Throughout her years she wept for the unlived life of her mother, only occasionally aware that she was weeping for her own:

> I cannot remember a time when I was not aware, and with what helpless pity, that her life had disappointed her...
> My terrible anxiety [was always] for her to be happy...
> I would have cut my hand off to give her another life.

These sentences, and many more like them running through *Journey from the North*, are alive to the touch; they color everything the narrative lights on;

make vivid the hold that domestic tragedy had on Jameson: 'Those seeds of guilt and responsibility, sown in me at the beginning, were not able to strangle [my involuntary egotism] but they have given it an atrociously uneasy life.'

Jameson understood well enough that while she saw clearly the *how* of things, she could not adequately penetrate the *why* of them. No matter. This was one time she wanted to give the reader the *feel* of things—the state of affairs one grasps not with the intellect but through the nerve endings—and toward this end she did what she should have been doing with all those novels behind her: she stretched her imagination to the limit.

In *Journey from the North*, as nowhere else in her work, Jameson's writing has the very thing she was always faulted for not achieving: the richness of texture necessary to bring a work of literature to fruition. The interesting question is why, when she was ready to dive deep, did Jameson not sit down to write the redemptive novel of her life? Why was it the memoir to which she turned? What was it about writing in her own naked voice that allowed her to make something indelible out of the lived experience that her novels had been exploiting, but not doing justice, all those years?

These questions, of course, are rhetorical. Perhaps the match between the appropriate genre and the release of the writer's imagination is something akin to the situation of a safecracker listening for just the right sound in the tumblers to make the door of the vault swing open. Clearly (that is, mysteriously), when Storm Jameson set out to write a memoir, the door of her safe opened wide, and she found literary gold in it. If she had died before she was ready to try that safe, she would never have composed the one book that admits her to the company of Gosse, De Quincey, and Baldwin—and I would never have written this appreciation.

# JOURNEY FROM THE NORTH, VOL. 1

# PART I

## *Avoid this Spring*

*So soon as ever your mazed spirit descends*
*From daylight into darkness, Man, remember*
*What you have suffered here in Samothrace*
*What you have suffered...*
*To the left hand there bubbles a black spring*
*Overshadowed with a great white cypress.*
*Avoid this spring, which is Forgetfulness;*
*Though all the common rout rush down to drink,*
*Avoid this spring!*

ROBERT GRAVES

# CHAPTER I

THERE ARE PEOPLE, there are even writers, whose lives were worth recording because they were passed in strange or exciting ways, or involved famous persons, or could be written as the story of a great mind in search of its beliefs. I have a good but not a great mind; my chances of meeting great men have been few and I have not sought them: the men and women who have come nearest slaking my curiosity about human nature have been obscure as well as alive with humours. The humours of the great are usually too well groomed.

What is a record of my life worth—the life of a writer treated with justice in circles where *camaraderie, cette plaie mortelle de la littérature*, is the merciful rule?

Perhaps little, except that as a life it spans three distinct ages: the middle class heyday before 1914, the *entre deux guerres*, and the present; three ages so disparate that to a person who knows only the third the others are unimaginable. Anyone born before 1900 can examine one civilization as if it were done with—as it is, but for noticing that a few of its ideas and traditions are still feebly active. Indeed, I can excavate two finished stages in society, since I remember sharply the one I rebelled against while continuing to live blindly by more than one of its rooted assumptions: that people of my class do not starve, that reticence in speech, and clean linen, are bare necessities, that books exist to be read. I ought to be able to describe them both.

Possibly I lack the coolness to give a dependable account of them to the ignorant. I can try.

That arrogant half-sarcastic phrase, *it can be tried*, is one I heard so often in my North Riding childhood that it has become an instinct. I seldom know when I am being led astray by it. It was a servant's saying, but a northern servant.

The span of my life is even longer than it seems, since its roots are twisted round hundreds of lives passed in the same place. Only a life starting from centuries of familiarity with the same few fields and streets is better than fragmentary. If there is any tenacity in me, any constancy, if there is an I under all the dissimilar I's seen by those who know or knew me as daughter, as young woman, undisciplined, confident, absurd, as wife, as friend, the debt is owed to obscure men and women born and dying in the same isolated place during hundreds of years.

All I could do to destroy the pattern, I have done.

What Pascal, writing about Montaigne, called 'his foolish project of painting his own portrait' is, after all, a book like any other. If it is dull, it will quickly be forgotten. Or, if it is not readable now, when there are people alive able to compare the portrait with the original and find it distorted or a lie, it may become readable when neither they nor I are here to protest.

How far can I hope to give a true account of an animal I know only from the inside? Nothing would have been easier for me than to write one of those charming poetic memoirs which offend no one and leave a pleasant impression of the author. I am trying to do something entirely different. Trying, in short, to eat away a double illusion: the face I show other people, and the illusion I have of myself—by which I live. Can I?

It is true that what one sees from the inside is the seams, the dark tangled roots of feeling and action, which may be just as misleading, as partial, as the charming poeticized version I am trying to reject. But it is *a* truth—known only to me.

I feel an ineffaceable repugnance to writing about close friends. Of the few people, men and women, I know intimately, I can bring myself to write down only the least intimate facts. This falsifies the record at once. But what can I do? Nothing.

'The real story of a life would consist in a recital of the experiences, few or many, in which the whole self was engaged. The greater part of such a book would be very dull, since as often as not our whole self turns its back contemptuously on the so-called great moments and emotions and engages itself in trivialities, the shape of a particular hill, a road known in infancy, the movement of the wind through grass. The things we shall take with us at the last will all be small.'

I wrote this, or something very like it, in a novel published thirty years ago. It is probably true. The pain and ecstasy of youth, the brief happiness, the long uncharted decline, can be summed up in the tune of a once popular waltz, of no merit, or the point in a country lane where the violence and hopelessness of a passion suddenly became obvious, or the moment when a word, a gesture, nothing in themselves, gave the most acute sensual pleasure. None of these can be written about.

It will be easy, too, to lose one's way in an underworld where time is no longer a succession of events, one damned thing after another, but a continuous present in which the dead, and the little I know about them, jostle the ghosts of the living. And where the antique chorus of frogs listened to in March 1935 in Spain is—at the same moment—distending the darkness above a lake in northern New York State fourteen years later.

The first thing I remember is the deck of a ship in sunlight. A lady, her face hidden from me by the parasol in her hand, is there in a low chair. My head, which does not reach above the arm of the chair, aches. I must just have told her so. Without turning her own, she answers, 'Nonsense. Children don't have headaches.'

She must have been mistaken. Some indefinite time later I am lying peaceably at the bottom of a crevasse, its walls densely white; two persons, indistinct, are looking over the edge, and one of them says, 'She's sinking.' The ship, I think. That the ship is sinking *out there* is no business of mine, and doesn't ruffle me.

My third memory is of a field of marguerites, so long-stemmed, or I at the time so short, that they and I were face to face, eye against incandescent eye. The whiteness seared, dazzled, blinded, a naked seething radiance, whiter than all whiteness, running out of sight.

Since beginning this book—that is, yesterday, Friday, the 11th of August 1961, the day of the new moon—I have realized what most intelligent people doubtless knew already: in any life a few, very few, key images turn up again and again, recognizable even though deformed by the changed light or the angle at which they reappear. This fierce whiteness is one of mine.

Another is the sound, a middling deep note, of the Whitby bell-buoy, ringing a mile off-shore, clearly audible at night or at any time when the wind blew off the sea.

And another sound, made, this one, by the fishermen's children when I was very young: it was like the screech of gulls—*Ahwa-a-ah!*—piercing, barely human, half summons, half warning. You could believe that every ship in the world was casting off at once. It was years before I knew enough to interpret it as *Away*!

In due course I shall come on the other two or three of these primitive or underworld images, voices out of sleep, out of a lost harbour, which are mine. They may indeed be the only things I ever, in the positive sense of the word, hear or see.

The voyage on which I so nearly died was one of my earliest, if not the first. It was certainly not my mother's first: in those days before human existence got out of hand, a sea-captain had the right to take his wife with him on any voyage, even as far as the River Plate or the Far East. She knew one or two older women, childless, who had no shore home; all they possessed, their clothes, family photographs, curling-tongs, shared the captain's cabin next the chart-room with his clothing and the ship's papers. She, I believe, envied these freed women while barely approving of them: life in a house of her own often bored her.

So long as she had only one child, she could go away easily, joining the ship in an English port or at Le Havre or Flushing. The first of these departures that I remember was in the early light; I see clearly the half-dark kitchen and taste the end crust of the loaf, soaked in scaldingly hot tea, she had given me: it was yeasty and exquisite. Were we going to Greenock, Harwich for Antwerp, Swansea? Once, in the last port, directed to it by the man in the ticket-office of the dock station, she and I found ourselves in a small hotel, in a bedroom immediately behind the bar, which was full of lascars. It was too late to seek farther, and while I slept in my clothes my mother spent the night sitting on the trunk she had dragged across the door.

The days at sea in a less than 3,000-ton ship were crushingly long and boring—it would not have entered anyone's head to amuse me—but the ports... ah!

Antwerp: tall yellow-faced houses behind a quay; the Place Verte with its flower-women; the rue de la Meir; the open trams; the zoo gardens at night, a band playing to sedately strolling families, the tall schoolboys in girlish socks and blouses, ridiculously bare-legged; the superb glove shop; the rough knife-edged grass of the ramparts; the open carriage clip-clopping us back to the docks.

It was Antwerp that gave me my first notion of an art. In a shop-window of the rue de la Meir there was a large painting of a garden, with two half-embraced figures in the foreground. It seized on my imagination and became for a few weeks my idea of sensual bliss. This had nothing to do with its merits as a painting, which doubtless did not exist.

One day when we came ashore—off the *Saxon Prince*?—the wharf was strewn with black brittle husks from some outlandish cargo; a man waiting to come aboard told us that Queen Victoria had died, news that made my mother pull a sorrowful face. So far as I knew, I had never heard of the woman, but a sense of her importance and the strange husks underfoot started up in me such a crazy excitement that to this day voyages and death resemble each other in my mind as one harbour is like another in another island.

So many journeys, begun before memory, so many half-obliterated departures, how could they fail to ruin my life?

Its pattern, if the word can be used of such a coil, was set by them at the start.

The impulse to go away has disturbed, delighted, mocked me, and is to blame for my failure to settle anywhere. I left one place with anguish, leaving behind half my soul, the less indifferent half: none of the many others I have lived in keep more than a thin paring of it, thinner and less persistent than the shadow I catch sight of in Bordeaux or Antwerp of my mother, pausing to stare in a shop-window at a hat she would buy if she could barely afford it, and were less arrogantly afraid of the foreign saleswoman: in those days she was an elegante—the word is not used now, but it fitted her—coveting finely simple dresses and beautiful gloves. I doubt whether she was content anywhere—any more than I am. I even doubt whether she felt the pleasure I rate higher than any other, that of being in a foreign town for the first time, free of its probably mediocre streets and cafés, its sounds, and the silence which encloses the stranger walking about in it, obliged to no one for her happiness.

The restlessness in my nerves and senses comes to me through her. Where did she get it? From sea-going ancestors, from the North Sea, from the stones themselves of the little port (already able in the seventh century to build a parish church and an Abbey to which the body of St Edwin, first Christian king of Northumbria, was brought at the end of the century: in the ninth, the Danes burned both church and Abbey), with its memories of loss, flight, violence?

Restless, adrift from the start, spiritually clumsy and imprudent, can I make sense of my life? Has it a meaning? If I can find the courage to stare coldly at its ghosts (including my own past selves, clumsy ungovernable young idiots), and as coldly at the moments of happiness as at griefs, blunders, sins, humiliating failures, will the meaning, if there is a meaning, emerge?

*It can be tried*. I am too old to be mortified by a failure.

And in a world so sharply menaced by destruction as ours, there is something friendly in the idea of going on gossiping to the last minute—if it is no more than to call a friend's attention to the exquisite yellow of a dying leaf or to ask for news of a child, the one who came last year to stay, and tethered an imaginary horse in every room in the house.


## CHAPTER 2

I HAVE A TRICK, when forced to make a speech—a folly I commit as seldom as possible—of repeating mentally: I am the last voice on earth of my grandfather George Gallilee and my mother Hannah Margaret Jameson.

This—call it what you like—this invocation has usually eased the ordeal. Once, on the 14th of December, 1943, it had an odd sequel. I had been speaking to the French Chamber of Commerce, at a luncheon, to please a friend, Pierre Maisonneuve, one of de Gaulle's Free French. Heaven knows what I talked about, and has mercifully erased the memory, but what happened afterwards is still entirely clear in my mind. An insignificant-looking Frenchman came up to me, smiling, and said: 'I have been sent to tell you that everything is all right. An old gentleman, very upright, with a great deal of white hair, was standing behind your chair when you spoke, and everything is all right.'

Taken completely aback, I made a stupid and ill-bred reply: 'That was George Gallilee, my grandfather; he was a severe man, with a bad temper.'

I don't pretend to explain the incident.

Possibly, when we talk of ourselves as being the only foothold the dead keep, the only channel for their voices, it is not nonsense or a sort of poetry

(I distrust poetic prose). They insist on living in us. They deflect our voices. They dictate our first choices, those which further or ruin our lives.

My grandfather, my mother's father, had the reputation of a hard stubborn man, arbitrary, incorruptibly honest, with a violent temper kept, for the most part, under control. I did not know him. How could I? By the time I might have made something of him he had begun his long death, and all I felt for him was the shocking aversion I feel from illness and sickrooms. I suspect him of strong feelings, brutally repressed: an egoist by instinct and training, he could not help regarding women as inferior creatures, mentally and morally. He had a degree of respect for my mother, the only one of his children who was at all like him in looks and temper. He believed with cold ferocity that Lloyd George should be hanged and the lower classes kept in their place: a workman repairing the roof was all but startled into falling off when my grandfather shouted at him from the nearest window to stop whistling or go home.

When I knew him, and until he died, he was handsome in a forbidding way: a head of hair as white as silk, springing strongly back from his forehead and temples, a thick white goatee, the long upper lip of his hard fine mouth clean-shaven, a splendid nose, and the formidably clear cold pale blue eyes he passed on to my mother and she to her last-born. (Not to me: mine are a darker clouded grey-blue: I fit badly into my skull, and while my eyes are taking you in my brain is trying to guess what you are thinking and what will keep you at a safe distance.)

He was bookish and extremely fastidious. He took daily ice-cold baths, dressed formally, and until his stroke held himself as straight as a bolt.

He had been a ship-owner. He sold out of shipping too early in life, and before it began to make money again. He married twice: his second wife was the one I knew as my grandmother: he married her to look after his seven children (seven living, out of I forget how many born) and entertain his friends; she was a middle-aged widow with three sons of her own; a rascally solicitor had bolted to Australia with the money left her by her husband: whenever, in street or church aisle, she saw one of his relatives she would ask loudly: 'Ha' ye heard from t' thief lately?'

It turned out that a fondness for fine old port unfitted her both as step-mother and hostess. My grandfather at once rearranged his life to conceal the blunder he had made. He put his children, five girls and two boys, into another house and visited them morning and evening: what social life he had was carried on outside his own house.

All his children were afraid of him, my mother, the youngest but one, less than the others: she had spirit and a hot temper, though at fifteen she was discovered to be 'in a decline,' that commonest of Victorian illnesses. The treatment ordered for her was the raw cod-liver oil brought by the whaling boats, and cold baths: she faithfully took both, carrying the cold water up every night to a hipbath in her room, and lived.

Her father was no gentler with her than with the others; she had orders to be practising the piano when he arrived at eight in the morning, and he beat time by clapping his hands loudly within an inch of her ear: in winter, since he refused to allow fires to be lit in the house in daylight, her fingers stiffened immovably on the keys (as mine did at the end of the icy train journey to Scarborough to take a music examination in the Imperial Hotel. In spite of having less music in me than a crow, I passed three of these before my mother resigned herself to the certainty that I should never, being now fourteen, acquire the ghost of an ear). He disapproved of pampering anyone, of any age or sex. During the years when he was only half alive, his youngest unmarried daughter, now in her fifties, dutifully sat with him an hour every day. Even on the bitterest days he refused to allow her near the fire—'Back, girl, back!'

Except under his eye, it was a lively household: the youngest two, my mother and my aunt Jenny, laughed at everything, at their sisters, at each other, even, under the name of Mr Bultitude, at their terrible father.

My aunt, who was actively pious—she was a deacon of the Congregational Church—with none of my mother's profound indifference (masked by habit), had the irrepressible laugh of a very young child. I remember an afternoon when they talked about graves. Neither of them can have been less than sixty-five, and my mother was sharply vexed that she had not been able to find out from my father how many people had been buried in the grave belonging to him.

'I told him, "We can't expect to stay very much longer," and he said, "But I *will*". I have no patience with him, Jenny! Let me think: his father was lost at sea, but there's his mother and her father and mother, and a child. I believe there will be nine to a grave. So there should be plenty of room for him.' Her eyes started with anger. 'I won't go into *his* grave, not on any account.'

'Ours has Mr Bultitude and our mother, and sister Ann and sister Mary, yes, and two children, Emily and Amy—I think they count as one.'

'And of course there's you to go in,' my mother said calmly. She frowned. 'It would be maddening to have to buy more land at the last minute.'

The absurdity of this conversation struck them both in the same instant and they went off into a fit of laughter; it lasted for minutes and was the gayest sound in the world.

As a very young child, I was mortally afraid of my grandfather. Yet the one time I had anything to do with him then, he behaved with great gentleness. My mother had been thrashing me. Made reckless by my fear of pain, I ran wildly round my bedroom, howling, trying to dodge the cane. Exhausted, she told me, 'I must bring your grandfather to deal with you.'

She left the house and I waited, in the state of self-induced apathy, a sort of stupor made up of dislike of showing distress, fear of being pitied, and a purely instinctive animal immobility, in which—so far—I have always been able to sink myself at will. Crouched on the landing outside my room, I watched my grandfather between the balusters as he came up the last flight: he halted half way up, stared at me for a moment and, to my great astonishment, said only, 'You shouldn't wear your mother out,' then turned and went down.

In those days it was the custom to thrash children. Few people imagined that they could be trained by any methods except those used on savagely unbroken horses. Whitby may have been backward in this respect (as in some others), still early Victorian, but not, I think, a great deal. My mother herself was impatient, easily bored, and perhaps more determined to bring her children up well than were some few of her contemporaries.

The cruelty of the method lay in its deliberateness. *I shall thrash you when we get home* had the ring of a death sentence. Any act of carelessness or disobedience outside the house merited it. If other people were present, the offender might get only a terrible glance, a warning what to expect. The pupil of my mother's eye seemed to send out a flash of light, like the discharge from a gun: I have never seen another such glance. The walk home might be short or long; no delay was long enough to ward off the assault on bared flesh and stretched nerves. And the business of forgiveness, which came hours later, was as emotionally racking as the punishment itself.

Only at this moment, as I write, sixty years after the event, I realize that when my grandfather halted and looked up, he saw a desperate little animal behind bars.

His second wife was my father's mother. The two familes were kept apart. My mother cannot have had even the most short-lived sense that she was marrying a stepbrother. Certainly she never regarded her mother-in-law as a stepmother. She disliked her. One day when she was an old woman herself, she spoke to me about her with all the bitterness of a high-spirited young girl.

'She was a wicked woman, malicious, a wilful liar, quite unscrupulous, and she had the tongue of a viper. I remember her saying to a servant who had just married, "I hope you'll ha' ten bairns and not a bite to put in their mouths." She was capable of any trick.'

She played evil tricks on her young daughter-in-law, and an amusing one. As a gesture of independence, my mother and her youngest sister had joined the Congregationalists, a sect the second Mrs George Gallilee considered not merely heretical but vulgar: she begged my mother to let me be decently baptized into the Church of England, promising to give 'the poor innocent bairn' a handsome christening present. The ceremony over, she presented an egg, a pinch of salt, and the smallest possible piece of silver, a threepenny bit.

I had no feeling for her, hardly even distaste. She handed out port and Christmas cake once a year, and pennies when we were taken to visit her on Sunday morning—'You'll ha' been to t'chapel,' she would say contemptuously—and occasionally begged one of us off a beating. She was then quince-yellow and shrunken, wearing lace caps over the sparse remains of black hair. In the end she, too, had a stroke and lay in the room next her husband's, speechless. The stroke paralysed her tongue.

My mother had one word for this. Justice.

## CHAPTER 3

O F THE UNCOUNTED PLACES I have lived in, for years or months, only one haunts me. Since I left it for good, I have been adrift, and shall drift to my death. Yet I cannot go back there—any more than a tree, cut down, could return to its roots left in the ground.

I cannot be sure that everything I remember about a now vanished Whitby is my own memory or my mother's. The most grotesque memories are probably hers. Isolation—before the opening of a railway line through the valley to Pickering in 1836—bred, in counterweight to its benefits, a crop of eccentrics, harmless fools, misers, house devils, despots, male and some female, who behaved towards their families with a severity even George Gallilee would never have allowed himself.

Talking to me about those obscure Catos, my mother's tone implied a certain respect. Later, when I came to study the Russian dramatist Ostrovski, I thought I recognized them in his plays of crushed lives and meaningless cruelties inflicted behind the bolted doors of provincial merchants' houses. Bitter tears must have been shed, decently, in strict secrecy, by the families of well-to-do men (and a few matriarchs), some of them only hard and miserly, some laughable, but all egotistical to the verge of madness, or so rigid with principles that they might as well have been lunatics.

In the early years of my childhood Whitby was still beautiful. It no longer built ships—sailing-ships, whalers, and, later, small steamships which had to be towed to Middlesbrough or Newcastle to fit their engines—but the skeletons of two of the old yards were rotting placidly, weeds thrusting between the stones and iron rings, on the edge of the upper harbour. I have a confused memory of a launching—the last?

I should admit at once that, for me, Yorkshire is Whitby—but not the town you will see if you go there now in search of a happiness which depends on a place.

Since my fortunate infancy, the high-hedged lanes and fields, the bare cliff-tops covered with short springing grass, have been disfigured by a brick rash, the ancient pier intolerably tawdrified, the splendid subscription library thrown away, and heaven knows what other outrage and perversion. Something remains. Impossible—unless there are no limits to insensitivity and contempt for what is only charming and dignified—to spoil the ruined Benedictine Abbey on the East cliff, or the quiet waters of the estuary. Or the Norman church crouched, pressed into the ground by the wind, between abbey and cliff-edge, and reached by a hundred and ninety-nine wide shallow stone steps from the harbour. The soul of an old ship inhabits this church and its three-decker pulpit: ships' carpenters put up the present roof, and the windows under it are so like cabin windows that on the rare Sundays when we occupied my grandfather's pew in one of the galleries I could only dream of voyages. Outside, the dust of Saxons, Danes, monks, ship-builders, master mariners, lies deep under the rank grass between wrinkled gravestones eaten by the salt.

Standing on the cliff-edge, three hundred or more feet above the sea, and looking north past the mouth of the harbour and the West cliff, you see a gently-curving coast-line, which moves me as music moves people who understand it.

In the narrow streets on both sides of the harbour, you may come on a child with the wiry reddish-gold hair of the Norsemen, harriers of this coast, driving their murderously beaked black boats into the sandy mouths of streams, and landing to kill, burn and, as they did at the mouth of the Esk, settle. (The first name I saw in Norway was *Storm*, on a doorway in Horten, a small town in the Oslo Fjord.)

Looking back, I seem to see the first step towards an inevitable deterioration in the re-naming—to please an enfeebled taste—of the Saloon. This was—you could not call it a cliff-garden, since there was only grass and paths or steps twisting half way down the West cliff to a theatre and a small reading-room and, built out above the sands some fifty feet below, a broad asphalted walk, with a bandstand in the open air: ticket-holders walked up and down during the concerts (as in Antwerp) or sat about on benches and iron chairs listening to Berlioz, Auber, Rossini, Weber, Strauss, and looking at the sea. It was re-named the Spa. Then the end of the walk was glassed in, to shelter orchestra and audience from the often cold sea wind; then... but why go on?

Or, perhaps, mark the beginning of the end by the humblest of graves— that of the last of the old fishwives who came round singing *vessel(wassail)-cups* in December. They carried a box lined with evergreens, holding a little cheap doll, and sang in quavering voices, as harsh as gulls,

God a-rest you, merry merry gentlemen...

The oldest of them died well before 1914.

Before 1914, too, the pier and the narrow street under the East cliff had superb jet-shops. If you own one of the elaborate necklaces cut by Whitby jet-workers, cherish it; there will be no more: a craft started in the Bronze Age no longer pays.

Not a great way beyond the upper harbour, the hills begin to fold in; a few miles inland they rise to a wide stretch of moor, by turns fox-red, purple, bone-grey, seamed by runnels of peaty water and narrow valleys filled with foxgloves, gorse, dog-roses, thyme, bracken, and a few self-possessed villages. In my childhood the moor road from Pickering to Whitby said all there is to say about the instinct for solitude, sharper than the impulse to herd: peewits, seagulls, a few grouse and, at a certain point, the first sight, piercing the heart, of the church and the Abbey clinging to the East cliff.

Eleven years ago, an unexpected glimpse of them from a lonely road running east brought tears to my eyes before I could check them, and I had to turn away to hide from my two companions my ridiculous anguish.

If I think of anything at the end of my life it will probably be the sea, the North Sea: the milky blue of summer, harmless ripples caressing the ankles of trippers and drawing slowly out to an air of Rossini's; the savagery of winter, waves rearing thirty feet to break against the pier lighthouse; suave, icy, gentle, enticing, treacherous, charging the air with splinters of light and the houses with exotic junk, shells from Vera Cruz, enormous dried seeds like the shrunken trophies of head-hunters, boxes and silk screens from Japan, eggshell china, elaborate French clocks, an African necklace, ostrich eggs on which I copied in oil-paint the birds and flowers from a great book of foreign birds.

Bringing in, too, a fever, a bacillus of restlessness and violence to creep into the veins. Not all veins; only those liable to catch the fever.


## CHAPTER 4

THERE IS A SENSE in which it is true that we only live in one house, one street, one town, all our lives. I have no memory of the first house I lived in, though I ought to be able to remember an afternoon in my sixth month when I began climbing its dangerously steep staircase on hands and knees: I set off six times, and was fetched back and whipped six times.

Have I been doing anything ever since except setting off again up those infernal stairs?

The first departure I remember was from our next house.

Whether reflected from the sea, or filtered as it crosses the moors, the light on this strip of the north-east coast has an unusual clarity. It may be this light—it could be flattered by the hand like a young horse—which sets 5 Park Terrace apart from the unnumbered houses I have lived in since. It was a terrace of Victorian houses, facing another on a lower level; from its end a very steep road, North Bank, dropped to Esk Terrace which faced, across a slope of rank grass, the upper harbour. Of what other house can I recall the satin-striped wallpaper in the upper sitting-room, the textures of its saddlebag chairs, the exact shape of the horsehair sofa in the dining-room, and the position, relative to each other, of bedrooms and attics? There was no bathroom: a wide hip-bath was filled for us in front of the kitchen range; I should be glad to forget a horrible night when I upset it.

At the farther end of the terrace, a cul-de-sac of four dull houses, moss and short fine grass pushing between its cobblestones, filled me, however often I entered it, with a voluptuous sense of strangeness—*le Pays sans Nom*.

This nameless country is now a few narrow streets, a harbour divided into upper and outer by a vanished swing-bridge, a naked cliff-top, the whole small enough to fit into a tiny flaw in my skull.

Do not believe that the earliest memories are anything but disguised choices. My first memory of injustice is attached to this house and this time: next door a family called Corney kept a school for very young children, to which I was sent a week after my fifth birthday: one morning I was accused of breaking a window and my truthful and passionate denials not believed. And my first memory of guilt and shame: I filled my infant brother's shoes with water from the yard tap and waited for him to be accused of the crime; my treachery must have been perfectly obvious, and, confronted with it, I could only take my whipping. And my first memory of lust, evil: two children my age, brother and sister, giving themselves up to some scandalous joining together of their bodies (I knew it was scandalous because they told me so, and made me swear not to talk about it).

Infantile eroticism is a very curious affair. It involves no sexual knowledge at all, and needs none. My ignorance was as complete as my want of curiosity. I was nine or ten before I learned—through watching a boy on the stern of a barge on the Scheldt—that male and female bodies are anatomically different. The discovery made an impression on me and led to day-dreams of childish indecency, savagely naive and absurd; I wove them round a story about two heroes of the Indian Mutiny, Generals Havelock and Outram—an innocent source, one would think, but there is no protecting the imagination from its power to corrupt itself.

Attached to this first house, too, are a handful of night dreams, the earliest one of pure fear: there were evil dwarfs in the streets; one touch from them would horribly twist your body, if not kill you. How did those chthonic gods, the Cabiri, get into a northern child's dream?

My so-called school taught a few children to write, count on their fingers, read, and learn by heart so many paragraphs a day of history, geography, grammar, poetry, the best method in the world, since it leaves the child's imagination severely alone. I could read before I went to this school; I taught myself, probably driven to it by boredom. No special books were given me, I read everything in the house. One evening my mother mocked me sharply for spelling out the word tobacco in Samuel Baker's *Albert N'yanza, Great Basin of the Nile.* I was sitting in the circle of light from the lamp in the centre of the red chenille cloth, absorbed in the hideous and fascinating journey shared by the devoted Mrs Baker. I was seven, or at most a year older. It was like my mother to expect me to recognize in print an object I had seen.

I still have the two volumes, published in 1886: the engravings are superb.

Forbidden to read before breakfast, I hid books under the mattress of my bed. They were discovered at once—I was either too young or too stupid to reflect that they would be—and I was thrashed, and did it again, and was thrashed again.

The year after her third child was born my mother went off on a long voyage. She put me to board with the Misses Corney. During the day I was unconcerned, but the moment I had been put to bed in the room I shared with the eldest Miss Corney, my tears started of themselves and flowed torrentially for more than an hour. This happened every night for three or four months. I could not explain my despair to the poor woman, and she had to let me cry myself into the sleep of exhaustion.

It was my first experience of loss, and my grief was as atrocious as any I have felt since.

I knew, with absolute certainty, that my mother would die at sea and I should not see her again—except in a way I could not imagine: before leaving she had said, 'If I'm drowned in a storm I'll come to you.'

This incomprehensible promise was the only hope I had.

My sister, three years old, and my brother, who was still in petticoats, had been left with a magnificent woman known as Mammy Fisher. I never saw them. With her husband and sons, she kept a greengrocer's shop: when a family in the neighbourhood was in trouble—sickness, a death, a hard birth—she was sent for. Fat and strong, with a voice ripened by years of advising, cajoling, soothing, seeing people into the world and seeing them out, she was sixteen stone of hard stubborn Yorkshire flesh, and a saint.

The second time my mother left on a long voyage I felt nothing. But at the station I pretended to cry, for fear she should be disappointed. Already, at the age of eight, I was an accomplished hypocrite.

This time my sister stayed at the school with me. It was nearly the death of her. The Misses Corney were young marriageable women, and after school hours left us with a servant: she let us do as we pleased, and one afternoon we walked into the country as far as the village of Ruswarp, two miles. The Esk was in spring flood, with a strong, fast current, and we amused ourselves on its bank until my sister lost her footing on a loose stone, and sank. I snatched at her desperately from the same jutting stone and dragged her out, drenched and shivering. We ran to a cottage, where a woman stripped her and dried her clothes.

For a week after this, to bring home to her the depth of her wickedness in coming within a hair's-breadth of drowning, she was made to stand on a stool before the roomful of grinning children, every morning for an hour. She was five, a little less.

I was not punished. Why? I had no idea, and a child does not try to understand the behaviour of his masters. The truth is, he does not think of himself as a child and of his elders as adults; he thinks in terms of rulers and ruled, helpless and powerful. Very much, I suppose, as the inhabitants of an occupied country feel towards an occupier, however benevolent.

Our brother had been sent to Mammy Fisher; she loved him fondly and gave him anything he asked for. When my mother fetched him home he refused to believe she was his mother, and rushed back scowling to his *real* mother. He was a singularly fierce child, with a frown that made people call him a 'black bairn.' A woman came one day to complain that he had torn her son's cap off his head and thrown it into the harbour. 'How old is your son?' my mother demanded.—'Nine.'—'My son is not yet five. I think little of a nine-year-old boy who lets a little child of four master him.'

My mother never allowed anyone, friend or stranger, to criticize her children.

Her passionate loyalty and devotion—she would without hesitation have stepped between one of us and an enraged tigress—and her severity (the merciless thrashings) sprang from one and the same impulse: we were to have everything she could get for us, and be everything she admired, upright, truthful, well-mannered, clever, quick, sincere.

How could it have entered her head that insincerity was one of the lessons I learned early and thoroughly, very early, very thoroughly?

## CHAPTER 5

FOR SEVERAL YEARS I had a recurring dream in which I was living with her in a badly-lit room: I knew that I should be forced to wake up and leave her there. I wept bitterly, I assured her over and over again that she, not *the other one*, was the mother I loved. I'll come back, I repeated, all the time struggling to stay asleep, but the room, the figure of my mother, became shadowy, wavered, vanished...

It seemed that a nerve led direct from my young mind to hers: I knew instantly what she wanted me to say, what it would please her to hear, what she wanted. She was curiously reluctant to say frankly: I want this, I want to do that. (I see, now, that she hated as I do *to be seen caring*.) When she coveted something she could not afford, I encouraged her to buy it. This habit became fixed: to the end of her life I encouraged her in extravagances, and spent recklessly on her. Even as children we somehow scraped up the money to give her a birthday present she would value. Once my brother refused to hand over his small savings, and gave her his own choice of present, a penny loaf with a tulip stuck in it. She did not thank him.

What she wanted she wanted blindly, unable for the time to see anything else in the world. I, too...

My terrible anxiety for her to be happy took in the most trivial events; playing bezique with her, I tried not to win; when she planned a day in the country I prayed feverishly for sun: a fiasco made me feel guilty.

I cannot remember a time when I was not aware, and with what helpless pity, that her life had disappointed her.

Those seeds of guilt and responsibility, sown in me at the beginning, were not able to strangle an egotism as involuntary as George Gallilee's, but they have given it an atrociously uneasy life.

In those days, how gay she could be! A fine day made her madly happy: she hurried us out of the house to walk the four or five miles to the moors, the road climbing, slowly, between stone fences; or, when my aunt Mary was still alive, to Carr Hill. (This aunt, the best-looking of the five Gallilee sisters, had married a small landowner who went mad, not violently, but tiresomely for his family: he used to turn his wife and my four cousins, two of whom went mad in their turn, out of the house at night, so that they had to take shelter in the nearest farm.) But she was rarely contented. How, given what she was, could she be? Take a young attractive woman, with a passion for change and movement, and shut her up with three unpredictably lively children in a house in a small town—even before the birth in 1906 of her fourth child she had given up long voyages—and what could come of it but boredom, an agonizing boredom?

I only understood years later, at a time when I was tempted to knock my own head against the wall, the fits of rage in which she jerked the Venetian blinds in her room up and down, up and down, for the relief of hearing the crash.

She had married—to get away from a house full of her sisters?—too young, a man inferior to her in breeding, sensitivity, warmth of heart and force of character. He had his own courage, tenacity, dreams, but she was too young, too uncompromising, to forgive him traits that vexed her and roused her contempt. She never understood or forgave him a habit of lying about himself—if you can call lies the instinct to appear clever or cunning, or to defend himself from her scathing tongue. She baffled and tormented him (and herself) for the disappointments and revulsions he made her suffer. Her passion for perfection—in everything she owned, a dress, the furniture of her room—scandalized him. No Whitby sea-captain's wife clothed herself and her children as she did, or bought Dresden china, costly rugs, Hepplewhite chairs, searching antique shops for bargains, bidding at auction sales. She spent on these things every penny that came into her hands, saving only in order to spend.

He did not like it any better when, on one of their first voyages, an old captain took her to be his daughter, though he was not more than nine years the elder. She was slender, with the complexion of a young child.

When they married he was not yet a captain, and they were pinched for money. I have her account book for that year, a little thin book with an olive-green cover. The first item runs: Cab and fare to Newport, and it ends on the 31st of December with the note that she had a Balance in Hand of *£6 10s 6d*. I doubt if she ever kept accounts again.

Before their marriage, she told me, he had begged her to correct his clumsiness and ignorance. (Of his mother's three sons, he was the one who suffered from the poverty into which the defaulting solicitor threw her; at the age of thirteen he was taken from school and sent as apprentice in a sailing-ship, to be schooled in bitter hardship and cruelty.) An eager haphazard reader, he mis-saw words—a geranium became a genarium on his tongue, and the like. His manners, unless he were able to condescend, were rough or too familiar. He made a cult of shabbiness and would let a new uniform moulder in his cabin, unworn, for years. (Like his mother with her dozens of boned silk bodices.) After their marriage, he would have nothing to do with her attempts to teach him a few graces. He was neither humble nor generous enough. Nor, I'll be bound, she adroit.

Used, in his ship, to the absolute authority of a captain, he might have bullied her and us if she had not, from the very start, been too much for him, too quick-witted, too lively, too stubborn and overbearing. He would have done better for himself to marry a stupider or an easy-going young woman. My mother's contempt for devious ways, her fastidiousness, her wilfulness and impatience, her (in his eyes) insane ambitions for her children, her love of beautiful things, vexed him, but he did not know how to deal with them. He was no match for her unconscious arrogance, the echo in hers of George Gallilee's intimidating voice.

Only in physical courage and a deep obstinacy was he her equal. Their long separations—months long—stretched the gap between them to an abyss. Before he had been home longer than a week they were quarrelling, bitterly. The bitterness, the impatience, were on her side, the stubborn incomprehension and lack of generosity his. But she was fully as stubborn as he; a quarrel might last days, and be followed by a reconciliation that must once have been eager, the passionate repentances of a quick-hearted young woman, but with the years became mere dry exhaustion.

The first years, of voyages to South America, France, Belgium, Norway, Vera Cruz, Odessa, must have been the least disappointing of her life: she loved strange cities, and from all of them her curiosity picked up new ideas, new recipes, new ways of setting a dinner-table, a new elegance. No doubt she was sometimes bored, shut up at sea for slow weeks with a husband whose ways jarred on her. But the one thing she respected in him was his seamanship.

In whatever else he fell short, as a sea-captain he had *arete* excellence in the highest degree. To the marrow of his bones and the smallest cell in his brain he was a good seaman. Not that this made him a just man: towards his officers he was neither considerate nor impartial.

On one voyage to the River Plate they ran into a storm, a *pampero*, of more than common violence, and were fourteen days overdue at Buenos Aires. 'We'd given you up, Captain,' the agent waiting on the wharf told him.

The ship lay on her side for three days and nights, and on the last of these nights he came down off the bridge to tell her, 'I daresay we s'll go down, she's lying right over, and the sea's very high now.' He would try, he added mildly, to get back to her, 'before aught happens.'

I try, and fail, to imagine the thoughts of the young woman waiting, alone, in the crazily-tilted cabin, in darkness.

Left to him—if we had been left to him—his children would have been poorly off. Years later, but only then, I understood his indifference to our education, his resentment of the money spent on us. The child who at thirteen was forced to endure, as if he were a man, cold, indifference, brutality, could not find in himself either the tenderness or the warmth to forgive other children, his own, their softer lives. He never spoke about his boyhood except when he was muttering over some—as he saw it—wicked extravagance. His wife could not bear him to pity himself, and cut such mutterings ruthlessly short.

'If I allowed it, he would ride roughshod over us,' she said to me.

It was true.

Not until he died did I see that he, too, was to be pitied and respected. He was brave, tortuous, full of mean resentments, grudging, naively vain, and patient. He had a streak of fantasy that in other circumstances might have changed his life. He kept a commonplace book into which he copied verses and anecdotes that impressed him. When he could, he took long solitary walks: I have a photograph he sent me when I was living in London in the thirties—he was then eighty—of a stretch of moorland with one signpost: on the back he had written: *Place for dreams.*

What dreams?

## CHAPTER 6

O NE EVENING when my mother was leaving the house in anger after a quarrel, I asked her when she would be back.

'Never!' she said drily.

I was much too young to reflect that one does not leave home for ever on foot, without so much as a dressing-case. In despair, I followed her. She took a road that after four miles or so would bring her to Aisalby moor, and we walked for an hour or longer, I keeping myself, as I imagined, out of sight. At last she turned round, took my hand, and we went back together, in the gathering darkness, in silence.

I shudder now when I think what unhappiness that silence of hers hid.

She had a terrible need to be in the right. It was impossible for her to admit that she had made a mistake, or been clumsy, or had acted from any but the highest motive. This was one of the traits that made living with her hazardous. But, as well as repeating itself in me, it taught me tact.

Is this really a benefit? I doubt it.

My anxiety to please, and my nakedness to all the winds blowing from other people's minds, start here. What a Frenchman who mistrusted me called '*la bouche fleurie de Madame Storm Jameson*' is nothing whatever but a gesture of propitiation, such as savages make to their gods. And a defence. To be noticed suffering, or even rejoicing too much—how frightful!

Some time between the wars, when I read *Souvenirs d'egotisme* for the first time, and came on the sentence which ends, 'with one idea in my mind: *not to be seen into* (*avec une seule idée; n'être pas deviné*)...' my heart leaped with joy, a stray dog recognizing its master.

That *nothing whatever* is too shallow. I fear punishment, I fear the pain of mockery, but I fear also to give pain. Too often, I see a naked quivering little creature behind the eyes of the person I am talking to, and cannot bring myself to disappoint it; I want passionately to give it the joy and reassurance of being approved. Anger can blind me to it and make me forget everything but the pleasure of striking. Or, if I feel a reasonable trust in the other person, I may risk frankness.

There are a few people, four or five, I feel no need to guard myself from— and no need to handle them as if they were fragile. One of these speaks, kindly, of 'your flunkey's tongue, dear Margaret.'

I see now that this double-stranded fear has been the strongest impulse in my life for as long as I remember.

Something that happened during my eighth year shows both her children's fear (in the Biblical sense) of my mother, and my own weak dislike of making myself unpleasant. The three of us had gone into the fields near Park Terrace and were playing there when a poorly-dressed boy, perhaps sixteen, came up and offered to teach us a new game. I did not like the look of him, he was obviously a low fellow, but I did not know how to get rid of him without hurting his feelings, the feelings of a wretchedly poor boy. I let him take us into the avenue of trees between one field and the next, and here he kneeled down and squeezed his hands round my throat; I was paralysed by astonishment, but the other two flung themselves on him, beating him with their fists, screaming. There was a group of picknickers in the next field: these must have shown signs of interest, because the lout made off in one direction and we in another, hoping fervently that no one would give us away.

It did not enter my head that my mother would not punish me if she found out. I hardly believed my luck when—the picnickers must have told her—she took me on her knee and in her gentlest voice asked me to tell her what had happened before ordering us in future to turn away if a stranger spoke to us.

She had two voices, the harsh penetrating one she used in anger—it could sharpen to a cruel mockery—and the other, her singing voice, strong and untrained but clear and perfectly true—

It's nothing but a shower
Just a quarter of-an hour
Don't you think you'd better shelter 'neath the chestnut tree,
For the wind is blowing sweet
And there are daisies at your feet
And if you'd like to dance I will pipe for you...

Here the voice breaks off, I strain after it, it swells on a note, falters, dies.

She had a third voice she used very rarely. No—it used her. It was the voice of a saucy smiling child. It echoes in my ears, which have forgotten the others.

When she sang hymns we bawled them with her. If anyone were to sing *God be with you till we meet again*, in my hearing, I should die of grief.

Another incident of that time when, fearing a scene, I behaved as I still instinctively do: just before leaving the house to go to school, I opened the *Daily Mail* and read a paragraph saying that the *Saxon Prince*, captain William Storm Jameson, had been seized by the Japanese—a war in which no one took any interest was going on—carrying contraband steel rails, and towed into Sasebo. I pushed the paper under the cushions of a chair, and hurried out. The letter from Newcastle, from the firm, came during the day. I pretended astonishment and concern.

My father spent several pleasant weeks in Japan and brought back a magnificent fold-fold silk screen (which, when he was an old man living alone, he destroyed), the antique God of Plenty I have, and various oddments. These included a photograph of himself in Japanese dress, with parasol and fan, at which my mother smiled drily.

Have I succeeded in drawing a portrait, however faint, of this warm passionate generous young woman, whose face I catch sight of only in sleep, and then uncertainly?

She expected and wanted so much and had so little.

She gave me more than my ludicrous conviction of being responsible for other people, and of being a laughing-stock. I have her bottomless weight of boredom, a never-appeased restlessness, which becomes torture in surroundings I dislike, and the jeering violence I keep out of sight. And, too, a deep, deeper than everything else, indifference—which may only be fear. My working patience and stubbornness I owe to that master mariner with the clouded blue eyes and a mind full of bits and pieces like a sea-chest.

The Yorkshire character has a monolithic appearance which in fact is a lie. Under that air of shrewd hard horse-sense it is complex in the extreme, even neurotic, one edge of its violence and irony turned inward. I have my full share of both, but some other strain in me mocks and bedevils the Yorkshireman—those Gallilees, perhaps? My grandfather, who felt a keen interest in his ancestors, never traced them farther back than their appearance, during the early eighteenth century, in a village on the coast a few miles north of Whitby. (In a document of that time, recording the births of six members of the family, the name is spelled *Gallaley*, and *Galliley*. Galileo?) It vexed him not to know certainly whether he came from gentlemen or a common stock...

Do not imagine that as children we were unhappy. Far from it. We were storing up sensuous wealth for a lifetime. We had everything that children brought up in large towns and cities, or with mechanical amusements, miss. Perhaps because my mother did not like having other people in her house, we had no friends of our own age. A closed society, we played endless ingenious games together. We sometimes fought; I was unkind and arbitrary, and the other two rebelled: my most powerful hold on them at this time was a trick of story-telling I found I had, week-long versions of books I had read, and fairy-tales—the trick deserted me when I was twelve and beginning to be serious about my future.

And we had the sea—endless days on the shore in summer, from nine in the morning until six or seven at night, by which hour we were alone, three children on the edge of an infinity of sand and water—enclosed in a boundless blue world, steeped in light, in a radiance of sun and salt, sauntering in and out of gently-breathing waves or racing in front of them, bare wet legs smarting from the sand-grains driven into the skin.

In spring and winter we went to the end of the pier to watch heavy seas breaking over the lighthouse—this was before extensions were built on to the ancient stone piers with their old mooring-posts, making the bar safe for fishing-boats and spoiling the storms. We stood close under the lighthouse, waiting, listening, for the next wave, and when it reared hissing and fuming overhead ran madly to be out of reach of the deluge; now and then one of us was caught and drenched; then it was a matter of drying off in the icy wind before daring to go home.

With my mother we learned a rhythm of country walks: in February the snowdrops in the woods of Mulgrave Castle, the pale yellow of primroses, scattered across the fields above the Carrs in April, thick oozing yellow of bog-buttercups, and an enormous bird-cherry, a dazzling cloud of white, in May, wild roses, orchids, foxgloves in the hot narrow June lanes below the moor; and in August and September the moors themselves, the intoxicating scent, the humming of flies and bees, the great cloud-shapes passing overhead—all, all belong to years before I knew the meaning of time, or that it was more than a word: time to leave the sands, already empty, the rock-pools darkened by the lengthening shadow of the cliffs, time to rush out of the house to school, to start for the Saloon before every sheltered bench has been filled, for the Saturday morning market before the scores of pounds of yellow butter vanish off the stalls, time to expect the reindeer tongues and small barrel of cranberries sent to my grandfather every year's end from Archangel, time to pick brambles in the abandoned quarry, time to look for mushrooms, wild daffodils, broom, time to dye the Easter eggs, to buy holly, time, time, time, a bell tolling to the beat of the deep-sea current, time gone.

I can live in it for a moment. For less than a moment—after that I only imagine, inventing echoes.

We kept anniversaries with religious happiness, from rolling Easter eggs down the steepest fields, through Whitsun and birthdays to Christmas, New Year and Twelfth Night. Birthdays began formally, with a tray known as the birthday tray, heaped with presents: it was large and square, with high edges, of gold and black lacquer from Sasebo. It must still be somewhere, it was strong as well as beautiful. Why—I have saved other things—did I not keep it?

One can't save everything.

## CHAPTER 7

I N THE SPRING OF 1903 we were living in a newly-built house on the West cliff, at that time two miles of fine turf, naked to the North Sea wind. The move brought us within hearing of the sea, close to the cliff-top and the zig-zag path leading to the sands. Not that we used it, preferring to climb down and up two hundred feet of slippery red clay and rocks. There was a very large yard at the back of the house, and my mother let me keep a young white rabbit a friend of hers offered me. She detested animals; when, in a week or two, I grew bored with looking after it, she was thankful to give it away. No sooner had it gone than I was filled with remorse, imagining its grief at being unwanted, and weeping bitter tears which started again each time I recalled its trick of springing from the ground upright, like a dancer.

'You should have cared when you had it,' my mother said, with dry justice.

This house was two miles from our new school; we did the walk four times a day, always late and always running. We became known for the habit. We ran to dancing-class, to the Spa fireworks and concerts, even, when we were alone, to church. No one was surprised to see us racing through the streets to my eldest aunt's funeral. She and my aunt Jane, eldest and youngest of the Gallilees, were the only ones not married, still living in the same house. My mother had gone early, leaving us to dress and follow. In the end we had to run like hares.

As it turned out, we need not have run. The funeral had been held up by the refusal of the undertaker's men to nail the coffin. Dr Mitchell had to be called to assure them that the old lady was dead: her gleaming white hair, rosy cheeks and wide-open blue eyes frightened them. Pray God she really was dead.

My mother this summer was out of all patience with her life, herself, us. She was going to have a child in November; she had not wanted another child, eight years after her son's birth, and her exasperation and weariness drove her to violent rages, which were really fits of despair.

During these weeks I went through a crisis of anxiety about her. Farther back than I can remember, this irrational anxiety had been growing in me:

it now reached a desperate climax. It woke me at night and sent me creeping downstairs from my room on the top floor to crouch outside the door of her bedroom: I sat there for two, three, four hours, until I was chilled to the bone, then went back to bed and fell asleep. During the days, too, when she locked herself in her room, to endure, out of our sight, the unhappiness we did not—how could we?—understand, I couldn't bring myself to carry away the tray of food she refused, but waited outside with it uselessly for an hour before giving up.

After this summer, my anxiety diminished slowly, overlaid by the energies and ambitions which, at the age of thirteen or earlier, began to take savage possession of me. Perhaps what is more nearly true is that I became able to ignore it, at least in its acute form.

My youngest sister, Dorothy, was born on the 13th of November, and became my mother's last and overwhelming passion. They were laughably alike.

I can fix the month, almost to the day, when I ceased to be a child. Soon after we moved to the new house, my mother went on the last of her long voyages. She went to Buenos Aires (pronounced by every Whitby sea-captain's family Bonnus-airs), leaving us as boarders in the private school we had been going to daily for a year. She was at sea when we went down with scarlet fever, all three of us. Rather than send us to the fever hospital, it was decided to open up the house and put us in it on the top floor, in charge of a nurse and an old woman called Nightingale. We spent six or seven weeks shut up here, we were not ill, and had nothing to amuse us except a number of cardboard dress-boxes that we turned into a fleet of liners and sailed in them about the rooms. On the fourth or fifth day when I woke, I glanced down at the ship moored alongside my bed, and realized in the same instant that I was an adult shut up with two children.

From this moment until we were released I endured an excruciating boredom, the worst of my life until I had to live in a house of my own—which was infinitely worse.

I had two books, no more—the nurse, a fool, had a theory that reading was bad for fever patients—*Kenilworth* and a copy of the *Arabian Nights* from which she had torn the opening pages as unfit for a child to read.

Neither was left in my hands for longer than half an hour. Every evening I prayed avidly that God would kill her in the night. A black mamba secretes less venom than a child's impotent hate.

The gap that separated me from the others widened at the speed of a galloping horse. I could no longer invent fairy-tales for them, I began to dream feverishly of *getting away*—away from Whitby, from a barren life without excitement or a chance to show that I was an exception.

Where did my ambition come from? The devil knows. Long before I spoke about it to anyone I was determined to get myself to a university. No pupil of the Misses Ingham had done such a thing; I doubt whether, at that time, there were more than two persons in the town attending any university. It was not the custom, even among the rich. There were several very rich shipping families, at some of whom my mother laughed because they spoke with a strong Whitby accent.

Many years later, J. B. Priestley laughed at me for having forgotten my Yorkshire accent: I took care not to tell him (because he would not have believed me) that I never had one; my voice is a thin poor echo of my mother's and George Gallilee's.

Each year from my thirteenth I took one of the Cambridge examinations, Preliminary, Junior, Senior. I prepared for them by learning enormously by heart: at that time I memorized a page of print by reading it through, and so long as I had a use for it, could summon it to appear in my mind as a printed page: after that I forgot it forever. I read extraordinarily fast, taking in three or four lines at a glance—as I still do. I learned the whole of *The Lady of the Lake*, *Marmion*, *Henry V*, the first book of *Paradise Lost*, pages of Macaulay, of Biblical commentary... On the long walk to and from school, I kept a book open, reading and muttering. For that matter, I read everything that came under my eye, from perniciously bad novels—pernicious to anyone, poison to a future writer—to the Encyclopaedia I stole paragraphs from for my essays. I did not know bad writing from good—then, nor for many a year.

When I look now at children of the age at which I began to be ambitious, I seem to myself never to have had a childhood. Not true: I had all the pleasures a child born between sea and moor could have. But already at this age I knew that I was responsible for myself, that the future existed, and depended on me alone.

I was ambitious without understanding, without even knowing it: it seemed perfectly natural that I should want to get away. So it was—*my* nature. I was a small cauldron of desires and longings, and ignorance. Infinitely more naïve than a normal child of my age now—or indeed then. And—I see this only today—my ambition was sharpened to an unknown degree by my social failure.

To say that I was not a success with children of my age is to say very little: there are no sharper mental torments in life than those endured by the child marked out to be ridiculed, left out of games—at which I was awkward and useless—and convinced of inferiority in the one field which matters at that age. It began, my sense of being different and inferior, when I started at Miss Ingham's. Here for the first time I was in a community of children a little older than I was. No doubt I am exaggerating the number of times when I drew on myself—without having the faintest notion why—the mockery of girls who at fourteen and fifteen were in my eyes self-assured and sophisticated adults.

I cannot see myself as I appeared to them. I try vainly to catch a glimpse of that child, so well-meaning and friendly, to detect what quality in her, what eccentricity, roused others to make her their hare, their mimic prey. I cannot see her, because the eyes with which I look at her are those of the child I was, and still, when I stumble over one of these derisive memories, am.

I shall die without understanding it. Thank goodness, there are no freaks in the grave.

I remember one occasion when mockery turned into a more savage form of baiting. I am in the yard behind the school (where one day a week a coast-guard drills us), and four or five older girls have twisted the skipping-rope round me below my knees; they have only to tighten the coils a fraction and I shall fall headlong on the flagstones. I recall their jeering laughter at my helplessness, and my terror of falling, and terror that they would notice it. How did it end? I don't know. The image does not tell me.

On the first day we moved to the new house, I stood in the large, extrav-agantly large scullery, cutting slices of bread on the table under the window, and listening with excitement to the voices of children playing on the other side of the seven-foot high wall dividing their garden from our yard. I did not know them, they went to a different private school. A new life, new friends who did not know that I was in some way ridiculous, were within reach. I had a few minutes of pure confidence.

They were two families of children, cousins, living side by side in houses which shared a very long garden. The larger family had four or five girls: the eldest, my age, was the best-looking, with yellow hair, blue eyes, a deliciously fresh skin. She had only one fault, she was bow-legged. She was amiable, perhaps stupid, and when we were alone together very friendly, and each time I believed that now, at last, I had been accepted.

This was an illusion.

I was never accepted. As soon as others joined us she abandoned me to them. (My experience of treachery, my own and others', is, as you see, very old.)

It was one of her cousins, a fat sharp-witted boy, who first spoke of me as 'a freak.' I pretended not to care, I was already able to give myself an air of stolid indifference.

What mark, invisible to the victim, appears on the forehead of the child who is a freak? Had I been naive enough to talk about myself and my absurd ambitions and opinions? I am certain not. I was naive, but not a complete fool.

It took me a long time to realize that my case was hopeless: any gesture of friendliness gave me fresh hope. Yet, from the time I was eight or nine I began assiduously, began or continued, to practise all kinds of reticences, evasions, hypocrisies and, above all, indifference.

This habit of indifference, painfully acquired, was extraordinarily useful later on. It was during these years that I began to teach myself a shallow stoicism: nothing lasts, the bitterest disappointment is endurable if kept at a reasonable distance. Tricks for keeping it at its distance can be learned as easily as other evasions.

It would be only natural if these humiliating scenes and the tears shed in secret were clearer than my other memories of that time. But I remember as sharply, and with a quivering happiness, the yellow sprays of broom, dazzling, sprinkling us with a cold dew, gathered on an embankment near the house; the exquisite smoky taste of peat-cakes (flat currant scones baked on a peat fire) in a moor farmhouse; the triumph of finding a bee orchis. And the sea, colours of deep sea, calm twittering of waves inshore, glittering salt-sharp air, returning then, now, and at the hour of my death.

The legacy my failure left me was a rooted mistrust. My lack of trust in human beings is as deep and ineradicable as any of my instincts, deeper than feeling, and I can trace its movements everywhere in my life.

I do not believe that human beings are evil; to not a few I owe an immense debt for kindness and happiness received. I cannot believe that they are to be depended on.

This has nothing to do with whether they are or are not trustworthy. It is a geological fault in me to be unable to trust people, and to expect them, if given the chance, to turn out malicious.

The other day a friend showed me a letter from that intolerant incorrigibly un-venal and uncompromising French writer, Ignace Legrand, in which he said: 'Ah, she's wise to the world, Margaret. She is too intelligent not to see that most people are idiots.'

This is barely just. I don't despise people, I crave their approval. Yet I am indifferent, too—which is a sin, *the* sin.

## CHAPTER 8

M Y MOTHER WAS ZEALOUS for my future. Was it she or I who discovered that three County Scholarships—worth sixty pounds— were awarded yearly, in each Riding, on the results of the Matriculation examination? Only three—and every school in the Riding would enter its scholars. It was my one chance. Sixty pounds would cover the fees at a provincial university—to our innocence all universities were equal—and she could, she said, find another pound or thirty shillings a week for my living expenses.

It occurred to neither of us to ask my father for help.

I had already passed the three Cambridge examinations: to take the third, the Senior, I had to spend the week in Scarborough, with two pupil-teachers who were sitting for it. I was in a fever of excitement and insisted on taking a hansom cab from the station to our lodging—the two young women thought me nearly insane. I can smell now the warm musty scent of vegetables from the shop under my bedroom, and feel the hard knot of blood rising to the back of my head when I came out of the hot examination room into the icy December street.

Miss Lily Ingham could not prepare me for Matriculation. My mother told her so, bluntly. I must leave at the end of the term, to go to the Municipal School at Scarborough. It meant a daily train journey of one hour and ten minutes, but neither of us thought that excessive. Only remained to arrange with the school to take me. My mother wrote to the headmaster to say that we should be calling on him on such and such a day: it did not enter her head that I might be refused.

A day in Scarborough was nothing new. We went five or six times a year, she and I, on the early train, ritual visits that began with coffee in Rowntree's, after which we combed every floor of the shop, from top to bottom; we went more cursorily through two other large shops; we sauntered along every one of the better streets, visited every antique dealer—my mother was known to them all—and the Valley and South Cliff gardens.

This day, except for the interview with Mr Tetley, was like any other. I have tried since to imagine his feelings when, after a sentence or two, my mother said coldly, 'My daughter will come to the school in September to take Matriculation next June, and get a County Scholarship.'

He glanced from her face to mine: at that time—I was sixteen—and for years after, I had a childishly round face and a habit of staring fixedly from wide-open unclear eyes. He must have thought us both a little mad.

'There are only three of them,' he said.

'Yes. She must take one of them.'

'I hope she will,' he said gently.

Smiling, my mother rose, and we went out into the bright day, to go through the ritual. As we went she said, 'Well, now you're started, my little dear.'

In Rowntree's, a young assistant in the fur department persuaded her to try on a sable coat. There was no question of her buying it, it was far beyond her purse, but she held its collar under her chin and looked at herself in the long glass with an intent fixed gaze, her invariable expression when she was trying on a dress or hat: it was as though she were seeking in her reflection someone not herself, some image the mirror held and, if she looked closely enough, would surrender. So, now, I seek her in a glass she used.

'One of these days,' I said to her, 'I'll buy you a fur coat.'

My ambition was personal and selfish but, twisted through it, a living nerve, was the anguished wish to please her by getting myself success and praise. Now that she is dead it no longer frets me to be without honours (in the plural).

A day in Scarborough like any other? No. We did all the proper things, without meeting a single failure; the sun shone, and a light wind lifted the Valley trees. A few words she said in the train marked the difference.

'I've taken many journeys with you, very long some of them.'

'We'll go many more journeys,' I answered.

'No. My time is over. You will go journeys, my little love, you're a Thursday's child—far to go.'

There was no trace of bitterness in her voice, yet she knew then—knew as the body knows these things, with a mute grief—that already I had my back to her.

'Vor daughters ha' mornen when mothers ha' night...'

For two terms, autumn, winter, spring, I travelled to and from school by train. A gleam of light out of these journeys will not vanish until I do. There was a moment in spring when, as we left Robin Hood's Bay, the just-risen sun passed behind a dark bank of cloud, and its rays descending stretched a thin silver line along the rim of the sea. (I saw it again—for the last time?—in 1965, in Portugal—looking across a sea as grey and lively as the North Sea in March but fuller of light, towards an horizon sweeping from east-southeast through south—a great hoop of silver let down below livid clouds from the sun behind them. Old image, old miracle, and infinitely moving.) And there was a moment in winter on the return journey when the train rounded a curve, and the little town sprang below it as a scatter of glittering points in the thick of darkness, the narrow streets invisible, only their gas-lamps and a few uncurtained windows alive. I have no idea why so ordinary a sight made my heart beat against my ribs like a fist, nor what name to give the pleasure that suffocated me.

A foretaste of voyages?

In my third and last term my mother allowed me to spend five days of the week in Scarborough. It was the first time I had lived alone in lodgings.

I took to freedom like a duck to water, or a monk to his cell. There was nothing monkly about the turbulence of my secret life.

Apart from the accident—no one's fault—that the habits and tastes of a vagabond and a solitary rooted themselves in me firmly, below a superficial neatness, I count my years in what its pupils called The Muni as good. At that time it was coeducational, girls' classrooms on one side of the great hall in which the whole school assembled for prayers and to bawl a hymn, boys' on the other. On the boys' side, a single class, the headstrong 5b, was mixed, boys and girls of fifteen and sixteen. After a brief try-out, I was sent to that.

Train scholars from Whitby were a quarter of an hour late in the morning. A short time ago a friend, my oldest, told me,

'The first day you came into 5b, I looked up when the door opened, and saw a country-faced lass walk in, taking her time about it, and staring round as though she owned the blooming place. Ha, I thought, thinks better than well of herself!'

I was a cold knot of fears and insane hopes. And able already to hide both.

None of my fears was realized. In 5b—a class approached with misgivings by a timid master—no one looked on me as a freak. I made my first friends, among them the two I think about as my other selves, with the blessed carelessness, ease, irresponsibility, that implies. One of the Harland brothers, the elder, became a famous geneticist: as a schoolboy he was taken to be the more eccentric of the two, he tumbled from scrape to scrape, once accidentally setting fire to a moor, at other times suspected of insolence, blasphemy, genius, heaven knows what. The eccentricity of the younger, Oswald, went deeper: he had, has, a strong arbitrary mind, a delight in the grotesque, the singular, a bigoted disdain of bigots, and a total inability to play tricks to get an audience: hence the unjust neglect of his few novels, and the reason why a man who would have been a great headmaster was not allowed the chance.

At the time—so ready was I to accept miracles as part of my new life—it did not surprise me that the Harlands chose to make a friend of a raw naively ignorant girl, no match for them in any way.

What did they see in me? An empty channel into which they could turn the torrent of ideas—socialism, atheism, anarchy—pouring through their restless brains? A willing disciple? A creature so obviously untamed that someone ought to put a hand on her?

None of us knew our luck in having A. S. Tetley as headmaster, a well-bred man and a humanist, with a genius for awakening enthusiasm in the minds of the barbarians he was condemned to teach. The afternoon he read *Lycidas* to us blinded me with the light that met Saul on the Damascus road: to this day I cannot read it without a shock of pleasure.

This year I fell in love for the first time—that is, with a living person, not with a hero of the Indian Mutiny or a character in one of the novels my mother brought, three at a time, from the subscription library on the pier. H.C. was a handsome, gentle, not at all intelligent boy of my own age: we took two or three silent walks together, but the affair, to call it that, took place in my imagination. *Le diable au corps*, mine, has always been the dupe of my imagination. Until the habit began to bore me, dreaming about a passion I might at any moment feel, or even rouse, gave me infinitely greater pleasure than the reality.

I see, but only now, that I have always fallen in love in the same way, by catching sight of a face which, for some inexplicable reason—since it was never even the same type of face—abruptly blotted out every other within sight and became, for a day, a month, an hour, the centre of an obsession. The duration of the folly was fixed by circumstances—a straw was enough to turn fervour to contempt. Nor could I go on admiring a person who showed no reciprocal interest: hence—after devoting myself silently for five days to a Swedish poet with the face of a Gothic gargoyle, tall, bony, really horribly unattractive, taking pains to sit where I could watch him unobserved, making careful written notes of his features—I lost all interest within five minutes of leaving Stockholm, and filed the notes for use in a novel.

I was never seriously in love, that is, for a stretch of months or years, except a few times, let us say three, in my life.

Each time the process was the same. I spent entire hours day-dreaming, recalling every detail of voice, gestures, looks, incapable of setting to any other occupation, contrived to be in places where I might catch sight of the obsessive object, schemed to hear his name spoken, to get news of him indirectly, without giving away my silliness, trembled when I caught a word connected with him, the name of his birthplace or of a writer he admired—in short, behind an apparent calm, behaved like a lunatic or a fever patient.

These fevers, fortunately, are rarely caught in their acute form. No harm is done by slight infections. In my thirty-third year, when I fell in love seriously for the last time, I became immunized, to all but the mildest disorders.

Alas, now that I no longer catch fevers, I find writing a lovescene intolerably boring.

What seems to me strange is that—with my inconceivable ignorance, no one having breathed a syllable to me about sex—I could experience, as it were in skeletal form, and for a rather stupid boy of sixteen, all the emotions that later on devastated my life...

I sat for the Matriculation in June, supremely confident with every paper except the mathematics. Figures baffle me—to this day my brain swoons in my head when it comes on a mathematical formula on the page of a book.

The County Scholarships were not announced until September: I was relieved to get one of them, but not much surprised. Why else had I come to Scarborough?

It had been decided that I should go to Leeds University, and I had already had an interview, of which I remember nothing. It was later that Professor C. E. Vaughan, who disliked female students, interviewed me: he asked what I had read, and I gave him in what I thought an impressive list of authors.

'Have you read Burke?' he asked drily.

'No.'

He frowned. 'None of you reads Burke, it's disgraceful.'

A Miss Douthwaite, who taught drawing in Whitby, an uncommonly cultivated woman, begged my mother to send me to Newnham. It was out of the question—even in 1910 sixty pounds was a pittance. We did not give Newnham a thought. But Cambridge might have steadied me and taught me to make better use of my mind. Or I might—why not?—have fulfilled my first and strongest ambition—to become a don.

## CHAPTER 9

A S THE DAY OF MY LEAVING for Leeds came near and nearer, my mother began to regret that I was going away. To console her—fool!—I bought her one of the gilt mesh purses fashionable that year. 'For you to have when I'm not here,' I told her.

'That won't comfort me in my lonely round.'

The day I left, she came as far as Scarborough with me. I see her, standing beside the Leeds train, looking up at me as it moved out: I was too well-trained to show more than a flicker of my pleasure in beginning a new life, but I did not, God forgive me, realize that the train was carrying off the last rag of her youth and its banners. For the first time in my life I hardened my heart, refusing to let myself feel her unhappiness.

I tell myself now that it is forbidden, on pain of death, to creep back to the mother. But the rejection, the victory, is a poor cold business at best. The hands I drew from hers were maimed.

When, years later, I read *Sinister Street*, I realized that in Leeds I had lived in another world and age. The difference did not lie in the disenchanting grime, the ring of steel furnaces and mills belching smoke by day and flames by night, the ceaseless beat of industry in our ears, the total lack of everything implied in talk of dreaming spires and punts idling between fields yellow with buttercups. It lay deeper—in a thin thread of spirit joining us tenuously to the mediaeval universities and their asperities, rough freedom, immersion in a harsh reality. For most of us, a degree was the only gateway to a tolerable life: an undergraduate who did not have this urgency biting him was a rare bird, probably the son of a steel or wool firm training in one of the admirable technical departments.

The rain of State scholarships that set in for good after the last war tamed the provincial universities, and opened the way to the rise of the meritocracy. I notice one trivial but curious effect. The Harlands and I emerged from our three starveling years with a lighthearted confidence that we were conquerors; we had none of the slightly sour grudge against society which today is usual: not only did we want nothing it could give us, but we felt certain of being equals in any social class. In those early years I had no *consciousness* of being shabby, I thought I could go anywhere, into any company. What paralysed me, and still does, is to know that I am an intellectual inferior. It was only later that I began to covet an elegance I had discovered I lacked—and that, after all, may have been a craving handed down to me.

Perhaps I am speaking only for myself and the Harlands. A pity that so few of a lively self-reliant sanguine generation lived to speak for itself. With one exception, the young men who were my friends at Leeds were all dead—Ypres, Loos, Passchendaele—within three or four years after they went down.

As did all undergraduates except those unfortunates who were able to live at home, I had to find rooms. There were then no hostels for women, and only one, I think, for men. The rest lived as near the university as they could, in streets that formed a graceless sooty Latin Quarter, without benefit of cafés, without a rag of charm. But there were few rules, and if you could get into the house without disturbing your landlady no reason why you should come in before three or four in the morning.

In my first two years I moved four times—until I had got myself near enough the university not to have to run for more than five minutes to my first lecture. Then I settled down; my mother began to send me each week thirty shillings instead of a pound and I could pay eighteen shillings for the tolerable discomfort of a sitting-room and dingy bedroom, with breakfast and a meagre supper. My landlady paid me the highest compliment in her power when she told me, 'You're as little trouble as a man.' She was deaf as well as amiable, which allowed me more freedom than—given my total lack of sense—was good for me.

Very soon, partly because of the time I spent idling in full sight, and partly because a charming senior with a reputation for being what then was called fast invited me to dine with her and two handsome and notoriously wild medicals in the Queen's Hotel—why? I had a round face and nothing to say for myself—I began to be thought irresponsible. I had no reverence for authority as such, and a manner that hid my profound uncertainty.

In my third year I was judged to have become responsible—this at a time when I was committing secretly my worst follies—and elected Secretary of the Women's Representative Council of the Union. This must have been the first incident in my life when I impressed people by what dear Michael Sadleir later called 'your specious air of competence.' (If I had had no aptitude for business, how much simpler my life would have been. I had enough to induce hard-headed people to employ me in jobs with which, after a few months, I became acutely bored.)

The Women's Representative Council had no funds, and our rooms, in a terrace of grey houses, were sordidly shabby. I decided to order a new carpet, and did, knowing that the Union would be forced to pay for it.

The professor of classics who was the Union Treasurer said that in his long experience no undergraduate, male or female, had acted in so unprincipled and profligate a way.

He was wrong in one particular. I had acted on principle—no doubt a rash principle, one which has bedevilled my life.

A life without ties suits me better than any. In spite of being poor—a misfortune at any age—I was madly happy, even during times when I was living through one of the ridiculous, unfeigned and groundless miseries proper to my age and nature, which even then was moody, passionately in love with gaiety and change, intolerant, horribly afraid of being mocked... that *n'être pas deviné*... impatient of control, nervously kind and deeply scoffing and pigheaded, fatally quickly bored and fatally certain in company to make the one remark that would damn me for ever in the eyes of sober right-thinking persons.

I was too young, even for my age, too deficient in prudence, in the most ordinary worldly sense, to realize that I was playing ducks and drakes with my whole life. Any sane person would expect that, with ambition biting me, I should take care not to waste a minute, or lose sight for a minute of the figure I might be cutting in the eyes of my world. Not a bit of it. I threw away hours every day, in delicious reveries, in lounging on the tennis-court watching a game I cannot play, in reading outside the curriculum, and dodging prescribed work. In those days I found it utterly impossible to hold my mind down to a book that bored me. The ferment of so-called advanced ideas in my brain came from many sources, none of them of any use to a scholar. Even my ambition was chaotic, and except for the idea of becoming a don, had neither direction nor singleness of mind. Nor did anyone attempt to direct it.

After the first weeks I began to cut lectures. I never cut Professor Vaughan's. For that severe woman-hating humanist, who must have found me pretentious and detestable, I had too much respect, not to say fear. The other honours students in my school—what a fool I was to choose to read English, with all its temptations to pass off ideas and invention as scholarship, but I had no one to give me advice—waited to see me come a cropper at the end of the first year. But I was working harder than they knew: in those days I could read until six in the morning, have a bath (in my wash-basin: there was no bathroom in the house) and breakfast, and go off to the university with the lightness of a young animal, as though my body had no weight. And I was a born examinee, a Napoleon in the marshalling of any facts I happened to have on hand, and—over ground that gave my imagination room to gallop—all but unbeatable. To their frank surprise and disappointment, I passed the Intermediate in the first three.

Two years later, in the Finals, I triumphed again, coming out at the top of the honours class. Much good this triumph did me.

If a ship that has slipped its moorings could think, it might have the illusion that it was free at the very moment when it was at the mercy of every wind and current. I did not even notice what, to make myself safe, I ought to be doing. It never crossed my mind that the erratic way I worked was unlikely to earn me the reputation I might have got by being overtly studious, attending every lecture, and slaving at Anglo-Saxon and the duller subjects of a course which was more of an endurance test than an education: it swept us from Beowulf as far as Keats, past Langland, past Chaucer, past Shakespeare and his forerunners to Sheridan and through a score or two of divines, essayists, pamphleteers, novelists, besides the history and theory of criticism, starting off in the *Poetics* and Longinus and marching through Sidney, Johnson, Dante, Dryden, Boileau, Pope, Wordsworth, Shelley and I forget what more. Oddly, this part of the course fascinated me, I read avidly, without acquiring the feeblest trace of self-criticism.

Years later, reviewing my third novel, Rebecca West noted that I had no taste, which, she went on, 'is incurable.' She was right about my lack of taste. I did, painfully, cure it, but not for several more years.


## CHAPTER 10


HONOURS STUDENTS were required to write a thesis, and I wrote eighty thousand words on William Blake, working in Leeds, in the admirable Public Library, all through a stiflingly hot July and August and a fortnight's feverish attack of some sort. At home, in Whitby, I copied it in my round hand. During the last week of the vacation, I worked on it most of the night, keeping myself awake with green tea my mother bought for me.

She put it in a little silver caddy I kept with my manuscript, and about three in the morning made myself a cup of the bitter stuff and went on copying.

I had no notion how to write, and the thesis was written in immensely long involved sentences. Moreover, I did not understand Blake. I supposed I did, but it was an illusion.

The manuscript had to be typed for the university authorities, and, later, two or three other persons read it. J. G. Wilson of Bumpus's bookshop, kind and zealous friend of young writers, was one: it is in my mind that he showed it to a publisher, but I forget. I kept the original handwritten manuscript for some years, in the corner of a shelf in my first house, then at the bottom of a trunk; it became shabbier and dustier, and at some point I must have torn it up.

The typescript I lost sight of, and after a time forgot what I had done with it, or when I had seen it last. My indifference to such things wiped it out of my mind. If asked, I should have said I had destroyed it. Only many years later, in 1941, did I discover that this would have been a lie.

I cannot see myself as my professors must have seen me. A photograph of that time shows a placid-faced schoolgirl. I must have seemed much more like an unbroken colt, with no manners.

In my first year I fell in love with a charming theological student. It was a safe thing to do, since these young men from the College of the Resurrection at Mirfield were dedicated to poverty, chastity and obedience, and I doubt if any one of them ever transgressed his vows. Apart from boring my closest female friend of that time by talking about him, the obsession did no damage. The one I fell into the following year was fatal.

After so long, can I tell the truth about it? From this distance I see much too clearly—in outline, not in the living tormenting detail—how disastrous it was, how unlucky. But I do not see how, given the circumstances and my own character, I could have avoided the trap laid for me by my senses and total lack of commonsense.

K., whom I later married, was in his third year, studying classics. He was very tall, with a narrow face and finely shaped mouth: his least attractive feature was a snub nose, which gave him a slightly impudent air, very marked when he was in a self-assertive or jaunty mood. Short-sighted, he disliked glasses and wore a pince-nez for reading: without it, his glance was kinder and less assured. He had, in my eyes, a maturity which was, I daresay, the effect of his quick tongue and the pleasure he took in supporting the unpopular side in any debate. I saw his self-assurance, his volubility, as enviable virtues, and was overwhelmingly flattered when he took notice of me during the journey of a delegation from the Debating Society to Liverpool University. My infatuation developed through all its stages. This time I said nothing about it, aware, without knowing why, that my friends disapproved of him. We took three or four long walks, during which I listened, tongue-tied, without a coherent idea in my head. At last, one February evening, the affair came to a head. I remember, exactly, the words K. used, because they were doubly revealing—of him, his comparative clearsight (compared with my immaturity and emotional imbecility), his lack of shyness, and of my dumb self-surrender.

'Poor Miss Jim,' he said calmly, 'you love me, don't you?'

'Why poor?' I stammered.

'Because I shall make you unhappy.'

Did he know what he was saying?

I was sensually and imaginatively obsessed, and as imprudent as possible. Several times, during the short nights of May and June, we walked far into the country, then closer to Leeds than it is now, and did not get back until after sunrise.

Some time during this year a friend who discovered my ignorance felt it a duty to instruct me, and did, astonished that she had to explain the most elementary facts of sexual life. The only effect on me of enlightenment was like the effect on a mill-race of stirring up the mud at the bottom. There was never anything sober or untroubled about the affair, I was often unhappy, without understanding why a slight argument turned almost at once into a quarrel, followed by fevered reconciliation, in which everything that had driven me near despair was resolved—or forced underground.

At the end of my second year K. went down, with a not very good degree. He went, I believe, to Cambridge, to take a diploma of some sort—in education?

Without him, I wasted less time. And—naturally without telling him, or feeling less involved with him, and without reflecting for a moment on the shocking ambiguity and bad faith it showed—I fell in love with yet another

Mirfield student. Together we trudged about the slums beyond the filthy River Aire during a strike which had been going on for several weeks or months—what strike was it?—carrying tins of cocoa and other oddments given us by the Charity Organisation Society. We walked about all day, and took back written reports to the Society: 'Room bare, all movable objects pawned, wife pregnant, needs bed linen, food.' What in decency's name can these half-starved women, sometimes lying in bed within a few hours of their time, have felt about the awkward smiling girl and the young man with a charmingly ascetic face who came in, set down the tin of cocoa and asked politely,

'Do you need anything at once? Have you pawned all you can pawn? Will this be your first, second, seventh child?'

As with the earlier infatuation, this broke down on the young man's unshakable probity and purpose.

I had forgotten—until this moment—another theological student, with an improbably Russian name, and money of his own, who proposed to me in form, five times, in my first year, embarrassing me: he was kind and good, and, to me, unattractive and a terrible bore.

I don't remember that I felt any disappointment that my nearest rival in the English Honours school, a man, was given a lectureship and I fobbed off with the John Rutson research scholarship, to be held at London University. My expectations had been too indefinite. Nor did I realize that this was a clear snub to my hopes, vague as these were, of an academic career.

No doubt the authorities knew me better than I knew myself. To these sensible experienced men I must have seemed thoroughly unstable, quite unfitted to be a don. But to this day I regret that life. Under direction, I should probably have grown to it. And certainly I should have been a great deal happier than as a novelist, an occupation for which I am even less suited.

When I left Leeds I was in debt to a bookseller. The temptation to buy books I could not afford was too strong. It took me four years to pay off a debt of less than fifteen pounds.

## CHAPTER 11

WHEN I COME TO STAND, as they say—used to say—before my Maker, the judgement on me will run: She did not love enough.

Every unforgivable act in my life may be explained by that flaw. Explained, not forgiven. For such a fault, no forgiveness.

During the years when I was living my self-absorbed and undisciplined life at the university, my young brother was stumbling about, trying to find his way. The 'black bairn' had grown into a clumsy silent boy, who disliked school, never opened a book for pleasure, spent all his time out of the house, where he was often sullen and disobedient, and never told anyone what he had been doing. Pressed, he might say, 'I went with some boys for a walk.' On one of these walks he let the others lower him over the cliff on a thin frayed rope they had, to take a gull's eggs.

I knew very little about him, and thought less. What room was there in my life for an inarticulate awkward boy, five years younger than I was?

Immediately after his fourteenth birthday he refused to go back to school, it was a waste of time—he wanted to get away. Encouraged to it by my father, he went off in another Prince Line ship as an apprentice, since there was no other way.

My mother tried to dissuade him, she knew too well what sort of life a boy had on tramp steamers. She knew, too, that he would dislike it for other reasons than its hardness: for all his fourteen years, he was still a child, with a child's blurred face and unmanageable body: the mind behind his clouded eyes was groping for something he would never find in that life. Utterly silent as he was about himself and his wishes, not able to explain anything, she knew that much about him.

'Your father,' she told me, with barely controlled savagery, 'maunders about his own misery at that age. Then why, I said, condemn your son to the same life? and he said: A hard life never did anyone any harm. Very well, let us hear a little less about yours, I told him.'

The first letter from my brother, and every succeeding letter, from New York, Santos, Rio, Victoria, Montevideo, Trinidad, gave away his disillusion and cruel loneliness. In his sprawling hand, he—who hated writing—wrote long letters, telling her all the details of his life, at sea and in port, and asking for news. 'Please write often and long, it is letters like yours which keep one going.'

She saw him distinctly, sitting on the edge of his berth, his hand moving slowly over the sheets of thin foreign paper, the clouded eyes downcast. To sit writing and writing his little news, he must, she knew, be lonely past all.

At last, after five months, he wrote at the end of a letter about Rio and Bahia: 'If it is possible I want to get something on shore, I know what you must feel about having me back after the life I led you before, but I think I have learned a few of the lessons of life, here where we all have to help one another and everyone is civil. If you think it better for me to stop out here I will, but I do want to come back and see if I can't do better. Now that we are only eight days' run from New York, I am wondering what it is going to be for me, for I do not want to make another trip down here if I can help it, so when you write will you tell me what you think about it. I miss you and everyone more every day now, and I would be glad to do anything. Your loving son, Harold.'

She felt an atrocious dismay. Never since he was born had he asked her, or anyone, for help. She could not afford to bring him home half way through the voyage, but she wrote promising to do what she could when he came back, and wrote at the same time to her husband, asking him not to discourage the boy. After another two months she had a letter ten pages long. Embedded in a laboriously detailed account of the museum in Buenos Aires, she read sentences that, when she repeated them to me, choked her.

'I had a letter from Father yesterday from Santos. He said I would be no good on shore, and that whatever I went to I would not stick at it. And that I would have no chance for anything except for an engineer or motor driver. Taking all together he made it clear that now I am at sea I have got to stop there. Perhaps he is right, there is very little in England for me, and nothing at all in Whitby. I have been wondering if it would not be better if it is possible to get work out of England somewhere, in the Colonies or the States. But I will think for a couple of months yet, for I find that the longer you let anything lie, the better are one's views on it...'

I saw her despair—not my brother's. In the blindness of my heart I did not see him. It never entered my head that he was as restless and ambitious as I was, and as profoundly uncertain. And even more desperate *not to be seen into*.

The ship was trading between New York and South American ports, and this, his first voyage, lasted nineteen months. His hands, when he came home, sickened my mother, they were shapeless lumps of scarred raw flesh.

She had no plan ready for him. At this time George Gallilee was still alive, a half-paralysed invalid. It was some years before her share of his money, severely diminished by the scoundrel Lloyd George, and by neglected investments, came to her. She had no money to train my brother for another career. It was useless—worse than useless—to ask his father for help. And, too, she was ill at the time, in pain.

Knowing that she had failed him—since he must have come home hoping against hope that he need not go back—she let his father arrange for him to be transferred to his own ship.

Her misgivings were cruelly justified. He came back again in October 1913, a week ahead of his father, thinner, and more silent than ever. During his first meal he dropped and broke a cup. She exclaimed, and he horrified her by bursting into a dreadful strangled sobbing. It went on and on. Since he had wept with rage as an infant she had never known him cry. In his sleep that night, he shouted horribly. Next day she called the doctor, a hard unsentimental Scotsman she liked and trusted. After looking my brother over, he told her that no boy of sixteen ought to be in so violently nervous a state. 'He has had a bad time, or a bad shock.'

'Did you,' she asked him that evening, 'have a hard time on this trip?'

He avoided her eyes. 'No. But I don't want to go back. Or perhaps I could get another ship.'

'You didn't like your father's ship?'

'No, not much,' he mumbled.

'Why not?'

'Well, I don't know. I didn't care for it.' He turned red. 'I'm not lazy, I'll work, I'm not a good-for-nothing, there must be *something* I can do.'

She got nothing more out of him, at any time.

I do not remember whether, even after this, I took any serious interest in his difficulties. I was not then at home, I did not see him, and my life which that autumn had run into a blind alley divorced me from my family as casually as if I had been living on the moon. What I remember is my mother's voice, cold and implacable, when, three months later, she told me about it.

'I don't know what his father did. But this finishes him with me.'

The words fell like a guillotine on the whole of her married life, its memories, and what gentleness, a mere sediment, remained.

## CHAPTER 12

I WAS TO HOLD my research scholarship at University College, working under W. P. Ker.

It did not surprise me at the time, but it has surprised me a little since that my mother raised no objection to my sharing rooms with the two Harlands, who were at King's College in the Strand. The elder, Sydney, my closest friend at that time, had taken his degree in geology, but he was still in London, and it was he who invited me to join them.

Nothing better could have happened to me, but why—in September 1912—did my conventionally-bred mother see nothing out of the way in letting me live in rooms with two young men she barely knew?

There were in fact three: the third was another Yorkshireman whom the Harlands had met at King's, Archie White.

The London I lived in as a poor scholar is as unlikely to rise again as Nineveh. Where is Appenrodt's Lager Hall, where is Maxim's? Where is the sixpenny gallery in the Coliseum from which we watched Reinhardt's *Scheherazade*, Polaire of the fifteen-inch waist, Florrie Forde, the ageing Bernhardt, the ageless Marie Lloyd? And those ladies with magnificent poops, navigating, with a wake of powerful scent, a far less crowded Leicester Square and Piccadilly? Where is the Vienna Café? At Maxim's, near the corner of Gerrard Street, the five-course dinner cost half-a-crown, at the smaller Boulogne next door, one and sixpence. The Vienna Café, in New Oxford Street, with its red plush benches and incomparable coffee and brioches, pleasures of a poor intellectual, has been replaced by a bank. A bank, God help us all!

I shall be accused of telling nostalgic lies if I write that those were the last years in which London was a town where young men could live happily on a pittance. Why let that abash me? It is true. To enjoy all we four *poure scolers* enjoyed easily, a young man today will need the income of, say, a bank manager.

Even at that he is forced to put up with streets so overcrowded that to walk in them he will have to overcome the nausea induced by the nearness of so many swarming bodies, eat worse meals at higher cost, and endure the intolerable boredom of having to *organize* his amusements, since every café, theatre, and even the Reading Room of the British Museum, is fuller of people than it will hold decently.

Under the simplicity and gaiety of this London lay an even simpler town, known to me as a child. My mother and I left my father's ship—lying where? Tidal Basin?—in the early morning, and went by train to Fenchurch Street and from there (Mark Lane Station) by underground to Hyde Park, Bond Street, Piccadilly, Regent Street, and all the squares and smaller more exquisite streets between, admiring the window-boxes and striped awnings of private houses—the eighteenth century had not yet been demolished—and shop windows filled with hats, gloves, jewels, fur coats, antiques. My pretence of interest in these was word-perfect.

The only thing my two Londons had in common was the endless walking I did in both. We four lodged in a small house in Herne Hill, and after breakfast walked over Denmark Hill to Camberwell, to get a bus: on days when it was a question of riding or eating, we walked the whole way—along the respectable squalor of Walworth Road, past the Elephant and Castle (now vanished) and over Waterloo Bridge to the Strand. Walking long distances, even on pavements, was no hardship to our countrybred muscles: on a few fine Sundays we spent the entire day walking about Epping Forest.

Half consciously, we remained a foreign body in this swarming city which did not know we existed. Did not recognize an occupying force sauntering in its streets, eating in the cheapest restaurants, waiting outside a music-hall for the early doors, and talking, my God, talking. A passer-by would sometimes look twice at Oswald Harland, but that was his hair, a flaming bush of the brightest possible red. His, too, was the most intractable tongue, he never gave way in an argument, and argued for the love of it and because any accepted belief, and most human beings, presented themselves to him at an angle.

His brother, Sydney, was intractable in another way. He was black-haired, with the face of a young smiling gargoyle: his mind was an active volcano of ideas and speculations—the label fixed to him at the time: *Brilliant but probably unsound*, turned out to be a lie when, after stumbling round for a year or two, he found his way into genetics. His brilliance had the soundest of bases. Emotionally, he was as irresponsible as I was, with fewer hesitations. He landed himself easily in impossible situations, and encouraged his brother, and me, to help him out of them. We did it with a comforting sense of our own greater steadiness and mother-wit.

Where I was concerned, this was an illusion.

The only one of us who was self-possessed, knew what he wanted, and had coolness, tenacity, and judgement to match his self-possession, was Archie. He had a passion for military history and spent more time on it than he should. Even that, as it turned out, had been the right thing. He kept his ambitions to himself: his tongue—he had his share and more of the jeering northern irony—was less loosely-hung than ours. Joining the O.T.C. struck us as an eccentricity, but to be eccentric was, after all, normal behaviour, and when he was given his first stripe I sewed it on for him, taking immense pains.

He had stronger nerves than the rest of us. Some time in December, a terrified landlady woke us in the dead of night, her husband, an old man, had had an internal haemorrhage: while Oswald and I, sickened by it and by the wretched man's groans, cowered on the staircase, Archie took charge calmly, quietening the poor woman and looking after the dying man until doctor and ambulance arrived.

A rehearsal...

Half way through my first term, I abandoned University College. I had taken a dislike to it, almost at sight: to my conceited ignorance it seemed to be a factory for turning out pedants; the two or three lectures I attended bored me, and after a few weeks, except for two visits to Professor Ker, I did not go near it. Instead, I registered myself at King's, which at that time had less than a dozen women students, and followed one of Israel Gollancz's brilliant and fantastic courses. It was no use to me, but then nothing I did at this time was useful, or even sensible.

When I allow myself the folly of thinking about it, a door opens on timeless limitless space, filled like an ash-can with bright scraps of sound, worthless songs, the noise of an orchestra tuning up, and with bat-flittering images, the Thames seen from Waterloo Bridge in early sunlight, a street now torn down or unrecognizable, vanished cafés, the first Cézannes shown in London, a fire blazing in the grate of shabby lodgings, in front of it the four of us eating—long after midnight—toasted muffins, split and filled with sardines: once, I think only once, we added a one-and-ninepenny bottle of Australian burgundy.

And talk—my God, how we talked. Generations since ours have talked as feverishly, but not with our confidence, or our illusions. The difference between them and us is that we *knew* we were at the frontier of a new age... of social justice, freedom, perpetual peace. *Because* of us—and the millions like us we felt on our heels—the world was facing towards it; there was really nothing much we need do, except think, talk, exist.

We were socialists of a sort—we disliked and distrusted Fabians, partly because those we saw and heard were middle-aged, even elderly, an order of brahmins. And, worse, smelled of a bureaucracy. We carried our Yorkshire distaste for officials into all our beliefs; a whiff of dogma drove us from the room.

I remain obstinately sure that if, thousand by thousand, our lot had not been slaughtered like animals and pushed quickly into the earth, there would now be fewer bureaucratic noses asking to be tweaked. Or more fingers able to tweak them.

About a year ago a young man wrote asking me to tell him when I had ceased to be a Communist, and why. Ceasing to be a Communist is, or was, a great opportunity, and since I was never one, I missed it. I told him so. He protested acidly at what he took to be a lie, and quoted a sentence from an essay written at a time when all but the most prudent or most astute English writers were violently anti-Fascist.

I may have told him about the Eikonoklasts.

A dozen or so young men, calling themselves by this name, met once a week in the men's common room at King's, to talk. By Sydney's insistence, I was allowed to join them. (I have since wondered what would have happened if the authorities had found me there.) I rarely opened my mouth. I had—have—no quickness in argument, unless I am angry. A serious social misfortune.

The Eikonoklasts—the spelling was an affectation, but a harmless one—were sceptics, unavowed anarchists, self-dedicated to the unmasking of hypocrites, politicians, clericals, reactionaries, bigots, and dogmatists of all ages and conditions. How the devil, after this fighting-cock start, could I have chosen to become a Communist and stomach the most rigid dogma the world has ever known? Anything, but not the dogma.

We admired certain people—Orage, H. G. Wells, Freud, the writer of *La Révolte des Anges*—so sincerely and blindly that we adopted their enemies. One of the very few moments when I found my tongue was to add an insolent phrase—well-received—to the jeering letter we were writing to the founders of the *New Statesman*: we had our philosophical reasons for rejecting this paper, but our real one was that Bernard Shaw, whom we suspected of having the mind of a puritanical rate-payer and no passions, supported it.

After these meetings, the four of us walked home across the bridge and through half-lit streets foreshortened by cold and darkness, still talking, I a little less tongue-tied now that we were again a foreign body with four heads. Four northern voices in a South London street, sounding, at this distance, like a single broken phrase of music, caught as it dies away. Now, as I write, after so many years, so many deaths, the echo brings tears to my eyes.

Our freedom intoxicated us; there was nothing we should not be able to attempt, no road not open to us, no barriers in the world that we children of farmers and seamen were going to walk about in as equals. Our certainty, our optimism, our illusions, are what mark our difference from every other generation which has talked its tongue off its roots since. No generation has ever been so naturally idealistic. Nor, perhaps, so happy, since of all the illusions on which young men get drunk the illusion of a future, a road running towards infinity, breeds happiness more surely and quickly than even a successful love-affair.

## CHAPTER 13

S OME TIME DURING THESE MONTHS I read (where?) an appeal
for someone to give free tutoring to the students of a newly-founded
Working Women's College in the Victorian limbo of Earl's Court. I went
there, and found a large house in one of those solid yellow terraces built
in not the worst manner in the world, its rooms almost bare of furniture,
unheated, and with two or perhaps three young women living on heaven
knows what scratched-up food, almost without books, and without other
help in their random studies.

The founder of this generous, courageously hopeful, preposterous and
foredoomed scheme for picking young women out of mills and factories
and giving them two or three months' education was Mrs Bridges Adams,
then elderly. She lived as Spartan a life as her protégées, in a room of which
I recall only the bed and a chest of drawers with a spirit lamp on which she
made tea for herself, and fried kippers: I doubt if she troubled to eat meals.

I went there on and off for a year. She told me a great many stories of her
young married life in a small community of other young well-bred social
revolutionaries living near London—I forget where, but the husbands travelled to London to work (not as conspirators) and the wives met the evening
train, hoping to hear that the revolution they expected daily had broken out.

In 1913, too, I had a moment of triumph. Orage's *New Age* was our
Bible, the source of half our ideas—the less anarchical half. On the 20th
of March it published an essay by an unknown writer, Storm Jameson, on
George Bernard Shaw, a joyous exercise in iconoclasm. After saying that his
work contained only one living character (Andrew Undershaft), it ended:

'In Mr Shaw's work there are no others—from the annoying Candida to
the futile Tanner they belong to an age that is passing and will pass with it.
To create them their author has spent much wit and little humour, much
mockery and little irony; much intellectual sky-rocketing and little truth;
no beauty, and hardly anything of inspiration.'

The other two—Sydney was by now in the West Indies—took my elated
jump-ahead well and coolly. They neither discouraged nor took me seriously.

On the other hand, they saw to it, kindly, that I did not get above myself—as
we say in Yorkshire. Was I in any danger? I doubt it. Even in those days I did
not expect to succeed without being whipped for it.

The impudent essay was an extract from the thesis I was writing. Before I
left Leeds, with my research scholarship in my pocket, I had agreed to write
on pantheism in French and German literature. Even today I cannot feel
that the subject was anything but academic flummery. But it was what had
been laid down for me, and I made another of my light-headed blunders in
not submitting.

I cannot remember when I decided that it was quite impossible to waste
time and energy on a boring exercise, but certainly before my first interview
with W. P. Ker. I told him frankly how little the official subject appealed to me.

'Then what would you like to work on?' he asked.

I had my answer ready. 'Modern European drama.'

He smiled and said, gently and drily, 'I hardly think you're old enough—or
wicked enough.'

He told me to go to the British Museum Reading Room and look at what
I should have to read: having done that, to prepare him a synopsis. Much
later I realized that he had been certain I should hand him in something so
confused that he would be able to turn me painlessly back to the safe path.

Little he knew me. If there is one thing I do easily it is to lay out the
ground-plan of a piece of work; I do it with method, enthusiasm, and the
purest enjoyment.

I worked for two months, and produced a synopsis, ten thousand
words long, of a critical study of European drama from before Ibsen to the
latest—latest in 1913—Russian (German, Spanish, French, English, Belgian,
Scandinavian, Italian) dramatist, lined up by nations, influences, heaven
knows what. It formed an exact chart of all I did not know about the subject.

I left this document with Professor Ker at the end of December, and
waited confidently.

He sent for me as soon as the term opened again in January, and with
the same dry kindness said,

'It's better than I expected. And now don't you think you had better
let your professors in Leeds know what you've been doing? You've rather
neglected pantheism, haven't you?'

With no lessening of my green confidence I wrote to Leeds—and was astonished by the rebuke I had so thoroughly deserved.

Since it was too late for me to start again, they let me go on. I daresay, though I heard nothing about it, that Professor Ker also wrote to them. I appreciated neither their forbearance nor my own blindness and levity. I had not the wit to see that I had simply confirmed them in their opinion of my irresponsibility and unfitness for any position.

I worked in feverish bouts followed by a day or days wasted in running about London.

Wasted? Nonsense. The waste time in a life is the days, weeks, years, spent living against the grain—all the social and domestic life, the thousand masks, the wearisome copybook filled even to the margins with unnecessary words. Dust in the mouth.

The gaiety and insouciance with which I wrote that thesis is unimaginable. Since I could read easily only French and English, the bulk of the dramatists who came within reach of my claws were translations, and all or almost all the dramatists I found worth praise were foreign—Ibsen, Strindberg, Hofmannsthal, Chekhov—I have not the courage to re-read the book and make a list. For the rest, I mocked, censured, rebuked, tore down, with reckless delight, Shaw, Yeats, Masefield, I forget who else.

It was the first—and last—time my natural violence and jeering northern malice was given its head. The shyness that paralysed me in the common room at King's disappeared as soon as I was seated in the Reading Room with a pen and a sheet of foolscap. I had no sense that my victims were flesh and blood.

Will anyone believe that I was imbecile enough to imagine I should be praised for my severity?

Some time before the end of that year, 1912, Sydney Harland made one of his sudden, apparently eccentric decisions, and applied for a post as schoolmaster in Santa Cruz. We went down to the docks to see him off on a Danish ship, and came home feeling that we had had a limb amputated. Morally speaking, we had. With him went part of the warmth and vivacity of our lives; none of the rest of us had his trick of conjuring exciting ideas out of the air, or his mercurial brilliance. Without him we were more sober, but not—or I was not—wiser.

We left Herne Hill, and in January went to live in Shepherd's Bush, in rooms I found for us. They were as freakish as Herne Hill had been dull and orderly. At first slightly dismayed by being expected to share the dusty sitting-room with ten canaries and two Spaniards, the others quickly took to them. The canaries belonged to our landlady, a thin bright-eyed, falsely yellow-haired and tolerant woman who had been a dresser in Sir Herbert Tree's company. It was for her sake I took the rooms. As soon as I set eyes on her, I knew we belonged to the same vagabond race.

As well as the canaries, she kept three dogs and an elderly wrinkled gnome of a German husband, who had once played the cat in *Dick Whittington*, and now mended clocks. (Later, during the war, he was interned: it broke his gentle heart and killed him.)

The Spaniards were an odd pair. They were travelling the world collecting the signatures of famous people; they had several hundreds already and expected to sell the haul for a vast sum. Now middle-aged, they began this strange life as young men. One of them was ill; he lay shivering, coughing, grumbling, on the shabby couch, nursed by the other with patient delicacy and gentleness. What became of their book of signatures? It may exist somewhere, a useless curiosity, though the two pairs of brown-fingered thin hands which held it jealously, turning the pages for our indifferent eyes, must long have vanished.

From that house, when our restless energy drove us out at night, Oswald and I could walk across Ealing Common as far as Kew without feeling that we were in a city: it was partly an illusion of the darkness, but partly, too, that the country had not yet been defeated in London; there were still rearguards holding out, where now all is lost.

I have forgotten too many details of my life then, but not the poverty and happiness.

No life I have led since has come so close to satisfying me—a life, that is, without possessions, above all without responsibility, to things or people. I was offended, sometimes, by the extreme shabbiness of my surroundings— they were pleasant compared with the house and street to which I sank a little later—but these moments of queasiness only roughened the surface. A little more money would have cured them.

I was completely unconscious, then, of the benefit to my mental and spiritual condition of living with intelligent boys rather than with girls or women. Even when they ignored some display of female silliness—or laughed only among themselves—the sense of their disapproval reached me sooner or later. Within reason, they treated me like a younger brother, with as much unconcern and good-temper. I don't recall being damned in any stronger words than: Don't be a calf. It was enough. Later in life I found attentions paid to me surprising and boring. I did not—do not—expect to have allowances made for me.

## 14th of January, 1963

The disadvantages of having been a member of Class 5b, and an Eikonoklast, were brought home to me today. I found myself the only person in the room not in ecstasies over a copy of *The Private Eye*. It was the second I had tried to read, almost sobbing with boredom, hardly able to believe that jokes so old and puerile were meant to be read by adults. All these irreverences, the rude nose-thumbing at middle-class idols, at religion, royalty, all manner of *idées reçues*, were going the rounds in 5b. We had not learned to talk of the Establishment, but that did not prevent us from being side-splittingly funny about the thing itself. I am stupefied, not by the titter of Kensington-bred ladies over a lewd joke… after all, poor dears… but by my worldly intelligent friends. How can they find these aged witticisms startling? Do they? Or are they afraid of seeming to have pieties? Or did they all, all, lead such sheltered lives in their youth that these jeers and mild blasphemies shake them?

I felt out of things, but took heart: it is not my fault, it is the fault of 5b and the Eikonoklasts.

## CHAPTER 14

I HAVE FORGOTTEN what K. was doing during this time: he came only once or twice to see us in London. The boys did not like him. They were less than frank with me about the reasons for their dislike, but I knew them too well to miss seeing it: I looked the other way and hoped that K. would not notice that he was being judged. I am sure he did not.

His visits had an unpleasantly disturbing effect on me. For a time, when he was with us, I saw through his eyes that we were an uncouth lot, slovenly provincials. I wished we had more elegance, a nicer knowledge of the world. When he left, my discontent and disquietude went with him.

I was still helplessly in love, but something, some submerged current, had begun to set against him in my mind, at a great depth. I knew, vaguely, that it was there. Given time, I should have become critical of him, and in the end my obsession would have died and I should have been free...

At some time in 1913 my mother read letters K. had written, which I had left in my room at home. Their language made her feel that the sooner I was married the better for my soul. She came up to London determined to save me.

So there I was, back where I had so often stood, cowered, as a child crushed by guilt for a half-realized crime. I was neither hard enough, nor adroit or single-minded enough, to withstand the force of her anger and grief. I had nothing to set against it except my deep inarticulate reluctance to be married, my profound instinct to keep my freedom. She swept this contemptuously aside. The strange thing—no, not strange; given her age and breeding, perfectly natural—was that she knew she was saving my moral being at the expense of my future, that future in which she had sunk so many of her own hopes: its collapse into a mere marriage was the cruellest of disappointments to her. But she knew she was right.

She is not to be blamed. I was responsible; the choice, after all, was mine. Letting others trap me, I trapped myself.

I had made blunders before this, plenty. This was the first crippling choice. All that can be said is that it harmed no one but myself—and K.

My memory for the details I ought in decency or politeness to remember is shockingly vague. I remember the names of Whitby shopkeepers long since dead, and the exact number of steps from the gate to the front door of a house left behind more than fifty years ago, and the exquisite taste of crusts soaked in warm tea, and the turnings to be taken from the Hotel de France in Nevers to reach the baker selling the finest bread, but I do not know whether K. and I began living together at once after our marriage, or if I went back for a time to my room above the sitting-room with the canaries and the ailing Spaniard.

I believe I did. But certainly in the late summer I was living with him in another room in Shepherd's Bush, a dreadfully dingy shabby room in a street of sordid little houses (in 1941 bombed to a pile of rubble) on the north side of the green—Caxton Street.

I cannot remember what we had to live on, unless my scholarship money still had a month or so to run. K. must have had a little money—from his parents? We paid six shillings each *a week* for bed and breakfast in this squalid room. I was still working on my thesis, of which I had written about two-thirds.

Every morning I walked from Shepherd's Bush to the British Museum, starting at half-past eight. When, in 1956, I went to live in a flat looking across Hyde Park near Marble Arch (before this edge of the park was barbarously and uselessly mutilated), I tried to catch sight of a carelessly-dressed girl walking past lightly, carrying an attaché case and a paper bag holding a half-pound of plums. I bought the plums in Shepherd's Bush to eat in the cloakroom of the Museum at midday. And there were little cafés in the streets near the Museum where, if I am not dreaming, in those innocent unorganized days the food, simple, tasted of itself.

For the evening meal there was a coffee stall at the Wood Lane end of Shepherd's Bush Green, where the man in charge was obliging enough to make me a ham sandwich without the pungent mustard he used. For the rest, I lived largely on energy and illusions of future greatness.

I was happier and unhappier here than seems possible—and not bored. London made my happiness. At that time I had a passion for it which neither poverty nor despair could dim.

For the life of me I cannot remember what K. did during the day. A little journalism? My egotistical absorption in my thesis made anything he may have been doing of little interest. It did not enter my head to rely on his earning anything.

The sum of two egoisms, two green vanities, does not add up to a placid life. Used to the boys' amiable wrangling, I was disconcerted by K.'s readiness to take offence. The discomforts of our way of living—neither of us noticed them except as one notices bad weather—cannot have helped. The young rarely have any mercy on each other—not that we thought of ourselves as young. We were two egoisms face to face, and incapable of seeing through each other's greeds, self-absorption, illusions, to the naked inner creature in need of kindness. I must too often have been madly stubborn. We quarrelled over trifles, bitter quarrels in which neither wanted to give way: I knew I was right and waited in anguish for K. to recognize it: then, only then, I could admit to being in the wrong.

One night, in despair and a reckless wish to be anywhere but where I was, I swallowed all the phenacetin tablets in a bottle I had just bought—in those days I knew only two remedies for any ailment, the ones my mother used: phenacetin and Eno's. I expected so much phenacetin to kill me. Feeling cold, I became afraid and told K. what I had done: to my grieved astonishment he flew into a sour rage, threatened to fetch the police to me, and did fetch a doctor who was anything but kind.

I begged him not to tell anyone what I had done. But he told the boys, who listened to him without comment.

At some time during this poverty-stricken autumn and winter his parents made him an offer. They were religious people, American Quakers, and before the marriage had made one or two gestures of lukewarm friendliness towards me: they could not like me, I was young, penniless, and not of their religion, but I think they saw my faults too clearly to notice that I had a virtue or two—among these, an eager goodwill; I responded to kindness like a puppy, licking hands, wagging my tail. I forget what they offered K., except that it was further training of some sort, I think at Cambridge. The condition, of course, was that he must give up the wretched wastrel life he was living with me.

I can sympathize, now, with their anxiety about their son, an only child. At the time, I rejected coldly the part of the offer which concerned me: they were willing, they said, to pay for a room in a women's hostel until I had finished my thesis. After that... probably they did not look further. The important thing was to save K. and separate him from a wife who was no good to him. Given enough rope, they may have reflected, I should hang myself. (Running off with an Italian organ-grinder was one of the things my father-in-law suggested I was likely to do at any minute.)

Did they expect me to oppose their plan? Far from that, I urged K. to seize the offer. When he had gone my only feeling was of excitement. I was alone, the world open to me. Later that afternoon, I went into a small café near Caxton Street (it is still there), to drink coffee and think what I had better do at once. Glancing up, I saw K. striding past, towards our lodgings. My heart leaped with surprise and disappointment.

Chance had brought him back. When he reached his parents' house in North London, they were both out, and he had time to regret leaving me. He left the house again at once, before they returned. As his mother wrote to him, 'If I had been at home, you would never have gone away.'

What a ridiculous accident, lighter than a touch on the shoulder, to alter the whole of my life.

Later that autumn my mother was in London with the ship, and came to see where I was living. She gave few signs that the place horrified her. Scarcely able to speak, she sat in the window, looking out on the sordid little street with its choked gutters and flea-bitten cats, her back turned to the room overfilled by the brass-knobbed bed, a chest of drawers, and the minute table covered by my books and papers, the whole an indeterminate rusty brown, the colour of age and grime. This room was scrupulously tidy—I hate disorder: any room I live in is properly ship-shape—but neatness did not hide its ingrained squalor and the musty smell of poverty. By now I was so used to it, and to washing from head to foot night and morning in a bowl of cold water (I have never dared ask a survivor of Ravensbrück what, apart from torture and hunger, was worse than not being able to keep a clean body), that I did not guess what she felt. I brought out the two cups and the spirit lamp, and made tea for her, and she drank it, trying to smile.

Years later, with a shudder of disgust, she told me, 'It made my heart ache to see you in that horrible room. I thought you were done for.'

At the end of the year I fell ill in this room: there was nothing wrong with me except semi-starvation and a touch of fever, but I did not recover and at last thought of going home for a time. My thesis was all but finished; there was only the summing-up to write, and the labour of copying it on the secondhand typewriter I had bought with my first money from the university.

I hung on until the first days of January. I had no money at all now, and arrived in Whitby with a single ha'penny in my purse.

K., too, went home. He had begun applying for a post as schoolmaster, in London.

## CHAPTER 15

'THANK GOODNESS YOU'VE COME,' my mother said, 'I'm going to be lonely.'

My middle sister was away, and a few days after I came my brother went off to Manchester, to a place calling itself the Northern School of Wireless: he knew nothing about it, but wireless was a new thing, and the fees at the school so low that my mother could afford it. She did not ask him how he was lodged: she expected all her children (except the youngest) to be able to survive anything.

The dominating person in the family now was this youngest, my sister Dorothy. She was eight, a very beautiful little creature, quick and graceful, warm-natured except in cross-grained moods when she was furiously intractable. My mother pretended to believe that these devilish moods could be traced back to a nearly fatal illness when she was six months old: an all but lifeless little skeleton, she had been given a glass of fresh blood, pressed from hunks of raw beef, every day for a long time. They gave it to her in a green Venetian glass and she drank it greedily, smacking colourless little lips over it.

In the middle of February my brother telegraphed: Have joined the Flying Corps, letter follows.

The letter next morning was almost as laconic: the Royal Flying Corps wanted wireless operators, he was eligible, it was a splendid chance, better than he had hoped for. But, since he was only seventeen, my mother must give her permission. Terribly agitated, she sent me to Manchester to stop him.

The imposingly-named Northern School turned out to be two small attics at the top of a shabby building. The thin young man who was running it talked with smiling enthusiasm about the Flying Corps: it was the coming thing, there were six squadrons, and there might soon be thirty, even more. 'It's a great piece of luck for your brother that they want men—by going in now he'll do very well for himself.'

Men! I thought, looking at my brother's short red childish hands. He was clenching them, and said, 'It's the only way I can get into the Flying Corps. If I had money I could go in for being a pilot, but——'

'What will you be?' I asked him.

'A Second-class Air Mechanic,' he said, scowling. 'But it's my chance. I *must* take it. You can tell her that.'

I don't think that, even now, I had the grace to take his ambitions wholly seriously. He was awkward and unformed—that I was both myself did not occur to me. Only his eyes, with their steady clouded stare, reflected an anxiety I recognized. The three of us in that shabby room were all young, seventeen, twenty-two, twenty-six, and at this distance from her my mother's fears seemed those of an old woman who knew nothing about the world.

I left promising to make her agree, and, without much trouble—after all, what else had she to offer him?—did.

Before this, I had missed a chance of my own. When I was in London, I had written two pieces of dramatic criticism for *The Egoist*, and met its founder, Harriet Shaw Weaver, and that remarkable woman, her friend Dora Marsden. I was not much given to respect in my first youth, but I knew enough to revere pure intellect when I met it. A small delicately-boned woman, Dora Marsden had a subtle and powerful mind and a passion for philosophy, I believe her only passion. She treated me with the most unmerited kindness and friendliness, and gave me the manuscript of her first book. I understood it only in the cloudiest way.

Soon after I went home, Harriet Shaw Weaver wrote offering me work on *The Egoist*, at a weekly salary of two pounds. My excitement when I was reading her letter is indescribable. I had not the wit to realize that she was inventing the job with the sole idea of giving a young provincial nobody the chance to make something of herself. The prospect of setting foot in a world of brilliantly clever and advanced men and women, who would, I thought, cure my worldly timidity and ignorance, made me wildly happy. I was a long way from knowing just how green and uncouth I was, and had no doubt at all that I should make my literary fortune.

It no more came into my head to refuse the offer than to cut my throat, and I wrote to Miss Weaver that I would come to London at once.

When I told my mother, she looked at me from eyes so remotely fixed that they appeared colourless. 'I thought you would be here at least until April,' she said; 'I shall be very sad and sorry without you.'

'But I should have had to go some time.'

'The money is very little.'

'It is a start. And I shall be in London.'

She said nothing more for the moment. I saw her pressing her lips together over her bitter sense of my eagerness to get away. A too familiar anxiety seized me, but I hardened my heart. Later in the day she said,

'This time next week you will be gone. I was planning a day in Scarborough, but not alone.'

'I shall be coming back.'

'That doesn't comfort me now, my little dear. It's dull here by myself. And no kind girl to go the round with me. It's not,' she added, smiling, 'as if you had a husband to go to. When K. has found work and sends for you, it will be a different affair altogether.'

The round was a walk we had taken so many times from this house that its rough flagstones and grass are sunk in my other life, the one in which I am innocent.

I might still have held out if she had not told me calmly, 'My body is not right, you know. Since Dorothy was born. It can't be put right.'

I did not know what she meant, but I had already noticed, and avoided thinking about it, that she had become, suddenly, older and heavier.

My heart dropped under its weight of regret, pity, despair. 'I needn't go,' I said, 'I can refuse.'

Her face changed slightly. 'I thought you had written accepting.'

'Yes. But I can write again.'

I wrote the next day, a clumsy letter of apology and refusal.

Cruelly disappointed as I was, I yet did not realize clearly what I had done. *Don't be to tell twice* is a sentence I heard so many times in my childhood that it ceased to make sense. Before experience teaches me anything, the lesson has had to be repeated not twice but a score of times. My whole life, if I had seized this offer, would have been different. When she got my second letter Miss Weaver passed the offer to another young woman, Rebecca West, who accepted it. Believe me, who should know, *The Egoist* and the world of letters got a better bargain.

At twenty-two, one expects to meet a chance round every corner. There was still my great work on European drama, from which I expected at least a living, if not fame. I worked on it, with no interruptions except my mother's demands on me, until April, then sent it, with a formal apology for the time it had taken me, to Leeds.

I had better finish with this at once. It was approved by the university, and I rewarded with the degree of Master of Arts. By this time I had other things on my mind, and we were in the middle of a war. I put my carbon copy away, and did not look at it again until the end of the war: then I added to it briefly, leaving my three-year-old son with my mother for a fortnight while I read feverishly in the British Museum, and sent it to a publisher. I did not confide to him—or anyone—what my hopes were.

I doubt whether Messrs Collins were less startled than I by what happened. The dramatic critics took me seriously and very hard. In a majestic column in *The Times*, A. B. Walkley spoke of 'a female Nietzsche': at even greater length, under the title 'The Young Person in Print', Mr St John Ervine dismembered the book with Ulster savagery; for good measure he said I ought to be spanked.

I was never more astonished in my life, and terribly mortified, feelings I hid from everybody—without exception. I felt that, even though they could not have known about all those pounds of plums eaten in vain, the brutes should at least have realized how hard I had worked.

For Mr Ervine I felt a violent dislike. Some months later I was standing in a crowded room where I knew nobody—one of Naomi Royde-Smith's Thursday evenings—when my hostess came up to me, and taking me by the arm said, 'St John Ervine is here, I think you ought to speak to him.' Nervously, but not at all unwilling—the idea of single combat did not alarm me—I went with her into the next room. The brute was not what I had expected: leaning on a stick, tired and hot, he appeared as tongue-tied as I was. Possibly he had not expected my too obvious simplicity and harmless looks.

A short time afterwards, hearing that I had written a novel, he offered to send it to an American publisher and, more usefully still, invited me to lunch. During the meal, he did all he could to advise me.

'What you need most,' he said emphatically, 'is discipline.'

To me then, discipline implied thrashings, hunger, poverty. I considered that I knew more than enough of all three, and saw no meaning whatever in his words.

His kindly-meant and fruitless advice, a small sum in royalties, and a critical article by Austin Harrison in the *English Review*—why did I not keep it?—were all the good that came of the book. Except an absurd memory of Austin Harrison himself. I see myself in his room at the offices of the review, my body hard with suppressed laughter. 'Look down,' he had said, 'now look up... Yes, I was right, you have perfect Oriental throwback!' What can he mean? I think: the man's daft... Daft or not, he was kind to me: he allowed me to write for the review an essay on Walter de la Mare which pleased that incomparable man, and two or more articles on, of all things, the United States, which must, since I was as ignorant as a calf, have been very queer.

I think I was before my time—before a time when impudence is a merit. Yet I really knew more about European drama than anyone but A. B. Walkley himself, and if I had been offered the chance should have made, softened by age and authority, an admirable dramatic critic.

This would, I am certain, have saved me from being tempted to write a novel.

## CHAPTER 16

IN APRIL 1914 I sealed and posted the package addressed to Leeds University, containing a great weight of confidence and ambition. I was without money, without a job, and I had heard from K. that, rejected for every London post he had applied for, he had taken one in a town in the Midlands. All I knew about Kettering was that it made boots and shoes. I was dismayed. There was no hope of my finding any work there, I should be dependent on K. This idea deeply offended me.

It did not come into my head that I could refuse to go.

At this time I was still bound to K. by ties which loosened only slowly, over the next four or five years and, if we had lived a retired life in the dead of the country—this supposes what is not true, that I was willing to live in such a way—would probably have needed half a lifetime to wear out completely: they were sensual and imaginative, like the grief I felt, as soon as I had abandoned it, for the white rabbit.

I meant to behave well, and set off with as many resolutions as misgivings.

At my first sight of Kettering I made a vow not to stay a day longer than I must. I refused to look for a house. We lived in a small commercial hotel near the station. No one else *lived* in it: no one except me would have dreamed of living there. We paid 16/6 a week each, for a bedroom, a small sitting-room and all our meals: I had a perpetual grudge against our landlady for her habit of mixing potato peelings with the little coal she allowed us; she did it to damp down the fire, but the smell was insidious and abominable. Had I complained she would gladly have got rid of us.

Shocked by what seemed to them my inexcusably disorderly life, the wives of other masters in the school were always telling me about small houses I could rent. I evaded them. Not only because of my secret determination not to stay in Kettering, and not even because of a loathing for these rows of human rabbit hutches without a shred of charm, to say nothing of dignity. My hatred of a settled domestic life was, is, an instinct, and borders on mania.

With my large ideas of what was barely necessary for life on a salary of less than fifty shillings a week, I took out a subscription to The Times Book Club. The discovery of Allen Upward's *The Divine Mystery*, and J. A. Symonds's *History of the Renaissance in Italy*, read volume by volume in that shabby room smelling of decayed vegetables, gave me the greatest pleasure I have ever had from books. I read in a fever of excitement, my cheeks burning, my mind in ferment.

These hours when I was alone, reading, sunk, were purely happy. Apart from them I was neither happy nor sensible. My mind behaved like a newly-trapped wild animal, throwing itself at the sides of its cage with undirected fury. I did not know where to turn to escape from a life which, the instant I shut my book, became an intolerable waste of energy and time. I must have been an uncomfortable companion, irritating K. as often as he disheartened and affronted me. I was changing as helplessly as a tadpole, and K. hardly at all. He was exactly as he had been in London, amiable and fond when he was pleased with me, rancorously ill-tempered when I vexed him, which I did too easily: I had only to be incautious enough to begin a sentence with the words: One of these days we'll buy... we'll go abroad... we'll see Greece...

I daresay that what he resented in me were changes he could not put his finger on but suspected. Under the features of the undeveloped girl, the tadpole, who had succumbed readily to his involuntary skill in playing on his own and her sensual curiosity, was faintly visible the confused outline of a young woman he could only see as detestable, foolishly unreasonable and splenetic. I was at times all these.

And no doubt I judged too harshly faults, a naive vanity and self-importance, at which a kinder or more sophisticated woman would have smiled.

All this is shocking egoism...

My only amusement was walking. No moors, no sea, only bird cries and the muffled sigh of wind in long grass, and, in the month of May, hedges full out in hawthorn, an unbroken torrent of whiteness reaching me along the same level as the marguerites of my infancy.

Twice I enticed K. farther afield. We spent a Saturday in Leicester. In a shop-window my eye was caught by a long green sofa: it reminded me of one at home, and the idea of buying it entered into me like a devil. I have never been able to see round or past what I want. Like my mother when she coveted something, I was *possessed*. But I was worse than she, stubborner and more cunning. There was room in our ugly sitting-room for the sofa and I persuaded K. to buy it on the never-never—13/6 a week for eighteen months. That evening when we got back, our landlady told us she would have to raise her weekly charges to 19/6 each—thirty-nine shillings. K. behaved nobly, leaving me to reproach myself.

My second extravagance was a day in London at half-term. Somehow we had saved thirty shillings and I could see no better use for it. The thought of even one day there made me insanely happy.

My brother was stationed near London, and my conscience, rather than any wish to see him, made me write and invite him to lunch with us in Soho. He came, a clumsy childish figure in his Air Mechanic's uniform. He had little to say, and that little had to be dragged out of him. Perhaps—I have just seen this—K. had on him the effect he had had on me when I saw him as a man of the world. After lunch, he mumbled something about 'going back now'. I knew he had the day off until evening, but, impatient to run about London, I made no attempt to keep him. We left him in Coventry Street and crossed the road. I glanced back. He was walking slowly, head down, and I saw—thank God for my long sight—that his face had turned red and he was struggling not to cry.

I rushed back across the road. Pretending not to see that there were tears in his eyes, I took hold of his arm.

'Can't you possibly stay longer? We only came up to see you, you know, and you're spoiling it by going off. Isn't there *something* we could do that would amuse you, a theatre, anything?'

Was he taken in? I shall never be certain. He muttered something about his frightful boots.

'What do your boots matter?' I said. 'In a theatre no one will see them, and we'll go to some small café for tea. Do stay.'

'Very well.'

Each time I recall this incident, I thank God for an uncovenanted mercy. Of all the escapes I have been allowed, all the deserved punishments I have been let off, this is the one I shall be as thankful for on the day I die as I am at this moment—after more than half a century.

## CHAPTER 17

SINCE THERE WAS NOTHING else I could do, I began to write a novel. It was a gloriously bad novel—perhaps not the worst I have written. It had no theme, only a riot of scenes and emotions, new characters brought on the whole time (and only one living breathing character among them), a great deal of talk, lively, cynical, jeering, images and ideas borrowed from the *New Age*, Anatole France, Upward, Symonds, thrown down in a style that dodged between curtness and the purest (most impure) Wardour Street. But the energy, the delighted playing with phrases and ideas, the irreverence, the reckless gaiety and enthusiasm of this frightful book—what happened to me to suppress them? I know. The double error of a settled life and the decline into writing for a living.

It is laughably clear that Nature was no more eager to make me a novelist than the university authorities to make a don of me. What did it intend me to be? What conceivable life would have satisfied my instincts of a *vagus* and my crying need of a sort of discipline I had no idea of?

I had emerged from an ill-found ill-considered academic course completely ignorant of contemporary writing, nothing in my head but echoes.

I have a strong patient brain, but it is myopic and slightly mad. It reminds me of a young horse I once rode, which was blind in one eye and under the delusion that it could jump walls.

I suppose that this first book had an awkward cleverness, mine at the time. No publisher or reviewer but took it for a young man's book. This suggests that at its worst it was crudely energetic.

With all the reading I did for pleasure, and my habit of day dreaming, and the outbreaks of restlessness when to sit in a room became unendurable, not much of it had been written when we left Kettering. Our leaving was my doing entirely. It was, I think, the first time I took on myself to manoeuvre another person's life. I discovered that I had a talent for *managing*. True, I only used it when my own life was involved.

Every week since we came to Kettering I had been going into the public library to read an educational journal, searching for a London school in need of a man to teach Latin. At last, at the end of May, a school in Liverpool advertised the post of junior classics master, and, Liverpool being at least a city, I used all my cunning to persuade K. to apply. He applied and was chosen.

Not long after, he caught a vicious form of influenza. My savage loathing of illness and sickrooms might have been the end of him if his mother had not travelled from London to nurse him. Reminding herself to be kind, she said gently, 'Don't feel that I want to push you aside.'

'Oh, but do!' I cried.

Not until he was recovering did I begin to feel anxious about him, and to think: Let us only get to Whitby and he will be safe. As soon as—at the end of July—he could travel, I took him there. All I did by way of preparing our future was to send the green sofa to a Liverpool warehouse.

My brother was at home on leave. For the first time, my mother caught a glimpse of his secret ambition. Sitting in her room, red short-fingered hands sprawled on his knees, feet in clumsy boots widely apart, he told her,

'I'm in the right thing. In the Corps you're not ordered about as if you were nothing, like we were in the ship. The officers talk to you, I've been up several times with one pilot; he said I ought to learn to fly, and he would help me if there was a chance for me learning.'

'How would there be a chance?' she asked.

His clouded eyes did not meet hers: he was ashamed of his ambitions. 'There's always changes. That's why it's lucky I went in now, when everything's possible.'

She felt the anguish of having no money, and under it a colder anguish, the fear that he would be disappointed. At other moments, she believed that he would distinguish himself in some way: she no longer expected anything of me, and placed all the hopes she had on this son who, for the first time, looking, with his round blurred face, an unformed boy, talked like a young man.

Suddenly—the suddenness was an illusion—the talk of a crisis in Europe leaped on to the front page of the newspaper. The telegram recalling my brother excited him so fiercely that he forgot to be ashamed.

'If there's a war,' he said, 'I might get a chance. It might be the very thing for me. You'll see, they'll be taking in new men, but us old ones will have the start. That officer I was telling you about said so to me—well, something of that.'

*Us old ones...* On the day war was declared my mother comforted herself with the certainty that *they* would not send him out of the country until he was eighteen. But he flew to France with the first English squadrons, on the 10th of August, and had his eighteenth birthday there.

He made his first stroke very early in November. My mother heard about it in a pencilled letter from him. He still wrote like a child, in sprawling uneven lines almost without stops.

'You will be pleased to hear that I got the medal which is called in France the Médaille Militaire, Medal Military, and seems to be very highly prized by them. I got it for working the wireless in a aeroplane over the German lines, a shell from one of their anti-aircraft guns exploded near us and blew part of our inlet valve away and cut the pilot's hand. This was on our great retreat of which you have read so much. The medal was given by the French government and presented by General Henderson. The war seems to be getting on slowly much slower than I expected. There is a heavy fog hanging about today and things are very quiet. I am still in the best of health and I am surprised to see how quickly we have got used to this kind of life. There is one thing when we do get back we will get a nice long holiday so let us hope it will be in the Spring. Looking at my pay book today I noticed I had over ten pounds to draw already...'

She noticed without surprise that he had not told her what he had done for the French army to deserve their medal. It was like him to say little. And she was not even faintly surprised that he had done well already. It was what she expected.

## CHAPTER 18

I HAD NO INTENTION, not the least in the world, when I urged K. to try for Liverpool, of becoming a householder and ratepayer—my term then for all that is dull, base, petty, in a word *Prudhommesque*. It came about inch by stumbling inch.

I took the first of these ill-judged steps before we left Whitby, when I accepted my mother's offer to lend me a hundred pounds to buy furniture. What she thought of as my disorderly life shocked and worried her; she was convinced that I must want a house of my own (accursed and nauseating phrase), it was what every decent normal young woman wanted. If it had crossed her mind that on this point I was neither decent nor normal, she would have been all the more anxious to whip the devil out of me. When I told her that I preferred living in rooms, with a landlady to keep them clean and cook, the flash of rage in her eyes reminded a child of an old terror. It had less effect on me now than my reluctance to disappoint her.

I might still have dodged but for the birth in me of a new guilty feeling— born since his illness—that I ought to look better after K. And the germ of another notion, one that went a very little way to justify my mother in her belief that I could not be entirely out of my mind: a weak stirring of greed to possess things I should not dislike looking at.

In the instant of saying, 'Thank you very much, you're being awfully kind,' I was seized by panic: I *knew* I had done the wrong thing. The sensation was familiar, but more piercing than I had ever known it; I felt emptied of all except panic.

There was still time to draw back. I was not morally brave enough.

A flat, I considered, would be a lighter burden than a house. I had not reckoned with the provincial barbarity of Liverpool. After two and a half months of living as paying guests in a respectable run-down house, and rejecting one unsavoury pseudo-flat after another in street after sallow dingy Victorian street, I was driven to rent a new house in the Garden Suburb, an estate, to my eyes raw and graceless, on the edge of Liverpool, in an unmade road of identical pairs of little houses, two small living-rooms and narrow kitchen downstairs, and two cramped bedrooms above. If I had been ordered to describe the kind of house which most nauseated me, I could not have found a more exact image.

We took this clean loathsome place from the 1st of December, handing the estate twenty-five pounds, to be given back to us when we left.

My mother came to Liverpool for a week, to help me to buy the furniture: she was delighted with the house, and even more delighted by the end of my disorderly life. In order not to hurt her, I kept up a pretence of happiness.

The evening before she left it broke down when I was face to face with the prospect of moving into the house as soon as its floors had been scrubbed. (Not that I object to scrubbing floors: I prefer it to a great many things—for instance, to speaking at a luncheon.)

The panic I had felt in Whitby was nothing compared with the mortal abhorrence I felt now, as much physical as moral, the sensations of a trapped human animal—a maelstrom of irrational disgust, despair, revolt. It was ridiculously out of proportion with its cause—I could not have felt a worse dread on my way to be hanged.

I tried to hide my demented state from my mother behind a stolid face. But I suppose that it was sullen as well as calm, and when I said that I would get the house ready but not live in it until January, her anger at what seemed my ingratitude and folly got the better of her. She spoke to me in her harshest voice, with violent contempt. After a minute I began to cry, and cried uncontrollably. My mother went up to bed, leaving me to my inexcusable misery. K., who had not said a word, was unexpectedly gentle with me. Neither of them had the faintest conception of my state of mind. I daresay I had none myself, all I knew was that I was trapped.

I cannot explain my pathological hatred of domestic life and frantic need to be free. Not free to write, or to be amused, or famous. To be free. To call it a spiritual nausea only pushes it farther out of reach. A crazily violent character, a tramp or a lunatic, shares my skin with a Yorkshire housewife.

In any event, in 1915 I was, all else apart, biologically trapped.

I kept the house dreadfully clean, washing, scrubbing, dusting, with feverish energy. I had forgotten, until the other day I opened a novel written in 1932, how K.'s shockingly meagre salary was spent. I cut and sewed a strip of while calico into four tiny bags, writing on each its name and the sum it was supposed to receive, and every Monday morning divided the week's money (£2 15s 6d, minus 13s 6d for the green sofa) between them. The Rent and Rates bag was remorseless in swallowing its 12s 9d, but the Coal, Light and Gas bag (4s 6d) and the one marked Food (25s) borrowed from each other with reckless optimism; there were many weeks when the miserable Coal, Light and Gas held nothing but a scrap of paper on which I had written: Owed by Food, 7s 8d. K. took ten shillings of the total to pay tram fares and his six two-course luncheons at school.

I had no skill in the knacks by which poor women make ends meet, and when the wife of one of K.'s older colleagues offered me a recipe for cooking an ox-heart I shuddered. In London I had contentedly eaten or gone without the cheapest meal, but now that I was cooking my own the only food I thought worth buying were things I had eaten as a child, smoked bacon, sirloin, fillet steak, English lamb, the finest country butter: each Saturday I bought a joint for the next day, and stretched it to make supper for K. during the week, pretending to eat midday dinner—not to spare him discomfort, but from an instinct to keep my clumsy shifts to myself.

Another young schoolmaster and his wife lived in the suburb. He was the first pacifist I had met. I hated the war, and swore with my tongue that I approved of his refusal to fight, but in fact I had neither sympathy nor respect for him. A letter from Archie, though heaven knows I did not understand it—he might as well have been writing to me in a foreign language, from a non-existent country ('I'm writing this in a field near a farm. We were relieved two days ago and brought back to this village for a rest. The men were dog-tired when they came in. For the last mile or so I was carrying three rifles and trying to encourage the weary. I was too tired to take my things off and the bed looked clean, a delusion, so I lay down on the floor and slept. We're all right now, as fresh as May. A small French child, about nine, is hanging round me as I write. I'm bound to say she's not attractive. I don't think war agrees with children.')—swung me violently round the compass. Without reflecting about it, I was on his side, and not on the side of the Fellowship of Reconciliation, which in theory I supported.

## CHAPTER 19

D URING THESE EARLY MONTHS of 1915, I tried in various child-ishly clumsy ways to find out what giving birth is like. Desperately unwilling to let K. see I was anxious, I waited several weeks before asking him what he knew about it—after all, he was a doctor's son. He advised me amiably to read *Anna Karenina*. The account of the birth of Levin's son terrified me. I became convinced that I was going to be tortured. Is anyone now so ignorant? In my first youth, these things were not talked of, no more than the sexual act, or abortion, or any of the body's daily habits.

What on earth would today's young novelists do if they were without these staples of their interest?

K. dealt drily with my awkwardly put questions. It may have been the instinct of a schoolmaster. And since I did not say I was afraid...

I did not think it strange that I was not treated gently: I had been well-taught in my first years that illness is nothing to make a fuss about. Looking back, I think that K. carried his lack of concern too far. Certain memories of those months are so bitter that the scars are alive. The young do not pity each other—or themselves. But the child who knew it had behaved badly *because* it was punished was too near me in time not to expect the consoling forgiveness that had always, sooner or later, followed the beating. It was usu-ally I who consoled K., but that is irrelevant. His repentances were sincere. And I have never been able to prevent myself melting like butter in hot sun the instant an enemy shows the faintest sign of remorse. It is a fault.

K. was not, or not consciously, my enemy. Neither was he my friend...

I had leisure during these months to write, and tried to finish my novel. I failed completely. My mind had lost its power to concentrate: the energy was still there, but the sap did not run. Surprised, I thought: It must be the child.

I loathed the deformation and heaviness of my body, and envied every thin young girl I saw, the poorest and plainest.

In spite of all this, in spite of everything, I never thought that I was done for. I would rather have died than tell K.—or anyone—that I still hoped. Hoped what? To escape, to become famous? Ashamed when I remembered my insane hopes and ambitions at the university and in London, I did not dare to make plans.

I had moments—when I was alone—of gaiety and confidence, when the life I was living seemed no worse than marking time, an interval to be got through. Miraculous mornings when, however exhausted I had been the night before, however unhappy or anxious, I woke, like a child or an animal, knowing instantly where I was, to a pure bubbling spring of energy, worth a fortune.

I had so much lightness of heart (or head) that it could not always be kept out of sight. Nor did I take myself seriously. But I should have liked others—K. especially—to do this.

Until I wrote them down, in 1932, in *That Was Yesterday*, I remembered almost every incident of the two and a quarter years I spent in that house. Writing them down freed me of the memory, but not of the lessons in distrust, dryness, patience.

My son was born in Whitby, in my mother's house, a little after eleven o'clock on the morning of Sunday the 20th of June, 1915. Two of my mother's friends looked in on their way from church (chapel, Mrs George Gallilee corrects me tartly) to enquire, and were shown a child whose eyes were able to focus on them steadily and directly, with none of the wavering vacancy of a new-born child's glance—blue eyes with long black lashes, and a smooth clear skin, not red or wrinkled.

The strangest things about the underworld through which I am travelling, trying to move backwards against the current, towards the sun of my setting-out, is that the darkness is not dark. None the less, there are areas, centres of total blackness, where my groping hands touch a reality I cannot understand. These centres attach themselves to an actual experience—so that I cannot recall it without running my head violently against the blackness, against a blackness filled with masks I do not understand, messages I cannot read. This happens to me when I remember my son's birth. I was unlucky, it is true; I had the misfortune to fall into the hands of a conceited mid-wife whose boast was that she needed neither anaesthetics nor a doctor to bring 'her' children into the world.

The moment I stumble into the blackness which streams away on all sides from this experience, my hands touch the masks. They cover the mystery which has haunted my life, and haunts it—the mystery of cruelty. During my day and night of agony I could not know that, in less than twenty years, torture would be in use again in Germany, and a little later in other countries of Western Europe: I did not know that the people I believed to be the most civilized in the world—they bore names like Molière, Stendhal, Mallarmé, Valéry, Giraudoux—would be not only enduring torture but inflicting it. The one thing I know is the moment when I should have broken down and blabbed all I knew—after only twelve hours of the extremes of pain.

What I do not know and cannot even hope to understand before I die, is why human beings are wilfully, coldly, matter-of-factly cruel to each other. What moves in the nerves of the men who bend over another man they have strapped to a table so that they can more easily make him suffer the most atrocious pain? In the nerves of concentration camp guards hurrying men, children, women carrying their smallest children, into gas-filled rooms to die of suffocation in agony and terror? In the nerves of men, soldiers, who are cutting the throats of children on the edge of the ditch into which their little bodies will be thrown ('*Sir, you're hurting me!*')? The ways to be cruel, to inflict pain, are countless: all have been or will be tried. Why? Why? What nerve has atrophied in the torturer, or—worse—is sensually moved?

I don't understand the masks, I don't understand them.

I am not, as are some of my closest friends, a believing and practising atheist. I should be very glad to believe that God is. But I cannot believe in a Creator who created man. Nor can I believe in the possibility of redemption for a race of beings capable of inventing gas-chambers for each other. When I remember these and the children lifting their hands to protect their throats, or in blind terror as they drown in their torpedoed ship, I think that the human kind is *damned*, it must, will and ought to perish. If there were a just God he could not forgive it. But what just God would have allowed it? Then who damned us? Ourselves, we damned ourselves.

Then perhaps we should forgive ourselves? Never, never.

Let everything be wiped out, the columns of the Parthenon in white sunlight, the foreign harbours, the plays of Sophocles and Shakespeare, the love of mothers for their young children, bird song, the stones of Chartres, vines, olive trees, the music of Mozart, the honeysuckle, the green tree, the rose, rather than keep alive a race without pity for itself.

Here must end a chapter which got out of hand. I shall hope, at the last second, to remember other things. What? The curve of a coast-line, of a gull's wing, the whiteness of a white petal, the sea, voyages.

## CHAPTER 20

TODAY, THE 4TH OF NOVEMBER, 1961, in Eric Linklater's *Roll of Honour*, I reached the phrase: 'The life he knew had blossomed like a great garden with brave young men.' Anyone, I thought, of our generation, his and mine, could write it. But, forty-six years ago, when I took my six-weeks-old son to the Liverpool house, I gave few thoughts, and those ignorant, to the young men of my age who were dying, thousands of them in one day, in another country.

If I try to find a way back to that absorbed self-willed young woman I see her, a thin gesticulating figure, half rubbed out, at the centre of an impalpable web of nerves stretched between her and her child.

Never have I worked harder. From the moment, before six, when I tore my eyelids open on another day, to the moment of dropping headlong into sleep as my head touched the pillow, it went on: I cleaned, washed linen and clothes, prepared the child's barley water, fed him, pushed him in his carriage the long walk to the shops or out into the flat country without horizons, two fields and a lane wide, beyond the Suburb, made bread from an old recipe I had, polished chairs, toiled angrily in that desert of a garden, filled with weeds, a disgrace, a menace to the gardens on either side of it.

That first autumn I planted it with potatoes, except for a square of grass under the window: when, in June, I lifted a root I found them covered with a black scum. Blight, the man next door said, pleased. Sorry for me, in spite of the weeds, he advised me to eat them at once, while I could still rub the blight off. 'You work hard, don't you', he said queerly.

I ate new potatoes three times a day for three weeks.

By this time I should have learned how to spend sensibly what little money I had. I never did and never have. Because of my upbringing, or from a shred of prudence, I pay as I go. But I have never been able to take money seriously, as a decent bourgeoise ought. I give it away or spend it—one folly equals the other—with reckless indifference. I have always lived, and still live, from my sixpence to my mouth, as a young German refugee said to me in 1934 of herself. I have saved nothing, and shall die on straw.

Not long before her death—before she let herself die, deliberately, out of disgust with life—I was with I. A. R. Wylie in her large handsome house near Princeton. We had been friendly for many years, and she asked me how much I had put aside against an imminent old age.

'Not a penny,' I told her.

She was sincerely horrified. Having made a great deal of money, far more than I have ever earned, she had a terrible fear of losing it. My imprudence saddened and irritated her. I might have dispelled the irritation at least if I had told her that, sometimes, between two and four in the morning, I endure an hour or more of sheer panic. Its effect never persists long enough to prevent my drawing my last pounds out of the bank.

In the days when I was truly poor, my only notion of saving was to go without inessentials such as dress and food. It was no hardship. When the middle of the week found me ashore for food, I lived on bread and tea, soaking the bread in the tea, delighted to find myself for a few minutes in the half-dark kitchen, safe, and on the edge of setting off.

Hunger did me no harm. I am so strong that if I had not persistently overworked and ill-used my body, the poor ass would have served me for a century—at least. Certainly I ill-used it then: one of the risks I made it run was a miscarriage I brought on myself, by inconceivable means: I remember sharply what I did, but I am not going to tell: I don't want either to harm some other young woman, as desperate as I was, who may read this book, or to pass for insane.

Always on the edge of nothing, I never for an instant thought that I could starve in real earnest. This was partly that I had been born in a class which did not—and, in spite of having seen its like in other countries wiped out like a weak pencil mark by inflation or revolution, still does not—expect to starve. But it was more my energy and blind hunger for living.

My only reason for hoping was hope, which, in those years, was a habit with me. Or an instinct, a memory in my body itself of voyages.

During the first months after I went back to Liverpool, I had no purpose more avid than my will, ferocious, to get my son the best of everything. No conscious purpose. Like my thesis on modern drama and the unfinished manuscript of my novel (both gathering dust on a shelf behind a coal-scuttle), my restlessness, my insane ambition, had been pushed out of sight. But they had sharp teeth and had sunk these into my stubborn mind below intention, below sense. While I ran from room to room, running the flesh off my bones, they waited their time, Eumenides watching a future victim—or a slow poison in my veins. After a few months they began to prick me. I became less stupefied by work and my new responsibilities, more impatient—and a more exasperating companion.

It is only by reflecting that I see K. as he might at the time have looked to older people or to anybody less close to him than I was. I was too close, and I suffered from his touchiness as often as he from my maddening need to be in the right and my moods of perfectly groundless gaiety. These were sure to earn me an irritable dressing-down. Then, raging against myself because I had been so idiotic as to talk to him about something that excited me, I became sullen or recklessly sarcastic.

One icy night in the winter of 1916 I exasperated him into throwing me out of the house. I had nothing over my sleeveless cotton overall, and I crouched against a hedge, shivering, raging helplessly, for two or three hours before the cold drove me back to the door he had now unlocked. He took no notice of me when I came in, not lifting his nose from his book.

Would I, if it had been possible, have left him after one of these mortifying incidents? I doubt it. I belong to a species of animal which endures a little death if it has to tear up roots it has put down in a human relationship. I have not a great deal of courage or will-power, and my confidence was not of the lasting indestructible kind, but I had the grip on life of a savage beast. Nothing subdued it for long.

And K. had moods when he was simple and pleasant. I could not count on them.

Today I see that he was trapped as much as I was. He could not have felt any sympathy with my unbearable sense of personal failure. It was not a disease he understood. He was only two years older than I was.

Too often I was little better than childish; I went on behaving badly—that is, grumbling and making useless plans—as a child persists in doing what it is told not to do, from the same puerile defiance. To make matters worse, when I was punished I cried with a child's maddening convulsive grief.

I had no dignity. I have little now, my character is no less awkward, but I put a much better face on it.

## CHAPTER 21

RESTLESS AS I WAS, my life had its fixed centre. In the first instant I set eyes on him, held out to me by my mother—before whom I took care to seem calm and stolid—my son became its only complete passion, its final meaning.

He was strong, and faultlessly beautiful. I brought him up on a strict method, learned, since I was totally ignorant, from the latest book, and because the book said that a missed meal was as dangerous as a brick pulled out of a wall, I roused him from sound sleep to drink his milk and barley water. (A cynical old woman told me: 'No mother ever woke her *second* child to make certain it had not died in its sleep.') I bought the most expensive baby soap and powder, the finest oranges, Jersey milk. As prices rose, I pinched in other ways. Possibly K. resented my silliness—to an unbeliever a religion must always seem grotesque. When the censorship department in Liverpool needed staff, he was infuriated by my refusal to apply. Baffled, too—here I was, detesting housework, strong as a horse, with better degrees than his own, and refusing a chance to earn money. I pointed out that the salary, about two pounds a week—though it would add seventy per cent to our income—was precisely what I should have to pay a woman to do my work: financially, we should be no better off. This argument was irrefutable. It was not, and he knew it, my reason for refusal. At that time I would have cut my hand off rather than give my son over to a woman who might—how could I know?—neglect or fumble one of the rites...

Curiously, I had no feeling of authority over my son—or not more than an older child has over the infant handed her to look after for an hour. When he laughed, I was filled by a hard light joy. If he cried, I tore myself in half to amuse him. My happiest moments were those between five and six, when I bathed him in front of the fire before putting him down for the night. He adored the warmth and the movement of the water on his body, and so long as I sang did not mind what I did with him. I have a thin voice and no ear. It is not that I am deaf, I hear as I see, acutely; my ear picks up the lightest sounds, shiver of a blade of grass on its fellow, distant voices, separate drops of rain. At some point between the nerves of my ear and my voice there is a barrier, uncrossable. A familiar tune, even complicated phrases of music, trace themselves in my brain with exquisite clarity, but I cannot turn the lines into sounds: I feel and see them, and hear nothing, except between the walls of my skull. The only notes I can sing are those I heard repeatedly as a child.

Over and over again, in my toneless voice, I sang *O dem golden slippers*, *In old Madrid*, and *By the blue Alsatian mountains*, ending with the air that obviously he liked best—

> There was an old woman
> Went up in a basket
> Ninety times as high as the moon
> And where she was going I couldn't but ask it
> For in her hand she carried a broom.
> Old woman, old woman, old woman, said I,
> Whither O whither away so high?
> To swe-e-ep the cobwebs out of the sky
> And I shall come back again bye and bye.

Sleep glazing his eyes, he forced his eyelids apart, pursing his small lips in the stubborn line which meant: Again.

Evening after evening I went through my brief act, enclosed in a bubble of light and warmth as clear as a wine-glass, and no stronger.

At the end of the year I took him—I have forgotten to say he was given three Christian names, Charles William Storm—to Whitby. At the last minute, when I was closing my suitcase, I picked up the manuscript of the novel and pushed it in, out of sight, at the bottom. (It may have been one of the moments when something heavy moved in me at a great depth and my mind formed words I had not even thought. *They think I'm finished, but I'm not, I'll do something.*)

The journey from Liverpool to Whitby passes through the corroded valleys of Lancashire and the West Riding of Yorkshire, vast troughs of solid grimy streets, mills, warehouses, chapels, sluggish canals, factory chimneys vomiting smoke over hillsides scarred by terraces of squat grey houses like out-croppings of stone: behind them the road climbs steeply between unmortared walls to the edge of the hill and beyond it to barren sooty moors: they excited me strangely, an excitement that deepened to pain, fingers pinching my heart, when the train ran under the viaduct a mile from Whitby, and slowed down past the upper harbour with its empty shipyards, old mooring-posts, grey gleaming water, ruined Abbey. If I took this route now, I should feel the same pain, useless, inescapable.

While we were there Bill caught whooping-cough from my young sister. At night I shut the windows in our bedroom and burned vapo-cresolene over a night-light. So that no one should know I was writing, I wrote then, kneeling on the floor against the chair that held the infuser: the tiny flame spread a circle on the paper, and I worked with an ear pricked to catch the first movement in the cot.

On one of these long nights, a character broke into my mind without any warning, from nowhere, from the darkness outside the weak ring of light. A round-faced disreputable little man, limping and voluble, called Poskett. I knew all about him: I knew that he had had trouble with his wife, and why. I knew his weaknesses, his shocking habits, his one endearing virtue. I scribbled like a maniac, my face burning. The child woke coughing, and was sick: I made him comfortable and went back to Poskett, who for that matter had never been out of my thoughts as I spoke soothingly to the child and watched his eyelids flutter for a moment, then close. I wrote until pain in my knees, cramped fingers, and the winter cold of the room drove me into bed.

Less than a fraction of what I knew about Poskett went into the book. It never occurred to me that this fraction was the one splinter of reality in the whole preposterous business. No one told me so, and no reviewer noticed him.

If I had been told at this time that I could not write—least of all, a novel—I should have been startled and angry. But I should have found some way of learning. I was an uncouth blundering simpleton, but shrewd and obstinate, with my father's patience in finishing what I had started.

I did not finish the novel in Whitby, but I went on with it in the spring of 1916, thinking about it at intervals during the day, and writing, unless I were too sleepy, after supper. At last I finished, and had only to type it, rapidly, with two fingers, on my rickety machine. I gave it a title I thought in every way fitting, *The Pot Boils and the Scum Rises*, and dedicated it—a fleering joke worthy of Class 5b—to the man who ran the Shepherd's Bush coffee stall.

Choosing a publisher at random—Messrs Duckworth—I sent it off. In the greatest secrecy.

## CHAPTER 22

SOME TIME DURING THE SPRING of 1916 my father's ship was sunk off the Irish coast by the German cruiser *Moewe*. The *Moewe* was on her way home at the time, and the *Saxon Prince* was the last of her victims. Her commander took the crew on board to join the crews of other ships, and landed the whole lot at Hamburg. From there they were sent first to a military camp, then to a concentration camp for civilians in Brandenburg. In the letter my mother wrote, telling me about it, there was an undercurrent of bitterness, as if she could not entirely forgive him for being safer than his son.

Harold was now a 2nd Lieutenant in the Flying Corps. He had done his pilot's training in France, in June 1915, after being given the D.C.M.—'For conspicuous coolness and gallantry on several occasions in connection with wireless work under fire.' (*London Gazette* 30.6.1915.)

A boy's hand moves slowly across the thin paper. It might be any one of the young unlined hands of that time, making their last signals to an indifferent world.

'In the Field

August 16th 1915

'... Some days out here it is stifling all day, then when night comes, cold, strange, a heavy dew.

'Myself and another chap are living in a small tent we made of old fabric off the aeroplanes, it is quite up to date. He fetched a stove back with him when he went on leave, my bed is of canvas slung on two sections of a wireless mast and my comrade's bed is of sacking between two old aeroplane skids.

'Our larder is an old cupboard off an aeroplane, the framework of the hut split struts and skids.

'The floor is earth kept dry by a trench dug round it.

'The table is a sheet of ebonite.

'One thing about active service you find out very soon there is nothing you can not do without.

'I think when the war is over I will put all my worldly goods in a pack and go and bury myself in Brazil.

'Well I will finish now as time is going about as quick as my candle.'

The following March he did a short spell at home, but refused a job at Netheravon, as instructor. He was not at ease in a position which would have forced him to lecture and make social gestures; nothing in his short life had prepared him for it—and nothing in his nature, which was like mine, solitary and diffident, without the social confidence I can pretend to when I must.

Besides, he was afraid that if he stayed in England he would be overlooked. 'You see, if I stop in England I might miss promotion. You never know what's going on, why some get ahead quickly and others are kept back. If you don't do something they forget about you. I have to make them notice me.'

He had no schooling, no useful relations behind him; he had only his ambition and his share of a courage which grows like grass in our country when it is needed. (In other countries, too, but let them celebrate it for themselves.) In April he went back to France, to No. 19 Squadron, and after four months was promoted to Flying Officer.

It must have been the late summer when I saw him again, in Whitby. He seemed little changed, still a broad-shouldered gawky boy in the R.F.C. tunic (why on earth was it called a maternity jacket?) with its wings and ribbons, no lines round his eyes, and no hardening of his slow shamefaced smile.

We grew from one stock, but I could not talk easily to him: in every member of my family there is—was—the same profound sense of being bound to near kinsmen in a duty overwhelmingly stronger than any dislike or resentment, the same that stretched between our marauding northern ancestors, and the same reluctance in speech. Moreover, he lived now in a country as closed to me as the country into which the dead go alone. But he was moved to make an attempt, out of his awkward young kindness, out of his experience, to do something for me, his elder.

One afternoon—he never spoke of K. by his Christian name, but always formally as Mr C—— he asked me in a neutral voice,

'What is Mr C—— doing?'

'Nothing,' I said. 'Schoolmastering. He's in London, with his parents, until the end of his holidays.'

'Does this conscription affect him?'

'I don't know. No. Schoolmasters are starred, you know, and he's B2.'

'That won't mean much in a few months. They lost a lot of men on the Somme.' He stared past me. 'Why doesn't he try for the Flying Corps?'

'He's shortsighted.'

'Oh, I don't mean as a pilot,' he said with a short laugh. 'He could be an Equipment Officer, y'know.'

A familiar excitement seized me. I kept a face as blank and stolid as his own, and asked him what an Equipment Officer did. He told me, and added, 'If he thought of trying for it, I could write to a friend of mine at Adastral House, Major R——.'

Was he pleased to be able to give advice and help? I must have thanked him, but was it well enough done to give him any feeling of satisfaction with himself?

His name was in the *London Gazette* again in December.

'Military Cross. For conspicuous gallantry in action. He attacked a hostile kite balloon under very heavy fire. Later, his machine descended to within 150 feet of the ground, when he got the engine going again and recrossed our lines at 1,300 feet and returned safely. He has on many occasions done fine work.'

That month my mother was staying with me in Liverpool, she and my young sister sharing the comfortless second bedroom. She was still there in the first week of January when the telegram came, forwarded from Whitby by my aunt Jenny, to whom, when he knew my mother was not at home, the postmaster sent it—these telegrams were no new thing now, but they moved bureaucracy itself to take a little trouble, sometimes. If they could have been laid down, each as it came, one on top of another, a great barren pile of death, growing and thickening as more and more young bodies were pushed into the ground, the shame and horror would have sickened us. Or so I think.

I stood in front of my mother with the telegram in my hand.

'*Open it.*'

I opened it and gave it to her... Deeply regret to inform you that 2nd Lt Harold Jameson Royal Flying Corps was killed in action January fifth the Army Council express their sympathy Secretary War Office... She made the inhuman sound women make when they lose a son, a cry torn from the empty womb, and turned blindly, to go to her bedroom. I did not try to comfort her. What use?

At this moment I knew, knew beyond any question, that I would sooner K. had died. This had nothing to do with love. I loved K. more warmly than I loved my brother. But—I realized it then, and if I have forgotten the feeling I have not forgotten that it existed—in certain families, not otherwise eccentric, love is a paltry emotion compared with the ties of blood. From nowhere, from a darkness, the figure as I imagined her of Antigone came into my mind, and I thought: Now I understand you, I know why your brother had this hold on your will; it was not piety.

There is no explaining this impulse. Reason has nothing to do with it, and nothing to say about it worth hearing.

Later we heard what happened. He had been ranging our guns on a German battery when he was attacked from behind. His machine fell in No Man's Land, and some brave souls of the infantry ran out and carried him into the trench: he was breathing but soon died.

When I read this in the letter from the major commanding No. 6 Squadron, I felt a dreadful sickness in the centre of my body, an uprush of deathly fear—it was what he had felt in the first moment of falling. The moment when he knew he had lost. We heard at the same time that he had been promoted to Flight Commander, a week earlier. Today (1961) I still feel glad he had that last small triumph.

All I could do for our mother was to listen without shutting myself off behind a wall of dullness, a trick I had learned young. I listened when she talked about his first leave after he became a pilot. She went with him to London. Once they were greeted in the street by an R.F.C. colonel who spoke with lively affection. 'Why, Jamie, my dear boy, it's you, is it? I'm delighted to see you. How are you, how are you getting on?' She had the same sense—a swelling pressure and lightness in her body—as when she read about him in the *London Gazette*. 'You could see how highly this older man thought of him. And when we were in Park Lane one morning he said: Mother, some day I'm going to have one of those houses. You shall live with me in it. You'll see. I shall be able to do something for you. If they'll let me I shall stay on in the Flying Corps. I might be a colonel then. You never know. This is only the beginning.'

I could scarcely bear her voice. It had the sound given back by a dry vase when you tap it. It was emptiness itself, the slow running out of meaning.

The frightful bitterness that came into it when she talked about my father was far more bearable.

'I asked him if he had written to his father to tell him about his second medal and his commission. Yes, he said, he had, and I asked: What did he say to you? And do you know what he wrote to the boy? He wrote: Don't think you've done anything, plenty of other men have done as well and fifty times better without getting a medal for it.' Her mouth worked in a way I could not look at. 'I shall never know what he did to the boy on that voyage. And then to tell him that he was nothing. I shall never forgive him for it, never. Never, never. I'm done with him.'

I listened. She was more capable of bitterness than I am, a simpler and more honest and straightforward human being. I gave a second's thought to my father in his German prison camp, but I don't remember that I had any pity to spare for him. Certainly she had none. The last flicker of kindness for him was dead. She would go on writing and sending parcels to Ruhleben. But give him, from now to her last day, a grain of warmth—no.

I understand that coldness.

Later, I saw that her son's death had been an end for her, a hard and bitter end of her deep life. From now on, for all she still had and was, it ran in colder shallower places, dwindling, in a drier country. At the time I did not see this. How could I, with my own life still quick and restless in me?

## CHAPTER 23

M Y BROTHER WAS NOT the only young man I knew for whom the war was a chance. In Archie's occasional letters from France my ear caught a ripple of excitement as far under the surface as the shadow thrown on the floor of a sea-pool by an unseen current, in every other way traceless.

'We are living in the cellars of an old brewery and across the road is the garden where D'Artagnan murdered somebody in an honourable quarrel. Did I tell you they had given me a decoration? I tried to find out why and had the correspondence returned. The party I sent to a saphead has just come back and the sergeant in charge reports the saphead full of Boches. I'm sure it can't be, because I was up there myself yesterday and found it full of water. Unless they are drowned Boches. I must go and look...'

The decoration was the V.C., given him, I found out later, for an act of prolonged cool courage. The coolness is a sleight-of-hand and real.

Another letter had an effect he had not intended, making me grit my teeth over the memory of years when I had been rebellious and confident. 'When I crawled out of my cellar yesterday morning I found a whole bed of white violets. Signs of the times—in a Staff Mess of eight people, the *New Age, New Witness*, and *New Statesman*, are on the side-table every week. And the General looks graver and more puzzled all the time. There's a war on, of course, to distract our minds—and heaven knows they need distraction after reading the home newspapers. Did I ever give or lend you my *Spirit of Man*? My stock of quotations is getting low... A funny thing happened the other day. You know there's a movement on foot to interest officers and men in social study with a view to simplifying adjustments after the war. The spirit of the thing is all right, but it's being run by generals and padres and people who still have to learn the rudiments. I say it's dilettante, and had better be run by omniscients from the School of Economics and sic-like people. I proposed a systematic education of padres and generals by the Central Labour College, and one red-faced High Priest got up and said, "You're little better than an Eikonoklast!" Truth will out, you see!'

The odds on K.'s being called up were shortening. I forgot that the mere idea of it used to dismay me. For one thing, I did not feel that he had any right to be safer than my young brother, and for another I was wryly certain that little harm would come to him on the ground. The excitement in my nerves was very like that I felt as a child, ankle deep in the sea, when far out the tide turns with a light all but imperceptible movement, which I could just feel. Also, I was shrewd enough to see what, for his own sake, K. ought to do now.

Early in February I persuaded him to write to Harold's friend in Adastral House: I drafted the letter for him, making it cool and urgent. It brought a reply at once—telling him to come to be looked over.

He came back delighted with himself. He had been accepted for training as an Equipment Officer, and was to go in the middle of March, to Reading.

I would follow at the end of March, after I had cleared up, and stored our furniture, and he had found rooms for us.

It never entered my head to wonder whether he would sooner have begun his new life without us. No more than it entered my head that I could stay on in Liverpool, in this detested house, waiting for the end of the war.

Duckworth returned my novel, but I took this lightly. A gaiety I tried to hide filled me, and, as soon as K. had left, an overwhelming energy. Confidence in my strength and cleverness swept away all the doubts I ought to have had about a reckless anarchic plunge forward, with a child less than two years old, into a future of which I saw nothing beyond the first step. My craving to get away blinded me. I was madly happy.

One day I decided to sell the furniture. Not only because I needed the money—desperately: K. had left me half his last month's salary, but had very quickly written asking me to send him part of it to help pay for his 2nd Lieutenant's uniform and the rest—but I had never liked it. The thought of getting rid of it delighted me. When I remembered that I still owed my mother the hundred pounds she had lent me to buy it I felt a momentary check, but a number of excellent reasons (all fallacious) for selling it jumped into my mind, any one of which might convince her. (And almost did.) I sold the whole lot for thirty pounds to an elderly dealer, a daughter of the horse leech, and told her to take it away on the morning of my last day in the house.

My middle sister was staying with me for a few days: she was resting in bed one afternoon when the door opened, she looked up and saw me coming in with a ferret-faced crone who began silently to rap the bed with her knuckles and drag the blankets aside to thrust her horrible fingers into the mattress.

'I've sold your bed,' I told her calmly. With equal calm, she said, 'I hope not before I get out of it.'

Another thing I did, of which I was proud, was to withhold a month's rent, so that, when I left and gave the statutory fortnight's notice, I should owe ten weeks' rent. A woman who left the suburb had told me that the £25 she expected would be returned to her had been held back, 'until necessary repairs are completed.' Since the woodwork was gaping away from the windows, and you had only to rap the corner of a wall for plaster to drop off, the whole of her money vanished.

I paid all but two small bills, both to tradesmen: these I put in my purse to be paid as soon as possible. (I paid them in time, and my mother's loans, too: I have a puritan and Yorkshire horror of debt.)

It was during these last days that an extraordinary change took place in the movement of time. It accelerated, suddenly, and began to run past at a rate which has never slackened. I can put my finger on the moment when this happened: I had taken Bill to a large store, to buy new clothes for him now that he was going into the world: he sat on a high chair at the counter, bored, while I fingered woollen tunics. A sudden anxiety seized me—Am I going to be late getting him back for his sleep?—and in the same instant, exactly in this instant, time began to rush away from me as, one day years later, in Norway, the horizon rushed past when I glanced up and saw the coast galloping off out of sight on the back of a long gleaming wave.

I thought: You have no time. But it was not a question of time to do this or that. It was a passage into another country. The moment when I looked, smiling, at my child's bored scowl was the same moment when, a child myself, I touched the smooth veined petals of Grass of Parnassus growing from the red clay of a cliff at the other side of England. Both moments existed in another sort of time—now lost. Run as I may, turn as I may, shielding eyes and ears, I cannot reach it; I can only remind myself that it existed.

On our last morning I got up long before daylight. By the time I had packed the last things, and lashed the dress basket filled with blankets, linen, my silver forks and spoons (from my grandfather's hoard), and the china tea-service, which I was sending to my mother to keep for me, a grey light was welling over the top of the blind. It came from that other time, from an earlier setting-out, from a darkened kitchen with one lamp on the table, and the shadowy figure near me of my young mother.

If a doubt plucked my skin it must have been now, but I don't recall feeling doubtful. There was no time—we were leaving on a one o'clock train. At nine, the railway van arrived to collect the dress-basket and, pulling at the knots in the rope, the drayman told me I was a good lasher, which pleased me.

On his heels came the horse-leech's daughter, with a handcart and a thin boy, and began dragging out the sofa (it must still be somewhere, poor thing), hacking wardrobes in half to get them through the door, and knocking great lumps of plaster off the walls of the staircase. Much I cared how she destroyed her own or the estate's property. She carted off one load, leaving the rest scattered like driftwood, outside. I swept and dusted the rooms after her, gave Bill his last meal in the house, and packed the basket holding all he would need on the journey, milk, raisins. His clothes filled his own zinc bath, mine and the rejected manuscript went into a shabby trunk, and these with his folding cot and his carriage were all we had.

The cab I had ordered came. I told the man to stop at the estate office, and ran in and told a startled clerk gaily that I had left, and he could pay himself two and a half months' rent out of the deposit money.

'Oh, I don't think we can do that,' he exclaimed.

'I don't know what else you can do,' I said with the greatest composure and confidence, and hurried out.

I'm free at last, I thought.

At this moment I knew that I could do anything. Anything.

I have had precisely this feeling at a few other times in my life. It is a splendid, ecstatic feeling and an illusion.

I was, of course, mad. No young woman in her right mind chooses for her carefully-nurtured infant the hazards of lodgings and wartime journeys. I don't want to sit in judgement on the young woman, but to tell the truth. The only anxiety in her mind when she stood on the main line platform with cot, bath, trunk and the rest—and a porter to whom she would give sixpence (and be thanked for it)—was about getting a corner seat in the train. There was nothing outrageous in her decision to follow her husband about England. Perfectly conventional and sensible women were doing the same thing.

The difference between these sensible women and me was that they had decent settled homes to which, the war over, they would return: I had cut myself and my child adrift—deliberately. If you can call deliberate what is little better than an explosion of energy, of an old passion for voyages, tides, another harbour, another sun.

A departure. The wolf's teeth of life.


# CHAPTER 24


I CARRIED INTO OUR LIFE as camp-followers all the anxiety about method and routine I had absorbed from my abominably enlightened book on the care of infants. Wherever we fetched up, I began by ingratiating myself with our landlady, so that I had the run of her kitchen to prepare my son's meals. It was this sacred routine, and my religious belief in it, and my ignorance, that almost killed him in Reading.

The book had so much to say about the supreme importance of fresh air that I was fairly convinced he would die, like a fish taken out of water, if I did not keep him in a current of air as often as he was not asleep. One day at the end of April the weather turned icy, showers of hail alternating with bursts of sunshine and a vividly blue sky. During one of these brilliant intervals I hurried him out into White Knights Park. On the way home a hailstorm caught us; he was warmly wrapped, but the treacherous cold must have reached him. At night when I was putting him to bed he was violently sick. He'll be all right after a night's sleep, I told myself. But in the morning he lay in his cot, waxen, with pinched nostrils and a faint blue shadow round his mouth. It was my first experience of the weak hold a very young child, even the strongest, has on his life; my heart turned over in me with fear—even though I did not yet know the danger.

He was saved by the accident that the doctor nearest us was an excellent children's doctor: when he came he ordered me, drily and quietly, to give him grape juice, or a tea made from raisins, but no milk, no animal food of any sort. I sent the landlady out to buy hot-house grapes and the best raisins, moved his cot into the warm living-room, and prepared stolidly to nurse him back to health. For all my agonized fear, strictly hidden, I did not think he was dying. The thought that he could die did not so much as brush my mind, not for one moment. Once an hour I gave him his spoonful of the warm raisin tea—he had rejected the grape juice by a weak pressure of his lips—but he still lay like a tiny marble statue.

The doctor came again in the evening: he said little to me, but—I knew this only later—he told K. not to leave me alone, the child would die any minute.

K. had been asked to dinner by another officer, and went, unable to face what was coming. I was immensely relieved to get him out of the way. As soon as he had gone, I made up the fire, pulled the curtains across the window, turned out every light except that of a feeble lamp, and settled myself to watch the child in the cot. I had the sense that a nerve in my body was joined to his. It was no effort to keep my entire attention on him; I should have had to make a conscious effort to turn it away. When, some time after midnight, K. came home and put his head round the door, I waited without patience for him to go and leave me alone with my child.

It would not be true to say that I concentrated on him the whole of my energy. It concentrated itself: the direction did not come from my conscious self, it came from a level far deeper than will. All through the night I had his life and spirit, as I had his small body, at the ends of my fingers.

At some moment in the first light I noticed that instead of simply letting me pour the drops of raisin tea between his lips, he was moving them to swallow. My heart turned in me again, this time with joy: I gave him a second spoonful, and another, and another. He opened his eyes and looked at me, a look as direct as a word—the first time for more than thirty hours.

When the light strengthened in the room I saw that there was no longer a bluish shadow round his mouth. He moved his hand in the light.

Today I see clearly that, although I kept him alive, the person who saved him was a doctor whose name and face I have completely forgotten. He must now be dead, or a very old man. If I were a Catholic I would have a Mass said for him. As it is—did I even thank him? I cannot remember.

If I did not, I deserve to be whipped. But I doubt whether I knew how narrowly I had escaped.

I had sent my rejected novel to Mr Fisher Unwin, and in the middle of June he wrote asking me to come and see him. Innocently, I supposed that he was going to take the book. By this time Bill was fat and well, and I could leave him with K. for an afternoon and go to London, less than an hour's journey. Before seeing Mr Fisher Unwin I saw his reader, who talked to me with great kindness, but did not tell me that the novel was no good: his kindness glanced off my specious self-confidence.

I have a clear image of Fisher Unwin himself, rosy cheeks, red palpitating scalp visible through his white hair, seated in his splendid room in an Adelphi which, thanks to the heroic work of our vandals, no longer exists. He, too, was amiable. He offered me—explaining that the novel I had sent him was unsuitable—a contract to show him my next six books. Innocent as I was, I saw that this committed him to nothing, and me to write an appalling number of novels on the off chance that he would approve one of them.

Politely—I am always polite unless I am angry—I replied that I would consider his offer. He walked with me to the door of his room, and at the last minute took a book from a shelf and gave it to me.

'Read this,' he said benignly, 'it will teach you how a novel should be written.'

I walked rapidly to the Strand, putting my rebuff in its place, the rejected manuscript under my arm, and there stopped to examine the book. The author was an E. M. Dell, and it was *The Way of an Eagle*. Somewhere between London and Reading, after trying to read it, I dropped it from the window of the train. I was tempted to throw the manuscript after it. Instead, I sent it out again, but I have forgotten where.

Shortly after this, K. was posted to Bradford. This time we travelled in comfort, since an officer in uniform could not be seen in the third class. Bradford was a disappointment. I had not the wit then to admire its hideous grandeur, streets plunging downhill into a cauldron of blackened mills and offices, a Wool Exchange in Venetian Gothic, and a Town Hall modelled on the Palazzo Vecchio in Florence (of which I had never heard). The moors were a few miles away, but I never got to them. And they were not *my* moors. I confounded the whole West Riding in my detestation of Bradford. Even today I find it impossible to think it as purely Yorkshire as the North Riding, or as handsome and arrogant.

Most of my time was spent in Manningham Park, pushing Bill's carriage up and down its asphalted paths; the weather was hot and airless, but if I tried to rest for a few minutes he flew into a rage until I set off again, down, round the lake, up, down. No doubt he was as bored as I was—I had not the least idea how to talk to a very young child. He was also lazy: when I took him out of his carriage and placed a ball in his hands he would throw it carelessly, then sit down and wait for me to fetch it back. Passersby would stand still to admire him—he was a beautiful, a perfect human creature—and I was torn between pride and superstitious terror.

Without admitting it I must have known that I had advanced myself very little by bolting from Liverpool. True, I was free of a house, but I was not doing anything with my freedom. I read a great deal, and, when I was alone, dreamed absurdly of a brilliant future—I did not realize how pleasantly corrosive this habit of day-dreaming is until I lost the talent for it. In the meantime I made no efforts towards any future at all.

I had no impulse to begin a second novel. What was the use, since the attempt had been a failure? Without reasoning about it, I felt that there was neither merit nor sense in repeating an effort that did not bring in money or fame. That a book is written at least partly for its own sake did not then strike me.

Imagine what an instinctive writer would have done with my long evenings in that grimly fermenting town—a D. H. Lawrence, or (if he had not at the moment been in France) J. B. Priestley, born in the West Riding and as shrewd, greedy, possessive, as, with half my mind, I am myself, but born to write.

At the beginning of September K. heard that he was being posted to a Stores Park in Lincoln, and I decided to go there at once, to a farm outside the town, where his parents happened to be staying, until I had found rooms for us. I detested his father as heartily as he disliked and disapproved of me, but I would have invited myself to live with Beelzebub himself to get my child into country air.

After a week there—during this week I was ill, in acute pain, hid it from my father-in-law, a doctor, and imagined I had recovered completely—I took half a small furnished house in Lincoln, near the Cathedral: I hated the idea of housework, but the town was crowded and I could find nothing else fit for a child, *my* child.

I paid a month's rent, and for the rest of the month went hungry. K. had been kept waiting in Bradford, and though he wrote a couple of affectionate letters did not send the money I asked for. Worse, when he came he was in high feather because the bank had credited him in error with a second kit allowance, fifty pounds. He had spent most of it on taking the chorus of a musical comedy out for a moonlight picnic, in hired cars. I made a terrible scene. I was furious with his, as I saw it, incurable frivolity. Illogically, I was also hurt because he had not thought of spending any of the money on me.

Weeks later, Messrs Cox discovered their mistake and proposed to put it right by deducting two months' pay, and now that we were really in trouble I remained calm. I sent K. up to London to see them and beg them to repay themselves at the more merciful rate of ten pounds a month. They agreed. No doubt it was not the first time a young officer had snatched at what looked like manna from heaven.

He had been in Lincoln less than a week when he was posted away again—this time to a Training Station in Hampshire, near Stockbridge.

## CHAPTER 25

H ERE BEGINS A PERIOD in my life when I was almost continuously happy. We had rooms in a farm on the edge of a small village called Broughton, three miles from the airfield. Immediately behind the farm a field rose steeply to the edge of the downs: a chalky track led up, through oaks and beech-trees, to a stretch of turf as fine and springing as the cliff-top at Whitby, under a sky no less wide and pure than the sky over the North Sea.

This is the only part of England I love as I love the memory of my own before it was so nearly ruined: it is English in a different and kinder mode, the hills rounded and smoothly grey-green, the names of the villages—Tytherly, Mottisfont, West Wellow—gentler, the air without salt, but clear and fine. A famous trout stream, the Test, runs along the valley, not like our peaty moor streams but green and glassy clear. At night it was easy to see the valley and the downs as the Romans—who planted the first beeches—and the Norman-French saw them, ghosts no gentler than our Vikings, but carrying the seeds of another, subtler, civilization.

Three other officers with their families lived in the village, but in rented houses: I was the only one living in rooms, they teased me about my easier life and were gratified and amused when the wife of the farmer had her second baby without a midwife and I found myself looking after the house, and cooking not only for her and her husband but for a dozen harvesters. In fact, I did much of my own cooking, and learned to make cheese and butter—and in return was able to buy all the butter I needed, game, and illicit joints of veal and lamb: no child in wartime England fed better than mine.

The cheese was made in the cool stone-walled dairy: when the solidified milk had been cut into squares my job was to keep them moving until they reached the proper leathery consistency. I stood for two, three hours, gently drawing a hand through the whey, like a fish in luke-warm yellowish water, and with the other turned the pages of a translation of the Book of the Dead, repeating to myself with obscure excitement such superb phrases as *Apes that sing at dawn* (what apes? what remote dawns?), and *He becometh brother to the decay which cometh upon him*, and wishing passionately that I had had the luck to become an Egyptologist or almost any sort of ancient historian.

The whey softened my finger-nails, so that they broke off at the quick.

I took Bill for long, almost silent walks in the empty lanes—that is, I walked. He refused to walk for more than a few minutes. He was extremely stubborn, and had just discovered the pleasure of breaking things. I had to move everything breakable out of his reach before leaving him alone. One day, with great ingenuity, he succeeded in getting hold of a jar of face cream, the first I ever bought in my life, and flung it out of the bedroom window on to flagstones. I was heartbroken at the waste of five shillings. But I did not know how to deal with his child's instinctive malice, or with violent rages when he stamped his foot, shouting, 'No, no, no,' the only word he knew. He had only to look at me with wide brilliant eyes and hold his arms up, and I forgave him instantly. At these times I felt faint and dizzy with love, and the fear that I was unfit to have a child if I could not train him to be good and obedient. But I was unable to punish him. The mere thought turned my bones to water.

The happiness of these months after October 1917 is not something I imagine. It rings in my head with the sound given out by a flawless glass. I have been happy at other times since, in other places, but never with this insouciance, this certainty that I should never age.

And this in spite of K.

When I was thinking coolly, I reflected that our marriage had been eaten away until only the husk remained, and a few weak roots. He was enjoying his life. He looked well in uniform: the cross-over tunic, breeches, high boots polished to within an inch of their lives, suited his long-legged figure. Adjusting his belt in front of the glass he looked at himself with a pleased smile which—depending on my mood—irritated or touched me. So far as he was concerned the war could go on. It had given him his first taste of a good life, with a man-servant, dinners in mess, and the flattering sense of his reputation, pinned on him by his C.O., as 'the finest wangler in the area.'

I doubt whether he thought of me as an enemy, but he treated me as one. He knew that the moment the war ended I should begin trying to arrange his life again. My passion for managing exasperated him: usually, he gave way in the end, worn down by my greater energy and stubbornness—and then bitterly resented it. Expecting the worst from me, he often got it. Yet I had more kindness for him than he for me, far more. There was something comical in my feeling of responsibility for him. Again and again—either because I had caught sight of a crack in his jaunty self-assurance, or had behaved badly, and was seized by remorse—I made efforts to bridge the gap widening between us.

Sincere as long as it lasted, my good-will never lasted very long. It was quickly killed by K.'s suspicions. What is the use, I asked myself drily, of swearing kindness to a husband who takes so much pleasure in *seeing through me*?

Towards the end of the year I began writing again—for an excellent reason. And this time I was not trying to be clever or ironical. I tried instead, inventing a lame story, to record, before it sank without trace, the colour of our life, mine and the three boys', before 1914, the mad hopes, the idealism, the messianic dream. I wrote in the evening, on sheets of foolscap, with a fool's confidence.

My excellent reason was that the first book had been taken. When it came back from whatever publisher I sent it to after Fisher Unwin, I gave it one last chance, sending it to Constable. I sent it in K.'s name, from 92 Squadron, Chattis Hill, with the unscrupulous idea that they would reply quickly to an officer of the R.F.C., who might be leading a dangerous life.

They replied early in November, inviting him to come to London to talk about the book. Not to be caught twice, I wrote a polite careful letter, asking whether they had any serious intention of publishing it.

I destroy everything, but I have their letter, dated the 6th of November 1917, beginning: 'Dear Sir, we certainly did not write regarding your manuscript *The Pot Boils* without seriously intending to publish the book provided we could agree on one or two alterations...'

I found this letter only last week, in the back of a book, together with three pages of suggested cuts. When I re-read the last paragraph, I remembered sharply the scepticism with which I read it at the time. I never find it easy to believe praise of my work; I consider, and always have considered it, as a substitute for something I might have done better. And this time I was right and Constable and Company ludicrously wrong—'All of which being said, we can only endorse our reader's judgement that the book is a remarkable one and in places really beautiful.'

The letter had not been signed.

I was ashamed to call on another London publisher in my proper person of a gauche young woman. I made K. ask for business leave, and sent him with strict orders not to give me away. Naturally, he did. But it was an impossible deception, and the writer of the letter, Michael Sadleir, had no trouble in getting the truth out of him.

Some little time later, I went up to London for a night, leaving Bill with the wife of the farmer, to dine with my publisher. I had only one so-called evening dress, the short one made for me by a sewing-woman in Whitby in my first year at the university.

The room I was shown into appeared a mile long. I crossed it, dazed, towards two figures standing motionless at the far end. They came into focus suddenly, a smiling attractive young man and his very young wife. Betty Sadleir was small, slender, with the narrow face of a mediaeval angel, and a smile I found again later in Rheims, subtle and naive, felicitous, very old: a thick plait of yellow hair crossed her head. Unless I am confusing this with a later evening she was wearing red-gold brocade. I cannot be certain of this: what is certain is that she was elegant in a simple way, and only mildly curious about a young woman in a shabby ridiculous dress, with reddened hands and nothing to say.

Like my mother when she went abroad, I took in avidly every detail of a dinner-table and rooms arranged with more elegance than I had known existed. They had a bad effect on me, rousing my latent greed to own beautiful things.

After dinner, Michael Sadleir brought out the now dog-eared manuscript of *The Pot Boils*—he had already deleted the rest of my title—and began tactfully going over passages he said were silly or injudicious. His tact was not needed. I seized the pencil he was holding, and ran it through every passage. This amused him. Turning to his wife, he said,

'She is the first author I ever knew to let herself be hacked to pieces without a murmur.'

What he took for submissiveness or timidity was nothing of the sort. It was a deep unrealized contempt for novel-writing as a serious use for energy and intellect.

This contempt still exists in me. It has nothing to do with reason. Rationally, I consider that the novel is one of the great arts, and I revere Tolstoy, Proust, Dostoevsky, Stendhal, as I revere, let us say, Mozart and Rembrandt, whom I understand much less. And I have given the greater part of my life and all my wits to learning to write well. But—under all this reverence, which is genuine—a perfectly irrational contempt, indifference, call it what you like, persists in murmuring in my ear, 'Only an artist without the wit to become a poet (or a sculptor, musician, painter) turns to writing novels.'

Well, there I was—launched. Or so, with part of my mind, I thought.

Some weeks later, after the contract was signed, I needed money. There was nothing new about this, but I had a new idea of how to deal with it. I wrote to Constable and asked them for a small advance on the sum I supposed the book would earn.

I was far from imagining that it was no asset, but a liability undertaken in the hope of my becoming, some day, a novelist.

Only wretches unable to believe in the existence of publishers who are recklessly generous and kind-hearted will be surprised to learn that they sent me the sum I asked for, ten pounds. It meant that their loss on the book was precisely ten pounds heavier than it would have been.

## CHAPTER 26

U NLIKE THE MASTER, who, to keep himself from lying, wrote his memoirs twenty pages at a sitting like a letter, beginning each day where he had left off, without looking back, I start every morning by tearing up part, much or little, of the previous day's work and rewriting it in the interests of dryness and accuracy. I doubt if the Master knew any better than I do whether he was telling the truth of this or that episode which had disturbed him.

In August 1953, when I was in Grenoble for two nights, I reproached the head waiter of the Bec Fin for the carelessness of his fellow-citizens in not taking the trouble to make it easy for me to find Stendhal's birthplace. Here you are, I said, with the supreme good fortune to own the greatest of novelists, and... He interrupted me gently,

'Oh, Madame, n'exagérez pas.'

Which goes to show that Stendhal's *horreur peu raisonnable pour Grenoble*, and for *l'esprit dauphinois*, was more or less justified.

What follows has been torn up and rewritten five times; I must finish with it, lying as little as possible.

In 1918 my tranquil happiness was broken into and destroyed by the only episode in my life which deserves to be called an affair of passion.

June was a hot month, the roads and hedges white with chalky dust, the wells drying up, and the ground parched. Great chestnut trees sent up thick unmoving flames of creamy white and red, and the short grass of the downs was warm under the hand and scented with thyme and the yellow cinquefoil.

That month a squadron of the American Air Force reached Chattis Hill. K. made a song about his American parents (he had been born in Ireland, in Belfast, but he made it sound like Richmond, Virginia), and was soon friendly enough with the commanding officer, a captain, to bring him to the farm one evening, without warning me. From my bedroom I watched them climb out of the R.F.C. tender, and cross the garden to the front door.

I did what I could, brushing my hair and powdering the end of my nose, to make myself presentable, and ran downstairs, only thankful that I had ready a cold chicken and cold gooseberry pie.

Frowning at me, K. said, 'I've brought a fellow-countryman of mine, an American——'

'A Texan, ma'am.'

'Oh, is there a difference?' I said.

After that, I said nothing. It has never embarrassed me to wear shabby clothes, but my lack of small talk was, is, a terrible embarrassment. The American talked easily, with an inoffensive irony, about his experiences since he landed his squadron in England. I listened, staring. He was strongly built, not tall, with a broad powerful head and noticeably small ears. He moved with a scarcely perceptible swing of the body, from his narrow hips, not, as most Englishmen walk, from the knees. He had a swarthy skin, eyes always narrowed, a direct guarded glance, and a short fine stubborn mouth. His expression was slightly arrogant, as though violence would be easier for him than argument, but he had a charming smile and a slow peremptory voice with more tones than an English voice.

Behind what I hoped was an air of intelligence, I was going through every sensation that the onset of an obsession—obsession-love—roused in me. It was so long since I had felt anything of the sort that I scarcely knew what was happening.

He must, I reflected, think me an imbecile.

When he got up to leave he said to K.,

'I certainly talk too much. Your wife is bored with me.'

'No,' I said, smiling warmly.

'Yes, ma'am. You were wondering if Texans are all as conceited. I've been talking about myself for three hours and a half.'

I had the sensation of jumping from a height, into total darkness: an astonishingly exhilarating feeling. 'It's an interesting subject,' I said, 'you could hardly have dealt with it in a shorter time. Not to do it justice.'

He took my mockery calmly, but K. scowled, and as soon as we were alone, said,

'If you had nothing sensible to say, why didn't you hold your tongue? You were damned rude.'

'Someone,' I said, 'should be rude to him. He thinks too well of himself.' My heart seemed to be beating in every corner of my body: I felt suffocated by it.

After this evening I thought about the Texan the whole time, whatever I was doing. When I sat down to write I was forced to drop my pen and give myself up to thinking about him, re-living, endlessly, tiny details, a tone of voice, a phrase. Now that I am incapable of behaving so fatuously, I regret the loss of a sensual trick so little harmful to anyone except myself, and so absurd and pleasant.

Ashamed to be wasting time, I made efforts not to think about him, not to stand looking out of the window in the hope of seeing him step out of K.'s tender. After a few minutes my mind rebelled violently and went back to its delirium.

The fear of mockery that froze me and drove me to silence in company vanished when he came into the room: I could say anything I felt. No need to pretend that I am a friendly harmless creature, no impulse to placate him. If I felt like jeering, I could jeer without fear of giving offence. The self I hide so carefully that few even of my intimate friends so much as suspect its existence, the fleering violent *northern* self, had met its brother. It was recognition—on a level below my absurd day-dreams. It did not brush my mind that so experienced and attractive a man would fall in love with me, but I had this other intimacy. It gave me the most acute pleasure.

My passion was a genuine one. It belonged to the same family as my delight in Marie Lloyd and all gross violent careless human beings. Is it possible that this derisive sceptical unpleasant self is my 'real' one, and that the moments when it gets free, the very few experiences it can take part in, are the only valid moments of my life?

It is quite possible. And that we begin dying, not when our body fails but much earlier, in the moment when we can no longer run the risk of a total folly.

One effect, good or bad, of my obsession was to ease my relations with K. The last of the quarrels in which he lost his temper savagely took place the week before he brought the American to the house. After that, nothing he said moved me, and when he left the house I forgot him.

Everything and everybody became unimportant to me except my son. He was and remained the changeless centre of my life.

## CHAPTER 27

THE TEXAN WAS EXACTLY MY AGE. Possibly he was inquisitive about a young woman who did not know that she was badly dressed, had never been trained to entertain a caller, and might at any moment insult him. He began coming to the farm three or four times a week. He talked to me about Texas, his father, the military school he was sent to when he was five, fence-riding, the Mexican expedition and, when I provoked him, about the English.

I had had no idea that the rest of the world did not humbly admire, and if not love at least fear us. I was astonished to hear him talk about our limited ideas, out-of-date traditions, laziness.

'But what can you possibly know about our traditions?' I exclaimed. 'Or our civilization.'

'Only that it's on its way out. Your traditions, whatever they are, won't be any use to you after the war, your people are tired, they don't want to work, we shall beat you to the trade of the world before you know what's happening.'

'How long have you been in England?' I asked.

'Four weeks, ma'am.'

'You have fine instincts.'

One day, when he had come up against the Wing Commander, he said with some sharpness that an Englishman's idea of cooperation is to decide what he intends to do, and leave the other fellow to think of a way to conform.

'But why,' I said, 'should you imagine you know what to do in a war that has been going on for three years while you Americans have been lending money at interest and writing pompous Notes?'

He looked at me for a moment. 'You have the tongue of a rattlesnake.'

Nothing in the world, not even to have him fall in love, could have given me a more sensuous pleasure than I got out of being able to say what I liked, no holds barred. It made up to me for my lack of all the qualities I knew he admired in women, elegance, social charm, the ability to ride and dance well.

I had few illusions about him. In any sense I could give to the word he was not educated. Behind his self-possessed politeness he was violent, with no desires or needs that could not be satisfied by intense physical excitements and money. If Stendhal could have made use of him in a novel he would have placed him in fifteenth-century Italy and made a soldier of fortune of him. (Later, he sold arms to both sides in the Sino-Japanese war, which shocked Michael Sadleir and struck me as typical of him.) He had curiosity and a hard brutal zest for living. This did not hinder him from being, in some ways, grossly sentimental: he had no moral sense, but a number of sentiments, unconsidered remnants of the idea of the Southern gentleman as it had come down to him, and as it concerned women, fighting, radicals. But—as Michael said of him—he made other people look like faint pencil-marks. He was violently alive, more alive than anyone I had ever known. And this was what infatuated me. I was half-dead, my energy, my mind, running to waste. He appealed to every impulse in me which sensible well-disciplined people either do not have or have had trained out of them. A part of me was gross, violent, sentimental, wanting change and excitement more than it wanted things in the end infinitely more important to me.

Good heavens, how is it possible to be so obsessed?

One evening K. came in with the look on his face, half-knowing, half-impudent, which meant that he had picked up a malicious story. It was about the Texan. The American squadron had given a dance to celebrate the building of their lavish recreation room. Ashamed of my poor dancing, I had left early, as soon as dinner ended.

'You remember the American nurses at the party last night? Remember the pretty red-head everyone called Oregon because she kept saying, "Y'know, I come from Oregon"? All our boys wanted to dance with her, but about one o'clock she disappeared with friend J., and spent the rest of the night until four o'clock in his hut. What a man, eh!'

A day or two later J. invited us to go into Winchester to one of the Saturday dances held in the Town Hall. I refused. 'I can't dance any of the new steps, and I have no proper dress.'

'There's no reason why we shouldn't go,' K. said. 'She's only showing off.'

His habit of taking me down in front of other people mortified me. To hide it, I said,

'Very well, we'll go.'

'Leave everything to me,' J. said.

At one o'clock on the day of the dance he sent a side-car and a gigantic sergeant-mechanic to drive me into Winchester, where he had taken a room for me at the Black Swan, so that I could dress in comfort. This I thought the height of luxury. When, late in the afternoon, he turned up in Winchester and asked my permission to bring two Americans from Pershing's H.Q. and a bottle of whiskey to the room for a drink, I felt doubtful—did he respect me?—and then exhilarated. This, surely, was the way people lived now.

Of the dance itself I remember nothing except one seductively silly waltz tune. The other day, a barrel-organ in a street off the Haymarket began croaking out the Missouri Waltz, and for a second or two I thought I should faint: it seemed that less than a breath separated me from a young woman in the claw of a ruinous passion, and that nothing, but nothing, equalled the loss of its agony and happiness.

None of this matters. What matters is to lose the power to regret.

We drove home after midnight, in an American tender, with K. and three English officers. Shivering in a thin coat, I leaned my head against the side to be able to watch the hard outline of J.'s head: he had gone to the front, to keep an eye on the tipsy driver. The officers, not very sober, were dropped off at the airfield, and he came with us to the farm. He and K. were hungry, I offered to boil eggs, and for fear of waking the household I went outside into the yard, to the great stone barn, where there was a fireplace. J. had followed me. We got a fire going with sticks and I hung over it the black iron pan that would have held a score of eggs. I forget what we talked about in low voices—trivialities—but the few minutes of quiet untroubled intimacy in a darkness scarcely broken into by the crackling fire are still somewhere in my mind, if I could lay a finger on them.

I have completely forgotten what, about this time, I wrote to Archie, but I must, with this one of my few friends, have been indiscreet. He replied early in September, a letter which ended with a sharp rap over the knuckles.

'You're too expository about the Texan. If you want to run away, my dear, why don't you? You're not a soldier, and I'm sure Broughton is a miserably dull place. By the way, why doesn't the man join the army and come to France? There really are Americans out here fighting, I've seen them...'

I pushed his contempt to the back of my mind—where it went on working.

K. had a week's leave due to him. He wanted to take it in London and, reluctantly, I agreed to trust Bill to our landlady for so long.

Two days before we were due to go, he came home from the airfield, pleased with himself, and announced that J. had invited us to be his guests in London, 'in return for your endless hospitality.'

'I let him see that I thought it was about time he did something of the sort,' he said complacently.

The rooms J. had taken were in the Piccadilly Hotel, a suite on the top floor, two large bedrooms and a bathroom: the door from the corridor led into a long inner hall, and the three rooms opened off this.

We had not been in this, to my eyes, luxurious place, longer than twenty minutes when K. was rung up by the Adjutant. The Equipment Officer of one of the squadrons had come down with appendicitis, and he must come and take his share of the extra work. Almost with relief, I began repacking my suitcase—no long job.

'Don't be an idiot,' K. said sharply. 'You'll stay here, of course, J. will look after you, and I'll be back the day after tomorrow. I know friend B., he loses his head if someone mis-counts a screw.'

J. took no part in the argument: his sexual vanity would make him careful not to say the wrong thing, or show surprise that an English husband thought it common form to leave his wife in an hotel with another man, and that man himself. I cannot be certain why K. was so eager for me to stay. The most likely answer is that he was showing off: one of his fantasies at the moment may have been to show how magnanimous, how nobly trusting, he was. He may even or also have been trusting.

My only clear feeling was that I should bore J. For the rest, I seemed to myself to be indifferent.

I went with K. to the station, then dawdled back to the hotel. To tell the truth, it alarmed me by its size, and the quantity of gay pretty women, smiling and well-dressed, sitting about everywhere. I caught sight of myself in a long glass, a thin shapeless figure in my five-year-old coat and skirt. Letting myself into the suite without a sound, I sat down in my room to wait until something happened. After a time, I had a vexed sense that this was no way to spend time in London. Not certain whether J. was even in the hotel, I ran across the hall and knocked on the door of his bedroom.

'Is that you, Margaret? Come in.'

I found him lying on his bed, a book he was not reading on the floor, and the obligatory jug of iced water within reach of his hand.

In five minutes we had quarrelled, I forget about what, but I had one of my rare paroxysms of rage when something like an explosion takes place behind my eyes, blinding me. In the same instant I was in his arms, abandoned to him, trembling, my throat hard, the veins of my body like straw in a fire. The next moment I was on my own side of a gulf, detached, cold. Why? Heaven knows.

I tried to move away.

'No,' he said, 'don't move.'

'Please let me go away.'

'I can't.'

A sentence jumped into my mind, and I said drily, 'You must think I'm Oregon and that this is your hut.'

He let me go at once, stepping back, and I walked out of the room to my own. I sat there wondering what cold devil had taken possession of my body and mind in the very moment when they were being offered all I had imagined and craved. I did not understand either why what I said had defeated him, but I had known it would: the words were put into my mind as though someone had slipped a knife into my hand. All I had to do was use it.

After a time, an hour or less, I heard J. in the hall. He knocked, and said,

'Don't you want to eat dinner?'

'In the hotel?'

'Why not?'

I opened my door. He looked at my outdoor clothes, and said in a gentler voice,

'Put your hat on, child, we'll go eat in the grill.'

He had realized that I had no idea that in a grill room (in those days) a hat was obligatory. In the crowded restaurant I felt dull and awkward, without an idea in my head. J. was gay and talkative, ordering for me things I had never eaten, *buîtres Mornay*, and drinking a great deal. At that time I never drank, not even wine. Naïvely, I expected him to make some remark about—what ought I to call it? the fiasco?—but he said nothing until I told him I was leaving the next morning.

'You don't have to do that,' he said. 'If you're afraid of me you can lock your door.'

Confused, I said, 'I'm not afraid.'

'It would be a hell of a silly thing to be. Things don't happen twice.'

'You meant it to happen. But it was partly my fault.'

'Listen. Only a fool worries about what happened yesterday. Tell yourself: That was yesterday. And forget it.'

He was a little drunk, not drunk enough to frighten me, as people who have lost control of themselves do. But the only thing I wanted was to get away, out of sight of the person who had seen me lose my head and behave badly. We finished dinner: he saw me into the lift, and went away in search of a more amusing companion.

In my room, I packed my suitcase: I meant to catch the first train, at six o'clock. Then, switching the lights off, I opened the window, thinking that if I couldn't run about London I might as well look at it.

The windows on this top floor were casements, neither high nor wide: a low parapet cut off the view. I pushed a chair under the window and climbed out on to the sill. It was of stone, fairly broad, and I sat there dangling my legs, and staring. I saw roofs and the black gulfs of streets, an alphabet I could not spell out, and behind them a sky with a veining of darker clouds like twisted roots.

Lifted up at this height above London, I began to feel self-possessed, and then coolly excited. This excitement had nothing to do with J. It sprang somewhere in the nerves of my mind. I shall do something, I thought; there is a way out, and I shall find it.

This was not Rastignac's cry, looking down over Paris from the Père Lachaise: *Et maintenant, à nous deux!* Alas, I am not so single-minded. I want, even then I wanted, too many things which cancel each other, solitude, a bare life, and the pleasures of theatre, concert hall, travel; honesty and a reputation; wealth without crawling to get it; to live like a monk and a foot-loose unbeholden eater of life.

Naturally, I achieve none of them. Nevertheless, when I come to die, among the minutes I shall remember gratefully will be the thirty or so I spent on a top-floor window-sill of the Piccadilly Hotel, in 1918, confident, and madly happy.

I began to feel cold, and scrambled stiffly back into the room. I was afraid I should over-sleep, but I had not the courage to ask a servant to call me. I lay down on the outside of the bed, half-dressed, sure in that way of being too uncomfortable to sleep long. I woke at four, dressed myself properly, and at five started to go downstairs, carrying my suitcase. Not only was I too ignorant to know whether, at that hour in the morning, the lifts would be running, but I dreaded the glances of servants.

Not until I was sitting in the train out of Waterloo station did I begin to wonder what I was doing, and why, without in the least intending it, I had refused a man for whom I felt a violent lust—no other word for it. I had only to watch him cross the room to feel myself on the edge of fainting.

All this will be incomprehensible to young women today, and seem very silly.

It may have been both—but I had not been able to help myself. An impulse stronger and deeper than the one that threw me into his arms had driven me to draw back, escaping by a trick, a jeer that stung him so sharply he would as soon have slept with an adder—or a rattlesnake.

What, as the train hurried me back to Stockbridge, baffled me was: Why? Why, involuntarily, had I failed to behave like the loose woman I obviously must be?

I had no feeling of guilt. I did not believe it would have been immoral to take what I wanted with such violence. Ungenerous towards K., yes, disloyal, not immoral.

It was partly caution—a shrewd hard sceptical Yorkshire caution—hating to be overreached, hating to give myself away. I could lose my head—to a point. That reached, I drew back.

My upbringing, too, a puritanism not mine, given me. But more, far more, my instinctive certainty that the American was uncontrollable, I should not have been in control of my own life. *And that would never have done.*

It turned out that all the qualities I most disliked in my family were stronger than I was.

I had a moment of overwhelming relief that, in spite of my grasping mind and desperate fatuous day-dreams, I had been too much for the alien he was—a crude greedy over-confident alien.

No doubt, Archie's contemptuous letter had reached in me a self I could no more repudiate than the colour of my eyes or my hard bones.

I decided not to tell K. about it. For two reasons, one more presentable than the other. In the first place, I could not trust him to hold his tongue. He would enjoy a public scandal in which he played the part of injured husband and friend, betrayed by a scoundrel.

The second reason was an instinct. The thought of giving one man away to another in an affair of this kind shocked me deeply.

I told him I had been worried about Bill, and let him suspect that I had made some sort of dumb fool of myself.

I see as plainly today as then that to give way to my obsession would have been a disaster. I see, too—what I did not then—that for moral health a sensual passion should be given in to at once, or strangled. During the next few months I did neither. I thought about J. day and night, sometimes with an agony of regret. To endure it, I reminded myself of his bad qualities—he was violent, uncontrolled, uncivilized. And then I thought: But with him I was alive, not as I am, half-dead.

I was out of my mind. In everything else I had self-control and good sense: I looked as carefully as usual after Bill, and when some malicious friendly woman spoke to me about 'your Texan' I kept a smooth face. It was a relief when, not long after this, he took his squadron to France.

At the same time, K. heard he was being moved—to Canterbury.

My heart sank. 'When?'

'In four weeks—at the end of October.'

The thought of moving to a town where, for all I knew, none of the things I gave Bill, cream, butter, fresh eggs, plump partridges and chickens, existed, horrified me.

I decided to take him and my all but finished novel to Whitby until K. had found us rooms at least half as comfortable as the farm.


CHAPTER 28


S OME TIME THIS SUMMER, the last of the war, my father benefited by the exchange of older civilian prisoners and was sent into Switzerland, where he was kept for a few weeks in hospital. I had not been at home many days when he returned. It was a strange homecoming. My mother met him in the hall, let him kiss her cheek, and asked coolly,

'Well, how are you?'

He gave his short laugh. 'Oh, I'm quite well.'

A few more words, and she went back into the sitting-room, closing the door. Tea had been laid for him in the breakfast-room, the first of many meals he would take there alone. Afterwards he drifted into the sitting-room and my mother talked to him, politely, as she might have talked to a not very welcome stranger. Perhaps trying to please her, he took notice of new things she had bought, a small old writing-table, a looking-glass, and she told him in an indifferent voice that she was going to Scarborough the next day to look at carpets for this room.

He lumbered away upstairs to his bedroom at the top of the house. When he came down again he went into the breakfast-room, and I followed him. Someone, I thought, should show interest in him.

The pity I felt was almost impersonal. None of William Storm Jameson's children had any liking for him; we scarcely knew him: as children we wrote brief empty duty letters to him, when told to, and fixed into albums the coloured postcards he sent us from the cities and harbours of a score of countries.

What became of these many hundreds of cards, fragments of a sunk world?

His youngest child could not stand him: her dislike of him had been born with her. I was the only one of his four children who felt a little sympathy for him, and that was a matter of nerves: his loneliness, his quick defensive lying when my mother accused or contradicted him, were the habits of a child lost at the age of thirteen. For a moment something infinitely baffled, tortuous, afraid, came close, and fell away again.

I tried to think of something to say to him. 'Were the Germans decent to you?'

'Oh, they were all right,' he said, indifferent. 'They knew what they had to deal with in us English. We didn't stand any nonsense.'

This was something he believed, as he believed in quinine. I saw him, gaunt, shabby, wolfish, shuffling about the camp, holding round himself the rags of his captain's authority, neither submissive nor defiant, preferring some of his German guards to some of his fellow-prisoners: he judged people solely by their attitude to him.

'I suppose there were all sorts in the camp.'

'Ha, yes. I didn't speak to many. Two or three was quite enough. The Brandenburg camp was worse than the other, they burned some of the prisoners.'

'What do you mean?'

'A hut caught fire and the men in it were burned to death,' he said carelessly. 'Queer people, them Germans.'

I did not know whether this were true, or something he had imagined. He said nothing more.

'Did you see the *Saxon Prince* sunk?' I asked.

For the first time he was roused.

'Yes. She went down very gracefully.' He laughed, a short nervous laugh. 'She didn't dive. She went down—down.'

He held his hand out, palm downwards, and moved it slowly down.

'What did they do? Did they torpedo her?'

'Yes. Two torpedoes.'

Between his son's death and the murder of his ship, there could be no doubt which went to his heart.

The breakfast-room had a french window opening on to a verandah and a small sunk garden. If a house keeps the impress of people who have lived in it, that is one of the two places where he still is, a tall shambling figure, head bent, fingers absently stuffing a pipe, eyes staring into the garden at a remote horizon. In later years, when he had left the sea for good, he lived in that room during the day. Once, for the sake of saying something to him, I complained of a large starling which drove the smaller birds from the crumbs I put out.

He frowned. 'I've been watching that bird,' he exclaimed. 'It's a very well-behaved bird. It's not a starling at all, it's an overgrown sparrow. I daresay it's the grandfather of the others. It's not greedy, it eats a lot because it needs more than they do, it's older.'

My bedroom was next my mother's now. On the night of his homecoming he was the last to come upstairs; I heard him cross the landing and hesitate outside her door for a moment before calling,

'Good-night.'

Silence. I held my breath. Isn't she going to answer him? He repeated it.
'Good-night.'

In a lifeless voice, dry, without warmth, barely audible, she said,
'Oh. Good-night.'

Listening with all my ears, I could not hear his footsteps going away up to
his room on the floor above. He walked like a bear, moving his heavy body
without a sound, in the way he crept up behind his officers on board ship.

The only person for whom my mother felt warmly anxious was her youngest. She had years ago given up trying to rule this child, as she had ruled the
others, by fear and pity. No punishments were any use. An appeal to her
emotions—which had brought me to grovelling remorse—only hardened
Dorothy, and a threat of whipping sent her into such frenzies of rage that
my mother withdrew in alarm. 'Go to your room and stay there until you
are sorry,' she ordered. Hours later, it was she herself who gave in, touched
by the sight of a small face closed against her like a fist.

She was too tired, spirit and body too worn, to master a young creature
so stubborn, so capable of a harshness like her own earlier harshness.

It was as if, at a moment when she no longer expected anything of her
life, she had turned a corner and come on her own younger self, pale with
revolt and anger. The hand lifted to punish dropped. How could she punish
herself in this last-born? How treat roughly a child for whom, now that she
knew what bestial cruelty life is capable of, she feared as never for anyone.

At twelve, Dorothy was tall, with thin supple limbs and an exquisitely
fair skin. Now that she always got her own way, her tempers were soon over:
she was generous and straightforward, a miracle of energy. My mother's face
changed when she spoke of her, softened by a half-foolish pride.

I saw that she had transferred her ambitions to this child. First it was I
who was to compensate her, I thought, then Harold, now Dorothy.

One day, she told me, 'I dreamed about Harold last night. We were
walking along a country road, and we came to a large house, with great trees
round it, and he said, Look, Mother, this is where we're going to live now.
The rooms were large and beautiful, like the trees—I've always wanted to
live near trees. And then he began going away, I tried to keep him, but he
was gone, and I woke up.'

My heart seemed to shrivel with pity. I did not know how to answer her. There were weeks when, my mind full of its own thoughts and wants, I did not give Harold a thought. I saw that there were no days when she did not think of him and the useless bitter waste of his life.

'One day you may have a house like that.'

'No.' She smiled unkindly. 'No. It's too late.'

The rawness of her grief scalded me. As did her reliance on her youngest child. I was afraid of another disappointment for her.

I did not resent it that she had written me off as no use. It certainly looked as if I were a failure.

During the first fortnight at home I expected every day to hear that K. had taken rooms for us in Canterbury. At last, when I had written to him twice, he replied that there were no rooms to be had, he might be moved again in a few weeks, I had better stay where I was. And be careful with money, since he had had to spend a good deal lately and wouldn't be able to send any of his October pay.

I felt something wrong with this letter, but could not put my finger on it.

That morning we were waiting for news of the armistice. If the Germans signed, a gun was to be fired from the cliff battery. We kept the windows open, and towards eleven I went outside into the road to listen.

I did not hear the gun, because suddenly all the ships' whistles and sirens sounded from the harbour, and then the bells, first from the church on the east cliff, then all the rest, peal on peal. A flag went up jerkily in the garden of a house farther down the hill, and another and another. I spoke to a man running past the gate.

'Is it the peace?'

He was beside himself with excitement, stuttering, waving his arms. 'Can't y'hear them? Can't y'hear t'whistles?'

Oh, pity, pity us and our weak useless hopes, the fraud, the treachery, the profit drawn from tears and death, the young dead, and the barren old carrying their bodies to the end. Or don't you hear them?

I went back into the house, trembling, scarcely able to speak quietly. 'It's the peace,' I said.

My mother's face was made ugly by her tears. 'What is the good of it to *me*?'

True—what good was it to her? I felt ashamed and helpless. In the same moment I was filled by an insensate excitement: I could not believe that this was not, for me, in some way a chance.

K. did not write again. He left unanswered the letter I wrote suggesting that he should approach his old headmaster in Liverpool and find out whether there were a place for him. Heaven knows I did not want to go back to the Suburb—but I would have gone. No question but I would have gone.

Nor did he answer another letter asking him to send me a little money, a pound, even ten shillings. I had nothing. There I was, twenty-seven, a married woman, and borrowing from my mother for our small daily needs, mine and Bill's.

Who wrote to me—Archie?—that he had heard there were openings in an advertising firm in London, the Carlton Agency. 'It might be something for K.?' I wrote to K. at once, begging him to apply.

This time he answered, a short letter. 'I'm quite capable, thank you, when the time comes, of arranging my own future. It's kind of you and all that, but I don't happen to need your help. Your letter made me smile. I fully appreciate what a disappointment I am to you, and you so clever and all. Don't get *too* clever. You'll go off in a cloud of hot air, and then what should I do?... I'm having an amusing time down here. Learning to dance...'

Had he not enclosed ten pounds from his November pay, I should have felt more mortified.

## CHAPTER 29

I CANNOT REMEMBER when the idea came to me to write to the Carlton Agency myself.

It is difficult to write, without distorting it, about a decision which, now, seems to me coldly unforgivable.

Horror at the thought of leaving Bill—where? how?—wrenched the nerves of my chest in the very instant of writing to the Agency. It was a sharp pain, purely physical. I carried the letter to the post, refusing to think what I was about.

He was now three and a half, a strangely self-contained child. He had begun to talk, with the greatest reluctance, using long words but rarely making a sentence of them. I knew how to care for him so that he would grow strong and handsome, but not how to amuse him.

I thought: *I can't go.* Behind everything I was doing, the senseless dialogue went on... I can't go, I must go. What thanks will he give you for staying with him, when he is older and you have no money to spend on him?... Dialogue? The chatter of apes or the insane.

As soon as I had an answer from the managing director of the firm, asking me to come and see him, I spoke to my mother about it. She listened with genuine interest.

'But it would mean leaving Bill,' I said.

She did not offer to keep him. She had no heart now, no energy, for such an effort. She was far too tired. He was very wilful, and her youngest child more than a little jealous of him.

She was not sorry to see me trying, after so many years, to make something of my life, but she could not go the lengths of burdening herself with my child. I don't remember that it so much as crossed my mind to hope. I was too sharply aware that he was *my* duty.

She looked meditatively at me from her clear pale Gallilee eyes, a glance that seemed to come from an immense distance.

'We'll think of something,' she said slowly. In the same slow absent voice, she added, 'K. isn't much good to you, my girl.'

Repeating to myself, even believing, that nothing would come of it, I went up to London on the early morning train, and saw the director that afternoon. He turned out to be a polite middle-aged man, with a yellow skin and quick nervously intelligent glance. Because with half my mind I hoped to be turned down, I felt neither anxiety nor embarrassment. The interview was not a long one. He asked—looking down at the letter in which I had set out my degrees—what work I had done.

'None.'

'No experience. And no training?'

'No.'

He smiled slightly. 'What do you think you're worth—in the way of salary?'

In the train I had decided to ask for five pounds a week. I lost courage, and said,

'Four pounds. At first.'

'Very well.'

I said nothing—and felt nothing.

'When can you start?'

'In January.'

'We're badly under-staffed. I should like you to come before then.'

'I can't come before Christmas,' I said.

'At the end of December, then.'

'Yes. I can manage that.'

He may have felt that I ought to show a little gratitude to him for taking on an entirely inexperienced young woman. It did not occur to me. He rose politely and walked to the door with me. Possibly he was amused.

I remember nothing between leaving him and getting into the night train. I spent the evening with Archie, who at ten o'clock put me into the train, and hired a pillow for me. I was unused to such attentions, which no doubt is why I remember it. The journey itself, huddled in the corner of a third-class compartment, my head slipping off the pillow, has run together with all the other night journeys I made between London and Whitby to see Bill for a few hours, the sooty comfortless carriage, the long wait in York station, from two o'clock until five, the cold dirty platforms, the light coming greyly through the glass of the roof, the phantoms of other solitary travellers.

I tried to think clearly. From a single moment of exultance in having landed the job I dropped into the blackest pit. To give up my child in return for four pounds a week in an advertising office was plain madness, a folly for which there was no rag of excuse. Don't go, I told myself, don't go, don't go, don't go—tolling of an undersea bell.

I must, I answered.

I was not reasoning with myself, I was adrift, driving before a wind out of the past.

I could have said—it would be true—that I felt responsible, solely responsible for our future. Justly or unjustly, I was quite certain now that K. would never do anything, for himself or us. I read his few letters with an eye that saw only their levity and what my grandfather would have called bombast. He has the mind, I thought cruelly, of a precocious schoolboy.

Some years ago, in a bus rattling towards Amiens, I overheard the woman in front of me, a small pale creature smelling strongly of cloves, talking to her friend about her husband: he was a miser, he tormented her and their daughters, etc etc: at the end, with a gently ironic smile, she said, '*Eh bien, que veux-tu, il est mon homme*.'

I am incapable of such unthinking unasking goodness.

My poverty and insecurity were a torment, and my blind wish to do the best I could for my son. (That this did not necessarily involve having money did not brush a mind haunted by too many hard-headed ghosts.) By keeping mum about my ambition, boredom, restlessness, I could make out an excellent case for myself. Any sensible jury would applaud it, and it would be a lie...

My mother did not advise me, for or against, but she helped me to go. She had remembered a Miss Geeson, a woman in her forties who ran a small morning school for very young children and was said to be kind and good. Perhaps she would take Bill to live with her. She lived in Ruswarp, a small village a mile out of Whitby—less, if you could have walked along the estuary.

I went to see her, and liked her—she was clearly a kind woman. She had brown hands and soft embarrassed brown eyes. Telling her that he must have the best of everything, the best milk, the best soap, I asked about her fees. With a little diffidence she wondered if two pounds a week would be too much.

'No,' I said, 'I can manage that.'

'Of course, his clothes...'

'Buy him anything he needs, I'll repay you at once.' By the time he grows out of what he has, I reflected, I shall be earning a great deal more money. Rashness for rashness, what was there to choose between me and K? Today I cannot imagine on what I rested my confidence. On energy and ignorance, no doubt.

K. wrote genially: 'Well, well. To think that you could nip in and sneak my job for yourself. Congratulations...' He said nothing about Bill.

In the short time between my interview at the Carlton Agency and the end of December I was very active, and stupefied, like a man walking through a thick fog. I had moments of frightful unhappiness, from which I rushed into activity, any activity. Methodically, I planned, added to the pile of Bill's clothes, drew up a list of my few debts, all without reflection. The truth is—is it the truth?—I was in the claws of a raging want. There is no arguing with a raging want; it can be hit on the head, but not by an argument.

Feelings of guilt and regret are nowadays in disgrace. One cannot be seen with them in intellectual circles. But no one is forced to read a book in which I am trying to write without lying.

Perhaps one day, when I am very old, and frozen, I shall be able to think coldly about this time.

The evening before I was due to go, packing my own and his clothes in our room, I began for the first time to cry. I have always refused to believe that mental agony is as intolerable as physical pain, but during these moments and in the years that followed, I became a little less certain. Flowing through the whole of my life, an icy current, running at a great depth, avoided as often as possible and stumbled on suddenly, at home or in the street, at receptions for the great, on journeys, in sleep.

When, after putting him to bed, I went downstairs, my stolid face must somehow have given me away.

'You know,' my mother said, 'you could still change your mind about going if you don't feel altogether happy about it.'

'Yes, I could,' I said calmly.

I had arranged for him to reach Miss Geeson's house at bedtime, so that he would fall asleep at once, and wake in his new life. I could not explain anything to him. It seemed better for him to come in from a walk and find me gone. So, in the morning, I dressed him and sent him out with a servant. I watched from the window. As they reached the top of the hill, the cab I had ordered crossed them on its way to the house. My mother was standing beside me.

'I was just thinking,' she said, 'he's very little, after all. I hope he'll be happy with her.'

'Oh, I expect so.'

'I wonder what he'll think, when he wakes up in the morning in a strange room.'

Does she know she is torturing me? I thought. When I stepped into the cab he was still in sight. My mother pointed to him from the house.

Turning my head away, I smiled at her. The cab jerked forward. I sat with a hand pressed to my throat. It was only a short distance to the station, I had no time left.

To write this makes me feel ill.

How ridiculous it will seem to...


# CHAPTER 30


WHY SHOULD I HAVE EXPECTED the London of January 1919 to bear even a family likeness to the London of three poor scholars? It did not. Of all the Londons, lying one below the other in my skull, from the streets known to the captain's wife and her little girl to the London of eyeless facades and heaps of rubble, it is the shoddiest and least generous. Under a grey sky it awaited the harvest of millions of fresh young bodies pushed hurriedly into the ground, their eyes and supplicating hands, out of sight.

I have a poor head for dates; my memories of the next six years, in which my life fell into the folds it has kept, are hopelessly fragmentary and confused, a fresco of vivid details and great gaps where line and colour have vanished.

I spent my first night in a small dingy temperance hotel in a shabby quarter of Bloomsbury. Not reflecting that London would be full of visitors crowding on President Wilson's heels, I had done nothing about reserving a room, and for some hours thought I should have to sleep in the crypt of St Martin-in-the-Fields, opened to the homeless. In despair I went into the blue Y.W.C.A. hut set up in Trafalgar Square; the kind soul in charge telephoned a dozen modest hotels before finding one.

The bedroom was penitential, and I spent one of the worst nights of my life, weeping tears as bitter as vitriol.

Next morning I presented myself at the Carlton Agency in Covent Garden, and said coolly that I must be allowed a day or two to find lodgings. Since I had never been a subordinate, it did not occur to me to behave like one. This attitude, completely involuntary, did me no harm. The managing director—call him Shaw-Thomas—was an educated and passably intelligent man, with, I now suspect, fewer commercial instincts than he needed for survival. On the few occasions when he called me into his room, he talked to me as though I were socially his equal, a civility I was ignorant enough to take for granted.

Some time during my first week, he gave me a brief lecture on the art of advertising.

'Let us call it the art of persuasion. One of the applied arts, Miss Jameson.' He smiled, pressing his hand down on his desk, stressing a great many words, and showing small very sharp teeth. 'How many novelists and poets manage to get themselves read by rich, poor, superior, ignorant, successful, happy, miserable, snobbish, unimaginative, resigned? Remember always that people *choose* to read a novel, but you must *trick* them into reading an *advertisement*. You can do it *only* if you *believe* what you are writing, if you believe whole*heartedly* in the virtue of the soap, the face cream, the tobacco, you are trying to sell. Avoid *cynicism*. It is incompatible with emotion—and great advertising is the expression of great emotional sincerity.'

I listened with all my ears. The trick, I told myself, is obviously to describe, as vividly as possible, the flawless skin, and to overlay this image with an image of the soap, the face cream. Persuasion is a matter of evoking the right images in the right order.

My cleverness enchanted me. In the same moment I was very slightly revolted, as if I had been made to swallow the skin of rice pudding.

During the time I worked in the Agency—much less than a year—this mute sense of outrage became loathing. It was not the fault of my colleagues. An edged gaiety made the days tolerable, and I think with affection of certain nameless faceless men, hardworking, sceptical, who took some trouble to teach an awkward provincial her job.

Apart from typists, I was the only woman on the staff. My immediate superior, Mr Foxe—I have forgotten his real name—was patient and friendly, a man of forty odd, slight, brisk, frankly concerned about his looks. 'In business, one can't afford to age,' he told me one day when we were both tired. 'D'you know what I do? At night before I get into bed, I stretch a narrow piece of sticking-plaster across the lines on my forehead and at the ends of my eyes, to smooth them out.'

'How clever,' I said falsely.

He smiled. 'You have no lines yet, Miss Jim, but you will, you know.'

This minute I could write an essay on the beauty and holiness of the art of advertising—forgive me, persuasion—and avoid calling up a single image which might rouse in its readers a suspicion of the truth: that the use of words with intent to sell something is simply the art of telling convincing lies. The accident that what you sell is harmless, or even useful, does not cancel the lie in the soul.

Great emotional sincerity! There is no polite word for it. Balderdash! (George Gallilee.) Modern advertising is a disease, a skin cancer galloping through the cells of society. Modern advertisers—highly-talented men and women, paid to lie.

Within limits (drawn by my profound boredom), I became a skilful copy-writer. Admirably persuasive about face cream, admirably succinct and convincing about roofing tiles and arc-welding lamps, charmed by type-faces, I could no more invent a slogan than sing. None the less, a career in advertising lay open to me if I had had the will to look for it. A more adroit or clear-sighted young woman would, without fuss, have split her mind, devoting one part to writing copy and preparing schemes, the other to honest work, and built a wall between them thick enough to keep one from contaminating the other.

This sort of inner duplicity—'controlled schizophrenia,' Klaus Fuchs called it—is too common a habit in our day to be noticed. Noticeable are only the rare exceptions, the one or two incorruptibles—like R. H. Tawney, that very great man and arbitrary saint. It is not to my credit that I resisted one form of the infection.

Ridiculous as it seems, I must have believed that I need only get myself back to London for all my unused energies and talents to flower at once. And here I was, doing work I knew to be worthless, making barely enough money to keep alive, and bored, bored, bored.

During those first weeks, I spent every evening, unless the weather were too abominable, walking about London from Oxford Street in the north to the Strand and the Embankment in the south. I was living in north-west London, I have forgotten where, in the house belonging to the widow of an officer killed in the war, a pleasant slightly *louche* young woman—I have a talent for finding landladies suitable to my condition. I had a small but not uncomfortable room, and would have done better to sit in it in the evening, since walking made me hungry.

I was singularly alone. None of my few friends were in London: Archie had (I think) already married his gay spirited Scotch girl, or was about to marry and go off to an Indian hill station, Sydney was in the West Indies, Oswald was marrying and beginning his career as schoolmaster in Yorkshire.

Why didn't I begin to write a novel? Because I lacked the sense to arrange my life sensibly. Because of the fever in my mind. And because I am a novelist *faute de mieux*.

I was dying of discontent with myself. And with London. This—these endless cold streets smelling of mud, sweat, petrol, these cafés and restaurants I could not afford to enter, these people with their flattened voices and faces, seeming to be nothing and nowhere, like shadows in water—was the London I had been praying to return to, and given up my son for it. Fool!

Wherever I went, at any moment, in the middle of a street, waiting to cross, crossing, in a cheap café before a scone and a cup of coffee, waking at two a.m., the same thought wounded me. Pressing its thumb into my brain, the image I had made for myself, of Bill looking for me in silence, became an illness. (I laugh like a dog when I think that these self-inflicted tortures belong to the same family as those I had felt thinking about the white rabbit.)

Walking along the Strand past Simpson's, I suddenly remembered that I had taken him there on our way to Hampshire. We had reached London at two o'clock, the two of us, and the train to Stockbridge did not leave until five. Carrying him down the long platform, I wondered anxiously where I could give him his lunch, and remembered that Simpson's, a place I had never been in, had a reputation for good English food. Nothing less would do for him. I took our luggage—cot, baby carriage, tin bath, dress-basket—to Waterloo station, and another taxi back to the Strand: I could never bring myself to risk him in the crowds and chance infections of bus or underground. (No wonder I never had two shillings to rub together!) When we reached Simpson's, it was three o'clock, and even in the doorway the place felt empty. We were directed up a flight of stairs. It took him a long time to climb them, and the large room was deserted. A man in a frock coat—I looked at him haughtily—led us to a table, and with his own hands placed a hassock on a chair to bring Bill's head above the edge. He gave me the menu—the prices were no worse than I had feared. I ordered lamb cutlets stewed in milk for Bill, and for myself mushrooms on toast—1/6. The cutlets were a long time coming, and meantime a round dozen of waiters gathered in the service doorway, smiling and pointing at the two-year-old customer who wanted stewed lamb at three in the afternoon. The chef brought it himself—no doubt he had heard the joke—and set it in front of Bill. A common waiter brought my mushrooms—two.

The memory of that afternoon only fifteen months ago caught me in the throat. Tears ran down my face in a stream I could not check, I stumbled along the street, praying that passers-by would take it I had been smitten by influenza. An elderly woman stopped and said hesitantly,

'Can I help?'

Scowling at her, I said, 'No!' in so foul and surly a voice that she stepped back. I hated her with such venom that it stopped my tears.

Hell, says Sartre, is the others. Nonsense. Nonsense prompted by a metaphysical vanity. Hell is five or six memories which are able occasionally to enter the intestines through the mind and tear them. That's all, that's all.


## CHAPTER 31


I AM WRITING THIS on the 17th of November, 1961. Yesterday I took the chair, with reluctance, at a dinner celebrating the 40th anniversary of the International P.E.N. About a hundred and fifty guests, including a charming old Dickensian professor from Moscow called Kirpotin. He had brought his interpreter, and throughout my speech—into which for his benefit I dropped the names of Pasternak and poor Ivinskaya—I was distracted by the muttered word-by-word translation going on in my left ear. Two other speakers, critics or dons, spoke amusingly: the second ended by calling for a toast 'to the distinguished women writers present, Dr Veronica Wedgwood, Dame Rebecca West, Miss Rosamund Lehmann.' This, I reflected with surprise, is the first time I have been publicly confronted by my own invisibility... I left the moment dinner ended, avoiding the kind of writers' talk which curdles my soul.

Dawdling along a cold brutally lighted Piccadilly towards my bed for the night, I made an effort to consider soberly the probable end of a freak.

It was no use—I could not keep my mind on my precarious future. Seizing the chance offered it at night, only at night, an older London tapped me on the shoulder. Friends, including one or two of whom I never now think, so undemanding are they, so withdrawn into their dark silence and peace, ranged themselves on either side of me, and we walked about unnoticed in streets no less immaterial than they were. I felt crazily exhilarated. My ghosts vanished, but, in spite of the cold, the gaiety stayed.

Why, I asked myself, do you write books? Not to be praised. There is not a single moment, during the many months or years of a book's conception and raising, when the thought: Will it be liked? Will it be damned? enters your mind. At this level, praise and dispraise are strictly irrelevant.

The person in my skin who flinches when damned or mocked is not the writer. The writer is deeply indifferent to opinion, fretted when she has not done her best, protected at other times by her ineradicable barely articulate conviction that novel-writing—or, more narrowly, her novels, for all the intense pains taken with them—are not serious, not worth a tear.

The one who flinches is the beaten child, afraid with an old fear. But there is no need to be sorry for her.

I walked about for an hour in my lost city, the happiest and no doubt the most foolish of its ghosts. No fine thoughts came to me, only lines I am certain of not forgetting.

> ... I said to Lord Nelson at three
> Pore devil, look at 'yer
> They built y' a stat'yer
> They built Piccadilly for me!

Some time in the spring of 1919 my first novel was published. Trying to grope a way back to what must surely have been a time, however brief, of intoxication and expectancy, I remember nothing. Nothing at all of the feelings of an obscure young woman. I was seeing no one to whom I could have talked about it. Not that I had the least wish to talk; I would rather run a mile than be seen caring about the fate of one of my books.

I was too ignorant to be surprised that it had a great many reviews. I kept them, good and bad, for some years before tearing them up. Nowadays, I destroy as I go. I have no intention of leaving driftwood.

Today, such a novel as *The Pot Boils* would not get itself published. Or if a rash publisher took it for its promise—what the devil did it promise?—it would not meet any such body of criticism. The room into which a young writer steps now is so overcrowded that he is lucky if he is not suffocated in the first five minutes. And even if he is noticed he can hope for useful advice from, at most, two quarters. The rest will be no good to him. Unless he has laid his lines beforehand—unless, that is, he has *friends*—the so-called serious journals will not notice him at all. In this way, his lot is harder than mine in 1919. So far as money goes, it could scarcely be harder. Ten pounds, and that not earned! (Unless I have forgotten.)

Mr Shaw-Thomas caught sight of a review and read the book. He called me into his room, to talk about a campaign for a new firm, and said, smiling, 'I had no idea we had a novelist on the staff. Nor that you were so intelligent.'

I smiled. But—as my grandfather would have done—I thought his remark impudent.


K. was still in Canterbury. If I had not been so engrossed by my exasperating work, I might have been surprised by the fewness and brevity of his letters. He turned up one evening without warning, and took me to dinner in the brasserie of the Café Royal.

Intoxicated by so much food and by the delicious warmth and liveliness of a place which—thanks to the mania for change of fools who cannot see to the ends of their noses—no longer exists, and pleased not to be alone, I was immensely grateful. An old tenderness woke in me. I would give a fortune, I thought, to be living with him and Bill in some quiet place. Rashly, I said so.

He said he might be moved to Netheravon.

'But I thought you would be demobilized any day now. Haven't you heard anything?'

'Not a word,' he said gaily.

'Would they release you if you applied?'

'My dear girl, why should I? I'm quite snug where I am, thank you.'

I had enough sense not to say: But the longer you stay in the Air Force, well-fed, going to dances, working easy hours, irresponsible because nothing depends on your efforts, with a servant to polish your beautiful boots, the less fit you will be for any other life.

'But you will have to leave in the end—and the longer you hang on the worse your chances of a job. Why not try at once for a school in London? We should both be earning, we could have a house and a nurse for Bill——'

'You dislike houses. How often have you told me that one room and a suitcase is all you want?'

'That's true,' I said, 'but Bill——'

'But any stick will do to beat a bad dog,' K. said, in an amused patronizing voice. 'How you enjoy managing my life for me. You're pricelessly funny when you imagine you're being subtle, my dear. But you don't impress me, you know. You always wanted to get away, you've got away, and blow me if you're not still dissatisfied! How'd you have liked it if I had rushed out of the Air Force, back to Liverpool and the Suburb?'

'I would have gone with you.'

'And made my life hell by grumbling!'

True enough, I thought. My hatred of a settled life, my unhappiness when I thought of Bill, started up in me in the same instant, throwing me back into the confusion I lived in. How unreasonable, how feeble, to wish that K. had settled the problem for me.

'Don't you want us to live together?' I exclaimed. I meant: have you no feeling for us as a family? No single impulse to make us safe?

'I knew we should come to that! And mark you, I didn't ask you to leave the boy and betake yourself to London. You did it entirely to please yourself. Don't try to blame me.'

I was only too ready to think everything my fault. When he had gone, leaving me in Regent Street, I reflected that, though I disliked my life in London, I had no great wish to live with K. To tell the truth, I thought, angrily, you don't know what you want or what to do next... I felt demoralized and incompetent. I did not believe in my talents as an advertiser—still less, as a novelist. The only person wholly important to me was my son, and I had left him to a Miss Geeson.

The cold night air sent a ball of blood to press at the roots of my brain. I walked home in a state near insanity. There seemed no way out of the confusion. The idea of going back to Whitby, a penniless failure, was intolerable.

I have failed at everything, I thought.

In May I took a night train to Whitby. Travelling both ways at night, I could spend two days with him in my mother's house, and be at my desk, heavy-eyed, on Monday morning.

Walking out to Ruswarp to fetch him, I prepared myself for everything but the shock of hearing his voice. He had not been warned I was coming: he was in the garden, hidden from me by the hedge, when I rang the bell.

In a high clear thin voice he called out, 'Is that my mother?'

*He has been learning to talk without me*, I thought.

We spent the day on the sands. Light-headed with happiness, I forgot that he had not had the practice in climbing of three other children, and brought him back up the face of the cliff. For most of the way it was easy enough, only the last ten or fifteen yards suddenly became steep, hard slippery clay. Here his feet slid under him and he looked up at me quickly in fear. Hiding my panic, I said, 'You're all right, son—use your hands and knees.'

He reached the top without help, and stood smiling.

Love crossed with pride gives birth to the most surprising sensation, of a sail furling and unfurling in the pit of the stomach.

When I took him back to Miss Geeson on Sunday evening he did not ask any questions—Are you going? When will you come back? I put him to bed, and waited until he fell asleep, one arm flung out, long dark thick lashes feathering his cheeks.

'Do you ever feel sorry you went away?' my mother asked.

'Something had to be done,' I said.

To this day, if I am incautious enough to go near her, the young woman I buried alive claws me.

Some short time after this, I told Mr Shaw-Thomas that I could not go on working for four pounds a week.

'Why do you want more money?' he asked kindly.

Without reflecting, I knew that it would be a mistake to say: Because I am always a little hungry, and because my son is growing out of his sandals and cotton smocks. I smiled at him.

'How can I hope to buy a new coat on four pounds?'

'Very well,' he said, 'we'll make it six. But you must give your whole mind to the job. You're not writing another novel, by any chance?'

'No.'

How easy it is to exaggerate. The habitual state of my mind when I am not working is one of happiness, or at least detachment. That year there were days, of superb weather, when it amused me to dawdle about London. My best moments were those I wasted day-dreaming. That I was famous, that I had written a masterpiece, or become a rich implacably clever business woman, or—equally consoling, and not a whit more absurd—that I had saved the life of a royal personage and been rewarded with a sinecure: better, the life of the director of the Ritz, who gave me two modest rooms looking across the Park, and the run of my teeth, for life.

Or I thought, less often now, of the Texan. The details of the scene in the Piccadilly Hotel, which had taken only a few minutes, lasted me through an entire evening spent under the trees of the Green Park, or walking slowly the length of Oxford Street, Regent Street, Piccadilly, St James's Street, the Mall, Constitution Hill, and Park Lane, dust everywhere, and the splintered voices and eyes of passers-by. I felt light and feverish, and deliciously free. Since I was not with him, I could give way safely to any delirium of my senses: the coolness, the vanity, needed to defeat him, were not needed.

It is when I recall the image of another person, or a place, that they give up to me the pleasure, even the ecstasy, missing at the time.

But there were moments that I really did see, did feel. I remember an evening in July when, walking across Trafalgar Square, I saw the pillars of St Martin-in-the-Fields as white as bones under a brilliantly blue sky; a sickle moon hung in it, and every object in sight, the edges of buildings, the fountains, Admiralty Arch, the pigeons, sprang out as clear as light. And there were innocent mornings when, even if the night before, in bed, alone, I had cried scalding tears, I woke certain that happiness was within reach of my outstretched hand.

The triumphs allowed the old are less insensate, less poignant, less ravishing.

## CHAPTER 32

THE IMAGE FOR MY LIFE in the years between 1919 and the end of 1923 is that of a vacant lot between crowded streets. I worked, idled, was poor, earned money, spent it recklessly, schemed, confided in no one, wasted time and strength, ignored opportunities—behaved, in short, with the utmost folly, while seeming to be responsible, reliable, intelligent. But give an account of it—impossible.

In contrast, my memory of the three days J. spent in London in the summer of 1919 is sharply clear.

He had not changed, voice, quick supple movements, energy. I felt all the happiness of coming, half-frozen, into a room alive with warmth and light. A gaiety I had forgotten—yet it was mine, natural to me—filled me: I had to use all my strength to speak in a cool voice. I forget where we dined; I forget at what point in a story he was telling me he broke off, and said, 'How long will it take you to get divorced in this country? A month? This is my last leave, I must go home and get myself demobilized. I don't want to have to wait when I come back for you. Your taste in husbands... couldn't you have found something else to keep you busy?'

Exasperated vanity must have had a great deal to do with his decision to marry a young woman with so few of the qualities he admired. He expected only legal delays. It did not cross his mind that I might find it no easier to be his wife than his mistress. As I always do when I am at a loss, I began an argument a little to the side.

He remained good-humoured. 'Don't you want to marry me and go live in a real country? This one's finished. Europe is finished. I'll say this for you that, without the war, you might have held out against us for another twenty years. But you've nothing left.'

His grotesque arrogance amused me. It was at least thirty years before I realized the crude truth in his boasts. (If this makes me seem to have been half-witted, reflect that only fifteen years before 1919 English imperialism had been at its glorious zenith. Merciful heavens, was there ever so rapid a descent!)

'I couldn't live in America.'

'Why not?'

'I would rather be poor and unsafe in this country than well off in yours.'

I said this thinking of my own poverty and uncertainty. But it was true. And had no relevance to what I felt. The thought of marrying him entered my head only to be ejected at once. I had no need even to hesitate. Put to it, I could have given reasons, excellent ones. The queerest thing about my destructive passion is that it was not blind. Or not more than half blind, half the dupe of my senses. I knew, I always knew, that there was no dignity in my obsession. In cold moments I saw him as any of my hard-minded upright forbears would have seen him.

The part of me neither blind nor duped judged him with shocking lucidity. The other part, the egotistical, ribald, unreliable, nihilistic part was wholly on his side. Had I been childless I might have gone off with him. It is possible. But I doubt it. I doubt whether any Gallilee woman could have brought herself to marry an ungovernable foreigner.

But what had reason to do with it? Devilish little. I discovered reasons for rejecting him after I had done it. At the bottom of every gentle or violent feeling I had for him, below lust, greed, liking, was quite simply fear. Not a physical fear—something older and harder. Fear is the wrong word. Why—unless our bodies are a great deal more intelligent than we give them credit for—should it have been my senses, obsessed with him, that warned me?

It occurs to me, but only now, that in rejecting him I rejected, once for all, my violent self. Not that this freed me of it. Good heavens, no.

At some moment in an argument that went on during three evenings, I said,

'The whole thing is impossible. You forget Bill.'

'I do not. We'd take him with us—of course.'

The bare notion of involving my child in so unpredictable a life put it beyond conjecture. This was so clear that I had the calmness to shrug my shoulders, and—in bad faith, since it was irrelevant—say that K. was vindictive enough to try to keep him.

'We won't talk about K. You'll have other children. D'you think I don't want sons?'

Heaven knows where my revulsion came from—some dry bodily pride, nothing to do with my reason.

'I'm sure you do,' I said drily. 'Americans have all the right sentiments.'

Thinking about it, I see, with a little astonishment, that during the whole of that brief time he behaved with great self-control, even kindness. Not until he was leaving did he put his arms round me. 'Why,' he said, 'must you give us both so much trouble? You're mine and you know it. When you decide to have me I'm yours, and I never told you lies—except about other people to amuse you. You don't want to be half dead for the rest of your life, do you?'

I thought that I was on the point of fainting. But I laughed.

How absurd this will seem to young women who fall into bed with a lover as simply as into a hot bath. And I am very willing to believe that the sensible (enlightened, free) young women of 1960 are wiser than I was. But not that they are the happier for behaving like commercial travellers with no time to waste between sales. With fewer unnecessary scruples, less naïveté, less tortuous minds, their lives may be simpler. But less boring? I doubt it. There is nothing like imagination for reducing the risks of boredom in a love-affair.

After he had gone back to France, my scepticism made me think it unlikely he wanted a wife. It must surely have been a mood. Then, a few weeks later, I had a letter from Texas, from his father, a kind polite simple letter, telling me that if I cared to come over at once I should be welcome in his house.

This surprised and pleased me, but did not change my mind. Given a second chance, I should have behaved with precisely the same stubbornness.

I knew it. I knew, too, that the fever would burn itself out. There are no incurable fevers. Oh, well, one.

During the next year he wrote a score of times, from China, South America, Texas, admirable letters, written in an idiom as sharp, lively and common as Elizabethan English, only now and then boastful. I answered some of them and destroyed all. In one he used a phrase—'the cleverest woman I ever owned'—that made me smile. Owned?

It was true in a sense.

## CHAPTER 33

T HIS YEAR (1919) I made a woman friend, the first since I left Leeds. Someone, possibly Sydney Harland, wrote to me that one of our group at King's, an Eikonoklast, was living in London in St John's Wood, married to a sister of the writer Stephen Graham: he had sent him my address. I was a little vexed. John Gleeson had not been a close friend: he was a medical student, an extremely ugly young man, lean, sallow, myopic—his eyes behind the thickest of lenses were like sea anemones—and a mystifier, always inventing stories about himself which amused us mildly and were, perhaps, now and then true. I had no wish to see him again.

When his letter came I delayed an indecent time, then, reluctantly, went. His wife opened the door of the flat, and said smiling,

'It's Margaret, isn't it? Come in.'

I walked straight into an intimacy which fitted me like a comfortable old glove... With my few close friends, it is always the same, no slow prudent growths, friendship at first sight. It is the only likeness between them.

She opened the door of the living-room. 'But what an enormous place,' I said, too horrified by the disorder, the eccentric poverty, the dust thick everywhere, on table, shelves, sofa, chairs, to hold my tongue.

Knowing perfectly well what I was thinking, Elizabeth only smiled.

We drank tea, and I learned that John was not practising as a doctor. When they had no money at all, he would answer an appeal for a locum, and pick up enough money to keep them alive for a few months. For the rest, he was writing stories, so grotesquely bad that again I was silenced. If he is as inept a doctor as a writer, I thought, he had better stick to writing.

They had a baby, a few months old, unbelievably sweet-tempered, who submitted placidly to being fastened in her bed in an empty room when they wanted to go out without her.

Elizabeth herself—ah, Elizabeth. She was not beautiful, her face was too long, her features, except for the eyes, too masculine, a wide sensual mouth, pale, its skin slightly rough, a strong nose: her eyes were long, narrow, a greenish grey and extraordinarily bright, their glance the flick through water of a fin: her hair, the colour of a brown fox, fell naturally into waves too coarse and heavy to be held by any comb. She was not intelligent—a certain quickness of understanding—the mind of a lively adolescent, but with reserves. The brilliant trivialities littering it distracted attention, even her own, from these reserves: she must have glanced into them as seldom as possible, for fear of finding there nothing reassuring—or nothing.

She was charming. Her charm was a sixth sense; she used it as a violinist his bow, without vanity, to give pleasure, and because it was what she could do better than anything else in the world. Without vanity... her certainty that she was charming might look like vanity, but was not—unless the sun rises or a nightingale sings out of vanity. Gaiety, a childishly natural gaiety and wit, rippled through her like light through a wave—in her smiling mouth a small jest became high comedy. And warmth—she was a fountain of warmth.

I thought their baby neglected—she crawled about the unswept floor, pushing fluff and fragments of coal into her mouth—but the warmth, in those days, covered her, too. One day when I came in with Elizabeth we heard her crying as we opened the door: in spite of the straps, she had managed to kick the blankets off her bed, she was cold and hungry. The instant her mother spoke to her, her cries ceased and she began laughing.

I am profoundly incurious about my friends' emotional habits and disorders. It ought to have struck me as strange that she had chosen to marry a penniless, eccentric, ugly man. I don't think it did for a moment.

She seemed radiantly happy. If she grumbled sometimes that John refused to do any steady work, it was lightly, with an amused smile, as she might have smiled at a child's clowning.

In the meantime she did not try to lead a good bourgeois life. She had not been used to cleaning or mending or cooking—therefore she did not clean, or mend, and cooked as rarely as possible.

The flat was large, much larger than they needed. After I had been visiting them for a week or two, they offered me one of the unused rooms—it held a bed, a chest of drawers, a cupboard and a glass dangling crookedly from a nail. It was ridiculous, they argued passionately, for me to pay a landlady when I could have a room for nothing. This last tempted me. On condition that I paid something into Elizabeth's famished purse, if no more than would cover the cost of my breakfast coffee, I agreed to come.

I hate disorder, and that flat really was squalid, but I lived in it for—how long? a year?—in exquisite ease of mind and heart.

I say nothing of body. John's indifferences to illness in his family—I now being part of it—was prodigious. One day, after I had been running about London in shoes that let the rain in, a pain started in my side, and after a few days I could not laugh or draw a quick breath without groaning. At the end of a week of this, I came back to the office from lunch to find that I could not climb the several flights of stairs, the pain was so frightful. A little alarmed, I got myself, on foot and by bus, to a woman doctor in the Harley Street quarter whose name I had picked up somewhere. Dr Aldrich-Blake was, though I did not know it, one of the great women doctors, and must have been mildly surprised to see me, ill and ill-dressed. She treated me with enormous kindness and gentleness, and diagnosed an inflammation of the gall bladder. I had a raging temperature. When I told her I was living in a doctor's household, she said drily,

'A male doctor, I suppose. Well—' writing quickly—'give him this when you get home. And take a cab.'

'What do I owe you?' I asked.

'Nothing.' She smiled. 'Since another doctor will, I hope, be looking after you.'

I spent a week in bed, looked after with loving inefficiency by Elizabeth— and recovered completely.

## CHAPTER 34

THE DAY WHEN I CEASE EXPECTING, slyly, to be saved from despair by some insignificant little miracle, I shall be really finished. By the summer of 1919, the miracle was overdue.

It astonishes me now that I kept my place in the Carlton Agency: more than half my energy and intellect was running to waste, dragging furiously against the other half—furiously and blindly. I was more discontented with myself than ever.

What would have become of me if it had not been for the *New Commonwealth*, that short-lived and hare-brained enterprise?

Some time in the early autumn, I had a letter from an F. Thoresby: the address was of a reputable city firm, and his name appeared among those of its directors. But for this I might, with the scepticism praise of my writing always starts in me, have thrown his letter away. He had read *The Pot Boils*, he said, it had impressed him, he would very much like to discuss it with me, if I would have the great kindness to lunch with him, at Romano's... I was ready to endure anything, even the boredom of talking about my novel, for the sake of a meal.

He turned out to be a not too elderly man, stout, friendly, evidently solid and respectable, and not a noodle. He talked less about my book than I had feared, and more, much more, about himself. This I could deal with: I had only to bring on my face an expression of alert attention and leave it there while I ate everything I was offered, like a starved boa-constrictor.

Besides, I enjoy listening to people talking about themselves as much as I detest being asked about myself.

After a time he surprised me into lively curiosity. He was, he said, about to retire, and had bought an old-established weekly paper, the *Christian Commonwealth*: he had plans for turning it, renamed the *New Commonwealth*, into a mouthpiece for his views. About these, although he went into them at great length, I remained uncertain. I imagine, now, that they were a form of *Poujadisme* before Poujade, but with more heart, an honest business man's vision of a society run on the lines of a good firm, reasonably generous to its workers. Neither then nor later did I take them seriously. In any event, he changed his views fairly often—and without noticing it.

He told me, too, that he was a theosophist. I had never heard of theosophy: I hid my ignorance, and afterwards looked it up in a public library. Like his politics, it seemed odd but harmless.

Throughout this long explanation I was waiting, without speculation, to hear what it had to do with me. Nothing very much, I thought. I was all the more startled—I took care not to show it—when he asked me to think over the idea of sub-editing his paper: he himself would edit it, and he needed, he said, a young sub-editor, whose mind was not cluttered up with rubbish.

Lucky you can't see my mind, I thought. I felt much less respect for him now that I knew I had impressed him with my—what? intelligence? competence? malleability?

He startled me again, by offering a salary of fifty pounds a month. At the same time he asked, smiling gently, for the year and hour of my birth, so that he could have his astrologer cast my horoscope. Later, he showed me five folio pages of incomprehensible jargon, of which I recall a single sentence: *The nearer the goat the nearer the god.* This struck me as unpleasant. Luckily, it did not seem to alarm him.

All this makes it seem incredible that he was a successful man of business, and not mad. In fact, he had been very successful, in a discreet way. Theosophy and astrology were an escape valve for a romanticism, a warmth of heart, an idealism, he could not use in business.

I hesitated over his offer. Not because I knew nothing about a sub-editor's duties—if he had raked London he could not have found a greater dunce. It struck my Gallilee shrewdness as unsafe. But fifty pounds a month!

In the end I told Mr Foxe about it, and asked his advice. He refused to advise me.

'You must decide for yourself. And I know what you will decide.'

'Well, then, tell me.'

'No. But I'll write it down, and when you tell me what you've done I'll show you what I've written.'

He scribbled a few words on a memorandum sheet, folded it into an envelope, sealed it, made me press my thumb on the wax, and put the envelope, at the back of his desk. Two weeks later I told him I had accepted.

He looked at me with a sharp smile. 'I was wrong.'

Opening the envelope, I read: Out of female loyalty, you will stay with Shaw-Thomas.

I burst out laughing. 'Perhaps I am less of a female than you think.'

The office of the renamed *New Commonwealth* was the top floor of a lean decrepit house in a square behind Fleet Street. The square itself was old and shabby, not a house in it but was on its deathbed. A narrow street, infested with lorries, led from one corner to the printers', and beyond that to the river. The floors of our two rooms sank deeply in the centre, so that chairs slid inward, and desks had to be stoutly wedged.

The middle-aged gentlewoman who had been a prop of the paper in its Christian era stayed on. It must have been galling to her to have an unlicked young woman set over her. I did not then realize what self-control, what patience, what desperate civility, she exercised. Whether out of good manners or despair, she did not teach me anything. The paper's printers did that. I was always behind time, and Mr Thoresby's habit of rewriting his editorial at the last minute—having changed his policy since the day before—did not help. On press nights I was at the printers' until two or three in the morning, reading pages as they came off the machines. A savage lighting painted the men's faces fish-belly white, and the clattering steel fingers unpicked the seams of my brain.

One night, when he brought me the ritual cup of deathly strong tea, a compositor suggested gently that there are less dull ways of making up a weekly review than by running articles straight on, three columns to a page, without changing type or lay-out. It had not occurred to me.

I thanked him, and thereafter produced a paper which looked a little less like a parish magazine.

At the end of these night sessions I walked home, from Fleet Street to St John's Wood, through blessedly empty streets—tubes and buses had stopped, and I could not afford a cab. Besides, I enjoyed the walk. It was the only hour of the twenty-four when London became human, when a clock striking in the city could be heard as clearly as if the sound travelled over fields and villages, when an air from the sea, or a ship's whistle, reminded me, innocently, of another life than this in which I made only mistakes.

I wrote a great deal of the paper myself: dramatic criticism, political notes, reviews, brief essays—all, except the first, with a lighthearted indifference to principles. Until the day when, between one minute and the next, I ran head on into a social conscience, into a passion, sudden and lasting.

I forget which newspaper I had bought to read over lunch: all I recall about it is the language it used to dismiss, as snivelling and a lie, the story (in another paper) of German and Austrian children dying of hunger. I did not know the facts, but the smell of hypocrisy and bad faith given off by the phrases themselves stank to heaven.

In those days we were almost innocent. Even the war, even the millions of young deaths, had not accustomed us to cruelty. The enemies this rancorous editorial wanted me to punish by starving them were infants, and I disliked the idea of an hereditary enemy with tiny stick-like arms and a swollen stomach.

For the first time in my life I had the sense, horribly familiar later, of a dark wave of pain, cruelty, fear, gathering force at the other side of Europe and about to rush down.

After this, no issue of the *New Commonwealth* lacked its paragraph—at least a paragraph—about Europe's famished children. Discovering the commonest of tricks for calling attention to an item of news by printing it inside a rectangular frame, I used it every week...

About this time we heard—John heard—that one of our King's College friends, a fellow Eikonoklast, was in a London hospital being treated for the cancer that had started in him at the end of the war. We went to see him, I with reluctance.

Red Smith—nicknamed for his romantic anarchism—was the youngest of us: he was very fair, with a childishly snub nose and clear blue eyes. Lying in bed in a small room, he greeted us with an indifference so unlike him that, although I did not know he was dying, I had the sense that he had half turned his back. He and I had shared a passion for *La Révolte des Anges*, and I remembered—I had never thought of it since that year—Nectaire's long account of himself and the other fallen angels as tutelary gods of Greece and Italy and their decline through the centuries to this moment when he was making a living as a gardener in a wood near Paris. It was all false, all nonsense, and a delicious sense of freshness, of marble gleaming in the sun, of the Mediterranean miracle of light, rose from it, intoxicating us both.

I was afraid to ask him if he remembered it. What could it mean to him in this bare little room, with the bed, the two chairs, the window facing a blank dark wall? His eyelids kept closing, and when he lifted them there was only an emptiness under them, shallow, clouded. I did not realize that he was drugged.

Suddenly he stretched a hand out and took hold of one of mine. Like any ignorant old countrywoman I believed that cancer is infectious. It was an effort to let my hand lie quietly in his. It lay there for the rest of the time, twenty or thirty minutes, that we stayed with him. I had to free it from his grasp when we left.

He mumbled a few words I did not catch.

'Goodbye, my dear, we'll come to see you again on Saturday,' I said.

It was not necessary to go again.

Early in life a death closes one door in an endless corridor of doors, all open. For a few minutes I thought about him, then left him, behind his shut door.

*And the night in its entirety turned its ear to Nectaire's flute...*

# CHAPTER 35

T HAT YEAR, 1920, my second novel was published—by Heinemann. Michael Sadleir had not liked it when I sent him the manuscript, and with all the indifference in the world I took it away from him. Nothing I could have done to it would have satisfied him, and the idea of throwing it away vexed my Yorkshire soul.

This book had two readers I know of—one of them John Galsworthy. Charles Evans of Heinemann sent it to him, and showed me his letter. 'I've finished *The Happy Highways*, and congratulate you on your choice. This authoress has done what none of the other torrential novelists of the last ten years has achieved—given us a convincing (if not picture, at least) summary of the effervescence, discontent, revolt, and unrest of youth; the heartache and beating of wings. I should like to meet her. She must have seen and felt things... To an old-fashioned brute like me, of course, the lack of form and line and the plethora of talk and philosophy pass a little stubbornly down the throat and stick a little in the gizzard, but the stuff is undeniable, and does not give me the hollow windy feeling I get from a German novel—say: nor do I feel suffocated by the crude ego that stalks through most of their novels.'

'I don't think we can ask him to let us quote it, do you?' Charles Evans said.

'Good heavens, no,' I said, shocked.

'I thought you would feel that.'

How innocent we both were. Today if I write a personal letter to a young writer who has sent me his book, I know perfectly well that he, and his publisher, will be outraged if I do not allow them to make use of it.

The second reader was in prison. One day my eye caught a newspaper item: a young American poet, Ralph Chaplin, condemned to a long term of years in the Federal Prison of Fort Leavenworth, Kansas, as a pacifist, had chosen an English novel, *The Happy Highways*, to take with him. Astonished—surely he should have something weightier?—and delighted, I wrote offering to send him books, and made a friend I never saw.

My conviction that novel-writing is no profession for a serious-minded pauper did not lessen.

I did not expect Michael to be angry with me for leaving his firm, nor was he. He was critical of me, an ugly duckling who never properly became a swan, and kind and sweet-tempered and loyal.

'Promise me on your honour that you will never put me in a novel,' he said once. I promised—and kept my promise.

Indeed, I knew too much and too little about him to draw his portrait. Like me, but without my violence and crudity, he was a flawed rebel. His mother came from a family of rich wool people, originally Quakers—not, I think, like my father-in-law, Evangelicals, but there was a certain Puritan rigidity, a strictness, which set its mark on him: he rebelled against it, but without conviction. Some—I have no idea what—feeling of disappointment, some failure or desertion of an original purpose (I am writing in the dark), remained in him, a grain of sand which grew smaller and smaller, but never disappeared. His good looks—he was extremely good-looking—had the softness enclosing a hard core which is noticeable in the portraits of certain priests. He was romantic and shrewd.

His young wife was an enchanting creature. Only the other day, when, after an interval of many years, she came to see me, I realized that her enduring quality is a simplicity in which there is nothing childish—although her smile still has the gaiety and irony, involuntary and guileless, of a very young child's. It is the simplicity of a heart without a single tortuous or calculating impulse.

A streak of worldly corruption in me, rising to the surface again and again, forced me, in those days, to covet an elegance to which, on another level, I am deeply indifferent. One year Betty Sadleir designed and made knitted dresses to sell to her friends. Because I should have liked to be a young woman who could afford it, I bought one. No sooner had I carried it away than I knew I had been a fool—I ought not to have spent the money. The dress did not even suit me.

I cried with grief, rage, shame. I could better have spared an ear than five guineas.

It seems to me that I have only to stretch a hand out to touch this young woman in her cold room, crying over a wasted five guineas tears which very quickly became tears for an infinitely heavier loss and error—also her own fault.

Nothing could be more ridiculous than this.

## CHAPTER 36

MICHAEL TOOK ME TO WHAT, only half joking, he called 'your baptism into the literary world.' It was not his fault that I am incapable of being sanctified by rose-water.

Naomi Royde-Smith was a power in what I now see to have been a soberly decent Establishment. She was editing, with tact and judgement, the *Saturday Westminster*, and had made it a forum for any talented writer—even, in Walter de la Mare, for genius—except the unpredictably new or eccentric. On Thursday evenings her drawing-room in Queen's Gate might hold as many as fifty or sixty people, friends and protégés, and protégés of friends, who came to talk to her and each other. Was there coffee? I cannot remember. Cocktails, which have murdered conversation, were not yet the rule. It was not a clique, not a restricted circle of close friends, not brilliantly intellectual. None of the currents setting towards the future troubled this urbane backwater. I could not have learned there that the world of 1913 was shrivelled and in ruins, like the forms of Georgian poetry. The great figures who sometimes glided through were none of them rebels—Arnold Bennett but not D. H. Lawrence, Eddie Marsh, not T. S. Eliot, not even a young Raymond Mortimer. No cold gusty breath ruffled this placid trough between two waves. It vanished, leaving no ripple.

Naomi I found a little formidable with her air of a younger more affable Queen Victoria. But Rose Macaulay, who shared the flat with her, had been kind on my first evening, and I had no fear of her, nor of her salty tongue. She was enchanting to watch, a narrow head covered with small curls, like a Greek head in a museum, with that way she had of speaking in arpeggios, and the lively hands, the small arched nose and pale deep-set eyes.

For the next twenty years I saw her in this way, unchanged. Then, in 1941, Arthur Koestler came up to me at a writers' conference and said with smiling energy, 'I've been talking to Rose Macaulay. But what a charming delightful old lady.' I felt a stupefying dismay, as if, walking behind her along a street, I had seen her swallowed up by a crack opening in the ground.

One Thursday evening, I watched her with Arnold Bennett. He hung over her, mouth slightly open, like a great fish mesmerized by the flickering tongue of a water-snake.

Another of these evenings remains in my mind almost intact, because it ended in my disgrace. The room, more crowded than usual, was frightfully hot. I cannot endure hot rooms. I stood about, with a false air of ease, wishing I had not come. Three or four young men and women—not many of Naomi's friends were young—discussed hotly the correct behaviour to be followed by a young wife whose husband, a poet, had brought his mistress into the family: they were very emphatic that she must not be jealous or give way to a narrow-minded respect for convention. They did not ask my opinion, and I doubt I should have been courageous enough to say that I thought their new orthodoxy no better or wiser than the old.

Suddenly, Naomi called me to sit, with two or three other people, beside a very well-known critic and patron of young writers. She meant it kindly, and I was thrown into an agony of diffidence. I could not have said a word to save my neck. I listened. When I listen blankly, like an idiot, what I hear is less the spoken words than the sense of the brain behind them, even its nature. Usually I am prudent enough to keep my impressions—which may be distorted by the medium—to myself.

I was leaving when Naomi asked me, 'Well, how did you get on with E.? If you have anything you would like him to read, let me have it.'

Startled by the idea, I lost my head completely, and said,

'Oh, I don't think he is interested in young women.'

Her friendly smile vanished. In a voice whose coldness terrified me, she said, 'Don't repeat foolish lying gossip.'

I fled—and lay awake half the night asking myself why the devil this innocent remark had brought such a rebuke on me. Unspeakably mortified, I wanted to hide, to run back to Whitby. I can endure, I told myself, the Yorkshire habit of rudeness and derision, but I can't endure *these* people, *la canaille littéraire*.

When, after several weeks, I dared show my face there again, she had forgotten my crime, and complained, smiling, of my neglect.

'Rose calls you a most likeable child. I doubt whether you're either likeable or a child, in spite of your voice.'

Those Thursday evenings should have cured me of going into company. When I got back to my room my mind was in a frightful disorder: fragments of it had been left lying on the floor of overheated drawing-rooms and in the limp hands of strangers; I had talked to a dozen people and said nothing that was not dull or indiscreet or at best meaningless: I had agreed eagerly with comments that aroused only hostility or derision in me, and made promises it would destroy me to keep. I was trembling with self-disgust. And there was nothing I could do about it—except turn the light off and sleep. Five hours of not-thinking, not-planning, not-regretting.

## 14th of January, 1962

Yesterday I was in Cambridge. Sun and ice-cold air, bare branches drawn with Indian ink on a cloudless sky, a light like brittle glass, the Granta running full and fast, and every college along its banks as white, sharp, radiant, as if new: a day of celestial energy, given once every hundred years. The evening before I had listened to arguments tossed between four or five enormously intelligent people, and had realized, suddenly, that I was not afraid of them. Remoteness had taken the place of diffidence and my instinctive fear of punishment.

It is because I am old, I thought, and because, when I dream *deeply*, it is of the young dead...

In 1920 I was still weaving blindly the pattern of my future. The dichotomy in my mind—it goes deeper, but the larger word frets me—was there to be seen, if I had had eyes to see it: the instinct to withdraw completely, and the desire to live a flashing life in the world.

How far back in the darkness must I force my way, to meet the self whose need was poverty, simplicity, solitude, freedom from possessions, and who was betrayed—oh, another of those large words—by the self hungry for a way of living which rests on money and power?

Come to that, they betrayed each other. In the part of the world I come from, we have a cruel saying: Let want be your master. My wants were completely irreconcilable, enemies of each other and me. In those days I ran about my life like a dog chasing a yellow leaf down a path, turning to chase another, and another. My busily wasteful days ended, not seldom, in useless tears.

There are plenty of people who can go into the world and take part in conversations and the business of a career without losing touch with themselves. Too late, I see that I am not one of them, I was only fit to live alone, in society I am worthless.

## CHAPTER 37

OUT OF A LIFETIME OF RECEIVING and writing a monstrous sum of letters, say, a hundred thousand, I have kept only a few—fifty, a hundred? (Apart from those tied together at the bottom of a deed-box, which, when a time comes, I shall destroy.) Kept for various reasons—not always for what they contained: the ones I tore up were often infinitely more important, that is, indiscreet, revealing, interesting—I re-read them with reluctance. The person I am afraid of meeting in them is not the writer of the letter, but myself—quite possibly, a self I no longer know anything about.

One evening at Naomi's I talked, for a long time, to Frank Swinnerton. The only thing I recall is his light smiling voice: 'You know, I don't regard myself as a writer at all!' But this letter from him, written, in 1937, to thank me for something, says: 'Well, I have always been fond of you from the evening when we first met at a funny party given by Rose Macaulay or N. Royde-Smith, and I was moved to the heart by your sympathy over our baby. I know that although we don't agree about some things it doesn't in the least matter; and you *are* my friend, and dear to me, though (as is the case with most of my true friends) we don't meet...'

Why not admit that the person I should like to catch sight of in this letter is not Frank Swinnerton but an unrecognizable young woman? Damn it all, this must have been a half-hour of reality in a desert of pretence, waste of time, inexistence. And I must, for once, have been talking with no impulse to protect myself. And the whole thing has gone—vanished—sunk.

Here are ten letters from Walter de la Mare, beginning in 1921, and in three of them, written twenty, thirty, years later, he describes the same incident of that year. 'Not so very long ago—to all seeming—I was sitting on the top of a tram with you, ascending, not Parnassus, but Sydenham Hill, en route for the Crystal Palace station one Sunday night—and you weren't wearing a hat.'

No doubt because my hat was agonizing on its deathbed.

I did not go often enough to 14 Thornsett Road, in South London, where he was living then, not so often as I might have gone—afraid of outwearing my welcome. A quiet street—its trees, lilac and laburnum, make signs to me from a yet more distant past—of houses with modest gardens at the back. The lunch, on summer Sundays, was always the same, cold beef, and an opulently fresh fruit salad in a wide deep bowl. There were four children; the eldest, Florence, was a thin graceful creature, who drew well. I have kept one image of their mother—she was nicknamed Friday—standing at the foot of the staircase with a smile of great sweetness on her colourless face: she seemed to me older than her husband—but was she? *Bonne ménagère*, as she needed to be, with two daughters and two schoolboy sons to feed, clothe, educate, and not a great deal of money. I should have liked to know better the younger girl, darker, silent, with—or did I imagine it?—a faint shadow of defiance across her face.

Walter de la Mare was only half a creature of the human world. What other he lived in, with that serenity, that air of looking steadily outward, into infinite space, I have no idea: it would be silly to speculate. Very young children have this same open remote glance, but there was nothing of the child in him. He was more adult, more unshakably himself, than any merely practical man.

He talked—I hear him—rapidly and lightly, with a detached curiosity about everything except people: if by chance he had to talk about a man or woman it was the lightest possible touch, without a flicker of malice. This was not because he was kind or a saint, but from a fathomless indifference to personalities. He saw everything, from the nearly imperceptible fold at the corner of an eye to the smallest wrinkle in a leaf or frost-tipped point of grass, and each of these tiny marks was one letter of a language he never stopped trying to read: his mind was too engaged in this effort to have time to be malicious, or bored or impolite. It had the quickness, the gaiety, of a young wild animal and the wisdom of—but I don't know of what. Certainly not of this world. He was in every sense—except in the sense of being rash, eccentric, extravagant—unworldly.

Some time in 1921 I wrote my essay on him for the *English Review*. It must have been printed a little later, in 1922: I have not the slightest recollection of it, and neither patience nor the courage to look it up anywhere, it is so improbable that it was better than superficial. But that it pleased and amused him I know from a long letter he wrote on the 27th of December, 1921.

'... it really is rather queer that in the first few pages of your paper you should have attacked the one problem that has been puzzling and fascinating me for months past. What *being* have imagined characters and places? I can distinguish no essential difference between them and the so-called real, except a partial uncorroboratible-ness [that extraordinary word, like others he invented in talking, had too many flying meanings]. Only partial, too, for Heathcliffe and Tess etc etc are mine now too. How can we find out; and what line shall we take? The odd thing is that the very instant such beings insinuate themselves (or arise) in "the imagination" they are as whole, infinitely explorable, pervasive and enduring as, say, Mr Janner or Miss Mule who may actually come to tea tomorrow afternoon. Indeed I rather fancy the prototypes of this real lady and gentleman may appear soon, some day—in a story! How Master Harrison can find the mind to suggest cutting this beginning out—well, I have never been an editor... Didn't I once tell you that you daunted me when we met at the J.D. [Beresford]'s? I thought you were an intellectual. And you are, of course. But then I didn't know there were different kinds. This is dreadful if you would prefer to be kind A. Do come and see us again soon, and tell me whether you really understand this misunderstanding. Friday sends her love... and I'm sending you a belated copy of *The Veil*. It was meant to come at Christmas; and now it will come at New Year. How strangely frigid and uninviting these portals always are...'

If he were alive now, I would ask him what happens to the selves we abandon in houses. Some of these must be at least as vigorous and enduring as the characters we imagine. I cannot believe that the house in Thornsett Road, Anerley, and the small garden behind it, have lost all touch with him or with them.

Places he lived in later would draw him less stubbornly. (When I went to see him in the larger house near Taplow, he complained, smiling, that he and Friday had been left alone in it. Had he expected that his children were, as he was, immune to time?) And, just as, so long as I am alive, he stands smiling and talking on a rectangle of grass in sunlight, so while he lived I was a hatless young woman on the top of an open tram at night.

Night, tram, poet, blown hair—the emotion stored in them must exist somewhere. But where? Frivolous speculations, of the sort he liked juggling with, infinitely saner than the Faustian speculations of nuclear scientists.

I have known two or three indisputably great men. Diffidence, the fear of boring, of not being equal to their scrutiny, the pressures of life, a broad streak of indolence, kept me from seeing them oftener, knowing them much better. I regret it sharply—but at least I have touched greatness with a finger. Say what you like, it adds a savour to life.

## CHAPTER 38

I CANNOT REMEMBER when K. was demobilized—I think late in 1920—nor where we lived: we had two rooms somewhere in north-west London, but where? Elizabeth and John had left London. Defeated by lack of money and Elizabeth's smiling refusal to lift a finger to make their poverty bearable, John had found a practice in a poor quarter of Portsmouth, where he kept hundreds of half-crowns in a large drawer in his consulting room. I missed Elizabeth, the one person with whom I felt completely safe and happy.

So much had happened to me since K. went to Canterbury, leaving me to shark for myself and Bill, that I imagined I was safe from being harmed by him.

What could he possibly say or do to me now—now that I had had two books published, and visited houses where no one knew anything about me before the moment when they saw me coming in behind my warm lying smile? I even felt ahead of him in worldly sense. If, without a word to me, he had left the country, I should have felt little except relief from a burden. But here he was, my husband, with the rights of a husband, and I still too much attached to him to wish him gone.

That is not true. I often wished him gone.

But I have an unlucky talent for clinging to what I once had, a frightful moral inertia, the other side of my restlessness. Or another self, a coward, unwilling to lose all she has invested in the past. And a little afraid to be alone.

There was also the part of gentleness, but how, at this distance, can I measure it?

He had his gratuity, and felt he could take his time about finding work. He did not want to leave London again. Nor—though I talked of living in a cottage and writing novels to supplement K.'s income as a schoolmaster—did I. I believed so little in my future as a novelist.

He had friends in what Michael Sadleir called 'the third-rate Fleet Street set,' and spent part of every day with them. It distracted him from his mortification, when he applied for posts in London schools, at being told politely that he had stayed in the Air Force too long; immediately after the war he could have had a dozen jobs, now there were younger men available, to be had cheaper.

As the months passed, his gratuity dwindling all the time, he became discouraged. From one of these interviews he came into my room with tears in his eyes.

'I'm the most miserable man in London, a useless failure. I shall never get a job, I'm not wanted. I ought to shoot myself.'

My mind is at its nimblest and most astigmatic, not to say insane, when it is making plans. The plan it produced, some time in March or April 1921, for saving K. and restoring his self-respect was no madder than others I have succumbed to. It was to give him my place as sub-editor (acting editor) of the *New Commonwealth*, and find some other job for myself.

At that time, I never had any fears that I might not be able, easily, to impress somebody or other with my talents.

To be strictly truthful, the only time I coveted a job was before I had got it, when I was leading an older experienced man to take my usefulness to him on trust. I enjoyed using my wits in this way. The appointment was no sooner in my hands than I began wondering whether I really wanted it after all. When it turned out to need the whole of my time and energy, so that I had none left for anything else—for the writing I still did not trust as a profession—I soon loathed it. Let a way of escape offer itself—if possible, without discredit—and I leaped at it.

What looked like the most quixotic generosity—stepping aside for K.—was very little either quixotic or generous.

Diplomacy was called for—first to persuade K. himself that I was *not* doing him a favour, then to convince Mr Thoresby that I was doing him a great one in resigning and offering him K. in my place. I have forgotten how I went about it. But when the time came for the final step, when K. was going to see Mr Thoresby for the third time, I made the mistake of trying to advise him.

'He enjoys the sound of his own voice,' I said. 'You must let him talk. If you listen attentively, you'll hear what he wants you to say. Don't argue with him. Let him tell you his ideas, but don't, don't remind him that last time he talked to you they were quite different.'

'Dear me'—he removed his pince-nez, polished them very deliberately, replaced them on his short nose and stared at me with something between hauteur and insolence—'it appals me to think that this is how I must have been handled, before I married you. I know you very well now, you'd like to arrange my life, you're as shockingly domineering as your mother. Perhaps you think I don't see it. I do—but usually I'm too amused by it to point it out. What a pity you have such a low opinion of me, it leads you into making a fool of yourself.'

I was atrociously hurt—and lucid enough to see that he was partly right. 'My mother has always been very kind to you,' I said.

He went off, and I sat trying to quell the storm raging in the pit of my stomach, hating the room I sat in, hating London for mocking my hopes of it.

I jumped up and went to the window. I can see now the nearly black leaves of a yew in the sooty garden, and the pale streak of yellow below it, a late crocus. In the distance a child—it must be a child—was striking slowly the notes of a piano.

> 'Parthenophil is lost and I would see him;
> For he is like to something I remember,
> A great while since, a long, long time ago...'

Why Ford's lines should have come into my head at that moment, I can't imagine. They gave me an intense physical pleasure, which cured me for the time of discouragement and the anguish of feeling that there was neither sense, purpose, nor dignity in my life now.

When K. returned, triumphant, having been accepted, I had a moment of panic—I must have been mad to give up a place where I was sure of earning money. My looks did not give it away.

It was precisely the same feeling as when, very young, I dropped a sixpence in the street and it rolled away and vanished through the bars of a drain. A lady who had seen the disaster bent down and said kindly, 'What did you lose, child?' She was opening her purse. When I said roughly, 'Nothing,' she shut it again.

I used my first weeks of freedom to go to Whitby to see Bill. The summer before this I had had him for several weeks near me, outside London, living with one of the officer's wives I had known in 1918. I saw him every weekend, but it was not altogether a satisfactory place for him, and at the end of the year I took him back to Miss Geeson. Since then he had had measles. Miss Geeson wrote to me every day, but I went through torments of fear—and shame. That another woman was nursing him through an illness humiliated me.

He had grown. He was now almost six, tall, with his wide forehead, fair skin and eyes of a deep pure blue, more beautiful than ever—so beautiful that I was afraid. When I was questioning her about him, Miss Geeson said, 'He is sometimes bad-tempered.' I looked at her in mute astonishment. 'He has fits of rage. I never know why. He lies on the floor and screams and bites the legs of chairs. I wait until it is over, then I ask him about it, quietly. It doesn't happen often. He's really a good child—kind and intelligent.'

It is my fault, I thought. It is because I left him.

When I had put him to bed that evening at home, my mother talked to me about him, repeating things he had said to her, and stories about his illness. For a long time, days, he had been listless, as though he felt no interest in getting well; then, about three one morning, when Miss Geeson went to look at him, he was awake, and she asked him, 'Is there anything you would like?' He said languidly, 'I should like a good cup of tea.'

'Then you shall have it, that good kind woman said, and there and then went downstairs and made it for him; he drank it and after that began to recover.'

Not for a fortune—not even to give her the satisfaction of knowing that she had touched me to the quick—could I show interest. Still less, tell her what I was thinking.

I listened with a polite absent smile. Behind it, my mind ran from room to room, scrabbled at doors, beat itself against the walls. There was nothing I could do, there was no going back—nothing, nothing.

My mother looked older than her years, and tired. When I saw her, sitting for hours in the window of her room, idle, her eyes empty, or fixed on a point so remote that it could only be her own youth she saw there, my heart moved painfully and quickly, and I began to talk about trifles, a dress she needed, a new hat.

'Nay, I can't afford it,' she would say, and wait smiling to be contradicted.

'I'll give it to you for your birthday!'

'We'll see.'

'When my ship comes in, I'll buy you a fur coat.'

When she laughed, her face changed and softened. 'Your presents!' she said gaily and ironically. 'You'd give away your own silly skin.'

## CHAPTER 39

WHEN I WENT BACK TO LONDON, to K.—as always, hopefully, but with a cynical readiness to be disappointed—I decided that before looking round for another job I would finish the novel I had begun. Miraculously, I had a little money in the bank, and in July I was offered fifty pounds for what was to be a month's research, but turned out to be much more exacting. Mrs Margaret Sanger, an American crusader for birth control, had written a book filled with statistics—of population, incomes, venereal disease, births per age, per profession, per year, I forget what more. They were all to do with the United States, and she wanted them replaced by the corresponding English figures for an English publisher.

I set out lightheartedly on a wild goose chase. More than half the statistics did not exist in England, and had to be made out by inference—invention is the correct term—from such facts as were on record. I ran about London, from library to institution and institution to the Reading Room of the British Museum—and once ran for my life from a place where, I realized suddenly, they supposed I had come to be medically examined: I did not wait to explain.

In August that year the heat became terrible: the grass in the parks turned yellow, then black, the commons caught fire and smouldered. At nine o'clock, when I left the house, it was already stifling, and by midday a white oily light poured over the buildings and turned the streets into so many scorching gullies sending out a breath of acid dust. I walked about in a state of half-drunkenness—drunk with heat and the black coffee that was all I could face—eyelids half closed against the searing light, wrists and temples throbbing. At the end of the day I reached a curious state of—I can only call it a mute delirium—in which I seemed to be moving in one world, and seeing in another, brittle and transparent.

K. had two weeks' holiday, and went away alone, to Dorset: I had neither time nor money to go with him; Mrs Sanger wanted her figures, I had already spent three weeks on them and they were less than half complete. (A generous woman—when at last I finished, she paid me a double fee.)

The day after K. came home, a letter to him, sent on from the hotel in Dorset, was laid with mine in my room. In the evening I gave it to him. In the instant of handing it over I noticed—with less interest than the eye gives to a flicker of light on the wall—a change in his face, almost imperceptible. I forgot it immediately.

Exhausted by the heat and my annoying task, I went to bed and fell asleep.

It was still dark, some time between one and two o'clock, when I woke suddenly. What had wakened me was a few words spoken, with the greatest distinctness, inside my skull—*That letter is important for you.*

There is no more earthy, stolid, less extra-mundane creature living than I am: visions, premonitions, rarely visit me. I cannot explain this solitary instance of—what am I to call it—clairaudience? divination?

I lay still for some minutes, vividly aware of the darkened room, the bed, my body lying in it. Then without reflection I got up and went into K.'s room at the other side of the landing. Groping my way across it to the chair near his bed, I put my hand in the pocket of his coat, found the letter, took it to my room, and read it. It was short, a fribble of a love-letter, and it took me a moment to realize that the writer had spent the first week of his holiday with him, and had been his mistress for a long time.

There will be other letters, I thought coolly. I went back into the other room, and without troubling at all to be quiet opened drawer after drawer until I came on a collar-box crammed with letters. K. half woke. I spoke to him, and he turned over and fell asleep again.

(The impulse—to know, to make sure—which moved me to this detestable act has in honesty to be told, but I wish it had not.)

For precisely the reasons that make it impossible for me to go on reading a bad novel, I could not read the letters, but I sifted through them rapidly until I found one signed in full, with an address in Kent.

Now, for the first time, I was seized by an overmastering excitement. I'm free, I thought, I'm free, I'm free. I felt I should go mad with joy and excitement.

Without warning, I began to tremble violently.

I was deathly cold, and could not get warm even in bed. Lying awake, I went over again and again, endlessly, the steps I must take when I got up.

Out of—bewilderment? fatigue?—I did nothing that day except take the train to Maidstone in Kent, and come back immediately. In London I walked about for a long time, until, feeling hungry, I went into a small café and ordered tea and bread and butter. My throat closed against the bread. I could, with difficulty, swallow the tea, but not eat. My tongue had thickened and become dry, like a strip of worn leather.

Intensely interested by these symptoms of an unknown illness, I made a note of them on the back of an envelope.

For five days I said nothing to K.—warned, I think, by the instinctive certainty that once I began to talk I should lose control of the situation. I had kept the letters, but, careless fellow, he did not miss them. On the evening of the fifth day—Sunday—I asked him abruptly, 'Why didn't you tell me you were in love with this girl?' He looked at me without replying. 'If you'll tell me about it, I can divorce you and you can have her in peace.'

One thing is certain. Had he said he wanted to marry her, I should have behaved well. Pride, vanity—call it what you like—would have guided me, I should have closed my mind at once to everything but relief, and the excitement of making plans for a new start.

He did nothing of the sort. His face worked in a very unpleasant way, and he said,

'Don't send me off, don't leave me.'

I see today that I was hoping for another answer. Taken aback, I began to ask questions. The story could not have been simpler: the girl had been a V.A.D. in Canterbury, his partner at dances—and when he took over the *New Commonwealth* from me, he had brought her into the office as a typist. At this point I remembered that one day when I called for him at the office I had been struck by the inquisitive glances of a new typist, and with a feeling of sickness I supposed that they had discussed me afterwards. Reason told me that they had not laughed at me and at their cleverness in pulling wool over my eyes, but I felt naked and ridiculous, a laughing-stock. One grotesque image after another rushed into my mind, detailed, lucid—and insane. And in the same instant a younger self, in the grip of all the ludicrous, unmanageable and laughably sincere emotions of that graceless age, clawed her way to the surface and took complete possession. She gave every sign of having returned for good, my tears of rage and despair were hers, my savage humiliation. This awkward young creature had never wanted to be rid of K., never prayed he would leave her so that without taking it on herself she could be rid of him. An incredulous grief at having been tricked filled her. There was no reasoning with her. Not that she had lost the power to reason: one of the oddest effects of sexual jealousy is to poison the intellect at the roots, so that it goes on arguing with impeccable logic, from a mad premise.

I did not fail to notice, at moments, that the greater part of my anguish was hurt vanity. To think that I had been hoodwinked, and for so long! It made no difference, there is no getting used to jealousy. Moreover, it was a blow to my self-confidence from which I never wholly recovered—all the more because treachery, to be made a fool of and lied to, was only what in the farthest recess of my heart I had expected. I suffered, too, because what had happened was irreparable. There was nothing I could do, I could not make a clever plan to reverse it, could not adroitly prevent the innocent past from being smirched and distorted by the present.

That first evening I asked so many questions, called up so many lacerating and ridiculous images, that I exhausted myself. When I got into bed I fell asleep instantly, sinking through layer on layer of darkness, a drowned body plummeting to the floor of the Atlantic. For a minute I heard dimly a knocking on my locked door: I would have roused if I could, but it was physically impossible, I could not move a finger.

In the morning K. said, smiling,

'You needn't have refused to open your door, I only wanted the book I left in your room.'

My behaviour during the next few weeks lacked elegance. I harried K. with questions, and when he told me that he had stayed with the young woman at the —— Hotel in Oxford, or at another in London, I went there and walked up and down outside, up and down, impervious to inquisitive glances, imagining their arrival in the cab, entering together, signing the register, going up the stairs to their room: the images I called up made a lunatic of me...

I had a resource which morally fastidious persons will find shocking. From the very beginning, I made careful notes. After an evening of questioning K. with imprudent cruelty, I hurried to my room and wrote down an accurate description of my emotions and of all I had been moved to say. A thrifty astute side of my mind knew that unless I recorded it alive, with the claws still in me, I should forget the exact taste.

I have a vague memory of reading that some famous writer made notes as he watched his child die. That revolts me... Surely, too, the only griefs needing to be recorded at the time are those which, however sharp, *do not go to the quick...*

Outwardly I was unchanged: I toiled over Mrs Sanger's statistics, inventing new and ingenious methods of hiding the gaps, worked in the Reading Room until it closed—it closes far too early—then went back to my room to go on working for another two or three hours. If K. were dining with his parents, I walked home, stopping on the way to drink coffee in a Corner House.

At these moments a familiar gaiety woke in me; the warm dusty air of the street touched my face with a friendly hand, stretched to me from my future, my happy future.

## CHAPTER 40

SOME TIME DURING THE FIVE DAYS before I made up my mind to speak to K., I made an appointment with a lawyer; I no longer recall his name, nor who gave it to me.

Carrying the package of letters, I went to see him. A kind dry man, he listened with an expressionless face when I told him, curtly, that I wanted to divorce my husband, showing neither interest nor boredom. But, good heavens, can anything in the world be more boring than listening, year after year, to the confidences of men and women with a grievance?

He began questioning me—Where did you live then? Just when did you begin to suspect that your husband...? A clerk sitting with his back to me wrote down all I said, now and then scratching an ear or his leg with his pen. I kept my voice cold, and watched my life slipping from me; the house in Liverpool with its neglected garden and the rosy-cheeked infant in his high chair; all the rented rooms since then, where I had left a ghost of myself, frowning over a sheet of manuscript-paper, rolling a naked child in warmed towels, day-dreaming.

Another minute of this and there will be nothing left, I thought.

'How did you gain possession of these letters?'

'I stole them.'

He smiled very slightly, and turned the pages with a finger-nail. 'Letters of this kind are all alike.' He handed them to the clerk, who tied round them a length of pink tape. 'They are not, I must tell you, evidence against your husband, although they are written to him. They are evidence only against the writer.'

This seemed to me no more idiotic than the legal procedure as he explained it to me. I must now write to my husband, asking him to return—my face did not, I think, give away the fact that he had never left—he would refuse and...

Here I interrupted to ask what I ought to say in my letter.

'Use your own best words, I don't want to put words into your head, that would destroy the spontaneity. Draft a letter, and let me see the draft.'

'And then?'

'Then we shall bring an action for restitution of conjugal rights; he will decline to comply with the order—giving you fresh evidence of adultery. Then we shall begin the action for divorce.'

I smiled. 'Conjugal is a ridiculous word.'

'You must not see or be seen with your husband.'

Outside, the heat tasted curiously of salt; I thought that the skin of my lips was cracked and tried moistening them with the tip of my tongue as I walked along Holborn and Oxford Street. I walked for a long time, feeling the heat of the pavement through my thin shoes. With an icy clarity, I blamed myself for everything; I had been selfish, disloyal, arrogant, without kindness. The gesture of the clerk's bony hand as he tied together in a small neat bundle all the days of my life with K., hopes, lies, unkindness, kindness, an empty calico bag labelled Coal, Light and Gas, a green sofa—what had become of it?—struck me as obscene.

The thought of turning K. out was singularly unpleasant. Where would he go? And how, in this heat, with the births per age of unmarried mothers still to be arranged (by me), could I find time and patience to separate my books from his? The trouble, no less than the callousness, of leaving him, bent my shoulders.

If anyone supposes that, in an emotional crisis, straws weigh less than iron, he is a fool.

When I told K. about the lawyer, he looked at me with an air of defeat. 'This is too much,' he said. 'I've had a miserable day. Your friend N. treated me abominably when I called there to ask her to let me review for her. From the way she spoke to me you'd think I was nobody. And I thought she was a friend of yours.' I felt angry that he had been snubbed. When he spoke in this voice, with this look of young unhappiness, my bowels melted. It reminded me of a time when I had admired him above anyone. It was in those days that he had discovered how to start in me a fever of anxiety. This habit of my nerves—surely only my nerves?—was the strongest hold he had over me.

I knew already that I had no heart for this business of letter-writing and pretending. I did not give way at once. As always when I am faced with what is in effect a moral decision to be made—and a tiresome upheaval—I fell back on doing nothing. I waited for a wind.

Moreover—how absurd this is—I felt ashamed to tell the lawyer, that dry correct man, that I had changed my mind.

I imagined him and his faceless clerk having a good laugh at me and my feebleness. When, after a few days, he sent me a long document he called my proof, I could not force myself to read it, only glancing through the pages to see whether it were recorded that I stole the letters. It was not.

In a note pinned to the document he reminded me that I was to draft a letter. I drafted it, and sent it to him. A day later it came back with two of my phrases corrected in a fine hand. This mortified me. Did the fellow know whose style he was correcting?

After another four or five weeks, I went to see him again, and told him, brusquely, that I could not go on. 'It takes too long, there are too many steps.'

'That is so,' he said.

'I am sorry to disappoint you.'

He gave me an impersonal glance. 'I'll have a parcel made of the letters.'

I had forgotten them. 'Oh, would you destroy them for me? If I have them, I might not destroy them, I might do something mean with them.'

'I can't destroy them,' he said calmly. 'I'll keep them in my safe for you if you like.'

I thanked him and left. Are they still at the back of a safe? Or did a bomb later get rid of them?

To punish K. for my want of hardness, I made an abominable scene. He endured it with some dignity, and I apologized, asking him to forgive me my indecent sarcasms. I then wrote them all down.

One promise K. made me at this time—for which I had not asked—was that if, later, I wanted to divorce him, he would take the whole thing on himself, invent evidence I could use, anything.

'Why?' I asked.

Clearing his throat, he said stiffly, 'I think I know what is expected of a gentleman.'

I had enough self-restraint to go into my own room to laugh. My laughter was an echo of my mother's at her harshest and most jeering.

If I had had any respect for him, I could not have laughed in that hateful way. But respect and admiration had long been dead, their place taken by pity—pity, a creeping plant, like bindweed, all but impossible to root up.

I am not naturally vindictive, I forget the names of contemptuous reviewers. If, for any peculiar reason, the injury some dog has done me stays in my mind, I never forgive him, but if a chance turns up to punish him, I don't take it. I am unforgiving, but not malicious. And I am lazy.

Since I am too lazy or indifferent to be tempted to avenge myself, I ought to have been able to forgive K. If only out of civility.

The truth is, a knife-thrust in one's vanity takes longer to heal than any.

During the day tranquil or happy, and hard at work, no sooner was I in bed and alone than the memory of this or that incident—with what I could invent—started up in my mind and drove me out of it. I have never been able to cry easily or with pleasure, or in public; my tears during these months were corrosive, as bitter as the aloes smeared on children's nails. But I did not only cry; I imagined biting phrases and wrote them in pencil on a sheet of paper I took care to have by my bed, and in the morning added to the pile of notes in my cupboard.

What a curious animal a writer is.

I remember an early morning, grey, very quiet, when something—the chorus of birds, a wandering scent of damp earth—flung me back six years to the bedroom of the house in Liverpool. The longing I felt was inarticulate—even I had no words for it: it was the craving for water of a man dying of thirst.

This time it was myself I laughed at, wryly.

## CHAPTER 41

IN 1922—or was it early in 1923?—the *New Commonwealth*, terribly emaciated, died. Mr Thoresby had lost rather more money than he was willing to lose on a hobby that came second in his heart to his theosophical studies.

He treated K. generously.

Before this money came to an end, his father made him the same offer he had made once before: to send him to a university—this time to take a Ph.D. at Oxford. Now that I have written this, I wonder whether it was not a small legacy that fell to K. at this time, which he proposed to spend in this way.

When he told me about it, and asked, not my advice but my opinion, I refused to give it. Partly because what I thought was, that at thirty-two, nearly thirty-three, he should have something more serious to do than go back to school with boys of nineteen and twenty. And partly—and even less avowably—I did not care in the least if he left me to make the best of things alone. It would put him in a poor light—and leave me free. Alone but free.

'If I go,' he asked, 'what will you do?'

I did not tell him that, for some reason, I no longer felt absolutely confident that I could pick up a salaried job. I had a moment's sickening panic. I have done nothing yet, achieved nothing, I thought. I swallowed my fear, and thought: But I will.

'I don't know.'

'You could go home. Your mother——'

'My mother will always take me in. But it is a little humiliating—married, with a child—to go back.'

'What can you do?'

So he means to go, I thought. I had the sensation of standing in the entry of one of the narrow openings we call *ghauts* in Whitby, flagged passages between houses on the east side, pitch black until you come out under the slope of the cliff. My heart sank, then flew up in a great arc, like a gull, up and away.

'I shall find something, I always do.'

'Very well, my dear. Since you want me to go to Oxford...'

I had finished my novel, the third. When, later this year, it was published, it got bad notices, no worse than it deserved. It was atrociously bad, far worse, far more pretentious, than *The Pot Boils*. The one person who praised it was my dear Michael; it pleased his romantic palate and he did not see that it was unspeakably overwritten and affected, the worst kind of fake. The letter he wrote to me ended: 'I can promise a frank welcome at Orange Street if and when you return to us. I hope it will be soon.'

I decided there and then to take him my next novel. I had already started it, and I intended to use my notes.

I took the quarter-written manuscript with me to Portsmouth, when we went to stay for a time with Elizabeth and John. They were renting a large house on the edge of the dirty clotted streets that supplied John with his hundreds of panel patients. It was dilapidated, furnished, like the London flat, with odds and ends picked up in sale-rooms, and smelled vilely of the brewery on to which it backed: they were living in the same eccentric disorder, but with two servants, and sherry in the place of beer.

I trusted no one with my unhappiness, not even Elizabeth. But K., who had sworn to me that he would hold his tongue, gave me away to her the first day. He could not resist telling me, with smiling condescension, that she felt I was making an hysterical fuss about a very usual incident.

'So you told her?'

'Of course. Why not? I'm not, let me tell you, afraid of the truth, I shall tell anyone I please.'

I did not reproach him for this slight case of treachery. What good would it be—since he would only confide in Elizabeth that I had made a scene? But my contempt for him deepened. I sat with a fixed smile, hating him.

Elizabeth I did not blame. I knew too well that, talking to a man, any man, she could not help trying to seduce him. Nor did I tell her that I knew she had joined K. in laughing at me.

My love for her remained, so far as I knew, intact.

It must, I think, have been April—May or April—in K.'s one year at Oxford that I stayed with him for a short time. He had made several friends among the young men—and one older friend, a man of his own age who had come to the university after years in his father's financial house. R. was a Jew, good-looking, intelligent, capable of clever and charming remarks: he courted me—no other word will do—with the same charm and thoughtfulness. I tried, vainly, to fall in love with him: it would, I thought, cure me quickly of my habit of wincing, a mere twitch of the nerves, every time I passed a hotel or a restaurant where K. had taken the girl. He made all the right gestures: for the first time I had a suitor who came with flowers and volumes of poems. It half embarrassed, half touched me. We spent long placid afternoons on the river, and he read the poems aloud, in his admirable voice. I could admire it, and his good looks, and the quickness of his mind, but I could not avoid moments when I was repelled by his romantic hedonism: he wallowed in delicate emotions.

One afternoon, in the very middle of a poem he was reading, his own this time, I yawned. It was not meant; I was simply caught out. Looking at me sorrowfully, he closed the book and took me home. On another occasion, he had drawn the punt into the bank of a meadow so thick with buttercups it was like glancing at the sun: under the opposite bank a canoe held four young men who climbed out and stood there, charming gawky figures, like the boys on a Greek vase. R. looked at them, and sighed.

'How I envy them. Their youth. It saddens me.'

'Why?' I asked, astonished.

'You must feel it as I do. Which of the four would you like to fall in love with?'

'None.'

I have never been able to understand how an intelligent woman can become infatuated with a much younger man. *Chéri*? Yes—but Léa is not presented to us as intelligent; a beautiful young animal would give her all she needed or craved. *Phèdre? But* do we know how old Phèdre is? Is she much older than her rather stupid stepson? In any event, what we are attending to is the poetry—

> Secret desire that once smoulder'd away
> Sees Venus fix'd in thrall upon her prey

—exactly as, listening to Lear's cries when he fumbles at his dead child's dress, we do not stop to reflect that she brought their unhappiness on him and herself by her priggish refusal to flatter an old man.

One of K.'s young friends, nineteen years old, caught an ill-humoured passion for me, as he might have caught a cold in the head or measles. I dislike hurting people—a scruple which has cost me dear—but his emotional crudity, the right emotions for his age, bored me.

The only one of K.'s undergraduate friends for whom I felt genuine liking reminded me of Boris Droubetzkoï as he appears in the first pages of *War and Peace*. B.J. was friendly, handsome in a cool way, poor, and scrupulously neat—he had, I think, only one suit, and when he was invited to a fancy-dress party he could go only because I lent him a blue crêpe-de-chine smock in which he looked charming. A hard worker, with no useful relations, and more conscience than Droubetzkoï, he became the secretary of a Colonial Governor.

I wrote R. three or four indiscreet letters, literary exercises, which I later took from his room. You can see that I have a talent for the theft of letters.

## CHAPTER 42

T OWARDS THE END of that year I finished writing *The Pitiful Wife*—
an admirable title for a novel spongy with emotion—and typed it
laboriously from the manuscript, working until all hours, without benefit of
green tea. Charles Evans of Heinemann was expecting it, but I had decided,
out of love of Michael, to send it to him. I could act in this unscrupulous
way because—in memory of Fisher Unwin, no doubt—I refused to sign
contracts for more than one book at a time.

I wrote to tell Charles Evans what I was doing: it says everything for
his patient kindness that he later took me back into Heinemann's bosom,
without reproaches. He was a good man, and my friend. He would never,
as did an elderly director of his firm, Mr Pawling, have taken me out to
lunch and lectured me solemnly on the duty of a young writer. This was, if
you believe me, to live for art, not money. It was too much for my—at the
time—famished stomach.

Michael was delighted with the book, and paid me a hundred pounds
in advance of royalties. I had not the slightest suspicion that it was a bad
novel: at this time, thoughts and feelings started a fever in my mind, and I
was under the delusion that this fever had some connection with literature.

Almost at the same time, K. sent me, unasked, a cheque for fifty pounds.
I hesitated—but not for very long: it went against the grain to throw away
money for a gesture, and I took it, with exaggerated thanks.

Now that I was so well-off, I decided to take rooms for myself and Bill—
near enough to Miss Geeson's for him to go there daily. To my great surprise,
my mother took it in bad part.

'The child is well enough where he is,' she said, in her coldest voice. 'You
may very well want to go away again, and you would have unsettled him
for nothing. And—you might find that Miss Geeson was not willing to
take him back.'

The tone of her voice, harsh and cutting, travelled by a short cut to the
child always expecting to be whipped for some misdeed. I flinched.

'But I'd rather have him with me.'

'You must do as you please.'

'I thought—I could write in the mornings and when he is asleep.'

'Miss Geeson has been getting him into good ways. You'll find he behaves much worse with you, I shouldn't be surprised if he begins his fits of bad-temper again.'

'He behaved well enough with me when he was a baby,' I said.

I have never been able to answer with dignity when I am castigated—unless I can feel angry. I hurried out of the room, up to my bedroom, trembling with resentment. She is perfectly right, I thought, but no one ought to speak to a grown woman in such a way, without a trace of respect.

It did not enter my head—it has done so only at this minute—that a jealous grief lay under my mother's words. Why should *I* be able to take my son back, when she...?

Downstairs, she struck a note or two on the piano in her room: her voice, for a moment clear and strong, rose in the first bars of *O Fair Dove*, weakened, missed the higher note, and broke off. A fury of love for her seized me. Why aren't you still young? I cried, Why was there so little for you?

Pressing my forehead against the window to cool it, I watched the wind rush down the field at the other side of the road, whitening the grass—then still a meadow, not yet groomed into the park where, when she was much older, I took her to sit staring at tulips and forget-me-nots with eyes as empty as an infant's. Grief caught me by the throat. Why must she die and lose sight of the wind in the grass? I saw her hands, fingers a little swollen, drop from the piano.

When I went downstairs, she was still in her room, talking now to a small lean bird-eyed woman in a thin coat, who listened with a guilty smile. The contrast between the two women struck me: my mother was older and frailer than her friend, yet had more life in her little finger than the other in her whole body.

'You shouldn't *do* it, Mary. *I* wouldn't. I wouldn't slave like that for any living soul. Visitors or *no* visitors, I wouldn't *do* it. Tell them you *won't*.'

For a moment I felt closer than their skin to all tired, anxious unattractive women, coming into rooms with propitiatory smiles, closing doors softly, opening and shutting windows, drawing blinds up, drawing them again at night or against the sun, turning down the sheets on beds, preparing trays, climbing with them up flights of stairs, hurrying to answer bells. The woman's thoughts rose in my mind in pale wisps and spirals...

I took rooms for us in a house on the edge of Miss Geeson's village: it stood alone in a field, and if I took the flagged path through this field, and through the next four, I came to the place where I was once nearly strangled by a lout, and so to Waterstead Lane and its mossy walls, and Park Terrace...

> Till down they swayed to sleep, the drowned, spreadeagled
> And, sundering the fine tendrils, floated me

The estuary, narrowing as it neared the first hills, lay beyond the house. In the afternoon we walked, I racking my brain for something to talk about to a child not yet eight: usually silent himself, he responded only when something I said amused him. He was quick, graceful and lazy, hating to exert himself. We had been living in these rooms for six months before I discovered that he was only pretending not to be able to read: he preferred to be read to.

In July that year there was an epidemic of diphtheria in Whitby, and one night he woke me to tell me that his throat hurt.

It was four o'clock: I got up, dressed, and spent the hours until I could summon the doctor, planning. I was determined not to let him go to the fever hospital. Nor did he. My calm certainty that she would allow us to stay in her house intimidated the poor woman. Like any other country wife, she was mortally afraid of infection, but I bore her down.

He had the illness lightly, but for the first two nights I did not dare to sleep. I floated a night-light in a chipped saucer, and placed it so that I could see the outline of his little body under the blanket. A dozen times in an hour I bent over him to make sure he was still alive. He slept through every night without moving.

Lying in bed, he drank milk and egg flip, and ate fish, white grapes, honey. He grew rosier daily. To hold the cup for him to drink suffocated me with joy. Told by the doctor that I must keep him lying flat, I read to him, hour after hour, until my penny whistle of a voice cracked and I had to lean close to make him hear me.

One day during the second week I remembered suddenly that my novel had been published a week earlier. I felt a pang of dismay. Clearly it was a failure. I drove it to the back of my mind. Nothing mattered but to go on pouring Valentine's meat juice, honey, milk, down my child's throat. Time enough when he recovered to look at the minor disaster.

The next morning I was reading aloud, as usual, when I heard my mother's voice in the field outside the house. 'Are you there, Daisy? I want you.'

I ran to the window and opened it. Because of her fears for my young sister, she would not come nearer than the flagged path. She stood there, a newspaper open in her hand, smiling.

'It says here that your book is fine and exquisite. A masterpiece. Wait, I'll read it to you.'

She was radiant, her eyes as blue and living as a girl's. I had never seen her so excited. A delicious feeling of warmth and confidence spread through me. Now at last I have done something, I thought; now she is pleased with me.

It was the feeling, half relief, half happiness, that I had when the news came of my scholarship, and when I could wire her that I had a First. Those other triumphs had led nowhere, disappointing her. Now something more splendid was beginning. A sense of power seized me, my energy starting up in my midriff like a famished wild beast. I laughed secretly.

Here, I thought, here begin the life and works of Daisy Jameson.

'Thank you for bringing it.'

'I always knew you would do well,' she said, smiling. 'Though I didn't expect anything so good as this.'

I could not endure to see her so pleased with this tiny success.

'It's only one review,' I said.

'There will be others.'

My courage came back, and I boasted,

'If it sells I'll buy you something you really want.'

There were other reviews, equally astonishing and fantastic. Nowadays when *The Times Literary Supplement*, as it has done for the last several years, treats me scurvily, I cannot help smiling when I think of the praise it gave a very bad novel.

One critic was not taken in: in a curt review Raymond Mortimer said that it was the silliest novel he had ever read. Since I am always willing to believe the worst of myself, this remark impressed me. Two or three years later I knew that he was right. The only real fragments in the book—the dialogue between husband and jealous wife—were not likely to appeal to a male intellectual. What could he know about the emotions of a violent and undisciplined young woman? He knew bad writing when he saw it, that was enough.

When Bill was convalescent I wrote to Michael and, hiding my diffidence, asked him whether any money had come in. I hoped for a hundred pounds. With a kindness I should have been obliged for—if I had not been too full of my own merits to notice his—he sent two hundred and fifty. 'There will be more to come,' he wrote, 'perhaps not a great deal more, but certainly something. You'll die rich!'

This prophecy delighted me.

A warning voice, my own or my grandfather's, said swiftly: *Not you!* You were born under an awkward star, and honesty will keep breaking in. Besides, you squander.

I am inclined, now, to think that it rested with me to become a rascally best-selling fake, a hypocritical success of some sort. If I had used my talents for Jesuitry consistently, I might have become rich.

I should still have squandered.

I had no trouble in persuading my mother that I was rich enough to give her a fur coat. Half her pleasure in it would come, I knew, from being able to say to friends: My daughter gave it to me; her books, you know, do very well... We went, of course, to Scarborough. The man in Rowntree's fur department had known her too long to feel impatient as she tried on coat after coat, always with an eye on the one she had coveted at sight. The ritual over, he said sweetly, 'You'll never be sorry if you take that one, Mrs Jameson: it will last you for years.'

'Do you like it?' she asked me, frowning. 'It's a lot of money.'

'No, no, it's not too much,' I lied. 'Is it what you want?'

Watching her run her hand over and over the sleeve, I felt the same piercing happiness as when I gave my son something he wanted very much and I could not afford.

It must have been the same day that she admired a hat so expensive that even I felt it was out of reach: separate strands of black osprey were sewn round the crown in four rows. 'You have an osprey at home,' I said, 'in the drawer with the ostrich feathers: I think I could copy it.'

I made my boast good. I am clumsier with a needle than any woman in the country, but when it was a question of getting her what she wanted I was without fear.

Dreams of supreme triumphs, of becoming rich, did not last: I was tormented by the sense that money earned by writing novels is less safe than the money my grandfather made out of ships. Except during a depression, the builders and owners of ships were sure of their tomorrow. Not so the writers of books. Between one novel and the next you could lose your wits and your audience.

Though I don't remember it, I must have written in this tone to Michael Sadleir. In September he wrote that an American publisher, Alfred Knopf, who was in London, wanted a young man or young woman to act as his representative in England, finding books and authors for him. 'I have told him that you are competent and unscrupulous, and—naturally—he wants to see you.'

Leaving Bill with my mother, I went up to London, and called on Mr Knopf. To my astonishment, he was not only young, he was a copy of the Spanish king, whose photograph in golfing clothes I had just seen in an illustrated weekly. This—and the smiling candour with which he remarked, 'I believe in giving people enough rope to hang themselves'—amused me so much that I felt there were worse ways of being hanged.

'I want my wife to see you,' he added. 'I never decide without her.'

The image I have kept of Blanche Knopf at this time is of a small golden-skinned young woman, enchantingly smooth and round like a Chinese idol.

I was not surprised to be given the job. Total ignorance of what is expected of me has never done me the harm that boredom does me every day.


## CHAPTER 43


WITH THE GREATEST NAÏVETÉ and coolness, I wrote to every publisher and literary agent in London and told them that I was in the market for authors, the best authors. Then, over my suppers of coffee and bread and honey, I tried to consider my tortuous life. I had lightheartedly promised Alfred Knopf that I would return to London to live. This

promise, and much else, ran head on into a moral—if it were no stronger—
obligation to live in Cornwall with K. With his Ph.D. thesis unfinished (he
never did finish it), he had left Oxford in July and taken a post in a school in
Launceston—encouraged to it by me. At the time I had thought Cornwall
as good a place as any to bring up a child.

Turning the saucer of my coffee cup, my hand came on a chipped place.
Instantly I was in the darkened room where a badly chipped saucer, a feeble
circle of light on the floor, and another on the ceiling immediately above
it, had kept me company as I held my breath to hear the breathing of a sick
child. An irrational fear seized me. The more radiant a living creature is,
the less use life has for him, I thought. If there were another war, I couldn't
save him. Panic drove me upstairs to make sure that he was asleep and safe.

In November, I gave up our rooms and went back to my mother's house,
putting off a little longer the moment when I should have to decide something.

After three days, I had a magnificent excuse for doing nothing: I fell ill.

I woke on the 11th with an aching throat and a body which seemed
made of equal parts of cottonwool and rusty iron. To get up and dress, I
had to fight off a nightmare weakness. My mother was expecting me to go
with her to the Armistice Day service in St Mary's—on the East cliff—and
it did not enter my head that I could disappoint her. The cold air, when we
set out, steadied me.

Luckily, my mother had to stop several times on our way up the one hundred and ninety-nine steps that climb from harbour level to the church. For
more than half the way the old houses went with us, one crouching above
the other, and I remembered the servant's story heard when I was four: one
rainy night part of the cliff fell away and in the morning the yards of houses
were found choked with bones and the crumbling wood of ancient coffins.

The top step, worn deepest because here many turn, ends in a narrow
flagged path twisting between the graves, with their seawrinkled stones, to
the church porch. We turned—and looked down at the harbour, and to the
hills drawn round it, and the great line of the coast curving north, and to
the pale sea. We walked towards the church, passing to one side, to climb an
outside staircase. The door stood open on a narrow passage running towards
the gallery. We trod softly between the wall and the high wooden walls of
pews. A little light came through low windows. The boards creaked.

To come this way, we passed my brother's memorial tablet—'To the memory of 2nd Lt. Harold Jameson, Médaille Militaire, D.C.M., M.C., Royal Flying Corps...' fastened to the wall of the gallery at eye-level—and came out between the walls to reach my grandfather's pew: a cushioned bench ran down its longer side, and the latch of the door was set high, above the reach of a child's hand.

I looked down, over the edge, into the well of the church, into pews like square roofless rooms. In the three-decker pulpit an old priest made the superb gesture I had watched him make when I was a child, flinging his white surplice over his head and bowing his face in it.

This church is part of my life: it speaks to my skeleton, which remembers clearly the worn places in stairs, the grain of old wood, the moment—each time as piercing as the first—when a man crossing the moors above Sleights sees the sea leaning against the sky, the edge of the cliff, and the church kneeling on it, waiting, beside the ruined Abbey. How could it forget, since those who live in me—and live nowhere else—have stared at it from the moors, from the harbour, from the sea, for eight hundred years? There is nothing here but what's mine.

I have read, in the logs of old ships, long since vanished, the handwriting on the page withered to the brown of a dry leaf: 'At eight in the morning Whitby church bore N.W.N. distant three miles...'

The winter sunlight crept round the wall to touch a corner of Harold's tablet. This wait for the Silence drew the cords of my stomach into a hard knot. How much longer? Leaning forward, I could see the soldiers drawn up facing the altar. I watched their officer: a narrow face, the cheekbones like knuckles, fair hair, hot quick eyes: he doesn't care who looks at him, I thought. The sergeant-major at his elbow did not expose himself in that way: his eyes, small and deep-set, gleamed, but it was the gleam of decaying matter, as though the mind at the back of them were dead. He had an air not so much cynical as over-used, and he was singularly quiet with it. He knows his officers like the back of his hand, I thought; their vanities, what each can do, their lusts. He would have known each time K. had his young woman...

The sailors filled three long rows. They were a different species of animal, and looked curiously naked in their tight uniform. Behind them the pews were filled with men and women to whom the war had brought gifts: a dead son, a new, more exciting life, money. Many Whitby people grew as fat as Eglon the king of Moab (look him up in Judges) on their war—like the elderly shipowner who allowed young officers to buy drinks for him on the first Armistice Day, and bought none himself. Perhaps these had come to give thanks.

Here it comes, I thought.

It came, the Silence, like the doom of God, like the sea rising between rocks. The great chandelier hung suspended in it; the tall pulpit, the galleries, the painted pillars, the bodies of men and women, were held upright in it. The great ball of air outside the old church contracted and pressed on it, and I thought that only the light, crossing and re-crossing between the windows, kept the shell of the roof from being crushed. I could hear my heart. I saw my young brother at the other side of a London street, his face bent down, scarlet; he thought he was not wanted. I ran across the road between the wheels of cabs. I called him. I touched nothing.

I thought briefly of other young men I had known until they were killed. I thought of Red Smith, not having thought of him since he died. I could not now remember the tones of his voice, nor anything he had said that was of the least importance.

The silence changed very slightly. Far out in the North Sea a wave gathered itself to fall, to send a green shock against the cliffs. No heads were lifted, no eyes that had been closed opened, the head of the old man bowed in the upper deck of the pulpit was not uncovered—yet there had been a change.

Nothing happened—except that a gun was fired outside, and at the back of the church a man lifted his arms and sounded the Last Post.

Dreadful, lacerating, unendurable sound.

The last note came to an end, slowly, passing over the rank grass of the cliff, over the harbour: it would be heard everywhere, except by my brother.

I gripped the edge of the pew. Standing beside my tearless mother, I was ashamed to make a sign of grief: her body heavy in its black coat did not move—when the trumpet flew up in the Reveille, it was a moment before she realized that all were not sitting. It would be indecent even to let myself imagine what she might be thinking, what she saw with that fixed remote glance. The frowning face of 'a black bairn'? A boy in clumsy khaki and thick army boots?

The old Canon lifted his head and sent his strong unpriestly voice through the church. My mother sat stiffly, hands lying on her knees. *It is raised in power; it is sown a natural body; it is raised a spiritual body.* What a mockery of the mother who wants nothing but the living body of her son.

I could do nothing for her. I thought—at this moment I thought—if by jumping from the edge of the cliff I could bring him back, I would... But how can I tell? Suppose I took a moment to reflect before jumping, I should draw back. Of course I should draw back.

Oh, my poor dear, I thought, you have no one for you, no one who cares more for you than for herself. It was for nothing, it was for this dry moment, that you endured your life, the births of children, heat and discomfort in foreign ports, illness, pain, anger, ambitions transferred to a daughter, to a son, disappointment, the new heaviness of your body. For nothing.

On the way home I felt confused and ill, the pain in my throat became worse, and as soon as we were inside the house I fainted.

It turned out that I had diphtheria. The doctor was convinced that I had had the infection since the time when, to read aloud to Bill, I was bending over him for hours at a stretch.

Little as she liked the thought of a fever patient in the house, my mother did not dream of sending me away. My middle sister was at home again and could nurse me. So, with a sheet soaked in some powerful disinfectant hung across the door of my bedroom, I had my diphtheria in comfort.

Ordered to lie flat because diphtheria puts a strain on the heart, I persuaded my sister to bring me my typewriter, and sat up in bed typing letters to publishers and writers. I did not dare interrupt the correspondence I had started. A qualm of conscience made me add a postscript to the letters: I have diphtheria, burn this if you are afraid of infection. This drew, from John Buchan, a copy of his *Lodge in the Wilderness*, which brought a breath of cold clear air into the room, and a letter from Middleton Murry, whom I barely knew, of such kindness that I almost wept: he wrote that Katherine Mansfield had been delighted, at a moment when she was feeling wretched, by a review I wrote of one of her stories, and if I needed money he would like to send me twenty pounds from her.

I refused the offer, but I must have written more than once. I have a letter dated the 23rd of July, 1953, in which he says: 'For some inscrutable reason I am tidying up the accumulation of years. In doing so I came across and re-read letters of yours, written in 1923. And they touched me so that I felt it was sad, and somehow wrong, that I should have entirely lost contact with you... I remember you as I first saw you, at a sort of party at J. D. Beresford's...'

I remember him at that party, a young man with dark eyes which never rested on the face of the person he was speaking to, but flinched aside. I had not taken to him—because of this glance. I thought it sly and evasive. Perhaps it was—but it masked a delicacy and a kindness I was never, after 1923, tempted to mock.

No sooner had I recovered strength than I began to plan my future, mine and Bill's. I had less scruple now in leaving K. alone in Cornwall: during my illness, by a piece of carelessness that was like him, one of his letters had given away that he was still seeing his young woman: he had folded into it a scribbled list of the things he must do during a visit to London, and among them was: Meet D. 6:30 Marylebone Hotel... I threw it away. I was humiliated, but I had the honesty to remind myself: There was a time when you hoped he would leave you.

Yes, yes, leave me—not stay to make a fool of me, not force me—me—to put an end to our marriage. If he had taken himself off, I should have been cured of him in the time it took to close the door on him.

If you think with enough energy about a hoped-for event, it will in the end happen. Not because you willed it. Because it was all the time in your nature. But this trick has one fatal flaw. The moment an imagined event emerges into the real world, time leaps on it and gives it a twist that deforms everything. A spring you had supposed dry overflows, the looked-for ground gives way, and down you go.

Jealousy is a disease we should catch as seldom as possible. It is incurable. All the same, one recovers from it...

Michael recommended a school for Bill near Weybridge—forty minutes by train from London—and I decided to go there in January.

The day before we left Whitby, I walked to the moor above Aisalby. From here the road ran north to the coast with its hardset fishing villages: inland, looking west, dark spongy peat, crossed by pale dry-stone walls and severed by deep valleys. The country of my heart's heart. Why am I going away? I wondered. I am a fool.

I thought a little about K. I felt absurdly sorry for him, because of his carelessness. In some inexplicable way, I was still bound to him. Am I a coward? I wondered. Am I afraid to be alone?

An extraordinary gaiety seized me. I shall do something with my life, I thought; who, what, could possibly defeat me?

## CHAPTER 44

COMPETENT AND UNSCRUPULOUS... I ACTED AS the Knopfs' representative for more than two years—until they had the fatal idea of starting their own firm in London. Nowadays, American publishers take a short and easier cut to a stall on our market; they buy an English firm, plump it out by methods known to every breeder of geese, and under cover of its name sell textbooks by the hundred thousand to peoples who are still anxious to pick our brains after getting rid of us as overlords.

As an agent I was a success. As well as being lightheartedly unscrupulous—doubtless there are pirates and wreckers among the honest smugglers in my ancestry—I was as green as I was bold. Riding light—without rules or ethics—I expected to win against the field. In fact the field was almost empty. There must have been older, staider agents at work, but I did not hear of them. It was, too, the Silver Age of English publishing, almost the age of innocence, when a publisher such as Victor Gollancz, who not only *meant business*, but said so, gave offence.

I ran about London like a dog, scarcely taking time to eat, pricking my ears in publishers' and agents' offices, my tongue dripping honey. For winter I had an excellent dark green coat, bought under the slightly disapproving eye of Betty Sadleir, who knew I could not afford it, and a hat I trimmed myself with a sweeping feather. Summer—well, in summer, let us be honest, I had the airs of a moulting sparrow.

I wrote to every well-known author under the age of fifty. I had a few civil phrases on the end of my pen... my profound admiration for your work... should you, at any time, consider changing your publisher in

America, I beg that you will give me the chance to... your reputation, your etc, etc...

The writer—more especially the novelist—who has not, at one moment or another, considered his publisher unworthy of him, has still to be conceived. And behold, waiting on the moment, a smiling young spider with the web stretched in sight of the fly.

Quite often, what I said was what I meant. When a writer caught my imagination, I was, in those days, only too respectful.

And I had my moments of long-sight, as well as moments when I fell in friendship with a writer and was prepared to risk my neck in the rope for him. (Let me say here that, for all his ferocious words, no hand was ever more reluctant to hang a sinner than Alfred Knopf's.) Any agent would have felt safe in buying Francis Brett Young, but I went farther on the road to being hanged. One day I read, before it was published, a novel called *My Name Is Legion*, by an unknown writer—unknown to me. As a novel it was impossible, with a streak of something wild and ambiguous—a smell of sulphur. Obviously it would sell two or three hundred copies and be ignored by any sensible agent of an American publisher.

I was instantly attracted. I wrote to the author, and went to see him—and at once felt for him and his young wife the sort of pleased love one can feel, at sight, for a fine landscape or a painting. Hilda Morgan was an enchanting creature, with red-gold hair and clear eyes, a flicker of malice pointing their gaiety. Charles himself was a portrait by either of the Cranachs: his face had that delicacy and energy, and, even then, a faint tracery of lines, like the surface, *craquelé*, of an old painting—more the shadow of it than the later reality.

After the failure of this novel there was a long gap before *Portrait in a Mirror*. Something, during this time, happened to the madman hiding in an obscure corner of *My Name Is Legion*: he was cured, exorcized, cast out, what you like. Possibly Charles had taken the measure of himself and his great talent: since he was the most reserved of men—and, which is more remarkable, of writers—who knows what he paid for the serenity and impeccable good manners of his writing from now on?

I forced him on the Knopfs, who did not keep him very long—incompatibility of species rather than any failure of Alfred Knopf's foresight.

'Alfred doesn't believe in the book [*Portrait in a Mirror*],' Charles wrote to me in 1929, 'though Macmillan's acceptance shook his unbelief a little; and even if I sent him all the reviews, he still wouldn't believe; only thousands of copies will convince him, I am afraid, and I don't hope for much in that line...'

This did Alfred Knopf an injustice. It was Charles himself in whom he could not believe—as if he were a hippogriff, or as if he were seeing him in a glass which reflected only Charles's more arrogant traits, his aloofness, his Platonic idealism, his distaste for anything that offended his style as a human being. The two men never met, however often they may have sat at the same table.

I think Alfred had moments when he believed that Charles was a figment of my feverish invention.

Yet no one was more acute, more open to reason, than Charles. Three years later, when *The Fountain* was an enormous success, he still hesitated to give up his position as dramatic critic of *The Times*. 'I'm frightened,' he wrote to me, 'of depending on novels for fear of being compelled to write them not in my own time, and with care for the financial result. Journalism is a guarantee against that and enables me never to spend a penny that comes from novels or to rely on them in any way. The question is whether it's better to keep this absolute independence and to write novels, as I wrote *The Fountain*, in holes and corners and scraps of odd time (which means endless rewriting to preserve continuity) or to throw up *The Times* and venture. I don't know. And I'm becoming desperate because I can't get a clear twenty-four hours anywhere to write even the first paragraph of a book that has been boiling in my mind for ages...'

It was not then (1932) too late for me to notice the implied warning, and profit by it. But it brushed past me at a moment when I had just taken the notion that I could learn to write well. For years I thought of little else.

Today I see too sharply the folly (blindness, recklessness, ignorance— choose your term) of relying on writing for a living. The model for a young writer is Stendhal, who became a consul, or Tolstoy who was a landowner, or even X, Y, or Z, niched snugly in a warm corner of the cultural factory. I am dubious about the last: cultural officials lead narrow etiolated lives.

Is there any more futile and pitiable career than that of the writer com- pelled, year after year, to do his tricks on the same scrap of threadbare carpet, only in order to eat, poor acrobat? I suppose a minor actor runs him close. Or a fifth-rate politician. But these two probably have thicker hides, and feel their ignominy less.

This is a terrible digression, which has taken me too far from the young Charles Morgan, and his not yet bridled and bitted demon. Perhaps I am inventing the demon. The copy of *My Name Is Legion* was stolen from me, together with that other early book on his experiences in the Navy, so that I cannot track down the whiff of sulphur.

## CHAPTER 45

A S A PUBLISHER Alfred Knopf has no equal in his country. True, publishing in the States had not then become what it is now, a vast industrial enterprise, heavily capitalized, employing an immense corps of editors, experts in publicity, professors of (God help us all) Creative Writing and, by a strange necessity, writers: unlike the others, and like commercial travellers on a commission basis, the last are paid by results. But in 1924 the current was already setting that way and away from the kind of firm, small, choosy, he had imagined when he began. This elegant ghost never let him alone, egging him on to publish some books because he liked them, though he had no hope of making money by them. Whether saleable or not, every book had to meet his exigent standards of printing and binding. Not, mind you, that he would ever have been content to become an honourable failure; he was too ambitious, too shrewd, too intelligent. Curiosity and a fine palate drove him and his equally ambitious wife to pick up writers in every country in Europe, from Poland to Spain—at a time when translations were neither fashionable nor obligatory. He had—I should write: has—a knowledge of publishing comparable only to that of an English publisher he admired greatly, and sometimes quarrelled with: they were both as stubborn as the devil.

I had been working for him about a year when one day I answered the telephone to hear a voice I knew well, because it imitated so precisely the fluttering gesture of his hands when he was talking—Stanley Unwin's.

'Miss Jameson, Alfred has called me a *pig*!'

What was I to say? 'I'm dreadfully sorry.'

'Oh, it's not your fault. But I'll have nothing more to do with him.'

I did not believe the estrangement would last. Nor did it. The respect, not to say affection, between these wholly dissimilar human beings was too strong to be ended by a tiff.

To my spiritual and moral profit, Stanley Unwin became my friend. Wise, knowledgeable, shrewd to a fault, incorruptible, he was kinder to me than I merited. There may have been something honest in me, even at that simian time in my life, which caught his sympathy; or his sharp twinkling eye noticed that 'this devil is but a Simpleton, after all.' I made excuses to go and see him in his somewhat shabby office in a quarter of which he owned a sizeable part. His mere physical lightness enchanted me, so much that sometimes, in the pleasure of watching his hands fly up his with voice, I forgot to listen and had to improvise my reply...

One warm light evening during the last war, I was walking towards Pall Mall, and came on the half-destroyed front of the Carlton Hotel. I did not know it had been bombed, and was startled into standing to gape at it—long enough to let the ghost of a young woman in a hurry slip past me between the broken walls into the dining-room not there. I knew her: she was expecting six guests—and they were all on time: two of them had simply to forget that they had died several years before, and the others to leave less than twenty years in the lobby with their hats, to be able to go straight to the long light room, where tables, chandeliers, waiters, and *supreme de volatile Montpensier* ordered by the young woman beforehand, needed only their goodwill to be waiting for them...

When I had been working for them for five or six months, the Knopfs arranged for me to sign the bill at the Carlton, so that I could—not too often—give lunch to their own writers, and writers I was angling for. I might—they trusted me enough not to ask for names—have fed every needy writer I knew, but I was at least scrupulous enough to stick to writers worth seducing, and only once or twice to slip in a poor unsaleable honest little lark with the peacocks.

With a clear conscience, I invited a critic or two with the clerisy. Today, most reviewers of novels would have to be invited to nursery tea, but in the 'twenties they were serious thoughtful adults: fiction was not then considered a sort of writing only fit for an apprentice to cut his teeth on.

During these years I came to know so many people that I almost died of it. I have, thank God, forgotten nine-tenths of them: those I remember clearly have stayed in my mind either because, like Charles and Hilda Morgan, they became my friends, or because they were eccentric or impressive or gave me far too much trouble.

Romer Wilson died young, of tuberculosis. The first time I met her was with Blanche Knopf, who had come to rely on me to cast out devils in writers she found unmanageable. She got a half-malicious amusement out of watching me make myself affable to a Swedish or a Spanish novelist, neither of us having a syllable of the other's language. Asking me to help her with Romer Wilson, she said,

'You'll be able to handle her. I can't talk to her at all, I think she is insane.'

When she came into the room, Romer Wilson's dark eyes were rolling like those of a nervous horse, but she was not insane. She was simply a self-consuming genius, not a great genius, but of the cloth.

An infinite number of accidents—a love of going much into company or disliking it, having a sensual robust body or a sickly crippled one, being brought up Catholic or Calvinist—decides the answer that the sensitized nerves of the writer (painter, musician) make to his world. In Romer Wilson, genius took the form of a short cut between her senses and her half-conscious mind. Read *Dragon's Blood*, written before 1926, for her prevision of the bitterness and insanity which served Hitler's purpose. It is easier to describe water than to give an account of genius. One of its needs, or effects, seems to be a tension or peculiar instability of the nerves.

It occurs to me that this is why there are so few women of genius—tension and nervous instability do not go with childbearing.

The condition of genius may begin to be as common in women as in men only after several generations in which enough women renounce their biological functions. (I offer the idea to feminists.)

Possibly, too, the instability explains why a male writer of genius can cut down to the quick of a woman: any talented writer can produce semblances of human beings to fill out his tale, but when it comes to touching the naked rage of their lives he can only make guesses—it takes a Tolstoy to *know* what drives a woman to suicide or adultery or self-sacrifice.

You have only to compare the male characters invented by that highly-talented writer Charlotte Brontë with the male presences in *Wuthering Heights*.

It is not an accident that so much genius dies young, either stiffening into talent in Picasso, extinguishing itself in Wordsworth, dying in the flesh in Mozart, Keats, Emily Brontë, an endless line of brutally snuffed-out candles. If it can find a way to feed on others it can go on living; if not, if all it can do is to offer itself to its dear vulture, it dies—of T.B., or syphilis, or a stroke, or…

When I saw her alone, I got on extremely well with Romer Wilson. We are both from Yorkshire, and I understood her form of honesty, her form of timidity (more than half arrogance), her form of insanity—which was partly a total indifference to appearances and partly the dangerous lucidity with which, when she was writing, she heard and saw.

She told me once that she did not write with the conscious or deliberate intention of writing what, when she came to read it through, was there on the page. For weeks, months, she felt no impulse to write at all; then the wish seized her, she shut herself away from everyone, husband, infant son, friends, and wrote until she was physically and mentally exhausted.

If Mr X or Miss Y had told me that their admirable mechanically-articulated novels were in this way *given*, I should not have believed a word of it. I believed Romer Wilson—if only because no fragment she left, however trivial, is less than alive.

# CHAPTER 46

I S IT TO MY DISCREDIT that so much I remember is laughable— even when the memory that makes me laugh is attached to a person I genuinely like, or admire, or respect? Perhaps if I had had the courage, or the impudence, to laugh aloud at the time, I should have fewer memories, but they would be less unsuitable to a work of this sort.

Am I lacking in reverence? I think not. There are many people I revere with heart and soul, not only men like R. H. Tawney—there is no one like R. H. Tawney, and never will be—and women like Q. D. Leavis, but certain of the exiles I know, who are, quite simply and without knowing it, heroic.

But, in spite of my respect for her as a poet, as a high-spirited rebel against an aristocratic insolence she nevertheless fell into whenever she or her brothers were attacked by a plebeian critic, and as a hater of cruelty (except to critics), when I want to recall Edith Sitwell as I saw her in 1924, what springs into my mind first is not the really impressive figure she made, sitting, in a dark dress and immensely wide black hat, upright against yellow cushions at the end of the sofa in my room, her hands, her incredibly long fine hands, folded in her lap. No, I see her in her own sitting-room in west London, and myself choking over the hideously dry bun I was foolish enough to take from the tea-tray and too intimidated to leave uneaten.

Just as I had made up my mind that I could leave, a young man, fair-haired, tolerably good-looking, came in.

'You know Peter Quennell, of course.'

I did not. And when he knelt on a hassock and looked up into her face with what I daresay was genuine adoration, I merely thought him affected—*a fond ape*, as the ill-conditioned member of 5b, never far below the surface, would have said. Later, when his essays on the French Symbolists came out, it was years before I brought myself to open the book and discover how admirable a critical work I had almost missed.

And here—saved from the fire by having been pushed inside his book on Einstein—are three letters from J. W. N. Sullivan. Alfred Knopf had written, urging me to get the manuscript from him, and I went to a house in Pond Street to ask when it would be finished. Misled by my awe of mathematics, I had supposed J.W.N.S. to be a very old gentleman, who should be waited on. I found a dark heavily-built man in his late thirties, who there and then invited me, very pleasantly, to become his mistress. He took my refusal pleasantly, too, adding that he felt sure he would very soon convince me that I was making a serious mistake. I was embarrassed and bored—and anxious not to seem *provincial*. Even if I had found him attractive—on the contrary, he very slightly repelled me—I was infinitely too calculating and fastidious to enjoy a casual affair.

Not long after, he came up to London from Surrey, where he had a cottage, and walked me about the Embankment a long time, two or three hours, talking brilliantly about music, Einstein, Katherine Mansfield

('You're very like her, you know.'), and the benefits a young woman from the provinces could look for in being 'educated', mentally and sexually, by himself.

The walk ended in Trafalgar Square, where we sat, in chilly sunshine, on the parapet of a fountain, and he said with energy,

'You are not a child. Why must you behave like one? Or like a cold-hearted Puritan. Here am I offering you the companionship for as many years as you like, and the devotion, of one of the great intellects of our day—I won't speak of my other talents—and you mock me.'

He was certainly vastly intelligent, not only able to argue in German with Einstein himself, but a learned and passionate lover of music. When, much later, I read the sentence in which Stendhal says he cannot understand why Méthilde rejected him as a lover—she was politically in disgrace, she had allowed him three years of intimate friendship, she loved him, and yet, yet, she refused to become his mistress—I thought at once of J. W. N. Sullivan. I understood Méthilde perfectly. With his brilliant mind, his youthful passion for mathematics, his wit, his knowledge of music, his apparent self-assurance, Stendhal must have been more than a little like him. My passion for Stendhal, as writer and human being, is barely this side idolatry—but I could not have fallen in love with him. There is a certain fatuity, physical not moral, not even spiritual...

The last letter from him (the last I kept) came—shade of Stendhal!—from Italy. '... why not run over here, straight into my outstretched arms? We have the *Spring* in Italy now. And living here is so cheap. Einstein will come along presently... And I have begun another NOVEL! I spend eight hours daily in writing. But that leaves time for other things. An Italian lady here tells me she never knew what happiness meant until I showed her... My dear little conscientious Northerner, come south for a while. *I mean it*, you know. You collect experiences, don't you? Well, I'm an experience (a delightful one, I'm told) and remember, *age* creeps on. And I know you. In your autobiography you will refer with veiled pride to your liaison (in Italy in the spring) with a certain well-known writer. And I will introduce you to Norman Douglas, a wise and charming blackguard...'

If I read this letter the first time with a detestably derisive smile for its fatuity, and if, re-read, it still strikes me as clumsy, ridiculous, insensitive—he was not insensitive—a little remorse seizes me: because he is dead and I have lived so long...

How carefully I cherish—between layers of blotting-paper—the youth of my friends! One young man's flaming hair, another's loud crowing laugh; Archie as a youthful lieutenant-colonel; the exquisite head, its line unmarred by its fleece of dark-red curls, of Amabel Williams-Ellis; Noel Streatfield, a lovely creature, tireless and witty, amused by her own preposterous life as a young actress *en tournée*; an absurdly thin Richard Hughes. He was living in a flat not far from the British Museum, with his mother, and I fell momentarily into disgrace with her when I went to see him in the hospital where he was recovering from appendicitis and told him a comical story about a poet we both knew which made him laugh, causing him exquisite pain.

Should I trouble the sleep of another ghost? One evening, at a large literary dinner-party—how I dislike these gatherings of enraged egoists— someone pointed out to me a small elderly woman sitting alone, neglected by chattering writers and camp-followers.

'May Sinclair. I wish you would talk to her.'

'But what shall I say?'

'Anything, anything.'

Her eyes were those of a very young child, incurious and a little unfocused. I stammered some phrase or other of admiration for the one of her novels I had read at the university. She made little or no answer. I went with her into the dining-room and helped her to find her place at the long table. From mine I could see her, with an empty chair on her left: the other, on her right, might as well have been empty, since its young male occupant ignored her throughout the meal. When coffee was served, Arnold Bennett, who was leaving, paused to speak a word to her as he passed behind her chair: after this, she sat silent, looking down at her cup. I turned over in my head the sentences I would run and say to her as soon as we rose, but before then she stood up alone and began to walk away. She had to walk the length of the room, and when she reached the door could not find her way through the curtains drawn across it. She glanced round, at a loss, then fumbled through them, distracted by her scarf. Too timid and self-conscious to get up and cross the room to help her, I watched her until she disappeared.

For weeks, I could not think of this episode without shame for my part in it.

I think it was this same evening, when I was standing near her, admiring her beautiful ruined face, that I overheard Violet Hunt say smilingly,

'My dear, Mary Borden sat all day at my husband's feet. He wrote her first novel for her. Many of the critics, I'm told, consider it her best.'

## CHAPTER 47

IN THE AUTUMN OF 1924, I took a large room in Sloane Street, and provided it with a sofa, a walnut tallboy, a kitchen table, and some oddments of Victorian furniture. I was pleased with it: one very large room is all I need to live happily alone.

In 1924 it was still possible to invite people to tea—I am talking, obviously, of a very distant time. Once in a while I invited—separately, I think—two young men who were close friends: they had been at Cambridge together after the war, and were living side by side, each with wife and a child or two, in the country near London. Of all the too many people I knew, turning my life into a cheap circus, they alone seemed familiar.

An illusion, the accident that they reminded me of three smiling poor scholars, innocent scoffers with whom I had felt more at ease than with any of my new friends.

I liked the two, Gerald Bullett and J. B. Priestley, very well. They were as dissimilar a pair of friends as ever was: Gerald appeared the simpler, only in the sense that he was simple enough to believe he need only write his best, and all else, recognition, a secure living, would be added unto him. His friend—even then—knew better. Years later, with regret and sharp humour, he said to me,

'The mistake our Gerald made was to bury himself in the country. I told him: Get out, do as I'm doing, get to know people, make yourself felt, go about. He didn't listen.'

The advice was useless. If Gerald had been able to take it, he would not have needed it. He had two traits that ruined him for a life of getting about and getting to know people: a sub-conscious lethargy, which may have been physical, a deeply-rooted indifference or carelessness, as if he had thrown himself once for all into a stream and was letting it carry him where it pleased. He struggled, did well the work offered him, broadcasting, reviewing; he wrote, with immense effort, novels which give an effect of ease and grace, even lightness; he had more than one of your serious novelist's virtues, ingenuity, an almost innocent eye for the lies, ruses, self-deception, the blundering decency and compassion of ordinary men and women, a distaste for rhetoric. And all the time he was drowning in the very current that held him up: it was a slow process, and, when I first knew him, had scarcely begun.

Would he, if he had been born able to choose, or if he had not had his friend's example inciting him, have written novels? His rather clumsy head and body housed a poet of extreme elegance, of an almost Chinese elegance, able to make complex statements as if they were simplicities, so acutely attentive to the dissonance of life that in a chaos of sounds he could pick out the single note of existence itself. One says Chinese, thinking of the delicacy and purity of his poetic language, but the word is misleading: in his verse he was an English mystic, one of God's honest stubborn lazy eternally youthful English: the landscape of his poems is a loving yet cool pattern of sensuous detail, English in its smallest strokes.

I loved him for his gentleness. Not that he was soft-spoken, still less bland. He was as capable of a tart or malicious speech as the rest of us miserable sinners. But he had more gentleness, more charity, more singleness of mind than was good for him if he had wanted success as much as he wanted—ah, what did he want? To be happy, to be a little better-known, to have time to write a few more poems, time to look longer and closer at a leaf, a child, the surface of a stream...

He was fond enough of me to forgive me—except when it exasperated him too much—what he called 'your abominable and inflexible energy.'

I did not like the other young man any less. In one sense I liked him, at that time, the better of the two—but my liking was not straightforward. Imagine yourself walking along an empty street, and suddenly met by yourself, coming the other way, in a mirror—the shock of recognition, the instinctive fear and refusal. Hence my instant sympathy, instant deep liking—that is, liking at a deep level—and all but instant rejection. I think coolly that it is not my fault we did not become friends. If I, without knowing it, rejected an image of myself, he did the same, with instinctive mistrust.

Here is an odd thing. When I think of Gerald, it is only the last glimpse of him which is clear in my mind. The others are blurred copies. A door opens, he comes in, moving slowly and a little heavily, his large head thrust forward, coming from nowhere, going—where? But my memory of my first meeting with J. B. Priestley in the summer of 1924 is curiously distinct.

He came to tea. I had taken it into my head that he might be even worse off than I was. This was certainly not true; I had no reason to think it, but I did—and offered him, in the Yorkshire phrase, an egg to his tea. (I think he refused it.) We talked—or rather, he talked and I listened.

The shadowy outline of a room in Herne Hill rose behind this more presentable one. I felt affection, warmth, ease and a wary scepticism. The thing most to be feared in a Yorkshireman is not his shrewdness, his black sense of humour, his scoffing disrespect for authority, his grudging temper—but his secret fear that he is not accepted at the price he puts on himself. Touch that in him, and you will not be forgiven.

I have always loathed and despised the grudging take-you-down-a-peg side of the Yorkshire character as heartily as I admire certain others of their virtues and vices: their brusque charity, tenacity, self-will, impatience of control, self-biting wit.

Nothing saves me from being the worst of Yorkshiremen except a profound indifference which comes from some other strain (Gallilee?). In my heart of hearts I do not care whether I am respected or disliked, or even injured, by *these people*.

'I had a look at your last book,' he said, smiling. 'I don't say it's bad, but all you women writers are the same, too careful or too violent. You s'd strike out something for yourself, not keep on hashing up all that old stuff. You haven't much invention, have you?'

Since my vanity does not lie in my writing, I took this for what it was, a nearly impersonal dressing-down. Moreover, I had begun to think he was right.

He talked to me about the book he was writing, and about himself. I listened. Later I discovered that he was carrying about with him a heavy weight of anxiety. True to his and my kind, he had no intention of showing it. His irony, his sardonic self-confidence, delighted me, and for a moment gave me the illusion that, with a cool blast of horse-sense, I could brush aside my mistakes, sins, follies. I was sorry when he got up to go.

Turning in the door, he smiled at me with the half derisive, half wary kindness familiar to me since my childhood.

'Well, you're not so bad,' he said. 'I thought you might be much worse.'

I tried hard to persuade the Knopfs that his novel was one they ought to snatch at once, without seeing it finished. Alfred Knopf did not agree—and lost *The Good Companions*. Just as well. The two of them would have been at outs in a year.

A few years later, when I was reviewing for A. R. Orage, I made him very angry by writing severely about his latest book. I have completely forgotten why I did it. The intellectual recklessness that seizes me when I am alone with a pen and a sheet of paper? A nearly impersonal Yorkshire malice?

I have never in my life altered my relations with a friend because he cursed or mocked my work—and I have had to take some pretty harsh comments. He is less indifferent, less sceptical about his writing, and—in a word—more honest. If I had imagined that my fault-finding would cut deeply I would have given my tongue to the cat...

This trivial incident tells nothing, or nothing of value, about a complex human being called Priestley. The person it reflects more or less accurately is a self-centred young woman, clever and imprudent.

# CHAPTER 48

THERE ARE MOMENTS when it seems impossible that I am coming to the end of my life—and with so little of all I intended to do done, and without knowing myself better than when I set out.

A psychologist might find in the confusion, the persistent *lack* of plan in the welter of plans masking the deep-rooted improvidence and incoherence of my life, a secret wish to be punished for my errors.

On this reasoning, Stendhal brought all his frustrations and disappointments on himself, even his dull life in Civitavecchia, as a punishment for having been in love with his mother, who died when he was seven... *But oh how I was as criminal as could be, how arduously I loved her charms...*

But, good heavens, how boring an account of the author of *Lucien Leuwen*!

When we went to Weybridge in 1924, I and my eight-year-old son, I meant to live quietly, write a fifth novel, and begin to save money to send him to school and the university, even—but this I avoided looking at closely—to be able to have a house of our own. The novel was a necessity: we could not go on living on my salary as Knopf's representative.

Nothing turned out as I meant. I wrote nothing—the other work demanded too much time and drained me of energy: to have to do with so many people exasperated me; they pulled my mind to pieces with their monkeys' fingers and at the end of the day I was in a state of distraction, as little able to sit down to write as sing in tune, always beyond me.

I am lying. In time I should have learned how to live two lives without cheating either. What scattered my plans like dry leaves in a wind was a personal crisis, the sharpest of my life, into which I fell as soon as I started to work in London.

I am not going to tell the story at length. Like my happy difficult second marriage, it is part of the nervous system of my mind: to draw it out would kill me. What little could safely be turned into phrases has been told once already.

Outwardly, as it unfolded under the amused half-sceptical eyes of two of my friends, Elizabeth Gleeson and Michael Sadleir, it seemed no more than an obsession. Michael refused frankly to believe that it was either deeply serious or final.

'You'll fall in love a dozen times!' he said smiling.

Quite possibly, had there been no great difficulties, it might not have been a mortal illness or lasted my life. But the difficulties drove it into my soul, like a stain driven through a piece of cloth. They were not only concrete—we were both married, though not living alone. The most paralysing difficulty, the one I was weeks, months, learning to recognize, was impenetrable by sense or reason.

I realized quickly that nothing made Guy happier than to talk about the war. Certain names of places, Bapaume, Gommecourt, Hannescamp, Arras, had more than the charm or excitement of poetry for him. They involved feelings I could never touch. With a little despair, I guessed that his five years of war and Occupation had used up too much of his energy. During those years the relationship between him and a few men, a few places, between him and a battalion, had been complete and satisfying, as no relationship would ever be again. He was *occupied territory*.

'Thank heaven,' he said once, 'that my personal life is finished. The only pleasures I want are all impersonal. To work until I can't think any longer. Music. A decent bottle of wine. I'm perfectly content.'

Like other soldiers I knew, whose war had been long, he became tired, suddenly grey in the face, between one minute and the next. Fatigue made him cruel. 'Work is more important to me than anything. If you, or my wife, were to get in my way I should have to leave you out, do you understand, my dear?... I don't like being driven. The idea that I'm being held down to any set of circumstances, makes me want to move *off, foutre le camp*, before it's too late.'

Where he was concerned, I had no vanity, no pride. Spoken to by two voices at once, one of them his exhaustion and fear of failure, I heard only the other one. Nothing convinced me that, dryness and impatience apart, I was not loved, not needed. My mind had fastened on him with all its tenacity, with a total imprudence, obeying, this time, an impulse engaging body, spirit, imagination. All the energy of my tortuous and, as it was then, domineering nature was bent to one end—for the most part I was, am, too lazy, too at a deep level indifferent, to use it in this single-pointed way. It would be a great deal truer to say that I was possessed rather than possessive.

I saw him two or three times a week, and he wrote as often. A small pile of letters accumulated in a corner of my cupboard in Weybridge.

K. had become remote, a shadow on the edge of my mind. I suppose he wrote to me, since he had fewer distractions in Cornwall, and I answered, as is my habit, at once. Then tore up his letter and forgot him.

One incident of this time slightly alarmed me. I had a letter from an elderly lady he had met in a train, to whom he had said that I was the daughter of an Admiral and closely related to Dr Jameson of the Raid. I was used to his casual inventions—they were a sort of involuntary play-acting, little more sophisticated than a child's day dreams of being heroic and witty. This seemed a little worse. And if I were to be involved in his myths... (This mythopoeic trick of his did become serious, and later in his life began to fringe mania. Some of his inventions were less innocent than this one; there must be several people in the world who know about me disagreeable things in which there is not a vestige of truth.)

Since I could not answer the lady's friendly letter without giving him away, I destroyed it.

## CHAPTER 49

S OME TIME IN MARCH OR APRIL I came home from London early in the afternoon and found K. in my sitting-room. From his air of sullen dignity I saw that I was in disgrace. Drawn stiffly to his height of over six feet, he scowled down at me. The whole thing was arranged, even to his gestures. I felt contemptuous and uneasy.

It was soon out. He had found and taken the bundle of Guy's letters.

'Where are they?' I asked calmly.

'They're not in this house.'

My heart dropped. He was perfectly capable of reading them aloud to his friends. He would make a laughing-stock of us both, almost without knowing he was doing it. As for scandal, he enjoyed it.

'You've sent them away? Where?'

'Never mind what I've done with them. May I ask if you meant to tell me about this—this sordid affair?'

'No.'

I felt unreasonably bitter, and sick and tired of him. Yet, when I looked at him standing there, solemn, peevish, the dignified husband victimized by a dishonest wife—which I was—I had an extraordinary feeling of pity, almost gentleness. He has never grown up, I thought: he understands nothing, neither himself, nor what he did to us.

The fear that he might use the letters to harm Guy turned me to steel: I was determined to get them from him—by any means.

'If you imagine I'll make things easy for you, you're entirely mistaken,' he said sarcastically. 'I'm not going to hand my son over to you, to be brought up by you and your admirer—don't think it.'

I felt an access of contempt. 'Are you by any chance going to bring him up yourself?' I asked him in my mother's harshest voice.

There was a silence. Then he sat down and began to speak sorrowfully.

'I never thought you were tired of me. I've been looking forward to living with you in Launceston—I meant to work, and try to make something of my life. It's almost funny—you might as well have taken a knife and cut my throat. I would never have believed it of you.'

His face worked, and he covered it with his hands.

It would not be true to say that the grief which tore its way through my body, wrenching it horribly, was for him: it was for the past, for what he had been to me, for the failure I, I, had made of our marriage, for all the mistakes, disappointments, defeats, still in the closed hand of the future. A hand twisted the nerves above my heart. Am I going to die? I thought.

My will had not died.

'If you will give me the letters back,' I said, 'I'll give him up.'

'Do you promise?' he said sternly.

'Yes, yes, I promise.'

'Very well. I trust to your generosity.'

No, don't trust me at all, I thought. So afraid was I of wakening his anger again that I spoke under my breath. 'Where are they?'

He had made a parcel of them and taken it to the Left Luggage office at the railway station. At once, so that he would have no time to change his mind, I went with him to get them. When I had them in my hands, my strength left me and I felt deathly tired and weak, hardly able to put one foot before the other. I forced myself to talk to him in a gentle flattering way. He told me he was writing a novel, very outspoken. 'Bolder than anything you can do,' he said, smiling, 'or Bennett or Wells either. You'll see—your little K. will astonish you.'

Pray heaven he does, I thought: I shall feel less responsible for him.

Did I, even at this moment, intend to keep my promise? Almost certainly not. I made it without reflection, as I would have clutched the blade of a knife to save myself falling over a cliff. I felt neither shame nor guilt. Afterwards, in a confused way, I thought: After all, I may lose Guy, and then nothing I have promised will matter...

Some time this month—it may have been later or earlier: my uncertainty about dates is a scandal—I saw one of my first friends, Oswald Harland. With him or with one of the others, I was always happy. What other happiness in the world equals that of being remembered from childhood, and approved or disapproved of without irony?

He had had what he called an impudent letter from K. He told me nothing about it, and I did not ask.

'K. did you a great deal of harm,' he grumbled.

'I'm very hard. I've lived through it without damage—as you can see.'

'The damage isn't obvious—except to me. I knew you, don't forget, when you were a schoolgirl, afraid of nothing and nobody.'

'Not true,' I said.

'Well, let's say that in those days you had enough self-confidence to take you to hell and back. You've lost it, and you don't trust anyone. D'you know what Archie and I said to each other when you married K.? We said: And that's the end of our Daisy Jameson... It damn' near has been... Why didn't you leave him years ago?' He scowled. 'I haven't forgotten one episode in Shepherd's Bush—I thought very seriously of killing him then.'

I knew he was thinking of my fatuous impulse to kill myself, and my mind turned tail and bolted.

'You only saw his worst side, he had others... I couldn't have walked out of the house lugging young Bill, and his clothes and travelling bath and the cot, and all my books and the silver spoons my mother gave me, and my grandmother's tea service.'

'I never heard such nonsense,' he said, grinning. 'You're a queer dishonest chap, you know.'

'Then why bother about me?'

'I have m'reasons. You have an honest mind. No call to look pleased— you can't help it, and in every other way you're as dishonest as be damned. I don't suppose you've told yourself a lie since you began to think, but you don't mind how many you tell other people. You like them to think well of you, don't you?'

'It's my great fault,' I said, mocking him.

It was myself I mocked. When I was thinking coldly I thought that my ambition and impatience were more to blame and K. less than this friend, looking at me from our careless past, imagined. My own disloyalties seemed—seem—inexcusable where those of others can be explained.

K. began sending me terrible letters. I read them with a sick heart—and pushed them aside, almost unanswered. The half of me that cringed was strangled by another which scarcely believed in his unhappiness. I had come to an end of regret. And if not—not yet—to an end of concern and pity, these were drowned in an indifference that rose, a cold tide, from depths I preferred not to look at.

That was not all. 'An emotion can neither be hindered nor removed save by a contrary emotion...' (Spinoza).

Whatever might come of it, my new love—more despotic than any simply erotic passion—had freed me, at last, from everything except a guilt which had older roots than those still twisted round the man who had taught me to distrust myself, suspected me, hurt me in anger, and given me my first adult lessons in solitude and the unseemliness of relying on the kindness of another human being.

To avoid thinking too much, I worked myself to exhaustion. After long days, a few hours' sleep gave me back a body as light as when I was one of four poor scholars.

In just the same way as, after a defeat, there came to my side all the hidden exultance, the gaiety, of the child resolved *to get away*.

## CHAPTER 50

I T NEVER STRUCK ME that hired rooms are no sort of life for a young child. Only very rarely, when he was more taciturn than usual, I asked myself whether Bill was happy living with me in Weybridge.

'What did you do today, my one?'

'Nothing.'

'No lessons?'

'Yes, I had lessons.'

'Do you like this school?'

'It's all right.'

'Do you like it better than living with Miss Geeson?'

'Yes,' he said, with indifference.

I saw that he could not tell me what he did during his days, because the repetition bored him, and because he had a profound dislike of answering questions. He answered them as shortly as he could, hoping there were no more to come.

With a little anxiety, I tried to hear myself as a child—and failed. It seemed that neither the streets and cafés of Antwerp, nor the ship's saloon, its air warm, stagnant, smelling of lamp oil and the steward's pantry, had been much troubled by my voice.

One day he left his composition book at home. The last two pages were filled, in his large straggling hand, by a piece entitled: How you write books. 'First you write what your book is going to be about, then you send it somewhere to be printed. Then if it is a good book it will be published and charged so much for, if it is a bad book it is Sent back. My mother Wrote a book each copy was so much money it took a very long time to Write. When it was finished it Was about one inch and ½ thick.'

Heaven be praised, he is not going to turn into a writer, I thought.

I spent too much time in London, taking the train as soon as he had gone to school and hurrying back in time to give him tea. Returning from one of these sorties I found Elizabeth in our sitting-room. She was playing with Bill, who for some reason had been sent home early, and she was on her hands and knees, her hair wildly in disorder, her eyes brilliant. I had never seen her look so beautiful. It startled me, and roused a little fear. With a wide sweet smile, she said,

'I have left John. Your landlady says she can let me have the bedroom next yours. Do you mind?'

I was overjoyed. The warmth, the gaiety, the ease she spread round her, without effort, in the movements of her large hands, in the tone, low and slightly rough—she smoked too much—of her voice, was what our life, mine and Bill's, lacked. I settled back into it as into my mother's house, with the same familiarity.

It did not surprise me that she had left John, but I was a little shocked that she had trusted her five-year-old Prue with the two servants. After Bill was in bed, she told me why she had left: she had fallen in love with the young doctor John had taken on as assistant, and John had found them together:

the same day the young man left for London, and she, after a few terrible days of scenes and arguments, had decided to follow him.

'What is going to happen?'

She lifted her hands, smiling. 'Oh, I don't know. A divorce, I suppose. I'm not going to make any plans. What happens, happens.'

I asked no more questions. She lived in these rooms exactly as she lived anywhere, with the instinctive lightness of a seagull balancing on a rope, perfectly at ease and ready to take off any second. Our sitting-room became untidy and lived-in, she dropped cigarette ash everywhere, borrowed my books and handed them back with coffee stains on the pages. Once or twice a week, not oftener, she went to London to see her lover, who had taken a post of some sort there.

She seemed content to idle through the other five or six days of the week, sleeping late, reading, talking to me when I had time to listen. She talked a great deal of Prue, rarely of John. It was not she who told me, years later, that he had caught her when she was unhappily in love with a young man too preoccupied to pay attention to her: from the start, their marriage was made false and brittle by the pretence that she loved him. She, I suppose, did not want to look at a humiliating mistake; she would rather pretend, even to herself, that she had married for love. Yes, even, for a time, to herself. As for him, he loved her with a sort of ferocity—then.

I exaggerate, perhaps. After all, I lived with them for months without suspecting that they were not, in their different ways, devoted. What went on below the sparkling surface—made to sparkle by Elizabeth—was probably out of sight in those years.

She talked about her childhood with an intelligent charming father, who flattered her, and later abandoned his wife, leaving her to bring up—on a wretchedly small income—five children, including the daughter he had seemed to admire and love. 'When I was still in my cradle,' she said, smiling, 'he looked at me and said: Perhaps she won't be at all beautiful, but she has charm and an intelligent body.'

She refused to admit his rejection of her: alone of his family, she called on him in his editorial office in London.

Some of the tales she told about herself were doubtless touched up or untrue, but in a strange way they were all innocent, like a very young child's efforts to draw attention to itself by smiling and clowning.

Now that she was here I made use of her. Knowing that Bill would be happy with her—what her child had lost, that incomparable gaiety and warmth, mine gained—I could sometimes stay in London with Guy until eleven, the last train.

On one of these evenings, at the end of a day when the June sun and the dry wind had between them made a desert of London, I had a curious experience. Guy and I were going to dine at the Café Royal. As I followed him into the brasserie, I saw the Texan.

He was at a table against the right-hand wall, with a companion, a woman neither very young nor elegant. My heart moved heavily. I turned my head aside, vexed by the exquisite line of the Hampshire downs wavering across a cloudless sky: of all creatures in the world I did not want to see a young woman staring at it from her window, her ears strained to catch the sound of an American lorry in the lane from the village... I walked past his table to the farther end of the room, and sat with my back to him, uncertain whether he had seen me. In my one glance from the doorway I had the impression that things were not going altogether well with him.

When we left, there was no one at his table. I stood for a moment outside the entrance to the brasserie, waiting for Guy to fetch his hat from the cloakroom. A waiter, a thin smile of connivance on his sallow face, stepped up to me, and handed me a folded sheet of paper.

'The gentleman left this for you.'

I put it into my pocket until I was in the train going home. Two lines. 'I wrote you yesterday, to Whitby. Call me at the Piccadilly, tonight or tomorrow morning—your J.'

I neither telephoned, nor, when the letter arrived, opened it. And when he came into my mind, I turned him out. I wanted *not* to know what he was doing. An instinct he himself would have recognized ordered me: Don't look behind you.

For some days I said nothing to Elizabeth. When I told her, she looked at me with an equivocal smile.

'Didn't you want to see him?'

'No.'

'Why not?'

'All that's finished.'

'Perhaps. But I don't think I ever knew you do anything callous—before this.'

I was surprised. 'Callous?'

'Incredibly callous. I don't understand you.'

I should have great trouble in understanding myself. Perhaps I was simply a coward. But the state of mind I recall is not timidity or nervousness: it is indifference, a dry deliberate rejection—of a self which no longer interested me, and, naturally, of the man involved with it.

That was the end—except for a letter, some years later, from his father, asking where his son was. I answered that I had not the faintest idea.

## CHAPTER 51

THINGS WERE NOT GOING well with Elizabeth. Though I did not notice it—I was too self-engrossed to see anything below the surface—she was adrift as she had never been in her life, and, perhaps without knowing it, afraid. I did not know that her love-affair was going wrong until an evening when I came back from London and found her in the sitting-room, not reading, seated against the wall, hands in her lap, head stretched back. She had an unusually long slender throat, with a barely noticeable swelling, and a long straight jaw. I noticed two things: she, who never used make-up of any sort, had covered her eyelids with oil, perhaps to disguise redness after tears, and she was deathly tired, the marked sensuality of her face softened by it.

She looked at me gaily. 'I never knew how many happy people there are in the world until I felt unhappy. This evening when I went out to the pillar-box, there were lovers in every gateway.'

I did not know what to say. I tried to hear her mind. 'Are you unhappy?'

'I'm usually very happy. When I'm dancing—and on warm fine mornings... Have you been dining with Guy?'

'Yes.' I did not say that he had been in a black negative mood.

'Well, you are luckier than I am,' she said lightly. 'D'you know, I have made the most humiliating mistake—he doesn't care for me any longer. I offered to live with him on any terms, and he refused.'

Pity would be another humiliation. 'Do you mind seriously?'

'Of course.'

She was smiling ironically. Her hands were perfectly steady. I thought: I shall never see her cry.

'I can't comfort you.'

'A stupider person would try,' she said quickly.

She lit another cigarette, and went on to tell me, in the greatest detail, how things had begun to go wrong from the moment she came to Weybridge, and repeated, calmly, even smiling a little, with the same fold of irony at the ends of her mouth, the insults vented on her by a young man who was clearly tired of her and afraid of scandal. I listened without speaking. I was slightly shocked that she could expose herself so nakedly.

I had no impulse to confide in her in my turn. There is no doubt, I thought, that I am showing as little self-respect in my own affairs, but I shan't speak about it or let anyone know what I am going through.

But, merely by listening with my entire mind, I drew so close to Elizabeth during this hour that there was no need for me to say anything. When she stood up to go to bed, I felt an impulse of pure love, a strange mixture of liking and identity with her. Neither of us was in the habit of caresses, but at this moment it seemed natural to lean forward and kiss her very gently on the lips. She smiled without speaking.

A week or two later, she went back to John. I never stayed with them again, and on the one or two occasions when she came to stay with me in London after I married Guy, there was a light sense of—not estrangement, but distance. We talked, laughed, were happy, across a small dried-up stream. In some way I made no effort to fathom, she had drawn back, her gaiety, her brilliance of life, very slightly blurred.

Guy was not charmed by her, and this itself set a curious no-man's-land between us, created by my anxiety that she should not notice it.

Possibly she only came once.

She died suddenly, in 1934, in her sleep. Of heart-failure? Perhaps.

After the shock of grief, I closed my mind against a smiling ghost. I preferred not to think about her life during the nine years after she went back to John. If I had thought about it, I should have been forced to see that she had been defeated—under my averted eyes. Forced to know that, for all her warmth, her charm, her hunger for safety and kindness, her deep reserve about the real things she felt, she was a swimmer in a strong stream clinging, with the strength of her fears, to a root in the bank.

With the strength of her fears... And I left her with them. Why?

I am old and she a ghost. Who are so unforgiving as the dead? It is useless to ask them to forgive.


# CHAPTER 52

AT THE END OF JULY I took Bill to Whitby for the summer. I was making plans to move to London, to the room in Sloane Street. I had a respectable reason—it had become very difficult to work for the Knopfs from Weybridge—but this was not the real reason.

Living in London, I could see Guy more easily, in a less hand-to-mouth and unsettling way. For this I was going to uproot Bill again and send him as a boarder to his school in Weybridge.

I knew—beyond any question I knew—that if K. were to stand on his legal rights and force me to decide between son and lover, I could only choose my son. That was as fixed and cold in me as iron. Did knowing this let me put him second in lesser choices?...

I have few memories more absurd and vivid than of the meeting, after I had asked K. to divorce me, between him and Guy. They met in my room. Guy turned up first: he was curt and distant, as though he were feeling ill. No doubt he was. I felt completely detached, a spectator of what, after all, concerned me gravely.

K. arrived on his heels, greeted me in a formal way, and Guy with what deserved nothing better than to be labelled stately courtesy. With a flicker of the jeering Yorkshire irony I detest, I thought that he had chosen the role of man of the world—a little spoiled by the shape of his nose.

They sat at opposite ends of my sofa. To give myself something to do, I took a number of papers and letters from my desk and began destroying some and sorting the rest into their kinds. After a moment's silence K. said haughtily,

'I understand that you wish to marry my wife, if it can be arranged.'

'Yes.'

A fit of laughter seized me. I did my best to stifle it, but it was too violent. Both men turned to look at me, K. gravely, Guy with surprise and displeasure. I was ashamed of my misplaced gaiety.

Which shrewd derisive forbear is it who takes possession of me at the very moments when I ought to be most moved or most dignified? For the rest of the interview, very short, I had no further temptation to laugh.

When Guy had gone, thankful to escape, K. dropped his sublimity.

'Don't send me off at once. Just think—I'm going to be alone for the rest of my life.'

Little likelihood of that, I thought. He was looking at me with a lamentable face. Not a line on it, not the faintest trace of a line; he was thirty-five or six, and except for a coarsening round the nostrils, his face was that of a man of twenty. For a disagreeable moment I saw the road we took out of Leeds on summer nights, stumbling over the roots of trees in the darkness, the spoiled runnel from the factory glittering in the moon. Disgusted by my folly, I thought: Forgive me, it was my fault—in the end I was the stronger and harder of us. I said stiffly,

'I haven't been honest with you these last months. I'm sorry.'

A look at once sly and bitter came into his face. 'Why should you assume that I'm going to let you keep Bill?'

This threat—the single indestructible hold he had over me—he repeated at intervals during the next few years. He never tried to carry it out, even when he could have done so. He was not unkind enough—and he did not for a moment want the responsibility and cost of a child. But the threat never failed to send a pang of fear and rage through me.

I steadied myself to answer coldly. 'For one reason, you have never, since the end of the war, kept him yourself. And for another, when I gave up my divorce, you promised that if at any time I wanted to leave you, you would take the whole thing on yourself. I am not asking you to do this. But you have no right to take Bill from me. Rather than lose him, I would call off the divorce—I tell you that frankly, so that you know where you stand. But it wouldn't do you any good—I don't dislike you, but I would never live with you again.'

'You're very hard.'

'Not until I'm forced to be.'

'I shan't take the boy from you,' he said. 'I'm finished, you've done for me... My girl, *must* you do this to me?'

I felt—not pity followed by indifference, but indifference, pity, contempt (for his asking to be pitied), sympathy, and an old habit of responsibility—all in the same breath.

I said nothing. He stood up, and looked round for his hat.

'Even now I can't believe you mean to get rid of me. I don't know what to do with my life. I feel like shooting myself... Sunday afternoon, too—it's awful, awful—not a thing to do and nowhere to go.'

The prospect of entertaining him for the rest of the day filled me with despair—as though I were agreeing to live with him again. 'Is there anywhere you would like to go?'

'Yes,' he said, 'yes. When I was coming up this morning I thought: How wonderful if a miracle happened, and instead of kicking me out she said: Hurry up, we're going to Richmond—just as we did, you remember...'

'Very well,' I said, 'let's go to Richmond.'

We spent four hours there, walking in the Park, gossiping, discussing his unfinished thesis, his novel, his social triumphs in Launceston, like old friends...

In November Guy's lawyer summoned us to his office, handed each of us a document, and made us stand against the window of his room, as close as possible to the glass. It looked out on a narrow yard, below the level of the street. Four figures in single file walked at the pace of a funeral across this yard, faces over their shoulders, like maladjusted puppets, staring at the window. K. first, in the overcoat I had given him on his last birthday; a large woman, with a grimly displeased face, the chambermaid from the hotel; a pustular bully in a navy suit, who was the inquiry agent; and a young wizened man, a solicitor's clerk.

This astonishing procession passed. I turned to Guy. He was no help to me: hurrying me out of the house, he said, 'I'll see you tomorrow,' and fairly ran from me.

I walked across the square, looked back, and saw K. striding towards me. I waited. The wind flattened his overcoat against his long thin legs; with his narrow head he looked more puppet-like than ever.

'Well,' he said jauntily, 'what are you doing this afternoon?'

No more able to disappoint him than if he had been a child, I said, 'Nothing. Would you like to have tea somewhere, and dance?'

'That suits me.'

The ball-room of the Piccadilly Hotel is a well-lighted overheated room below the ground. We drank hotel tea, and danced—since that was why we had come here—and talked. He was in a boastful mood, and I felt the old impulse to encourage him, for my own comfort more than his. His mood changed suddenly. With a mocking glance at me, he said, 'You look older, my dear. He didn't wait to see you home, your new lover. Well, if you change your mind about him, you can always come back, I shall welcome you with cheers. No doubt when I'm sixty I shall give up feeling. At present I still think about you.'

I acknowledged his right to mock. It struck me that, unreliable and useless as he was, he had never wanted to convince me that I was less necessary to him than other things. I neither liked nor respected him, but I was not, not yet, free of him in my mind. Should I ever be?

When the dancing ended, at six, I shook him off, as gently as I could, and set off to walk home. I was in a fever of impatience. It's not even true, I thought, with despair, that I am doing what I choose... My brain seemed to be boiling in my skull; I thought I was becoming insane... I could be living with Bill, simply, I don't like London now, in another ten years it will be uninhabitable by anyone with a nose and ears. I don't want to know people, or be known—that at least is true. And this, this, is the moment I choose to lose my wits again, for a difficult self-centred lover. Well, I must do as I can—sit still in my bones...

I caught sight of my morose face in a strip of glass between two lighted windows, and laughed out.

For an instant I felt free and light, as though I were beginning again, with no hand on me to turn me this way or that, no son, no lover, no abandoned husband. I hurried on, breathing the cold damp earth-scented air of the Park, towards the illusion of safety in a room empty of ghosts, without thoughts, without anxiety, without plans.

## CHAPTER 53

I DECIDED—THE WRONG WORD, it was simply the next step along a road I was following like a sleepwalker—that it was time we lived together: a life of meetings and letter-writing was a distracting compromise.

As soon as it was decided, I felt qualms—and ignored them. I daresay that, used as he had become to the life of a bachelor with a good club, Guy had his own unspoken doubts. These, too, I ignored. I knew, how well I knew, that doubt, even hostility, can exist at the same time, towards the same creature, as an irrevocable love and dependence.

He left everything to me, and I found a small furnished flat, the attics of a house at the top of Primrose Hill. At night it was suspended over London like a lighthouse; lines drawn by the street-lamps crossed the hill in all directions, the circles of light becoming smaller and smaller until the last point merged into the half-darkness, thinly-sown with blades and tendrils of light, stretching to an invisible horizon.

I will not say that I lived here easily. Guy was at times unapproachable, sunk in his work or his dry thoughts. And all I feared and disliked, disliked in my bones, a domestic life, was nailed to me again. I had brought it on myself. Alone, as I often was, in the flat, trying to write, I was mocked by a jeering northern voice asking me what I imagined I had gained by my headstrong folly.

My worst moments had to do with Bill. I cannot—that is, will not—try to decipher what kept me from carrying out any of the foolish plans I made to bring him to London.

*No man is an island...* what nonsense! The one certain thing we know about a human being is that he is an island, becoming smaller, colder, more sterile: the wildness of first love, the lovely ease of youth, the pleasures of hate, all slowly failing, until the day when only a habit of caring remains.

Guy's wife had put an end to their marriage in the most humiliating way imaginable. I understood her—no one can be so brutal, so blindly callous, as a woman in the grip of an infatuation. He had no conscious wish to redress the balance at my cost. In good faith he told himself, and me, that he was used-up, incapable of meeting the demands of an exacting love, unwilling to risk a second failure.

Possibly, I told myself, it is true. Possibly, as well as being naturally self-centred and self-absorbed, he really is incapable of self-surrender. Having once, without noticing it, given his whole confidence, with the recklessness, the happiness and torment, of first love, he is now half tired and half a coward.

I could not accept this. Hope is one of my vices. Beaten off at one edge, my fingers close round another—to this day.

Moreover, he was not consistent. There were moments or days when I was completely, madly, happy.

Like the Master, *I feared I should taint the happy moments that I have known by describing them, by dissecting them...*

I shall not try. A decade of disorder and bitterness was behind me; I even felt an acute pleasure in the certainty that my life would be far from easy. I had done well to risk myself with Guy. I knew it—even at times when I lost confidence.

A year ago, at our first meeting, he had said, 'I couldn't read your novel. Do you mind? It's too emotional.'

A crack that was to become an avalanche opened in my mind. There and then I determined that, whatever else, henceforth I would write as drily as Euclid.

This was as far as my wits took me then—not far.

I should like to know whether I am eccentric in remembering places infinitely more vividly than I recall people. My skull is the walls of a vast museum of roads, streets, harbours, in foreign countries. And, if an incident I remember for other reasons took place in Whitby, I see it with every gesture, every tone of voice, every colour, as distinct and sharp as if it had happened this morning... As soon as his school term ended, I took Bill to Whitby, promising Guy not to stay longer than the end of the month.

On the first evening, my mother settled herself in her fireside chair, her dress turned back over her black satin petticoat, the palms of her hands resting on her knees, and prepared to astonish me with Whitby news. Her life, once rich in exotic memories, had narrowed to the streets and a few houses of a small port, and the doings of her youngest child.

I hated to deprive her of a familiar pleasure, but I had to tell her about Guy, of whom she knew nothing yet.

There was a long silence: she stared into the fire, her mouth working as it did when she was troubled or angry. The fear always at the back of my mind since I was a child, the fear of punishment, needled me. But she spoke gently.

'What is going to happen?'

'K. has agreed to divorce me. I shall keep Bill—of course. K. would not want to bother with him. He has taken a job now, but I don't suppose he'll do anything very much.'

'Not he,' my mother said contemptuously, 'he's lazy to his very bones, a good-for-nothing. A rare soft sit-down he's had of it all these years. I can't be anything but relieved that you have got rid of him.'

Ashamed to have thrown K. to the wolves only to make things easier for myself, I went on,

'The divorce won't be heard before May. And then there are six months before the decree is absolute. I thought—I can't see the sense of waiting a year—I thought we might begin living together at once. It would be more economical...'

'Everything is changing,' she said calmly, 'you must do as you think best.' Her face softened. 'You know that whatever you do you are still my little good child. You have always had courage for anything. You deserve to be happier.'

Relief, love, surprise, suffocated me. I could not put them into words. In my family there were few spontaneous gestures, few easy familiar words of tenderness.

'I couldn't have done anything but for you,' I said.

She seemed satisfied, her blue eyes less remote than usual. 'When you were a little girl, you were restless and patient—I used to think, how can she be both? And unbelievably stubborn. You don't take enough care of yourself, you live as if you were made of iron, and there is an end to that.'

'I haven't reached it,' I said.

Bill supposed I was going to spend the whole of his holidays in Whitby. I had told him, 'Ten days,' but, as children do, he put this aside.

Unless he wanted to do or be given something, he rarely began a conversation. I felt a blind ditch between our minds. Was it only because he had been so often away from me during the last six years? I had a heavy sense of guilt, of time rushing past. I want him with me, I thought: he is the centre of my life, and Guy is an indulgence: I am a wicked woman.

When the day came to leave, I helped him to arrange his Christmas presents on a shelf in his room. 'As soon as I can I'm going to find us a house to live in. You shall have a fine large room in it.'

He did not answer. He had been talking, and now he had nothing to say, and, it seemed, no wish to listen.

'Shall you like that?' I asked.

'Yes.'

He doesn't notice whether I'm here or in London, I thought. I was going back on the night train. When I was giving him his bath, he said,

'Don't go.'

I no longer remember what, in my despair, I said. His face changed. He began to cry.

'You could stay here.'

'I must go, it's to get money for us, this isn't our house, you know, my little love, I'll come back for you in two weeks, I'll...'

Heaven knows what words I forced past the hard knot in my chest. He let himself be comforted and began laughing. When I was taking him upstairs, he said,

'I wish these stairs would never end.'

He had his wish. For ever and ever, as long as I live, I climb them behind him in the darkness, between the second and third floors of my mother's house.

The station at Whitby is alongside the harbour; I was early and had time to walk along the quay for a minute. It was full moon. The sky was a cold blue, as pale as the line of the water; above the skeleton of the abbey on the east cliff lay motionless feathers of cloud. The tide was out, and the harbour a stretch of bronzed mud divided by threads of beaten silver.

As always, my mind began throwing up plans, dykes against despair.

If, at the last instant, a soul is able to glance back over its life, what I shall see in the ambiguous moonlight will be a great bronze plain, crossed by threads of bright water and crumbling broken-off dykes which held back no destructive tides.

# CHAPTER 54

I DOUBT WHETHER I SHALL ever know what has forced me to live as if the one unbearable fate were to be settled anywhere. Imbecile.

Once, in the country between Bordeaux and St Emilion, I saw on the rough lawn in front of a small manor-house a young cockerel tied by a leg to an iron stake, and a boy watching its struggles to free itself; it rushed away, the length of the cord, returned, rushed off in another direction, returned, collapsed, rushed away again, now and then uttering cries more like a frog than a young bird. Its cord was seven or eight yards long; all the silly creature had to do was keep calm and peck where it could reach.

All I had to do was to keep quiet, bring up my child, cook, entertain my friends, learn to talk easily, cherish my husband, and cultivate my mental garden with patience and gaiety...

At Easter (1925), when I fetched Bill from Weybridge to take him to Whitby for the holidays, I thought he looked pale. Panic-stricken, I decided to persuade my mother into offering to let him live with her. A boys' school had just been started in Whitby by a woman I knew to be cultivated, warm-hearted, and a born teacher. My middle sister was at home now, and could take any trouble he might be off my mother's hands.

This sister, four years younger than I, began trying to escape from the family when she was three years old. Time after time, neighbours would meet her trudging up Waterstead Lane into the country and bring her back. Once she stationed herself with her doll's-carriage at the end of a line of horse-drawn cabs waiting to be hired. When she was seventeen, she began again. Each effort failed and she came home to be our mother's companion, housekeeper, nurse, depended on without mercy, scolded if she stayed out late. It would not occur to my mother—nor did it to me—to ask her whether she resented having a ten-year-old boy added to the household. Nor would it occur to her to protest: she had too much warmth, and the habit of obedience—and she had not given up all hope of escape. (She escaped after our mother's death—to New York.)

My younger sister was now nineteen, in her second year at a provincial university. Tall, immensely attractive with her cold clear blue eyes and marvellously fair skin, she was still the one creature my mother loved with passion. She was restlessly energetic, moving as quickly as a young lizard, and very impatient, except with her short-fingered hands. She said what she thought, without fear or mercy. Even a friend who had vexed her might be flayed and cast out for good. But she was as generous as implacable, and her malice was honest malice; the victim had not to fear an arrow in the back as he fled.

After all, I had no need to be jesuitical with my mother. She agreed almost at once that, yes, the boy could live at home now—why not? She may have regretted the moment when, weighed down by her body and her loss, and afraid—she who never in her life hesitated to scold and subdue even a married daughter—of the jealous temper of her youngest, she had let me send him to a stranger. Or was it a simpler impulse?

'He can have Harold's room,' she said, slowly.

Filled with heavy oak furniture—a wardrobe in which hung one of his flying jackets and his fleece-lined boots, two large chests of drawers, a bookcase, a desk—it was not a child's room, but Bill was pleased with it. To have a room of his own gave him a sense of safety and dignity.

The camera I gave him before I left was only one extravagance among others. He had seen it in the window of a chemist's, and asked me for it. So long as I had any money at all in my pocket, I had not the strength of mind to refuse him anything. Inside the shop, the man laid it in his hand. It was dearer than I expected. Seeing my hesitation, the man brought out a cheaper one, much cheaper, much larger, and, as he said, much more suitable. Glancing at Bill, I saw his face change: he said nothing, only stared at the engagingly small camera in his hand.

'No, I'll take the first one,' I said, sighing.

My son gave me one of his dazzling smiles, his eyes brilliant with excitement and satisfaction. I felt the happiness a woman is said to feel when she conceives, and that I felt only when I could give him something he coveted.

That evening, speaking about the camera, my mother said harshly,

'You spoil him. You're bringing him up to think he has only to ask and get. He asks, and you give. You'll ruin the boy.'

I had no answer. I lacked the courage, or the insolence, to tell her that she spoiled her youngest at least as crazily and without forethought as I my son, spending on her every penny she could get into her hands. And without my impulse to make up to a child for his loss of a settled life. The reserves of tenderness, indulgence, weakness, she lavished on her last-born child had accumulated during a lifetime. I did not feel sure of having a life-time to indulge mine. There might be another war, then what good would strictness have been?

And—what had my mother's done for me except make me distrustful, of life itself?

I looked at her. As so often, she was staring in front of her—at what? My heart contracted with an old feeling of helplessness, an old rage, and I began to think: What can I give her before I go that she would really like?

## CHAPTER 55

GUY, A GREAT-NEPHEW of Dickens's publisher, had as a boy two passions—history and publishing. His parents over-rode both. Prudent elderly Victorians, middle-aged at his birth, they wanted to see their only child safely niched in the Civil Service, and from Westminster sent him to study law at Oxford. The War, and his father's death, cut him loose. In 1924, with a derisory sum of money, he started his publishing firm.

It was at least twenty or thirty years too late for the kind of firm he had wanted—a short list of scholarly works, translations (even of a few novel-ists, Paul Morand, Claude Anet), and minor classics of literature, superbly produced. Martin Secker in his young days as a publisher could indulge his polite tastes and live. (It is said, with malice, that when he was asked to send a book abroad, rather than fill in the many forms demanded, he dropped the order in the waste-paper-basket.) In 1924, a young man with scholarly notions and no money worth counting might, with luck, be taken on as an editor by some well-found firm. He had no other chance of survival.

From his two-roomed office in Adelphi, he published a few books of immense elegance (they included the *Historiettes de Tallemant des Réaux* translated by Hamish Miles, Charles Scott-Moncrieff's translation of the *Letters of Heloise and Abelard*, and the *Book of Wine* Morton Shand wrote at his suggestion).

He had as staff a secretary, Mrs B., a good-natured florid Cockney, so devoted that she was willing to work half the night, and so slow and conscientious—to all appearance—that she now and then did.

Some time in 1925 he took a pupil, Dennis Cohen, an uncommonly handsome young man, very like the fifteenth century portrait of the Emperor Maximilian I by (I think) Bernhard Strigel, but gayer.

In the autumn of that year it became clear that he could not carry on without running into debt.

He had two offers, one from Dennis Cohen, who wanted to start publishing and had a great deal of money, the other from Alfred Knopf. What Alfred wanted was his own English house. Impossible, after nearly forty years, to recall how we persuaded ourselves that he would be freer as a London manager for Alfred Knopf than as Dennis Cohen's partner. It was so obviously the wrong choice that I must have been responsible; it bears all the marks of one of my blind plunges. Or, I may only have wanted to please Alfred.

I have half erased the memory of my folly. As always, what I remember distinctly happened not in London but in Whitby.

In December, the negotiations with the Knopfs reached a stage when they asked us to come to New York for ten days, over Christmas. It was unthinkable that I should spend Christmas anywhere but with Bill. I sent Guy off to New York alone and went to Whitby.

My first glance—I had not seen him since the end of summer—gave me a child taller and stronger, his cheeks glowing, lips a clear crimson; even his eyes seemed bluer and more brilliant. An overwhelming relief consoled me: for once I had done a wise thing.

My father was at home between voyages, and vexing my mother by talking about two pound notes he insisted had been taken from his room. 'He makes these stories up,' my mother told me drily.

The second evening, when I was drying Bill after his bath, he began to cry, with shocking violence, shaking from head to foot; he told me that he had taken the money to buy, of all useless things, a gramophone pick-up he had seen in a shop, and coveted—heaven knows why, since he could never use it. My heart turned over. I recognized a trait of my own, the thing I wanted becoming an obsession, blinding me to every effect and every other impulse of my mind or body.

What was I to do with this child ravaged by remorse? By the code of my upbringing, he ought to confess his crime and hand over his pocket-money week after week until he had wiped out the debt... I could not inflict such humiliation on him—no more than I had ever been able to punish him except by the sort of angry remonstrance one child might use with another, younger... If I am doing the wrong thing, I thought, I can't help it—let it be on my head.

I forget what I said to him in the way of comfort and warning. I remember what I did. I tucked two pounds between my father's bed and the wall. When he found it, he told my mother triumphantly, 'You see? *She* took it. If I had said nothing she would never have brought it back.' *She* was the daily woman, whom for some reason he disliked.

'You never lost it,' my mother said ironically...

Without thinking about it, moved by an impulse which had nothing to do with my will or my reason, I tried blindly to guard my son from any of the feelings of responsibility, anxiety, guilt, with which I, a child, had been burdened. Even revolt against them is sterile...

I had been at home only four days when the Knopfs cabled that unless I came to New York nothing could be arranged. A fast boat, the *Homeric*, was leaving on the 23rd; I must catch it.

I had three days in which to get a berth and a visa, and get myself to Southampton. Somehow I managed it, and laid up for myself an agony still, if I am rash enough to lay a finger on it, searingly alive.

'I've been missing you so much,' Bill said, 'and now you're going.'

Neither time nor familiarity mitigate it. I should avoid touching it.

In the train I sat with my body clenched over the pain. Why am I going? I asked myself: no good will come of it.

I was not even sure that I had a berth on the *Homeric*. I had—a minute cabin on the lowest deck of the first class. I had never slept in what felt like the bottom of a hold, with the terrible weight of the Atlantic pressing against its sides. But neither had I sailed in any ship larger than three thousand tons. In spite of myself, in spite of an involuntary contempt for so much space and luxury in what passed for a ship, my spirits rose. When I walked into the vast comfortable drawing-room—an orchestra playing, waiters bringing elaborate teas to the small tables—I felt drunk with excitement.

For the space of a few minutes, it wiped out the burdened years separating me, as I stood there, from the child determined *to be someone*. Smiling, the two of us touched hands.

This exultance did not last very long. I am like my mother, for whom the sea was always only a boring hiatus between ports.

As for New York, I spent nine days there and did not see it.

Days in the Knopf office, that miracle of suave efficiency, were followed by evenings at parties where certainly I impressed no one by my wit or my one dinner-dress. It was the Prohibition era. Everybody—everybody we met—drank enormously and talked enormously about ways of getting hold of non-lethal alcohol. One evening, stupefied by the frightful heat and luxury of an apartment I had been taken to after a concert of Gershwin's music, stupefied, too, by the powerful voices of two coloured singers invited as guest-entertainers—it was also the era of Carl van Vechten and *Nigger Heaven*—I left silently, abandoning Guy, and walked a short distance, exasperated by the thought that I was being cheated of America.

I had no idea where I was. I seemed to be the single living creature in a wide tunnel driven between stone cliffs, open to the night sky, lit by two rows of street-lamps dwindling into the distance, and void—except of cars following each other endlessly and all but noiselessly. The cold cut my breath off at the lungs. I was forced to get into a taxi and listen to an account of the driver's troubles with a faithless wife. The garrulity, or inventiveness, of New York cab-drivers has to be endured to be believed.

Another evening, at a party given by the writer Fanny Hurst, eighty or a hundred people stood about chattering and drinking in a room filled with ikons and church hangings: a long buffet held twice as many bottles as there were guests: there was also a samovar of ink-black tea—thicker than ink. Lady Colefax's black and white dress drew cries of admiration.

'Surely—Paris?' Carl van Vechten said.

'Yes. Worten. Designed for me.'

Five minutes later Alma Gluck, the singer, came in, wearing the same dress: before either could escape his malice, Carl van Vechten had seated them one on each side of him, to enjoy their absurd discomfiture.

Miss Hurst enchanted me. Under a long crimson silk shawl, heavily fringed, she was wearing what in my childhood I knew as 'dancing-class knickers'—row on row of white lace from waistband to knee: when she moved, the fringe parted to show them above black silk stockings.

I left New York thankfully, as ignorant as a carp, even of New York.

The English house of A. A. Knopf lasted three years. We left it six months before the end, without rancour: with characteristic reluctance to use the knife, Alfred allowed the rope to fray itself; I have never known anyone in whom generosity, kindness, acumen, a loyal warmth, and ferocity of purpose, were so inextricably mixed.

Both sides, we and the Knopfs, had been misled, or had misled ourselves: Guy supposed he was free to create a small wholly English firm; the Knopfs—more insistently after Alfred's father, a man to be respected and in his genial moods liked, his brain fitted with the tentacles of an octopus, began taking an interest in the firm—wanted something more rapidly profitable, and able to swallow at least a slice of their American list. Little of this admirable list was better than a dead weight on us. Two things might have saved the new firm: luck with an English author or authors, and a manager with less cultivated tastes and a great deal more commercial sense.

In New York it had been arranged that I should work half the week, with a salary half Guy's. In the event I worked five full days in the office. But—fatal circumstance, one the Knopfs could not have foreseen—I was bored. When the elder Knopf said to me, 'My idea of you is that you will want more and more to concentrate on business, and become less and less a writer,' I felt a violent revulsion.

It was less that I wanted to write novels than dislike of being tied down. Yet he was right to suspect me of an instinct for business. One side of me was pure Gallilee. By some freak—yes, freak—it had been yoked to an anarchist, a tramp, a *révolté*. The two cut each other's throats.


## CHAPTER 56


I HAVE FEW MEMORIES of this wasted time. One day—I was alone in the office—an old gentleman came in with a letter of introduction from I forget whom: he hoped we could give him a French book to translate. I eyed him stealthily while I read the letter; he was sitting expectantly, with all the air of a child waiting to be spoken to, too well-trained to speak first.

His name, Charles Roche, was not known to me. He was one of eighteen elderly journalists sacked from the *Morning Post* when it changed hands.

'Just think,' he said, smiling at me, 'eighteen of us were sacked at once, all those over sixty—without pension. I am seventy-two.'

'You look younger than that,' I said.

He was pleased. 'Do you think so? I ought not to take your time, but you are kindness itself. I'll tell you why I need money. My wife, my dear Annie, is dying. She doesn't know. I told her last week, "Annie, I've got the best job I ever had and as soon as you're strong again we'll go to France." Yesterday the doctor said, "I suggest giving a little stimulant." "I know what you'd like," I said to her, "you'd like some champagne." She only looked at me. Well, I went to my wine merchant, and I said, "Let me have one bottle of Moet '06; I'll pay you for it as soon as I can." And what do you think, he sent round half a dozen bottles that evening!'

'*How* long were you on the *Morning Post*?'

'Forty-two years, my dear Miss Jameson.'

I had to tell him we had no book he could translate, and promised him the first we had.

'You're too kind. Just think, eighteen of us in the same minute. An execution! One of us committed suicide.' He spoke with an innocent pride, like the survivor of an earthquake. 'I shouldn't like to blame him, but I shall not do that. Fortunately, it's forbidden. My religion is perfectly clear on the point.'

He rose to go. Trying to think of something I could say to please him, I said,

'I'll pray for your wife.'

'Oh, you're a Catholic!'

'No. But perhaps even a heretic's prayers may be a little use.'

'Oh, don't think I am such a bigot as that,' he cried, distressed. 'It's just that I never heard a Protestant speak of praying.'

I saw him two or three times again, then lost sight of him. He found some way of getting his Annie to France. A year after we left the firm, he sent me a photograph of her grave at Le Portel, near Boulogne. He cannot have survived her long enough to be chased out again, this time by the Germans...

I had a letter from Blanche Knopf asking me to see Wyndham Lewis (the painter and writer): we were not publishing him in London, but he had promised her his next book—whether a novel or literary polemics I forget—and now, in the way of very intelligent writers, in whom conscience is often in inverse ratio to intelligence, he had promised it elsewhere.

He came into the room and sat scowling at me across my desk, in a wet dirty mackintosh—the day was as vile as his temper—with a drop forming at the end of his nose: his eyes, furious, gored me. Politely and warily, I asked him why he had disappointed Mrs Knopf.

'Blast Mrs Knopf's soul,' he exclaimed, 'she hasn't said a word to me about the book for six months. How was I to know she still wanted it?'

Loud voices frighten me as much as bulls. 'But surely you realize how important any book of yours is?'

'Then why the devil didn't she write to me?'

'Why do you think? We were anxious not to annoy you by asking questions. But we expected the book, and the firm—the New York office—has been making every sort of preparation for it, talking to critics—' so far as I knew, this was pure invention, but it was what they ought to have been doing—'doing everything possible to make sure that when it came it was recognized as important.'

His terrible eyes shifted a point. Suddenly I felt his mind at the end of my own.

'I suppose you're talking sense,' he grumbled.

I smiled at him. 'I don't know. But I know how a book of yours ought to be treated, and how the Knopfs will in fact treat it... Can nothing be done? Have you the manuscript in your hands still?'

'I'll see what I can do.'

He stood up and began tying the greasy belt of his mackintosh, snatching a dubious handkerchief from the pocket to blow his nose dangerously. Spiritually arm in arm, we walked to the door together...

We, Guy and I, made one pure gain from our two and a half years' servitude—the friendship of Edward Thompson. We published his first two novels, *An Indian Day*, and *These Men Thy Friends*, two of the finest novels of a generation, and worked for them with the devotion they, and he, deserved. If at the Last Judgement, I were the 'prisoner's friend', allowed to put forward two, only two, of the Englishmen of my time as an example of the best we can do, they would be R. H. Tawney and Edward Thompson. The two of them were in ways alike: both had a consuming passion for justice, both were incapable of lying, both were loyal without flaw, generous without flaw. Both, without intending it, a little intimidated, or offended in their vanity, small mean men of power, who repaid them by neglect.

Dear Edward was like Tawney, too, in that the war (the first) gave him more than the bitterness and anger roused by its abominable side—I begin to believe that there is no state in which the minds and hearts of good men ripen so quickly as the state of war.

Tawney was the more arbitrary, with the involuntary arrogance of a man who is entirely indifferent to what other people may think of him and his merits. This in Edward became the fine muted rigidity of your bred-in-the-bone Nonconformist. His creed plagued him a little: to balance it he was a poet, with an innocent eye for all that can reach and touch the senses—only a poet could write the last twenty-five pages of *These Men Thy Friends*, or see the Indian scene as he saw and evoked it in *An Indian Day*. And *In Araby in Orion*, brief and elegiac, fine-boned, is one of the few nearly perfect *contes* of all time.

He loved his fellows, without sentimentality, with a singular clear-sight, indeed with irony.

He married the one woman he should have married, an American, the serenely beautiful child of American missionaries in Syria. They bred two sons as brave and honest as themselves. Frank, the elder, fought with the Bulgarian partisans, and was caught in May 1944 and executed. Left—of this splendid Puritan stock—a second Edward, as intransigent an idealist as the other...

As he grew older, Edward was a little humiliated by the retreat into which he had been forced. A letter he wrote in 1942—I had written to him about a volume of poetry, *The New Recessional*—gives out when I touch it a smiling bitterness.

'... I know the poem is good, but people whom I imagined friendly have not even acknowledged it, it seems to have shocked them; and in three months the sole reviewing has been three brief and all contemptuous notices... Brailsford and David Low privately have been enthusiastic. But when after hesitation I asked David, who has long been rather pleasantly friendly, if he would mind telling the publisher only that he found it readable, he has not answered. So that's that. Anyhow, I know that such passages as "By the Waters of Babylon" will last, if they ever get read at all... Frank after a year at the front is now in sub-caucasian Persia. He knows Russian, so may go further afield: I think, will. Palmer is training in the tanks... I do little and have been vetoed for India repeatedly... About your work: and mine: a lot you have had to put in former days into newspaper articles ought to have gone into criticism... But neither of us, my dear, have any right to blame ourselves, for what we have done has had to be done from necessity—my Indian scribbling was laid on me as a job for this incarnation, and my novels were an accident and then were a necessity to help pay one's way. We did what we had to do, and some of it was good...'

As always, he does himself a great deal less than justice—that 'Indian scribbling' covers historical works of high seriousness and importance as well as the enchantment of *An Indian Day*. And no war novel—of either war—is more worth remembering than *In Araby in Orion* and *These Men Thy Friends*. Oblivion, being blind, makes too many mistakes.

By a lucky accident, I re-read *In Araby in Orion* a week after a struggle, only partly successful, with one of the better artificers of *le nouveau roman*, Alain Robbe-Grillet. Suddenly as I read, a window was thrown up and I saw why, for all their virtues, intelligence, poetic double-sight, a visual imagination of peculiar intensity, Robbe-Grillet's novels are unsatisfactory, and, at a deep level, unauthentic. The writer who says mockingly, '*Ah, vous croyez encore à la nature humaine, vous!*' is condemned to work at a more superficial level than the one on which are conceived the great novels, French, Russian, English, and the miniature of *In Araby in Orion*, all of them resting in the affirmation that, by way of love and compassion—and, alas, of cruelty—men can, though imperfectly, communicate with each other. Without this single possibility of communication there *is* no human nature, no continuity of being. *Le nouveau roman* pushes to a limit the existentialist view of man as a project of action, immersed in becoming, disqualified from being. The characters in any of Robbe-Grillet's novels are a kaleidoscope of moods, no value judgements on their acts, thoughts, feelings, are possible or permitted. An axe is laid to the roots of any rational grasp of reality.

Clearly, all too clearly, this a-rational philosophy, this diminishing of the human person, this effacement of the classical-Christian-humanist idea of the individual, is as much a product of our mechanical civilization as Shell House and computers.

Two extraordinary paradoxes, two jacks-in-the-box, appear. Robbe-Grillet's scorn of 'bourgeois humanism' and of the pathetic human habit of 'appropriating' the non-human world by injecting emotions into it (the sad sky, the cruel sea) is mocked by his own intensely emotional link with natural objects. He seems not to know that his descriptions quiver and burn with sensual emotion. It is what saves his novels from dissolving in tedium.

And then his romanticism—like Sartre's—with its plumes from Kierkegaard, Rilke, even Byron! Lonely in the world into which he has been thrown, climbing with Rilke 'the mountains of primaeval sorrow', the solitary sport of moods, enduring *Angst* before the horror of the abyss, never in all literature was there a more relentlessly romantic figure than that imagined by the existentialist writers and their cousins.

Robbe-Grillet is a painter who has amputated his hands in order to prove how brilliantly he can lay on his colours without them.

## CHAPTER 57

I WAS BROUGHT UP TO THINK that illness is shameful, and a doctor the last resort of a feeble mind. The body must do its best unaided until the moment when it surrenders unconditionally. For several years now I had been enduring an intermittent pain which grew more and more nearly unendurable until at last, in July 1927, I took myself to a doctor and discovered that I had waited too long.

On my first night in the nursing home—the operation was at eleven o'clock the next day—I had a vivid dream. I was walking slowly up North Bank, the steep straight road that leads from the harbour to 5 Park Terrace: it was night, I was naked, alone between the walls of the houses, feeling the cold and roughness of the stones under my feet. As I neared the top, the houses became unsubstantial and remote; I became aware of a shadow behind me, it took something of K.'s form, and his voice or another's said, 'Poor thrawn girl, come back again.'

In the dream, I wondered what on earth 'thrawn' meant. I half turned my head. The hill, the night, the voice, lapsed into vapour, into an overwhelming regret and longing.

I woke in the unfamiliar room and lay watching the leaves of a tree in the garden outside the window until the day nurse brought me breakfast I refused to eat. It was no use her telling me, and bringing the Sister to confirm it, that experience in the war had proved that soldiers who had been fed beforehand did better in an operation than men who had fasted. I knew better. It was my only victory over authority, which from now on did its worst.

I was furious with my body: it had been as soundly and strongly built as a ship or a tree, and ought not to have succumbed to my neglect. I could not forgive it.

Left alone for two hours, I began on one of the five books I had brought with me. It must be vanity that makes it easy for me not merely to ignore panic at these times, but not even feel it. I read placidly and carefully.

'And as the many tribes of feathered birds, wild geese or cranes or long-necked swans, on the Asian mead by Kaystrios' stream, fly hither and thither joying in their plumage, and with loud cries settle ever onwards, and the mead resounds; even so poured forth the many tribes of warriors from ships and huts into the Skamandrian plain.'

The list of captains and ships in this part of the Iliad had always bored me to yawning, and now gave me the most acute pleasure. Why? I suppose that terror is kept at bay by what is both serious and concrete in literature, where it would instantly break through a charming or flimsy or merely amusing book.

I had been told that people coming out of an anaesthetic talk wildly and give away their secret soul. Determined not to give mine away, I had written—on the piece of paper I was using as a bookmark—a sentence of which I had forgotten the origin; but that I had often used before when I was dejected. I hoped, by recalling it at the last minute, that it would come to my helpless tongue and save me from disgrace—'The last peaks of the world, beyond all seas, well-springs of night and gleams of opened heavens, the garden of the Sun.'

The nurse startled me when she came in at five minutes to eleven. 'Oh, is it time?' I asked.

'Yes.' She smiled. 'Nervous?'

'Not yet.'

She annoyed me by making me get into a wheeled chair, which a grinning boy held steady in the lift.

'I could have walked up the stairs in half the time,' I said.

'You'll be heavier when you come down again,' she retorted.

The operating room was large and light. To my first glance it seemed full of people, all women: surgeon, doctor, middle-aged anaesthetist, four or five nurses. When I lay down on the table, all I could see through the window was an elongated box, shaped like a coffin, of brilliantly blue sky. I thought: I must look carefully at everything. The surgeon's big white-clad body and brown face came between me and the light. *Last peaks of the world, beyond all seas...*

The anaesthetist looked down at me, smiling. 'Well, you look like a little girl,' she said.

Someone I could not see adjusted the mask over my face. This was the moment I feared—the choking. I made myself breathe gently. My doctor had come close to me: she took my right hand and held it in one of hers, and I gripped hers, so that they would know I was still conscious and not begin to cut me. My sight was failing. The outline of the window withdrew to a great distance, the waiting figures of the nurses dimmed. The silence became a presence. Shadows moved past my eyes. I lost the sensation of the doctor's fingers against mine.

Now an extraordinary thing happened. A thought—*I must signal to the last man*—pierced me. Why on earth should the scene in Giraudoux's *Bella* when Fontranges visits the disgraced Dubardeau brothers, read months before, float to the surface of my mind precisely at this moment? I had the impression that I was raising my arm and holding it straight out. I may have moved it, or my body on the table, because someone indistinct said in a quiet voice,

'Everything is all right, Miss Jameson.'

I was almost blind now, stubbornly widening my eyes to see the blurred form of a woman near me.

In darkness, for less than a second, I saw the figure of a woman bending over, something in her hands. Then, in terror, I hung in a black whirling flood, shot with red flecks, and supposed I was dying. Then I was fully conscious, of shadowy room, feeble night-light close to me, canvas straps holding me in a sitting posture, and at the other, the darkest end of the room, a nurse. I moved slightly, and the movement tore open my body.

I must have whimpered. The woman came and bent over the bed.

'Time?' I whispered. I was ashamed to ask her whether or not I was dying.

'After nine o'clock.'

I am a good sleeper, I can sleep through storms, in trains, sunlight, strange beds. The only sleepless nights of my life before this were during my child's illnesses. This one was sleepless with a difference. The pain in my body was shocking. I kept my eyes on the square of the door, outlined by a thread of light. My watch was lying in the weak glow of the lamp, and as my sight strengthened I could read the figures. It was five minutes to ten. Several hours passed, and I looked again. This time it wanted a minute of ten o'clock.

Once or twice the nurse spoke to me in a soft Welsh voice. When, without meaning to, I whimpered, she said, 'Poor rabbit,' and told me the surgeon had forbidden them to give me morphia.

'Why?'

'She said she didn't think you ought to have it. I'm sure I'm sorry. I would give you something, I would indeed, if I could.'

'Never mind.'

I walked through every room in 5 Park Terrace, noticing the wicker blind over the lower half of the kitchen window, of a sort no longer made, the horsehair sofa and chairs in the dining-room, the satin-striped wallpaper of my mother's sitting-room, the heavy furniture in her bedroom: next to my own room under the attics my brother slept, soundly and heavily, in his bed beside the small window, his doubled hands on the quilt.

I walked out of Whitby, through fields of buttercups to the Carrs, the river sleek in sunlight, the white dust, to Briggaswath and Sleights, climbed through the village past the old houses to Blue Bank, up which I toiled slowly, and turned away from the moors to follow the road leading down, down, to the lane with its foxgloves and honeysuckle, and the warm sound of bees. But not even here was sleep.

I never knew light so slow in coming, or bird to cry so clearly, piercing me to the bone with a moment's pure pleasure.

When the nurse was preparing me for the day, she patted my hand and chuckled.

'Do you know what you said when we were putting you into bed yesterday afternoon? You fought and struggled, we had to bring a third nurse in to help hold you. Sister was afraid you would open the wound. To think you could fight like that! And you kept on saying: "I must go home now, I must go home." We had as much as we could do to quiet you. My, you're strong.'

Weeks later, when I got home, I looked up *thrawn* in a large dictionary. It is a northern word, meaning: twisted, crooked, bent from the straight.

## CHAPTER 58

DURING THESE YEARS I finished a novel barely started in Weybridge, and wrote two more. I was trying, fumblingly, to write honestly.

I did not know what the word meant. I supposed it meant writing without affectation or uncontrolled emotion. I became hideously self-conscious, and touched an adjective as if it were venomous.

As a novelist I had for me only energy, curiosity, and my passion for looking. It is not enough. I read little modern fiction, and the chance I threw away in 1914 of making friends among people reaching out to new literary forms did not recur. I did not so much as suspect that the gulf between Tolstoy (or Stendhal, Balzac, Dostoevsky) and Joyce is one of intention, a choice between two ways of using language. Had I been told to define 'great novelist', I should have replied that a few novelists are great by virtue of an exceptionally profound understanding of human passions and a bold vision of man the social and political animal. In short: great novels are written by great men, acutely interested in the human comedy and able to animate it in depth.

That there is an entirely different species of novelist, interested first in what he can do with language, brushed my mind without penetrating it. The fragments of *Ulysses* I had read in *The Egoist* struck me as *de la blague sérieuse*. I read them with pleasure only because, in the absence of a living 'great novelist', *la blague sérieuse* was infinitely preferable to the swill of stock reflections and counterfeit emotions that go to make the bladdernovel, that great modern industry.

'The sole excuse that a man has for writing is to write himself... to be original. He must say that which has yet to be said, and say it in a form that has yet to be formulated; he must create his own aesthetic.' (Rémy de Gourmont.) This was the only thing I read which put under my eyes the case for the experimental novel, for the growing impulse to break the traditional mould, achieve a new fluidity, new and personal symbols for human experience. I thought about it a little, and concluded that it was almost certainly impossible for a novelist to combine in himself the passions of a Tolstoy and a Joyce. The two impulses, I reflected, must diverge in the mind at an unseizably great depth, and the choice is inwardly dictated.

Today I am much nearer seeing Joyce as a purely disintegrating force, a sacred monster, uprooting established forms to create a waste land, a great anti-humanist, the destroyer by his devilish skill and persistence of the thin walls against barbarism. Writers who give themselves up to the disintegration of language are, so far as they know, innocent of the impulse to destroy civilization. But the roots of the impulse run underground a long way, to the point where the smoke from burning books becomes the smoke issuing from the ovens of death camps...

In 1926, when I was writing *The Lovely Ship*, I was even more ignorant, more out of date, than I knew. Fascinated by a past, still, in my fortunate childhood, within reach of my finger-tips, I wanted to record the Whitby that built ships and sailed them, a Whitby peopled by the great eccentrics of my mother's memory, men and women larger, more fiercely individual, harder, less light-minded than their successors who pull down decent houses to put up rubbish and vulgarize everything they touch. It took me three novels to write the life of Mary Hansyke, who became Mary Hervey, from her birth in 1841 to her death in 1923, and follow shipbuilding from sail to steam to turbines to her sell-out at the height of the war boom in shipping. This was something I knew all about. The three novels are like prehistoric animals reconstructed in a museum from clay and a few real bones.

When I sent the manuscript of the first to Michael, I told him I wanted an advance of three hundred pounds, a hundred more than he had ever paid.

At the end of a month I had not yet heard from him. I thought about it at odd moments every day, but said nothing.

Although, at this time, I was writing highly-paid articles for a newspaper—far too highly paid for their deserts—I needed money. I am one of those unfortunates for whom money has no *real* value. When I have it I spend it, seldom enough on my back—to my Yorkshire conscience, waste and extravagance only describe such inessentials as clothes and fashionable restaurants.

In those days, and, alas, still, the more I earned the faster I spent, and the end of every month found me ashore for money.

When at last it came, Michael's letter was a long one. '... I think I had better say at once that I don't feel this novel is very satisfactory. My chief feeling is that you are trying to do something for which you are not fitted. I don't know why you have chosen to experiment in this method, which contrives to be dry and violent in the same moment. Your natural romanticism suited you better, and if you'll forgive me for writing bluntly—after all, the question of money does enter into it, since you are asking us to pay half as much again as we paid for your last novel—had a much better chance of succeeding...'

I put the letter away hurriedly, without re-reading, and without showing it to anyone. I had a sick feeling of disgrace.

The idea that I was almost penniless whetted my mind; it began its familiar trick of throwing out lines on all sides. I became a Yorkshireman with something to sell.

A short time before this, I had run into Charles Evans at a party, and he had said, smiling, that he hoped I would come back to Heinemann. Almost without reflection I telephoned to him, and asked,

'Do you still want to publish my next book?'

'Certainly I do,' he said at once.

'If I tell you that it is better, much better, than the last, would you be willing to pay me four hundred pounds advance?'

'Are you offering me the book?' he asked.

'I'm thinking of offering it to you.'

There was a brief silence, then Charles said calmly, 'Four hundred pounds sounds reasonable.'

My mind jumped a peg. 'I'll write to you or come to see you.'

Still without deciding, I felt stiffened to talk to Michael. But when I walked into his room, in the ramshackle house in Orange Street, and he greeted me with his familiar smiling affection, I felt a cold worm of fear in my belly. Fear and grief. I dreaded his possible anger, and shrank from the idea of hurting him, however lightly.

'Well, my dear?' he said.

'I can't alter the writing,' I said roughly. 'Or the book itself.'

'What do you want us to do? We'll publish it, of course. But I don't see how we can pay more than two hundred on this book, altered or not altered. What do you feel about it?'

At this moment, in one of those dangerous and deceitful flashes of lightning it was subject to, my mind cleared. I realized that when, reading the manuscript, Michael had caught sight of the real Storm Jameson, he did not like her—his S.J. was the author of that neo-Gothic abortion, *The Pitiful Wife*. He had not the slightest idea what, blindly, I was trying to do, and if he had, would detest it.

This conviction drove every other feeling—gratitude, affection, diffidence—out of my sight. Every scruple, too. I had only one thought—to escape from his uncomprehending hands as quickly as possible and, if possible, without vexing him. Feeling my way, I said,

'I would rather you did not publish a book you don't like.'

What I meant was: I am going to take my manuscript away with me, now, and do what I can to throw the blame of the break on you... It had ceased to be a question of two or four hundred pounds, and become a question of freedom from a kindly critic who was in my way. We argued for thirty minutes. My stubbornness and lack of submissiveness surprised Michael: he was friendly and baffled, and I in the state of mind of a ship's captain with a crew of lascars.

I was too sunk in my purpose to have the faintest notion how I appeared to him. At last I said,

'Let me take the manuscript away to look through it again.'

'Very well—but don't decide now. Frankly, my dear, we'd rather publish the novel as it stands than let you go to another publisher.'

In my satisfaction at having got the book into my hands again, without a quarrel, I forgot to be politic.

'Thank you,' I said, smiling.

'For what?' he asked ironically.

'For being patient.'

Hurrying away along Orange Street, filled with remorse and a con-scienceless gaiety, I turned over the phrases of the letter I would write, telling him—but in such a tone that I should not lose his affection—that I had gone back to Heinemann.

Friendship, affection—I have always placed a higher value on them than on love—*tout le corps, moins un sens...*

(*'Alors, décrie-moi ton amitié. C'est une passion?*

*Folle.*

*Quel est son sens?*

*Son sens? Tout le corps moins un sense... Elle accouple les créatures les plus dissemblables et les rend égales.'...*)

I could not have acted otherwise than I did but, I see now, it was only one broken-off thread among dozens. There was less continuity in my life in those years than at any time since—though heaven knows how incoherent it still is. After its owner demanded back the flat on Primrose Hill we lived in four places before the end of 1928. We stayed for months in The Spread Eagle, in Thame, and made a friend of its eccentric proprietor, John Fothergill. Then we gathered my scattered pieces of furniture into a large flat in the fading late-Victorian gentility of Belsize Park in north-west London—the covetous side of my nature, momentarily unleashed, had laid hands on several antiques, chairs, tallboys, chests of drawers.

After a year, avid for country air, we moved to another flat, in a wing of a house near London. Designed by the architect of the House of Commons, it was grotesque, but it had caught the eye and heart of a gentle little City man—he fell madly in love with it, and it tyrannized over him like a rapacious kept woman, driving him to ruin himself to save it from the demolition it merited. The house itself had every discomfort, its only charm—to a cold eye—the large half-derelict park.

I brought Bill here, and sent him to the nearest preparatory school as a day-boy.

Why did I never think with misgiving of the confusion these many shifts must create in his mind? Small thanks to me that he grew up intelligent, brave, authoritative, to become an airline pilot of all-round excellence (*arete*), and cross the Atlantic both ways in a twenty-nine-ton yacht with, for crew, his wife and two very young children. That particular tenacity and indifference to danger he owes to a number of forgotten men and women—and first to one shabby taciturn old sea-captain...

Some nerve of my brain, an inner ear, was always, still is, on the alert to hear him breathe. I had an odd proof of this in the spring of 1929, when the three of us were staying in an hotel in Tunbridge Wells. He left my room on the fourth floor to go downstairs: the lift, an old-fashioned one, was at the far end of the corridor, and a minute after he had closed my door I heard the faintest of sighs. Nothing more—it might have been a leaf fluttering down. I knew in the instant what had happened. I ran from the room and along the corridor, running blindly. The door of the empty lift-shaft was open. I called—and his voice came back from the bottom of the shaft.

His only hurt, apart from shock, was a twisted ankle and the palms of his hands laid open. Without noticing that the lift was not there, he had stepped through the open doorway and fallen five floors on to the roof of the lift waiting in the basement: as he fell he clutched the rope running from top to bottom of the shaft; it tore his hands but saved him from breaking all his limbs or his neck.

'What in heaven's name were you thinking of?' I asked later—hours later.

He gave me the coldest of cold glances. 'I was thinking.'

'Did you call out?'

'No. I hadn't time.'

After one year in Harrow Weald Park, Guy and I went back to London, and Bill to Whitby again...

This unsettled life at a time when, if either one of us had had a grain of worldly sense, we should have been, as they say, *making ourselves a position*, was not entirely my fault. I had married a man as impatient as myself, and as unwilling to lift a finger to draw attention to himself. In love not with war, but with the conditions of war—sudden changes, no responsibility save to a few men—he took indifferently ill to the benefits of civilization. Except for a few of these—libraries, bookshops, a decent claret, the Savile Club. Turning the pages of those letters I must tear up before I die, I come, in every one of them, on phrases of exasperated discontent and boredom.—We must clear out soon—I wish we could travel together for a year—Do let us run away—I feel more and more impatient to get out and away from the Knopfs...

By the middle of 1928, the Knopfs were as eager to get rid of us as we to escape from an impossible situation. They could see Guy's total unfitness for the sort of publishing firm they wanted. What they did not suspect—or they mistook its cause—was my boredom, abysmal.

There was no quarrel. We parted so peaceably that my friendship with Alfred and Blanche survived, and with years became a solid faithful affection.

We had taken with us into the new firm the warm-hearted devoted Mrs B. Just when we left it was discovered that she had been robbing both the Knopfs and Guy for years, by an ingenious method known in the world of fraud as teeming and lading.

No one wanted the trouble of prosecuting her: she disappeared silently— like a cat slipping out of the larder.

# CHAPTER 59

FOR ALL MY, as I thought it, cynical understanding of human beings, I was still, when I married again, emotionally and intellectually a clever savage. My second marriage was a slow education, in many things. In trust first. Very slow, this—it was many years, a great many, before I even had the courage to say frankly that I wanted to do this or have that, I was so used to going by tortuous paths to avoid being seen, and perhaps mocked. Slow and not easy. I had more to learn and unlearn than Guy, whose life, the war apart, had been infinitely more secure, more polite, than mine.

In short, I was a savage, at best well-meaning, at worst pigheaded and lacking discipline.

If I have learned one thing about love, it is that no love endures very long, not even the most passionate, unless it is mortared by shared suffering. The birth of an enduring love is as hard and painful as any natural birth, and its growth attended by as many accidents. There is a passage at the end of one of Chekhov's tales which, when I read it as a girl, I did not understand: indeed I thought it nonsense. What the devil, I scoffed, have bitterness and pity to do with being, as Chekhov has it, 'properly, really in love?'

'... they forgave each other for what they were ashamed of in their past, they forgave everything in the present, and felt that this love of theirs had changed them both. In moments of depression in the past he had comforted himself with any arguments that came into his mind, but now he no longer cared for arguments; he felt profound compassion, he wanted to be sincere and tender... it seemed as though in a little while the solution would be found, and then a new and splendid life would begin; it was clear to both of them they had still a long long way to go, and that the most difficult and complicated part of it was only just beginning.'

Any marriage worth the name is no better than a series of beginnings— many of them abortive.

I was happy—that is, madly alive and interested—but my deepest coldest fears and hatreds coiled and uncoiled themselves, unchanged, below the happiness. My mania against domestic life was at its height. At one time in those first years we were the tenants of two places we never lived in, a large flat in Richmond and a house near Tunbridge Wells. I really meant to live in the house, lead a settled sensible life there, send Bill to Tunbridge as a day-boy, write, educate myself. And then, on my first visit to it after the contract had been signed, I was seized by the worst most unmanageable panic of my life and fled from it with the devil on my heels.

The flat was easily re-let, but the house remained on our hands for a long time.

Some time after the incident of the lift, in the summer of 1929, I made one of my sudden decisions. Less sudden than they look, no doubt—I imagine that my mind reaches a pitch of repressed fury when any decision is better than none. This one was almost sensible.

I went up to Whitby alone and arranged to buy a small house on what was then an edge of the town, on a road leading to Aisalby and the moors. As a house it was nothing, but, from the wide windows of the workroom I built on at the back, I looked across fields and the unseen valley of the Esk to the steep hill climbing to another moor. A road, up which I had often walked as a child, stretched across it, marked at night by the lighted window of a solitary farm.

The edge of the hill, where it met the sky, was a fine bounding line, as hard and pure as the line of the coast, as satisfying, giving me as sharp a thrust of pleasure.

For three years this was the view I had in my eyes when I lifted them from the paper under my hand. Since then I have lived in scores of places, without catching a glimpse, even in sleep, of the world bounded by a hillside, a dark belt of trees, a road climbing and turning, gleaming in rain and sunlight like a snake, in which, only in which, a freak, a savage, a child of one now marred edge of a province, is better than a stranger.

This was, too, the first and last time I had a room only to sit and write in.

As housekeeper I had a fifty-year-old villager from Ruswarp. She was completely illiterate, and at the beginning of winter drenched her short sturdy body in oil of evergreen and sewed it into a number of under-garments she did not take off again until May. As soon as she left the house at night, I opened the kitchen windows to clear the air which had become, as she would have said, *ram*, rank. But she was an admirable cook, and tireless, walking her two miles to and from the house in all weathers. She had innumerable skills, and a splendid natural eye for form and colour: the canvas-work seat covers she made, designing them herself, for my Chippendale chairs are still in use. Her life was one of continual excitement: any accidental touch, or a piece of string dropped in her path, might be a trick of Satan or an enemy. It was easy to see her accusing her neighbour of witchcraft and watching her burn with the liveliest most innocent curiosity.

A young niece lived with her in her cottage: she was always bragging to me about her as a *scolard*, who could read the newspaper, write, curl her hair, dance. This girl was a nincompoop, not worth her aunt's little finger.

For the time being, I was as tranquil here as in 1918 at Broughton. There are always these lulls, even during a typhoon.

One fine acid spring day, moved by heaven knows what pre-monition of change, I went out of my way to walk along Park Terrace. The life had ebbed from its faded narrow houses, and gardens filled with pampas grass and half-opened lilacs. I hurried past No 5 with a half-glance not quick enough to see the captain's young wife on her knees pushing a plant into the bed edged by exotic shells picked up on beaches at the other side of the world, and turned down North Bank. The tide was out, and in the harbour the gulls stepped delicately on mud goffered by their feet. On the other side a small shipyard was dying in its sleep, peaceably, after a brief flicker of life during the war.

Everything, I thought, has gone. But, resting for a moment on an old wall warmed by the sun, my hand let escape from me the child who stood there on just such a day, tasting the salt and honey of early light. For a moment, the gaiety, the simplicity, the modesty, of an older Whitby came close...

## CHAPTER 60

A T SIXTY-SIX, my mother's life was withdrawing from her as modestly as its life from the old shipyard. But I refused to believe it. Indeed, she herself did not believe it, or was surprised. Her heart was weakened, but she went up and down the steep streets every day. Why not? Her life was there, in the cobblestones and the dark older shops, smelling of cinnamon, yeast, coffee, malt vinegar, dry rot in the wood, calico, new bread. She would stand still to look fixedly into the window of some shop which, now, held nothing she would have as a gift.

'I bought my first pair of sheets here,' she told me. 'In those days every captain's wife knew decent linen when she fingered it. Now there's nothing.'

But she went on staring into the window as though it might be keeping from her in its depths a young woman who, if she looked long enough, would step forward to speak to her.

'Do you remember Crane's Christmas show?' she asked.

'Yes.'

Be sure I remembered it. For a week before Christmas Eve a blind shrouded the main window: the moment when it was drawn away to reveal a cottonwool snow scene, or dummies dressed as angels, or, one year, a Flight into Egypt with a Joseph so like the old Canon that he might have sat for it in his surplice with a drunken halo leaning over one ear, started in me a sensation that was purely voluptuous.

There was no essential difference between it and the pleasure to be got from looking at an El Greco: all was already there, even to the subtle distortions of art.

My mother spoke in the gay railing voice that broke from her when she forgot that she was an old woman. 'They don't take any trouble now, but why should they? Look at that—does that care about good linen?'

*That* was a young woman in Russian boots, hanging on the arm of a boy in the uniform of a third mate: a short skirt uncovered plump knees. After the age of thirteen, the human female knee is commonly an ugly joint, which doubtless is why in all classical statues and in paintings earlier than the nineteenth century, naked women are given the knees of a young Hermes.

'How long have I had this fur coat?' she asked suddenly.

'Seven or eight years. Full time I bought you a new one.'

'Oh, it will last me out,' she said. But she smiled, a quick, pleased smile.

Going up the steepest part of Flowergate, she had to stand still. She was breathing with difficulty, and her lips had a bluish tinge.

'What is the matter?'

'Nothing—except that my heart is a certain age.'

I felt furious with her for growing old, and for taking so little care of herself. 'You ought not to climb these hills.'

Her eyes flashed in the old way, the eyes of a girl in her lined heavy face. 'Nonsense,' she said sharply. 'If I can't come out, I might as well be in my grave.'

Her life revolved more and more narrowly round my younger sister, a lapwing circling its nest. It was the last and, I believe, the overwhelming passion of her life. She thought of this youngest child day and night, and talked about her—to me—endlessly, since I was the one person she could count on to listen with an attentive smile, and make the right answers. With me she had not to ignore an un-spoken disapproval, or invent a good reason for spending money, recklessly. Anything Do asked for she got, and one year of her school in Lausanne cost more than the whole of my education. So far as I was concerned, this obsession was no different from lesser things she had set her heart on and I had encouraged her to buy, or tried to get for her. So I smiled approvingly when she broached another extravagance. It was, I thought, a harmless vice...

I see her stepping out of the London express in York station: she had been visiting Do, now married, and I had travelled from Whitby to meet her in York and see her through the rest of the journey, with its two changes of train. She looked at me with a young heartless flame of gaiety in her eyes, and before she had set foot on the platform cried the words that had been boiling in her throughout the journey.

'She is going to build a house, and I am going to help her as much as I can. What do you think of that?'

'I think it's wonderful...'

Did it for an instant enter her mind that she was treating unjustly the daughter, the other daughter, who lived with her and on whom, without even thinking about it, she depended? (My father, to mark his indifference to them, always spoke of Winifred as *that other one*, and of Do as *that one*: if he remembered my name it was because I was the eldest, the one in whom he had seen, perhaps, a thin reflection of himself.) If it did, she chased the unwanted thought out easily: there was no room in her mind for anything but this last passion...

When, at the end of her second year at the university, my young sister refused to stay up any longer and demanded to be sent to a secretarial college, my mother was disappointed. I set myself to put this right for her.

'Why not let her go?'

'I think she's much too young to be in London.'

'Not younger than I was when I went.'

'True, but she's not strong.'

At nineteen Do was as strong as a foal, but even to herself my mother would not admit that she was infinitely more careful of her than she had been of her other children.

'She can be secretary to a publisher or an editor. I'm certain I can find something for her.'

'Oh,' my mother exclaimed, 'she'll do well—of course. She's exceptionally clever, you know.'

'Yes, she is,' I said warmly.

As soon as she had trained I ran about London to find a suitable post for her. I should have been ashamed to fail, but in fact it was not difficult. She was attractive, tireless, and quick-witted, and had more sense in her little finger than I in my whole body.

This year, 1929, she married a young man she had known at the university, a scientist who had moved to the managerial side of a large factory in Reading. There she set up house, in a tiny flat, keeping her job in London.

When I saw her in her flat, self-confident, gay, delighted with her few possessions—'my good cups,' she would say, caressing one of them—her husband, her status as a wife, I thought: I am seeing Hannah Margaret Jameson in her first house, the one I don't remember.

## CHAPTER 61

A BOUT THIS TIME my father sent in his resignation to the Prince Line. He did it without consulting my mother, who was bitterly vexed. She told me scornfully,

'I heard from your father this morning. He's retiring. After this voyage. He has written to the office already: they've promised him a yearly pension of three hundred—a grace pension, they call it. They're not bound to pay him a ha'penny. Grace!' Her mouth twitched with annoyance. 'The fool he is! And why retire now—at his age? He'll be bored to death hanging about the house for the rest of his life.'

'How old is he?'

'Seventy-four—seventy-five in October. Any number of older captains are still at sea. After all these years of being waited on hand and foot, he won't like it... But he has never taken my advice. Before the war, when shipping shares were going begging in the town, and he had a little money saved, I advised him to buy. If he had, he'd have been a rich man. As it is, the shares he did buy—because some man, a stranger, a Sir William Somebody, told him about them—are completely valueless. That's the kind of witless fool he is.'

'Thank goodness,' I said, to distract her, 'that you have a little money of your own now.'

I have in my ears, as I write, the terrible voice in which she cried,

'Too late! If I'd had it in time to help Harold when he was a boy!'

At this moment I would have cut my hand off to give her another life, which might turn out better.

The one my father led, when he came home for good, will be incredible to anyone born after 1900. During the early weeks my mother made a few careless efforts to accept him as a member of the family, but soon dropped them. Now that he was going to be in the house every day, for the rest of their lives, she lost the remnants of her patience. Quite simply, she could not endure him. The way he had treated his son was a living bitterness in her: after that time she had cut him off finally. To see him, to speak to him, cost her more effort than speaking to a stranger, and she hated strangers. His habits, his very voice, his presence in the same room, were insupportable.

If she were forced to talk to him, perhaps thank him for the Christmas and birthday presents he never failed to give her—anniversaries meant everything to her: she even expected her children to give her flowers on the anniversary of her wedding!—or to comment on the basketful of brambles or primroses he brought back from his solitary walks, she could not manage more than a dry, 'Thanks,' or a, 'Yes, very pretty.' Meeting him on the staircase, she would say, 'Good morning, Will,' in the detached polite voice she kept for a total stranger.

Mumbling, 'Good morning,' he hurried past, eyes averted.

Once I came out of her sitting-room where she and my aunt had been laughing like two schoolgirls over a memory of their terrible father, to find him close to the door, listening. What did her clear gay laugh remind him of? Furious at being caught, he rushed away, head down, walking softly and heavily, like a bear on two legs.

After those first weeks, he never entered either of her rooms except for chance minutes. He lived between his bedroom at the top of the house, the breakfast-room in which his meals were laid for him, and the kitchen where, at night, he smoked the strong American tobacco my mother detested, sitting for an hour or more staring at the stove—through it, rather, with his longsighted eyes, drained of their blue by the sun. At what?

Sixty-one years at sea, from the age of thirteen, must provide anyone with as many horizons as he needs.

Or, in his clear slow back-hand writing, he filled another page in the latest of the large folio diaries he had been keeping for the past thirty or more years. He had no longer the incidents of a voyage to describe, but he recorded weather in a seaman's precise terms, and what his wife called cruelly 'his maundering notions': now and then he would leave spread open a page on which he had written a complaint meant for our eyes. He did not dare say openly what he thought about the way the house was run, or about Do's visits with her husband and their departure laden with gifts.

*The sooner that one leaves, the better I shall like it*, he would write. Or: *I don't care for living in a show house such as this. My idea if I should be left*—he was nine years older than my mother, but he expected to outlive her—*would be a small place clear of the town, and then I think I should write a book on people I have never met but would like to meet.*

Unafraid of hurricanes or fighting-drunk lascars with knives—looking down from the bridge on to the lower deck, I once saw him separate two and shake them until the knives dropped from their hands—he was afraid of my mother, and full of impotent resentment when he thought of her extravagance and wilful half-conscious arrogance.

'She's always done as she likes,' he said to me in an unguarded moment—or did he trust me not to tell tales? 'There was all that furniture of m'mother's she sold—I daresay it wasn't worth much, but... and then buying more and telling me, That's mine. And Mr Gallilee's money—y'know, I never saw a penny of it. I didn't want it—not I—but she always said, If I'm left any money it will come in for our old age... Well, if it does, with *that one* about, I shall be surprised... Sixty-one years at sea—it was snowing when I saw my first ship—I was thirteen... Well, I've lived long enough not to expect anything.'

His short nervous laugh was an arm lifted to protect a thirteen-year-old boy's head.

When, as he sometimes did, he spoke to me in a genial voice, it did not seem incredible, that, a long time ago, there had been a handsome well-set-up captain who sang, not to his wife,

> Said the young Obadiah to the old Obadiah
> I am dry, Obadiah, I am dry.
> Said the old Obadiah to the young Obadiah,
> Are you dry, Obadiah? So am I...

Shall I be thought a monster if I admit that I had no affection for him? Since I had not to live with him, I could make myself seem friendly. And—perhaps only because I was born before my mother began turning away from him—I did not dislike him. What is more, I knew, very well, why he told absurd lies and bragged about the famous people who had made him the most astonishing confidences.

I don't think he was unhappy. After all, what difference is there between being solitary at sea, as the captain of a ship, shut in his authority, must be, and solitary at home—unless he had expected something better? His real life was lived outside the house, yarning with other old sea-captains, who may not have swallowed all his stories, but respected him as an experienced seaman, who did not find them grotesque—they, too, had heads crammed with foreign wharves, tropical scents, tempests—and in the long days he spent walking about the moors and lanes.

The blow that fell on him in the 'thirties still, to this day, fills me with anger.

How long had he captained Prince Line ships? Thirty, forty, years? The Line had become part of another larger firm, Furness Withy, and, finding no doubt that he was living too long, it reduced his pension abruptly to two hundred a year. And not very long after to a mere hundred.

True, shipping was in a bad way again, but I should not like to be the man who could bring himself to tell the oldest captain of the Line that he was worth less than two pounds a week to it at the end of his life.

When the first letter came, he brought it into the sitting-room and laid it in front of his wife with a nervous,

'Look at that, will you?'

She read it, and said drily, 'You were too eager to leave. If you hadn't been in such a foolish hurry, you might have got better than a promise they're not bound to keep... Economies! It's a rich firm, it pays a dividend. I'd dearly like to know what the man who signed that letter is sacrificing.'

She was as angry with my father as with the Line, and not surprised—it was a commonplace in Whitby to begin a sentence with: If there is a meaner creature on earth than a shipowner...

The second and savage cut woke in her something like pity for him. It vexed her to see him ashamed.

He was not going to starve, nor stand in a dole line. He had his house, and the few savings he had been able to make and would be forced to spend now. But he was pitiably ashamed. And behind that, behind the humiliation and bewilderment, was a real grief. To have endured at sea more than sixty years—forty-five of them as master—and to discover, with brutal suddenness, what the men who smiled and shook his hand when he walked into the office at the end of another voyage—'Well, Captain, had a good trip?'—really thought of him. Nothing.

Nothing at all. He had less to be proud of than the thirteen-year-old child blubbering secretly in his bunk.

My mother said warmly,

'It's a mean act. They've treated you abominably.'

But this stung him worse than her familiar coldness.

'No, no,' he muttered, 'they'll put it back later. It'll only be for a time. They'll make it right when they can. You'll see.'

When, some ten years later, the Line sent the usual letter of sympathy in the death of an old and valued etc etc, the acknowledgement I forced myself to write was barely civil.

Hypocrisy of this respectable sort is only the small change of our society: it was simple-minded of me to be nauseated by their letter.


## CHAPTER 62

A FEW DAYS AGO, talking with an intelligent nineteen-year-old, I discovered, with surprise and some sadness, that the abyss between his and my generation was even wider than I imagined. I had been telling him about the confrontation between France and Germany which, during the twenties and thirties, took place not only before our eyes in events, but in our deeper consciousness, each country standing there not for a geographical area with a different climate, architecture, language, manners, customs, wines, but for a different state of soul. To him this antinomy, this once mortal contrast, was completely without meaning.

In the exterior world as in the dialectical one, nothing had interest or importance for him except the confrontation, material, intellectual, spiritual, between Europe and America or Russia, two giants of equal size.

'But surely you can feel the tension between two ways of thinking and feeling so different as France and Germany? And the need to choose between them?'

He was only puzzled. 'Why? Aren't they both part of Europe? And isn't Europe, which includes us, going to have to choose between uniting or being Americanized or communized?'

'Do your friends think that?'

'Of course.'

This sponge passed casually over the feverish obsessions and ferment of years when—so we felt—the whole future of the world was being played for disconcerts me. Who will now believe that there was a time, to be measured in heartbeats, when, with anguish, we watched the conqueror of 1918 stumble from one moral surrender to the next, and a crushed defeated Germany becoming every day stronger, more openly aggressive, more of a threat? And when nothing else seemed as important?

I have two countries, the Whitby of my birth, and France, the first secreted like a salt in my blood, bone marrow, and the cells of my brain, the other nursed by my foolish heart. The one lost, vanished, the other too large to be completely disfigured and spoiled.

My liking for France, for the country itself, is peculiarly English, a store of humble love, unasked-for by the recipient, unwanted, even mocked. Like all love—and all travel which is not simply globetrotting—it traces the map of my heart rather than the contours of the country itself. At my first sight of it France became an idea I cherish, the idea of a habit of living which leaves room for more real pleasures than any we English have practised for at least a hundred years: the butter tastes of butter, the bread varies from one village to the next between toughness and an exquisite texture and savour, a village of a few poor streets grows its own wine, the stench of a cracked drain is followed at once by the smell of cooking herbs or the scent of lime-trees in bloom alive with bees. It is the country itself I love—I am neither naïve nor impudent enough to want to embrace its people—its fields, chestnut trees, olives, vines, its old houses, its country roads and village streets, even hideous. Part, no doubt, of my happiness in France comes from being where I am not known, but the greater part is the gift of the country itself.

(Nowadays, my happiness, no less acute, no less naive than it always was, is edged by the bitterness of having been excluded from Europe by the will of one stiff-necked old man with the ideas of Charlemagne and the pride and vanity of the devil himself. To feel this about General de Gaulle is not to deny his physical and moral energy, suppleness, wit. He is a great man and it would have been better for Europe if he had been born in, let's say, Pennsylvania: a nature like his needs to be diluted by as many millions of men and acres as possible.)

If I were ordered to give reasons for my passion for France I could find plenty, and very respectable. France is the country where *le tact des choses possibles*, the instinctive knowledge of what is humanly possible and the refusal to strain beyond it, is least likely to be killed by an inventiveness which is taking not only the drudgery but the zest out of life. France may (pray heaven) have kept in reserve enough inefficiency to save its people from dying of boredom, enough modest households where the choice between buying a book or a bottle of wine and paying the first instalment on a washing-up machine is decided in favour of the wine or an edition of Stendhal's letters. Its provincial cities and towns have not yet been sterilized by the nearness of the capital; the life in its villages, on a working day so concentrated that they seem empty, suddenly breaks into a joyous childlike energy, perhaps a cycle race which brings out whole families for miles round and stops all other traffic, however serious. It is still, for God knows how short a time, the non-standardized country, the country where a mechanic enjoys repairing a foreign car with an inch or two of wire coaxed into shape by fingers that might be those of the anonymous builders of Chartres or the cave artists of the Vézère, where the *agent* bawls you out today for precisely the offence which, tomorrow, will move him to cover his face with one hand in mock grief and with the other wave you on, where museums are closed on Monday in one town and on Thursday in its nearest neighbour, where regulations are enforced or broken by an official's whim.

One day in 1931—it was the day after the abdication and flight of the king of Spain—I took my young son to see the flooded caves near Sare, right on the Spanish frontier: they stretch, in fact, between the two frontier posts. To his disappointment, they were closed, the season had not started. Ignoring rules, the gaunt middle-aged peasant in charge took us through them in his boat and provided from his own larder a meal of splendid bread, butter, cheese, and a bottle of strong unnamed wine. As we ate it with him, he talked with sharp gaiety about the fall of kings.

'For me,' he said, smiling, 'they cannot drop off too quickly.'

Lifting a hand the colour and texture of a ripe walnut, he wiped them off the end of his long Basque nose.

*My* France, yes—a lover's illusion of France, a country laid up in my memory. I do not offer it as a true image. It leaves out entirely an evil side of the very virtues which—for a lover—are the essence, the perpetually renewed miracle of France. Speaking in a secret session of the House of Commons in November 1942—and leaving little doubt in the minds of his hearers which of the two images he considered likely to please a God who at that moment seriously needed His good slow-witted English—Churchill said, 'The Almighty in His infinite wisdom did not see fit to create Frenchmen in the image of Englishmen.' The fact that, sitting at the side of a road in the Landes, eating French bread and cheese and drinking a bottle of Corbières, I say, 'And thank God He didn't,' does not prevent me from noticing that no more insular people exists, no people so innocently convinced that they belong to the greatest nation in the world, incomparably more intelligent, shrewder, more cultured, than any other, and speaking the only language worth the trouble of learning.

It is not possible that *my* France, still only half industrialized, out of step with less sane, less human neighbours, can keep the savour of a civilization founded on good bread, four hundred different cheeses, and heaven knows how many different wines (including the strong delicate *vin sable* a peasant in the Landes grows for himself and his family alone); can survive the monstrous deformation of our instincts forced on us by our own ingenuity and irrational conviction that we have an absolute right to indulge our intellectual curiosity about the universe to the point where, at any moment, we may annihilate it and ourselves; can keep its delight in *making*; can for many more years avoid being demoralized by the speed, the nervous tension, the efficiency, the growing incoherence of modern life; can keep a middle way between order and freedom, between the mechanized and the natural. Can look to a future which is largely a repetition of the past, so that a man is likely to die in the bed he was born in. Can enjoy a civilization predictable and subject to time. Modern technological civilization is almost wholly unpredictable (who knows where he will be this time next year?), unsettled, rootless, alarmingly subject to space. The former may bore the senses or the mind; the second plants a deeper boredom in the very spirit. No doubt it is an advance, but to what?

I suppose that soon the last traces of a backward France will have been effaced, the country will have been dragged up to date and saved for—heaven help us, for what? The long miracle of France will be over.

A Frenchman, highly intelligent, to whom I put my fears, said,

'What you are pleased to call our sanity, our civilization of the possible, brought us to the edge of the grave. Much good it did us in 1939 to be saner, more modestly creative, with, as you would say, more *nature* than the Germans. God forbid that we should ever again rely on our habits.'

'All the same, we need *that* France, we need, my God how we need the idea that bread, wine, and a margin of inefficiency are at least as necessary as speed and a sterilized efficiency. Water in a dry land—it might keep us just inside the humanly bearable.'

He laughed. 'Are you by any chance a poet? Come back in ten, five years' time, and exactly here, where a miserable couple of familes has been scratching a living from lavender and a few olives, I'll show you a magnificent factory for electronic machines, employing hundreds of men and women and offering them, and the whole district, an ease, security, interests, they never had. Thank heaven that the future of this country is not in your hands.'

All right, thank heaven. Thank heaven I am old and shall die. Meantime I keep what are for me the living memories. The strange thing—is it so strange?—is that these are not, as you would expect, of Chartres, of Albi smouldering in hot sunlight, of Chenonceaux, of the naked brutality of Les Baux, but, returning only for me, of some unpaved square shaded by immense chestnuts in flower, some insignificant Café du Centre in a village with nothing to commend it but the age and strength of its houses (to an English eye stupefyingly shabby and neglected), of the dark shop, barely room to turn, in which, one torrid Sunday noon, I bought the finest bread in the world, of meadows where, as in a mediaeval tapestry, or as in fields I knew as a child, there are as many wild flowers as blades of grass, yellow ladies'-fingers, pink clover and ragged robin, red and purple vetch, pale mauve cuckoo-pint, blue speedwell, white bird's-eye, tall blazingly white marguerites, and innumerable creeping plants of all colours.

What have we done, in the past thirty years, to our English meadows?

And the rivers. Only the cold narrow Esk, flowing into the North Sea at Whitby, runs in me at a deeper level than Loire, Garonne, Dordogne, Lot.

My France, I say humbly, is these images and unnumbered others, and with them a few signs—again I daren't imply that they equal the reality— standing in my life for Stendhal, Péguy, and, yes, Jean Giraudoux.

In my green years I read Giraudoux with unfailing pleasure in a style which hovers between the baroque and the deceptively simple (a style full of paradox and half-relevant images, as fascinating as the movements of a skilled dancer), and a loyal refusal to notice his fiascos. I must be the only Englishman who has read all his published writing, parts of it half a dozen times. In Zurich, in 1947, I was impolite enough to correct a French writer on a detail in one of the lesser-known novels. He took it calmly since he knew, about Giraudoux, personal details he hoped would disconcert me. When I showed no interest, he went on,

'And, after all, as a writer he is an escapist. How like an Englishman to admire that!'

What nonsense. Escapist, the writer who returned again and again to the themes of treachery, madness, disappointment, death? He was escapist only in the sense in which Mallarmé escapes from the real world by substituting an image for a real event or emotion. And as Picasso deforms the reality in order to imply a truth about it. No writer ever came closer to dissolving in words the ambiguous and disturbing Greek smile, or the least reassuring Mozart.

I am very close to the moment when I shall be too dry of mind to re-read even those of his books in which the images had the freshness of a jet of water in sunlight, but I hope never to be so disloyal as to turn them off my shelves.

Older, much tougher, certain to last as long as I do, my passion for Stendhal is less easy to account for. (Can one account for a passion?) *That Stendhal, both tender and disturbing*, Paul Léautaud wrote in his diary on the 18th of March, 1901, and at another time: *When it comes to Stendhal, the man is so particular that there is no middle ground: one either loves him or hates him.*

It is true.

His dry phrases, often careless, limpid to a fault, quivering with emotion below the surface, made a confused secretive adolescent free of a lively world, open on all sides, where any question could be asked, and no pretence was made of knowing every answer. A world exactly the opposite of the appalling closed world of Mauriac's novels with their final sense that everything has been exposed, and their suppressed pleasure in the defeat, pain, ugliness, of ugly defeated men and women.

But that is not the single reason for my abiding passion for Stendhal. There is no one adequate reason. It was instinctive. An instinct led me to the only writer who could explain to me, because he shared them, my hatred of authority, my inborn restlessness, my profound happiness in foreign places, fear of ridicule, distrust of human beings, my insanity. All these have their roots in my childhood, but they brought me, a masterless dog, to the feet of the one person I recognized.

Not that the instinct was a wholly fortunate one. Years ago Denis Saurat told me,

'You should read less French. French literature is poison to an English writer.'

I took this to be one of his sceptical quips until the day when I realized that I had caught an incurable disease, the taste for lucidity.

## CHAPTER 63

WHAT IN THE 'THIRTIES I felt for Germans was not dislike, not fear, it was a cold passion of curiosity. I began to think it useless to look in my dear France for an answer to questions about the future. If anywhere, they were in Germany—about which I knew nothing except that my mother, as a young woman in Bremen with my father's ship, had seen a wife walking three paces behind her husband, carrying his heavy overcoat and what seemed to be a lightning conductor. No doubt he was expecting a thunderstorm.

In February 1932, we went to Berlin.

I lived there some weeks, fascinated, repelled, amused, above all disconcerted by a city unlike any I knew. Every other foreign city offers an image of itself in the first days, which may turn out to be incomplete or a downright lie, but is at least coherent. Berlin contradicted itself at every moment, and with the utmost violence. It did not even look like a capital city: there was scarcely a building anyone would cross the street to look at. Yes, one—the old guardhouse on Unter den Linden which housed the tomb of the Unknown Soldier, a square of black lightless stone, with the date, topped by a great copper wreath; nothing else except the wreaths and two thin bronze pillars supporting thinner flames: the place was open to the sky, and the day I went snow was drifting down on to the tomb.

Other public buildings and most of the streets made an impression of middle-class sobriety and immovability, Victorian in its complacence. They evoked the most respectable feelings, but the writers and painters in vogue all belonged to an avant-garde devoid of any feeling livelier than disgust with life. Buttoned up to the neck in thick garments—it was bitterly cold everywhere—angry young men and women stripped themselves of conventional ideas and emotions, practising total evacuation as a moral hygiene.

A play that had been running for months, staged by a group of young out-of-work actors calling themselves Truppe 1931, was about the Marxian theory of value.

There was—this was not contradicted—a feeling of public tension such as exists in England only in the last few hours before the outbreak of a war.

As commonplace as a Baptist chapel to look at, with few trees, a wretched river, monuments of stupefying banality, Berlin at that time was conscientiously corrupt and gross, with misery, grey hunger, uncertainty, in the background—not so far in the background, either—but fascinating and heady, boiling like a crater.

An alienated city, living—it was impossible not to feel this—on borrowed time.

It fascinated because—where other capital cities are full of a past still living in their old houses or the wharves of their river or their bakers' shops—here what you saw was the future waiting in the wings for the curtain to rise. If I were to pretend that I guessed what the play was going to be about, it would be a lie. All I saw, tasted, felt, was the nervous gaiety, the eager abandonment and deriding of morals, the threat of social collapse, the paralysis of all ideals—including the ideal of freedom, squeezed to death between two extremes.

The first thing I saw when I came out of a dull declamatory meeting of the Stalhelm, a memorial service for the dead of the Great War, was a frieze of posters plastered on kiosks and bare trees: they gave the names (with dates) of people who had been killed by the Nazis during the month. On the other side of each tree, each kiosk, was a Nazi poster, with the list, much shorter, of their dead. Either the communists are worse shots than their opponents, I thought, or less savage. The young German with me said,

'It is a new war, yes?'

'As useless as the last.'

'No. This one is to defend our freedom.'

That same Sunday, in the evening, another German took us to the Bock-Bier-Fest in a working-class quarter. Cheaper and a great deal less comfortable than Haus Vaterland—where for a few shillings the clerk and his girl, the elderly official and his fat smiling wife, could choose between the scenery and eating habits of some dozen countries—it seethed with an animal gaiety: mountains of sausages and sauerkohl, tuns of new beer, singing to split the ear-drum, wall-paintings of innocent indecency and vulgarity, a Love Boat...

> *Einmal ist keinmal, drum trink' mit mir*
> *Und morgen ist alles vorbei...*

When we left, our German companion, shouting because I was temporarily deaf, nudging me in the ribs because I was wiping smoke-blinded eyes, said,

'See this street? Last week during a fight between our chaps and Hitler's swine, a child ran out of that doorway and got a bullet through its head from both sides. Absurd, eh?'

Nothing seemed absurd in a country where all contraries were equally possible, and where an inexhaustible vitality threw up in the same jet order and disorder, the most brutal theories of collective discipline and a reckless anarchy in personal life, energies as dangerous as Luther, Fichte, Marx, but also Meister Eckart, Beethoven, Goethe, themselves a little too much of a good thing...

Alfred Knopf was in Berlin for a week. He invited us to lunch at Horcher's. The small room with its faded olive-green panelling had seen and forgotten more princes and personages than other fashionable German restaurants remembered. I watched the waiter prepare a sauce, using double cream, an egg yolk, brandy, and a cupful of rich stock: he stirred them in a shallow dish over a flame, arranged in it the slices of venison, and let them simmer. As he passed, Herr Horcher gave the dish a glance from faded blue eyes. The vegetables were asparagus tips, kohlrabi cooked in cream, and potatoes dissolving in butter. I have forgotten whether I felt a little ashamed—perhaps not, since it was certain I should never sit in Horcher's again—but I ate everything. And I seized the chance to make a new contract for my novels which, as I expected it would, gave me the benefit of movements in the pound-dollar exchange.

'A much too shrewd businessman was lost when you took to writing novels,' Alfred said later. 'That's twice you've played the exchange against us.'

Outside in the street, the cold drove the breath back down my throat. It came straight from Siberia, and flayed the skin. Oddly enough, it did not destroy a petal of the snowdrops, narcissi, violets and feathery mimosa bunched together on stalls at the corner of a dull lumpish square.

If this nakedly pitiless wind made me flinch, what did it do to the unemployed who in the district north and south-east of Alexanderplatz outnumbered the employed? Face after face, the flesh sunk into ravines, had the waxen colour of hunger, but none of these skeletons was less than carefully shaved and very neat in his threadbare suit.

'When one of them loses hope completely, which may happen in his second year out of work—a man with wife and children is then allowed fifty shillings a month—he kills himself; his self-respect draws the line at dirt and rags,' my German friend said...

We were living in a boarding-house on the Kurfürstendamm. I could not call it an ugly street, since ugliness is itself a distinction, and these houses were as vacantly unattractive as a pile of rubble. At the lower end, the little cabarets and restaurants were simple and friendly, but one in every three shops was empty: here as in other streets the most noticeable object was the To Let signs.

On my fourth or fifth evening I was rash enough to ask whether anyone at the table took Herr Hitler seriously. The only person who did was a thin elderly spinster. She was put brutally in her place by our landlady.

Frau Broesike, a Saxon with the voice and moustache of a sergeant-major, was the widow of a professor of history; her boarders kept her alive, and she despised and bullied them. Striking her mouth with her hand, she cried,

'Fräulein Schön, if that fool should win in the election, you never eat in my house again!'

Did she later pay for this insult? Decent old virago that she was, I hope not.

'And Dr Goebbels?' I asked.

'Ah. He is not a fool, he is a devil. But he is not, as some say, a Jew. When he married, he offered to show his wife to any genuine enquirer, to prove that she was not Jewish.'

I burst out laughing. No one else thought the offer comic, and I reflected that what divides one tribe from another is less likely to be religion or politics, or a lack of oil or harbours, than different ideas of the ridiculous. To cover up my discomfiture, I asked,

'But who does support the Führer?'

'Apart from our sentimental Fräulein Schön?' Frau Broesike said spitefully. 'I will tell you. Small shopkeepers ruined by the crisis. And young men, trained doctors, who are glad to earn a few marks addressing envelopes. Do you know what we call our university in Berlin? *Wartehalle für Unbeschäftigte*—waiting-rooms for the work-less. The lecture-rooms are so crowded that students pin to the floor scraps of paper with their names, to reserve a few inches of standing-room. But, when we are on our feet again— and we shall be—you'll hear no more of Fräulein Schön's vulgar little friend.' She laughed like a mastiff. 'Do you know what she said about him the other day? That he was Frederick Barbarossa himself, come back to save us, ha, ha!'

I winced for the wretched Schön. It was unnecessary. After supper she drew me into a corner to ask if I had seen anything of 'our crusaders, our young archangels?'

I said I had. 'You have a song—I mean, they have—which begins something like: How fine to see the blood of Jews spurting under the knife.'

Her gentle face remained placid, smiling. 'Yes. Yes, it is a song. Like other songs.'

'Well, I don't know,' I said. 'It's not like any English song.'

'No?' A gleam of satisfaction came into her pale eyes. 'Much more lordly, no doubt.'...

I had a friend in Berlin. Some months before this, in the autumn of 1931, I was in Scarborough at the Labour Party Conference. It was a dispiriting affair, both delegates and Executive wry-mouthed from swallowing MacDonald's 'betrayal'. Some at least of the dejected men and women on the platform must have seen it coming, but they were adrift and out of heart. I was standing outside the hall, watching their faces, when the secretary of the local party came up to me.

'I have a very young German here, a Miss Linke, I wish you'd speak to her.'

Turning, I saw what I took to be a schoolgirl in a shabby coat and a soft hat pulled down over her eyes. Reluctantly—I dislike getting involved with people—I went over to her and found myself looking at the goose-girl of the German fairy-tales, tall and slender, with a flawless skin, pale rose on white, red unpainted mouth, hair like fine yellow silk, eyes of a clear blue, the shape and colour of a kitten's. With some derisory sum in marks she had come to England 'to find out what my English comrades are thinking and doing.' Everywhere she had found friends, and shelter for a night or a week. In poor people's houses she shared a bed with the children, as contented as when she could be given a room to herself. In the morning her hosts sent her on her way with advice and another address.

But of course, I thought. She is the Youngest Brother, whom everybody, peasant, old crone, swineherd, emperor, recognizes at sight and is compelled to help.

This was not her first journey. A year before, with two friends, boys as poor as she was, she had been to France. They visited the battlefields, and at Douaumont promised each other 'to be friends with all, to forget our losses, to build the future.'

Her English was eccentric, she was learning it as she had learned French, by ear.

'For months I, what do you say?, am scratching together pennies to come to England. I am happy here, *le bonheur fou*. But why is your Labour Party sitting glum and sad, repeating like old women: We must be calm, do not let us be excited, keep very quiet and all will be well? Why don't they wave their arms and shout: We are socialists, let us fight?'

'Perhaps because they are English.'

'Oh, no.' Her smile showed strong perfect teeth, very white. 'This four weeks I am talking with people of all classes, and they are not as if dead since years.'

In the few hours she spent with me in Whitby next day, I discovered her complete lack of self-consciousness. Words, gestures, actions, sprang directly from her nature, without vanity or calculation. I have never, before or since, known a man or woman of whom this is true. Born in East Berlin, the second child of a very minor civil servant, she learned during the War anything the Youngest Brother needs to know about hunger. After the War, a skinny fifteen-year-old with her first job, she learned to snatch her wages and run like a hare to buy the dress which in the meantime had centupled in price, so that it was as far out of her reach as ever. To say that she was a rebel against the stiff respectability of her lower middle-class family would be absurd; their ideas and teaching had no meaning for her, none at all. Her father's dull anger when she joined the young socialists, the tears and scolding of her mother, made her yawn.

She had been born without a sense of guilt. It did not occur to her to refuse to sleep with the young comrade she fell in love with at sixteen. To make any fuss about so simple a gesture!

The most common human vices—malice, envy, timidity, greed, jealousy, hypocrisy, fear—had been left out of her entirely. But her sense of responsibility was full-grown.

'What do you want most?' I asked her. The answer I expected was: To have the money to travel. Or: To be heard of.

In a serious voice she said, 'To live, to work, to build a world where is freedom and bread for all.'

Just as she was leaving, my mother came in, and without reflecting I said, 'This is Lilo Linke, she has come from Berlin.'

There was a silence. Then my mother said in a strange voice,

'I'm glad you are in England, we must forgive and forget the past.'

The words struck me as exaggerated. Surely, thirteen years after the war, a young German could be thought of as an ordinary visitor?

I had not the wit to feel the enormous effort with which my mother lifted her few words and laid them in front of the smiling young German. Who accepted them with polite simplicity. And why not? But I ought to have guessed that, only to be able to see distinctly, to reach the German girl, she had had to step over the body, its hands clenched, of her dead son.

In Berlin, Lilo was living in a two-roomed flat, not far from the Kurfürstendamm. She was immensely proud of it. It was so small that four pairs of legs filled the living-room, and so new that the plaster had barely set. Her few possessions stood to attention against the walls or on shelves: to balance her passion to be independent and free, she had a Prussian love of order.

'How,' I asked, 'can you afford this?'

The rent was very low, much lower than it would have been in London, but even at that little was left of her salary from the *Deutsche Volkswirt* (a journal she said was the Berlin equivalent of the *Economist*). The meal she had got ready for us was sparse, but I wondered anxiously whether we were eating next day's supper, too.

An efficient staff officer, she had drawn up a time-table for the next weeks, and I saw that I was going to have trouble to make room in it for what I enjoy in a foreign city, walking without aim, searching at the back of a café, between the half-closed shutters of a house, for the excitement, the sense of a mysterious other life, that when I was a child I got from the lights of houses rising suddenly out of blackness. The smiling fair-haired young man she introduced as one of her comrades in some Social Democratic youth front had been called up for duty to show us places she didn't want to see herself. His name was Werner. When Lilo was telling us how, as a child during the War, she had fainted in one of the endless queues and been charitably carried to the head of it, and after that, until she was found out, had pretended to faint in queues, happy to have stumbled accidentally on the right trick, he said,

'The only thing I remember about the War is my mother crying. She had hold of my arm and she was saying: Oh, your poor thin arm, where shall I get milk for you? Oh your arms, your arms!... But it was *after* the War, she had thought the blockade would stop, and when it was the same, still the blockade and no food, she cried. During the War—no tears. After the War, tears every day. That was very funny—yes?'

'It won't happen again,' Lilo said fiercely, '*we* shall see to that.'

Already I had my doubts about her leaders. Little turbulent as our Labour leaders were, I could not see them tolerating brutes like the Nazi storm troopers, encouraging judges to treat them with fatherly mildness, and allowing schoolmasters to sneer at the Republic and preach a violent nationalism to their young pupils.

Maliciously, I told Lilo that I had been listening to speeches by her Social Democratic leaders. 'Why do they go on repeating: We must be calm, do not let us be excited, keep quiet and all will be well? You blamed our people, but yours seem far timider, far more cautious and eager to show how correct and respectable they are. And we're not in danger, our streets aren't full of potential dictators. Why don't your leaders wave their arms and shout: We are socialists, let us fight? Anyone would think they are ashamed of having given birth to a Republic and want to keep it dark.'

'That's not true, you've been listening to old men. Who cares about them? *We* shall fight. Listen...'

She talked in a laughing authoritative voice about the new age, egged on by the smiling Werner. So long ago as it is, and Lilo dead, all I remember now is that suddenly I was madly happy. For the first time since 1914, 1 had the feeling of the years immediately before that war, the night-long talks about the future, the blazing excitement. It was like one of those dreams in which, ravished with joy, one is young and strong. These young Germans were talking with our confidence and gaiety, our mockery of the old, our rage against injustice. At one moment I could have sworn I heard a voice not heard since 1916—but that was too good to be true.

There were differences. Behind us in 1913 stretched years of solid peace, behind Lilo and her friends lay defeat, hunger, anarchy.

In a few months they discovered—as we had—how little the future was theirs, and how indifferently their leaders, not out of any ill-will, not for want of courage, had led them. Like ours, their new age died by default, surrendered by decent cautious men too much of whose energies ran away in oiling the machinery of a party: the machine functioned beautifully to reproduce itself, and broke down the moment it ran against passions it had no idea how to evoke on its own behalf and never came within worlds of controlling in its enemies.

The really surprising thing about the Weimar Republic is not that it lasted only fourteen years, but that it lasted so long. True, the rest of us did not do a great deal to help it elude its murderers.

Rather late, someone knocked at the door of the flat. 'That will be my boss,' Lilo said, smiling.

'Your——?'

'My editor. Dr Stolper. He said they would come—they want to meet you.'

But it was an elderly man—elderly or middle-aged, impossible to guess the age of these faces denatured by hunger. So ashamed to be begging that he was nearly inaudible, he asked for a pfennig. At most doors in the building he would have been lucky to get just that. The boy gave him ten, and Lilo—waving me fiercely back—another ten. She began to question him. Her candour reassured him, he poured out a torrent of words, cried a little, and stumbled away, his money in one hand, the other wiping his grey cheeks.

'What did he say?' I asked.

'Eight months ago he got a chance of work and lost it because he couldn't raise the fifteen shillings to buy a waiter's third-hand tailcoat. He cries because he doesn't understand how this could happen to him, he has always been a good waiter.'

Werner left. Soon afterwards, the Stolpers came: they had been to the theatre and were in evening dress, he a strongly-built middle-aged man, with a fine intelligent head and a smile at once friendly and arrogant, the unconscious arrogance, more an air of authority and success, of a man who knows he is better informed than anyone he is likely to meet. His wife had one of those narrow Jewish faces which suggest a Greek coin, an extreme delicacy and strength, dark hair, immense dark eyes with a flicker of gaiety in their depths, and the gentlest voice in the world.

Both treated Lilo with the indulgent interest they might have shown a young relative. At one moment, when she shook her head, refusing to do something Dr Stolper wanted her to do, his wife said quietly,

'But you must obey him, he is your boss—he is mine, too.'

Lilo gave her a brilliant smile. 'No. He is my boss in the office, but not outside. Outside I am my own boss.'

Her total lack of subservience was one of her most surprising virtues. Where had this East Berlin child, less than half educated, learned to defend herself and her opinions in any company, politely, but with unshakable self-will? No authority as such, no difference of age or class, made the faintest impression on her. She was never defiant. She was simply, in all times and places, her own boss.

Gustav Stolper and his wife lived in a society where intelligence, good manners, tolerance, uncommon sense, wit, worldly knowledge, join to quicken a cell which can only exist in a capital city, and there only at certain times on certain conditions. Their house in a suburb of Berlin, among pine-trees, was an instance of the new moneyed simplicity: the interior walls of four living-rooms could be rolled back to form a vast central square with immense windows and an invisible source of warmth: the nursery, which I saw when Mrs Stolper took me with her to say goodnight to her two young children, was divided at night by a sliding wall. The furniture in all the rooms was light and strong; there were admirable modern paintings, and, lying about, weeklies and monthlies in three languages. Had you wanted an example of the Berlin farthest from the one brawling in the streets, here it was, cultured, cosmopolitan—on the edge.

The talk at dinner was at first about politics—it could not begin anywhere else. A member of one of the centre parties, a liberal, Stolper refused, with a fierce controlled passion, to believe that Hitler would come to anything.

'No, no, everything is against it, every sane force, economic, financial, even social. Even philosophic—you can't found a society on a doctrine which is entirely irrational. But entirely.'

One of his guests—the American journalist Edgar Mowrer—said soberly, 'Don't be too sure that what looks irrational isn't viable. This country smells of trouble, as if somebody had buried a rat under the boards. If my experience of people—and countries—has taught me any one thing it is that if a man or a party can tap irrational energies they'll blow up Everest, let alone a single country.'

'Not this country,' Stolper said, with his fine smile.

Mowrer turned to his neighbour—banker or industrialist (I forget). 'What's your opinion?'

'Mine? Don't be too shocked if I tell you that, supposing he can take over the government—by any means—Herr Hitler will find more economists, bankers, diplomats, civil servants, field-marshals, even clerics falling over each other to work for him than he needs. The fact that he's insane—if he is—won't deter them for a moment when they're offered a chance to get their hands on the levers.'

Still smiling, Stolper shook his head. 'You're quite wrong. In the end unreason always destroys itself.'

Mowrer threw his hands up. 'Oh, in the end!'

The fourth man at the table—was he the banker?—had the face of an ecclesiastical official, perhaps a member of the Curia, smooth except for a few deep lines, all curved, widely-curved nostrils, downward-curving thin lips, a full womanly chin.

'My dear friend, my dear Gustl,' he said, laughing, 'you live in an unreasonable world. My cousin, who is a millionaire, has been placing money, gold, in half a dozen capitals. He can't get at any of it. How's that for lunacy! Europe is more than half off its head, and if all the statesmen, diplomats, economists like yourself, and financiers who are not mad, have neither will nor power to drag it back to sanity, why on earth do you put any trust in reason? Reason! My advice to you——'

He broke off abruptly, as if he thought his advice had better be given behind doors.

One of the others began to talk about a book he had been sent from Paris: from this, by way of Rilke and an argument about translating poetry, the talk was steered into thinner unpolitical air.

When I left, Mrs Stolper laid in mine a hand as light as a leaf and almost as narrow.

'I am glad that Lilo has made a good English friend,' she said. 'Perhaps she will need you.'

'Don't you agree with your husband about Hitler?' I asked.

'Of course I agree with him,' she said, smiling. 'He is always right.'

Later I discovered that this small dignified charming woman, often silent—who lived in and for her husband, believed what he believed, accepted as irrefutable all his opinions—had a mind little less cultivated and acute than his, and, as well, an instinctive wisdom which sometimes showed itself in a word or a gesture slipping from her unnoticed by her conscious mind...

What happened, later, to the Sportpalast, that monstrous building which served equally well for the six-day cycle race, memorial services, the stream of vitriol pouring from Dr Goebbels, and Communist rallies? The programme Lilo had laid down covered all these. The Communist evening was colder than any I remember, flurries of frozen snow and a wind like a flail. Over ten thousand people crowded into the place, solid patient faces of older workers, faces of nakedly angry youths, pinched faces of anxious women, children holding banners in their blue hands. A woman recited her husband's poems; the police had forbidden him to recite them himself. I tried to imagine which of our poets would be dangerous to public order. The words of songs were thrown on the screen. The one that fetched them all to their feet, bellowing, was about defending the USSR—it reminded me of the old maid in my boarding-house with her *leibliche Friedrich Barbarossa*. Why this passion for a Messiah, shared by both extremes? The last we had was Cromwell, an experiment never repeated.

Except when he halted the torrent long enough to ask, 'And who did this to you?' I could not follow the speaker. A roar answered him. '*Polizei!*'

Outside, arm-linked lines of the *Polizei* broke the crowd up into twos and threes as it came out into the brutal cold. The wind wrapped a piece of paper round my ankle—Vote for Hindenburg.

'Are you going to vote for him?' I asked Lilo.

'Of course. He is a decent old fellow, he will keep that devil Hitler in his place.'

The following evening—all part of my education—she and Werner took us to see a friend who was a Communist. He was also a scholar of sixteenth-century music and a composer. He and his wife had a flat even smaller than Lilo's, a room and half a room in one of the huge new blocks of workers' flats in north Berlin: luckily they were both very thin as well as young and very poor, and the room held only the essential minimum of furniture.

The conversation began politely, with a question Ernst Meyer asked about Dolmetsch, but in less than ten minutes a furious argument broke out between him and Lilo. Turning to me, he said,

'If she tells you that the Social Democrats are socialists, don't believe her. In 1916 they called out the army to shoot down the only honest socialists in the country, and they've been selling out to the Right ever since. In every crisis. All they think about is their jobs. Thanks to their treachery we——'

Eyes like a spitting cat's, Lilo cut him short. 'He has no right to talk about treachery. When I tell you that on the 9th of August last year his Party voted with the Nazis against Brüning! Think of it—*they voted with the Nazis!*'

'You know less about politics than this table leg,' Ernst retorted. 'The last time your people had an idea was 1848. Do you want a social revolution or don't you? If you did, you'd see that the only one way to it now is by backing Hitler against your shuffling old women who think about nothing but staving it off.'

'You're out of your mind,' Lilo said with contempt.

We were so jammed together that it was impossible to wave an arm; yelling was the only outlet. The gentle Werner, sitting beside me, turned out to have a drill-sergeant's voice behind his quiet one.

'No, he is not,' he bawled, 'but he has nothing in his mind except orders from Moscow. Fight the Democrats! Yes, sir. Vote Nazi! Yessir, yessir.'

In the foolish hope of pouring oil, I said,

'I admit I don't understand why the government allows the Nazis to preach murder, and plot, quite openly, against the Republic. It seems an odd way to defend yourself.'

Werner smiled. 'Ah, I'll tell you why. We must get the Treaty revised. So—if your English government sees that the Nazis threaten us, they will help us—yes?'

Taken aback, I said, 'Do your leaders really believe that?'

'Of course. I think it is sensible.'

'And do *you* believe it?'

Ernst said drily, 'No, he doesn't believe it, he's not an idiot. Nor do they. The fact is they don't know what to do, so they do nothing and pretend they're being very clever and cunning. And let me tell you——'

'Let me *tell you*, if you think that you can bolshevize us you're mistaken. We shall fight you.'

It struck me, even then, as ominous that they thought they could quarrel with each other, using the Nazis as a weapon. I must have shown my discomfort. Ernst smiled charmingly and said,

'We have not made you feel at home. Wait a minute.'

He fiddled with the wireless set. Through a screeching storm of noises, a few words were suddenly audible: This afternoon their Majesties left London for... Everyone burst out laughing. Ilse Meyer, who had not opened her mouth during the quarrel, went out of the room and came back with a few sandwiches on a plate and handed them round, with a little air of anxiety...

For all her eagerness to embrace the world, Lilo was a loyal child of Berlin. She talked about it as though it were the centre of Europe, all roads led to it; it had the only swimming bath in which the artificial waves were as rough as at sea, the only museum with a complete reconstruction of an Assyrian palace, the only restaurant where each table was linked by telephone to all the others, the only production of the *Tales of Hoffmann* with a real horse and cab on the stage, standing outside a faithful model of the café where Hoffmann himself (or was it Offenbach?) spent his evenings, the only night club, open to all, whose habitués were inverts.

Werner was told off to take us there. He led us to a respectably ugly house, and into a room which would have been considered a little dull for a

Methodist tea. I had supposed that these places were kept up for the benefit of foreigners who had been assured that Berlin was the most immoral capital in Europe. Not a bit of it: the small tables round the dance floor were all occupied by stolid Germans and their wives or secretaries, 'negroes', Werner said: provincials. The cabaret began at half-past eleven, with a plump woman in blue satin, opulent shoulders and arms bare and powdered, dancing politely with another, younger. But for their rouge and carefully plucked eyebrows they might have been a schoolgirl and her dancing-mistress—and but for the final gesture which revealed them, very delicately, as men. The next turn was a slender girlish creature, all but naked, her dress cut down at the back to the cleft of narrow white buttocks. She, he, danced alone, showing rounded thighs.

'He is alone,' the head waiter said, 'because his lover does not allow him a partner. See, he is here every night, watching.'

The elderly gentleman who might have been a civil servant rose at the end of the dance, bent to kiss the young man's hand, and escorted him to a table. My boredom was now intolerable, and I insisted on going home. Werner was distressed.

'Oh, but you haven't seen the other place, where the women wear men's clothes!'

Heaven forbid. Outside, his back against the wall, the man was still holding out the limp copy of a magazine he had been holding—how long? all day?—for several days. He made no effort to attract attention: perhaps the effort needed to stand upright in the icy wind absorbed all his energy, even the energy to move, to turn towards us eyes, I saw now, covered with a grey film, like frost...

'This evening,' Lilo said, 'I am going to show you the true Germany. Well, perhaps it is the true Germany. You will see.'

As I stepped inside it, the flat in Charlottenburg greeted me like an old friend. For some moments I could not imagine why it was so warmly reassuringly familiar. Suddenly, I realized how I knew it and where I had seen it before—not I, but my mother. It was one she had described to me, belonging to the German agent of the Prince Line in—was it Odessa?—where, a very young woman, she spent several afternoons. It was her first voyage, and everything amused her, so that she forgot none of it, the German woman herself, so dowdy and submissive and good-humoured, the living-room where all that could be was overstuffed, cushions, quilted curtains, sandwiches, and the room itself so crammed with chairs, tables, sideboards, a piano, whole services of china on the walls, every plate and jug carrying its warning— Gluttony is a vice of the eyes—Drink only with friends—Discretion gives long life—that once seated you could not rise without disturbing a table loaded to the edge with family photographs, or a brass bowl, or a lampstand in the form of a Nubian slave or a shepherdess embracing her shepherd.

Nothing was missing here except the warning signals and the Nubian.

My mother must, I reckoned, have been in Odessa for the first time in the eighteen-eighties, half a century ago.

It was a delicious evening. Dr Walter, an elderly professor of music, and his plump lively wife had chosen among their friends the three who could entertain us without needing a word of English: the young Jewish violinist from the Schauspielhaus orchestra who liked playing Bach, the old singer who could take the top notes in the Jewel Song almost without faltering, the not very young actress who was still—a little affair of jealousy—being given only minor parts but could, and did, recite long passages of Schiller with all the pleasure in the world.

A table had been covered with plates of sausages, salad, cream cakes. Between Schiller, Bach, a good-tempered debate about Webern with explanatory passages on piano or violin, noisy gossip about the theatre, and roars of homeric laughter, they ran to the table to swallow another mouthful, sang, shouted, and slapped each other on the bottom. The room was over-heated, shabbier than when my young mother knew it in Odessa (or Hamburg), but the gaiety, good humour, gluttony, that vice of the eyes, the sentiments, the un-spiritual spiritual values, the pieties, were unchanged.

The true Germany? Well, perhaps—but fifty or a hundred years out of its time.

They had a past, these warm-hearted friendly people, but had they a future? Hadn't I, that very afternoon, seen the future in the form of a boy of twelve or thirteen, glaring at me, hands clenched, repeating furiously,

'We young ones didn't sign that Treaty. No!'

'He's only been like this since he passed into High School,' his mother sighed. 'I try to teach him better.'

The true Germany? No other capital city I knew gave me this sense of improvisation and uncertainty: it was like a house the week before the family is due to move out because of an impending bankruptcy or divorce—dust, cracks in the ceiling, nothing quite in its proper place, an ugly feeling of exposure. As in a cubist portrait, all the fragments of a dismembered body were there. The disorder, the chaos, the distortion, had its significance, like a fever patient's chart.

It never entered my head that a people so in love with exaggeration, so quick to turn everything into an object of hatred or worship, so little in possession of itself, might begin to dream of possessing Europe.

Nor that the young ghosts haunting the fields on either side of the Marne would shortly be outnumbered by millions of ghosts—even of children, of women hushing a child as they carried it into the gas chamber. (But who could have imagined Auschwitz?)

Nor that the separate wills murdering each other in the Berlin streets were the shadow thrown by the passion for collective self-assertion, the romantic distaste for tolerance, compromise, individual freedom, which tolls through German history. Nor that that history has been made up of stupefyingly sudden changes, splendour to misery, empire to the most wretched anarchy. But I knew no history. Anyone knows more now who has seen the defeated despairing Germany of the twenties turn itself by an immense effort of cunning, tenacity, hypocrisy, moral and physical energy, shameless brutality, into the Reich which dictated to Europe, drove the Russian army to the suburbs of Moscow, only to collapse in ruins. And in fifteen years rise again, still mutilated, but rich and proud of itself. A country of diabolical energy where anything, any contrast, any self-contradiction, is to be expected.

On the 13th of March a mixed lot of Germans, Americans, English, waited in the offices of the *Chicago Daily News* in Berlin for the results of the Presidential election. The Germans, all members of the Centre or the moderate Left, were praying for Hindenburg. During the day I had noticed Communists and Nazis standing together outside the polling booths, almost arm in arm, shaking collecting boxes. This truce was not reassuring. The patient might die even if the operation were a success.

Sitting at an end of the long crowded room, as close as she could get to the loud-speaker, Lilo took down the figures as they came through, her cheeks flaming, red on white. She was by many years the youngest creature in the room.

'Ah—' a radiant smile—'*absolute Mehrheit*'—a frown and a heavy heaving sigh like a puppy—'*keine absolute Mehrheit.*'

One of the English journalists, Harrison Brown—humane, single-minded, pleasantly selfish and, except for Lilo, the happiest adult I have ever known—teased her.

'Your socialist comrade Hindenburg! Doesn't it ever occur to you that there is something very wrong with your party when it has to call out its followers in support of a reactionary old general, as stupid as a boot, and in the pockets of the East Prussian Junkers? Step by step you've retreated—into their arms! How do you like going to the poll hand in hand with Junkers? What good do you expect it to do you?'

Pushing her yellow hair back, Lilo said vehemently,

'He has sworn to uphold the constitution, he is a German general, not a devil.'

When we left, at two in the morning, Hindenburg's election was certain. A wind from the steppes was driving livid clouds overhead. The streets were empty, even of shadows, since the lights had been turned off. We groped our way in darkness.

'Are you sure,' I asked, 'that you can trust Hindenburg?'

'Of course. He has *sworn.*'

I was leaving Berlin next day. 'Well—you can always come to England.'

She laughed. 'What do you think can happen here? This good old man is a rock. Perhaps, as H.B. says, he is stupid, but what does that matter when there are a hundred men to be clever for him, and millions like me to prop him up. I'm not afraid.'


## CHAPTER 64


FROM BERLIN, the rootless alienated city, to my quiet house on the edge of Whitby, a long step backwards in time. If I had had the sense I should have seen it—correctly—as a rocky ledge out of reach of the tide racing to cut us all off.

I am absolutely convinced that I became a novelist owing to a serious misunderstanding with myself. But I doubt whether I can now find my way back to the source of the profound sense of failure, of spiritual dishonesty—in a word, treachery—that seizes me when I think about my novels. It lies a great way farther back than 1930, though that was the year it rose to the surface—a tormenting sense of dryness, *accidie*, futility. My mind, that clumsy dancing bear, went on inventing incidents and characters with fluent ease, but the labour of writing them down filled me with such mortal boredom that but for my insane obstinacy I should have given up.

Obstinacy and an equally insane belief that I had been born to be happy. Since I was no good now for anything but writing novels I decided, with a ridiculous excitement, that I must write better ones.

In civilizing a barbarian the danger is that something, some vital energy, irreplaceable, will be enervated at the same time as the barbarism. Possibly I educated myself above my intellectual level—*quelle blague pas sérieuse*!

A note in the margin of a book reminds me that it was on the 25th of October, 1930, that I began my first attempt to write well—that is, with unromantic plainness. *That Was Yesterday* was meant to be an account of what happened to me between going to Kettering in the autumn of 1913 and setting off to London at the end of 1918, a little over five years. To avoid the odium of I, I, I, I wrote it in the third person, and omitted or changed the order of events to give it the form of a work of imagination. But I did not leave out events humiliating to me, and did not try to soften my own follies, failures, and the atrocious flaws in my character.

Timid and dishonest in company, the mere act of writing, alone in a room, forces me to be honest, and unconcerned to the point of recklessness.

The effort to discover what, during these five years, I had become, gave me back, for the time being, my pleasure in writing. It would disturb me to re-read this so-called novel, but it is a good book, one of the few in which I feel pride.

(Gingerly turning the pages, I have been hooked by this paragraph: 'At this moment, she felt sure that she would do something in the world. "Deliver us from temptation" should run: Make us to grow old, and our muscles to slacken, and our conceit to drop from us. Cause the young men to sharpen their wits on us. Bind burdens on us and make us afraid to run. Make one day like another and the nights the divisions between the days. Make us not to care.')

At last, I told myself gaily, I am on the right road.

It did not occur to me that I was on the point of disciplining myself out of one market without earning the attention and respect of my equals.

With smiling kindness, Charles Morgan told me,

'My dear Margaret, you know far too much about human nature, and too little about making what you know palatable. You don't give your imagination room to breathe, you dissect, and you write too many books too quickly.'

True, true. But I have no private income and I am a spendthrift. The worst of an income that rises and falls with the fury of a spring tide is that it is fatally easy to give away five hundred pounds, or spend it on going to France, since the next tide may—or may not—cover the rocks again.

None of this adds up to unhappiness. I have been madly happy for days at a time, and placidly engrossed for months or weeks. If only, I shall say to myself, when I am dying of not being able to stay alive any longer, you had had a little more coolness and foresight.

*That Was Yesterday* ran to nearly two hundred thousand words. (Who would have thought that my veins had so much blood in them?) In a recoil, I turned to the idea of writing a series of very short novels (*nouvelles* or *récits*, depending on the manner: we have no term for these forms), tenuously linked. Each was to be a portrait of a woman at the turning point, early or late, of her life, composed with the utmost scepticism about the feelings (love, friendship, loyalty, etc) we all profess, the self-deceptions on which we all depend: each was to convey through its form the essence of the character.

I wrote the first, *A Day Off*, with intense pleasure—pleasure in doing what I could do better than anything else, creep through the corridors of a brain and the veins of a heart. And unfailing pleasure in the view from my window. I had only to lift my eyes from the sheet of ruled paper under my hand to see the hill, the road climbing it, the edge of the moor, the wind-bitten trees on the horizon. No other scene in the world has, as that did, filled every crevice of my soul.

Ah, fool that I was to leave it and make an alienated city of my life.

It was not the first time that my craving for change, for a worldly life (something for which I have not a rag of talent) kicked my far deeper need of solitude into the cellar. Nor the last.

Was it about *A Day Off* or about a second *récit*, *Delicate Monster*, that R. H. Tawney said to me, 'You write like a devil!'

The second, I think, but I am no longer sure, although I could not have been better pleased if I had been given the O.M.

*A Day Off* is perhaps the only genuinely imaginative book I have written. No, there is one other, published under a false name. Both were failures.

Telling myself that I had been rash to suppose I was capable of great things as a novelist, I began to write an account of my near ancestry and youth: I wanted, before it was covered by the sand, to record a world that had been destroyed in 1914. Begun in my room in Whitby, *No Time Like The Present* was finished in a London flat. But by the time I reached 1914 in it, I had had a change of mind or heart, and I filled the rest of a short book with my opinions. These were nothing if not violent, and it was an error in tactics to add them to an otherwise innocent book which had every chance of pleasing by its polite simplicity.


# CHAPTER 65


BEFORE WE HAD BEEN LIVING in Whitby six months, Guy was writing from London: 'It is a fatal thing to settle down... I don't like London, but I think we must come back.' Yet in Whitby he worked no less hard than I. He was writing *A Passionate Prodigality*—one of the half-dozen finest books about the first war—planning his admirable life of Beckford, and editing a series of fine editions for Eyre and Spottiswoode. None of this satisfied him. I did not, then, realize that he would never be content, never be less than dissatisfied with himself and his work, a maniac for perfection as I for changes. Had I realized it, I might not have been infected so easily by his discontent with Whitby. It is just possible. Heaven knows I need very little to start up my restlessness. But Whitby is in my bones.

And, I had my view, that incomparable view of hill and moor road.

The surface began cracking in all directions. After many enquiries I had started Bill at a new public school, chosen because it was going to pay attention to biology, in which at this time he was interested, and because its founder had been the ruling genius of an older school. Genius he was and, I think, a bit of a humbug. None the worse for that—a touch of the charlatan is as necessary to a great schoolmaster as to an eloquent preacher or a politician.

In the summer of 1930 when he came home, I thought him wretchedly thin and listless; the panic always at the back of my mind started up, and although I listened calmly when the doctor advised keeping him at home for a term and talked about over-strain, overgrowth, and a threatened lung, I lost what little common-sense I had about him, not much, and decided to send him to Switzerland. It was a bad move. The English school in Switzerland was expensive and not even good. It made him strong and tough, and taught him to ski, but little else. What side of his intellect went on growing grew of itself—acute powers of observation, a habit of accuracy. For the rest, it became the mind of a healthy savage. I could have found some more sensible way of toughening him.

One of my misfortunes is that air of competence which persuades all but my most malicious friends that I know what I am about, when in fact I am totally without sense of direction, or much other sense. Very soon after I had taken my fifteen-year-old son to his Swiss school, I began planning, with suppressed impatience, another change. Guy was turning back to his first love, history, and my scheming brain threw up the idea that to work for a degree at the London School of Economics would give him the solid training he lacked. As an idea, it was suspiciously reasonable.

In the autumn of 1932 I rented a small flat in London, in St John's Wood, for three years. At the end of that time, I told myself airily, I can think again.

My mother, half resigned to the restlessness of her first-born, half sad-dened, pretended to believe that it was only a passing upheaval. When I took her her pre-publication copy of *That Was Yesterday*, she wished it luck, warmly—no more than I do could she feel that novel-writing is a safe way of living—and began to talk about Dorothy.

Without warning, she said,

'I wish you weren't going to London. I shall miss you, terribly.'

I hardened my heart against the pain that made a child of me. 'We must go, for Guy's work. I'm not selling the house, remember. We'll come back every vacation.'

'Yes, I know,' she said in an absent voice.

Her eyes stared through me. I had a sensation of emptiness, as when, at night, the darkness on one side of the road you are climbing begins to be the darkness of an unseen precipice. Her voice sent back an echo from it. What did she think about during the hours she sat in her window, hands folded? Not all the time about my young sister? About Harold? About voyages—the wild strawberries growing by the fjord in Norway, the beggar in Alicante, without arms or legs, rolling to her feet in a ball of rags, the agent's wife in Odessa, at whose submissiveness she had laughed unkindly, Vera Cruz and the scorching plague-carrying heat?

To distract her from the thought of my leaving her, I asked,

'Did you enjoy voyages?'

'I didn't care for the ship,' she said in a simple voice. 'And the long weeks at sea, often a bad time of the year, and no fresh milk, and quite often towards the middle of the trip there were maggots in the food, and your father hating fresh air, keeping the port closed and smoking his vile cigars. What I liked was going ashore.' Her voice changed, became younger, the smiling insolent voice of a girl. 'I liked Antwerp. I shall never see it again.'

'I'll take you there next May.'

'No. I'm too tired now.'

'We can travel comfortably, you know. Not like we used to.'

She smiled. 'We'll see,' she said, without belief.

She was right. We never did go to Antwerp again together. And when after thirty years I went there to look for her she was nowhere to be found. I counted on my body to recognize the corner of a street, a café, a shop window reflecting the silhouette of the captain's young wife, but for once it failed me.

The September day we left for London was cold and cloudily sunny. In the few minutes as the train drew out past the harbour, I felt myself isolated by a barrier of ice from every living human being, including the husband facing me. Like a knot of adders uncoiling themselves, one departure slid from another behind my eyes—journeys made feverish by unmanageable longings and ambitions, night journeys in war-time, the darkened corridors crammed with young men in clumsy khaki, smoking, falling asleep, journeys with a heavy baby in one arm. At last I came to the child sitting in a corner of a third-class carriage, waiting, silent, tense with anxiety, for the captain's wife to return from the ticket-office. A bearded gentleman in a frock-coat—the stationmaster—saunters up to the open door and says, smiling, something she makes no attempt to hear. Her mother walks lightly across the platform. 'Ah, there you are, Mrs Jameson. Your little girl was afraid you weren't coming,' he said amiably. Nothing less amiable than Mrs Jameson's coldly blue eyes turned on him, and cold voice.

'Nonsense. My child is never afraid.'

Not true...

# PART II
## *The Glittering Fountains*

*O play the glittering fountains of the heart.*
*Here music ends...*

H. B. MALLALIEU

# CHAPTER I

IN LONDON I RUSHED headlong into a life of seeing people, a great many people. I had taken a service flat, with a restaurant downstairs. Nothing simpler than to lift the telephone and tell the head waiter, 'I shall have four, six, eight, guests to dinner.' In the minuscule kitchen, barely room for me to stand inside and close the door, I prepared our breakfast and made coffee for our dinner guests. The food in the restaurant was frightful—like the bills at the end of the month.

Of the twenty-four hours in the day I may have slept for six; the rest were terribly occupied: writing a novel, reviewing (without pay) for A. R. Orage, running about London to political meetings, reading, to educate myself, economics and books on foreign affairs, and talking—no, not talking, listening.

It was at this time that I began the habit, kept up for many years, until it began to bore me, of writing down every night the conversations I had listened to during the day. Only certain conversations. Not any that were merely scandalous (these I buried in a corner of my mind, not deeply, but with no idea of resurrection). Only those attached to one of my obsessions.

Over twenty years or so I recorded many thousands of spoken words. I shall destroy the lot when I have finished this book. (Destroyed on the 26th of March, 1965.)

Lying awake—now that I am old—listening in the first light to a bird singing alone, I feel that only the thinnest least material of veils hangs between me and a meadow of my childhood; the wet grass bright with orchis and cuckoo-pint, the running stream, the clear pale northern sky and cool air, are within a single step.

To turn back into the thirties is infinitely less easy.

The survivors of my generation did not—then—realize that they had also survived an age and a world. Between us and that vanished world stretched four years of completely useless butchery, a wide furrow driven across Europe, crushing out bloodily the energy, genius, intentions and plain decent hopes of millions of young men. Those left were survivors in a strict sense, men living *beyond*—at the other side of a closed frontier. They lived, most of them, ordinary, sometimes highly successful lives, on this side of a country peopled only by ghosts, this side of a nearly incommunicable experience seared into their brains. The few who made the effort to force their experience into words would be the first to say that their account was incomplete.

Neither did we realize that what we were living through was an interregnum, not a new age.

The interregnum lasted some twenty years, traversed a series of conferences held all over Europe, where ageing men made the decisions which decided little except the death a few years later of their sons and the collapse into scorched rubble of their cities, saw the revival of torture as a method of government and the establishment of police states, broke down into another prolonged slaughter, and came to a sudden stop in 1945. Then, only then, the new age opened.

Looked at from this distance (1963), the interregnum itself splits in half. The twenties, for all their disorder, were lively with ideas, dreams, hopes, experiments. The illusion of freedom was intoxicating. When the change came it was like nothing so much as waking up in a grey light, with memories, half dream, half real, of a gay party, the only signs of it a deplorable muddle and a great many used wineglasses.

It was not so abrupt. But a moment did come—roughly at the end of the feverishly energetic twenties—when the moral and intellectual climate changed. Almost before they knew what was happening to them, writers found themselves being summoned on to platforms and into committee-rooms to defend society against its enemies. Writers in Defence of Freedom, Writers' Committee of the Anti-War Council, Congress of Writers for the Defence of Culture, Writers' Section of the World Council against Fascism... I forget the names.

The impulse that turned so many of us into pamphleteers and amateur politicians was neither mean nor trivial. The evil we were told off to fight was really evil, the threat to human decency a real threat. I doubt whether any of us believed that books would be burned in England, or eminent English scholars, scientists, writers, forced to beg hospitality in some other country. Or that, like Lorca, we might be murdered. Or tortured and then killed in concentration camps. But all these things were happening abroad, and intellectuals who refused to protest were in effect blacklegs. In this latest quarrel between Galileo and the Inquisition they were on the side of the Inquisition.

During the same decade, the cancerous poverty of the unemployed became, for many writers, what Quakers call a concern. (It still seems to me that there is little to choose between the ancient custom of exposing unwanted babies and ours of allowing an accident of birth to decide which child shall be carefully nurtured and which grow up in a slum.) Social historians of 2930 will ask why it should have stung the consciences of writers and other artists just when it did. Why, after all, should they fret about social justice? The savage injustices and cruelty of classical Greece, Elizabethan England, Renaissance Europe, did not distract them from their work.

Where energy and salt have not been choked out of a society, the writer can breathe freely. In the thirties, millions of half-fed hopeless men, eating their hearts out, gave off a moral stench which became suffocating.

There really was a stench. On one side Dachau, on the other the 'distressed areas' with their ashamed workless men and despairing women. Not many English writers had the hardness of heart, the frivolity, the religious certainty, the (why not?) noble egoism—noble or ignoble, the gesture is precisely the same—to hurry past, handkerchief to nose, intoning, 'My concern is with my art, what troubles are troubling the world are not my business; let those whose business it is attend to it, I must be about my own...'

By coming to London when I did, I moved from the margin into the centre at the very moment when the current dragging writers into active politics was gathering force. It was my road to Damascus. The heavens opened, and I saw that two principles were struggling for mastery of the future. On one side the idea of the Absolute State, with its insistence on total loyalty to the words and gestures of authority, its belief in the moral beauty of war, its appeal to the *canaille*: Germany awake, kill, hate, Sieg Heil, and the rest of it. On the other all that was still hidden in the hard green seed of a democracy which allowed me freedom to write and other women freedom to live starved lives on the dole.

In 1933 this explained for me everything in sight. I had no need to think further about the future, the destiny of man, or my own. I had my key.

The error—mine—was that I tried to open everything with it, beginning with my novels.

Moreover, I never succeeded in stifling in myself completely the promptings of a shrewd nonconformist.

For a long time, several years, I lived in a condition of violent self-contradiction. I was clear in my mind about the enemy. And absolutely clear that I was being urged to defend freedom by (among others) persons who knew much less about freedom than the policemen standing on the fringes of our meetings eyeing with the same stolid curiosity the political virgins and their seducers.

The fingers of the puppet-masters and the strings jerking us were perfectly visible. I knew I was being used. I knew I was wanted on committees because a pen in competent hands is a tool. When I stood on a platform and sang the Internationale—or would have sung it if I had not been as tuneless as a crow—I had no delusions about the doctrine of Communism as practised in Russia. In this I was more clear-sighted than some of my friends.

(Do not let us forget that the puppets could bleed: there were writers among the five hundred volunteers of the International Brigade killed in Spain—John Cornford, Julian Bell, Christopher Caudwell, Ralph Fox. True, these—since they had no prudence about risking their talents and their skins—might have died in the greater war they hoped to avert. But, at the age they were, a few more years is a long time.)

'Do you know,' an awed fellow-writer said to me, 'that Leonov and two other well-known Soviet writers were ordered to report to a factory in Siberia last month?'

'Why?'

'To write in praise of it, of course.'

'And you approve that? How is it better and less debauching than being ordered to write advertisements?'

(Or for that matter, I thought, than sitting in this damned room trying to draft a manifesto.)

'To have the privilege of working for the only free and rationally governed country in the world! You're being perverse, my dear.'

She was perfectly sincere. And certainly Leonov's was a more tolerable servitude than being ordered to hate liberals and Jews and acquiesce in their death by torture. (I knew less than I thought about Stalin's Russia.) And less sickening than the way politicians were refusing to *see* the barbarians on the move again at the other side of the Rhine. So—one of my counterfeit selves went on dumbly mouthing the Internationale on anti-Fascist platforms.

Put to it, I might have said that if my throat must be cut I had sooner it were done on behalf of Communism than by a Fascist. (This state of mind shows how little faith I had then in the triumph of that liberal humanism under whose banner I had enlisted.)

If I looked closely enough, I might see that what made me loathe Fascism was only my hatred of authority, only a mute rebellion against my violently feared and loved mother.

Perhaps the coldly precise reasons for rejecting a vile doctrine came after the instinctive revulsion? But does that invalidate them? Not at all. It is seldom that writers have so plain and comprehensible, if vile, bestial, and bloodyminded an enemy as Fascism.

The amount of time and energy I spent on reading and writing pamphlets, and attending committees and political meetings, was prodigious. And they bored me! I felt asphyxiated by the jargon that was beginning to take the place of criticism: it made the noise in my ears of water running over stones. Heaven knows how many hours I spent swallowing yawns in the company of writers talking about the materialist conception of history—familiarly, the M.C.H.—as if it were a formula for judging and even writing books.

A friend not to be suspected of liking Fascism, Henry Harwood, tried by smiling mockery to convince me that I was wasting my time.

'What good do you think you're doing with your politics compared with the good you might do by getting on with your own job? Your conscience? You haven't a conscience, my dear, you simply like interfering.'

He was right—and unjust—and (since he was talking rationally to a monster of unreason) might have saved his breath. My own hard mistrustful Yorkshire nature, my upbringing in a society hostile to change, convinced me, secretly, that our protests were completely futile and certain to be defeated. An irrational instinct, a voice out of my childhood, deeper in me, tougher, older, than scepticism and *Angst*, retorted: Useless? Yes, if you say so. *But it can be tried.*

The loathing I felt for what was being done by barbarians who had taken over the Europe of Goethe, Dante, Vico, the very heart of Christian humanism and the classical Renaissance, was genuine. Concern may be only another name for the passion to interfere, but—such as I am—I could have done no other.

During those years I did not speak my whole mind either to friends or political allies. I recall—I have forgotten the date—a meeting between English writers and four Russians who had been brought to London by the organizers of friendship between our countries. Friendship has as many faces as uses. The face turned by the English wore a smile of eager good faith, curiosity and naive willingness to make amiable signs to the country of Tolstoy, Chekhov, and the rest. The Russians did not converse, even through their interpreter. They made statements. Alexander Fadayev, author of a novel which had sold, he said, smiling, five million copies, made a speech. He told us that the qualities demanded of a Russian novel were realism and optimism; in Soviet Russia, since a society which is advancing has only hopes, this means that he need only report truthfully on the life round him. Subjective literature is bad, because distorted by personal ties, and in any case egotistical—that is, worthless.

One of our exiled writers, a German, was simple or malicious enough to say, 'Surely it is sometimes difficult? For me—to be forced to write in a particular attitude, however noble, or socially useful—would be boring. At the best. At the worst it would choke me.'

'On the contrary,' said Fadayev, 'I feel boundlessly free; I have a continent to write about, and the exciting advance in it of socialism, new cities are being built, a new happiness, new progressive men and women.' He spread his arms. 'With thousands of miles of progress to move round in, I am infinitely freer than any English writer.'

I had been nerving myself to ask him about a writer fewer people, at that time, knew. I stood up.

'What is Boris Pasternak writing now?'

Fadayev turned on me eyes so clear that they seemed holes, through which I saw a thousand miles—at least a thousand—of a dry cold country.

'Oh, Pasternak doesn't write now, he is busy on translations. He is very much happier.'

Even supposing I had had the contumacy to argue in face of the dis-approval of the organizers of the meeting, it seemed, for Pasternak's sake, imprudent: I sat down, and closed my ears.

In twenty-five or thirty years' time, I thought, either I shall be translating (or telling hopeful lies in five million copies) for a living, or the whole of this debate will seem meaningless. No one in 1960 will believe that an English writer in his senses could ever ask himself whether literature ought to serve the projects of the State and its Jesuitical priest, the M.C.H., or whether on the contrary he is bound, by a fierce inner command, to indulge his cruelly egotistical passion for uncovering the motives, stratagems, comic, foolish or agonizing thoughts of single human beings in the act of love, hate, treachery, murder, rejoicing, lust, death, ecstasy.

I had an impulse to get up and bolt... What the devil am I doing here?...

Apart from being secretly bored, I had other reasons for feeling uncom-fortable in the company of politicizing poets and novelists. I shared their views about war and Fascism, but what they said often outraged me, or woke an uncouth jeering self I was too timid to let loose. I was shocked when a well-to-do novelist said at a dinner-party that one advantage of doing socialist propaganda was the chances it offered to get inside workers' houses—'to get the background right'. It's not her fault, I reflected, that she doesn't know and can't imagine what her kitchen looks and smells like to a poor woman when she lifts the blind at six in the morning on a dirty grate and the ring of rust on the stove, and can't *see* the woman's nail scraping the inside of a pan, or the gesture of her hand sifting ashes or setting on the table the little cake she has bought her ill-fed child for a treat. Not her fault, but, my God, the abysmal ignorance and silliness of supposing that she will discover anything by going to stare.

But I did not say this. I sat as dumb as a carp.

I did not even say that I saw no virtue in the much talked-of 'proletarian novel', that latest weakest version of the naturalist's 'slice of life'.

A comfortably placed poet, fifteen years younger than I was, explaining that when he thought of the poor he felt guilty, made me grin in my sleeve. The misery and injustice of poverty, the slums, the mean dole, made me blazingly angry. But guilt? I had brushed the edges of poverty myself, and his metaphysical distress bored me.

The one occasion when I spoke frankly did me no good. It was at a meeting, in a private house, of some committee summoned to draft a pamphlet in
support of... to protest against... I forget. One of the young men I suspected
of carrying a copy of *The Boy's Book of Civil War, or How to Build a Barricade*
was talking about the benefits to a writer of joining the Communist Party.
(He joined it himself—for a few days.)

'One will have the moral satisfaction of being able to look a comrade
in the eye instead of skulking, head down, past chaps standing in the rain
selling the *Daily Worker*, or picketing a factory.'

Exasperated beyond the diffidence which makes me incapable of sustained
argument among people I know too little to be certain they are harmless—
my brain moves only when I am alone, pen in hand, and three or four clear
hours in front of me—I said,

'Is that what you think? Don't deceive yourself. Communism is no go in
this middle class country, and even if it were they don't want your help. Nor
mine. Don't imagine you'll turn into a revolutionary by going to meetings
in shabby rooms and addressing the others as comrade. You're not their
comrade.'

'I'm afraid you rather miss the point,' he said kindly.

I shut up.

Walking home, I passed through all the stages, very familiar, of discontent
with myself. My heart beat so quickly that I felt suffocated. The truth, I told
myself, is that you are not fit to go into company...

As I always do at these moments, I retreated into the last time in my life
when I was wholly at ease—as a poor student in London. What do these
solemn neo-romantics matter to me? Whom do I love? My son, my husband,
my mother, at most three others. The rest of the world can hang itself.

I felt the crazy gaiety that always follows my black moments.

That night I had one of the dreams I remember. I was in a room, vaguely
a café, with someone indistinct. I knew that he was dead. Class 1914, he said
smiling. I had a terrible feeling of anxiety. We ought to keep together, I told
him. He laughed and said: What is left of the company will advance in loose
formation—or not advance. I shall advance, I said. But he laughed again, with
heartbreaking kindness, and said gaily: Count on me in any personal way,
but don't expect me to turn socialist with you. That's all moonshine. You're

not their comrade, you're mine but not theirs... In the dream, I thought: But *I* said that... The light gay friendly voice went on: A new age is no good to me, my dearest. I shan't understand it and I shan't like it; Class 1914 was a damned fine class and it lived in a fine world. Hear me, I'm bragging, I know what England was like in 1913. You can keep the change. Comrades! I've s-seen comrades! I'll tell you something: the world you're part of, bone of, is finished. You believe in reason, you believe you can argue people into tolerance and goodwill. I tell you, my girl, that dream is as dead as I am. The new age is being prepared by unreason, to be brought in with violence. In that day reasonable people will be swept aside. This is something you don't know yet; you'll know it soon enough and you won't like it. This isn't the world I was born into, you'll say. Nor will it be. My love, your world's finished.

For less than a minute I saw his hands on the edge of the table. Then the dream vanished. I found I had been crying in my sleep...

The young Left-wing writers of the thirties were unlucky in so far as, thanks to the Second War, they became middle-aged and prudent without passing through a normal period of maturing powers: one to become a virtuoso in voluntary exile, another bedding down in academic exercises, a third in the barren world of international conferences and semi-literary politics. Today's respected *conférencier* is not as quixotic and engaging a human being as yesterday's histrionic young ass, but he is not more of a defaulter than the rest of us.

It would be neither perceptive nor decent to mock the comrades of the thirties. Their attraction to Communism was better than a literary fashion— although it was that, too. It was the outward and visible sign of a spiritual discomfort, distantly kin to that which drove Tolstoy into trying to live like a peasant, and, in every generation, drives a few generous-minded or thin-skinned members of the comfortable classes to give practical effect to their disgust with injustice and misery.

Why Communism? A complex of reasons: the *grande lueur de l'est*; the obvious weakness of social democracy; the greater logic and vigour of Marxism compared with the pliant doctrines of official English socialism; the attraction of a discipline (I offer you blood, sweat, tears, and the rest of it).

When the Spanish war broke in July 1936, and the democracies trimmed and lost the wind, Communism seemed *the* opponent of Fascism. In effect...

in effect the fierce enthusiasm, the brave generous hopes, the courage, the young deaths, are not cancelled by the ugliness of the Party's tactics in Spain and elsewhere.

## CHAPTER 2

T HE SUDDEN—only apparently sudden—volte-face of leaving Whitby did not only plunge me into politics; it swung me round the compass as a writer.

After my Damascus vision, when I 'understood' everything, I understood that the two novels, *That Was Yesterday*, and *A Day Off*, which I had imagined were the start for me of a new truthful way of writing, were no good. Not that they were worthless, but they lacked, heaven help me, *social significance*.

This portentous phrase stupefied me. I had enough sense left not to translate it as the proletarian novel (that abortion), but it distracted me from my own narrow ravishingly subjective (egotistical) road.

Not that I should ever have drifted into the fashionable—is it still fashionable?—heresy of the 'pure' novel, in which form, composition, have the supreme importance they have in a painting. Brought up on the northern sagas and Dickens, I could not have swallowed anything so prudish and genteel as a theory of criticism which demonstrated that Tolstoy, author of 'large loose baggy monsters', full of 'queer elements of the accidental and the arbitrary' is a lesser artist than Henry James. Since the conclusion was absurd, there was a flaw in the argument. I felt certain that any novelist who starts from the impulse to create a style, to impose *himself, se créer sa propre esthétique*, has begun to separate himself from his age. And that, carried too far, this separation must end in sterility and the breakdown of communication. But between this respectable belief and my new passionate conviction that only society, only the crisis, was worth writing about lay an abyss I did not even see.

Like all reformers (including self-reformers), I set about hacking down the idols. No more atmosphere, I said, no evocations of rain and moonlight, even by a word, no 'inward landscapes', no peeling of the onion to reach the core of an emotion, no stream of consciousness, that famous stream we pretend to see flowing as we pretend that the water moves under Lohengrin's swan, no aesthetic, moral, or philosophical comment.

This neo-naturalism was as suited to me as his false nose to a clown.

The paradox of my life, which I am only now (1963) learning to see through, is that the genuine passions I indulged (hatred of war and injustice) did me as much damage as those I suppressed (violent hatred of a domestic life, love of change and gaiety). I was genuinely fascinated by the spectacle of a society in transition and convulsions. Even by its ugliness. From that I concluded passionately and blindly that the novelist ought to be a receiving station for voices rising from every level of society: he must be like the magi who heard of a birth and set off in the dead of winter, the way long and the roads hard, to find the place. The modern novelist's country, I said, *is* this new birth and the hard bitter death it involves: in one way or another its disorder must show through his words—or else he is a literary deserter and a coxcomb, a liar.

From this year, 1932, I began to *construct* myself as a writer.

I was no longer satisfied to try modestly, sceptically, to find the quick of a human being. I thought of *A Day Off* as a self-indulgence.

I was seized by the ambition to write a *roman fleuve*. I had its title: *The Mirror in Darkness*, and my brain spawned like a salmon scores of characters, politicians, ex-soldiers, financier, industrialist, newspaper proprietor, scientist, writers, labour leader, embryo Fascist, the rich, the very humble, the ambitious who knew where they were going, and the confused, the ruined, the lost. They pressed on me so thickly that I was sure I should die before I had given each of them his drop of blood.

I had not noticed that a *roman fleuve* is not the same thing as a human comedy, that Proust and Balzac start from two clearly opposed modes of the imagination. My conception was flawed from the beginning. At times the mirror itself—identified with that Hervey Russell who is and is not myself—supplied the images and ideas; at others, a character unfolded independently, alone or in a web of action. Because of this initial failure of awareness, no single novel of the series had a clear centre, and a far from despicable mass of knowledge, energy, insight, foundered—sunk without trace...

Possibly the cold bestiality of the immediate past would today defeat even a Dostoevsky. Nothing in the liberal humanism we were taught to revere prepared us for it. No earlier novelist, when he looked attentively at the life of his time, or when he strained his ears to catch the note of the future, was faced by chaos. There were fixed points, or which seemed fixed. Language itself did not break in his hands. Words had not been emptied of their meaning: if prisoners were tortured it was not called re-education; the term *final solution* did not imply the methodical killing by slow suffocation of six million human beings, old and young. Even in war certain acts were held to be too obscene. Certain principles still had enough force in them to restrain men able to read Goethe and enjoy Mozart from conceiving and administering Auschwitz.

It would need an inhuman detachment to forget that we have barely emerged from the smoke of burning flesh hanging over Auschwitz into the shadow of the nuclear age. But the intimate movements of the heart, the torments of sexual jealousy, the pain of betrayal, the secret stratagems of ambition, the private hell of lovers, dreamers, and neurotics, are the disguise the serious novelist must adopt before he begins to write about his time.

In 1932 I did not know this...

I am plagued by memories I have not had the courage—or the immodesty—to try to manifest. In November 1945 I was in Prague, and saw an exhibition of drawings made, in Terezín, by the artist Bedrich Fritta, who died there. And I listened for two hours to a young Czech doctor who went into Terezín with a few officials of the International Red Cross on the 4th of May, 1945, while the Nazi guards were still in charge. He risked going in because he had heard there was typhus in the place. Afraid of the typhus, the guards let them in and fled—after shooting some sixty people as a last gesture of authority.

I have twenty photographs taken by the young doctor. They are not more ghastly than others I was shown earlier that year in Warsaw, but they record, a needle turning in the brain, a cruelty, an indifference, so atrocious that the imagination cannot bear for more than a short time what men, women, children suffered—some of them for years. The images—a pile of bodies caught in the indecent attitudes naked and half-clothed limbs take when they are thrown down like butchered pieces of flesh, a hand covering the ruined sex, a mouth open on the blackness of corruption, the bones of a young woman's body standing out in the purulent skin, the tiny limbs of a child drawn into its body—remain.

Terezín—Theresienstadt—was not a concentration camp, it was something differently unimaginable, a decent little garrison town which was turned into a transit camp for convoys of victims from all over Nazi Europe. It remained the simulacrum of a town—with hospital, mad-house, streets of barracks and houses, a baker's shop, a dress shop where second-hand clothes were bought and sold, lime trees, Town Hall, a restaurant, a coffee-house, a cinema, a theatre with numbered benches, a synagogue, a music-hall with singers, acrobats, a clown.

One day—for a day—it was given a new face, with flowers, whitewashed house-fronts, a welfare centre, a shop selling perfume, a *Lebensmittel*. For the benefit of a visitor from the Swiss Red Cross.

The convoys were halted at a station a mile away. From here the passengers walked, carrying their baggage. In a large badly-lit hall names were taken down before some of the newcomers were sent on to Auschwitz to be gassed, or to Mauthausen to be used up quickly in exhaustion and filth. Others were allowed to stay in the town, for a short or longer time. Or, if they were singularly lucky or rich enough to buy their reprieve, to the end. There are degrees of degradation even in hell: the few rich were allowed, encouraged, to use their money: they lived, as a very intelligent and charming young Jewish woman—her name, which I have forgotten, began with K—said, 'as at Deauville', in their own rooms, with some penniless inmate as a servant, buying food from the thriving black market. When it was known that, to make room, another batch of men and women—once, four thousand at a blow—was to be sent off to be exterminated, they could buy themselves off the list. Always at least one of the Jewish officials making the selection was corruptible.

'For money,' K. said, smiling, 'you could buy many things in Terezín, even life.'

The wages she earned as a servant bought a touch of comfort for her mother and young brother. Then she was sent to Auschwitz and her brother to Mauthausen. There was something she recalled with great pride, some trifle, I cannot remember it, a stroke of integrity in the man she fell in love with in Terezín and married three days before he, too, was sent to die in Mauthausen. Something he could not bring himself to do...

Like the *univers concentrationnaire* itself, Terezín would make sense to me if I could believe that it was devised by a wholly evil scientist anxious to fill out his knowledge of human nature by exposing millions of men and women to the extremity of pain and fear, to see what, to defend themselves, they would do. And what, finally, one of them chose to defend *in* himself by a refusal.

I looked long and closely at Fritta's forty-two drawings. The one that ran me through was of his infant daughter on her pot. It summed up what, in the bestiality of our age, is totally unforgivable—the violation of the innocent.

It is Dostoevsky's theme, I thought. How dare I touch it?

None the less, for a long time, years, I brooded over a book or a play laid in Terezín. It—Terezín—is, or was, an image of the human condition, a sealed world in which all the human virtues and vices, from the most abject treachery to the most genuinely modest self-sacrifice—doomed to be forgotten—had their chance to reach perfection. This book took possession of a whole level of my mind. For hours, days, I lived in a crowd, life-size, of its characters, not only the main personages of the drama, but the unnumbered others which no novel or play would have room for, but which existed. They became my familiars, I saw their eyes, their mouths, their gestures: the two women in the secondhand dress shop, the elder fingering hungrily a shabby fur, the other describing, for herself more than for her listener, the evening dress made for her eight years ago in Frankfurt by a half-French dressmaker, silver net, eighteen yards in the skirt alone, but a tight bodice, with no back, and a second dress in pinkish grey velvet she wore in winter that year; the girl and the skinny desperate boy looking for some place where they could join their bodies without being discovered; the mad mother of the little child on the pot; the bearded Jewish elder miserably or cunningly making his terms with the S.S. guard who lived, with his newly-married wife, in a villa near the ramparts and had two servants picked from a convoy for their air of vigour; the well-known clown making his jokes in the music-hall the evening before he was being sent to Auschwitz; the gesture of the man (moustache, yellowish face, long bony hands) piling the bodies on to the curiously shaped carts: they had sloping sides like the carts in French vineyards. And K. and her mother. The old woman survived Terezín. And because her young son had died in Mauthausen she could not forgive K. for coming back from Auschwitz.

'She has Terezín in her stomach,' K. said.

Why did I never write it?

Not because it was difficult and I was afraid of distorting an event almost past imagining. From a sort of shame. From pudor.

Had anyone who had not lived in that world the moral right to stare at it? Had I any right to press so much as a finger on the despair and nonchalance of the young, the panic-stricken baseness of the few rich, the courage of one woman, the creeping tide of insanity in another, the furtive sex, the innocence of the child on its little pot? I could not convince myself that I had.

Some future writer will be driven, as Dostoevsky was, to lay open in a novel unfathomed depths of the human possibility, led to them by what he is able to learn about Terezín and Auschwitz and the rest. I shall not now write it. Perhaps, surviving the death of my brain, a thought of mine will find its way into a cell of his.

## CHAPTER 3

EARLY IN 1933 I decided that at seventeen my son had wasted more than enough time in his Anglo-Swiss school, and I sent him, with some misgiving, to Göttingen, to live in the family of a retired professor. He stayed there until the end of May. Then—disturbed by a snapshot of him with a lock of hair across his forehead in imitation of the Führer's—I brought him home to be tutored for a year, although he insisted that nothing was happening at Göttingen, no one there had been persecuted. At that time, probably true.

There were only two bedrooms in the flat: I gave him mine, and slept in the living-room on an old Dutch day-bed, a very elegant piece of marquetry, too short to stretch out in comfort. For his six feet it would have been torment.

Even now, I cannot explain why I was never at ease with the idea that I had a child who was my own, not simply handed to me to cherish and bring up. By the time he was seven, he had learned that silence and a frown were enough to set me wondering anxiously what I could do to amuse him. He was an amiable child, but he would have been unnatural or a saint if he had not used his whip hand to get his own way. Almost always he got it. A vein of timidity ran through my love. In a moment of discouragement I tried to fathom why I felt this diffidence towards my own child. Because I want him to be pleased with me, I thought. Because of my unappeasable sense of an unfulfilled obligation.

He had rare bursts of talk when I caught sight of a speculative intellect hidden behind his one enduring passion. He wanted to fly.

He was going up to Cambridge in the autumn of 1934—to Trinity, which had accepted him after an interview, without an examination. In the meantime he wanted to take flying lessons.

'Now?'

'Why not? I'd like to have my A licence before I'm eighteen.'

I gave in. He was pleased. For less than an instant a child looked at me through his eyes, made a signal I could not read, and was gone.

For several hours I have been trying to compare our fear of war now (1963) with the fear that slowly submerged our minds during the thirties. (In 1934 an American reviewer, a woman, complained that 'like so many English writers, Storm Jameson seems unable to outgrow the war.' I retorted that the war we could not outgrow was not the one we had survived but the one we were expecting.) There is one overwhelming difference. The climate of fear is much the same, for at least three decades, but in the thirties we were facing an imaginable terror, one we could look at without falling, like Christian in Giant Despair's stinking dungeon, into a swoon. Today the imagination is stunned, paralysed. We look into a darkness without issue. What lies at the other side of nuclear war? A human remnant, mutilated in its seed?

As a writer with a mortal distaste for exaggeration I can find little that is fit to say.

In October I attended the first—was it the first?—meeting of The Writers' Committee of the Anti-War Council, in a shabby flat near Buckingham Palace. A very prosperous writer took the chair: he was willing, he said amiably, to do anything, he would even put aside his art, or adapt it to writing propaganda.

I looked from his smooth, healthy, wholly sincere and almost meaningless face to two others, the thin tired twisted face of the middle-aged Communist who was there to keep us straight, and W. H. Auden's heavy face, with its extraordinary patina of age. I have never seen so old a young face, it might have been overhanging a mediaeval cathedral during centuries of frost and sun. He scarcely spoke. Nor did our Communist, except when a writer said, in all seriousness,

'We need a great deal of training. I shouldn't have an *idea* how to set about pushing over a tram.'

'Don't let's talk nonsense,' the older man said icily.

As always in committees, my attention drifted. If no one else saw the two young men in stained khaki come into the room, that is not to say they were less alive than anyone there. The boy with the blunt nose, thatch of flaxen hair, and pale clear blue eyes, looked right through me to the worm under my breastbone. The other had kept his trick of waiting for the right moment to stutter a derisive comment.

I was seized by an indefensible gaiety.

So you have come back, I said.

They burst out laughing. We never moved, it was you who left us.

That's true, I thought. What is left of Class 1914 has forgotten almost everything it once knew and felt...

Every person in that shabby room was against war and against Fascism. Only the middle-aged Communist with the nose like a spiral of discoloured flesh separating his tired eyes knew that this was a contradiction in terms. For him, there was no dilemma. He was against Fascism and against any war *not fought by or in defence of Soviet Russia.* What intellectual muddle we others were in did not even amuse him.

I walked away from the meeting behind the strange shambling figure, dusty bear on two legs, of Auden, wishing I had the courage to say to him: Is this any use?

What a relief I should have felt if he had said: No use at all, but that's not the point: like you, I am prepared to protest uselessly against war, in dubious company.

(I suspect that Auden always had in reserve, even when young, the inviolable egotism of the born writer, and an instinct for self-preservation as dependable as Goethe's. One can divide writers into self-preservers, like Goethe, and the self-squanderers, Stendhal, etc, etc.)

## CHAPTER 4

ALL THROUGH 1932 Lilo's letters from Berlin traced, without a sign of panic, the graph of a defeat. Writing about friends of her own age, she said,

'Our whole outlook was directed towards the future, only the future. We are like children forced to grow up in a week.'

In February 1933 these children began to be afraid, and her letters sounded like a child talking, to reassure itself, at the top of its voice. 'We are all here desperate, our hopes gone, only expecting dictatorship or civil war or even both. I feel confused and in some way deceived. Who deceived me, the others or myself? Since ten days I am trying to be calm. Marches, demonstrations, flags, my neighbours' wireless, voices shouting through the walls, a people mad, crying a thousand at a time "heil, heil", like wild animals. Every notice in the paper a provocation, every march hurts the heart. In the office we are working hard to record every event and every decree, for the future to read, and every word I write down is bitter to me. In the end one must either commit suicide or try to handle the situation, but I am too without experience to learn it quickly. There is not one of my friends who is not involved with it. That is the worst—this uncertainty which does not allow to see three hours ahead. Every ring of the telephone, every knock on the door, may begin that which would not be bearable. The faces of my friends are white, shadows under their eyes, even if we speak of something pleasant or indifferent, our minds are going on behind this conversation with fear. We are like strangers here, the people's festivals are not ours, the songs, the speeches, the words, the future. Suddenly we are cut off from everything round us, life has been taken out of our hands, we feel old and tired and do not have the comfort that those coming after us will carry on our work and ideas.'

This discouraged mood was not one she could live in. A month later, in March, she wrote, 'I was thinking very often of England... Now I am making a plan. When the fate of our paper is decided I shall rather soon come to England to look for a chance to live. Shall I not be able to write little articles in English? And so I hope to go on. Well, I shall fear nothing for the future, having here no present and the past wasted. I promise already not to show myself to you if I am once being afraid or dull.'

She stayed on in Berlin for two or three months after the *Deutsche Volkswirt* had been suppressed. When, in October, she came to London, Bill had gone away for a short time and I had a bed to give her in the flat. I was a little dreading her arrival; she would need more than a bed, I should have to do this, say that, to give her courage to pick up her life.

How little I knew her! She turned up at the flat when I was out; I came into the living-room and there, smiling her wide brilliant smile, stood the Youngest Brother. Delighted to have a story to tell, she neither expected nor wanted comfort.

I have known a great many people. I know no one more remarkable than this child of East Berlin. Not so much for her courage, gaiety, superb energy, refusal of boredom and despair, as for her indestructible self-possession. She was born free. As others may live in a state of grace, she lived in a state of freedom. In her way of looking at life and people, she was like a swift young animal, without the cruelty; there was not a cold fibre in her, nor (to come to purely human vices) a mercenary one. Her instinctive refusal to be shackled, emotionally, morally, intellectually, shocked some people—me, never. She herself said, smiling,

'I make no demands, I come and go, I am selfish, yes, but I don't ask anyone to give up for me one shred of himself.'

Some months ago, reading a new novel by a very intelligent woman (*The Golden Notebook*, by Doris Lessing), I was struck by its involuntary and complete misconception, parody, of the very thing it was supposed to be about—freedom, 'free women'. No human being was ever less free than these women struggling in the sticky web of their sexual needs like flies in a pool of treacle. They do not begin to know the taste, colour, shape of freedom. With no more trouble than a child takes reaching for a berry, Lilo took lovers, fought them sometimes, went through emotional storms if the weather set that way and came out smiling and heart-free. Perhaps the quality she possessed, and these other hopelessly un-free women had not, was innocence. Her intense sexuality had nothing complex or sombre in it. I almost wrote: nothing erotic. Her innocence leapt at any experience, but it was uncorrupted and incorruptible. Free of doubts, free of sin.

Possibly, the 'free woman' cannot be self-made. Like any other type of genius, she is born. With the necessary egoism and energy.

A race of free women would be the end of humanity, since freedom and childbearing are incompatible.

I am drawn irresistibly to all I am not and would like to have been, to the gross reckless vitality of a Marie Lloyd, violently herself, as quickly as to this German girl's energy, essential innocence, fearlessness, invincible gaiety.

From the beginning Lilo refused to fall into what she called, with smiling contempt, 'the refugee mentality'.

'They bore me with their talk about the past. Why waste energy on regrets when they have the whole world except Germany to look at? However long I live I shan't be bored.'

She had a little money with her, and she lived in my flat only a few weeks, long enough to find herself a room of her own, at a very low rent, with some woman friend, I forget the name. She made a new friend at every turn in the road.

Utterly unafraid, she would have argued with the devil. She wanted to meet R. H. Tawney, and I asked him to dinner. After dinner, when he made some statement she could not accept, she said so, with polite smiling vehemence, and refused to be shaken. If Tawney had told me the moon was made of green cheese, I would never have dared contradict him. He smiled at Lilo's want of subservience—but it took him a little aback.

She talked to me about the last few months, about her childhood, her friends in the excitable Berlin of the late twenties, and her first frugal journey abroad, to France. Among other things she did then, she persuaded the skipper and crew of a Marseilles fishing-boat to take her with them on a trip lasting several days. No one could tell a story better than she did, no detail, no touch of humour or poetry missed or blurred. I began to harry her to write down this French adventure, as a start.

After a few weeks she brought me the manuscript of *Tale Without End*, written in what she imagined was English. Everything was there, as vivid and racy as you please, but the language was no known language. I set to work on it. I had the idea that by making her follow every change I made, I could teach her correct English.

She would attend for a few sentences; then, seized by a fit of yawns, get up and go away, saying,

'Do it as you like, dear Margaret.'

I suppose I rewrote every sentence in the book. It remained un-alienably her work, her own voice.

The instinct that made her avoid my attempt to teach her was sound. In a few months, merely by listening, talking, reading (a little), she wrote clear lively English, as later in South America she learned to write Spanish.

I sent the revised manuscript to the firm of Constable, and Lilo after it. Enchanted by her—'How,' he said to me, 'could I refuse anyone with that smile and that face?'—Michael Sadleir took it.

After this, she wrote a longer book, *Restless Flags*, about a young Germany now stone dead. Then a novel, not a bad novel, but the trouble it gave her convinced her that she was no novelist. So, in search of something to work on, she went, with a few pounds in her pocket, to Turkey, and travelled in the hardest way, staying where she was invited, questioning any man, woman or child who could tell her anything. No one rebuffed her: the candour and smiling goodwill of the Youngest Brother served her here as again and again in strange countries, all her life.

The book she wrote when she came home, *Allah Dethroned*, drew an invitation to lecture on modern Turkey to the Institute of International Affairs. I trembled for her, but she spoke with the greatest simplicity and coolness to an audience which listened with respect.

When I say that no one ever rebuffed her, I don't mean that everyone liked her. Some of her fellow-exiles did not forgive either her energy or her frank contempt for their attitude.

'What the devil do you see in this half-educated conceited guttersnipe with her intolerable airs of knowing better?' one of them said to me.

Would it have been any use telling him that a fresh spring is gayer than a stagnant marsh? Or that conceit is easily forgivable when it takes the form of courage and lighthearted egoism? He himself was intelligent and conceited, and unable to forgive a gaiety and success which seemed as undeserved as the Youngest Brother's good fortune always does—to the others.

Some time in 1938 she began planning to travel through the whole of
South America, to write 'a splendid book, really truthful.'

'How long,' I asked, 'would you be away?'

'A year. Fifteen months.'

'If war breaks out next spring, you'll be trapped there.'

'There isn't going to be war.' She gave me a clear look, without a hint of
derision. 'The English and French democracies won't fight, you know that.'

She had a German passport. When it ran out of date she had walked into
the consulate and demanded a renewal. Glancing at her yellow hair, frank
smile, and innocently blue eyes, the clerk gave it to her without asking a
question. She was delighted by the success of her bluff, which convinced
some of her fellow-exiles that she was not and never had been a refugee.
Their suspicions amused her.

'I shan't be able to trick the devils again, but why shouldn't I do it this
time? Without a proper passport I can't travel.'

With the one you have, I reflected, you'll be interned the day war starts.
I took care to say nothing to dissuade her from leaving.

The outbreak of the war caught her in Ecuador, in Quito. She kept herself
alive by teaching English in a boys' school. (I pity any young Latin male who
imagined he could outface Lilo.) Soon she began writing—in Spanish—for a
liberal newspaper. I have forgotten how soon after the war she decided to stay
in South America, and became an Ecuadorian citizen. Nor am I sure when she
began to be the personage in liberal circles she became. She wrote regularly on
social and political affairs, visiting journalists and economists consulted her
as an authority; she travelled enormously, she would go anywhere she could
persuade her newspaper or an institution to send her. Many of these journeys,
in the Andes, through the jungle, on the Amazon, were hair-raisingly hard
and dangerous. They were her abiding passion—they and one other: her
hunger to see justice done to the humble and oppressed. In her new country
this became an assault, patient and vehement, on the frightful poverty and
ignorance of the Indians. She loathed the oppressor and spent herself to
drag and coax the oppressed out of their lethargy. As a passion it went back
to her hard childhood and rebellious adolescence, a thread she never let go.

It was the most generous of passions. It was also the managing Prussian
in her—the liking for order and authority that ruled her tempestuous life

as it might have ruled any honest little workgirl. She detested and despised grime, untidiness, incompetence, weakness. In her shabby London room, the furniture and her books and clothes were always ranged *garde à vous*.

In 1937 when she and I were in Paris, it infuriated her that I paid no attention to the street-map. After we had walked for an hour in a strange quarter, she would halt and say,

'Now what is this square?'

'Heaven knows.'

'Margaret, you are absolutely intolerable, only last week I brought you to this very place and told you all the names. Don't you notice anything?'

'Only what interests me,' I said.

This struck her as a vice, as did my inability to keep money in my hands, and my willingness to tell lies to please people. Any lies she told were to please herself, and—she would have given her last shilling to a hungry man or woman—she never wasted a penny, and foresaw with horror and grief my end in a workhouse.

She came back to England from Ecuador, three, four, five times. Except that the yellow of her hair became tarnished, I saw little change in her: the gleam of white teeth, of cornflower blue eyes, remained that of the young girl. Her letters, long and marvellously vivid, charted a life which ran deeper and more calmly, but not any slower. I answered all of them, and did not keep one.

In May this year (1963) she was in a plane between Athens and London (coming to England as the guest of the Central Office of Information) when her heart—which I and all her friends imagined to be the soundest in the world—stopped.

Impossible, I said, impossible. I still say it.

## CHAPTER 5

'ENGLISH WRITERS,' a French novelist stranded in London during the late war said to me, 'do not exchange ideas. I find this surprising—a little, what do you say?, debilitating.'

'Perhaps they have none to spare.'

'Perhaps,' he said reflectively, 'I ought to read some English novels. Thus I should discover for myself.'

I doubt he carried out a plan clearly distasteful to him.

He would have been just as disappointed if he had arrived in peace time. There is no literary society in London, in the meaning of the words: groups form and dissolve, like the tiny circular ripple an insect makes on the surface of a stagnant pond, nothing more serious. There is no room and I think no wish for the café society of a Place St Germain des Prés where new ideas and gibberish keep the air moving and dissipate the fog which had thickened round my poor Frenchman as he crossed the Channel.

During my years of seeing a great many people, I saw few writers. My close friends in the thirties were almost all politicians, usually of the Left, journalists, foreign correspondents, with a light sprinkling of historians and economists. It happened because my eyes and ears were fixed on the spectacle of Europe, and the only people I wanted to see were those who could tell me what was going on in a theatre where innumerable scenes were being played simultaneously, side by side and one above the other.

The past, even so vivid a past as the thirties, is a mural of which only fragments remain intact—a face, a gesture, a phrase. Philip Jordan's face had a very startling delicacy, like a Chinese painting: he had almost no eyebrows, clear pale eyes, a pale skin, and a trick of sending the point of his tongue rapidly across colourless and very fine lips, like the flickering movement of a lizard across a stone, when he made one of his sharp comments. He did it when he described an editor, Kingsley Martin, conscious of his exposed position on the Left, going into a theatrical wig-makers to order himself a crown of thorns.

He was the wittiest talker I have ever known, a fountain of intellectual malice, and incorruptible. He was also one of the kindest of men. He had, I think, fewer skins over his mind than other people, no protective layer of indifference, not enough moral egoism to keep him going for more than a short life.

A mind as thin-skinned as his could, perhaps, have been jarred into dying, suddenly, with no obvious physical cause.

After the aeroplane taking him to Jugoslavia during the war was brought down in flames he had bad nightmares, but can nightmares kill?

At dinner it amused me to place his deceptively transparent face next to the head—equally striking and equally not meant for long use—of the correspondent of two Scandinavian newspapers, Bjarne Braatoy. Bjarne's immense arched forehead seemed dragged backwards by very fair hair like a wig of tightly curled wire. The son of a Norwegian pastor, he was incorrigibly restless, ambitious, very intelligent, without stability or fore-thought—Peer Gynt in the flesh. Peel off his outer self, and another as lively, clever, and mercurially boastful, appeared: a hundred identical selves and no identity.

(Or was it reached at the last minute? Years of disappointment and fail-ures in America, during and after the war, divorce, plan after plan falling to pieces in his hands, and then—at the very moment when the tide turned and he was given the position in the international Labour machine that he had craved and was well fitted for—he died, in a London hospital, alone. Perhaps he had no time to summon one of his English friends. Perhaps he had none left—or had wanted to establish himself before reappearing. He was vain, with the innocent vanity of Peer Gynt, one lie, one blunder, one misdeed effacing the last, leaving his mind swept clean for the next to be written on it. As his wife I could not have borne with him. Simply as a friend, I found it impossible to condemn him out of hand.)

He had married a young German woman from a cultivated, liberal, upper middle class family, the most charming creature in the world, polite, spirited, naturally elegant. She had the slenderly rounded body of a dancer, and hieratic good looks as indestructible as her air of race: arched nose, high cheekbones, wide straight sensuous mouth, hair like curled feathers springing strongly back from her forehead and small ears. One of her habitual movements, hands lifted in a gesture of tolerance and indifference, had a Mozartian wit and gaiety.

One evening in, I think, 1934, I invited together Philip, Lilo, and Aneurin Bevan. In a small room Aneurin's quicksilver energy was almost alarming, I felt that I was sharing his cage with a powerful wild animal. When Nye was telling a malicious story, which he could not do without miming it, gestures and voices, he was a great cat poised for a bound, claws unsheathed, eyes gleaming with savage amusement. He had a rich caressing voice, but there was no caress in his eloquence. Always double-edged, it could be corrosive. It secreted an unappeased bitterness—much as what some of his colleagues at this time thought his laziness secreted contempt and a turbulent ambition.

I had friends for whom he was the devil himself. They were off the mark. He was an earthy Welsh rebel, generous, likeable, pleasure-loving, highly intelligent, born a kicker against the pricks, a good hater who would have hesitated to guillotine a mouse. Since I had reached an age to distrust politicians of every breed, and since all breeds are forced, except in countries where power has congealed in a few hands, to promise their followers happiness, and no party has the courage to try to create a society in which the individual will see to his own happiness—the single chance of a civilized future for the human race, and probably humanly impossible—I could admire him without caring whether his eloquence were trustworthy or not. When his speculations about the future were based on reason and logic they were usually worthless, bound to be contradicted by the event. But so far as any politician is, he was honest—every politician is forced for his political health's sake to tell a number of lies. He might, seen eating and drinking in the Ivy, look like any well-off politician mixing sans-culotte sentiments with a good claret, but he remained furiously a rebel to the moment he died.

At the last minute Lilo rang up and said she would like to bring a friend she had just made, a writer, Ralph Bates.

All I knew about him was that he was the author of a volume of short stories, laid in Spain. Admirable stories, written, obviously, by a man who knew and loved an austere poverty-stricken Spain of workers and peasants tilling a handful of earth. They were, I think, the first notable re-appearance in our day of the Spanish myth—or metaphor—in which even before the civil war, before Guernica, Spain began to be identified with contempt for luxury and death, and the instinct to revolt.

'Of course bring him,' I said.

I expected a haggard Quixote. The well-fleshed young man—twenty-seven or eight?—who followed Lilo into the room looked like a responsible workman, a foreman come to weld a broken pipe.

He was self-assured and amiable. 'I've heard of you,' he told Nye.

He ate with extraordinary rapidity, and as he ate talked about himself. He was remarkable enough. Bored by his life as a railway-worker, he had cleared off to Spain, learned the language, and made friends among socialist workers.

'It's the only country,' he said, 'where the movement has kept its soul. Poverty and hard living—that's the secret. You won't see any labour leaders there stuffing themselves in the Ivy.'

'You enjoy your food, though,' Nye said, smiling.

'I can go anywhere I like,' he said calmly, 'food's the same to me wherever I eat it. What you have to remember about me is that I'm not only a writer, I'm a trained mechanic. I'm better off than any of your middle class novelists—I can always go back to that. And mark you, it's skilled work, it takes learning.'

Philip gave him a coldly ironic glance. 'Not like writing novels. Any fool can write.'

Not in the least disconcerted, the skilled man did not take the trouble to answer.

He was no fool, and not naïve. He had energy, the energy of imagination. About that, it is impossible to be deceived; either a writer, a painter, a musician, has it or he is merely clever: it may be a thin vein, soon exhausted, but there is no mistaking it.

When we went back to the flat, someone spoke of Oswald Mosley's 'amateur Fascism'.

'Let me tell you how that started,' Nye said.

Smiling cruelly, he described a meeting of the Parliamentary Labour Party, called early in 1931 to discuss a proposal, put forward by Mosley and backed by John Strachey, Nye himself, and one or two others, for a special conference to deal with the appalling unemployment. As he talked, his face lengthened and became Ramsay MacDonald's face, and his voice took on the softly unctuous tones of an old gentleman of failing mind and unshakable self-confidence. It may have been a caricature, but it was brilliant.

'Everyone of good faith knows that my government is doing its tireless best. Some of you are making speeches you should be ashamed of. It's an ill bird... You young ones don't understand how in the past some of us toiled and sacrificed, yes, sacrificed ourselves, for the cause. In those days we learned to put first principles first, we learned that everything must be done gradually, first one step, then another, and that each step has one behind it, that effects spring from causes, and causes produce effects, that if you drink too much in the evening you will have a headache the morning after, and if you have a headache the morning after it is because you were drinking too much

the evening before. And that, friends, is the whole meaning of socialism...
And he opened his arms—' Nye opened his—'and without blessing us he
was parted from us and carried up into Park Lane to sit on the right hand
of Lady Londonderry. The other so-called leaders went away, too, leaving
four or five of us gaping at the empty platform. I knew then that Mosley
would go. He was too impatient to realize that he was making headway in
the country and had only to wait. X. gave him eighty thousand pounds, and
he asked me to see the fellow. I refused, and left him.'

'The one of the three rats I don't understand,' Philip began, 'is Snowden——'
Nye grinned with amused contempt. 'He is eaten up by his own acid,'
he said lightly.

A short time before this, my American agent, Carol Brandt, had asked
me if I could take her to see Philip Snowden. I forget why—she may have
been told that he was writing.

Out of politeness or habit, she dressed for the occasion as for an Embassy
party, and Snowden was fascinated by the tassel of her small hat, dangling
over one eye. We sat round a lace-edged tablecloth set with scones, sandwiches, a large fruit cake, plates of bread and butter, jam, a proper Yorkshire
high tea. Snowden looked very old, frail and twisted, no flesh on his bones.
I had been afraid he would sit silent, but he talked freely in his edged voice,
and even laughed. Obviously he liked looking at Carol, who is a beautiful
woman. Suddenly, when the ironic smile left his pale Yorkshire eyes, I saw
the skinny white-faced child, shivering with cold, and hungry. I knew I could
never dislike him, never condemn him, never not feel for him a sympathy
of the nerves and the northern ice in my veins...

I was neither bold nor quick enough to try to defend him from Philip's
forked tongue and Nye's contempt. How find defensible words for what is
foolishly emotional and irrational?

When he left, Ralph Bates shook hands with me in the friendliest way,
and said,

'You might ask me here again. I like you.'

Well, I liked him—but without sympathy or warmth...

The after-dinner gossip of foreign correspondents is the best in the world.
Writers—and politicians—can be at one and the same moment intelligent
and imposters, self-deceiving humbugs. A foreign correspondent is rarely a

charlatan, his day-to-day work brings him into acid touch with too many events, physical and moral, of more than passing significance. No talker, and ignorant, I listened to them with passionate attention. I could live happily in a cell, I told myself, so long as the messages continued to come in from all sides.

Inevitably, during these years, from wherever a conversation started, in a short time it came back to our chances of escaping war. Of one such evening, I remember only the angry Dutchman, a friend of Bjarne's, who had been travelling for his paper in Germany and had collected evidence—a quantity of evidence—that the Germans were preparing for war.

'With enthusiasm,' he said, stammering a little, 'with enormous enthusiasm. And I come here and find that decent intelligent men would rather walk naked down Whitehall than believe it. Are you all raving mad? Something worse than ignorance is driving you to suicide—sheep following each other over a cliff. God knows your shepherds are ignorant, they can't read German, they know nothing about history, nothing about Europe, but it isn't ignorance, it isn't for want of being told and told again, with proof and archi-proof. They *refuse* to know. Why? Why do they run up to Hitler with their silly throats stretched for the knife? Why do they believe he will say: I must spare these poor gentle hens? Why do they think that the sensible way to handle a thug is to give him everything he asks for? My dear fellow, we must redress your grievances, they say, take what you want... You know, I am baffled. I can't see any reason in what you are doing. It is somehow irrational. Your Halifax and Chamberlain are like those poor elderly gentlemen who ask girls to whip them.'

He laughed. I was surprised and embarrassed to see that there were tears in his eyes. I said diffidently,

'You say that the German government, that Hitler, is preparing to make war. Do you mean he wants to conquer England and France? Isn't that rather a mouthful—even for a dictator?'

His wide heavy face took on an extraordinary look of grief. 'You will see,' he said softly. 'When your decent pious respectable politicians—and *The Times*—have betrayed all the little countries to him, you will see how he will respect you.'

His voice dropped still lower. 'I am screaming with anxiety and despair,' he said in a whisper.

I must write this down, I thought (and did, as soon as he left). As usual, my ambiguous mind was thinking two things at once. I lived now in dread of another war, and by a sleight of mind believed it possible and impossible, in the same breath, with the same rage.

'I hope you are wrong,' I said.

This infuriated him again. 'You are not any better than your Cabinet Ministers and your dear deluded liberals. You shout: Down with armaments and God bless the League of Nations. Good, good! You are against Fascism, of course you are against Fascism, you are an English radical, you detest tyrants, you are going to fight them. With what? With some old guns left over from 1918? Madness. You are mad. I must go, I shall insult you, and as soon as I have gone you will say: These Dutchmen have no sense of proportion and no manners, obviously he is out of his mind... Well, forgive me, I *am* mad.'

He turned with his hand on the door, to say, smiling,

'But, of course, if you believe that *nothing* is worth fighting for...'

He waited for me to answer. I said nothing. His smile broadened end-lessly, and he went off.

I was too afraid of what I might see to look closely into the confusion in my mind...

I had the sensation, often, of listening to footsteps outside my room, drawing slowly nearer. If they stopped for a few minutes, it was only to make a bound and start up again closer. At moments the tension of listening became unbearable, as on the afternoon when for two or more hours I listened to Dorothy Thompson's account of the 30th of June, 1934, one of the coldest of Hitler's bouts of murder, when he saw personally to the killing of a friend and followers he had no further use for. It was stiflingly hot in the room. I sat without moving a muscle, as cold as a stone, sweat running down my spine, my stomach contracted in nervous anguish. When I stood up I found that my whole body had become as rigid as a clenched fist, and I could scarcely move it. Something in the incident—not, I think, the deaths—paralysed me with fear and curiosity. The curiosity of the writer. And perhaps fear of human nature itself.

I recall only one other time in my life when this strange physical rigid-ity seized me. That was an occasion in the brasserie of the Café Royal: I was listening to Harrison Brown who had come back from Berlin with evidence—at that time new and barely credible—of what Hitler planned to do to the Jews living in Germany.

I was still (in 1933) naïve enough to think that he had only to lay it before the editor of *The Times* to blow away for good every hopeful illusion about the Nazi regime. During the next two years that good man, Ebbutt, the paper's Berlin correspondent, broke himself against his editor's wilful delusions...

I should be lying if I pretended that I spent much time feeling anxious. Incidents like these were icy jets rising to the surface from an underlying terror. The surface itself was as lively as a June sea, splinters of light piercing the water, leaping, breaking, re-forming. What I remember about unnumbered evenings at this time is, first of all, an immense liveliness and gaiety.

I have never been so gay since, in any society.

## CHAPTER 6

THE CONFERENCE of the Labour Party at Hastings in 1933 was haunted by the ghost of German Social Democracy, in the shape usually of a young doctor or lawyer, with a pale intelligent face, and no money. What did these *revenants* hope from their assembled English 'comrades'?

I attended this conference as the delegate of the Whitby branch of the Labour Party, the first, and for all I know the last time that penniless branch sent one. I sat faithfully through every session, and shocked dear Philip Noel-Baker by raising my hand on his left in favour of workers' control in factories. He rebuked me very gravely. I assured him that I was only obeying the orders of my committee. In truth, like the group of born rebels it was, it had told me to vote as I pleased on every point. I had no principles and my instincts were those of an anarchist.

Every evening I wrote a racily detailed report for the famished and delighted eyes of a branch no one had ever heard of. None of the moments I remember most clearly found their way into the report.

One day at the end of the afternoon session, a gentle guttural voice—during the next few years this voice, in all its varieties, became very familiar—said in my ear,

'I think you are helping me. You are Storm Jameson, yes? I am—' I have forgotten his name—'from Berlin, a friend of Miss Linke. I am a lawyer, I have here very important messages and a letter from some Trades Union officials for Mr Arthur Henderson. One of them is his friend for a long time. The letter tells him how he can help. I think you are taking me to him—perhaps now?'

With the desperation of the timid, I marched him across the lobby to the great man.

'Mr Henderson,' I said, 'this German has messages for you from a friend of yours in Berlin.'

I drew back a few steps and watched. For all I know, Mr Henderson was feeling an agony of grief. Nothing, no emotion of any sort, warmed a face the colour of a fishmonger's slab. I heard him say stiffly,

'What do you expect me to do?'

Pilate number thirty million, I thought, and hurried away.

I walked clumsily into old George Lansbury. He spoke kindly to me, and we sauntered together along the sea front in the last of the cool light. Outside one of the richer hotels, he halted me to watch three of his colleagues going in.

'Look at them,' he said, smiling. 'And all on the pennies of the workers. We ought to be ashamed.'

After this I avoided the German. On the last day he caught me as I stood watching the better sort, arms linked the length of the platform, singing *Auld Lang Syne*. Hugh Dalton, large gleaming head tilted back, only the whites of his eyes visible, smiling, at once cold and hearty, resembled nothing so much as a Chinese executioner. The guttural murmur began in my ear.

'This song, it has some significance, yes?'

'It has indeed. It signifies that no revolution will happen here, ever. Fortunately.'

Behind us a ragged handful led by Bill Mellor was trying to start *The Red Flag*.

'And this also you do not sing? Yourself?'

'I can't sing a note,' I said.

One can make literature of anything, even—or especially—of the cancer of violence, cruelty, despair, exile, eating into the thirties. As for exile, possibly only a writer who has suffered it has the right to try. The rest of us, with our guesses, are clumsy intruders. We do not know sharply enough what takes place in the brain and nerves of the man turning his back, not on possessions—within measure replaceable—but on the street he crosses to reach a certain café table, on his habit of pausing on his way home from work to watch a man fishing from a narrow quay, on a plane-tree always the last in his street to show green in spring, on the death he intended to die in his own place and time, on a worn-out school satchel kicking about in an attic with other rubbish.

Because of one incident in my life, I know a little about these losses. But not what it means to a writer to cut his writing hand off at the wrist, to lose by the same brutal stroke a country and his language, his own word for bread, house, sleep, child.

Departures are in my blood—voluntary departures. I belong to a country I left. Not quite the same thing as exile. Not the sensation of crossing a frontier into an alien language, an alien death. Still less the agony of being pushed on to the lower deck of a rotten ship, to be turned back from strange harbours, to drown in darkness, clutching the little terrified body of a child.

None the less, I never felt separated from an exile by more than a thin membrane. The refugees I began to be friendly with in 1933 were not destitute—or they would not have reached London. They still had something by which to hope, a cousin in Wisconsin who was going to send for them, a profession they might, in time, be able to use. (But I have never known what became of the old magistrate who had had the honesty to give a decision against two Nazi killers only a month before Hitler's triumph. Or what passed through the mind of the elderly Jewish woman who killed herself after arranging on the table in her room a strand of seaweed and a few shells in the shape of a bird.)

The evenings when I invited three or four of them to dinner had a taste my tongue recognized at once—the pleasure of being in a foreign town where I am limitlessly free. They were also exhausting: so many insoluble problems, so many hopes foundering, the icy sense—Henderson no doubt had felt it—of being responsible and helpless.

I had no idea how some of them were living, on what dole. And here is a curious thing I noticed. For all the weight of anxiety, discomfort, poverty, certain exiles I knew kept into late middle-age a sort of youth—as if begin-ning life again in another country had reduced the sum of their years. The eyes remained innocent.

Ilse Meyer's, for instance.

I have a sharp image of her, sitting, very silent, in a corner of the sofa while her husband argued with Lilo and the lawyer I had met at Hastings.

(The one object of value the young Meyers brought with them from Berlin was the manuscript of Ernst's scholarly work on English Chamber Music from the Middle Ages to Purcell: he expected to make his reputation by it. During the war, after I had written innumerable letters, and with the help of some fund or other, it was at last published, and praised at length and unequivocally by the *Times Literary Supplement* for its 'great learning'. Was that all he got out of it?)

Speaking to me—no doubt he thought I needed telling—the lawyer said, 'Some cruelty shall accompany naturally the establishment of a dictator-ship. If minds and bodies are to fill a mould, some must be broken to fit, yes? Is then the opportunity of scoundrels—such as in my country flog political prisoners with steel rods, castrate, blind, or arrest usually at night.' He lifted a short broken-nailed hand. 'Without extravagance, one may suppose national instincts. One nation prefers to use castor oil and exile, another simple shooting, another inclines to mutilation of the parts or other tortures. One may even suppose that here, in England, brutality should be kept low and the choice be of moral and economic pressure. What do you say?'

I had nothing to say.

He went on, smiling, 'I am sure you will not, like your Labour leaders, say: What do you expect me to do?' His chin worked in a very unpleasant way. 'His friend writes: For God's sake help us. And he answers, coldly: *What do you expect me to do?*'

'Well, what *did* you expect?' Ernst Meyer asked in his soft voice. He had one of the most charming speaking voices I ever heard. 'First, he can't save everyone. Second, you ought to know that a democrat is a man who bends before he is broken.'

Lilo turned on him a vindictive smile.

'And a Communist is a man who makes mistakes in order not to learn from them——'

The quarrel raged for more than an hour. I effaced myself and went to talk to the silent Ilse. It was hard work. The magnificent dark eyes in her small face had a look of blindness or absence. She is still, I thought, living in the tiny room in the Jäckelstrasse, she hasn't yet let go of the life broken off short at a point she can still, by looking obstinately back, see.

After a long time I felt her mind move at the end of mine. It was not courage she needed from me; she had enough (and showed it twelve years later, at the end of the war, when Ernst, still a faithful Communist, left her and their five-year-old daughter in London and went back to East Berlin with the English girl he had fallen in love with). What she needed was some assurance that she existed. She smiled a little. Her hand moved from her lap to the arm of my chair.

Lilo beckoned me from the other end of the room. When I went to her, she said fiercely,

'Why do you trouble with her? She is mad.'

'Nonsense,' I said coldly, 'she is as sane as you are.'

'Well, there is no need to talk to her, she is not used to being noticed.'

Three more people arrived, a musician and his gently anxious wife, and a younger man, a poet. The musician I knew as one of those with a cousin in America; he was so certain of the future that he had recklessly given away part of the money they had brought with them. I made a great deal of fresh coffee, and hoped that the air of intelligence with which I listened to an argument about surrealist writing hid my exhaustion. I was so bored by it that when the poet said that surrealism is a new birth, I made my only comment.

'It looks to me much more like an abortion. The death by a thousand yawns of any literature worth the name.'

They fell on me in a body.

'I never dreamed you were reactionary,' Lilo said, with reproach.

'How is this? You hate what is new and damn it already out of fear?'

'Have it your own way,' I said.

Long before the last of them left, towards one o'clock, I was emptier of virtue than a husk. As I shut the front door, my furiously exasperated husband stamped out of his bedroom. He had stayed with the party—he was very fond of Lilo and liked the young Meyers—until the onset of surrealism. Then he could bear it no longer and shut himself in his room to work. He watched me stonily as I carried coffee cups into the ridiculous kitchen, emptied ashtrays, and straightened chairs. In reality I was collecting the scattered fragments of myself from all over the room.

'Why the hell didn't you turn them out sooner?'

I had a vision of the drab curtains and thin dusty carpet of an un-heated bed-sitting-room in West Hampstead.

'They were enjoying themselves talking.'

'No reason why you should kill yourself.'

I knew that my energy was inexhaustible. It might for the moment have vanished, but I could count on its return in a few hours, asking to be squandered.

## CHAPTER 7

FOR SOME YEARS after 1933 I lived in equivocal amity with pacifists and combative supporters of the League of Nations, adjusting my feelings, in good and bad faith, to the person I happened to be with. I swayed between the two like a tightrope walker, or a politician. My only immoveable conviction was my loathing of war.

In the autumn of 1933 this shocking indecision led me into more trouble than usual. Philip Noel-Baker asked me to help him to recruit well-known writers in defence of collective security and against war. His plan was to invite a number to dinner and talk to them. Then he decided that the dinner should be given by Viscount Cecil, and asked me to choose and invite the guests.

I was incapable of risking his disapproval by refusing. My respect for his courage and goodness, and admiration of his flawless profile, were both too great.

I brushed out of my way the uncomfortable reflection that a pacifist could support the idea of an armed League only if she assumed that the bombs of the International Air Force would never be dropped. My mind was far too divided to reject one more ambiguity.

What worried me much more was the all too likely behaviour of the well-known writers. I knew my fellows too well to share his confidence that they only needed a call to arms to come running. We shall eat Lord Cecil's salt, I thought, and nothing will come of it. Already I felt myself disgraced by a humiliating fiasco.

Racking my brains for a way to avoid it, I came on a half-formed idea that we might write a symposium on the danger of another war. Secretly I was convinced that we should be wasting our time, children throwing sand against the wind. I am rarely taken in by rhetoric, even my own, and I can never believe that anyone else is less sceptical.

Looking back, I see that in 1933 I was blinder than a bat to the real tragedy of our time.

What I saw then as an attempt of the reason, of reasonable men, to divert irrational forces driving us to war was not that, not that at all. It was a struggle of the human spirit *against* the intellect. Our intellect has betrayed us. Has set ajar the door of hell with a cruelty as frigid as that of German administrators and technicians opening the gas chambers. Today, Faust, in the person of the dedicated nuclear scientist, has prepared the extinction of human kind.

I chose a score of glittering names, and wrote my letters of invitation with tactful cunning, trying without frightening them to warn Lord Cecil's guests that they were going to be asked to do something.

The Wellington Club, where the dinner was held, was as imposing and reticent as any noble London club. Nothing could have been better suited to a gathering of distinguished minds and stomachs. The only faces I now see distinctly are those of Lord Cecil himself—great domed head and forehead, deeply-sunk eyes, superb beak of a nose, long prominent upper lip—and, flanking him on either side, Rebecca West and Rose Macaulay. (I have forgotten how I settled the problem which of them to place on his right: I think I tossed for it.) He looked like one of Jove's eagles overtopping two smaller vivid birds.

Towards the end of dinner, cold with the fear of ridicule, I suggested that we might write a book for him. I should have been certain that the task of editing it would be thrust on me. My heart sank. But food, wine, and the splendour of Lord Cecil had put our writers in a foolish state of goodwill, and rather than risk losing a fair wind I agreed.

It turned out a frightful labour—the writing with my own hand of a couple of hundred letters, cajoling, explaining, persuading, encouraging;

not to speak of putting together the skeleton of the animal and struggling endlessly against the natural impulse of writers to promise one thing and write another—or not write at all.

Few of those I attacked had the hardness of heart—moral courage or sense—to refuse. One or two accepted out of vanity, the others from decency or sincere hatred of war. The greater the writer, the less trouble he gave. Edmund Blunden gave me none at all.

'It is very kind of you to invite me into the Disarmament Ring, and I hope I can produce something worthy of the occasion and the company. Some floating ideas might form a poem of say 100 or 150 verses, if you would take in so many. How long do you allow your Bards? I should like a little time. Can you invent a machine to reproduce the Menin Rd Battle for instance, so that some of our young may just look in at practical war? I could show them the way out of Hedge St, and eastward.'

The long poem he wrote, *War Cemetery*, is the single part of the book still living, still, as it was at the time, the only fragment of literature, a jet of truth from the heart and nerves of a poet.

My own opening essay on the revolt from reason was a fine piece of rhetoric and could have been written either by a devout supporter of the League or an out-and-out pacifist. Both of them were admirably clear about the normal man's ambivalent attitude to war, and the nonsense of believing that fear or hatred of war has the slightest effect in preventing it. And about the banality of evil. (I was then far from imagining that sane men, with cultivated senses, can conceive and keep going an Auschwitz.) I wrote fluently about the Hegelian roots of Etatism, and the paradox of a rational theory breeding the irrationalism of the Absolute State. No one, I was sure, would notice the logical gap I skipped across to touch in lightly the idea of an armed League. No one did.

After trying in vain to persuade various better-found writers to provide the final essay, I wrote it myself. It contained—in 1933—an eloquent plea for a united Europe.

A splendid polemist was lost when I took to writing novels.

The book was published by Constable. It had the effect I expected—none.

This year, too, in November, I finished the first volume of the *roman fleuve* from which I expected so much, *Company Parade*. It was a good book. Yes, really a good book, crowded with men, women and a child or two, who are still breathing in a recess of my brain, though I have abandoned them. There is a great deal in it about Hervey Russell and her ambitions, blunders, joys, griefs; there are ex-soldiers, industrialists, a Jewish newspaper proprietor and his family, writers, a segment of the literary *panier à crabes* of the twenties, a Marie Lloyd figure, a young Labour politician and his wife—I forget the others, and have not the heart to look into a book into which so much energy, passion, intellect, and faith and hope disappeared.

The second volume, *Love in Winter*, took me another year, until November 1934. More characters forced their way into it, with ruthless energy, and truthful and sometimes bitter episodes from my own life in London in those years—Lord knows what more—the economic web, the social web.

I am coolly certain that, *fleuve* for *fleuve*, it ran faster and deeper than any flowering now, in the sixties.

But what a devil of an idea to set myself up as a Balzac. I must have been mad.

At the same time I was reviewing for A. R. Orage in the *New English Weekly*. Why add that to my other labours? For a reason, completely irresistible, which went back to 1913 and my joyous life then. Orage's *New Age* was the Bible of my generation. We would far sooner go hungry than miss buying it. We quoted it, argued with it, formed ourselves on it. I suppose he had a sharper influence on intelligent young Englishmen of that time—compare Alain's influence on a generation of Frenchmen killed in the War—than anyone else, and writers whom no one suspected of recklessness in money matters wrote for the *New Age* for nothing, simply because he asked them.

In March 1913, when he printed my first piece of writing, the gaily impudent essay on George Bernard Shaw, I would have gone to prison for him.

I did not meet him then. The idea of presenting myself to him never entered my head, I was infinitely too timid, I could not imagine that he would welcome a shabby student with nothing to say for herself.

All but twenty years later, in March 1932, standing in an icy Berlin street, I bought an English paper and read that he had come back to England and started a new weekly paper. I must have written to him, since he invited me to see him on my way through London.

He took me to drink tea in a small shabby café near his office in Cursitor Street. I had heard him spoken of as an intelligent charlatan, and came prepared to be disillusioned. He turned out to be direct, entirely without airs of importance, as easy as if I had known him a long time, and naturally charming, with a flicker of ironic gaiety that was rarely out of sight. It showed itself when he said calmly,

'Young writers are a great deal more commercially-minded than they were before the War.'

I supposed that our successors were not showing themselves very willing to write for nothing. In 1913... I didn't need to dip Proust's madeleine in my strong tea to taste the gaiety, the causeless springing happiness, the feverish expectations and certainties of that year. Warm and alive, they were waiting in me to be discovered, as they will be waiting at the end of my life. Because of them, and to please more than one young ghost, I agreed to review for him. The idea of reading every month more novels than I care to read in twelve dismayed me, but I did not dream of refusing.

I kept it up for a time something short of two years, until too many other tasks made it impossible. When, with genuine shame, I told Orage I could not go on, he sent me the bound volumes of the *New Age*—would I had kept them!—and a comforting letter: 'My dear Storm, dear, you've served your time for a dozen volumes, so I still feel in your debt...'

Later I wrote a pamphlet for him on The Soul of Man Under Leisure. I have lost or thrown away my copy of this exercise. Did I believe what I wrote? Possibly. Certainly I wrote what, from so long a discipleship, I knew he believed. In those days I was an excellent mimic.

Three months later, on the 6th of November, I opened an evening paper in the street, and read of his death. It seemed that everything, the traffic, the thin bitter wind, ceased. This death, I thought uncertainly, is the end of more than a man, it ends a story, and the story of my youth. I had a sharp image of him, smiling. I felt in some way silenced and stopped.

None of these words is real. The shock and the silencing were real.

# CHAPTER 8

O NE FIGURE DETACHES itself from the dissolving phantasmago-
ria of my years in the St John's Wood flat. My younger sister steps
forward smiling.

I saw her two or three times a week; either she came to the flat, or, oftener, I
met her somewhere in the City, near the offices of the Amalgamated Press—
she was on the staff of a magazine—and gave her lunch. Afterwards, if there
was time, we walked about the City, looking at old squares and churches
she wanted to see. In 1940 most of these disappeared; I could not now go
back there to look for her.

At twenty-seven she seemed no more than sixteen, her very fair skin
smoothly unblemished, like a young child's, the natural scarlet of her lips
undimmed. She had my grandfather's and my mother's coldly blue eyes; one
man or woman in every generation of my family has these eyes, a clear pale
blue, without a shadow.

Intensely practical, quick-tempered and quick-witted, she had none of my
fear of other people, none of my anxious need to be approved, no wish at all
to please; sharp-tongued, frank, pitiless in her dislikes, wholly loyal where
she loved. She loved only very few persons. She had some contempt for my
extravagance, restlessness, and what she called my softness (with people),
but she would have used her tongue on an outsider who criticized me, with
very much the annoyance she showed if one of her possessions were belittled.

I should be put to it to explain the compulsive need I felt to give her
anything I knew she wanted. It was not caused by the fifteen years between
us, making her as much my child as my sister... Why are we afraid to talk
about foreknowledge?...

Her name for me, Dear Dog, was half affection, of a rough unemotional
family sort, and half mockery. The writing on a scrap of paper in the back
of a notebook begins:

'Dear Dog, if you are coming to Reading on Saturday I'll make a fruit
cake for you to take back, and some fresh eggs. The garden has suddenly

exploded with roses, I have mowed and weeded, we are painting the kitchen, and it is all—'

There it breaks off, the light quick voice, full of pride in a small house in a street of small decent houses. There was not a single thread in her of my hatred of domestic life or any itch for change and foreign countries. She was never bored, never inactive, never tired.

At some time in the autumn of 1934 she told me she had learned that she could only have a child if she were operated on to correct a serious internal deformity. It was not an easy operation, nor entirely certain.

'Do you want to have children?' I asked.

She stared at me coldly from those far too direct eyes. 'Of course.'

'I'll take you to a London specialist.'

'The specialist in Reading is quite good enough,' she said impatiently. 'Don't let's have any fuss.'

The first time I saw her after the operation, she was still drowsy. Looking down at her, I had an extraordinary sense that she was separated from me by an immense distance in time, the half-closed eyes, flawless skin, short-fingered hands lying idle on the sheet, the slender body, were remote, something I remembered. She roused herself to ask a question, and my momentary discomfort vanished.

Outside her room, I asked the sister in charge, 'Is she all right?'

'Oh, yes.' She smiled slightly. 'When I saw her just before the operation I thought how calm and self-possessed she was for a little girl. I was astonished when I knew her age.'

## CHAPTER 9

A T THE END of that year I sold the Whitby house. Clearly we should never want to live in it again, there was nothing for Guy in a remote little coast town, neither future nor, for him, past. It was my past I rejected when we left it, finally, on the 9th of January, 1935.

The light that morning had a familiar clarity, at once cold and gentle, almost voluptuous. Looking, for the last time, at the view from the window of my working-room I felt a mortal grief. 'I shall never see you again, old road, old hillside. You are scored on my heart, to be found again, perhaps, at the last minute—*on n'arrive jamais à la mort sans dot*—but so long as I live, nothing, no view, will remind me of you. I am a fool to go.'

I was speaking in the emptiness of the room already stripped of its few pieces, the old chair, the long well-scrubbed table, a desperate cry, heard only by my own inner ear. No one had forced me to go, I chose to uproot myself from the one place where I am not a stranger—happy or unhappy, but not a stranger. The few primordial images I see my way by start here: the colour, in all weathers and seasons, of the North Sea, the enchantment of distant lights, the hard curve of the coast.

There was no room in the London flat for my table, nor for the rest of the furniture. It would have to be stored. I have never had the courage to get rid of certain objects some woman of my family chose years ago. For all my dislike of possessions, I drag about with me heavy tallboys, old chairs, old clocks, as if it were they who would suffer if I abandoned them. Or as if such capacity for loyalty and stability I have has taken refuge in them.

Explain why I threw away the piercing happiness my Whitby view gave me every time I lifted my head from my desk—no, I can't, though there must be a reason, other than insanity, why I arrange to drift like an anchorless ship, moving myself and my pieties from place to place.

Until this year the fear of another war had been balanced by a naïve incredulity. ('It's not possible, after the hideous lesson of 1914–18, for even a Hitler to risk war.') In 1935 it began to flicker continuously, just below the horizon, a lightning flash, a sudden thinning of the clouds, another flash, another.

In March and April we lived for five weeks in a village on the Spanish coast north of Barcelona. Since then, that coast has been, as they say, developed—that is, its mediaeval poverty, dignity, bigotry, and crust of old habits broken into. In 1935, the signs of civilization were a handful of German refugees living on—mercy, what were they living on?—and a school of young female artists, English, their trousers, bangles, and high screaming laughter so out of time and place that the Catalan women in their black dresses looked at them without seeing them. There was a harbour, a lighthouse on a headland, a beach given up to fishermen and their nets—the few visitors walked half a mile along the rocky coast to a narrow bay, the sea rough and ice-cold—four or five thin dusty streets of secretive houses and a few dark small shops where the owner began by offering the cheapest thing he had, and dry hills covered sparsely with scented herbs and shrubs. The single hotel was a large Catalan house owned by (I think) a Swiss, and furnished in the barest way. Our rooms were two cells, the stone floor and immensely thick walls meant to defeat the sun. After five o'clock in the afternoon they were bitterly cold, and the stove, burning green wood, filled them with a choking acrid smoke, without giving off warmth. Meals were eaten in a small courtyard round a wind-bent orange tree. A single Catalan waiter, with the face and bony elegance of Dürer's 'Death', did everything: without him, and without the pale smiling German-Jewish secretary, sitting in a cell at the back of the courtyard, gentle and exhausted, apparently unsleeping ('You want to leave at three tomorrow morning? I call you, I bring coffee. Of course I am awake, why not?') the place could not have existed.

A few hours, in the middle of the day, were hot, with a violent white light and a wind that exasperated the nerves and drove sharp grains of dust into the skin and under closed eyelids. After five it dropped, and we walked across the land side of a headland, following a path upwards between tall dry thorns and shrubs; these crackled like the snapping of innumerable tiny bones, on a note a degree sharper than the continuous creaking of the cicadas. There were no other sounds and even these ceased during minutes when the path crossed a naked slope, burned to the bone and eaten away deeply between distorted pillars of rock and dry earth. The path climbed interminably, rounding one headland only to twist across another; in the end we had to leave it and force our way down steeply between the crackling shrubs, two or three hundred feet, to the coast road; on the left the dark sea, the powerful acetylene lights of the fishing boats floating on it like comets, their tails lying across the ripples. Outside the village a man was still patiently turning over the few feet of dry stony soil on which he and his family—you could not say, lived—existed. A chorus of frogs made more noise than a dozen double-basses tuning up. The streets were empty, cold, silent.

My writing brain is at its easiest and most energetic abroad, or when I live in an hotel. If I could travel perpetually, only pausing for a few months in the impersonality of a hired room with a view, I should write with all the pleasure in the world. And write less, because I should not be bored.

My notion of perfect happiness as a writer is a foreign hotel of a decent simple bourgeois sort—I know a score of them, where I could be happy for a lifetime—a wooden table in a window looking out at the sea, a garden, hills, roof-tops, any expanse you like, coffee and croissants in bed, the morning and afternoon spent writing, the rest of the day sauntering, sitting in cafés, hearing music, seeing friends, reading, staring, making a few notes, while the next day's work ripens peacefully in the mind behind my eyes and ears.

During these weeks I thought constantly about a novel I had been meditating for several months, ever since listening to Dorothy Thompson's account of Hitler's 30th of June murders. What I wanted to do was to expose why a dictator is forced, almost always, to kill the very men who fought for him when he was only a brutal adventurer. I thought I knew why, and I could imagine an English Fascism, the brutality half-masked and devious, with streaks of a Methodist virtue. I saw scenes, landscapes, figures, but did not yet see clearly the figures of the dictator and his friend.

One night, between dusk and dark, I glanced from my window into the courtyard. It was empty except for two men, Spaniards, sitting at one of the small iron tables, drinking. The light from a single weak lamp fell across their hands lying on the table, and over the face of the older of the two. I had an extraordinary sense of the tension between them, a tension which was part of a deep wordless attachment. It struck me that there is a homosexual relationship infinitely subtler and more powerful than the physical one, subtler than any merely sexual intimacy, or than intimacy between men and women. The two men I was watching knew each other at a deep level: there was attachment and hostility, both a little dangerous.

I had my English dictator and his friend, the man he would have murdered.

Now I had only to write the novel. I began it in June, on a Norwegian island, Tjømø, in the Oslo fjord, so much more charming and likeable than the fjords on the west coast, which are a shade too handsome, and know it.

I was only retracing the voyage my remote ancestors had made—there are still Storms in Norway, and a vein of my mind is open to the older blood and the tart sceptical northern humour. It is certainly from them that I get my naïve belief in freedom as the supreme good... No Mediterranean warmth is as deliciously exciting as the brief summers of the true north; they don't soothe, they rouse. Tjømø is a small island, a wharf, a few houses and farms, fields broken by fantastic grey rocks. The water off-shore was like the air, as clear as the finest glass, and in the hot sun the pines gave off a heady scent of wild raspberries. There was a shabby friendly hotel, built of wood. Writing the whole morning, looking across a garden of long grass and fruit trees at a sky of astonishing purity, I was continually happy. Exquisitely happy.

*In The Second Year* has admirable passages. Since my interest, as always if I please myself, was in the extraordinary way human beings behave when they imagine they are being simple, heroic, truthful, generous, it was a disappointment to my friends on the far Left, who expected a direct attack on Fascism, with a Communist hero, and the rest of it.

In August we moved to Oslo, to an hotel half way up the wooded hill immediately behind the city, the most charming capital city in the world; it was small enough to be held in the hand, and contained all a capital city should, and once for all proved, if proof were needed, that the real horror of modern life is size, the inflation of everything, including cities. I hope it is still possible to leave the wide street running from the simple dignified royal palace in Oslo to the harbour, and, three-quarters of an hour later, follow a mountain path between wild strawberries and pines. A recipe for happiness—too simple to have any merit in the eyes of economists and politicians.

I am not suggesting that the Norwegians are simple people. On the contrary. The farther south you go in Europe, the simpler life becomes, and human beings. The endless winters of the north, the corrosive cold, the long hours of darkness, encourage people to live an intensely self-regarding life, and—of course—the more they live inside themselves, the madder and more complex they become.

One evening in Oslo we dined with Bjarne Braatoy's brother, who was a medical psychiatrist, and four of his friends, two Norwegians, a shipowner and his young attractive wife, a Dane, and a Swedish novelist. It was a superb dinner, afloat on aquavit and ending with a vast bowl of cloudberries. The talk never stopped, immense good-humour, violent arguments, outbreaks of crazy laughter, and not a trace of vanity or the reserve noticeable in any gathering of intellectuals in London ('Am I giving myself away to a competitor? Am I being impressive, witty, intelligent?').

Provoked by something Trygve Braatoy said, the Swede began a half-serious half-mocking analysis of the Norwegian character.

'You think,' he said to me, 'that Norwegians are candid, simple, spontane-ous. Nothing of the sort. In the first place, they are all mad or half-mad—the incidence of lunacy is the highest in Europe. How many writers do you know in England who have been psychoanalysed? One? Not more. Every one of my Norwegian friends has been or is being analysed. It is an occupational disease. I tell you, that old brute Ibsen knew what he was doing when he created Brand and Peer Gynt, the monomaniac, all or nothing, and the self-destroying braggart, the split man, imagination and no reality. At this moment, yes, at this moment, what you are seeing is not a meeting of simple souls, but a roomful of barbarians who have never been happy or content since they were forced to give up raiding and stay at home.'

'Then that goes for you, too,' his host retorted. He had the same ear-splitting high-pitched laugh as his brother.

'No. We have civilized ourselves. We don't go mad, we drink to be happy, and commit suicide when we are sober.'

Inevitably, the talk turned on the threat of war. Frowning, the young Norwegian woman said,

'When I look at my two children I feel a little guilty because they are safe, and yours are in danger.'

'Are you sure you are safe?'

'Why, of course, who would gain anything by attacking us?'

'Now, the Germans are a simple people,' the Swedish writer said, 'if you like. They are still in the amoeboid phase of humanity, an active outer layer taking in food and ideas from all sides, an inner layer which is still fluid. The day when they split into two cells, ah, that will be the day.'

At midnight, I stood up and said we must go, we should miss the last funicular to our hotel.

'You can't go yet,' Trygve exclaimed. 'We are just going to eat—if this much-talking Swede will hold his tongue for five minutes.'

I forget how, after eating a great many thin rolled-up slices of almost raw beef, and swallowing more aquavit, we got home...

Back in England in the first week of September, with the finished man-uscript of *In The Second Year*, I felt an irrational gaiety and hope. The Abyssinian crisis was in spate, and I ought to have felt anxious. In fact, I was convinced that there was no need to be anxious. Not because of what I learned from a friend who had been staying at Chequers, but from a purely irrational sense, born of the clear Norwegian air, the scent of pines and salt, the shiver of long sun-bleached grass in a light wind, that war was an insanity impossible in Europe.

When I saw my young sister she told me that she was going to have a child next year, in February. There was still a risk for her in child-birth, but she brushed it aside as not worth a thought. To speak of her courage misses the point. She was brave, yes, and without being conscious of it for a single instant: what was at work in her was her will, she wanted this child, therefore it was not only possible but safe for her to have it.

She asked me about the crisis. 'When I told S—— that I was going to have a child she said she would be afraid to bring children into such a world.' She laughed contemptuously. 'Can you imagine anyone being so *soft*.'

'There isn't going to be trouble yet,' I said. I repeated what my friend had told me. 'We shall give Mussolini no cause to make war on us, rather than do that we are going to let down the Abyssinians and all the small nations.'

'Are you sure?'

'Absolutely.' I wanted to reassure her. 'The Italian government has spent seventy-five million—francs or lire, I can't remember—on seducing the French press, which asks nothing better, and the Banque de France has been financing the Italian war credit. They are all rascals.'

The eyes she turned on me had the same remote look as my mother's, as if she were raking a distant horizon from the bridge of a ship.

At this moment I decided that when the London lease fell in I would move to Reading to be near her, and in November we found a flat of fine large rooms, the upper floor of a house on the edge of Reading.

I took immense pains to arrange these rooms, setting out in them all my possessions, as if for a lifetime of peaceful mediocre existence. I found a housekeeper who had been kitchenmaid, then a year in the still-room, then under-cook, then cook in an aristocratic household, and now wanted an easier life. To all appearance I was as near being perfectly settled as possible.

On a sunny windless day, the North Sea is an image of calm enjoyment, not a cat's-paw of disquiet, above an unfathomed depth of restlessness and treachery.

When I visited my young sister during this time I was moved by her happiness and pride in the least of her possessions. She and her like are the salt of the earth, I thought: I am a wastrel. As her thin body became heavier, her face took on a serenity and an innocence it had not had when she was a child—as though she were no longer seeking anything other than she already had. Remembering the impatient rage my distorted body had roused in me when I was carrying a child, I thought that something essential had been left out of my nature, or some foreign body lodged in it, a grain of sand in a joint. No use to be sorry now.

Her son was born on the 17th of February, 1936. She called him Nicholas.

## CHAPTER 10

AFTER THE 7TH OF MARCH, the day Hitler sent his soldiers into the Rhineland, I seemed always to be listening to the sound of approaching footsteps and counting stairs.

One evening I had arranged to meet Guy and Philip Jordan in the brasserie of the Café Royal. The large room, when I came in blinking from the cold wind, was a chaos of fragments, a waiter sliced in half, carrying a bottle and two glasses in his one hand, a decapitated head with small malicious eyes and black whiskers, splinters of light, a woman's face, mouth open in a grimace of alarm, another mouth laughing brutally without a sound.

I saw a face I knew, Thomas Balogh, and paused to speak to him. The League Council was still discussing the Rhineland affair, he knew a great many people, financiers, politicians, journalists, and might have heard something.

He is the nearest thing to a heartless intellect I know. Not that he is without heart, but his brain functions with no interference by that refractory organ. This detachment is not unusual among genuine intellectuals, the Central European variety of the species particularly, but he must have begun as a child to bring it to a fine point of dry rationalism, logic, malice, acid wit. He told me once that one of his early memories was that of looking curiously at a dead body as he crossed a bridge in Budapest on his way from school, during the revolution. 'What revolution?' I asked. He shrugged his shoulders. 'Oh, my God, why ask? You wouldn't know anything about it.'

'Tell me in one word what has happened or is going to happen,' I said.

'There isn't going to be war. The Council is going to adjourn indefinitely, without waiting for that scoundrel Ribbentrop. The French get nothing, not even a military agreement with us, there may be an agreement with Germany, there will be no sanctions. The League is finished.'

'Are you sure?'

'Of course I am sure.' He smiled sharply. 'Yesterday I talked to a German in the Embassy, not a friend, but I know him very well. He was very cock-a-hoop. He said: We've let you kick our backsides from conference to conference for a number of years, now we're showing you other parts of our anatomy, you won't kick us again, that phase is over... He's right, but the truth is, all those victims of hardened arteries and renal disease in the Cabinet are too timid and prudent to kick a louse. It's amusing to watch them.'

'If one had no children,' I said.

'My dear girl, don't let your imagination run away with you. Keep it for a novel. I suggest you write one about a Czech or a Pole—one of those nice countries with nothing to brag about but their past—running from one international conference to the next, watching Europe collapse. Call it: Useful Spade Work Has Been Done... If you are hoping to judge affairs in Europe by any form of reason or sane thinking, you had better hang yourself. It is a bloody laughter, my dear, and you are wrong to take it seriously.'

'Thank you,' I said.

Philip had brought a friend with him, a Foreign Office official, one of those exaggeratedly lean, tall, well-bred Englishmen who look young well into their forties: the only mark of his age was a groove running from the sides of his blade of a nose to the corners of a thin mouth. Call him X. I repeated what Thomas Balogh had said, and asked if it were true.

X. knew him slightly.

'These Central Europeans are too clever by half,' he said lightly. 'There is no agreement with Germany, only pressure for it in some quarters; the political ground is too spongy for it to hold up. Otherwise he is right—to a point.'

'Why only to a point?'

'Because he knows, we all know, that there will be demands and crises and demands and crises, and a superb operatic performance, Hitler as Wotan— do I mean Wotan? the fellow who sings bass and is a bore—reciting his sad story, and prophesying the downfall of Europe if we don't all join him in crushing the Bolshies. A lot of chaps who ought to know better, important chaps, will applaud, and he'll begin to think he needn't manoeuvre us and can go straight ahead. What Tom Balogh and his kind don't know is the point when this will be too much for us to swallow.'

'Do you know?' I asked.

'Of course not.'

I had an inarticulate sense that this picture of us as short on logic, that dubious continental trick, and saved at the last moment by sound English instincts, was one of our vanities. But I held my clumsy tongue.

'By the time we reach that point,' Philip said drily, 'there may be nothing left to stand on, and nothing to do but invite Hitler to take over Covent Garden. And I detest Wagner.' His tongue flickered across his upper lip. 'They say Flandin blubbered like a calf in the Council.'

'My God, how would you expect him to cry? Like a film star?'

'The people I loathe,' Guy said, 'are the Liberals. When *The Times* says we mustn't offend the Germans it's only doing its duty as the last voice of Queen Victoria and some distinguished birdwatcher or other. But the Liberal newspapers make me vomit.'

At this moment, the finger I was running round the stem of my glass came on a slightly chipped edge, and before I could stop myself I was fingering the chipped saucer I had used to float a night-light when my son had diphtheria. Something like a ball of blood exploded in my brain, I felt deaf and blind with fear and an insane anger. I stammered stupidly,

'Someone should assassinate Hitler now.'

I must really have looked insane. X. gave me a sweet condescending smile. I drew my shaking hand out of sight and tried to control my mind... The images in it were those any woman in any country might see, thinking of her child's brains spilled on the ground. In the 1914 war I had not felt this mortal anxiety for my friends who were being killed in France. Now, when I thought about my son, I became frenzied with fear. An irrational fear. But there was nothing irrational about my horror of killing, of the impulse, premeditated or blind, which sends men out to slaughter each other. Call it what you like—war, human butchery—nothing, not even the courage or docility of the soldiers, makes it less sickening.

I thought: And it will be no use. It will be like the battle of the Somme which went on for more than four months and killed the best in our country...

> The many men so beautiful
> And they all dead did lie...

If I believe that concentration camps, the torture of Jews and political opponents, is less vile than war, I must say so plainly, not pretend that the price is something less... With physical nausea, I thought: I can't say it.

I came back suddenly to the crowded over-warm room. Philip was talking, with a smile which curiously accentuated an air of transparence and bitterness.

'These Hoares and Simons would sell their own offspring to save their places and skins.'

'You're wrong,' X. said easily, 'they're all very decent public-spirited types, who wouldn't lie or cheat—except as a political duty. Or allow the Prayer Book to be messed about. In fact, that's one reason why they back the sober industrious tax-paying Boches against the corrupt immoral French. They may be limited and self-righteous, but they mean well——'

Philip interrupted, smiling. 'Yes, I know. If you talk to them about Dachau and all that, they think it's your dirty mind.'

I felt the instinct of an animal to bolt from my dilemma. Ashamed, I said, 'I couldn't go on living in England if we allied ourselves with these brutes.'

Philip raised nearly invisible eyebrows. 'Could you live in America?'

The pure line of the coast running north, seen from the East cliff, wavered behind my eyes. A stone leaning sideways in the rank grass had had its inscription eaten by the salt in the air, all but five words... *master mariner of this parish.* I felt an intense savage joy and pride in being one of the fraternity of master mariners.

'No.'

Guy said, 'The Germans have some virtues, but they're not house-trained—*sales Boches tout de même.* I'd join up again at once, to fight for France.'

But you were happy in the army, I thought without kindness: you were young then, and you enjoy not being responsible for yourself.

We drove back to Reading very late. Ahead of us on the Great West Road the shifting line of lights quickened an old excitement in me. A dark bubble formed of sea and sky closed round me; I had a sense, familiar and consoling, of time as a plain running out of sight on all sides, where in the same breath I was a child and dead, a phantom. I felt detached even from Guy. I thought: I've had several minutes of an absolute happiness in my life. In a final count, what matters more?

## CHAPTER 11

I WAS WRITING far too much. I told myself so at intervals. You are writing far far too much. And went on doing it. Was it at this time that I had a letter from Laura Riding ordering me to contribute to a volume of some sort? It would have involved hard work—I should have been ashamed to do less than I could—and I refused, explaining that I was already over my ears. I had a letter from Robert Graves, rebuking me sharply for not being delighted to put everything else aside when Laura had done me the honour of an order.

I could not feel about her, as he clearly did, and as she felt about herself, that she was quasi-divine, but, sceptic that I am, I had no impulse to jeer. She was as hard on herself as on others.

I finished (7th of March, 1963) *None Turn Back*, the third in the *Mirror of Darkness* series. In a long review in the *Listener*, Edwin Muir explained carefully why the book was an imaginative failure, 'because Miss Jameson's real theme is society, and all these people are seen as conditional responses to society; with the result that they must remain conditional, that they can never speak to us: society is their ventriloquist. The ventriloquist is brilliant and sometimes moving, but...' etc etc. At the end of his long analysis, with every word of which I agreed, passionately, as I read it, he said: 'The generous passion and the complete honesty of the story are beyond praise. The writing is sometimes exquisite, and always has the directness and candour of good prose. In spite of its faults, therefore, this is a novel which no contemporary reader can afford to neglect.'

Most of them none the less neglected it. And I knew he was right about the imaginative defect. I knew, too, that the effort I had been making for the last three years, to uncover the social web of the thirties and the men and women caught in it and struggling, was not contemptible. There are honest and moving things in all three books, and, what is worth more—part of an aesthetic creed too lightly decried now—they are, so to speak, built to be lived in. But, though certain of the characters refused stubbornly to die, and became central characters in later novels, I could not go on. Edwin Muir's criticism did no more than confirm in me my own frightful sense of dryness, *accidie*, when I thought about it. Dryness or spleen? I gave myself sensible reasons. That I was writing in a vacuum—not enough people were interested, and one cannot write without the complicity of at least a generation. That no one could write the sort of novels I had planned at the pace forced on me. What you need, I said, is a private income, time to spend several years brooding, rewriting, with no pressure to finish a book and be paid for it.

(When you come to think of it, the life of a professional writer is as horrible as would be the life of a politician condemned to offer himself to the public every year for re-election.)

All damnably true. But... to do what I wanted to do, give life and a form to the vision of England moving cloudily in my brain, I needed—what? The daemonic energy that drove a Balzac to empty himself to create a world, the egoism of a great writer, a Tolstoy, a Proust, forcing him to put everything, every human being, family, friends, himself, a bad second to his task.

The deep reason why I abandoned *The Mirror in Darkness*—but I see it only now—was a stifled instinct warning me that I was working against the grain of my talent. The restlessness and dryness were eddies, rising briefly to the surface from a subterranean river which was *my* truth, *my* reality.

I refuse to regret the energy spent writing polemics against war and Fascism. Still less the energy given to helping a few, too few, men and women to escape the hell of German concentration camps, and then to keep them alive. Nothing in me is fiercer, more obsessive, more nearly involuntary, than my loathing of the cruelty that issued in Auschwitz, except the sense that exile is only the human condition pushed to its farthest limit.

These images have burned me to the bone.

I could not have held aloof. No regrets. A concern with politics, a conviction that political activity was obligatory at that time, was right. Wrong as wrong was the fallacy that political passions I could not ignore had somehow to be pressed directly into my novels. I confused an inescapable personal commitment with a totally mistaken and crude literary one.

After *None Turn Back* I had an impulse to efface Storm Jameson altogether. Not that I had the wit to realize that my profound boredom with her was due to an obscure instinct that she was making a fool of herself.

Instead of turning the poor animal round to find her right road, I left her, and wrote two short books, and then a third long one, under two other names.

The first two, written this same year, were *récits*.

I began *Loving Memory*, by James Hill, on the 10th of March, an ironical story of a man's relationship with two women, one of them his dead wife. This—and James Hill's full length novel—were published by Collins, who loyally kept my secret.

The other short book, *The World Ends*, was a very different affair. I wrote it with intense care and the most acute pleasure—a story of the drowning of the world except for a fragment of Yorkshire moorland, an edge of the high moor springing abruptly from the plain west of Thirsk.

It was written slowly, through the summer and early autumn. I finished it on the nth of October, and began an absurd intrigue to get it published. I decided to send it to the firm of J. M. Dent, only because I knew that one man there, Richard Church, would like it. The letter I sent with it was signed William Lamb. I don't now remember whether I intended to deceive Richard, but, when he wrote asking William Lamb to come and see him, I found that I could not, absolutely could not, bring myself to unmask.

I sent my young sister to see Richard Church.

The game amused her. I don't think he was taken in: he guessed, I think, that this slender blue-eyed woman was not the book's author, but he could not shake her self-possession.

He sent her a contract, which I have, signed by William Lamb in a fine sloping hand.

A few weeks later, I went to a dinner given by the P.E.N. Club, and found myself placed next to J. B. Priestley. Over dinner we became reconciled—so far, that is, as any Yorkshireman is ever reconciled to having been treated with less than the respect due to him. We left together, and on the way out, were stopped by Richard Church.

Going into company makes me reckless; I talk too much or I listen in silence, with approving smiles, to opinions that curdle my soul. Richard talked about publishing, and I asked him whether Dent's had any interesting books to come.

'Yes, one,' he said, 'an extraordinarily fine book by a new writer, William Lamb.'

'Ah,' I said, 'I'll read it.'

'I'll send you a copy,' he promised. 'We're going to make a handsome book of it, with engravings by John Farleigh.'

'I'll read it,' I repeated.

As he walked off, J. B. Priestley called over his shoulder, 'She'll cheat you, you know.'

What made him say it? A resentful memory of that harsh review? An atavistic instinct—one astute ironical Yorkshireman seeing right through to another's guile?

*The World Ends* finished, I turned back to Storm Jameson—I needed her—and wrote a long novel which was in reality a retreat. Into my mother's past and my own. *The Moon Is Making* was a Brueghel-like novel about the violently individual men and women, obscure eccentrics, dreamers, saints, their veins filled with the strangest fluids, whom my mother remembered from her childhood. Some of them were still alive in mine, in particular one, a Unitarian minister called Haydn Williams. His hatred of poverty and injustice devoured him. In an earlier century he would have been a Chartist, earlier still, a Leveller. When what had been a piece of commonland on the West cliff was enclosed to become part of the Spa gardens, he went there and tore down the iron railings. He was fined, jailed, and as soon as he was free, tore them down again, and again. The police lost patience and began to handle him roughly, and the common people he wanted to protect came out to laugh and jeer at him. A freak is a gift to men and women who have, after all, hard narrow lives and few amusements.

I was very young then, and I assumed that he was mad and said so to my mother. To my astonishment and mortification, she said contemptuously, 'You don't know what you're talking about, you little fool. What he does is useless and silly, but he's a brave good man.'

I daresay that few of her sharp speeches struck me harder. I don't say that it alone is responsible for my respect for rebels—which in turn is partly responsible for what I have made of my life.

## CHAPTER 12

IN MAY THAT YEAR MY MOTHER stayed with me in Reading. It was a superb spring, the lilacs and chestnuts so full that each tree was a single massive flower, dazzling.

She could not walk far. I drove her about the countryside to look, with that blue fixed stare, at an inordinate beauty, almost too much, too cruel and insistent an energy.

'I shan't see them again,' she said suddenly.

To hear her say it angered me sharply, and I said, 'Of course you will, you'll be here next May and I'll bring you to see them.'

She looked at me without answering; she had wanted to be reassured and was not.

In August, my middle sister wrote from Whitby that she had had 'an attack', and was very ill. All the way in the train, an eight-hour journey, I was nagged by anxiety, and then impatient when I thought of the book I had had to abandon, and must finish soon: I needed the money.

'She thinks she has had a heart attack,' my sister said, 'so be careful.'

When I went into her room and saw her lying in bed on her side, my heart shrank; her face, her soft hair screwed into a plait, her eyes, all had in some way given up, as if this time she were really defeated. She spoke in a voice I had never heard from her, slow, slurred, coming from a great distance.

'I'm glad you're feeling better,' I said.

She was a long time answering. 'Am I?' she said at last, like a child who has been told by an adult something it can't take in.

I was both anguished and numbed, I refused to believe what I could see. Deliberately and yet as if blind and deaf, refused. She must not be dying—that was not thinkable. And, if she were, I could not leave her and go back to my life and my work.

Her recovery was very slow. Time confused her terribly. The kind thing would have been to let her live in her own time, waking and sleeping as she pleased. But she had to live by others' time, and it was a torment to her. She slept, and woke bewildered; or she forgot she had just eaten, and demanded her lunch, and then begged us to give it to her, half weeping. Sometimes the railing voice of a lively self-willed child broke from her; sometimes it was the strong full voice of a young woman I could just recall.

I knew when she was living in the past, because her mouth shut in a hard stubborn line; she was thinking of her dead son, and my father's unkindness to him, or of some other bitter cause she had for not forgiving her husband. She forgave him nothing. The dry indifference she had come to feel broke, and now she could not endure him. When he came into her room—as once a day he did, and stood awkwardly, looking down at her, for a minute—she closed her eyes.

'How are you feeling?' he asked, pretending ease.

'Better,' she said icily, and waited, clenched, until he had hurried away.

I think that now she hated him simply because she had married him, not for anything he had done. He stood for the disappointment her life had been, for the absence of all an ardent quick-witted young woman had expected from it and had not had.

We talked about my young sister, and her house and her baby, end-lessly, since I was the one person who would listen endlessly. Even this was not completely safe, and once, as she had said about the chestnuts, she said,

'I shan't see Do and Nicholas again. I shall never be well enough.'

'You'll be as well as ever,' I said lightly. 'You've had a bad heart attack, but if you're careful you won't have any more.'

There was a long silence. Then she said slowly,

'I don't remember the heart attack.'

It shamed me that I, her child, was deceiving her. And that perhaps she was not really deceived.

One evening when she and I were alone in her room—she was strong enough now to sit in the window, looking, looking, looking—she said in a hesitant voice,

'Sometimes, in the night, Daisy, I feel afraid.'

I shut away, at once, the agony of grief. 'Why should you be afraid?'

'I don't know. But I am afraid.'

'There is something you could say to yourself; you could say: *In quietness and in confidence shall be my strength*. It's what *I* say when I'm afraid.'

I would not let her fear reach me. Would not. I kept it away from me, I would not know or feel what was taking place in her. She was not going to die, so why think about it, why suffer? I shut both mind and heart against what, if I let it in, would destroy too many of my defences and pretences. There were moments when I thought it would be better for us all if she died. And this, too, I did not look at.

Days and weeks went by. When she was strong enough to walk the short distance to the nearest shops, though not alone, I prepared to go back to Reading, to Guy and my unfinished novel. She did not want me to go.

It was like all the other times I had left her. I had to go, I had to get away—back into my life, into the world. As I had done at these other times, I hardened my heart.

To catch the only train that would get me to Reading that evening, I had to leave the house very early, at half-past six, and when I went into her room to say goodbye, she was half asleep: she was lying in the bed as though she were sinking in it, her eyes closed. I could scarcely hear her when she spoke.

'Don't go.'

For less than a moment I knew that I should hear that remote barely audible voice in the deepest recesses of my brain, and those two words, all the rest of my life. Then I closed my ears.

'I *must* go,' I said. 'But I'll come back—I'll come as soon as I can.'

She did not answer or lift her eyelids to look at me—as though she had lost interest. Or as though she had known all along that she could not count on me, had known I would fail her, and were turning away from me.

I did not go again until, in February, my sister wired me to come. Because, in winter, there were fewer trains to Whitby, the journey was endlessly roundabout, and I was tormented by the thought that I might not get there in time. Time for what? My mind drew back sharply from that edge.

The dark, the cold North Sea wind, the empty streets—it could have been any of the evenings when I jumped out of the school train from Scarborough and hurried home.

'Do didn't think of coming with you?' my sister said.

'How could she? She can't leave the baby.'

'Well, it doesn't matter,' my sister said wearily, 'she's forgotten her.'

'What do you mean?'

'Last week, when Do's box of snowdrops came and I took them in to her and told her Do had sent them, she asked: Who is Do?'

For all these years the abiding passion of every moment, and it had dropped out of her hand. Why, then you have had nothing, I thought, oh, my poor love, nothing.

She was reared up on pillows, her face empty, a skull, not a face, the cheeks sunk, the eyes a blue absence of sight: she was the image of her father, my hard grandfather: nothing of her was left except the life of her Gallilee tribe.

I bent down, thinking I should be able to reach her.

'Here I am, Mother.'

Slowly, almost imperceptibly, her eyes turned towards my voice. For less than a second.

'She's going fast on her journey,' the nurse said loudly. She saw my frown, and said, 'Oh, she's completely unconscious, y'know.'

I no longer remember whether she was two days or three finishing that journey. I slept through the nights. During the day, whenever I could be alone with her, I bent over her and said softly, 'Don't be afraid, I'm here.' But she made no sign that she heard me. Once I said, 'Don't worry, I'll look after Do for you.' I was forced to believe that, somewhere in the silence, she must remember her youngest. My breath was cut off in my throat by the knot of pain. Tears came against the hard effort I made; I could not bear it that she did not know I was there.

'You and I have been on so many journeys,' I said, 'and now you are going alone.'

I was ashamed to be crying, afraid that I was crying over myself, and ashamed to be seen crying. When the nurse came into the room, I hurried out.

On the second or was it the third evening my sister said that we had better begin to destroy or put out of reach things she would not want my father to touch.

She lay in her bed in the lighted room, seeming asleep, breathing lightly and rapidly, while her daughters turned out drawers and looked into cupboards. I came on the box full of my brother's letters from France. I began destroying them, then stopped. They can live with me, I thought: let someone else destroy them. I took the photographs of him, the young blurred image, a boy still, in the uniform of the Flying Corps, and the parchment *au nom du Président de la République*, awarding him his *Médaille Militaire*.

Laid under gloves in a drawer there was a letter from my father, written thirty-three years ago, in 1904. 'My darling wife, this wishes you Many Happy Returns on your Birthday. I am enclosing you £5 (five pounds) cheque to buy yourself something as a present. Well my Dear your welcome letter to hand well I am sorry you have such hard work and trouble with the children. You should let them run wild like animals that is what they are. It doesn't do any good making a fuss of them spending money on their clothes all they want is enough to cover them never mind looks. I don't give myself trouble about clothes and none the worse for it. Well we have had a lovely week. Sunshine all day and a smooth sea and this morning the sun is shining and a blue sky and 60° in the shade. I am happy and in good health and the air here is beautiful coming in the berth. Well my Dear I trust you are feeling alright and get all the sunshine you can for it will be best for you both for health and happiness. Now I will close with best love and best wishes and take care of yourself. Your loving husband Will.'

Very distinctly I saw the sea captain in his shabby uniform bent over the table in his cabin writing, in his backward-sloping hand... Why did she keep this single letter out of hundreds? Is it silly to think that, perhaps, under the bitterness, a single flicker, of warmth, regret, was still alive?... I put the letter in my pocket without showing it to my sister.

We found a large crudely coloured photograph of the three of us as very young children, my middle sister and Harold—he still in petticoats—smiling like idiots, I looking sullen and stolid. We laughed over it madly, and tore it up. I remembered suddenly that it used to stand in my father's cabin in the *Saxon Prince*. He must have brought it home, or it would have been sunk by the German cruiser in 1916, with his other possessions.

The night nurse came in as we were finishing. She looked closely at my mother and said quietly,

'She's going home.'

I would not take this in. Mechanically, without conscious effort, I refused. I went to bed and slept, in the next room, leaving her with the nurse.

Towards one o'clock the woman roused me. I went in. She died so quickly that even if I had cared to speak to her with other people in the room there would not have been time.

When I saw her again, it was daylight. Between them, the two nurses had made an image of her, lips upturned as never in life, an almost suave smile, not hers at all, her face ivory, small, ice-cold, fine soft hair drawn back from her arched forehead. Now I knew that she had really gone. It was a purely physical agony, a nerve being ripped out of me, slowly.

Downstairs in the hall I came on my father, standing at the foot of the staircase, crying. He was wearing the frightful suit, soiled and green with age, he insisted on wearing in the morning until he went out. I spoke to him awkwardly, with a false pity, and he turned his back on me, vexed. He cheered up later, and went out to be shaved in the town, first asking me if I had seen the chequebook of the joint account. I gave it to him and he took it away to his room. What a time he'll have going through the counterfoils, I thought.

When he came back, shaved, he handed me a paper bag. 'Here's something for you and the other one,' he said, smiling pleasantly. There were two grapefruit in it. He always bought these at Christmas, one for each person in the house. I suppose he had felt this was a day to be marked, and since the nurses had taken on all the business of a death, he had nothing to occupy him.

I kept going into her room to speak to her, when I could do it without anyone noticing. The cold of her cheeks shocked me, and the silence, but I could not let her lie there alone all day. (Why—since I had slept during her last night?) Each time, another piece of my life was ripped slowly out.

'I'm here,' I told her, 'I'm here, you're not alone.'

The agony came up again, tears poured down my face: I forced them back, and went away. No one must see me.

When she was alive, my father never entered her sitting-room. This evening, when the men brought the coffin, he came in. He was shivering with cold. He stood in the middle of the room, throwing quick glances round him, and said,

'I'll go out. I'll go out at the back.'

'Why?' I asked. 'Why go out? You're better here. Do sit down.'

He sat down in one of the armchairs, and began to talk about a pain in his chest. 'I shan't last long,' he said.

I despised him for trying to get attention and sympathy. Besides, he did not mean it; he had every intention now of living for ever. The men were walking about in the room overhead. I knelt and poked the fire noisily.

'Are you warmer?'

'Oh, I'm warm enough,' he said jauntily. 'I don't believe in warm rooms. Hers were always too warm for me. I've been forty-eight hours on the bridge in bad weather without so much as a hot drink. That's nothing, that's nothing.'

He laughed his short defensive laugh and went on talking about himself until the steps overhead ceased. Then he shambled away.

Later that night when I went into the kitchen, he had put aside his endless newspaper competitions—he never won anything—and was turning the pages of his scrap-book, and crying.

'Look,' he said, 'look what I've found.'

He pressed a long brown knotted finger on a yellowed cutting from some Australian paper. 'Y'see?'

I read the lines, shutting my mind against them.

> 'Then home, get her home, where the drunken rollers comb,
> And the shouting seas drive by,
> And the engines stamp and ring, and the wet bows reel and swing,
> And the Southern Cross rides high!
> Yes, the old lost stars wheel back, dear lass,
> That blaze in the velvet blue...'

'All them voyages,' he said.

What does he see? I wondered. A foreign quay that no longer exists as he knew it, blinding sunlight in a street in Vera Cruz, in Santos, in Montevideo, and a young woman who holds a sunshade over her as she walks with that light step towards the corner and the waiting cab, and is gone.

I left him sitting there. I had been sorry for him for a minute.

Shut in my room, I waited for him to come upstairs. When he had come and gone, padding quickly, almost silently, across the landing and up the further stairs, I went in to say goodnight to her.

'You're so cold,' I said to her.

I touched her hands, her cheek. The skin was soft.

'Goodnight, my love, goodnight, goodnight. Don't think about anything. The journey is over. Oh, my love, my love.'

Bitter grief hardened my throat and scalded my eyelids, and it was all no use.

The next day when I went in I saw that a faint colour had come into her cheeks. She seemed younger and vulnerable, and yet more nearly serene. This new image of her, this tranquil, inconceivably tranquil face, masked, at least for now, the tormented skull of the last days, and wiped out the image of the last few years, the blue fixed stare, the face which had become shapeless because her mind had given up bothering to mould it. Yet the last was what I ought not to forget.

I tried to recall other images of her. They must, each of them, have been familiar—the very young woman, tireless, the woman touched by time but still so eager to live. But nothing would come except an image drawn from a photograph, shallow and meaningless.

This smiling tranquil dead woman threatened to efface all the others. I turned away. Suddenly and piercingly, I saw her standing before the long glass in her other bedroom; she was trying on a new hat and looking at herself with such intentness that she seemed to be willing another self to step out from behind the one she saw.

My only chance of seeing her again is to catch her off guard in moments like this, I thought. And in sleep.

My father had been standing outside the room, waiting to say something. He was holding a painting on silk, made by a Japanese artist from the coloured photograph my sister and I had torn up. He gave it to me.

'It's no use keeping this,' he said hurriedly, 'since you're all going.'

I preferred not to glance at the abyss under the words—all but hidden from him, too. I am like him in the cowardice with which, when I can, I dodge an unpleasant reality.

It was her last day and night in her house. I went in and out of her room, and talked to her. The delicately flushed cheeks, the smooth rounded forehead, the smiling mouth, the rigid body, dreamed their own dream, indifferent to us, the living.

I stood there in the dark, alone as I had never been.

'This is your last night with us,' I said. 'Forgive me for all I have thought against you in vile moments, forgive me for all I did not do for you. Remember me only as the child I was, wholly in your hands.'

The searing grief ran over me. I felt drained of life, naked, and defenceless. Help me, I thought, help me.

That is a long time ago, many years. All but a few of the things she saw every day, and liked, have disappeared from my life. I keep a few. It is a long time, too, since I made the effort to see with her eyes the harbour, the old houses crouched against the side of the cliff, the abandoned shipyard, the old church, landmark for sailors, the fields and woods she knew. On the rare, very rare, occasions when I go back, no shadow comes to meet me. But—at any time since then I could have said this—the story is not at an end. Her life did not end then; it goes on echoing through mine, and will echo there until it and I are both silenced.

## CHAPTER 13

FOR A LONG TIME I used to catch sight of her easily: she seated herself in a certain chair in her bedroom in my flat and looked with pleasure at the reflections of a vivid sunset in the tallboy (made in 1799 of mahogany for a Whitby shipowner and sent to China in one of his sailing-ships to be lacquered and brought back), or she came towards me from an old mildewed glass I had taken from her room. Objects have a long memory of their owners: her leather and silver travelling flask, when I touched it, had that instant been laid down by a hand swollen with age. These memories were wholly involuntary. I never sought them. A scene, a colour, a sound, split open as I brushed past it, and for an instant she was there.

In June, we went to France, and on our way to Royan stayed three nights in Bordeaux. The heat in that opulent city—which still, in some remote way, belongs to the English—was so heavy that it ran like a yellow oil down the old buildings on the quays, over the lighthouse columns, over the tracery of ships' cranes, and lay like a fog above the surface of the Garonne. I learned as a child the habits of a sea-captain's wife; it takes more than a violent sun to keep me from running about the streets of a foreign city, staring. I slept

little—like Bordeaux itself that month. It seemed that only a few minutes
separated the moment when I was looking at the Monument des Girondins,
a white finger poked through the dusk, from the next when the rising chatter
of scores of birds under my window in the Place des Quinconces woke me,
and I got up to watch colour come rapidly into the sky over the harbour,
obliterating first the street-lamps, then the single brilliant star.

On the second day we took a tram along the right bank of the river as
far as a small village called Cambes. There was a very small hotel with a
lawn of rough grass going down to the river and big coarse marigolds, and
tables under the trees and on a wooden platform built out over the water.
Barges passed very close, going downstream. At a table nearer the house,
were three people who caught my eye, a boy and two middle-aged women,
one in black silk with a great many old-fashioned gold chains and rings,
dark-fleshed, her hair dressed in tightly-rolled curls over her whole head,
the other also in black, shabby, leaning forward with an ingratiating smile,
much too eager to please, or hoping for something. But it was the boy who
attracted me. He was perhaps ten or eleven, very pale, with a head a little too
big for him, the hair springing back stiffly, like fine wire. His hands, laid on
his thin knees, were remarkable. He was frowning: obviously, I thought, he
is both ashamed of his mother's anxiety and sorry for her, and a little anxious
himself.

He and his mother were people I and James Hill had been looking for.
The other woman, well-to-do and fleshy, I did not know yet, but I knew a
little about her house in this village and its grotesquely ugly furniture and
ornaments...

At that time—two years before the war in which it was flattened into
piles of rubble—Royan was a little town of enchanting simplicity: a front,
two beaches of clear sand, a street or two, a pleasant unassuming casino, a
few hotels. The visitors were all French, no Germans, no English—bearded
papa, plump vigilant mamma, children making no more and no less noise
than birds, girls and sunburned youths playing ball. My bedroom in a modest
friendly hotel faced the sea, and after my coffee and croissants—served by the
lean smiling overworked and completely indefatigable Joseph, who waited
at table, ran up and downstairs with trays, swept, dusted—I sat up in bed
and made notes for the full-length novel James Hill was writing, and read

(since the central character was a musician) a life of Busoni, a volume of his letters, Berlioz's memoirs, and an account of van Dieren.

I have never known, and cannot imagine, a life of greater, more exquisite happiness.

On our way home in July we drove from Rouen to Arras through country which has been fought over so often that the dust must be more than half human, and certain names of rivers and villages are fixed in the brains of a great many living, and of a great many of the half-living—and who knows anything about the dead?—like nails. The country itself did not mean very much to me, but what I saw as a mere empty grass-filled depression between two fields, Guy saw alive with young bodies, restless with life. Many of them had now no other life. But there was one village—I have forgotten its name—where a few graceless new houses had been set down hurriedly in the middle of fields which still looked shabby and vacant: there were a great many coarse nettles and no trees. A long and unnecessary action had been fought here; it lasted for two days and a night, a short night, and some thousands of young men, English, were uselessly killed. Did the present inhabitants of this uncouth village ever feel that they were hopelessly outnumbered?

As soon as we were at home, I had to arrange for my son to start his training as a civilian air pilot, at Hamble. (Nowadays, that *air* before the word pilot seems superfluous. Not to me. When someone speaks to me of a pilot, I have first to rid my mind of a weatherbeaten face and robust body coming up the side of the ship, hand over hand, to take her into dock or to the mouth of the river.) He was twenty-two, tall, remarkably good-looking with his fair skin and speedwell-blue eyes: except that he had finer eyes and a long narrow head, he looked much as my father would have looked had he been carefully nurtured instead of starting at sea at the age of thirteen. Both had a northern look.

His single ambition was to fly. His career—what a word for so careless a passage—at Cambridge had been irretrievably altered by it. He went there to read for the Mechanical Sciences Tripos: in his first year, since he has a good brain, he did very well. Then, in October 1935, he was allowed to join the Air Squadron and thereafter did little except fly, and fall in love with a young woman a few years older than he was, a lively handsome creature, with whom he spent the time when he was not flying or making casual efforts to work a little. He listened amiably to his tutor's reproaches and complaints, agreed that he must do better, and continued to do as he pleased.

Very soon he was forced, with no regret, to give up hope of the Tripos. He did a little work, enough to earn a pass degree and lend him, for an hour or two, the disguise of a student. The rest of his time he spent, very happily, amusing himself and flying. He left Cambridge this year, when we were in Bordeaux, with his degree, a number of debts, and the young woman—she would have made a splendid wife to a less absorbed or more ambitious young man.

In my eyes he had changed little: looking at him I saw easily the engagingly beautiful child, amiable and quietly self-willed. The degree to which I was responsible for his indifference to success—no, his active rejection of anything except the one thing he wanted to do—is too clear. My restlessness, my profound loathing of a settled life, were being played through in another key...

The training at Hamble would take two years. He agreed readily—why not?—that it was impracticable to think of marrying before he had finished it. Now that he had got his way about flying, he was happy; he would wait, the young woman would wait; there were mitigations. I had no hope that a marriage I knew in my bones must end badly would not take place.

## CHAPTER 14

EARLY IN SEPTEMBER, when Guy went to Spain to stay with his old friend Peter Chalmers Mitchell, I went with Lilo to Paris, taking with me—of course—a half-finished manuscript. I had agreed to live at the rate of her purse—she refused to help herself from mine—and she went ahead to find an hotel. She found it—a place meant for students—in the rue de l'Abbé de l'Epée, and engaged two attics. The rent in English money worked out at less than one and four-pence a night. You can easily imagine what, at that price, our rooms were like: low, narrow, a thin bed, a chair, a decrepit small table, a sort of wardrobe, all of the roughest sort and depraved by years of ill-usage, a strip of worn-out carpet, a cracked bowl and jug of cold water for washing. On my first evening I looked round it with unspoken dismay.

No, this is too squalid, I told myself, I'm not young enough to live like this again. Lying down gingerly between the coarse sheets, I pushed from me a blanket which might be clean but did not look it—just as the stairs, polished by a servant who spent the whole day on her knees, had acquired a second membrane of hard ingrained dirt.

In the morning I saw that from my window I could look across the roofs of even shabbier houses to the dome of the Panthéon. In a strict light, the absence of all softness, all blurred lines, was suddenly exciting. Less than a quarter of a century ago I had been living, in London, in no better or more reassuring a room, without caring. I turned back quickly to rejoin a penniless young scholar hurrying to offer me her tireless body and joyously inquisitive mind.

I can live here easily for two months, I thought, oh, easily.

To say of Paris that it is cruel is a generalization for the simple. No city I know is so determined to endure, so clenched on an old root which reaches down, unbroken and still sappy—not only in carefully-preserved great buildings—in narrow foetid streets with overflowing gutters, squeezed between houses which have not had a sou spent on them in five hundred years, to the twelfth century. To stay alive for so long requires, no, involves, a certain detachment, not to say contempt for things and persons which are *not of the family*. Yet this city, this face stony with age, at moments wears a smile purely enchanting and as young as the infant born five minutes ago in a room of one of these ill-smelling dilapidated houses. Neither its hideous poverty nor its beauty contain it. At its coldest and most sordid it keeps a certain air of breeding, a suavity, little shaken by the barbarism of our age.

We breakfasted—a single cup of coffee (abominable) and a roll—in a small dark low-ceilinged bistro at a corner of the rue St Jacques—Abelard's rue St Jacques to the life and slippery gutter. A few workmen at the counter, taking their first drink of the day, had an air of unhurried enjoyment. Sometimes we lunched there, on another roll and a glass of yellow Anjou wine, cheap and instantly intoxicating—but the effect wore off before we reached the end of the street. This quarter was full of cafés, Chinese, White Russian, so cheap that Lilo was reluctant to dine anywhere else. Certain that I was being poisoned, I ate these appalling meals with a calm which went unadmired—except by myself.

To her overwhelming energy and curiosity, Lilo joined a ruthless dis-cipline. We did not saunter through Paris, we walked, briskly, miles, vis-iting, quarter by quarter, museums, old squares, churches, palaces, the Louvre, modern painting in the Petit Palais, markets, the outer boulevards, Montmartre, parks. To save myself from dying of suffocation I took care, wherever we went, to look—that is, look—at only one or two objects. This is why to this day I remember every line and delicate feature of a thirteenth-century oak figure of an angel, in (I think) the Musée de Cluny—long slender nose, curled hair, strong childishly thin neck, closed lips turned up at the ends in a smile of pure malice, which spread to the eyes with their suggestion of a pupil, and fine springing eyebrows. I remember it, too, for another reason.

One morning, when we were in a café near the Halles, a young porter came in, a magnificent animal, filthy and sweating. Lilo looked at him with naive admiration and greed.

'Look at that strong sunburned fellow,' she said gravely, 'I should like to have him as my lover.'

'He'd probably beat you.'

'No, no, I should make him wash and teach him to respect me.'

'Never,' I said. 'Prussian though you are, he would defeat you.'

She laughed without resentment, a flash of her strong very white teeth. 'Well, you are always right.'

It was the year of the Exhibition. We went several times, and walked, in the torrid sun, from pavilion to pavilion, bored by the loud-mouthed effrontery, smugness, or swaggering efficiency of the great nations: only the smaller peoples know, or had remembered, that a polite host effaces himself before his guests, does not bawl at them, or insist on their admiring his wealth; again and again we went back to the fountain of rose-water in the Bulgarian pavilion: the man in charge of this unpretentious building, almost always empty, recognized us and came forward with a pleased smile. He had so little French that he could only beckon us with gestures from one to another of his few treasures, but he flattered each with his small muscular hands, watching our faces to make sure we shared his delight. Except for the enchanting fountain there was really very little to see, but it had been arranged with intelligence, perhaps with tenderness, and the effect, in the middle of so much that was alarming or intolerably noisy, was very reassuring. After all, how young Europe is.

Lilo had friends in Paris, an odd assortment. Where had she met and impressed the Turkish writer, Halide Edib? We sat in the Deux Magots with her for a long time, eating croissant after croissant, for which she was going to pay, while she talked about her life in Kemal Attatürk's army.

'I was a soldier, you understand me, I wore uniform, I fought as infantrymen fight. I was Kemal's friend, but when he made himself dictator afterwards, I turned against him, and left him and Turkey. Since then I am only a writer.'

Another afternoon it was a Jugoslav, a Professor Jovanović, who invited us to the café at the corner of the rue Soufflot. To explain his politics to us, he raced through a history of Europe from the tenth century, smiling joyously as he presented first one and then another triumph of civilization—'*Donc, les autobus! Donc, les avions!*'—until he reached the crowning evidence, the Parti Paysan of Jugoslavia.

These were incidents: her closest friends, who became mine, were a lycée professor and his wife, Henriette and André Buffard. Any Englishman who has the luck to be invited by a cultivated Frenchman to his house or flat finds himself with delight in an atmosphere he has met only in the memoirs and letters of two or three finely cultured families of the late Victorian age. The affluence is missing, but the assured intelligence, the ease with which ideas are passed from hand to hand, the inborn goodwill and politeness of heart are there, as if these were still the only criteria of civilization. And with them a play of light, a gaiety, a cutting edge, which is not English at all, of any age.

Not only does André Buffard look as though one of his ancestors may have been a quick-tempered cat, he has a wholly feline independence of spirit, a little savage. Add that he is—there is no English phrase for it—*un coeur sensible*, an almost reckless sensibility, passionate to a fault—and you have, crudely drawn, the portrait of a natural anarchist, incapable of taking on trust an idea or a creed, instinctively mistrustful of received opinions, not because they vex him, but because they are hypocritical.

He was a close friend of another relentless individualist, Alain.

His contempt for the politicians of the Third Republic was vitriolic. He mocked me smilingly when I said that another war was unthinkable except as a paroxysm of irrational fears.

'Why delude yourself that rational ideas have any place in politics? Certainly there may be war—there are enough idiots in all countries—and this time, this time, it will not unite France. You'll see.'

What I had seen or felt already was the curious difference between the war fear here and in England. I explained it to myself by the mere existence of frontiers: the Spanish war, now over a year old, roused violent feelings in England, but we did not feel the ground move under our feet. Open on three sides to Europe, the French were less able to work off their fears in speeches from platforms.

Even the refugees from Germany—we knew several of these—living, many of them, in rooms shabbier and poorer than our attics, were tenser and more anxious. And this was not only because often they were really more insecure than their fellow-countrymen in London. One of them explained to me,

'It's infinitely more difficult to get into England than to get here, but once in England you are not continually harried, you have your papers. Here—' he spread his hands—'you can sneak in here without them, and then you spend your whole life trying to scratch together as many francs as will make all the difference between living, however uncomfortably, as a human being or as a louse, always in danger of being trodden on by the police, by a neighbour who dislikes Germans, by anyone.'

He was a gentle good elderly man, a painter of landscapes so innocently orthodox that he could, if he had chosen to close his eyes and ears, have gone on living comfortably in Munich: he was not a Jew. Here he lived in the city cellar of a house sinking under the weight of its age and filth, eating little but potatoes.

'They are cheap, and even more important, clean,' he said, smiling.

His closest friend was a young Berlin Jew called Emil, living, at the other side of Paris, in much the same conditions, except that his room was large and almost completely bare. One evening when we went there, the painter had carried across Paris the large water-colour he had just—a true miracle—sold. It was to be delivered, packed, to the buyer—a former patron, on a visit to Paris from Munich, who had accidentally discovered him here—at the Ritz next morning, and he was sure he could not make a decent parcel of it. Swathing it delicately in the clean remnants of a shirt, and paper he had begged from a shop, Emil said to me,

'Do you know what the fellow paid for it? I'll tell you.'

It was a very small sum.

He was whispering, but his friend overheard him and said reproachfully, 'Emil, you are still grumbling. And on a day when I am divinely happy.'

'He could have given you the proper price.'

'But,' the painter said gaily, 'he came to see me in my room, and he saw how little I spend. Why should he give me more?'

Both these men had the precious papers they needed not to be chased from their pitiful foothold; but they did not, for that, feel secure. Emil was working feverishly, like a spider, or like an old woman piecing together fragments of string, to get himself to America. It tormented him that he could not persuade the painter to move.

'You know, you can't trust the French,' he said urgently, 'at any moment they may round on us, they'd care as little what became of us as if we were stray cats.'

'I know, I know,' the other said, with his old man's innocent smile. 'But I can't run away any further, you must go, you have young legs. I'll take my chance here.'

No one in this room had better reason than I to be convinced that they were perhaps right to fear for their safety. The house I had just come from, to meet Lilo here, between Emil's bare cracked walls, had shaken more than one of my illusions. Listening to André Buffard's sarcasms about 'the other France', I had put down part of his savagery to an intellect which was all sharp edges. This afternoon I had with my own eyes seen 'the other France'—in a house in the seventh arrondissement. Impossible not to admire, coldly, the nearly inconceivable elegance of the women, an elegance no other country, even much wealthier, is able to bring off—I daresay unable to hit on the exact proportions of genius and hard-hearted insolence—and impossible to imagine anything more magnificent, more opulent, more imposing, brilliant, flawless, than the drawing-room itself, its rococo scrolls, curves, mirrors, chandeliers, and the rest.

I should have breathed easier in this room if it had been what it seemed, an incredibly lavish stage set.

The only person, apart from my half-American hostess, to whom I talked, a little, was a Madame de C., indecently rich, related by marriage to a

Guermantes family. She introduced me to a middle-aged politician, slender, sinuous, bull-voiced, a human organ-pipe. I listened, at first idly, then with an astonished attention, to what they were saying to each other. Until this moment—although I had been told, not only by Buffard, that rich Frenchmen had only one emotion, the fear of losing their money, and would go to any extreme to muzzle persons and classes they suspected of being Reds—I had not believed that this feeling, if it existed, was strong enough to make two people, intelligent, without a drop of any but French blood in their veins, talk of Hitler as a Messiah and of an alliance with Nazi Germany as the quickest way—the politician's phrase—'to castrate socialism and the Red swine once and for all.'

Madame de C.'s fine eyes softened as though she were going into an ecstasy over a painting or a symphony.

'Castrate,' she echoed. 'Figuratively, of course. Why not?'

I had not the courage to say a word. I left them and wormed my way towards the anteroom.

They are not, I said to myself, France.

I reached the arched doorway into the anteroom in time to see a guest arriving alone. It was a long room. Two rows of footmen, tall splendidly healthy young men, in silver and sky-blue, formed a lane stretching its whole length. Along this lane the guest, a man, walked rather slowly, the footmen bending before him like Lombardy poplars in a wind. The two nearest the door, speaking together, announced him, but I did not catch the name.

I watched him being politely mobbed. The celebrated writer who, in the hour I had been there, had not altered by an eyelid his pose of bored distinction, dropped it instantly, and began a deferential sentence of which I understood only the first words.

'If your Excellency will allow me to...'

I had the curiosity to go back to Madame de C. and ask, 'Who is it?'

She raised her eyebrows. 'Surely, you have met the German ambassador?'

I thought: It is a rehearsal.

I did not entirely believe what I supposed I had seen. Certainly, I told myself, if they could, these people would carelessly hand over Emil and his friend and all the other refugees to be 'castrated' (figuratively). But had they any power—except to live as the very rich live?

After considering it uneasily for some time, I thought not...

The next day, we dined with Edgar Mowrer. I had not seen him since the evening of the Hindenburg election in Berlin in 1932. He and his wife had a fine apartment near the Chamber of Deputies, and as we walked up the wide staircase I thought that these intelligent Americans moving about Europe from one threatened country to the other must have a vision of it which it would be interesting to compare with that of a fifth-century monk meditating on the sack of Rome.

With this in my mind, I was enchanted by his third guest, another journalist. Helen Kirkpatrick had the head, on a slender American body, of the thirteenth-century angel in the Musée de Cluny, the same firm delicacy of line, the same finely ironical smile.

During dinner I described yesterday's reception, no doubt exaggerating its flamboyance. 'But of course,' I said lightly, 'these people have no real influence or power.'

'Don't be too sure,' Edgar Mowrer said. 'Your Proustian epigones are a bad joke, but there are at least as many better-placed men and women, bankers, rich industrialists, politicians, who ardently admire and respect Hitler, here as in London. Monsieur X. may be more corrupt than most of them—no one believes that he cleans up less than a hundred thousand francs out of the Budget in the week before the new taxes are announced—but he isn't the only politician I have heard saying that he would rather give Chartres to Germany than see a socialist France. These people would feel *safer* as vassals of Hitler. Naturally they'd rather not go so far, but if they had to...'

'What has happened to this country?' Helen Kirkpatrick said, smiling. 'The French used to be fighters.'

I felt a prick of anger. 'Have you any idea how many Frenchmen were killed in the last war?'

'I'm only now beginning to realize *how* deeply that war weakened France,' Mowrer said. 'The standard of the reservists is very poor, and as for their generals! Weygand is so out of date it's not believable.'

I was experiencing a familiar difficulty in saying clearly what I thought; somewhere between my brain and my tongue the words fell into a helpless disorder. I said stuttering,

'I don't believe we, or the French, can be defeated by a people quite so intellectually repellent as the Germans... that frightful cold mysticism of theirs that makes them turn everything into abstractions—trees, the Rhine, human beings... They don't *see*, I mean, either things or people, they see abstractions they call the Volk, or the Jewish infection, or *Brutalität*, or... Our minds may be slow and untidy, but at least they're still in touch with the real world.'

'But there *is* something wrong with the democracies,' Mowrer said gravely. 'They didn't defend themselves in Spain—that war is lost, you know. Stalin doesn't give a damn about his Spanish friends—why should he, when neither your government nor the French can make up its mind which stinks worse, Hitler or Republican Spain?'

'England isn't France,' I said. 'We are still sound.'

'You may be right. But you threw away your last chance to trip up Master Hitler two years ago. If he had three divisions in the Rhineland that was the most. The French had four times as many behind the Maginot Line. My belief is they never had the faintest intention of trying to hold him off—they knew they couldn't. Now, the Germans are so strong that if you want to contain them you'll really risk a war. *Which you may very well lose.*'

If I had dared I would have said: Nonsense, the English don't lose wars. It was what I thought.

I had a sudden uprush of fury—no doubt humiliated annoyance with myself and my tongue.

'If there is another war,' I said, 'we ought to scatter the Germans over the face of the earth afterwards.' I controlled myself. Looking across the table at Lilo, I said, 'I'm sorry.'

She gave me a warm brilliant glance. 'Perhaps five just men will be saved,' she said, smiling.

She left Paris a week before I did. The weather changed: overnight the bland honeyed warmth of September withdrew itself, and in the last days of October a cold west wind drove heavy clouds like Atlantic rollers across the whole sky.

I am never happier than when I am alone in a foreign city; it is as if I had become invisible.

The evening before I left I sat outside a café in the Place Théâtre-Français, watching the blown jets of the fountains and shivering a little: a fine rain, more mist than rain, more a cold breath than mist, clung round the street-lamps. If

I were to stay another month, I thought, or if tomorrow morning I were to go south to Bordeaux, I could finish James Hill's novel... The daily business of living, about to close round me, would delay it.

If, I said to myself, you thought this or any novel more important than other things, you would not live as you do...

Before I could save myself, the finger of mist on my cheek had swept me as far north as Whitby: glancing over my shoulder I saw the flagged path across the fields behind her house, the line of bare trees, and on the left, across a valley, the hill rising steeply to the moors. How long before I cease to see this path and the two figures moving along it? Never. Unseen, unheard, unending, her life, like mine, turns at the same point, on the same path, between the same hill and thin pale line of sea.

Yet somewhere I had lost my way...

It was too cold to go on sitting here. I paid, and walked back to my attic in the rue de l'Abbé de l'Epée. Refusing to think that it was my last evening of freedom, I was very happy.

## CHAPTER 15

THE TENSION OF THE WEEKS after Hitler's triumphant march—a parody of Wagner—into Vienna. Imagine a steel coil round the brain which is slowly contracting. Or smoke thickening in the air from an approaching fire. Any trivial incident reported in the papers, a frontier shooting, a dictator's access of vanity, a speech by some maniac, could mean that it had started and would go on from here.

On the afternoon of the 22nd of May I was with my young sister. She was to go into a nursing home that evening, to have her second child. The news was bad: Hitler had moved troops to the Czech frontier and the Czechs were calling up their reserves, and the rest of it and the rest of it. She said, casually,

'I suppose we shall be at war very soon.'

I supposed it too, but I said,

'It's not all that certain.'

She hesitated and with the same air of indifference—she would cut her hand off rather than show fear—said,

'If it happens at once, where could we take the children—Nick and the baby?'

'Perhaps to Canada? I know some people there.'

'Oh, no.' She shook her head. 'I didn't mean take them out of the country... You don't know anyone who could tell you how serious it is?'

'Yes, I do.'

With her watching me, I rang up Philip Jordan in London and asked him what the journalists and foreign correspondents he knew thought about the crisis. He was reassuring.

'If you'd asked me last night I'd have answered differently, but now the feeling is, strongly, that this isn't it, it's going to simmer down.'

I told Do. She smiled vaguely and calmly, without making any comment. Looking at her closely, I thought that she was too deeply absorbed in what was going on in her body, the child's movements there, to be much disturbed by anything outside. At thirty-one, she still seemed a girl of twenty—at most twenty. Her air of delicacy, the pure outline of her face, its brilliantly clear skin, hid a toughness, a northern toughness, that I had yet to see shaken.

Her daughter was born the next morning. In the afternoon when I went in to see her in the home, she said,

'I counted twenty-seven heavy planes flying over us about an hour ago.'

'Yes, it's an Air Day.'

Her expression changed very slightly. 'D'you know what I thought? I thought war had been declared and the Government was trying to reassure us.'

'Didn't you ask the nurses?'

'Of course not. They would have told me some silly lie. I waited for you.'

In June, as English delegate to the P.E.N. Congress to be held in Prague at the end of the month, I had to attend the dinner-party given by the London Centre before one of these affairs. I went with a light heart. The guest of honour was the Czech ambassador, Jan Masaryk, and, if nothing else, I thought, I can watch him.

Jan was an entertainment in himself, Elizabethan in its daemonic vigour and cheerful bawdiness, a miracle of wit and energy. He had more energy in his little finger than most of us in our whole bodies. Perhaps he enjoyed good food, wine, talk, and women, a little too much, but they did not destroy him. He enjoyed his life as might a fine animal who had been endowed with a human mind of the liveliest most acute sort. Even when he was unhappy, his dejection was shot through with an ironical gaiety as likely as not to issue in jokes that would have been in place in a barrack-room and did not endear him to the more formal of his diplomatic fellows.

'An outrageous buffoon,' one of these exclaimed.

'What,' I asked, 'outrages you more? That he sometimes plays the buffoon, or that he is not one?'

All I remember about the dinner itself is the speech made by old Henry Nevinson. In his nearly inaudible voice he talked about international decency and good faith, about Czechoslovakia, and the duty laid on us to help a small democratic country to defend itself against the lies, abuse, and threats heaped on it by a bully. I think he knew already that, for decent and indecent reasons, our statesmen had decided to try to buy peace by encouraging the bully to sate himself on this small country, and he was using up the last jet of his life's passion for justice, as, without thinking about it, he would have used the last drop of blood in his old veins. As I listened, I felt the deepest reverence for him.

After dinner, H. G. Wells, who was taking Masaryk and Baroness Budberg, a woman I admired very much, to his house in Hanover Gate, asked me to come with them. Afraid as I am of not being equal to the talk of very intelligent people, I was pleased. Not simply flattered. I would have gone anywhere to listen to Moura Budberg's voice. It is the most enchanting female voice I know, rather deep, but not too deep, with a double note in it which is indescribably moving. Goodness knows how many times, in a novel, I have tried and failed to describe it.

I suppose she was then in her middle forties, but she might have been any age; she was heavily-built and cared nothing about her looks—she had been beautiful—and dressed with lazy indifference. Why not? She has spiritual elegance. She belongs to a very rare class of human beings—if one can call a class that which is strictly a handful of unlike men and women who may lead lives of the greatest saintliness or the greatest amorality, without in either case ceasing to be given love and respect, since at no moment will they act against their nature, which is essentially good, sensitive, generous, and supremely tactful—that is, devoid, within human limits, of egoism.

H.G. loved and depended on her. His dependence took the form that evening of not wanting to let her out of his sight. When she left the room for a minute he followed her to the door, calling,

'Don't run away from us, my dear Moura. Where are you going? Don't be long. I want you here.'

She put up with his insistence as unselfconsciously as a child. Not that she was or is in any degree childish. It would be truer to say of her: She is a gentleman. There are honest gentlemen without a rag of charm: she charms as she breathes, naturally.

No doubt there are flaws in her—I certainly hope so—but what can they matter by the side of so much courage, warmth, nature, openness to life?

H.G. wanted to provoke Jan into indiscretions, the easiest thing in the world.

'D'y'know,' he said in his high weak voice, 'what a Conservative Member of Parliament, a woman, said to me the other day? "*After Chechoslovakia*, we may have to put our foot down." My dear fellow, there are men, powerful men, in this country who detest you and Beneš.'

Jan was in a ribald mood. Walking up and down the long room, twitching his lips like a clown, and drinking, he amused himself by imitating the Foreign Secretary.

'Oh, I know, I know. When I got the news about the German troop movements on the 20th of May, I went to Halifax with it and told him he must have enquiries made in Berlin. Halifax said, "You're always making us ask questions and we don't like it." I trembled, of course, but I insisted. I must know what the Germans are up to, I told him, because everything depends on me, and it's me they're attacking, not you. So Halifax told Henderson to ask Ribbentrop in Berlin.' He stood still, staring at us with eyes as impudent and lively as a schoolboy's. 'Your ambassador in Berlin is a scoundrel and a Fascist,' he said, smiling. 'Ribbentrop told him: Oh, just manoeuvres. And Henderson telephoned the Foreign Office that it was only the bloody Czechs trying to stir up trouble. Then more news came in, and back I went to Halifax and got him to tell Henderson to ask again. In the meantime we moved some troops, and this threw Hitler in a rage he worked off on Ribbentrop. So, when Henderson came in, Ribbentrop banged the table and spoke to him in language which has never been used in diplomacy. Not even by me. "What the hell do you mean by coming to me with this crazy stuff? Go and look after your ramshackle empire, which we're going to crack like a nut." So Henderson was annoyed and said, "What the hell do *you* mean by speaking to me like this. I'm His Majesty's representative, etc," and left. That helped us. Ribbentrop sent for our Minister in Berlin and told him, "Take your troops away, take them away, I say.'"

He made a gesture I liked, scattering a pinch of dust with his fingers. 'Ah, if only he had said it to me!'

'You don't understand,' H.G. said maliciously. 'You think you're an outpost of western democracy, wonderfully civilized and all that. You don't torture your political prisoners. You have no concentration camps. You don't give anyone any trouble. If you did, we should begin to respect you, and write to *The Times* warning people to try to understand your proud, frank, loyal nature.'

Jan brought his hand down on the table with a single obscene word.

'I'm devoted to you, all of you, you're the nicest people in Europe. But why in God's name are you so afraid of—whatever you are afraid of? Why do you let Hitler go on making a balls of Europe? Are you hoping he'll leave you alone and attack Russia? Would you? Would you go after a bear, with a fat sow of a British Empire within reach of your foot? You're mad. No, no, I don't mean you or old Nevinson, God rest his soul. But what the devil is your pious candlestick of a Halifax telling the Nazis behind our backs? What does he think would happen if Hitler were able to swallow us? Peace and——everlasting?'

The malice in H.G.'s voice sharpened to the squeal of a hacksaw. 'Not Halifax—another member of the Cabinet—said a week or two ago in my hearing: The Czechs are a nuisance in Europe, that fellow Beneš is a nuisance, a common adventurer. If Hitler goes in we shan't stop him.'

Jan shook with laughter, fingers splayed out on either side of his stomach. He had a stomach. 'I'm delighted to hear that your Cabinet finds Hitler well-bred and dependable, it must console them when he kicks their backsides. We poor Czechs—so ill-bred we even keep our promises—of course we stink.'

Without giving myself time to lose my nerve, I said,

'No, it's nonsense. We can't afford to drop you overboard. For our own sake.'

He rolled his eyes at me. 'Why not? You let the fellow march into the Rhineland, re-arm, grab Austria, threaten. Why not my poor ill-bred little country? You'll ask him to promise not to do it again, of course. And Halifax... oh, my God, Halifax. You know, my dear girl, you English really are too awful, too supercilious. I happen to think Heine the greatest poet in the world, also I was brought up on the Bible, and I told Halifax, "Listen. If the Germans tried to take away my Heine and my Bible, well, I'm afraid I should fight." And he said mildly and casually, "Yes, old boy, yes, old boy, that would be awful." I started to be riled, and said, "Well, if the Germans came here and took away your Shakespeare and your Bible, you wouldn't like that, would you?" He got excited at once and said, "By God, that would be terrible, terrible." I said, "You see? It doesn't matter a damn about my little Heine and my little Czech Bible, but your Shakespeare and your Bible, that's terrible! You don't care what happens to my soul, only about your own."'

He began to laugh at himself, and said sweetly,

'Halifax is a good sort of a man. He rides and he prays... He is even a sportsman. Y'know, he shoots birds. So, when one of our policemen killed those two Sudeten chaps in Eger with one bullet, and I went to tell Halifax, and he sat there trembling and wringing one hand—the other is paralysed— and repeating, "The fat is in the fire, the fat is in the fire," in a shaking voice, I said, "Well, after all, Halifax, he got a double."'

He roared with laughter. His excitement was beginning to run away with him pleasantly.

'Our mobilization in May went off without a hitch,' he said, shouting, 'two hours quicker than we expected. And you know what? There isn't a Prussian second lieutenant who isn't ashamed to his guts of the march into Austria. The bloody fools drove tanks from Munich, three hundred miles, they were ditched all along the road. Why didn't they take the train or come by steamer like sensible people?'

For some time H.G. had been fidgeting in his chair as though he were tired of listening. He said in the strongest voice he could manage,

'I take it that, in Prague, I shall have a chance to talk to Beneš alone?'

Jan stared at him. 'Certainly. I'll arrange it.'

'I shall tell him the exact truth. Whether he likes it or not. I shall say, "Don't delude yourself, the men who have all the power in London and

Paris don't love you. Or democracy. Their bank credits matter to them, nothing else. If you're relying on us to lift a finger to help you you're off your head. We haven't the slightest intention of risking trouble. If you'll take my advice you'll make terms with Russia. Now. Before the worst. It's your only chance—a risk, of course, but safer than trusting us. Or France." If he won't listen to me... well...'

He opened his hands and let Beneš fall to the floor.

'Ah, to hell,' Jan said, grinning. 'Of course the Germans are going to march in. We know it, and we shall fight. And lick them. Every Czech man, woman and child, is ready to fight. In Prague last week I was talking to the archbishop. He said, "Though I am an archbishop"—y'know, he had all his robes on and you could see he wasn't Pavlova—"if Hitler came into this room now I would strangle him with these hands."'

He rocked from side to side, ready to burst with pride in his country, and so confident that I was tempted to tell him to knock on wood. Why didn't I?

When we left, at midnight, it was still warm in the streets. London was wide awake, people sauntering, standing under lamp-posts, and in doorways in each other's arms. The searchlights were closing in on an aeroplane, so high up there was no sound from the engines: caught in them in the dark sky, it looked like a very small weak moth.

Masaryk drove the large open car as though he enjoyed it, with terrific energy, talking all the time.

'Y'know, he's not a joke, Hitler, but when he says that as a passionate architect he can't bear the thought of Prague abandoned to the Czechs, you laugh, my God, you laugh.'

He put an arm round my shoulders. 'Who cares if you rat on us?' He laughed pleasantly. 'We have our army.'

## CHAPTER 16

WHEN WE REACHED PRAGUE it was already dark. My bedroom in the hotel in the Václavské Náměstí—the names were a reminder that we had crossed a frontier into another Europe—looked down on to a restaurant in the courtyard of an old building, not more than five or six small tables, a lamp on each, no other light: it had the look of a stage set, the opening scene of a ballet; at any moment the next to principal dancer would come on and begin his delicate lively steps between the tables with their motionless couples. It was deeply exciting, an old memory, its start far off at the very beginning of my life.

In the morning, after sitting for two hours, oppressed and silent, through a meeting of the Executive Committee, delegates from all over Europe under the chairmanship of an imposing Punch figure, Jules Romains, I walked about Prague, alone. The hot dry light-fingered sun made me feel that I could walk here forever. That and the exquisite pleasure of being in a city where the past is still confidently alive. A double past, mediaeval and Baroque. Other capital cities, as splendid, as careful to preserve their old buildings, are in comparison stiff and wrinkled. In Prague the seventeenth century has kept the ease, the supple limbs, the smile, the amiable boldness, of a young man. This week, too, the streets were full of the Sokol striplings, carelessly lively and free-stepping, the girls hardly less broad-shouldered than the boys, and older men in red shirts, with the Sokol coat flung across a shoulder, like soldiers off duty. Trained in groups, in villages and small towns, to the same music, when they came together for the first time in the Stadium they moved as a single body, a vast ballet.

To look at these confident children, brought up to the free use of their bodies and minds, and remember whose hand was reached out to strangle their country—oh, intolerable.

Later that day I watched a score of them, fresh from their village, marching through the streets as lightly as if they were at home in this superb city. As they were. Jiřina Tůmová, the secretary of the Czech centre, was with me, a small slender young woman; her face, colourless from exhaustion, was so small and narrow you could have cupped it in a hand, and she had a quick ravishing smile.

'See how gay they are,' she murmured, 'and proud, like dancers. When we train them for the Sokols we take care they are not stiff like Germans. It is a *free* discipline. They must be as if springing from their soles on the ground. You see?'

In the garden of the Ministry for Foreign Affairs that evening, she slipped from one group of chattering writers to another, listened for a minute, and moved on. With their instinct for what is perfect in itself, the Czechs had not brought out lights. In the half-luminous June night, the seventeenth century, smiling, vigorous, suavely self-possessed, had the Černín palace and its garden to itself.

'They are happy?' she asked me anxiously.

'You can see they are.'

'Yes—' she laid on my arm a light cold hand—'but do they know how madly hard we are working, so that no one shall be ignorant or too poor? When they go home will they tell the truth about us? Don't mistake me, my darling—' listening to the English, she had taken the word to mean 'my friend'—'I know that none of you will tell lies. You will write that Prague is beautiful, that we are kind and stubborn and eat a great deal of goose and dumplings. But... tell me, please, why does your Government not say to Hitler, "These dull sober obstinate Czechs are our friends, do not threaten them"? Why?'

'We can't let Germany overrun you,' I said uncomfortably. 'For our own sake. We're as selfish as any other nation, but we're not out of our minds.'

I could just see her face, paler than usual. She was not smiling.

'I hope you are truthful, my darling, as well as kind and clever. And I must tell you—if our friends refuse to help us, we shall fight without them. But I am sure you will not refuse. And France—' her voice rose to a bird note—'the French will never fail us. They have promised.'

'Do great nations always keep their promises to small ones?'

She was more than a little shocked. 'You are talking about France!'

She and Jan Masaryk, I thought, are two unlike faces of the same coin, the same country. I suspected that there was another Czech, shrewd, hard, with the hidden malice of a peasant, subtler than he seemed, and capable of a simple brutality as unlike the planned bestiality of his enemy as possible.

She and her husband, a doctor, took me back to the hotel in an open car. In the darkness I could only see that he was young, with a calm friendly face. He stopped the car at the other side of the river and told me to look back. The castle had been flood-lit, with the utmost delicacy and subtlety. Lifted up by its hill as by a dark wave, Hradčany rode at anchor above six hundred fathoms. I looked at it with joy, my God, what joy—and grief because in

six minutes an airman could wipe out an angelic beauty that had stood for
six hundred years.

'You have a superb country,' I said.

'And we shall keep it,' Jiřina said very calmly.

The next afternoon I was with her in the Street of the Alchemists, a narrow
lane close to Hradčany. Its absurdly small mediaeval houses leaned against
each other in the sunlight. H. G. Wells and Jules Romains had asked for an
interview with Beneš, and were with him in the castle now.

'What are they going to say to him?'

The warmth and the light made me reckless. 'I can tell you. They are
saying that the only people in France and England who admire you for your
reasonableness and honesty are middle class liberals and intellectuals, of no
importance and without any influence. If you murdered Jews and socialists,
and had a great many aristocratic families and powerful financiers, you would
have many more useful friends.'

She shrugged her thin shoulders. 'You are joking, my dearest.'

'Not entirely.'

'Well, we are not afraid,' she said lightly. 'If we are forced to fight we shall.
All the children you have seen will fight. And all the old. And we shall win.'

Later, Moura Budberg told me that H. G. Wells had said what he intended
to say. Had warned Beneš not to trust too much in his English ally. And
Beneš had smiled. It was impossible, he said, smiling, that self-interest, if
nothing else, would not compel a rich civilized country to protest against
international robbery with violence.

What Jules Romains had said she did not know, or did not tell me. No
doubt he had been diplomatic and eloquent.

The P.E.N.'s International President had eloquence to spare. Behind a
table or a rostrum, the shortness of his body was less noticeable; his large
head, its features at once heavy, wooden, and delicate, impressed, even
while it made an English listener think of Punch (without his friendly
hunchback).

From where I sat to hear his speech when he addressed the Congress, I
could see Jiřina: she was listening gravely, but with so clear and delighted
a satisfaction that I began to listen to him more attentively. It is what the
reporters scribbling at their table will call just and moving eloquence, I

thought. Very just about the dangers facing the world, very eloquent about the deaths of civilizations, and with a curious echo—the sound a finger-nail would make tapping an empty vase.

*'Be wise, moderate, supported by a wholly good conscience, fair to the point of generosity. Beware of clumsiness—so much goes without saying—but beware in at least equal measure of excessive competence—of that excessive competence which has done so much harm wherever you turn these past few years...'*

Did he, I wondered, think that a good conscience would serve in place of allies? Had he advised Beneš to be generous? To whom?

Such an abundance of crypto-clichés seemed excessive even for a French rhetorician...

I had looked at the baroque sculptures in the superb Valdštejn palace and noticed, for the first time, that there is a trace of cruelty in the smiles and bossed eyelids of these voluptuous angels, and in the delight certain monks and priests were taking in their own sufferings. This evening, the Minister of Education had arranged for *Romeo and Juliet* to be played, in Czech, in the garden room of the palace. There can be no more beautiful room in the world. Giovanni Marini built it, a few years after Shakespeare's death, at a moment when the energy of the century was approaching the height of its exquisite curve. We sat in darkness in the garden and watched the dancers move quickly and lightly up the shallow steps, and through the triple archway of white columns into the great room. The young men ran, fought, argued, with ravishing energy and boldness. Words I could not understand rang like gold coins, so new and un-handled that they might have been only just written down in time for the first performance. It was shockingly new. There was a moment when Mercutio, who must at that moment have cried out 'I was hurt under your arm,' turned his head towards a foreign audience he could not see with an extraordinary air of contempt. It reminded me of Jiřina saying, 'We shall keep it,' and my spine felt cold.

I was sitting beside Henry Nevinson. In one of the brief intervals, tired and a little sunk, he glanced round him—black trees, a sky the colour of blackish plums, swallows and flittering bats. Suddenly he took hold of my arm in a painful grip, long dry fingers.

'To think, Storm, that all this will go on and on, and in a few years I shan't be alive to see it.'

I don't remember what I answered. What answer could I have made to staunch *that* wound?

Are there left such men as Henry Nevinson was? Passionate quixotes who feel injustice anywhere in the world as a nail driven into their own flesh?

After we got home, he wrote three or four times a month in a hand which over the years became more and more broken and thread-like. I answered every letter and kept a few, out of piety. His house was damaged in an air-raid, he had to leave London, and his letters became the bitter complaints of 'a useless old man'.

'Can it be possible that we must spend another winter in exile? I had hoped to patch up our house, but it would be too expensive for the risk of another blast. I fear now that I shall die far from the centre, my inward life, and you. I look at the churchyard here and I don't like it, I should so much prefer a chariot of fire. I don't think even you can imagine what joy two days in battered London gave me. Here in Campden all is beautiful, but on every side an angel with a burning sword stops me and asks, "What dost thou here, Elijah?" I am saying goodbye to all my friends, but I will not say it to you yet...'

To whom were these scores of letters written? Not to me, not to any flesh and blood woman. To an echo, to the answers his own youth sent him.

It saddened me to watch this incomparable fire burning out, shielded by Evelyn Sharp's thin gentle hand. When he died in 1941 it was a ghost who withdrew from all the places he loved. Sitting immediately in front of me in the chapel, Evelyn looked too small and slight for so many heaped-up flowers, such a weight of death. When, to watch the coffin disappear, she stood up, she made the movement with her arms that a tired woman makes at the end of a hard day.

The Czechs had arranged a journey for us across the country to a summer hotel in the High Tatras, the mountains and mountain lakes on the Polish frontier. That was for the English. With a fine tact, they arranged for the French delegation something less spectacular and slightly more sophisticated and, above all, in another place. We travelled together as far as a Slovakian village.

A memorial service was being held there, in the single street. In 1918 four hundred Slovakian soldiers had refused to fire on a company of Serbs; their colonel, an Austrian, ordered the company to be decimated, and one of the forty young men on whom the lot fell came from this village.

There was a tablet, a file of soldiers, and a handful of peasants, men and women. An officer and the Lutheran pastor shared the clumsy platform.

Standing in the hot sun, we listened to the preacher's trumpet of a voice. Suddenly he spoke in bad English.

'Do not be afraid, Englishmen. We do not fear.' He smiled at us sternly. 'N'ayez pas peur. Nous, nous sommes heureux.'

The officer, too, was clearly a peasant, with a great beaked nose and large hands. He spoke in a curt voice, each word a blow. The Czech writer who was standing behind me muttered,

'He says: This soldier who was murdered by Austria is your lesson. All of you, men and women, get it by heart.'

The officer stepped back, and a big lean man in a shabby French uniform sprang forward and began to speak with a strong American accent.

'English friends, I love America, I lived there honourably when I was young. I say to you that we, peasants, have no time for things of the spirit. You must enjoy them for us, you must keep them alive same as we for three hundred years kept our freedom alive in our hearts. Thank you. Glad you came.'

Climbing into our motor-coaches, we rushed away to a town smaller than many English villages. The town band met us and played us in, and we sat down in a great barn to a feast—soup, roast goose and pork, cabbage with carraway seeds, dumplings, roast chicken, salad, strawberries and thick cream, rich cakes, eight sorts of bread—the whole grown, reared, given and prepared by the women of the little town. It was a divine feast; I have never eaten a meal like it, not in Paris. A torrent of fine white Mělník wine and powerful home-made slivovitz poured down our throats. My tongue loosened by it, I made an emotional speech, followed by one of the French writers. Would we help them to defend Czechoslovakia? No question, we were their allies, we would fight with them. Roars of *Na Zdar* and, 'Come again!'

'Come again—you are our friends!'

'Next time,' shouted a young Slovak, 'bring your rifles with you.'

He laughed, his French and English friends laughed, the musicians fiddling for dear life laughed. A troop of peasant cavalry had been waiting, and galloped beside the motor-coaches for a mile, then turned back, laughing and waving. I had the strongest possible impression that there was nothing to laugh about.

In Bratislava the Slovak P.E.N. was waiting to entertain us. I have forgotten how they did it—no doubt the Danube was called in to help. I remember two things. The face, charmingly serene, a little the Flemish madonna, of the chairman of the Slovak P.E.N., Marina Pauliny—I sat next to her at dinner, we talked about the Czechs, and for the first time I realized that they were not one but two nations.

'They are a fine people,' she said carefully, 'but they look on us as their young brothers, who must be taught. We are less cautious, less—what shall I say?—*serviable*, but we are a nation.'

(Rather more than a year after this evening, she reached London through France, and in 1942, when I was living there, came several times to see me. She was so confident of returning to Bratislava that there were hours, days, when she forgot that, turning a corner, she would not see the Danube. Immediately after the war, she contrived to get herself a seat in one of the first aeroplanes going back; it crashed as it left the ground and caught fire.

It happens sometimes that I drive past Blackbushe airfield. I don't forget to pray shortly for the soul of Marina Pauliny, as she would expect of a friend. Not that her spirit would hang about that desolate place, it would go back directly to a country untouched by cruelty or violence, the only one it remembered.)

The other thing I recall was the walk I took, after dinner, with a professor of the Komensky university, Otakar Vočadlo. We sauntered along an embankment, the Danube moving with us silently in the darkness. Almost silently. Now and then an underwater sigh or whisper interrupted for a moment what my companion was saying. He was in love with England and English literature, and he spoke very simply about the time he saw coming when his fluency in the language would be useful to English soldiers.

I—even I—was exhausted by the travelling, the long days, and the effort of enjoying banquets where I was forced to make a speech. The kind of lucid penetration fatigue gives the brain before numbing it made me notice that there was nothing forced about his confidence in us: he believed—as a man believes in the friend he has known all his life—that, when Hitler attacked his country, we should come to its help. He did not rest his certainty on the sensible idea that, in our own interest, we could not let one of our friends be murdered. He *knew* that Chaucer, Shakespeare, Keats, Byron and the others would not let him down.

Shortly after Munich, in October, I had two letters from him, written without emphasis, his anger and disillusion well in control. In the first there was even a flicker of humour: he wrote on the paper of the Anglo-American Club of Slovakia, of which he had been president, and noted, 'This club is dead now, but I have to use up the stationery!'

'... across the Danube, where I walked with you after the P.E.N. banquet, I could see tonight a huge swastika made of electric bulbs. The Nazis have occupied the right bank and they don't let us forget it. But that is nothing compared with the invasion of purely Czech towns and villages. However I shall spare your feelings. It's according to the old *vae victis* formula. The difference is that we were *not* defeated but betrayed and, what is worse, prevented from defending ourselves, by our allies and friends...'

He went on calmly, giving me news of writers I had met, and of his plans. He had convinced himself that, whoever had betrayed him, it was neither Chaucer nor Byron.

On that June evening several of his sentences began with the words, 'I foresee...' Neither of us foresaw the moment, not many weeks in the future, when an English journalist, stopped on the Hungarian frontier by a single Czech guard, almost a boy, asked, 'Can we cross into Hungary?' and was answered, with a contempt that cut to the bone,

'You're English? Then you won't have heard—we Czechs haven't any frontiers now. Go where you like.'

## CHAPTER 17

AFTER BRATISLAVA the English were alone for three days in an hotel in the mountains—almost completely alone; it was not the season.

I was born and bred by the sea. To be surrounded by jagged peaks of mountains cutting off the horizon keeps me awake. I feel that I should keep an eye on them. It was all I did—from the edge of the truly splendid lake. I could see them twice—when I lifted my eyes and again when I looked at the water; every rock and snow-veined crest was engraved in it as by an acid. The more energetic climbed to a pass where they could stand and look down into Poland; one of them, on the way down, took her shoes off on a smooth path; a solitary German tourist stopped her, pointing at her feet, and asked with grave eagerness, 'On what system do you walk bare?'

When the others left Czechoslovakia to go home, I took the train to Vienna. I was to stay a few days with Toni Stolper's sister, Anna. I went reluctantly—surely, I thought, they could not have wanted the trouble of a visitor now, when they are preparing to leave the country.

My first sight of Anna Jerusalem, in the doorway of the pleasant shabby house in the nineteenth district—Paradisgasse 20—reassured me. A human being of such goodness, such simplicity—not naïve—would not resent me, even now.

In her late middle-age Anna had kept the thin angular body of a schoolgirl, quick, a little awkward, direct. The clearest sign of age in her sallow face was in her eyes, large and dark, a little sunk; they were far older than she was, with the age and half-tragic half-humorous wisdom of her people. There are times when I feel that only Jews and Chinese are really civilized: no doubt each of them has, as a people, grave faults, but they are incontestably more philosophic than the rest of us.

When I asked her, Anna said that yes, they were arranging to leave, the children first, then perhaps, no probably, she and her husband, a professor of history, retired. The eldest daughter, the most brilliant, had already settled in Palestine, and the tall young son was on his way there. Time was running out, a Nazi official had been twice to look over the house, and...

'And we have been lucky,' she said, smiling. 'One morning not long since a storm-trooper came here and took away Leni and her sister to clean the Nazi barracks. I begged and implored him to take me instead. And do you know what he said to me, that boy? He said, "But would *you* let your mother go in your place?" He was shocked!'

'What happened?'

'Oh, in less than an hour they were back. I had a servant for years—until the order forbidding Aryans to work for Jews. She heard about it, and rushed off to the barracks, and rated the Nazis until they were thankful to send the girls away.' She smiled, her sad clown's smile. 'I don't think that would happen anywhere but in Vienna. But I must get them away as soon as I can. Next time we might not be lucky.'

I followed the glance she sent round the room. It caressed lightly, one after another, without showing any unjust preference, all the things, the old chairs, tables, a pile of linen sheets, worn thin, the set of small gilt and white coffee cups, she had loved and served all her married life with the gentleness, pride, and essential innocence of her love for her family. It seemed at the moment only absurd that the paranoia of an Austrian-born ex-corporal should deprive them of her.

Not she, a secretary of our Embassy, warned me not to be taken in by the dull surface, dulled by a foul breath, of Nazi Vienna. Under the surface, unpleasant things were happening, an unknown number of suicides, many arrests, a few known incidents of torture—a great many brutal confiscations. 'There is always the Danube,' an official told the young Jewish surgeon whose hands they had deformed beyond repair after taking away all his other possessions. He had asked, 'What shall I do?'

I told him I had to go to our Consulate.

He frowned. 'You won't enjoy it.'

When I went into the courtyard I understood him. It was filled to suffocation by men and women, Jews, hoping for visas: they stood, pressed closely together, some patiently, others angry and scolding; there were even children, gripping the skirts of mothers they hardly knew any longer, so changed were they by waiting and fear. Some of them had been coming day after day without getting near the stone steps leading up. A harassed consular staff was forced to keep the door locked on the inner courtyard, letting in two or three at a time. The instant the door opened, an eddy set towards it, like the dead eddying and whirling about the blood poured out by Odysseus. I was ashamed to have thought this. What right had literature, even the greatest, here? And even more ashamed, after hesitating for a long time, of holding up my English passport when the door opened again, so that I was let in at once. I had promised one of the German refugee writers in London to ask if a young Viennese actress about whom he was anxious had passed through their hands.

The clerk who searched rapidly through the lists for her name did not find it. 'That doesn't mean she is still in the country. There are other ways of getting out.'

'How many of these people get a visa?'

He shrugged his shoulders. 'Not a great many.'

'What will happen to the rest?'

'Oh, if I knew! Probably nothing. Perhaps they will go back to the days of the ghetto. After all, they can't be killed off, can they?'

I spent hours every day walking about Vienna. After only four months of German occupation it had become a dull provincial city, the cafés half empty, the shops disfigured by paintings and blown-up photographs of Hitler and placards announcing that they were—or were not—in Aryan hands. The Germans could not be blamed for the unseasonable rainy cold, but like the notices forbidding Jews to enter parks and museums it seemed part of the spreading tide of pus.

And yet, and yet... With every step I took in the streets between Kärntnerstrasse and the Graben, another Vienna came briefly to life. June in Vienna in 1930 was cloudless and very hot. Walking about these same streets, then rippling with light, I stared into every shop in search of the right present to take my mother. It was always the same when I was abroad; until I had found her present I was anxious and fretted. What in 1930 I found, after days of looking, precisely in this small shop, in this narrow lane still blessedly free of obscene notices, was a bed-jacket of soft white wool, cunningly knitted, and almost weightless. She liked it—so much that she kept it between layers of soft paper and rarely wore it. I found it after she died and gave it to the two women who were dressing her, telling them to put it on her.

I stood there, in the fine chill rain, letting the threefold images dissolve into one behind my eyes—then, now, always—always the same moment, in which I was drawn backwards by so many threads that I knew as little where I was going as a sleepwalker.

I meant to lunch in the Hofkeller. Eight years ago we had taken most of our meals there. The food was admirable: a door at the back of the inner room led into the old Imperial cellars, and on our last day we bought six bottles of strong Tokay and two of yellow Chartreuse. The manager had become our friend, he told us where to go in the city and out of it, and one blistering Sunday took us by train and cable-car up the Raxalpe and made us walk down it into the valley. Long before we reached the bottom, my knees were on the point of collapse. To encourage me, Rudi pranced ahead on the steep path, jerking his broad middle-aged body from side to side, crying, 'Look at me, I am a horse, a little horse!'

He sat with us evening after evening, talking about himself with endless vivacity. In 1914 he was a waiter in a London restaurant: interned, he escaped in the last year of the war, stowed away in a Dutch boat, and walked across Holland and Germany to Austria, where he was put in jail. I asked why. He spread his hands. 'Why not? I might have been a scoundrel. I was lucky. "You are unfit for the army," they told me, "find yourself a job." So I apply to the Imperial Hotel. "Yes, you can have a job, but you must first get a dress suit." "Where?" By now, in 1918, there is nothing to buy in Vienna. "Perhaps you get some clothes from someone who has died." I look round and I hear of a woman whose husband is killed, and I buy collars and two shirts from her. Then I hear of another woman whose husband was a waiter and he has just been killed, and from her I buy, cheap, his suit. So in June 1918 I start in the chauffeurs' room, then outside, then in the dining-room. In November I give notice, not enough money—no tips. The manager sends for me and says if I stay now he will give me a good place later. So I stay. In 1919 I am afraid to leave. The other hotels have closed their restaurants, only in the Imperial is there food, plenty of food, white bread, meat, at terrible prices. Because of it, because if people knew, don't you see, they had to be very careful who they took as waiters. There was one very old waiter—Fürst. He knew all the Archdukes from children, he used to force them to order the most expensive dishes, lobster at fifty shillings a tiny slice and so on, nagging at them until they gave in, cursing. He was an idiot. One day at my table the customer said to him, "Fürst, I don't feel very well in my stomach, I want something very light." "Well, Excellency, we have some fine boiled beef and cabbage." "Get out, you fool!" So Fürst brings him the beef. The man doesn't touch it. "Did he pay?" Fürst asks me. "Yes, and he is very angry." "So long as he paid!" Then, in 1924, an industrialist I served every evening asks me to manage a hotel he has bought. The manager of the Imperial is so furious he almost strangles himself, but after two years he sends for me again and offers me the job of managing the dining-room. The industrialist has died, and I play a trick on his widow to release me from my contract. Then, last year, it is the Hofrat who sends for me. I know what he wants, but I go into his room and ask, "Well, Hofrat, what do you want with me?" "There is something wrong with the Hofkeller," he says, "it loses money. Do you know what is wrong?" "Yes, I know, and when I am employed I tell you. But first, what terms do you offer me?" Well, we argue a little, and in the end I make my own terms, perfectly fair good terms, I am an honest man: he must employ my wife, and he must give us a room in the Hofburg. So—here I am—as you see me, safe, well-off, as safe as the Hofrat himself. I crack my fingers—' he cracked them with a noise of tearing calico—'at the manager of the Imperial, at the politicians, at generals. No more changes. I know exactly what will happen in the world—that is, in Vienna, that is, to Rudi Göldner—for the next thirty years. Nothing. Nothing!'

He laughed, throwing his arms out. 'Look at me. An absolutely free happy man.'

I went, more than a little reluctant, ready to turn back, down the steps from the narrow Schauflergasse into the outer room. Rudi was there. He knew me, but spoke without a trace of friendliness, and sent a boy to serve me. I ate a dull uninspired meal, drawing it out until I was alone in the place, so that as I passed him on my way out I could say quietly,

'Vienna has changed.'

He gave me a sullen cold glance. 'Yes. For the better. Everything is better.'

The rain had stopped, but it was still cold. I walked through the outer courtyards into the Josefs-Platz and stood, my back to the Pallavicini palace, looking towards the corner between the Redouten-Säle and the great Library, where, in 1930, an improvised platform with a single lamp held the singers. It had been dark, a soft warm night. Three or four rows of chairs faced the narrow platform: waiting behind them for the opening notes of the Nachtmusik, a silent crowd of Viennese, too poor to pay to sit down: some had bare feet. Windows had been opened in the palace and in a few of them an oil lamp, turned to its lowest, did no more than thicken the shadows round a listening figure. In those years Vienna, still shabby and straitened, brought to its sharpest pitch one of the oldest pleasures in the world: music heard in the open air, at night. At no other time, in no other place, have I listened to anything more moving. And contrived by the simplest means. Showing that, thrown back on themselves for the essentials, most people do not need to be told how to live. (In 1945 I saw this again in the rubble of Warsaw.)

I was alone in the Josefs-Platz with, coming towards me from a low doorway, the ghost of an exquisite happiness. What was happening in Vienna did not disturb it.

Egoist!

## CHAPTER 18

AT THE END OF THE WEEK I went to Budapest. On the Hungarian side of the frontier, the uniforms became sadder and dirtier, and the young man who checked my passport had the face of a diseased rat. Suddenly, pressing a yellow finger on the first page, he glanced up at me with a smile of astonishing sweetness.

'Ah,' he said, '*Orter!*'

Was he an author himself?

In the hotel I was given a room on the fourth floor with a narrow stone balcony. It looked across a noisy square and across the Danube to Pest. In the evening light without sun, the river ran grey and oily. There were barges. Looking down into one of them as I crossed the bridge, I saw two, no, three naked children lying asleep, knotted together like little snakes. Farther along the embankment there were large buildings and cafés, but I was afraid to go into one of them. Besides, I was running short of money. I chose an unpretentious café near the bridge and ordered coffee and rolls: since I had eaten nothing since breakfast in Vienna I was hungry, but the happiness of being alone in a strange city was all I needed to satisfy me, and the coffee was very good: so were the rolls. Pretending to be absorbed in a German newspaper, I made these last out.

When I had finished it was fully dark, but I could not bring myself to go back to the hotel without at least glancing at Pest. The street-lamps along the embankment, and the lighted cafés and hotels, made it seem any capital city, but in the streets like walled drains open to the sky, running away from the river at this end, there were few lights. The black gaping mouths of courtyards

gave out a sour breath—earth, sweat, excreta, and another pungent spicy
smell I could not identify. I turned back. This place stank of violence in a
way Vienna, for all its Nazi jails and barracks, did not.

The next day was very warm, light pressing down on the streets from
a white-hot sky. I decided that coffee and bread every two or three hours
was an excellent diet in such heat. Both were very good here, even in the
smallest cafés; the bread was the best I have ever eaten, better than French
bread. I spent the day sitting in the gardens and bastion of the Royal Palace
near the top of the ugly dolomitic hill behind the hotel, making notes for a
novel. Two, three, novels. Between a slight hunger and the delicious ease I
feel when I can live a completely irresponsible life, my brain raced ahead of
me like a colt. I walked a little in the dusty quiet square outside the gardens,
drank more coffee, and went back to my notes. When I closed my eyelids,
the sun drew on them a black sinuous line which was the Danube.

I had brought two letters of introduction, one to a journalist, the correspondent in Budapest of the *News Chronicle*, another to a Madame F——
K——, from a friend in London who had asked me to take her a tin of Earl
Grey tea. Reluctantly, I had posted them in Vienna, and when I went back
to the hotel about seven o'clock, the hall porter handed me a letter from
Madame F—— K——, and a visiting card. *Baneth Alexander, Correspondent
of the London News Chronicle. Hungarian Chamber of Commerce.* The last
words had been crossed out in pencil.

'The gentleman is waiting for you.'

Turning, I saw a short middle-aged man buttoned into a thick overcoat.
He had black hair, black very bright eyes, a creased white face the texture
of soft india-rubber, perfectly round. He was wearing grey kid gloves and a
monocle on a broad moiré ribbon.

He smiled and bowed. 'I got your letter from Vienna this morning only
and I telephoned at once, but you had gone out, you are very active, the
English are all active. I am charmed to find you at last.'

'It is kind of you to come, Mr Alexander.'

'Baneth. In this country we place the surname before the other names.
It is absurd, of course. I tell you because you will wish to know everything
about me. How long have you been in Budapest? Today only? Good, good.
What have you done already? Have you seen some people?'

He had a clear soft voice, and his eyes never moved from my face. 'What are you going to do this evening?'

'Nothing.'

'Then you will have dinner with me? No, it is a pleasure for me to meet a friend of the editor of the *News Chronicle*. I shall take you to my club, it is fortunate I have no engagement for this evening. You have just come in and wish to go to your room. I shall wait as long as you wish, I am not in a hurry. Though I am a Jew I do not run everywhere.'

With my indifference to people's looks, I had not noticed that he was a Jew. Now that he had told me, I saw it in the blunted softness of his features and long fine womanish mouth. He had very small soft hands.

We took a tram in the square outside the hotel, and crossed the bridge. He went on questioning me, with a gentle insistence.

'What is your position on the *News Chronicle*?'

I realized that if I told the truth he would be bitterly disappointed. 'I am a writer, I have written many articles for the paper.'

'Oh, you have written articles. I am sorry, I have missed them. But you are a friend of the editor? You know everyone in London? Why have you come to Budapest? You must not go back and say I am in despair. You can see I am not in despair. I am objective. After the war, Count Bethlen—you have heard of him—told me, "I can ask your opinion because I am sure you will give it without fear or politics." He asked me to do certain things for him.'

He broke off, to speak to the conductor with the same smiling energy.

'I know everyone. Not only Count Bethlen. I know the tram conductors and the dirty little newspaper boys. They are all my friends.'

Sitting opposite us in the tram was a remarkably handsome little boy, shabbily dressed, nursing on his bare knees a school satchel and a bunch of lavender. Leaning across, Baneth talked to him for a moment, then chose a stem of lavender.

'Please take this,' he said to me.

I gave the child an apologetic smile. Smiling back, he handed me several pieces of his lavender, whispering to Baneth.

'He says he would give you all of it, but it is for his mother.'

'In Hungary even the schoolboys are charming,' I said ridiculously.

'Well, he is a nicely brought-up little Jewish boy.'

Impulsively—it seemed the right thing to do—I gave Baneth a piece of my lavender. He took it, looking at me gravely, and throughout the evening kept on taking it from his pocketbook to smell.

We were now well into Pest. 'Here we arrive,' he said merrily. 'We are almost at my club. But first we shall walk a few steps, I want to show you something.'

We were in a wide square, scarcely lit by a lamp or two. Trees, possibly a park, stood about at the far side: in front of them a massive stone column rose into the blackness—the Great War memorial.

None of these memorials move me except those with no aesthetic merits, on the edge of a village or in the busy street of some small town, where it is possible to imagine that the dead young men crossed here between the narrow pavements or stood there, idly breaking a branch from the hedge. Great marble monuments mock the obscure dead. Who, looking at them, remembers a boy with unformed features and large clumsy hands?

Baneth was talking in a lively voice. 'Andrássy Street, behind you, is the finest street in Europe. It will be to let when they have got rid of the dirty Jews. Please look only at the base of the column—at the statue of Arpád. He was a savage who founded Hungary. I must tell you only the truth—he was not a Jew. But he chose the Jewish religion. He had all the others explained to him and decided on the Jewish. Repeat this, please, to a Hungarian who is not a dirty old Jew. Very likely he will not be a Hungarian either, he'll be a Slav or a Swabian, or a mongrel. I, I am pure Hungarian, my family has been living in Buda for hundreds of years.'

He smiled finely. 'Now, this way, please.'

We dined in the lighted garden of his club. I was the only woman there and the only Gentile. The other diners glanced at me inquisitively as they passed the table. Baneth fixed each of them with his single eyeglass, and answered their greetings with the greatest affability and the reserve of an important diplomat.

As delicately as I could, I asked him whether the Jews in Hungary feared trouble. He shrugged his shoulders.

'After Béla Kun a great many poor lower-class Jews were killed a little brutally. An old friend of mine, a Christian and a Conservative Nationalist, what you call a Tory, of very good family, made speeches saying that every

Jew, rich and poor, must be stripped and driven out. I went to this man, and I asked him, "Why do you say these things? You know me. Do I deserve to be murdered?" He said, "Well, you Jews live at a swifter pace than we Hungarians. You are going to say that since the treaty the country is ruined and can't afford not to work quickly. Please don't be silly. To live as you do is against our Hungarian character—it offends us." Very well. I understand. I agree that the five percent of Jews in Hungary ought to give way to the ninety-five percent of Hungarians. But it ought to be arranged in a decent way, not in the cruel way they do it in Germany and soon will here.' In a meditative voice he added,

'I try to be objective.'

He held the stem of lavender under his nose. 'Do you see that man with grey hair?' His eyes sparkled with a youthful malice. 'He is one of the Jews I dislike. During the war he made clothes, rotten clothes, and became rottenly rich. He decided to be baptized. I asked him, "Why have you been baptized?" He replied, "We Jews ought to be assimilated. We must assimilate ourselves." I answered him, "If you mean by it turning a bad Jew into a bad Christian, then you are assimilated already."' He laughed gently. 'Some of these spoiled Jews do not like me. I make jokes about them. Before the war a schoolfellow of mine became a nobleman—I don't imagine what it cost him. You know—I explained you—we put the Christian name after the surname; his first name is Andreas, it sounds a little like Andrássy, and foreigners take him for one of that family. Do you believe he corrects them? One day he came into the restaurant of the Szent Margitsziget; there was no room for him, he made a row about it, and the head waiter suggested, "Perhaps you can sit for a few minutes at a table where there is only one gentleman." Very well, my assimilated friend looked round the room and saw a young man lunching alone; he went up to him, bowed like an officer, and said in German, "Baron etc etc etc von Nimburg. May I give myself the honour etc etc of sitting here?" The young man looked at him once politely and said, "Esterházy. Please sit down." You know what that means here, to be an Esterházy? Perhaps the story isn't true. I hope it is. When I am feeling sad about all these threats and assimilations, I remember it and laugh... What do you think?'

I thought that I had never seen malice allied to so much gentleness and serene smiling philosophy. I thought that, as a human being, he was probably

worth a dozen Esterházys. Before I could say anything—I had no idea what
to say—he went on with energy,

'Don't think that we Jews are wise. Our rich clever leaders are making
frightful mistakes, for which we others shall pay with our teeth.' He smiled
sweetly. 'But I am not consulted.'

Outside the hotel, he asked me,

'What will you do tomorrow?'

I had an appointment, I told him.

'Then you know some people in Budapest?'

'One or two.'

'They are journalists?'

'No—private persons.'

He swallowed his curiosity. Holding my hand between both his small
paws, he said warmly,

'If you will be here another two or three days at least I shall ask my friend
Count K—— H—— to dinner. He is of old family. You will like him.'

Sighing—I infinitely prefer to be alone in a foreign place—I asked him
to come to the hotel tomorrow about five and drink coffee with me, on the
terrace of the *Wellenbad*. Then I went upstairs to my room and patiently
transcribed all he had said—no, all I thought worth remembering.

The St Gellért had two fine baths, one in the hotel where powerful sulphur
springs lifted all but the heaviest bodies out of the water, and another outside,
with artificial waves and a wide double terrace. It was again a day of stifling
heat, but Baneth was muffled in his overcoat. In the strong light I saw that
it was turning green, and worn down to the thread on the carefully-brushed
cuffs and shoulders.

Stirring his coffee absently, he said,

'Yesterday you asked me how things are here. I shall tell you. The country
is being driven to an abyss—' he pronounced it *ábbiss*—'I don't even know
whether it can escape. I will tell you another story—this Baneth, you will
say, is always telling stories. When I was a boy an old journalist—he was
a Jew, of course—told me, "If our mother has bad servants, she is still our
mother. It is wrong to write what Hungary does against her Jews." Well,
I want only that other nations should leave us alone and not write about

us.' He paused and went on in a still gentler voice. 'How could the *News Chronicle* understand what is necessary for us, for Hungary? They do not understand—I must send *only* news which helps Hungary. They have been complaining of me in London?'

I did not immediately realize that he hoped I could put him right with the newspaper. Nor did I realize his position. Under a new law Jews were being thrown out of work in Budapest. His job as correspondent of an English paper was safe—exactly as long as he was able to send the sort of news they wanted.

'Things are difficult?'

'A short time ago something happened which I shall explain. A man came here. I did not speak to him, I avoided him on purpose. He talked to a great many people, and he got a fair idea of what is going on. His article in the *News Chronicle* did not tell lies. But he told things I would never have told. Certain people here were angry, they thought I had given him his facts. A question was asked in Parliament, there were even letters in the press. No one gave my name. No one said, "Baneth the dirty Jew is sending out anti-Hungarian propaganda." But wait, please.'

He drew from his pocket a shabby note-book. Moving aside the stem of lavender carefully he took out a frayed newspaper cutting.

'Listen. It is written in a bad style—rotten—I shan't read much of it. "How long are we going to allow a dirty animal from the ghetto jungle to send lies about Hungary to an English newspaper? Somebody should slit the pig's throat. He would squeal on another note." I went to a friend of mine in the Government and told him, "I had nothing to do with the article in the *News Chronicle*. I would not write such things about Hungary." He was polite, but I ask myself did he believe me? In any case he could do nothing. Nothing.'

His black eyes sparkled. 'I told you I am objective. It is my religion. Religion of a dirty little ghetto animal.'

He stood up, and bowed to an almost naked young woman sitting at the next table. She waved carelessly.

'She is the wife of my friend Count K—— H——. I think he is bathing. When he comes, I shall bring him to speak with you. He is of very old family—excuse me, I told you already. He is also well-known.'

The air, absolutely still and as if wadded, muted the cries and laughter from the bath. There was a smell of geraniums and heavily oiled bodies.

Fully-clothed dancers crowded the narrow space between the tables and white wicker chairs. In spite of the heat, old gentlemen in high-heeled shoes leaped like goats, hands on the shoulders of young women who must have been more enduring than they looked. Averting his glance from them, Baneth said,

'Like every country which is on its way down, we are governed by a sick man. It has been so for years. In 1936 Gömboes was with a shrunken kidney already, and last year Dáranyi is a thyroid-deficient. It is very sad.'

'You have a new Prime Minister,' I said.

A smile ran through the creases of his face. 'Dr Imredy—I know his doctor—has an ulcerated stomach. My theory is proved. I hope he will recover. But he will not save Hungary from—what will they call it this time? A spiritual regeneration... Excuse me, I shall bring my friends.'

Followed by a yawning reluctant wife, the count was smiling vaguely. He sat down between her and Baneth, and became absorbed in pinching his body in its cotton wrap.

'You are cold?' Baneth said anxiously. 'The water is too cold for you? Why do you bathe? Your wife is wiser, she never bathes.'

'The water is unpleasantly warm, but my blood is slow,' his friend said, smiling.

'The K—— H—— family,' Baneth said to me, 'is one of the oldest Hungarian families. You need only to visit the crypt of their palace at Esztergom to see in stone nine centuries of our history. The count will give you his permission.'

'Certainly. Do you wish to go there?'

'I should be delighted,' I said. I had no intention of going. The count knew it without glancing at me. 'My wife adores England,' he murmured.

She looked at me for the first time. 'We go to London as often as we can afford it.'

Her body was a dark gleaming brown. A strip of thin blue cotton drawn tightly across her breasts drew the eye to them. Another strip shaped into narrow drawers vanished when she crossed her legs. Behind dark lashes her eyes were bored and greedy, the eyes of a clever slut. Her toe nails had been painted a black-red and trimmed into points. She yawned, showing narrow white teeth like a little animal's.

'You are tired?' her husband said gently.

'Yes. We must go. But give me a cigarette first.'

I don't smoke, but I was carrying English cigarettes to give away. I offered her the case.

'Oh,' she cried, 'wonderful. They are too expensive to buy here. I make my English friends bring them.'

'I have a friend coming in September,' I said. 'If you'll give me your address, I'll send some by him.'

The only reason I made the offer was to show Baneth that I admired his friends. Smiling innocently, he watched the young woman scrawl her name in my notebook, 'Margit K—— H——,' and said,

'She will not tell you herself because she is polite, but I can say it for her. On the envelope you must put: The Countess K—— H——.'

She grimaced. She stood up, and ran a finger under the edge of her drawers: a thin paring of white showed, exactly below the cheek. Baneth bowed deeply.

When they had gone he asked,

'Do you like the countess?'

'She is very pretty.'

'I don't like her nails,' he said in a gentle voice. 'And I am sorry I must tell you they are the only genuine thing about her. I don't like to say what would hurt the Count, who is my friend, but I don't know anything good about her. He—I love him—he is intelligent. It is a great pity... But I must make you amused. You are invited to dinner?'

Only for a drink, but if I said so he would certainly ask me to dine with him, and quite apart from preferring my own company I did not care to take so much from him: he was certainly not well-off.

'I was invited for seven o'clock,' I said.

'It is twenty past. You will be in good time for Budapest.' He stood up. 'But you must go. I shall take you. What is the address, please?'

'Malna Utca. It is on this side. I shall take a cab.'

'It is not necessary. There is a tram along the embankment. You will be there quickly. It gives me pleasure to come with you.'

We crossed the square to the tram. Baneth smiled at me. 'You see? I have arranged everything for you. This is the right tram. Not even a moment to wait. Please sit here. And now tell me. You do not know these friends? Perhaps I know them?'

I did not answer. For no reason whatever, I felt sure that, if he knew the F—— K——'s, they were people he would rather I did not meet.

In the poorly-lit tram, he looked yellow and downcast. Rousing himself, he said,

'If I tell you what is in my mind you will laugh at me. All these troubles in the world are caused by sun spots. Thunder disturbs horses, and we are a very little, only a little, more intelligent. The sun erupts and destroys seeds in the earth, the brain, the womb. It is written in the Talmud, *When spots appear on the sun the Jew should be afraid*. You know in the Talmud one sentence often needs many pages of commentary. The commentary on this sentence asks: Why are the Jews to be afraid? And the answer: Because when the rod is brought out it is those children who have been beaten before who must fear.' He looked into my face. 'It is true,' he said softly, almost gaily.

We left the tram and I followed him through dark streets. It was still very warm, and a light breath from the Danube did no more than thicken the darkness.

'This is Malna Street. Do you know the number?'

I peered at the nearest door. 'This is it.'

'You see,' he said, with smiling triumph, 'you were right to trust me.'

'It was good of you to bring me.'

'It is my greatest happiness. I shall telephone to you in the morning.'

Madame F—— K—— was young and amiable. We sat in the courtyard, at a wooden table on which were glasses and an oil lamp. She thanked me for bringing the tea, and went on quickly,

'What a pity you came after dark. This house would amuse you if you could see it, it is small and very old. My parents bought it in 1918 when they came here from what is now Slovakia. My father said, "We must only buy a small place; we shall be going back in six months, this nonsense can't last, and we shall need our money." I was four years old. In six months we had lost both money and estate. I and my husband and my brother all live here. We didn't do anything to the house and at last it was so uncomfortable I said, "We must do something, we can't squat here any longer like Czechs." So now it is not so bad.'

Her brother came in from the street carrying a suitcase. He had been to look at a summer hotel in the mountains, and his sister asked him about it. Turning to me, she explained,

'Since the Tatras were stolen from us, we have to find other places for holidays.'

'The place was lovely,' her brother said, 'lovely, lovely. But the hotel was full of old post-office girls who went to bed every night at eight o'clock. Ferenc and I bought four bottles of wine and sang songs. In the morning they said, "You mustn't disturb the other guests." I said, "Excuse me, what is this? A hospital?"'

I had fallen, as one falls asleep, into a state of mind a great deal too familiar. The small courtyard, the weak ring of light in the centre of the table, the three young Hungarians—her husband had arrived and kissed my hand carelessly—the glass of wine in my hand, lost reality: it ran out of them as air seeps through a puncture. It became difficult to feel that they existed, in the vital sense of the word. They were there, dwindled, and drained of substance, I could make them out, but not add myself to them. Then the feeling of estrangement spread to my hands, my body. I began to lose touch with myself. (I imagine that dying, if one dies rather slowly, must be much the same sensation of withdrawal from the living and from oneself. A withdrawal of reality, and from it.) I have learned that to struggle against this annoying condition is worse than useless. It is, though, easy enough to keep up an air of being present—and wait for it to take itself off.

'Where have you come from?' F—— K—— asked me.

'Prague.'

'How do you like the Czechs?'

'They are very decent people.'

Both young men shouted at once. The brother's voice rang like brass.

'Oh, so you think that! Well, Mrs—I can't remember your name—I will tell you. In September there will be no Czechs. Hitler will march in, and we shall march into Slovakia at the same time. It will be after the harvest. These damned swine of Czechs have lived too long already. Look here, every Saturday I go into Slovakia to see my wife. They know me at the frontier, they know my wife is with her parents, ill. And every Saturday for a year they make me strip to my skin and search me like a thief. They do it to everybody. Every Hungarian.

It's nice to have your shoes ripped off their soles. Once they smashed my watch and handed me a paper to sign that I did it myself, I was so gay I jumped on it. I said, "No, I don't sign, I don't sign nothing written in Czech." Very well, they put me in a room with nothing, no chair, no fire, it is winter, and say, "See how you like that." So in the morning I sign—or I would be there now. You think they are decent? Yes, you have an English passport. The swine smile at you.' He shouted with laughter. 'If I had *just once* an English passport!'

'He is telling the truth,' F—— K—— said. He told a long story about the meanly savage treatment of two Hungarian schoolboys, and exclaimed, 'It *must* finish. There *must* be war.'

'Perhaps you are shocked,' his wife said to me. 'But, after all, we must get our country back.'

Her brother laughed again. 'Now *I* will shock her. Mrs, there is a Hungarian officer going into Czechoslovakia, he is a spy, and they play a trick on him with an old lady. She asks him, "Please look after my luggage for a minute." Well, there is something, I don't know what, in the luggage. They arrest him. They beat him. They inject caffeine in him to bring him alive. They beat him again. Then caffeine. Then beating. He is unconscious. They throw cold water over him. They take a piece of wood and scrape the flesh of his leg, to the shin bone. He is unconscious again. Again injections. At the end they empty him into a coffin full of nails, and roll and roll it until he is all, all, all, wounds, and throw him away, he is finished, dead, in a railway siding. Another Hungarian, a spy, gets to him, he is still breathing, and this fellow puts him in a truck, you know, covered up with coal. He is safely over the frontier and is in hospital for eighteen months. I know him.'

He waited for me to show my horror. I did not disbelieve him, but he might have been talking about puppets for all I felt or cared.

'But, Mrs, look here,' he said sharply. 'We don't act no different ourselves. Our soldiers captured a Czech captain two weeks ago. He was spying. My friend who was there told me, "Although his feet were broken, twice, and his arms and legs all broken, we didn't get anything out of him." Look here, that was a pity!'

'Never mind,' F—— K—— said, smiling. 'In September we march. In less than two weeks it is over. The French, pooh! The English—' he stretched his neck from side to side—'cluck, cluck, in Parliament.'

'The Czechs will fight,' I said.

His brother-in-law kicked his legs up like a schoolboy. 'Fight? They'll run when they see us. Look here, you're mad. They're all peasants and cowards.'

'And you've forgotten Russia,' I said.

'Russia has no officers! Stalin has shot them. There is only Jugoslavia. Look here, we don't want to fight the Serbs, they are tough!'

'Miss Storm Jameson will think you are both savages,' Madame F——K—— said, smiling at me. She filled my glass.

'Tell me one thing,' her husband, said, almost quietly. 'Why doesn't your country make friends with the Germans? You won't be able to do anything against them, they're marvellous. Lions! That man Hitler is like God, he makes men. The German air force is magnificent: in Vienna they dropped thousands of men by parachute, with full equipment, on the Aspern aerodrome. The other day I went to see a news film, and there was your king, King George six, reviewing his troops. I was shocked. They held their bayonets up anyhow, as sloppy as girls. Then directly after, German troops simply majestic—every bayonet in line. I was in Vienna when they marched in—with the goose-step—whack, whack, *bang*. Tears ran over my face, and I thought: Oh, my poor country, what could we do against these fellows?'

You talking ape, I thought remotely. I was not offended by his contempt for England. It did not occur to me for a moment to take him seriously. A dog lifting his leg against a lamp-post.

'You know,' Madame F—— K—— said, 'it's true. I dislike Germans, they are mannerless bullies. But our only chance is to march *with* them. If we don't, they'll squeeze us to death.'

They'll do that anyway, I thought. I made some polite meaningless answer, and looked at my watch.

'Don't go yet,' she said warmly. 'We're not really savages. How long will you stay in Budapest? You ought to see the country. Lake Balaton is very beautiful. We could drive you to see my husband's parents on Sunday.'

'My parents are mad,' her husband said calmly. 'They keep twenty-five indoor servants and my mother never buys a new dress. The whole of that generation is the same. Every soul in Hungary could be dying of hunger and they wouldn't know what to do. When we begin running the country we're going to break up the big estates and give the peasants some of the land.'

'But, look here, half Hungary really is starving,' the brother shouted. 'Go into the country and offer a child sweets—he'll think they're marbles. There are hundreds of young men, doctors, students, lawyers, thankful to address envelopes. If you speak about it to one of these damned old idiots, he'll whistle a song. Bah! We shall kick them our of the way.'

I stood up. The sense of unreality and absence was beginning to wear off, and the only thing I wanted was to escape. I thought: I don't understand these people. If there is such a thing as civilization, they haven't yet been *assimilated*.

'We should show her at least something,' F—— K—— said. 'Have you been to the Kakuk? No? No gipsies? Oh, but you must. Tomorrow night— we'll take you tomorrow night.'

I hesitated over an excuse. His wife said quickly,

'Please do come. You have no engagement. I am sure you have none.'

Vexed by my clumsiness—I should have lied quickly—I said,

'Thank you, I should like it.'

In the morning, the telephone rang before I had finished drinking my coffee and reading through the notes I had made the night before. My heart sank a little. Although I was not responsible for the uncertainty of Baneth's life, and the dangers—these were certain—hanging over him, he made me feel guilty.

'Baneth Alexander. It is you? Good morning. How are you? I hope you will dine with me this evening at my club—if you do not dislike my club. I shall ask a friend——'

'Your club is delightful,' I said. 'But I am very sorry, I am going out to dinner.'

There was a brief silence. Since I had withheld the name of my Malna Utca acquaintances, he must be feeling certain they were the wrong sort of Hungarian, the sort which describes Jews as animals from a ghetto jungle.

'When are you leaving? I am afraid you will go soon. I am glad for you that you have friends here, but I wish you had none.'

'Tomorrow,' I said, 'I'm leaving tomorrow.'

The silence this time was longer. 'Your letter said four days. Perhaps I have miscounted.'

'Today is the fourth day,' I made my voice as affectionate as possible. 'Perhaps you could come here for coffee—if you can spare the time.'

'After six I have all the time,' he said quietly. 'I shall come.'

He came punctually. 'We will go out,' he said. 'I hope you did not come to Budapest to sit indoors. Besides, I have an appointment.'

'Surely——'

He interrupted me, smiling. 'Shall I tell you what Count Bethan said to me? He said that when he wants to know what everyone in Budapest—not a few people, but everyone—is thinking, he asks me to come and see him.' We were crossing the street, and he took my arm. 'This tram will move now. Please be careful.'

'Where is your appointment?' I asked.

'Here.'

We stopped at a dilapidated newspaper kiosk. The middle-aged woman inside, worn to a rag of grey flesh, looked at us without interest. Baneth glanced at his watch.

'It's later than I thought,' he said, grieved. He poked his head into the kiosk. His politeness forced him to repeat in English anything he said in Hungarian, even to waiters.

'I am asking her: Do you know that dirty little boy who comes here?'

The woman said something in a scrannel voice.

'No, no, I know it is not your son. Your son is smaller and dirtier. The boy I mean fetches your copies of the *Magyarsag*. He asked me for a paper fan, like the one I gave your son. I promised to bring it. Please give it to him when he comes tomorrow.'

He handed her the fan and turned to me with his sweet smile. 'Now we shall go to a place I know which is comfortable, and drink coffee.'

The café, a large one, was filled with Jews, and after a moment I realized that they were speaking German to each other. Baneth looked at them with a gentle malice.

'It is sad, but I can't help remembering what a French Rabbi said about the German refugees in Paris. *Ils sont nos frères, mais ils sont Boches*. These are all rich men, and I only like rich Jews when I remember they are in danger.'

'Are they really in danger?'

'The Jews in Hungary are done for,' he said softly. 'Perhaps Hungary is done for. For the Jews there is no perhaps. It is only a question of how many months.'

His face took on the look of a mischievous child it had when he was going to make one of his quips.

'There is a Press Control Board now, which is going to have a small percentage of Jews. One of my friends, a Christian, said to me, "Of course you will be on it." I told him, "No, I shall refuse." He asked, "Why?" "Because," I said, "if I take this place I am depriving some other Jew, with a wife and family, of a chance of safety. I will sell bootlaces. And I hope you have many many pairs of boots, because I am sure you will buy your bootlaces from me. But I am afraid you will not have any boots, and I shall not be able to live."' He lifted his hands. 'To be a poor Jew in a rich city is not a bad thing. To be a poor Jew in a poor city! They are going to ruin Budapest. All these restrictions on the Jews means ruin—for a simple reason. Only the Jews understand banking and business. Other Hungarians despised these professions. There was no law to forbid Gentiles to be bankers, journalists, business men. They chose not to be! Now they have lost their estates and they see the rich dirty old Jews, and want to step into their place. Why not? you say. I shall tell you. They are not fitted for this work. After they have killed the Jews they will kill Hungary. Even if I am dead or half-dead, I shall be in pain for the country... But now I sadden you. Forgive it, please.' He began smiling again. 'I am luckier than most of my friends. I have no wife or family. It is my only fortune now.'

His eyes sparkled. 'I couldn't speak of my salary from the *News Chronicle* as a fortune. They allow me so little that one of my friends said to me, "Other men keep an actress, you keep the *News Chronicle*." I laughed. I shall try to laugh—I am objective—when the *News Chronicle* writes to me they must find a correspondent who is not a Jew, because a Jew cannot send the news.'

'Why not come to England at once?' I said. 'You have friends in London. If you wait until there are hundreds of refugees from Hungary, it won't be easy.'

My conscience was speaking. My heart sank at the thought of being obliged to think about him in London.

'You are too kind.'

'Good. You'll come.'

'No.'

'Why not? You would be safe in England.'

'I am so much a Hungarian—since I am a Jew—that I would rather starve in Budapest. It proves how tactless we Jews are!'

He told me several more stories, some amusing. When we left the café, and were sauntering along the embankment, I thought that the Danube is one of the cruellest rivers. Running out of the darkness of the past, it has heard so many cries, closed over so many victims like the man talking beside me, that it should be called Acheron. With a sudden real grief, I said,

'Do think again about coming to London.'

He laughed gently. 'How kind you are to think of me.'

When we reached the hotel, he asked,

'You are dining with the same friends?'

'Yes.'

'Where are you going tomorrow, when you leave?'

'To France.'

'Ah.' He sighed and smiled. 'I don't care for the French but I admire them. They refuse to believe that they have no longer any power over what happens to them... You are leaving by the morning train?'

'Yes—alas.'


I stood a minute and watched him walk away, with his short quick step, holding round him the folds of his absurd overcoat...

I do not know what it is that gives to almost any continental night club a gaiety lacking in the determined efforts of the English to enjoy themselves by paying through the nose for inferior wine, carelessly served, in a stuffy overcrowded room. I once put this question to an old Frenchwoman who had been, in the greatest respectability, the mistress of two well-known writers and was the widow of a third. Narrowing wrinkled eyelids in a smile, she said, 'My dear child, the emanations.'

'What can you mean?'

'Put one of us—' she meant her countrymen—'down in a *boîte*, even a stupidly fashionable one, and at once his mind begins to give off little wisps of amusement and interest and curiosity and malice, so that the air in the room is alive with them. You, your men and young women, when they come out for the night, leave their minds at home. We have come here to enjoy ourselves! they say. So that what they give off is only animal spirits. Like horses.'

She may be right.

There was nothing much about the Kakuk: a small discreetly lighted courtyard, overlooked by a balcony as well-screened—from its single window the occupants could look down into the courtyard without being seen themselves—as any Moorish room, a few tables, the gipsies. And the conversation was not gay, or intelligent. And yet there was in fact gaiety, a smiling movement of the air—those emanations, no doubt.

'He has had a boring day,' Madame F—— K—— said, smiling at her husband. 'He needed to come here.'

His position in a Jewish banking house was, I suspected, a minor one. It was interesting only as a portent. His was the first generation of landowners' sons to go into business.

'The head of my firm is a terrible fellow,' he said to me. 'He drinks coffee. He pulls the saccharine out of his pocket—so—he has diabetes—then stirs it with his pen. Then—excuse me for telling you—he cleans his ear with the pen. Then he says, "Did I put sugar in?" and sticks the pen back in the coffee. Then he wipes it on his sleeve.'

'Look here, Mrs. Before the war people of our class didn't go into trade or banking. Such a thing was unheard of. We left that to the Jews to do for us. But we are learning. In a few months we shall turn every Jew out and run Hungary ourselves. You'll see then!'

F—— K—— burst out laughing. 'You should have stayed here to meet my father. You know, he could bathe in the lake—Lake Balaton—from his own land. But he won't. Why? Because, miles farther on, anyone can bathe, Jews can bathe! So he has a bath filled from a well, and sits in it in his bathing drawers.'

'He is absurd,' Madame F—— K—— said, smiling.

'I daresay, but——'

'But with these hands,' her brother cried merrily, holding them up, 'I am going to strangle every Jew I meet. When the time comes... If you are so fond of Jews in England, why don't you give them Shanghai? Let them fight a little for once.'

'There were many Jews fighting in the war,' I said.

Both young men went off into fits of laughter. 'What did they do? Sell the others their bootlaces?'

I felt savagely angry with myself. Since I hadn't the wit to be able to deal with their unpleasant obsession without incivility, I should not have put myself in this position. I was ashamed.

F—— K—— took from his pocket a photograph of the Nazi leader, Franz Szálasi. Gazing at it with ingenuous devotion, he handed it to me.

'Isn't he in prison?' I asked.

'Yes. But we'll have him out. A few months. And then—well, wait, you wait!'

Jumping up, now perfectly good-humoured, he went over to the gipsies and ordered them to play his favourite song, and conducted them in it with long fine hands. His face was altered and softened by a childlike happiness.

'You must never say *you* to these fellows,' his brother-in-law instructed me. 'Always *thou*. Or they won't respect you. Ah, what do I need more from life than gipsy music and a bottle of wine! No money. The Jews started that filthy habit here.'

Thank God I am leaving tomorrow, I thought. All my pleasure in being here was poisoned by—ah, be honest, I told myself, by your own stupidity and clumsiness.

In the morning, I as near as a touch missed my train. A score of peasants, women, their faces blackened and withered by the sun, close-plaited hair, bare feet, came into the station. I turned to watch them. An elderly man was herding them in front of him like a flock of goats, and their bare feet on the platform made exactly the sound of pattering hooves. One woman had her child with her, a little boy, so skinny, legs like a bird's, and so anxious, that to look at him drained the meaning out of life. What are we worth if only one child is born to know only hunger and fear?

The porter with my luggage had vanished. After a minute's suppressed panic—I was alone on this platform—I saw, two platforms away, a train which looked important enough to be the express from Bucharest, and ran to it across the rails, dodging between two shabbier trains.

My porter was there—and Baneth.

He was staring at the carriages with a blank face. In one hand he held
a bunch of pale feathery grasses; they were like something I remembered,
something out of childhood. He must, I suppose, have been thinking that I
had lied to him. When he caught sight of me his expression changed to one
of the liveliest gaiety and affection. He gave me the bunch of grass.

'Why did you come at this hour?' I exclaimed.

'We have frightened ourselves yesterday,' he said softly, 'with the idea
that Budapest will be destroyed, or I shall be killed. Thinking of it, I came
to say goodbye.'

'Ah, do come to London.'

'I am afraid you will miss your train,' he said, smiling. 'Get in now, please.
It leaves suddenly.'

I felt the greatest respect for him—and relief. Only another minute or
two, I thought.

As the train moved out he stood, smiling, a hand raised holding the
monocle on its black ribbon. Dwindling quickly, he disappeared. I laid the
grasses on the rack, meaning to forget them when I got out.

Guy was waiting for me in Basle, with the car, and we drove across
France to Talloires, on Lake Annecy. Need I say that I was madly happy?
I do not go to France for any other reason than to be happy, and am. And
lighthearted and sane. Even when I was writing down, not to forget them,
scenes and things said there, the images of Budapest in my brain began to
seem unreal; the faces, even Baneth's, became bloodless and spectral, drifting
at the back of my mind like the clouds of dead and dying moths I saw a few
weeks later on the edge of the Saône at Mâcon, a million slender transparent
bodies, visible only as a network of thread-like veins, a dry whisper in the
river breath—*Mânes*, the porter at the Hôtel de l'Europe et de l'Angleterre
called them: manes, ghosts, spirits of the dead. Well, why not? A river bank
is the right place for the dead to collect.

It struck me as I made my notes that Vienna is as far east as an Englishman
can go without losing touch completely with a tradition, only partly
Christian, which holds in one and the same hand even countries hostile
to each other.

Mâcon, Saulieu, Bourges, Troyes, Rheims, St Quentin, Abbeville—so
many white stones on a road stretched between the beginning and the end

of my life, so many streets seen for the first time, with such delight, with such deep contentment, so many old walls still warm under the hand laid on them.

July 1938: I was happy to be alive...

After the war, I tried to find out what had happened to Baneth. In vain— no one could tell me. Many years later, my friend Paul Tabori told me he had been killed in an air raid.

There were many worse ways he could have died in Budapest then.


## CHAPTER 19


W HAT HAPPENED AT MUNICH in 1938 is spoken of as a respite for France and England. In effect it was more like a syncope, a failure of the heart which might have ended in the death of both countries. No one word exists to describe the curious taste of those weeks: it was bitter, rough, puckering the mouth like a green fruit, and as indigestible.

Helen Kirkpatrick was in London and I had invited her to lunch with me on the 5th of September. That day *The Times* carried a leader on the benefits of ceding the Sudetenland to Hitler, and started a great fluttering of the stool pigeons. When I walked into the Ivy and saw, at the farther end of the room, her head of a thirteenth-century angel, I wished I were going to have to listen to anyone but an American.

Naturally we talked only of the crisis—back and forth, over bones already picked clean and dry. Is Hitler now absolutely certain that he can have his war without being hindered by France and England (*cluck, cluck, in Parliament...*)? What will Russia do? What did a high-ranking French officer say last week? What, who, when? She was as well-informed as anyone, any foreign correspondent, intelligent, very charming. I began to think it had been foolish to dread meeting her.

Towards the end of the meal she said, with a fine ironical smile,

'I think the time has come for your Government to send yet another questionnaire to Berlin. It should run: Now that we have given you Czechoslovakia, how can we help you to (a) Poland (b) anything else you want? Which bit of the Empire would you like first?'

Her irony was completely justified. And since to show my insane rage would give away that I had been stung, I laughed.

That same day or the next I dined with Bjarne Braatoy and a man, a Danish industrialist, whose name I have forgotten. Bjarne this evening was more than ever Peer Gynt at his most excitable and irreverent. As we sat down, I began, 'Do you suppose war——'

He interrupted me with his loud high abrasive laugh. 'There isn't going to be war in this country.'

'Why not?'

'Either Hitler will be intimidated. Or your Government won't fight. Either way there will be no war.'

The Dane, a dry man, with an ironic smile that spread until it twitched his black eyebrows, said,

'You are right, my friend——'

'Of course I'm right!'

'——in Paris yesterday I asked the head of the firm we do business with, a great deal of business, it is a large firm: What about your treaty with the Czechs? He is a nice fellow, but he was ready to spit in my face. He said, "First, that crazy treaty is no longer valid, and second, if it is, no government, not even that *sale coquin* Blum, would dare to ask us to sacrifice another generation. This country is sick to death of war, we must, yes, must save our young men, *je me fous de la Tchécoslovaquie, elle m'emmerde*, Beneš is a crook, he wants to drag us into war and we shan't let him!'

'Neither of your countries is in danger,' I said.

Bjarne looked at me mockingly. 'Don't be too sure that yours is.'

'Why should Hitler take the trouble to invade my country?' the Dane said smiling. 'He has only to come to the front door.'

As the days passed I began to avoid foreigners. Talking about the crisis became as unpleasant as discussing the disgrace of a friend. So much has happened since, to erase the memory of those weeks of fear and sick shame, that it will seem an exaggeration to say that the handing over of the Czechs to Hitler is the worst, most corrosive shock the European mind—is there such a thing?—has suffered. It relegated to the museums the millenial image of European civilization which now, in the sixties, the rest of the world treats with indifference. Or should I say that it began the relegation made final in August 1945?

I worked. I finished James Hill's long novel, *No Victory for the Soldier*. It was a solid lively book, the story of John Knox from the day when, a Busoni of seven, he played in his first concert, to the day when he was killed in the Spanish civil war, and an effort at a portrait of the thirties, with a great many characters and a great many scenes in England and Europe.

After that I wrote rapidly a novel of the greatest ingenuity. *Here Comes a Candle* was a film never, alas, made. When I try to make money I always fail, all my successes of that kind have been accidents.

On the 22nd of September I had the briefest of letters from Jiřina Tůmová, enclosing an appeal signed by Czech writers. I read it, skipping sentences—it was not long—much as one avoids reading carefully the letter a friend has written to reproach us for a mean act.

'TO THE CONSCIENCE OF THE WORLD

> In this fateful moment, when a decision between war and peace is being reached, we, the undersigned Czech authors address this solemn appeal to all those who form the conscience of the world... truth... freedom... spirit' and the rest of it and the rest of it.

It had been sent out on the 14th, exactly a day before Chamberlain flew to Germany, to see how much or little of Jiřina's body would sate Hitler.

Very distinctly I saw her hand, as thin and weak as a child's, serenely folding the single page. Whoever else *took account of realities*, as the leader-writers say, she, when they offended her sense of decency and justice, would not. My poor friend, I thought with anguish, if the Germans invade your country, what will they do to you?

There are people who say that the nearly unbearable tension of the next few days, the distribution of gas-masks, the politicians' deathbed speeches, which sent a number of people, rich enough to pay through the nose for a funk-hole, scurrying out of London, were part of an adroit deception. That at no single moment during the negotiations—if you can use that term of a knock-down argument—was there the least intention on our part of risking war. The precautions were a political comedy.

I do not believe in so accomplished a cynicism. Our old gentlemen were not cynics, not even ironists. Even Chamberlain, fluttering, an elderly dove, between London and the vulture's nest, knew that he was dealing with a ruthless fellow, no compromising fellow Tory. A falling-out among the comedians, and the gas-masks would be needed.

The next day, after the last (near midnight) news on the wireless, I tuned into Prague—the B.B.C. announcer had just said that telephonic communication with Prague had ceased. For a few seconds a strong unhurried voice came into the room from the other side of Europe. I could not understand anything except the word for 'mobilization', which came several times. In a darkened city, lorries crammed with reservists were moving across the bridges, with some old legionary in what might be a French or a Czarist uniform waving them on. We may never hear a voice from Prague again, I thought. Jiřina...

I hope that records exist of the speeches made by Hitler and his creatures. Otherwise no one will be able to imagine their obscene energy. (I suppose that the sounds emitted during a lynching might match them, on a small scale.) I listened on Radio Paris to a meeting in the Sportpalast in Berlin— bestial howls from the audience and Hitler screaming like a trumpet and a horse... 'Herr Beneš lied... this fellow Beneš squatting in Prague... *Beneš und ich*... the liar and murderer, Beneš... Sieg Heil! Sieg Heil! Sieg Heil!...'

Divorced from their bodies, his voice and that of Goebbels revealed an odd thing. Even at his most obscene, Hitler did not cease to be a human being: hatred and cruelty are human. The other voice, Goebbels, convinced me that an abstraction, evil, *exists*, and that when the authors of the scriptures speak of the devil entering into a man, they knew what they were writing about.

Against these two energies, a human pitilessness and an inhuman one, what hope had our champion, a vain, obstinate, decent-minded old man? Chamberlain's voice when he broadcast about the Czechs gave away all his distaste for a small democratic people standing between him and his determination to prove that he knew better about the rulers of Germany than those unrealistic persons who babbled about torture, concentration camps, perjury, killings. Allowed, at Godesberg, to see maps prepared showing a dismembered Czechoslovakia, he said nothing about them. Neither his virtues of sincerity and stubbornness, nor his crippling absence of vision, were any use against unscrupulous greedy men who knew exactly what they were going to do as soon as the old gentleman left the room.

At his age, after a prudent life, he could expect that he was safe, that he need fear nothing in this world or the next, that great tragic events had no place in his career of a patient reasonable politician. He was parochial, not sinister. Loving his English parish, he would sacrifice any weaker country to have peace in it. Was it his fault that he had no more imagination than a French peasant unable to see over the top of his splendid dung-hill?

Ambiguous, two-faced, as were my feelings and thoughts during all this time, had I any right to curse him and his fellows? Yes, but *only* for allowing a venomous animal to grow to unmanageable maturity.

'Is it safe to take the children to Pevensey for two weeks?' my sister asked me.

'Yes, why not? After all, it's not the first place they'll bomb.'

She said calmly, 'I would rather be in my own house when a war starts.'

'Well, go. If I hear any certain news I'll telephone to you.'

On the afternoon of the 27th, I went round to her empty house to take in the gas-masks being distributed. The woman handed over three, a small one for Nicholas. I signed for them.

'There's also a four-months-old baby,' I said. 'What have you for her?'

'I'm afraid—nothing. You must wrap a blanket round her and run with her to the nearest gas-shelter.'

'Oh. Where is it?'

That it did not exist was part of the lunacy, no more insane than the rest.

The 9.40 news that evening was frightful. In the middle of it, my sister rang up from Pevensey.

'What does it mean, Dear Dog? Ought we to come home?'

'I don't know what it means. I suppose that Beneš is making up his mind now whether to give in or not.'

I felt absurdly at fault that her holiday was threatened.

Her light voice went on. 'I just thought you might know. I'm sorry for the poor Czechs, but, you know...'

'Exactly! In any case, it's not for tomorrow. Stay where you are.'

She rang off, and I went back to the wireless. 'We pray especially for those who bear the heaviest burdens at this time, the Chancellor of the German Reich... And we pray for ourselves, for the common people, that is, in every land...' A hymn and the benediction, and then, not a breath between them, 'This is the National Programme. A Comedian's Dream.' A salvo of voices bawling *Down at the old Bull and Bush* and other songs of innocence brought into the room my mother's strong gay scornful voice... *As I walked along the Bois de Boulogne, with an independent air...* My brother, his small round body, as hard as a green apple, convulsed with laughter he could not contain, rolled across the floor between the piano and the horsehair sofa... Ah, let me go back, I begged. Nothing got since is worth a minute of that infinite world, the sharpness and salt air of its morning, the cold dew scattered by its yellow gorse, the more than light on its hills, the sea wind, the small curled waves under the floating gull, the harbour.

I switched the wireless off, so that her voice had it all its own way in the room...

After Munich, Jiřina sent out two more documents. Did it never cross her mind that no one cares to hear from the dead?

The first was short.

### 'TO THE CONSCIENCE OF THE WORLD

On this day when, by the decision of four statesmen, our country has been abandoned and delivered to injustice, with its hands bound, we remember your declaration of friendship, in the sincerity of which we believe.' At this point, the writer's real voice failed him. The trombones took over. 'Even in the difficulties of our present position, we remain and we shall remain in the forefront of humanity's common struggle for truth and justice. We stand by our President and without despair we fix our eyes on the tasks of the future and still remain faithful to the moral and spiritual ideals of our nation. Sacrificed, but not con-quered, we charge you, who for the present have escaped our lot, to persevere in the common struggle of mankind.'

A vast no-man's-land separates truth from the rhetoric composed in anguish and good faith by people used to handling words. I could have written the document myself, meaning every syllable of it, and weighing the effect of each word on its readers.

A Czech who left Prague two or three weeks later told me that Jewish and German refugees, forced into trains by Czech soldiers, were being taken to the occupied areas, where they were jailed or sent off to Dachau. Looking at me coldly, he went on,

'We can't hide them. What else can we do except try to satisfy the Germans?'

(These appeals to the conscience of the world must be an instinct with writers, a nervous reflex. The fact that they are addressed to what obviously does not exist is of no importance. The acid applied, the nerve twitches. On the 21st of June, 1964, in Oslo, I listened to an elderly Israeli writer reading, to a committee of fellow-writers from I forget how many nations, a statement—he had been refused leave to present it in the form of a res- olution—about the employment 'by a neighbouring country' of scientists preparing nuclear weapons for an attack on his people. Trembling, he read it in a low voice. The effort he was making to keep his anguish within bounds almost suffocated him. There was no comment. The briefest possible spatter of applause and, with relief, the committee passed to the next item.)

Jiřina's second document was longer and very bitter. She enclosed with it one of the three letters she wrote during this time to reassure me that, whatever the documents said to the contrary, I, she knew, had not betrayed her and her country.

'... no, no, my darling, we need your pen and your strong heart, we are suffering still beyond measure, but there is so much hope in my heart that I can give you part of it...'

After the Germans marched into Prague, I had a postcard from her. She had chosen it carefully—a narrow window barred by a grill of Renaissance ironwork; behind it, a single lamp. The first lines were clear—'My darling, thanks for your kind words, they have been a comfort in my illness. It is receding now and I hope to be soon my old courageous self. But you, my love, be careful, your health is so uncertain.' The rest concealed a message I could not, to my grief, decode.

After this, nothing.

# CHAPTER 20

I KNOW ONE RATIONAL HUMAN BEING—one, that is, to whom the term 'man of reason' applies in a sense wholly unlike its meaning when applied, say, to Beneš, whose reasonableness drove him into seeking formula after formula to paper over the most gaping cracks in his policy, or when we mean by it a man temperamentally incapable, as Beneš himself was, of meeting violence by violence.

My one rational human being, one of the most remarkable men I know, Basil Liddell Hart, is governed, or governs himself, by an extreme distaste for the human vices of intolerance and prejudice. This discipline, self-applied by an intelligence at once lucid and solid, would make him inhuman if he were not the most loyal, the friendliest and most humane person in the world, the gayest of pessimists, and the best company.

Lean and tall, he has a head by Goya, tempered by an air of amusement and kindness. I believe he respects the rights even of fools. Certainly he only recognizes two sins—cruelty and intellectual dishonesty.

One of his most disconcerting traits is the mental flexibility which allows him to think an opponent's thoughts for him. The week after Chamberlain returned from Munich he told me that the next crisis would come in March.

'Why March?'

'Six months, not less and probably not much longer, is the time Hitler will need to prepare his next move against the Czechs.'

'Isn't there any hope that he'll be content with what he's got?'

'My dear Storm, no military adventurer could refrain from taking over a defenceless neighbour—we've just made Czechoslovakia completely defenceless and given him notice that we shan't try to stop him. In fact, we can't.'

It would be idiotic not to believe him. I believed that the Czechs that is, Jiřina—had until March. I believed at the same time that he was wrong.

A few weeks later, in October or November, he told me that a small group which included Duncan Sandys and himself was meditating a non-party movement—to be called The Hundred Thousand. Its aims: to broaden the government, begin urgent social reforms, put the country on a war footing as rapidly as possible, and stop the catastrophic retreat before Hitler.

As a Yorkshireman, I felt the strongest doubts. Not about him. He was one of the first persons an English nationalist-socialist party, if it turned into that, would silence. I was too diffident to say a word.

Besides, the only thing I wanted to ask him was: Is there going to be war? Afraid to seem naïve, I did not ask outright. I said,

'A war footing? Do you mean conscription?'

'No, certainly not. Militarily it would be useless, and another step towards the Totalitarian State in this country.'

'Then what do you mean?'

One has to listen with desperate attention to hear what he says in his low rapid voice. 'The next crisis may shock our incorrigibly hand-to-mouth government into making promises to the next victim, Poland—an insanely rash thing to do unless we have an alliance with Russia. So far as I know, nothing of the sort is being planned; in the end we shall be forced into one—in the teeth of men who care nothing about the country and only want to keep their power and profits—and the Russians will then be able to impose terms on us. A detestable state of affairs. Almost as unpleasant as the mess our military and civil preparations are in, thanks only in part to the Treasury.' He added with something as close to bitterness as he allowed himself, 'My worst fear is that the government will panic: the War Office and the General Staff would then, by force of habit, swing into the ghastly 1914–18 policy of flinging in masses of men. If they do, half a million young men will be sacrificed before they learn.'

'Do you really think there will be war?' I said.

'I put our chances of avoiding it as almost negligible. It's too late.'

Forgetting to pretend that I was calm and rational, I stammered,

'Because of one vain inhuman old man.'

'No, no, no, Chamberlain is well-meaning. He has no imagination, he doesn't believe that a fellow like Hitler exists. More remarkable, my dear Storm, he doesn't know the most elementary facts of European history.'

He looked at me with a kind half mocking smile. 'He's not a pacifist, you know—though he wants their votes and shares some of their illusions.'

That evening, I repeated to my sister what he had said about the near-certainty of war. She sent a slow glance round her room, resting it longest on a Wedgwood bowl and a small old table of which she was proud. So had Anna Jerusalem looked at possessions that were as much part of her as her hands. Neither for my young sister were her things only a table, a chest, a cup. They were a living portion of her life and her children's lives, a promise she had made to the future. If she had cried out, I should not have felt this searing anger against the adventurers who dishonour all these millions of humble promises.

'If I had more of a garden I could grow enough food for Nick and Judy,' she said, scowling.

'You couldn't grow very much here,' I said.

'I know that,' she said sharply. 'I must think.'

I suppose that in the discussions she and her husband had, evening after evening, it was she who decided that they would let this precious house and rent one with enough ground to keep a family alive. In November she told me that they had looked at one in an isolated village some eight miles out of Reading; it was a large shabby Victorian place, standing in three or four acres, with fruit trees and a greenhouse.

'It's far too big for us,' she said, staring at me. 'We can only take it if you and Guy will share it with us.'

The idea of refusing her did not cross my mind.

It will be a bad war, I thought. Worse than the last. We'll go through it as a family.

# JOURNEY FROM THE NORTH, VOL. 2

*For Guy*

# PART I

## *Turn as You May*

*Turn as you may, lap after lap, in front of the black
Eumenides who are bored and cannot forgive.*

GEORGE SEFERIS

# CHAPTER I

THE DEVIATE APPROACH of a war many can see coming is a hand clapped over the eyes. Ridiculous to look back, over the waste months, to a time already irrelevant when some current of action might have set in and swept us past the teeth of the rock. And though this can still happen, we don't look forward, we have lost the sense that the future is our business.

In the early spring of that year I moved us to the house we were to share with my young sister, her husband and her two very young children. It was a big house, solid, and dignified in a pleasantly shabby way, like a plainly-bred Victorian dowager. It had lawns and a great many old trees and an orchard, and this, with the large kitchen garden, was what we counted on to see us through the war. My room on the first floor was vast, with windows looking down towards the high south wall of the garden; there were nectarines on this wall. Guy's room downstairs was equally large, but darkened by the elms and a strong old yewtree. The village itself was small and unspoiled, in the middle of open heath.

I have never been happier.

The autumn before we moved, in the middle of the Czech crisis, I began writing a novel that had been knocking on my skull to get out. It was about Europe—portraits of Europe seen in this and that light, from this and that angle, as a painter might go on trying to get at the truth of a man or woman, looking for it both in himself and his model. I wrote it with consummate pleasure, without a moment's boredom. For once I was too sure of the probity of what I was writing to feel either bored or impatient.

I know well that to be perfectly happy all I need is an unearned eight hundred a year, or its equivalent in our depreciated money, and the courage to live abroad and write a book every seven or ten years.

There were to be four portraits, long *nouvelles* or *récits*. I wrote the last first—'The Children Must Fear'—about Budapest, and finished it in November. But already, in October, I had begun writing another novel, completely different in kind, and just as determined to get itself written.

This one, which I meant to call *The Captain's Wife*, was the story, after her wilful marriage, of Sylvia Russell, one of Mary Hervey's daughters—Mary Hervey being the central figure in three novels about shipbuilding I wrote in my green twenties. It sprang from a deep nostalgia for a life I knew only through my mother, and through my childhood in a society of captains' wives of the old sort, as much at home in small cargo boats as in their own houses. Sylvia Russell is not my mother. But I drew from that powerful ghost and from all I had absorbed, consciously and unconsciously, from her memories, the portrait of *a* captain's wife who resembled her in looks and gestures. (When, in the underworld, Odysseus tried to take his dead mother in his arms, she slipped through his grasp.)

At the same time another of the stories of *Europe to Let* was nagging me. This was 'The Hour of Prague'. I began it, and after writing ten and eleven hours a day for a fortnight dropped it to get on with *The Captain's Wife*, which I finished in February—to my grief I had to find another tide for it in England—and went back at once to 'The Hour of Prague'.

In April and May I spent five weeks in Paris, alone. My mind has saved only one image of what must have been at least a near approach to complete happiness, that of the evening when Benjamin Crémieux took me to the *répétition générale* of Giraudoux's *Ondine*. At that time I still adored Giraudoux, and would have listened to Jouvet's incomparably moving voice with equal pleasure had he been reciting a time-table. I was madly happy—in spite of the ironical surprise I felt that, at this moment, when, Vienna lost, Prague lost, Paris was really in danger, we should be applauding fervently this piece of enchanting nonsense about a German knight. The work of a rather tired enchanter.

'Would you like to speak to Giraudoux?' Crémieux asked.

If I had had the courage I should have refused: I knew that I should be too timid to utter two consecutive words. We climbed a mean dusty staircase to an even meaner room, and I listened dumbly for ten minutes while Crémieux talked amiably and volubly to Giraudoux, who was grey-faced and smiling, and looked for all the world like a Foreign Office clerk.

Over supper in Weber's, Crémieux described the scene there after Munich, men and women in evening dress, sweating violently with relief, excitement, and too much wine, waving their arms and parts of garments, and shouting, '*Merci, Daladier! Vive Daladier!*'

'Too many Frenchmen are less afraid of the Nazis than of socialism,' he said harshly, with a harsh grief.

Simply out of politeness, I answered, 'They have their counterparts in England, eminent respectable men and politicians who believe that Hitler is no threat to their interests and so need not be opposed.'

This was true, but I had not said what I thought, which was that in any event we were sounder than the French, and more likely, at the last minute to stand. Or were we only less intelligent?

After that night I did not see Crémieux again. When, some time in 1944 I was told he had died in Buchenwald I felt only a conventional regret, and for twenty years never gave him a thought. Then, on the 29th of March 1964, I was reading the fifteenth volume of Paul Léautaud's *Journal Littéraire*, and came on the entry of Wednesday the 19th of May 1943.

'Paulhan spoke to me again of Benjamin Crémieux. Alerted by friends that they were going to arrest him and hurrying to slip away and hide. He has been arrested in a little bistro where he was living in secret, by two Gestapo agents, revolvers in hand. At this point, Paulhan, with a pained sort of expression on his face, said: "They're going to torture him." He tells me that Benjamin Crémieux, a lieutenant in the French army, took the reins in forming a sort of armed resistance group.' Léautaud has no use for such senseless gestures, and says so. Paulhan answers that Crémieux is 'one of those people who does not take things lying down, who does not yield'. Strangely, this touches Léautaud, who had always liked Crémieux, although he did not like Jews. 'What,' he reflects, 'is better, more commendable, more noble (if we dare use such a word, and I must admit that when I write this word *noble*, the word *foolish* comes equally to mind)—is it to not yield, to not give in, to fight, to continue to act, with all the resources available, despite every risk you run in doing so (and which nevertheless gives the act a certain character)? Or is it to be like me, caring scarcely a jot about how things are or what is happening, refusing to be duped by the rhetoric of events?...'

Suddenly I was seized by a piercing grief for Crémieux, seeing him very distinctly, a ridiculous figure with his black Assyrian beard and short clumsy body, playing tennis, in shapeless white trousers on the point of falling down—he invariably hitched them up at the last second, in time to save himself from disgrace—and in P.E.N. committee meetings watching the

English with a savage determination not to be tricked by us, and applauding one of Giraudoux's more sterile plays because Giraudoux was part of the literary establishment to which he himself, urbane conscientious critic that he was, belonged. This middle-aged Jew, the last person in the world to be, in Léautaud's phrase, duped by the rhetoric of events, to turn into a hero of the Resistance—I had tears in my eyes. Why had I laughed at him so often?

When I returned to England in May, Ria Braatoy, who had just come back from visiting her father in Germany, told me that the highly-placed Nazis who were his business friends and associates had amused themselves by telling her that a Russian-German treaty was as good as signed, the British Isles would very soon become untenable as one European country after another fell to Hitler, the King and members of the government and the aristocracy would bolt to Canada, the remaining English would be serfs in a German Gau.

'What did you tell them?' I asked.

'All I said was: Don't be too sure,' she said, with her fine smile.

'But you, Ria, what do you think?'

She shrugged her shoulders. 'Your ambassador in Berlin is an incredible fool, and your people haven't the faintest idea how arrogant, how brutal, the Nazis are. When you realize it you'll fight back. One can only hope it won't be too late.'

'They say God watches over fools,' I said. 'No doubt He'll look after us.'

After six weeks, I was too restless to sit writing all day waiting for war to break out, and went back to France with Guy. The mortal certainty that we were seeing France for the last time heightened every colour, every image, every sensation. In Saumur, a little drunk from reading too much Péguy— the eve of a second war had seemed the moment for him—I saw the Loire, 'notre blonde Loire', as he might have seen it, in a ravishingly gentle light, a benediction of light; every shadow of leaf or stone, every bank of sand, every crumbling strong old house, recovered in it the innocence of man before he learned—or had learned only a little—how to be cruel. Bordeaux was unbearably hot, the sky a sheet of blistering white metal. Without looking it up I don't know whether the Gironde is masculine, but certainly it is a male river where the Loire, even in a sullen mood, is as unmistakably feminine. Despite the heat, I walked from end to end of the quays and in crowded streets, gathering up a café table, a crane, an old woman with a head from some *jolly* Dance of Death, if you can imagine that, every wrinkle a toothless smile, a scent of limes, a small child lifting its single garment over a gutter, and putting them away against a dry future. Except in Bordeaux, the days were only gently warm, and the light a caress.

I am never unhappy in France. This time it was happiness, gaiety, a lively contentment, above a thin cold current. How much of this would exist after the war?

Still lower, colder, as cold as ice, the narrow stream into which, again and again, without meaning to do it, I dipped a finger. The shop windows in Bordeaux were full of things, gloves, handbags, scarves, any one of which would have pleased my mother. Even here there were times, even in France, when the whole world, its June sunlight, its lime-trees, was only the form taken by my grief, nothing, an absence of her.

## CHAPTER 2

S IX MONTHS BEFORE I had made one of my more insane blunders, tricked into it by the comedian in my skin who again and again in these confused middle years led me farther and farther out of my way. I ought, when its International Secretary, Hermon Ould, invited me to become president of the English Centre of P.E.N., to have rejected instantly an office that would involve me in the anguish of making speeches and meeting people. For six years, from 1938 to 1944, my life was bedevilled by this folly. But for one circumstance I should have invented a reason for resigning at the end of a year.

As an establishment, P.E.N. has one indubious virtue: no one is forced to join it and it has no power to bind or loose, even though its centres—except the amiable well-meaning English—are wormholed with literary politics. European writers, from Erasmus to Sartre, are political animals. The politics run a different fever in each capital. In Czechoslovakia, say, or Indonesia, they are likely to be ferociously nationalist. What do you expect of countries which have had to plot and struggle for their right to become or remain a nation? In these countries a writer is held to be as accountable for his actions as a financier or a baker.

In Paris an active member has his eyes fixed on the next stage in his career—a literary prize or the Academy—and cannot lift an eyebrow without asking himself whether it will do him good or harm.

'Now that I am *académisable*,' a French writer I like and respect said to me, 'I must be a little careful what I do.'

I felt no impulse to laugh. To be *académisable*... frightful, but is it worse than the disorganized struggles, vanities, discretions, of English writers?

I began my presidency by writing a long letter to the *Manchester Guardian* on the duty of writers to abhor racial intolerance. A most worthy letter. Any good Victorian liberal could have written it. None of my hard-tempered sceptical ancestors would have dreamed of doing so. I daresay that is why I wrote it.

The circumstance that kept me from resigning was not political. In 1938 the gas-ovens for disposing of human beings had not been invented, but Hitler's bloody harrow had been at work for five years, and in the thin stream of refugees able to reach England were a number of writers, German and Austrian Jews and non-Jewish liberals and socialists. Now, after Munich, many more began trying to escape it. Letters—from Vienna, Prague, Brno— poured into our shabby office, and since we had only one half-trained typist, Hermon and I were in the situation of a man with a piece of frayed rope trying to save hundreds sinking in a quicksand.

There were too many of them.

We answered every letter, we tried to get the visas needed, an effort involving us in hundreds of letters to the Home Office and visits to overworked refugee organizations. For one person we got out, ten, fifty, five hundred sank.

On the day when the German troops entered Prague, I came into the office and found a Czech writer, a big man, standing there: when he fled he had had to leave his wife to follow: her visa did not come and she was trapped. Until he put his hand over his face he did not know he was crying. Surprised, he stammered, 'What is happening? Excuse, please, I don't sleep. She is alone. What can I do?'

If he had been flayed, he would have been less exposed.

An exile understands the words *solitude*, and *death*, in a sense to which an Englishman is deaf. I realized this again twenty years later, in November 1959, when I was sitting, the only English writer who had taken the trouble to come, in a room full of exiles. As one after the other, Albanian, Czech, Estonian, Hungarian, Latvian, Lithuanian, Polish, Roumanian, Ukrainian, recited the names of the writers in his country who had been imprisoned, deported, murdered, an icy cold came from him. I felt a useless familiar despair and anger.

'There is only one way to help people,' A. R. Orage once said to me, 'and that is to give them money.'

At the time I was surprised to find him cynical: I realized now that he was absolutely right.

'We *must* get hold of some money,' I said.

Hermon looked at me wearily. 'Where on earth do you imagine it can come from?'

'We can try.'

I drafted two letters, paying attention to every word. One we sent to the Centres in every non-European country, asking the secretary to send it out to newspapers; the other went to English publishers.

It did not surprise me that the richest firms sent the smallest amounts. The rich are often mean, it is one reason why they remain rich.

From one source and another we raised almost three thousand pounds, not a great sum. Had we been appealing for some superb cause... but our exiles were not famous writers—these could make shift to live anywhere—and they had been victimized by their own people, a suspicious circumstance. My grandfather used to say, 'A man who says he has been ill-used by his family doubtless deserved it.'

After a time I knew that I would rather go out scrubbing floors than write any more begging letters.


# CHAPTER 3


THE SWEDISH CENTRE had arranged to hold a Congress in Stockholm, in the first week of September. All through July and the first week of August we went on preparing for it in London, as though there were no Polish crisis. In a civilization which is fundamentally insane, always liable to fits of homicidal mania, it is the only way to live. I knew, when I sat down to draft a motion to submit to the Congress, that it would never be submitted, that the English delegate, E. M. Forster, would never present it, never make the speech he was preparing. I took no less pains over it.

It was a fine motion, plumped out with the rhetoric of events like a stuffed partridge, every word of it sincere and useless. 'We, the members of the English P.E.N., hold it advisable now to call the attention of all Centres to the need to remind their members of their pledge, which forbids them to disseminate hatred in any cause; that they owe a duty to truth and reason and that if they allow truth to be destroyed and hatred to triumph they will be betraying their own country, other countries, civilization itself.'

'It will be a great pleasure,' E. M. Forster wrote, 'to speak to a resolution which is so sympathetic to me, and so sympathetically phrased... I had thought of a reference to the Antigone and an (unfavourable) one to Plato just to show that the problem isn't a new one, but coeval with civilization...'

The same day I ran into the writer and Liberal journalist J. L. Hodson and asked him whether he thought there were any chance of our going to Stockholm.

He smiled his good gentle ironical smile. 'I never prophesy. But I visited Holloway prison this week, and found the women busy making thousands of red ties for the wounded.'

This very minor symptom of our insanity shocked me, and I stammered something about the frightful wickedness of people so obsessed by their idea of Hitler as a barrier against socialism that they forgave him the concentration camps, the invasion of Prague, everything.

'That isn't the whole of it,' he said. 'It's difficult for an essentially dull decent man like Chamberlain to believe that anyone is so paranoically ambitious as to want to dominate Europe. It's very difficult for anyone to believe in the reality of evil men. If Hitler were patient and subtle he would wait to swallow the Poles very slowly, and we should probably turn away our eyes. For good reasons—horror of war is a good reason—as well as bad. Luckily or unluckily he's neither patient nor subtle.'

'Do you believe that war is the worst thing that can happen?'

If he had said yes, I should, I think, have closed my mind to every other conviction. He was a good man, very brave, a natural Christian.

'No, I don't,' he said, smiling. 'We have to die sooner or later. To surrender and let the country fall into the hands of men capable of inventing artificial hells, Dachau, Buchenwald, would be far worse than anything I remember about war.'

'For men,' I said, 'even young men. But children?'

'The price of fighting for what you believe gets higher all the time, I don't blame anyone for deciding that it's too high. But you were asking me if I believe that death is the worst thing that can happen. I don't.'

My most grotesque memory of those days is of arguing with H. G. Wells. I am astonished that I was able to argue with him in his arbitrary and bad-tempered moods. The credit was his. I did not suddenly become morally brave, I was still anxious to say what would please, but from the time I came to know him fairly well I was never tempted to placate him.

My feeling for him swung between two extremes. At times I believed that he was a crystallized mass of vanity and self-will. Again and again our arguments deteriorated into an unseemly wrangle before witnesses. On my way to a committee in August, I saw the first Air Raid Warning notice pasted on the colonnade of the Ritz, and decided that nothing was more ridiculous than to talk of going to Stockholm on the 30th. I had just told the committee so when the door opened and in walked H.G., very jaunty, always, with him, a sign of intransigence.

'Of course we are going,' he said brusquely. 'We're going there to prove that we're not afraid of the Germans and to defend the dignity of English letters. It's no good your consulting the French, they're all bureaucrats, afraid to call their souls their own. *We* must go, and speak for freedom in a voice that will be heard all over the world.'

Vexed by this gasconading, I said recklessly, 'The world isn't interested in hearing from us at this moment, and we shan't impress anyone with our courage in being out of England when a war starts.'

The others waited dumbly for the teeth to close on my head, but he remained good-humoured and smiling. 'Very well,' he said, 'if you're afraid, I shall go alone, and while the rest of you are cowering in England—'

'The war is not going to be fought in Sweden,' I said.

'—I shall be in Stockholm, telling the Swedish writers that you are all cowards.'

'They may cancel the Congress.'

'Short of their turning out to be as weak-kneed as you are, I shall be at Tilbury on Thursday to sail in the *Suecia*.'

I corrected him. 'Wednesday.'

Delighted to be able to quip, he began turning the pages of his pocket diary. 'It would be strange,' he said, chuckling, 'if I were saved by a subterfuge while you all sailed to a Swedish concentration camp.'

This was one of the moments when I loved him.

'We'll meet here again the day after tomorrow,' he said to me genially, 'and you'll have the pleasure of agreeing that I'm right.'

In his old half-inaudible voice, shaking with passion, Henry Nevinson said, 'I must tell you all and Storm that I have written to the Italian Centre to protest against a poem in their journal. It's a very bad poem but that's not the point. It runs like this: We thank our Duce for the joy of machine-gunning the Abyssinians from the air like black ants... Abominable. I couldn't wait to consult Storm before protesting.'

'What was the phrase?' H.G. asked.

'Like black ants.'

'Black—? Oh, yes, ants. Well, Italians...'

He was in a less amiable mood at our next meeting, and told me sharply that it was not only his duty but mine to go to Stockholm 'to speak for freedom.'

Feeling like Alice trying to reason with one of the incomprehensible and specious monsters of her dream I said, 'Your metaphors might be misleading; a speech made about freedom in Stockholm won't be worth a snap of the fingers.'

'Your feebleness shocks me,' he retorted. 'I've worked very hard to put a little self-respect into the French, they spend their time on their knees to the Quai d'Orsay, and now I see that you're just as much under the thumb of our rascally Cabinet.'

The next morning I heard from the Swedish embassy that their government would much rather we did not hold a meeting there now. When I told H.G. he said drily that he would go alone, as a private person, not as a member of a society of cowards.

He sees himself, I thought, standing up on the eve of war, demonstrating, with the world listening. He is an ape.

In the same breath I thought that he was one of the most generous of men, with no vanity in him. Or he would not allow me, a nobody, to quarrel with him.

I thought: I should write and tell him so.

He answered my letter at once, in his small firm hand. 'Don't you worry. About values there is no argument. We go our several ways and no doubt we shall find ourselves in alliance again later.'

As we did. In 1941 I let myself get involved in a prolonged time-wasting argument with Jules Romains, who had gone off to New York and there, exasperating to blind fury the European writers sitting it out in London, formed what he named 'The European P.E.N. in America'. Certainly he did not expect the London exiles to take offence. As for the English—he held suavely the common French view of England as a hypoborean island of dubious origins.

Talking to H.G. at a luncheon we were giving the Greeks, in Frascati's, I asked, 'Have I your support if I am driven in the end to try to rid us of this turbulent Frenchman?'

'Certainly.'

'Will you take his place as International President? If you won't, what will be the use of my fighting him?'

'Sooner than leave him in charge, I would even agree to that.'

After the lunch, when Hermon and I came down the staircase into the wide foyer, we saw him sitting there with Moura Budberg. He looked small and tired.

'You really will take Romains's place?' I said to him.

'I'll do all I can,' he answered, 'though I am an old worn-out man, and may die at any moment. What would you do if I dropped dead now?'

Without reflecting, I said,

'I should cry for my lost youth.'

'Ah.'

I could not read his expression, but I had the sense that he was not vexed...

Six months after this we quarrelled violently. It was at a meeting of the International Executive. He attacked me at once, savagely. What he said was too grotesque to be disproved.

'It has become obvious to me that you are an agent of the Foreign Office. You're plotting with the rascals to bring P.E.N. under government control.'

His voice rose to a high-pitched scream. 'You want to make it an instrument of Foreign Office propaganda. I won't have it!'

I glanced round the long table, at the dozen or so foreigners, half of them presidents of the several Centres-in-exile in London. Only five faces have stayed in my memory: William Kielhau, the Norwegian, whose ordinary speaking voice was the screech of a gull; the smooth diplomatic face of the Swedish delegate; the Catalan's small black eyes set in old yellowed ivory; Antoni Slonimski's delicate Polish features, and Salvador de Madariaga, his delicate lips stretched in a finely mocking smile.

Which of us is he mocking? I wondered: me, or H.G. in the part of an unscrupulous bully? None of them would come to my help. Except for Madariaga, their respect for H.G. kept them silent—that, and their sense that it was an Anglo-Saxon quarrel—whatever sympathy they might feel for me. My own poor forces were all I had.

I (or my grandfather) thought: I'm damned if I'll give way in front of a lot of foreigners.

'What you're saying is absurd,' I said. 'There's not a word of truth in it.'

'I don't believe you,' he retorted.

'You'll do as you please,' I said calmly, 'but the truth is that we have never been asked to do propaganda, for any Ministry. If we were asked, I should refuse.'

I have forgotten the rest—and lost the notes I made afterwards. The more violent a scene, the harder it is to recall it clearly.

A fortnight later he repeated his accusation.

'I've been lunching with the Minister of Information,' he said, eyeing me. 'He left me in no doubt that he considers you one of his errand-boys.'

'I have never met him.'

'He believes he can do as he likes with you—you. You're not experienced enough to deal with these people. I daresay you mean well, but I don't like the way you're going.'

Before I could check myself I said, 'You talk like my mother.'

He looked at me with such malevolence that I felt momentarily excited. 'I shall leave the society,' he said. 'I've done my best to keep you straight and you have abandoned me.'

'It's you who are abandoning us,' I protested.

'No, no, this is a parting.'

He stood up. I got up at once, none of the others moved, and stood while slowly he put on his overcoat and adjusted the straps of his gas-mask. Smiling round at the silent committee, he said, 'I notice that some of you are not carrying your masks, it's foolish and very anti-social, you should be setting an example, as I am.'

I opened the door for him, we shook hands, and he went. No one seemed sorry. I was so sad I could have wept. He had been behaving badly, but my respect for him was too great to be destroyed by a fit of hectoring, and I regretted our quarrel bitterly. Why, I asked myself, did you choose him, of all the people in the world, to prove that you are not timid?

When I was adolescent he had a prodigious influence on me and on all my friends. He formed a whole generation, throwing himself at us in a rage of energy, overwhelming us with his ideas, some absurd, all explosively liberating. Unlike Bernard Shaw, who did no more than instruct and amuse us, he changed our lives. A pity that so many of us were killed before we had time to do him credit or discredit, and without knowing what the world he had been trying to shape would be like. It died between 1914 and 1918, with several millions of half-formed young creatures.

To share the bitterness of my regret now you would have to be twenty or less in 1913, living in cheap lodgings in London, poor and continuously happy.

Short of apostasy, I could not mend things. I could do nothing.

Suddenly I felt certain he would not leave. He won't, I thought, cut himself off from the body he still dominates. Next week, he'll turn up as though nothing had happened.

He did. Smiling and in the best of tempers.

## CHAPTER 4

IT MUST HAVE GIVEN George Fox enormous satisfaction to run through the streets of Lichfield crying, 'Woe, woe, to this bloody town.' More satisfying than waiting, in an atmosphere which is that of a painting by Bosch, full of unrelated objects, each as sharp as a nail and casually distorted: a web of letters secreting useless hopes, fears, defensive evasions; voices repeating the mobilization order, notices about food hoarding and the evacuation of children from the most threatened areas; an eloquent speech by Daladier—oh, the eloquence of these comedians who used none of the powers they had to avert war—about honour (the honour of an adroit politician), liberty, the judgement of history, *la chère patrie*, and the rest of it and the rest of it, raising in advance a memorial to young men who are still alive.

I went on working at 'The Hour of Prague', which was turning out to be the longest and most difficult of the *récits* making up *Europe to Let*. After a few minutes, I was sunk in it, and—to be honest—perfectly happy. The air coming through the widely open window was warm and soft, and there was a scent of leaves and scythed grass. As soon as I dropped my pen, the voice started again in the darkness at the back of my skull: You may not see your son again... It was seven weeks and two days since he had written.

These icy thoughts went on below the pleasure of sitting writing in this large tranquil room, *and did not alter or destroy it*. So long as I knew he was alive, I could not only go on sinking myself over my eyes in a half-written book, but feel this intense happiness.

A writer, even a minor writer, is something of a monster.

The war began on a day of unusual beauty, clear hot sun, dazzlingly white clouds below a blue zenith, a high soft wind. An old man's dry croaking voice, full of bitterness—more, it seemed, because he had been duped than for any other reason—reached us in the garden.

'Consequently we are at war with Germany...'

We were filling sacks with earth to protect the windows of the cellars. Nothing could be more naked than my sister's glance at her two children. For less than a moment. Then her face closed: she would not give herself away. I helped her to carry down the stone stairs, into the largest of the four cellars, a table, chairs, rugs, a box of toys. In another cellar a huge frog squatted in the middle of the floor. Startled, she clutched me, laughing wildly, herself a child.

I went up to my room and began to draft an article for *The Times Literary Supplement*. It was not due until October, but I wanted it out of the way. In effect it was a genuflexion before the ghost of Erasmus, one of the idols of my adolescence, and his Europe. I set down the tide: *Writing in the Margin, 1939*, and then another ghost, living, this one, tapped me on the shoulder and I went to look for my copy of the letter 'A soldier' wrote to the *Spectator* in 1916.

'... You seem ashamed, as if they were a kind of weakness, of the ideas which sent us to France, and for which thousands of sons and lovers have died... You make us feel that the country to which we've returned is not the country for which we went out to fight... We are strengthened by reflections which you have abandoned. Our minds differ from yours, both because they are more exposed to change, and because they are less changeable. While you seem—forgive me if I am rude—to have been surrendering your creeds with the nervous facility of a Tudor official, our foreground may be different, but our background is the same. It is that of August 1914. We are your ghosts.'

A few persons, even in 1916, must have recognized the voice, made hard by contempt, of Sergeant R. H. Tawney.

He at least, I thought, will not tell me that when half the world is in agony it is indecent to sit writing about the need to save a few ideas, the idea of brotherly respect, the common man's instinctive mistrust of authority, the need to doubt. If only I can avoid rhetoric...

I see now that it is only possible to avoid it when the first person for whom one writes, to whom one writes, is oneself. The double effort, to recall the past without inventing forgotten details, and to see clearly one's own failures, lies, hypocrisy, illusions, cuts the throat of rhetoric. Wherever I detect its traces in this manuscript, I know that they hide a failure of attention or honesty, or of both.

Writing to a crowd of people, even to a narrow or friendly crowd, rhetoric is probably almost a form of politeness. The long eloquent Statement I wrote in the middle of September, to go out to the Centres in all allied and neutral countries—I have forgotten why we sent it as well to bishops and archbishops—is full of a modest rhetoric.

I believe that rhetoric in war time has another use—as an incantation. As a savage makes his most ceremonious gestures before a menace he cannot face nakedly...

In September 1939 it seemed highly unlikely, as well as slightly indecent, to think of earning a living as a novelist. I wrote to Humbert Wolfe, my one friend in the upper reaches of the civil service, and asked him to help me find other work.

I had known him for years, well enough to see as real and solid a man very many people saw as unreal, an assiduous player of parts he invented for himself. He had been born in Yorkshire, of an Italian mother and a German father, into one of those continental families which gave nineteenth century Bradford its distinctive colour among the dark cluster of textile cities in the West Riding—not my Yorkshire. His mother when I knew her was a formidable old lady, as slender and straight as a rod—as she was to her dying day—a foreigner, uncompromising in her refusal to take on the protective colouring of a native. She was a very Calvin of morals, without any intention to be cruel. She set a mark on Humbert he never effaced.

He spends his life, I thought, effacing the mark of Bradford.

For all its intake of continentals, Bradford is West Riding to a monstrous degree, a trough of smoke-blackened stone, majestic Victorian Gothic, factory chimneys, mills, steep grimy streets. The child a good half Italian set down in this dark place might, by a miracle of adaptation, of mimicry, have been happy. Humbert chose—at what age?—to mimic instead everything that Bradford was not. His body seemed to have learned its gestures by heart, and his voice to have studied its inflections under a master unwilling to leave anything to chance. The first creative effort of his mind, carried out with unbelievable thoroughness, was one of self-creation. The creation of a self whom no one, not even Humbert Wolfe, could accuse of a Bradford virtue or vice. Hence the ceaseless spinning round an invisible centre, the play of impudence and irony, the underlying melancholy, the amused invention of personae, which made him so gay and often disconcerting a companion.

There are many people, especially bureaucrats, whom no one, not the most miserable, dreams of asking for help, because it is manifestly useless and ridiculous. At the opposite pole are those it would be ridiculous not to beg from, since they as manifestly lack the self-importance to defend themselves. Humbert was incapable of learning the simple creed of the bureaucrat, for whom human beings are the raw material of an experiment which can only be a complete success if the human beings are dead or witless. Objectively, he was an immensely competent civil servant; morally, he had never been a member of the sect, he had been too early saddled with a sense of responsibility for other people, their unhappiness, disappointments, mistakes, cruelties.

Perhaps it was on this side that my mind was able to touch his and discover that he was real.

He used himself mercilessly, living his two lives, as official and writer, as though each had a right to the whole of his nervous energy.

Absurd to talk of his two selves. He had a score of selves, each quick-witted, adroit, and well able to defend itself. It would have been stupid to think that there was nobody at the centre except the puppet-master, too busy inventing the play to have time to reconcile himself to himself.

His kindness was the first paradox of this most paradoxical of men. He handled misfortune and unhappiness with the greatest delicacy, and took an intense pleasure in annoying and mocking self-important and respected persons, with whom his tongue did him as much harm as did what they called his affectations.

They would have forgiven these more easily if he had not been affecting an intelligence, a wit, a shrewdness, which were genuine.

A few days after I wrote to him, an editor invited me to lunch in the Ivy. Ridiculously, I expected that three weeks of being at war would have transformed a restaurant which was a habit with the better-known or better-off actors, writers, journalists, politicians. Looking round when I came in, I was surprised that nothing had changed; there was not a uniform in the place, not one of the young men I half expected—foolishly, since they were dead or no longer young. My eye caught one after another of the faces seen on other visits: two middle-aged writers lunching with their publishers; Princess Bibesco; Aneurin Bevan with the political editor of one of our less polite newspapers; a celebrated actor with a very young man whose hand he kept touching; and Humbert with Pamela Frankau. Even in repose, or in the act of attention, Humbert's face had the look of a mask. An impressive mask, haggard, strongly drawn, bony, the eyes remarkable, the eyes of a comedian, perhaps a great clown, made more remarkable by the circle drawn round the pupil with a fine pen dipped in Indian ink.

After a minute I realized that my first impression of the place had been an illusion. With a light shock, as if a skin were being peeled from it, or from my eyes, I saw that it had in fact changed, in a very odd way. It was not the famous scene at the end of Proust, there had not been time for any of these people to become deformed or old; but they had suddenly, even Humbert, even Pamela, young, elegant, witty, become old-fashioned. A hand passed across them had effaced colours and displaced the figures themselves into a colder distant background.

A few of them, I thought, will be able to catch up again with their time, the others will one day notice suddenly that they have ceased to exist.

It did not cross my mind that I should be among these.

Towards the end of the meal Humbert came across the room to speak to me.

'How soon do you need a job?'

'I'd like to finish the book I'm writing.'

'Of course. How long will it take you?'

'Until the end of the year.'

'Very well,' he said lightly, 'I'll ring you up then. Don't worry, I can certainly do something.'

Watching him as he made his way, moving with practised negligence, between the tables, pausing to speak to Elizabeth Bibesco, my host said, 'Extraordinary fellow he is. I can never believe he's real.'

'He's really kind,' I said.

This was not the place, nor had I the quickness to say that his immense skill in impersonation sprang from the fact that, for as long as it amused him, he was, wholly—almost wholly, leaving aside the part of him reserved, as we say, to God—whoever he happened at any moment to be impersonating, the witty diner-out, the tactful handler of a social crisis or its deliberately unscrupulous provoker, the malicious story-teller, the poet...

## CHAPTER 5

I WAS WRITING 'The Young Men Dance' for *Europe to Let*. Set in Cologne in 1923, it twisted three cords, the short-lived separatist movement in the Rhineland, that strange bitter episode, the friendship of two young men, and a foreshadow of the German damnation in the form of a young Goebbels. It is probably the best, because the only purely imagined, of the four nouvelles, and I enjoyed writing it.

I wrote through every sort of interruption, letters and telephone calls from and about our exiles, anxious letters from English writers about Alain and Jean Giono, who had been jailed as subversive characters—the first indeed was, as subversive and unmanageable as Socrates.

A minor symptom of wars is the cancerous growth of committees. I have deliberately wiped out my memories of all those I was trapped in, including one, secret and high-powered, formed to save a few young writers from the slaughter to be expected—which I admired coldly. Did anything come of it? I have completely forgotten. It remains in my mind as a noble torso, shoulders and a pelvis, but no limbs...

A hard-working writer can count as one of the benefits of his obsessed life his trick of living simultaneously, with equal intensity, in two scenes. Driving through Hyde Park, a few minutes after nine o'clock on the morning of the 8th of November, I saw vividly the dirty grey-green balloons resting their hindquarters on the ground between the air-raid shelters for their crews, the lounging groups of soldiers, sea-gulls, cavalry in steel helmets exercising their restless horses: the day before there had been a violent thunderstorm, long tearing claps, flashes of lightning across a livid sky, and torrential rain; now, in the mild sun, the grass was a luminous green, fleecy clouds grazed the pale freshly washed blue of the sky, and a few yellow leaves, very precisely drawn, clung to the branches between drops of water or mist. In the same instant of time I watched the Czech actors on the evening of the 27th of June 1938 playing *Romeo and Juliet* in a seventeenth century palace. The illusion was complete, the white pillars of the garden-room, the darkening sky, the swallows, the superb freshness and vigour of the young men and their word-play, were as solidly present as the actual scene, not imposed on it or seen behind it, but reflected with it on the sides of the bubble formed by sky and grass.

I did not know then that the man, Dr Franke, Minister of Education in Beneš's government, who had had the lyrical idea of playing *Romeo and Juliet* in a room built when Shakespeare was alive, was in the hands of the Gestapo in Prague; he died a month later, of the tortures they were using on him.

(I have been sitting for an hour, staring at that sentence. To go on writing seems impossible, if not indecent.)

Some time that month I finished the fourth nouvelle for *Europe to Let*, the last—'Between March and April'—set in Vienna, immediately before and after it fell into the same hands. There is a portrait of the young Lilo in it, too ingenuous but fairly accurate: the story itself and the other characters I invented, *after* the truth, as one says of a painting that it is after Rubens. All I had heard, seen, felt in Vienna in July 1938, went into it, in some form.

As soon as I had sent the manuscript to the publisher I began making notes for a novel which had been at the back of my mind, half patiently waiting its turn, ever since the day when, reading Wheeler-Bennett's *Hindenburg, the Wooden Titan*, I felt, with the indescribable excitement a woman is said to feel when her unborn child moves for the first time, theme and plot move in my brain. I conceived my Hindenburg as the head of a family of Alsatian wine-growers—somewhere I found an old book on the history and methods of wine-growing and read it with passionate interest and enjoyment—and characters and scenes germinated in my mind with delicious ease. Nothing in this novel came from my own life, yet to speak of it as an improvisation would be absurd, since no other novel I have written was, as this was, lived intensely in the writing.

I had written less than a chapter when, opening *The Times* on the 8th of January, I read that Humbert had died the day or was it two days before, in his sleep.

In the first moment it was difficult not to think that this was another of his half-malicious, half-mischievous jokes, another mask invented and slipped on to mystify, amuse, and disconcert friends as well as enemies: behind it he was surely smiling, delighted by the success of his latest deception, delighted to have created an effect, even of dismay.

It is the first time he ever gave up, I thought.

I remembered a fellow Yorkshireman, J. B. Priestley, speaking of him as 'a damned show-off', and thought: Imbecile! Couldn't he see that this supple worldly mercurial figure was terribly vulnerable, this teller of malicious stories considerate to a fault, this damned show-off a man with no image of himself as admirable, no vanity, and no egoism, if egoism consists in thinking of oneself as more important than the obscure, the young, the weak?

How dull the world is beginning to be, I thought...

After a time I reflected that my chances of a war-time job had vanished. I felt completely indifferent to this, even relieved, and went back to *Cousin Honoré*.

\*

On the 28th of January, as if to ape the immobility of the armies, the earth itself turned to ice. The day before, after several weeks of intense cold, with thick frost, there was a thaw, and torrential rain. The temperature must have dropped again suddenly. Towards midnight, opening a window in my bedroom, I noticed the curious sound a very light wind was making in the trees. In the morning every blade of grass, thin branch, weed, telegraph wire, had its thick sheath of ice. Each single leaf of the privet hedge was encased in ice, and the separate sprays of the evergreens; the grass stood erect in fine lancets of ice, each veined by a thin greenish-brown blade; every reed, dry thistle, bare twig and branch of the trees in the orchard was enclosed in a cyst of ice; the ground was covered with ice to the depth of more than an inch, and wherever a wall had been still wet it was masked by a dark clear film, curiously striated. The sound I had listened to at midnight was made by the slight movement of all these ice-imprisoned leaves and twigs, a chinking or creaking note, strangely dull.

... rat's feet over broken glass
In our dry cellar.

During the day the wind strengthened a little, and the creaking sound became louder.

Snow fell during the night, so that leaves and branches now had a thick double sheath, snow on ice, and the ground was inches deep in snow. The electricity failed; we dressed and ate breakfast by the light of candles, and then tried to ring up the town, but the wires were down. Outside, the cold forced the breath back into the lungs. No sun, no thaw.

The next day a heavier fall of snow began to crack the branches. The big rhododendrons turned into a strange form of cactus, each leaf swollen by the ice to monstrous thickness, looking like limbs of grey green-tinged dead flesh. Ornamental shrubs round the lawn, frozen to the brittleness of glass, broke at a touch.

It crossed my mind that Europe might be dying under this ice, and the war would be stopped by famine.

I had accepted, I forget why, an invitation to a party, given by a publisher, in the Café Royal. On my way across the hall, I caught sight of J. L. Hodson disappearing into the brasserie, and ran after him. He was not going to the party, and I sat down with him on one of the plush benches. He had been in France as a war correspondent. He said he was trying to make up his mind whether, since he could write so little about what he saw, he could in honesty go back.

'What *is* happening?' I asked.

'Very little—except to the Finns. It makes me uneasy and I don't feel any easier here. No one has any sense that we're fighting for anything except to patch up the kind of world where the same few are comfortable and privileged and the rest remain half-educated and half-fed. The country will go bad if it isn't given a hope for the future: the old men who got us into this—out of their natural sympathy with the Nazis and anxiety for themselves—are fighting it without a rag of energy or vision. There's no moral basis, our leaders have none, they can't see outside their class—one or two of them would make terms with Goering now if he promised them a gentlemanly capitalist Germany and a war on Russia. The Labour bosses have accepted the ends and means of a mechanical civilization and don't offer anything more. Hence the feeling that nothing is worth a fight. And yet how decent our people are! We went into this war with no lift, but our young men are magnificent—believe me. Give us hope and a faith, and you'll see...'

He smiled. 'Don't think I'm a pessimist. I'm not... Are you writing?'

'I began a novel. But isn't it wrong to sit writing now?'

'Good God, no. Write as long as you can. This interlude isn't going to last, the Germans aren't in it for a joke, or for what—when it was a question of a few muddy yards a month—we used to call a limited objective.'

I left him, with reluctance, and went upstairs to the party. The immense room was so brilliantly lit, and there were so many people, hundreds, not counting the scores of waiters running about with a surfeit of food and champagne, that I almost turned back from the door, cowed by the numbers and the tearing rattling noise of voices. It was exactly the sound, enormously magnified, made by the branches with their membrane of ice.

A man I knew slightly, an eminently successful novelist, spoke to me and I asked him, 'Are all these people writers?'

'My dear girl, of course not, they're reviewers and journalists and broadcasters and civil servants, and an ambassador or two—and a few writers like you and me who are still, as they say, in full production.'

I thanked him for comparing me with himself. We talked for a few minutes about 'the novel', with a certain delicacy, as if it were a disreputable relative of his or mine. He moved away and I left at once, knowing that if I stayed I should say the most idiotic things to people who had no more wish to talk to me than I to them. I am not an imbecile, but slowness of mind, and boredom, often make me talk like one. I had been a fool to come. If you must talk and drink, I said to myself, let it be with one or at most two others, friends.

The fourth day of the ice began in thick mist, a grey wall behind the lines of spectral trees. A large old acacia, the tallest tree in the garden, had every one of its main branches split down the middle. Smaller trees and bushes had snapped off at the roots. The lawn was an extraordinary sight; in places, spikes of ice, each the sheath of a blade of grass, thrust above the snow, looking for all the world like miniature tank-traps. The children amused themselves by running against shrubs and trees in a clatter of glass rods and cracked branches.

In London I had picked up from Hachette's dwindling stocks a copy of Valéry's *Variétés 2*. Cutting the leaves this evening, I had a few minutes of piercing happiness; it contained essays on Stendhal, Baudelaire, Mallarmé, and for a moment this seemed worth the trouble of living.

A slow thaw began, and went on during the night. On a branch of yew under my window stems and ice-sheath had parted company, the leaves fell to the ground, but the sprays of ice clung to the tree, still marked by the fine veins of the leaves they had killed.

Paul Morand was in London that week, and P.E.N. gave a luncheon for him at the Café Royal. We asked E. M. Forster to take the chair, and I found that I should have to sit between him and the First Secretary of the French Embassy. Never had I felt less sure of being able to entertain either of these distinguished men, and I asked Denis Saurat to stand with me in the doorway and help me through the first moments with the Frenchman. He was called away, and said, 'You won't have any trouble recognizing him. He has spent years trying to look like Proust, but I think he has given it up as a bad job.'

A minute later I saw, coming up the staircase, a man who did not look more than thirty, but in every other way fitted Saurat's malicious description: he was slight, elegant, with heavy eyelids, and moved languidly.

'Monsieur de Charbonnières,' I said.

When we were seated, he asked, 'How did you know me? Do I look so like a diplomat?'

I said recklessly, 'Professor Saurat told me that when I saw someone coming in who looked as though Proust might have written about him, it would be Monsieur de Charbonnières.'

'That is a compliment,' he said, without a smile.

But he was not displeased, and roused himself to speak, in a faintly animated way, about the news. With *Cousin Honoré* in mind I had been reading the lately published French Yellow Book, and I made a polite remark about the difference between Neville Henderson's reports, clumsy and full of self-justification, and those of the French Ambassador. 'Perhaps under Federal Union, we might educate our diplomats in Paris to write with that splendid clarity.'

'But everyone knows that your late Ambassador to Berlin is a fool,' he said, without a trace of irony. 'They are not all like him.'

Somehow I found myself talking about the failure of intellectuals. 'My only criticism of your English intellectuals, he said, 'is that they are not serious. I see H. G. Wells here. He has drawn up a Declaration of the Rights of Man, and is debating it in the *Daily Herald*. Why doesn't he write about what is happening to these famous Rights in Poland now?' He went on with the same limpid nonchalance, 'The information we have is so frightful that much of it can't be printed. The Germans are systematically shooting professional and educated men and women, with the idea of reducing Poland to a nation of peasants and workers, uneducated men without leaders. They hand the women of these classes to their soldiers. They have emptied whole towns and villages of their inhabitants, turning them out to die in forty degrees of frost. They bring in a Baltic German, show him round the house, ask him if he likes it, then tell the Polish owner he has two hours to clear out. "This is not your house any longer, it belongs to this man."—"Where am I to go?"—"That is not our business."—"What can I take?"—"What you can carry in your hand." There is no other house for him to go to. He and his family join the thousands dying on the icy roads.'

'What are we to do with the Germans?' I exclaimed. 'What can one do with a European nation which has no respect for the individual?'

He lifted a small finely shaped hand. 'I don't know. We can't hold them down forcibly for ever, we can do it for a time, but then people get tired.'

'The English get tired first,' I said.

He smiled for the first time. I reflected that I was doing a little better than I could have hoped. His neighbour on the other side spoke to him, and I turned to E. M. Forster. I admired him so much that what confidence I had froze again into timidity, and I could not think of anything fit to say. He helped me by asking about Monsieur de Charbonnières.

'Mr Morand tells me he never speaks, I am afraid you must be working very hard.'

'He has been talking a great deal about Poland,' I said. I repeated what I had been told.

The great writer moved his hands in a light gesture, very charming. 'But is there any evidence?'

I was taken aback. It had not crossed my mind that I was showing myself eager to believe in atrocities. I assured him hurriedly and untruthfully that I knew there was evidence. He did not dispute it and talked about something else. I had been quietly reproved. Shocked out of its confusion and diffidence, my mind fell into its trick of attending to what was not said, and I thought: He is good, honest, cares a great deal about justice, and is very slightly cruel, in a feminine way...

After the luncheon, with an hour to wait for my train, I sat in Paddington station and listened to a shabbily-dressed woman talking to her friend. She repeated the same phrases over and over, as though to make them harmless.

From thinking about Poland and wondering whether I had been misled, I tumbled into a black pit of despair about the war itself. Oh, God, I prayed, let it end, now, quickly, and set us. free from this nightmare, this fear. Anyone who justifies it is forgetting or pushing out of sight the misery of poor women unable to pay their rent, the children running loose in London with gas-masks knocking against their skinny shoulder-blades, the anger of young men, the useless deaths.

I told myself, and I believed, that to accept, as genuine pacifists do, any-thing rather than war, total disrespect for freedom, the systematic crushing or deformation of the spirit, is to accept a death as final as the death of the body. Even in hell, one could not give up fighting for freedom of mind.

But this was merely reason. My black despair came from another source, and did not lift until I was giving the children their bath that evening. Then it lifted—for no reason.

During these months I came to know President Beneš a little. I felt for him an affection—I dislike politicians on principle—I never felt for any other public figure. He had the failings and weakness of a man of reason who believes that reason *ought* to prevail. In a crisis he asked himself involuntarily: How would Thomas Masaryk act? His desperate struggle to bend together two extremes, two utterly incompatible ways of thinking and living, Masaryk's solid nineteenth century idealism and good sense, and the hideous violence of his own time, drove him into expedients and into devising ambiguous formulas which gave the impression, sometimes, of slyness and cunning. But the dislike, no, hatred felt for him by a number of powerful men in London and Paris was not based on this. It was based entirely on their sense of being confronted by a decent sober-minded reasonable man who was hindering them from coming quickly to terms with his would-be murderer. They actually spoke of him as ill-bred and unreliable, transferring to him the epithets that applied with complete accuracy to Hitler. It would have been interesting as a semantic irony if it had not been a disaster.

One day near the end of February there was a memorial service in London for Karel Capek. Henry Nevinson made a speech, and Jan Masaryk, and Czech actors put on scenes from his plays. The whole performance was anything but polished, even shabby. When one of the young women lifted her arms on the stage, you saw that none of them shaved their arm-pits, and the Czech folk-song sung during the recital of Capek's superb prayer for his betrayed country almost drowned it. Yet I had to keep back tears.

I was sitting between Beneš and Madame Beneš, and he talked about his long friendship with Capek. 'After a difficult day, I would go and sit with him for an hour, two hours, three, we did not speak much, but it was a great help to me.'

'The time you will miss him most is when you go back,' I said.

'Yes. How did you know?' he said.

In fact I had only wanted to bring on the idea that he would go back. He sat for a minute, sunk in himself, then said abruptly, 'I can give Germany three narrow strips of country and still keep a defensible frontier, but that way I shall get rid of two out of our three million Germans. Half the remaining million will have been killed off by our people before I get back. Those left can be given their choice of going to Germany or becoming Czechs. There will be no more German schools, no German language used, no parliamentary representation—this time we shall be drastic.'

His calmness when he spoke of the killings gave me a strange muffled shock. Not that I had the impudence to approve or disapprove. And I understood sharply enough that his countrymen would want to efface in blood the memory of humiliation and worse. But what was this future that threw its shadow backwards over streets lively with the springing feet and clear candid faces of the Sokol children and over the free village women heaping a table with food and wine for their foreign guests, and over Jiřina's tranquil confidence? And who said that justice can be more bitter in the belly than it was honeyed in the mouth?

## CHAPTER 6

THERE WAS SOMETHING peculiarly horrible about the invasion of Norway. Why? I think because it was like seeing that a cancer which is killing the older members of the family has begun to work in the children. Listening to the first news on the wireless I was shaken and afraid as at no other time in the war, not even during the air-raids.

When we went to Norway, in 1935, the ship put us off at a tiny port in the Oslo fjord at four o'clock in the morning, a June morning as clear as fine glass, sun, a light wind off the water, silence. Not a cat was awake. Walking along a narrow street, past the door with my name, Storm, over it, I caught the sharp hemp smell of new rope and felt not only a keen pleasure but relief, as though a weight had suddenly been lifted from me—as indeed it had, a weight of years, of regret and errors, letting me go back into one of countless mornings in Whitby when I was walking with my mother in a narrow street in the oldest part of the town, the air cool, the salt wind from the harbour light and friendly: if, on our errand, we went as far as a large ramshackle storehouse and loft she always said, 'Your grandfather's sail loft was here, I used to like the smell of tar and rope,' and I would answer, 'There is still a smell of rope,' which was not true, but it pleased her and made her smile. I was not conscious then of being safe and happy, but now, in the empty Norwegian street, glancing into a flagged passage which might be any one of the dark narrow alleys in Whitby called ghauts, an exquisite sense of freshness and lightness of mind and body seized me. It was not mine, it belonged by right to the child who was still living in a Whitby I had long left, but it was I who felt it.

This defenceless little port, Horten, the Germans had bombed. It seemed an appalling irrelevance, even in war time, and the shock of grief I felt was sharpened by an instant when I saw the bombs wipe out my grandfather's sail loft and the old, very old street with one foot in the upper harbour and another in the roots of the cliff. Not knowing how much or little damage had been done to Horten, I tried, walking up and down my room, to hold it in my mind exactly as it had been when I saw it for a moment with the senses, new, intact, of a child...

After the endless winter, spring was late. The first warm day came at the end of April, with a gentle wind and rain as fine as blown hair.

I spent the last week of the month in a country hotel near the Liddell Harts. During those days I understood, for the first time, the intense fascination of the study of strategy, a logical or mathematical exercise of which the terms are living bodies and minds and geographical features (as in *Alice Through the Looking-glass*), with the subconscious bite of danger. There was something criminal in the pleasure with which I listened to his lucid account of what was happening in Norway, an account completely different from those we were being offered in the newspapers. On the fourth evening I was there, the B.B.C. announced, as though it were an unimportant item, that our troops were withdrawing from a position covering a town of which I have forgotten the name—Dombaas?—but it was one Basil Liddell Hart had pointed to on the map, four days earlier, and explained why it was essential to hold this insignificant place and why, unless our people moved very quickly and were lucky, they would not be able to hold it.

Delighted to show myself off in the role of attentive pupil, I said, 'I suppose it means we shall leave Norway.'

'Yes,' he said, 'I give us three days, perhaps only two.' In his quiet only half audible voice he went on, with no emphasis of any kind, to explain why the situation was serious, far more serious than we were being allowed to know. 'The truth is we were never in so dangerous a position in the last war as we are in this, and we have never been so threatened. Compared with the Germans we are ill-equipped, and'—he hesitated and went on with a half-smiling grief—'the French are not altogether dependable allies. From all I can gather they're in a worse muddle than we are.'

It was on the tip of my tongue to ask: You mean we may lose the war?

I said nothing. For two reasons. I was as reluctant to talk about the possibility of defeat as if England were a member of my family who had disgraced himself. And equally diffident about saying that I did not believe we could possibly be defeated, it wasn't one of our habits.

I felt that it would be impudent to ask him what he felt. Possibly—the most English as well as the most rational of men—he was able to contemplate the idea of defeat with the whole of his mind where mine lost the power to think or understand as soon as it was a question of our losing the war (not, after all, an impossibility: other countries had been defeated, Poland, France in 1870, Germany in 1918).

On the 2nd of May I went, rashly, to see the Braatoys. Bjarne was not there, but two other Norwegians were in the small living-room with Ria, a man now at the Legation who had crossed into Sweden and left his wife in Stockholm: the second, whose name was Rytter, had been a broadcaster in Oslo. Ria, who loved heat and spent any sunny day on the dusty ledge miscalled a balcony overhanging Albany Street, was looking particularly handsome, her bare arms and shoulders a smooth dark brown like oiled teak.

'We're waiting for Bjarne to ring up from the *Herald*,' she said, 'there may be news.'

Rytter was unable to keep still or be silent. Walking, with difficulty, about the room in the few feet between Ria's bed and the table, he answered her polite question by a torrent. 'We began getting queer news on the night of the 7th of April, about ten, that German warships were moving up the fjord, we didn't understand it, then air-raid warnings, we gave these out, over and over, and then, about midnight, the order to mobilize, and we gave that out. We didn't know at all what was happening. Some time after four we heard that a German warship had been sunk in the fjord, and we said: Ah, the English have come, thank God. Suddenly, about seven, the Nazi planes were overhead. Then about half-past nine we were ordered to leave Oslo at once, we packed a lorry with stuff and went off, passing the aerodrome where we saw German planes landing, we got to Hamar, Haakon was there, and after a time the Nazi planes began to hunt for him, and we went with him into the wood—it was the only wood they bombed. Who, I ask you, had given away his whereabouts? There were only five traitors among well-placed Norwegians. Five.' He stopped abruptly in front of me. Staring into my face he said, 'How many would it need to betray England? Do you know?'

The other Norwegian smiled. 'I haven't reached that point of despair yet.'

Picking up a newspaper, Rytter demanded, 'Who is this R. H. Tawney who wants your Air Force to bomb the Ruhr?'

'My God, it wouldn't be so bad,' Ria said, smiling, 'why should only Norwegian towns be bombed?'

At this moment the telephone rang. We watched her as she listened. Her face, under its tan, paled, and I knew that Basil had been right even to the day. She put the receiver down and stood frowning for a moment.

'Are we retreating?' I asked.

'Yes. Chamberlain has just told the house that we—your troops—are evacuating all southern Norway.'

Neither of the others looked at me, and Rytter said hurriedly, 'I was not anxious about my father—he is a strong socialist—and the others, because, although they lived near the Oslo aerodrome they had a hut in Hallendal and they got away there. This means that the country will be overrun by the Nazis, and they will be caught.'

'I don't understand very clearly,' Ria said. 'What does it mean?'

'It means,' the Legation man said calmly, 'that Scandinavia is gone, Sweden will have to make terms, Italy will come in on the German side, the Balkans will capitulate...'

Rytter looked at me. 'Let me say this, please. We knew quite well, if we resisted, it meant that Norway would be a battlefield. All right—we put it at your disposal as a battlefield. Fight the Germans here, we said, and you'll never be invaded. Now they can sit down behind the Siegfried Line and build a magnificent fleet, and attack you directly. Your Prime Minister talked about Germany losing our iron ore. Not at all, *you* have lost it, it will pour out through Lulea, the Swedes won't resist.' He laughed. 'Does your poor Chamberlain think that the ice lasts all year up there?'

'That's enough,' the other man murmured.

I had nothing to say. Rytter went on, with the same dry anger, 'If you had only landed enough men and supplies *in time*, and gone straight for Trondheim, risking your ships, we should have pushed the Germans out.'

'You won't be a battlefield,' I said.

'Listen. If every town in Norway had been destroyed and the Germans thrown out, we should still be happy. But if you are leaving us we are finished, we can't fight alone.'

'Enough, enough,' his friend said.

When Bjarne came in he went straight to the wireless set and switched it on. 'Chamberlain will be on the news,' he said, smiling sharply. 'It would be a pity to miss it'.

I have rarely heard a more adroit or vainer speech, or of worse quality. He implied that Norway was a trap, and almost gave the impression that we had been extremely clever to go there in order to be able to withdraw so skilfully. It was painful hearing. I felt sure he would not lie in his private life: as a politician he lied without noticing it, and that was surely much worse than the lies everyone tells privately.

'Will he get the country on this?' Rytter asked.

'Almost certainly,' Bjarne said, with his mad laugh.

'The Swedes will be able to exercise their splendid talent for neutrality.'

After a few minutes, Bjarne took both men away to dine in town, and as soon as we were alone, Ria asked, 'Have you made any plans? I mean, if we lose the war.'

If she had not said *we* I should not have remembered at this moment that she was German. 'We can only keep very cool, and our eyes open,' I said. 'If we are occupied, the Germans will kill some of us: If we make terms'—I had been going to say: If we capitulate... I could not get it out—'I shall try to get the children and ourselves to America. But I won't be an exiled writer, it's a ghastly life, I'll char, or get a job as housemaid.'

Ria smiled, showing the edge of magnificent white teeth.

'I shall kill myself before they can touch me,' she said calmly, almost gaily.

I reflected that there was no doubt she would. At this moment she looked as though she had been very narrowly bred, a look of race, like a fine animal. Beside her, I was slow and inelegant. I doubted whether I should kill myself.

I left her and walked up the hot shabby street towards the underground station. Grief and a feeling of shame raged in me. And yet... There is a sharp old northern saying: No man dies of another's wounds... *We* are not defeated, I thought.

Is it absurd to say that I have never felt the life of England stronger in me and in the people I passed in the street and sat opposite in the underground than on that evening of the 2nd of May 1940?

## CHAPTER 7

P EOPLE LIVED SHARPLY THAT MAY, with the double sense of being driven by time as by a strong following wind, and of each minute of this scudding time being dilated to infinity.

On the ninth I was in London. We were giving one of our refugee parties that evening: they cost us a little money, but they (we hoped) gave the exiled writers a brief sense of being still part of a community. The greater number of our guests were German or Austrian, and most of these were Jewish. Walking about the long room in the New Burlington Galleries, I picked out the dark-skinned skeletal face of one of our Catalans, and the two or three Czechs—what had become of the young writer who sent us desperate letters from Brno, whom we had failed to get out? The thought of the speech I should be forced to make was nearly intolerable. I detest making speeches, and to have to make one to people for whom the present was an insoluble riddle and the past a kaleidoscope of fears, anguish, and the deaths of friends, shamed me. Moreover, not many of them would be able to hear my light voice. Perhaps more heard than I could have expected, they were so quiet when I got up on a chair and began speaking that I felt their attention like a hand clutching my arm. I said what I could about the difficulties of their lives, I said I knew we could not give them back their lost certainties, their lost streets, cafés, friends, I said that our friendship for them was a plank thrown across an abyss, I tried to warn them not to show anger and impatience when they met, as, if the war took a bad turn they would meet, suspicion and injustice... It does not matter a toss what I said. If I had had the tongues of men and of angels I could not have lightened their obsessions for longer than a breath.

I was staying the night with Noel Streatfeild in Bolton Street, within a step or two of Green Park. When I knew her first in the twenties, this daughter of the vicarage was a lovely and charming young rake of an actress (I daresay an indifferent one): she dropped acting to write gay well-mannered novels and lively sensible quick-witted children's books, and without losing a feather of her gaiety arranged for herself a hard-working and eminently well-run life. It ought not to have surprised me that she turned out to have an active social conscience; she was not a descendant of Elizabeth Fry for nothing.

In the morning, Nellie, her shrewd friendly housekeeper, a Londoner to her ill-fitting teeth, brought my coffee to me in bed. I was taking it from her when Noel came in, smiling, merry as a grig.

'Well, girls, we're on. The Germans invaded Holland and Belgium this morning. I've just heard it on the French wireless.'

'I suppose they would know,' I said.

'They certainly do.'

'I've a sharp kitchen knife out there for any parachutists who land in the Park,' Nellie said pleasantly.

'You won't,' Noel told her, 'need it this morning. Later, perhaps.'

I listened with pleasure to her strong self-possessed voice as she talked on the telephone to some knowledgeable friend. Like the well-born women of a much earlier generation she spoke with traces of a tart accent, learned in the nursery.

'Yes, yes, but what *sort* of help are we giving them? The sort we gave the Poles?... My cue? Yes, of course. Anything is better than waiting...'

She had been training as an air-raid warden since the first week of the war. Laying down the telephone, she sent a quick smiling glance round the room. 'I wonder how long all this will be here.'

(It disappeared one night during the Blitz, with parts of Piccadilly and Jermyn Street. Noel was on duty outside—or was it one of the nights when she toured Deptford during raids with a mobile canteen? She worked in Deptford to the end of the war: what she saw and heard there—with her acuity about people, even the barely articulate—made her contradict me sharply when I said, of the crowds cheering their throats raw for Churchill one day in June 1945, 'They'll keep him in power.'

'Don't you believe it, my sweet. They're saying goodbye to him.')

It was a deliciously warm clear day. Unwilling to go back to Reading, I dawdled about London. A news poster had it that Antwerp had been bombed, and I walked attentively about the streets round the Cathedral rearing above the old houses squatted at its feet, and looked with love at shabby buildings on the near-by wharf which could not be expected, without my help, to stand up to bombs. Antwerp gave me my first foreign memories, my first taste for departures. Did my restlessness, my impotent hatred of being settled, start there? No, earlier—long before I was born...

During the next fortnight the speed of the German advance across Belgium and northern France numbed a part of the mind while keeping another listening intently, whatever else it was busy with, and even in sleep, to sounds too distant to be audible: voices that were and were not the voices of young men, my friends, killed in 1914 and heard now for the last time below the voices of young men I didn't know and thought about with an anxiety I was incapable of feeling in 1914; sounds of wheels grinding to a stop on hot dusty roads crowded with refugees; cries of terrified children.

'Is it true,' I asked one of our airmen, 'that the Germans make a habit of flying low enough to machine-gun the refugees?'

'Perfectly true.' He added reflectively, 'I don't know that habit is the right word, it seems more like a game they play.'

What sort of boys were they who played this game? Perhaps Hitler's only unforgivable sin is to have turned a generation into robots, or conscienceless *routiers*, who killed, as the guards in the extermination camps did later, not mindlessly, but with minds bent to a pattern and anaesthetized to feelings that might disturb it.

The one of us to whom listening became anguish was Guy. As the names of the first war succeeded each other in the bulletins, Vimy Ridge, St Quentin, Amiens, Arras, Abbeville—dear timeworn Abbeville—a buried landscape, an area of grotesque corruption, its clusters of splintered houses, corridors, tunnels, stench, obese rats, treacherous parapets, rose again in his mind, and he sickened with a fever which was only a poisoned abscess of memory.

I realized what I had always known. For its survivors that war did not end on a day in 1918: they are the survivors of themselves.

## CHAPTER 8

FROM THE MOMENT the Germans broke into France, May had been superb, skies without a cloud, clear dawns widening to a day-long bright warmth, springs, fountains, rivers of hawthorn, chestnut, lilac, apple blossom, cherry: the acacias were more splendid than I ever saw them, large old trees heavy with ivory-white flowers, scenting the air for a distance of twenty yards.

On one of these cloudless days I went to a reception in the Chinese Embassy. To step from the hot street into the coolness of the hall was like walking into the sea, a sea without waves, and the staircase was noticeably quiet and cool. It was only when I reached the top that the voices came out, like so many crossed tentacles. The large rooms were crowded. I recognized some of the faces; at a first glance it seemed that all Dr Quo's English guests were Left-minded intellectuals, writers, journalists, publishers, politicians— likely enough. A few Chinese women, young exquisite creatures, stood about in the eddies of nervous excitement, unmoved by them, holding plates of sandwiches, minute, very delicate, and bowls of strawberries.

After some minutes I thought that everyone in the room was saying the same thing, circling round it like a hen round a knife lying on the ground.

'It's a question of time, the French are completely demoralized, completely unable to stop the German advance units, and they—the Germans, of course—are magnificently equipped. Their parachute troops are firing villages behind the French lines——'

'If there are any lines now.'

'—smoking ruins, and no one knows what the civilian casualties are, but they must run to a hundred thousand. The first German troops will reach the coast facing us in less than a week.'

'A nice prospect.'

'My dear fellow—' a short laugh—'you haven't been attacked in the *Völkischer Beobachter* as often as I have. I don't mind telling you that I've made my doctor supply me with poison, I couldn't stand being tortured. I know too much about it.'

'Why don't you go to America?'

'I can't do that, I should be discredited: all I've worked for would be discredited.'

'Have you heard the latest? The Ninth Army has been captured.'

'Whose Ninth?'

'The French, of course. Giraud's army. So far they haven't admitted it, but it's certainly true.'

'Surely you know *why* Churchill went to Paris? It was to back Reynaud in dismissing Gamelin and giving Weygand the job.'

'Too late. The capitulation party is too strong. Influential people there are already in touch with the German Foreign Office.' 'You see how ridiculous it was to depend on France, and how sensible *The Times* was in the days when it was advising us to make friends with the Germans. What we ought to have done—I said so at the time, to several people, including Attlee—in 1933, was to hold out a friendly hand to Herr Hitler, and join him in reorganizing Europe. We shouldn't, if I'd been listened to, be in this mess now.'

*Herr* Hitler? Why this respect?

'... a Gauleiter taking the place of the Lord Lieutenant of the county, and German administrators—but no doubt the civil servants will stay in their jobs. After all, the country must be run.'

I stood knee-deep in the currents converging from all sides. I felt stupid. I was not taking in what I heard. Because of this protective stupidity—a habit—I believe in a disaster only *after* it has happened. Did all these people believe we were defeated? They seemed to... I had not spoken to my host; I had never seen him in my life, and I asked Kingsley Martin to point him out to me.

'You don't know him? Come and talk to him, he's a splendid fellow, you'll like him.'

Certainly he had a splendid, sculptured, serenely intelligent face: one could look at it for a long time, as at a wide landscape, without coming to an end of it. Fortunately I had no need to talk, Kingsley talked. He, like the others, assumed that France was lost and that the Germans would assault England in a matter of weeks. Politely drawing me in, Dr Quo said: 'What do you think?'

'Surely,' I said, stammering, 'the Fleet—so long as the Fleet is intact we can't be invaded?'

'Absurd,' Kingsley said kindly. 'We could be devastated from the air before they risk landing troop-carrying planes and parachutists.'

'But are you sure the French are going to give in? Defeat—it isn't my idea of France.'

'We all know how infatuated you are with France,' Kingsley said, laughing.

'I think they're done for,' Dr Quo said. 'This isn't the sort of war they're equipped to fight, their generals are too old, it's not a war for old men.'

Coming from him, this shook me as nothing and no one else had. But it did not penetrate far into the fog of stupidity. Nor did even Kingsley's account of the situation, now, of our soldiers: in the next two or three days, he explained, they would be caught in a triangle of the coast with a choice between surrendering or being massacred when they tried to get away.

'Couldn't they fight their way through?' I asked.

'My dear girl, three hundred thousand of them—at the most—and the Germans have eight million men under arms!'

With the least noticeable of smiles, Dr Quo said, 'It reminds me of an incident in northern China in the fifth century. One of our poets...'

I have forgotten, I believe I did not catch, the name and most of the details. The episode seemed to belong to the fifth century B.C., and I had the impression that he was trying, out of kindness, to reassure a barbarian that a break in the short and brutish history of her country would not be the end of civilization.

I watched him carry his smiling calm from one to another of the groups of excited, too well-informed men and women. I was certain that, if the worst happened, they, or all but one of them, would behave as well as the dullest and simplest, but I wished sharply that they would keep quiet in front of the politely undisturbed Chinese.

If the worst happened—like a dog shaking itself after a plunge into the sea, my mind shook off any image attached to the words. I was staying the night with the Kingsley Martins. My son had given me a Hendon telephone number, no use, he warned me, before half-past eight or nine at night. To please Susan Lawrence I had agreed to speak at—of all absurd things—a Fabian dinner, and I gave Kingsley the number and begged him to go on ringing up until he got an answer. I went off, distracted between the fear of missing Bill and fury at having, once again, been too weak to say No. The dinner was being held in the ballroom of a Bloomsbury hotel, a place of purgatorial decency and gloom. A number of silent, noticeably square-bodied men were sitting about the comfortless hall. I was told that they had crossed from Holland in fishing-boats. My spirits rose. At least one of our allies was worth having. In two rooms I crossed to reach the ballroom, furniture and wall-mirrors were shrouded in dust-sheets, as for a funeral. Surely a little premature? Susan Lawrence was in the chair; I sat between her and Margaret Cole, and saw with despair and rage that it was already eight o'clock. You fool, I thought, you ineffable fool, what a way to spend one of your last evenings! I was not the chief speaker, but as the dinner, which was atrocious, dragged on, I lost patience and my manners, and said that I must be allowed to speak first. As soon as I had made my speech, I fled.

Opening the door of the flat to me, Kingsley said quickly, 'It's all right, my dear, I got the boy. He's on his way in.'

He arrived almost at once. Kingsley went away to make a telephone call, and I had a few minutes with him alone. For all my inability to direct or discipline him, or tell him any of the dull truths about the way sensible worldly people live, I had never told him lies. I saw no excuse for starting now, and I told him brusquely that many people believed we were going to lose the war.

'Do you believe it?' he asked.

'No. Yes. I don't know.'

'Not very clear of you.'

'Thank God you and I haven't the same name.'

'Do you think the Germans are as dumb as that?' he said, smiling.

Kingsley had come back. 'Quo says he very much wants to meet Dr Jameson again, and though he's very tired, he'll come round.'

I did not believe this, but I was enchanted that it had been said in Bill's hearing. Some sorts of vanity are innocent. Almost innocent. That, for instance, of appearing in a good light before one's children.

Dorothy Woodman came in from a committee meeting, something to do with help for China, bringing with her an attractive young man who was Stafford Cripps's secretary. Behind her warm placid looks and soft voice, she is the perpetual revolutionary: impossible to imagine a society in which she could not find an under-dog to defend. When Dr Quo came he began questioning the young man about an affair not yet in the papers: Cripps was being sent to Moscow, with plenary powers.

'Why Cripps?' I asked.

'Because,' said Kingsley, 'he is *persona grata* there, hates the Labour Party, and can't possibly be considered an Imperialist.'

'I spoke about it to Maisky two days ago,' Dr Quo said, 'and asked him what chance there is of the approach succeeding. Maisky said: I don't know, it's late, it's late.'

My only reaction to this startling piece of news was, again, pleasure that my son was listening to it. He must, surely, find the conversation entertaining, worth the trouble of coming into town to hear. I felt modestly pleased with myself.

It will seem fantastic, I thought, if we *are* defeated, that we sat here, in this quiet pleasantly untidy room, with the Chinese Ambassador, and discussed the reasons why France is collapsing, the strength of the French Fifth Column, the abject failure of social democracy in Europe, the length of time, days or weeks, we can hold out, the meagre chance that America might help us. I tried and failed to imagine a German-occupied England in which such gatherings had become unthinkable. Instead, a ludicrous image flickered at the back of my mind—myself haring across the fields at the back of our house, a little ahead of the Germans, dragging with me a large canvas bag stuffed with unfinished manuscripts and notebooks.

When Bill was leaving, to go back to Hendon, Kingsley said, 'Can't you get Storm away in an aeroplane? As a known anti-Nazi she'll be in real danger.'

I said swiftly, 'He has a wife.'

'You must get them both away,' Kingsley said with energy.

It was two o'clock before I went to my room. I lay awake a long time, thinking of Bill, of my young sister and her children, and of the novel I was writing. The thought that, if we were invaded, I should not have time to finish it vexed me.

## CHAPTER 9

I N THE MORNING I sent a telegram to Amabel Williams-Ellis, asking her whether, if it became necessary, she could find lodgings for Do and her children in her North Welsh village. I expected and got the answer: Yes, of course.

The internment of B class aliens was under way, and some of our exiled writers had been taken, among them the Austrian writer, Robert Neumann: he had been in England since 1934 and I knew him and his second wife very well. That is, I knew the amiable side of a complex character; I suspected that in private he used his witty tongue, sharpened in the literary café society of Vienna, on his English friends, whom he found provincial, but I believed him to be kind, and I was truly vexed that we had thought it necessary to intern this quick-tongued soft-bodied friendly intellectual. I felt more anxious about his young wife, Rolly, left alone in their cottage in a small Buckinghamshire village.

I was to see her this afternoon. Waiting for her in the United University Club, I was greeted by a man I knew very slightly, a youngish diplomat; he had been at the Hague and was not yet tired of talking about the ease with which troops, guns, and even small tanks are landed from planes or by parachute on aerodromes and arterial roads. I reflected that our house in Berkshire was ringed by aerodromes. Ought I to hurry Do and the children off to North Wales now, at once?

'Are we going to be invaded?' I asked.

He laughed. 'Who knows? Churchill has gone to Paris again to try to stiffen the dear French. How do you stiffen a puppet that has lost all its sawdust? France is finished.'

I had the civility, or the servility, to smile.

When Rolly came into the room, I thought she had shrunk. She is small and slender, a Rhinelander, gay and very stubborn: that afternoon she looked smaller than ever, her gaiety pinched out like a candle. Since Robert left with the friendly policeman who came for him, she had heard nothing, not a word. She had been to see every English friend they had who might help to get him released. Some of these had made excuses not to see her. H. G. Wells, although he allowed her to come to the house, had said drily that he didn't know enough about Robert to speak for him.

'I said, "But you have known him for four years! You know he is an anti-Nazi," and he said, "Yes, but how do I know whether he is reliable or not? He could be blackmailed by them." Margaret, what can I do now? I am defeated. And what are they doing to him that he doesn't write to me?'

She spoke evenly, without raising her voice, using as few words as possible. I did not say what I thought: that Robert's worst or only suffering would be metaphysical.

'It's extremely likely that his letters are lying on some official's desk, with a great many more, waiting for someone to decide whether they are to be posted or censored first.'

'They ought to know how frightful it is to hear nothing.'

I caught sight for a moment of the anguish of the stateless, accepted on sufferance for a time, and rejected abruptly as *not one of the family.*

'The worst of all,' she went on, 'the thing that really frightens me is—if the Germans land—the Government may hand the refugees over to them.'

'Oh, no, that's impossible,' I said, shocked.

'You say that because you wouldn't do it yourself. But that doesn't mean a defeated Government wouldn't do it. One can't trust any politician.'

I did not argue the point, which struck me as absurd—we did not then know about the German political exiles in France who were handed over, in many instances deliberately, in others out of a brutal indifference, to the Nazis. Instead I wrote down all the details she could give me about herself and Robert, to use in writing to the Home Office.

'Promise me one thing,' she said. 'If I am arrested, will you go on trying to get him out? It doesn't matter about me, I can stand it, but please don't forget him.'

'I promise. On condition that you tell me when you are short of money.'

Her small face closed as though she had suddenly gone blind. 'I don't need any money, the garden is full of vegetables I planted, and I put down twelve dozen eggs in water-glass when they were cheap; I can live on them for a long time.'

I hardly knew which made me feel clumsier, her look of brittleness or her stubborn pride.

She was swept into internment long before she came to the end of her preserved eggs.

I was hoping against hope to see my son again this evening, and at eight I began to ring his number: I rang at intervals of ten minutes until at last a man's voice said, 'They were late leaving.'

'What did you say?'

'They were late leaving.'

This time I understood what I was being told. There was no point in staying a second night in town, we caught the last train and I sat staring at a sky so abnormally still and clear that it was menacing, as though the darkness were a mask. This unreal darkness thickened when a huge violently yellow moon rose on the left; the water of the Thames near Reading was absolutely still, as if turned to ice, the reflections of the trees imprisoned in it like the naked branches during the four-day ice at the sterile beginning of this year.

Do must have been awake, listening. As we came in she appeared at the head of the staircase, her hair falling about her shoulders; she may have hoped it was her husband, who was working a twenty-hour day at his biscuit factory to replace the supplies lost in France.

I had forgotten, I thought absurdly, that she is beautiful: excitement had laid a patina of soft brilliance over her face and darkened her eyes. For a moment the thought that she would grow old, and tired, and lose her air of fineness and perpetual youth, was shocking.

'Is there any news, Dear Dog?'

I told her what there was, and said, 'Perhaps you had better take the children to Llanfrothen for a few days, until we know what's going to happen.'

She shook her head. 'I can't go now, with the fruit ready to pick and bottle. We shall need it.'

'Well—we'll see.'

'The French are going to give in,' she said contemptuously.

Suddenly convinced that it was impossible, I cried, '*No!* Not France.'

Two or three days after this, on the 14th of May, *Europe to Let* was published. I did not notice it at the time, nor, so far as I recall, did anyone else.

Except, perhaps, the Czech exile who later gave up his allotted period on the B.B.C. to telling his listeners in Czechoslovakia about 'The Hour of Prague'. And except, oddly, a Soviet writer called Rokotov who translated 'Between March and April' for some Russian journal and cabled to the Ministry of Information in October 1941 to tell me that a sum in roubles was owing to me. I answered telling him to give them to the Russian Red Cross. Possibly he did.

Through the Ministry at this time I used to exchange passionate telegrams and letters with the secretary of the official body (VOX) of Russian writers, he exhorting me to stand shoulder to shoulder with them against the bloodthirsty (debased, treacherous, abject) tyrant (traitor, fascist hyena), and I replying, a little more austerely, in the same spirit—I had small hope that any adjective I used was better than abjectly counter-revolutionary.

On the 24th of May, between errands to the village shop, picking our gooseberries, and bandaging Nicholas's cut knee, I drafted a long and eloquent appeal 'To the Conscience of the World'. We had it signed by a score of our most important writers, and sent it to all the neutrals.

Who received it in silence. It drew a single reply, a finely sincere letter from the woman librarian of the Dallas (Texas) public library.

Anyone, especially any young man, reading it today, twenty-four years after the hot bright day when it was written, would jeer not only at the naïveté of the sentiments, but, if his ear is fine enough (unlikely), at their profound unreality. These well-cut sentences are not the real sentiments of a human being who may or may not be in danger, they are phrases which float to the surface from the level where simple feeling comes up against the debris from a lifetime of reading, and is deflected into speech.

The young man would be deluding himself if he believed that the sacred cows of rhetoric are less sacred than they were. Their bones may be sticking through the hide, but they can't be killed.

It is now (1964) nearly a quarter of a century since our soldiers, trapped in a corner of the French coast, were brought back. Nothing during this quarter-century has come anywhere near the intense excitement of those few days, starting in anguish and rising on this side of the Channel to a pitch of exultation no one could expect to feel more than once in a lifetime.

I shall begin to tell lies if I try to describe this feeling to anyone who was not there.

## CHAPTER 10

To be thought well of, I should imply that the fears and anxieties of these weeks made it impossible to write a novel. The truth is, I have never, as a writer, been so voluptuously contented as I was during this time.

There was nothing I could do to stop the barbarians invading us. I might just as well go on with my ordinary life. Better in any event than bolting, or wringing my hands.

Except on days when I had to go to London, I wrote from early in the morning until six at night, whatever the news I had swallowed with my breakfast coffee—heaven be praised that coffee was never rationed during the war. Mantes had been bombed, Paris was in mortal danger: I recalled briefly the evening in Mantes less than a year ago when we sat drinking, glasses of cheap yellow wine, at a trestle table outside one of the two small cafés in the dusty square; it was the evening of the 14th of July, and young men swung their girls across the cobblestones, round the dry cracked fountain, to the music of a concertina and two drums: the Seine was a short walk away. ('You have your coasts to protect you,' a Frenchman said to me, 'we rely on our rivers.' This year not even the Marne kept its word.) Think about all that this evening, I told myself obscurely, when you are bathing the children, or in the half-dark garden watching low-flying swallows, but now write.

This was not only the invincible egoism of the writer—when it comes off, his trick of pressing the marrow of feelings, sights, sounds, into language gives him such astonishing pleasure that only an immediate shock, a disaster taking place under his eye, can distract him from it. But, as well, I was driven by a subconscious wish to pretend to safety, and a stubborn need to finish what I had begun.

I was working at *Cousin Honoré*. Not only because, at this moment, nothing was worth doing except the best I could do, but because it had been living on a deep level of my mind too long, the process of *crystallization* had gone much too far: to abandon it now was impossible.

This one of my too many novels is the one in which it is easy to watch the maturing of an honest book—one, that is, which exists as an organism, not as a construction, a neat scheme. The actual source or sources of such a book may differ widely; the process of growth is the same. As soon as I had transposed the Germany of Wheeler-Bennett's life of Hindenburg into an estate in Alsace, the characters began transposing themselves. Honoré Burckheim revealed the strengths and weaknesses Hindenburg might have shown if he had been the head of an Alsatian family of ironmasters and winegrowers, with a modest Renaissance house in Strasbourg and a château and vineyard in the village, Burckheim, which had belonged to his family for six centuries. In turn this Alsatian Hindenburg merged with my idea of Stanley Baldwin, and the two together fused into the complex figure of Cousin Honoré. I was not for a moment concerned with the real Baldwin, of whom I knew no more than I knew about the real Hindenburg (less, since Wheeler-Bennett is an admirable analyst, and what little I knew of the Conservative statesman came from the gossip of his colleagues and opponents), but with an imagined human being able to absorb all I felt about the men who had led us to disaster, politicians for the most part, obsessed with the need to safeguard not only the spiritual values of their class (as much an instinct in the rather stupid Hindenburg as in the astute Englishman) but its possessions, self-satisfied, disingenuous to the point of lying, eminently respectable, with respectable emotions and an actor's ability to use them to create an impression, solid men, pragmatists, not ill-willed or in the worldly sense inexperienced.

The process bears no resemblance to the act—the folly, rather—of copying a living model. What takes place is a crystallization of feelings, insights, memories, ideas, round the bare outline, the germ, of a character: a living model, a man or woman known to the writer, can only hinder the process: his imagination is embarrassed by irrelevant facts instead of working freely and easily on the unknown, the half-seen, the half-begotten, the barely conceived.

Other characters in the book were born by the same double process of crystallization and the fusion of two or many persons. Wheeler-Bennett's Brüning attracted to himself the little I knew of Beneš and became Edward Berthelin; Schleicher offered the germ of Sigenau, and Sigenau and his

English wife took on the physical, only the physical, likenesses of two people I knew and admired, so that he became a more likeable character than the slippery opportunist, General Kurt von Schleicher; Henry Eschelmer, Burckheim's illegitimate son by a peasant mistress, who murdered both Sigenaus, drew life from the idea of a young Goebbels; and Jules Reuss from the equivocal figure of Otto Meissner who served both Hindenburg and Hitler. A few of the characters were invented—but what is invention?—the peasant farmer, Dietrich; the two young people, for whom I felt indulgence and liking; Burckheim's second wife, an American; Anne-Marie Eschelmer...

The change of milieu produces its own complexities and depths of meaning, one change involving another, and another, until the original chain of events is completely overlaid. The personages move farther and farther from their point of origin and become truly autonomous, and are enriched, complicated, changed in depth, by the working on them of circumstance.

And, of course, the fusion of all these many elements is fed and animated by personal memories and emotions entering it spontaneously at every level.

This digression will be of interest only to a writer, and one who cares more about his writing than about the impression he is making.

I wrote *Cousin Honoré* with unfailing happiness, no feeling, not a trace, that I had set myself a task, only the exquisite pleasure of following the action as it unfolded and the self-revelation of the characters. A pleasure without anxiety, an angelic pleasure. No insoluble problems. Everything I knew or could learn about French politics and society between the wars offered itself willingly to be used or discarded, and my passion for walking about foreign cities (and anger at being deprived of it) sharpened the image of an Alsace I had not, at that time, seen. I worked surrounded by photographs and engravings of Alsatian towns and villages quickened into life by the breath of a remembered France. Remembered with love, with grief.

Years of hard work had suppled my writing brain, and I was—I realize it now—at the peak of such intellectual and emotional energy as I possess. *Cousin Honoré* was one of the last novels I wrote with pleasure. It was written, too, in what, for me, are the only satisfactory conditions, a quiet room, looking over a wide view or a garden, and—the one really essential thing—no responsibility for running a household, the one task in life I loathe and resent. My young sister ran the house for both families, hers and mine.

I had duties, as might a child in its home—I made beds, washed clothes and dishes, picked fruit for jam—but no responsibility. My mind was free.

Looking back at those months, across the errors, restlessness, drifting, of succeeding years, I see that I was being offered a sample of my real life as a writer. At the time I did not see this clearly.

No one, unless he is of the family of Goethe or Tolstoy, stays on his peak long. The moment of greatest energy reached, a descent begins. All I can say is that if I had had the sense or the luck to go on living as I lived then, I should have put off my moral and spiritual old age ten or even twenty years.

I wrote the last lines on the 15th of June. The Germans had been marching into Paris since the day before, and the book ended in a Strasbourg emptied of all but a handful of its citizens.

'It seemed to Berthelin that he was walking through any moment, it might be as distant in the past as the first Roman fort set here, in which the city was in danger, and through his own life, and the life at this time of every man in Europe. Streets, houses, the Cathedral itself, with its spire and pinnacles of endurance, were the thoughts and fears, the solitude, the endless curiosity, the sins, the crowded estate of pain and helplessness, the unconquered mind, all he is, all he has lost the habit of, all that is only habit, proper to a Frenchman. He remembered that Péguy said, "Christendom will come back in the hour of distress." Would it, when it came back to France, find all this untouched, this body made lightly of stone? Or would these be broken, the past smouldering, and the future a weight lying across the living bones of a hand? Of whose hands?

'Let there be French hands and feet and a brain, Berthelin prayed. Risen behind the spire, the sun promised at least that.'

Who would have guessed that the answer to this lyricism was General de Gaulle?...

A minute or two after I had laid my pen down and stretched, I was called downstairs to the telephone. With a slightly crazy gaiety Bjarne Braatoy told me they were leaving in four days, for New York.

'And listen. An American journalist tells me he saw your name on a Nazi black-list in Berlin. You're in as much danger as anyone, and it would be only sensible to leave now.'

'Let me speak to her.' Ria's voice had kept its undercurrent of laughter. 'The sensible reason why we are going is that a German woman married to a Norwegian socialist would be a fool to stay here, the real reason is that I couldn't bear to drown in that Nazi filth, my father might be able to save me, but I should have to live with it.'

'Of course you must get away,' I exclaimed.

'Come with us.'

The revulsion I felt had nothing to do with my will. I did not answer at once, and after a moment she said gently, 'Forgive us for going.'

'But it would be idiotic to stay,' I said. 'You must go.'

'Yes.'

'I'll come up to see you before you leave.'

My sister was waiting to talk to me. Something in her clear look, a certain hardness and fixity, struck me.

'What's the matter?' I asked.

'Nothing. Nothing really. I've been thinking, I've talked about it to Robert, and we think, I think, if you know someone who would be the right person to keep them I'd take Nick and Judy to America, now.'

She had spoken simply, coldly. Without hesitation, without asking myself whether to send them away was the right or the wise thing to do, I said—as I would have said to my mother about something she wanted, 'Yes, of course. I am sure I can find someone—if you're sure you want them to go.'

Her face did not change. Still looking at me fixedly she said, with the same coldness, 'If we're going to be invaded... they're so small... and even if we're not invaded this autumn there won't be any food.'

The fear that it was already too late to arrange anything seized me, but I said calmly, 'I'll get advice.'

'All right.'

She turned quickly and went away. Afraid, perhaps, that I was going to say something that would trick her into giving away feelings she would think it shameful, indecent, to show to anyone, except her husband.

That same evening or the next I had a visitor, a middle-aged German woman I had met in Berlin, a cultivated warm-natured woman, half-Jewish, talkative and very gay, earning a tolerable living as a translator from English. She came to London in 1935, bringing with her a little money,

enough to rent the ugly house in north-west London she had turned into
a boarding-house.

It was another of the warm velvety evenings of that inconceivably generous summer. We sat in the garden and she told me why she had come. To
my astonishment, it was only to beg me to go to America while there was
time. I interrupted the flood of words to say, 'But, my dear Sophy, you're in
worse danger than I am. Why don't you go?'

She began to cry. 'I'm tired of running away, I ran to San Remo in 1933,
and then to London, I can't run any farther. But you can go, you must. I beg
you to go. Go now. You don't know what they're like, the Nazis, they can
do worse than kill you, other English writers have gone, Auden, Isherwood,
if they weren't ashamed to leave why should you be? And they were right!
Think of the German writers—Erich Kästner—who didn't leave when Brecht
and Thomas Mann did, even if they're still alive what good are they doing?
Oh, I'm right, you know I'm right.'

'Probably you are,' I said, 'but—'

'But what, in God's name?'

'But there is a difference in kind between running away from your own
countrymen who are trying to murder you, and running away from an invader,
when millions of your innocent fellow-countrymen can't. And don't think
I haven't considered doing it.'

She shook a wildly dishevelled head. 'The Gestapo can't kill everyone,
but they'll kill you.'

I tried to clear my mind. There is no logical reason, I thought, why I should
feel this mild contempt for young men who remove themselves from the
danger of a violent death—and not only themselves, their unwritten books.
No one need be ashamed of fearing air-raids, and no writer can help feeling
a mad exasperation at the prospect of dying before he has finished his work.
In the last war I felt a cold respect for conscientious objectors who bore
witness to their hatred of war in prison, and contempt only for the obscene
women safe in England who handed white feathers to young men in civilian
clothes. It is harder to feel respect for a witness living two thousand miles out
of danger. Moreover, a clever young minor novelist is scarcely worth saving,
though a good poet may be—if he feels that the most important thing is to
survive. Nor is there any good reason to save a middle-aged woman novelist.

My flesh shrivelled at the thought of falling into the hands of the Gestapo, but... between the wars I had been a pacifist, and I had not had the moral firmness to stand by my pacifism in this war. To run away would make this worse.

I looked at poor Sophy, sitting, snuffling, her imploring eyes fixed on me like a gentle untidy intelligent dog, and felt for her suddenly all the respect, all the love, all the sympathy I could not feel for our prudent intellectuals.

I patted her arm. 'Dear Sophy, we're not going to be invaded.'

'You are mad,' she said, sighing.

But for the time it took me to say it, I believed it. And, without better reason, how could I leave the country which held my son, my young sister, my husband?

## CHAPTER 11

IN THE MORNING, I went up to London to give lunch to the Oldens. What set Rudolf Olden apart among our exiled writers was not that he was a scholar and a humanist where the rest were novelists, journalists, critics, but the almost impersonal nature of his hatred of tyranny; he hated it with every fibre of a fastidious intellect rather than for its disruption of his own life. Living since his arrival in England in a cottage near Oxford, on Boar's Hill, belonging to his friend Gilbert Murray, he could have been almost content, but for the war, to use himself up in writing—himself and his passion of hatred. He took two things for granted, the English care for freedom and the unfailing quiet devotion of his young wife. They had a two-year-old daughter, born in England, and her birth had opened in him a spring of pure happiness, something he had never, I think, known; he was too complex and self-lacerating an egoist.

It took the first internments to shake his belief in English justice. At the beginning of the war his sole anxiety was to find ways of using exiled writers, of every nation. He had almost forgotten that, officially, he was an enemy.

'I regretted deeply,' he wrote to me, 'the postponement of the Stockholm Congress. There would have been the very occasion to show to the world that the writers of the world are not divided into different camps, that they are not "enemies". This is the great difference between 1914 and 1939. Then they said: My country right or wrong. Not so this time. Poor Hitler who does not know the value and weight of spiritual things saved us from so terrible a mistake...'

This was the first moment when I caught sight of a naive innocence behind the delicate, ironical, and ambiguous smile with which he watched the workings of vanity and ambition in his fellow-writers.

When the internments started he began writing to me about his idea that the American government could be persuaded to invite the German writers in France and England to carry on 'the great struggle' in the States. They might even, he thought, found a publishing house there to save the tradition of Goethe and Heine.

This was worse than naïve.

'No one would wish to give the appearance as if he run away from potential dangers.' (No one, dear Rudi?) 'I should say almost all of these men living in France or here would have had the possibility to go to the States in past years and they remained deliberately in Europe although they foresaw the coming war with certainty. Some of them just wanted to remain nearer the great decision, some of them did it for love of Europe, some felt sure they would be used and wanted to fight the Nazi. This was perhaps foolish but it was so... The trouble of being interned is not so much to live for some time without the usual comfort and liberty used to—but it is this: to be entirely idle whilst one hoped for utter activity...'

Before leaving to go to London, I turned on the seven o'clock news. Reynaud had resigned. So, I thought instantly—and instantly strangled the thought—the French do mean to give in.

In the drawing-room of the United University I listened to the lively conversation of two men—one I knew to be a War Office official—about 'the latest plan'—whose?—'to fight a retreat across France, evacuate the French army to English and French North Africa, make this country impregnable, blockade Europe, and wait for the Yankees.'

The Oldens cut short my eavesdropping—not to overhear I should have had to move away or put my hands over my ears.

Rudolf's friendly twisted half-smile was a thin mask: behind it, the tense knot of anger, refusal, and under everything else, hope. His face was thinner than ever, and more deeply lined, as though the bones were working inside it, like the wood of a tree, to age him rapidly. As always, Ika showed none of her anxiety. Was there a nerve in her body which was not vowed to him?

He talked for some time about his schemes, and I tried to imagine the quickest way of helping him to approach what he called the two *hommes de lettres* in the government. (Who were these two mythical animals? I have forgotten.) Then, abruptly, he told me they had decided to send their child, the little lively Kutzi, to a friend in Canada.

'It is better—I may not have much time.'

'Our English subject,' Ika said, smiling. She had a low even voice, comforting the ear. 'I must tell you that the clerk in your passport office treated me with such kindness as if I were the child. My troubles only started now, this morning, in the American consulate; I went to ask if they would give her a visa so that, if necessary, I could send her in an American ship, and the man I saw when I went in was brutal. I told him I wanted to make an enquiry. "What's the passport?" he said. I told him, "British nationality."—"Parents' nationality?"——"Stateless." He looked at me like a stone and said, "She'll go on the quota of her parents' nation."—"That seems hard," I said, and he said, very rudely, "We don't give visas on compassionate grounds." I said, "But I'm not asking you for compassion, I came to make enquiries."—"Come at 9.30 tomorrow, I'll give you another chance," he said, and pushed me to the door.'

'Let me go for you tomorrow,' I said.

'Oh, no,' she said calmly, 'I'm not afraid. You forget, I'm half English.' She smiled. 'I told them that, when they said I couldn't be an Air Raid Warden any longer, and they said sweetly, "We trust both your halves, but..."'

'Nothing would matter if they would allow us to work,' Rudolf said, with polite anguish.

'I am sorry,' I said. 'But that's no comfort. Try to forgive us.'

'Don't think it is not comfort,' he said swiftly. 'And don't speak about forgiving. You are one of the great assets of the world, found on the way through many countries. *Eine Frau mit einem grossen Herzen*—excuse my talking in my own language—what great, rare, reassuring comforting occurrence.'

I have rarely felt more ashamed. How had I deceived him to this extent about myself? Hurriedly, to distract his notice, I repeated the gossip about 'the latest plan'.

'But you have no troops in France, nothing you can fight with,' Rudolf exclaimed. 'And the French—my God!'

Now what peered through the mask was the Prussian gentleman's wholly involuntary contempt for a Latin race: I had seen it before, when he was watching Jules Romains give his arrogance and vanity a run in committee.

'Surely,' I said, 'if they meant to surrender they wouldn't have called on Pétain?'

This had only just occurred to me. Rudolf looked at me with aloof amusement, and said softly, 'For a really dirty trick they would be sure to call in a general.'

When I went to the back of the room to pay the bill, the head waiter whispered, 'The French have ratted, it was on the one o'clock news.'

I let the Oldens go away without telling them. A minute or two later, the hall porter brought me up an evening paper with the news headlined; Ika had bought it in the street outside the club and told him to take it to me.

In the village that evening, I went with Do to order wood at the store. There were other women waiting, from the cottages, and they talked calmly among themselves about our going on alone. One said, 'All I hope is they'll get the children away.' Later, an old man fetched the logs to the house. I helped him to carry them from his handcart and stack them in a shed. He smiled at me toothlessly.

'Now we got rid of them foreigners we s'll be as right as rain,' he said.

He had not the slightest idea what he was talking about, it was the sort of thing my father, with his unthinking distrust of every other nation except the Scandinavians, would have said. But he was a consoling contrast with the agitated intellectuals in the Chinese Embassy. So was Churchill's grim short speech. He made no appeal to the Americans. Thank God—that would have been unbearable... His style as a writer sets my teeth on edge, I detest inflated eloquence, but again and again during these years, as at this moment, he thrust his strong harsh voice to the roots of our hearts.

The light striking on my thin eyelids woke me at five a.m., and—I must have been thinking it in my sleep—I thought: They're going to let us down... This must have been how the Czechs felt after Munich, and I wondered whether the French would turn against us as they turned against the Czechs as soon as they had given them away.

I had a few moments of soaring exhilaration, worth a lifetime of sober existence.

During the next four or five days I worked frenziedly to finish typing *Cousin Honoré* from the manuscript, to get it to New York before we were cut off.

Never, I shall never forget the opulent summer of 1940; no single thread of cold in the air, a sky without a flaw; the branches of the trees in the orchard were dragged to the earth by their weight of pears and green plums; on the long south wall nectarines offered themselves by scores, by hundreds. The sun roared overhead like a young lion, the grass of the lawn became as brittle as ash, and wide cracks opened in the dry iron-hard earth.

I interrupted my typing once, to go up to London and stand for almost three hours in a queue in the passport office to get an application form for my sister's passport. I finished it two days later, in time to hear the wireless news at nine p.m. Listening to the armistice terms the French had brought themselves to accept, I did not look at her—I felt sure we had left it too late.

Day followed rainless day, with a light dry hot wind. We were now so certain that the Germans would invade—and the French had not even sent us their Fleet—that we expected the first landing every mortal day of that time. Troops arrived in the village to dig emplacements for machine-guns and deep trenches at the side of the roads. The barricades of barbed wire and wood looked crazily homemade, like the chains of crochet-work which were all I ever learned to make as a child.

I spent the last day of June reading the typescript which he had just sent me, of *The Behaviour of Nations*, by that tortured old Quixote, Morley Roberts. I read it in the garden. In spite of its strength, the sun had not bleached the sky; intensely blue, with towering white clouds too large, too swollen, to be moved by a gusty south wind. No book could have been more apt to a day expecting violence than this bleak hard work, written (as I knew) in conditions of mental and physical stress which did not so much as crack the clear surface. It was an examination of the social conduct of nations, of their behaviour among themselves, made in the light of his conception of the world as 'the great nutritional field of hostile hungry nations', leaving aside questions of morality and dignity, and looking at the naturally morbid state of Europe as a surgeon would look at his patient.

'Man in the mass,' I read, 'is not man, but a low organism of gross instincts and irresistible tropisms, an animal incapable of reason... Such an organism recognizes no effective claim but the power to hold... Ideas of right and even righteousness, morality and moral laws, the sacredness of treaties, honour, kindness, mercy and nobility found only in a very few units among the animal mass have no meaning for the threatened or aggressive organism.'

There was something astonishingly exhilarating in the company, at this time, in this moment, of a modern Hobbes.

He was the embodiment—a lean hard embodiment, graceful even in extreme old age—of nineteenth century materialism and humanism. The book was written with coolness, lucidity, a natural elegance and a courteous avoidance of all ambiguity. Who could believe that it had been written by a man over eighty, in bad health, enduring, without a thread of comfort or consoling hope, an agony of grief for his dying step-daughter?

Planes, fighters, began to pass in formation across the blue gulfs overhead. Surely, I thought after a time, many more than usual. Had it begun?

It struck me that if the country were occupied I should have to leave this house for the sake of the others. Moreover, I mustn't leave anything behind, any letter or paper, that could compromise them or any friend or any of our exiles. I had heard too many stories about the meticulous work of the Gestapo to think it absurd that they might come here.

I keep very few letters or documents. I don't understand my own passion for destroying these things since, unless they are cracked or broken (I detest all scarred and defective things and only want to get them out of my sight), I cherish any number of useless objects. On the day when, in a final desperate effort to free myself, I sell all my possessions, long heavy bookcases, antique tallboys, old china and tables, I shall for sure keep my mother's small exquisitely useless Chinese cabinet, the case of war medals, scores of photographs, the parchment from the République Française conferring his Médaille Militaire on my brother, and a round dozen more things no more good to me than the confusion in the rag and bone shop of my mind, its darkness broken into by shafts of light picking out a lace table-cloth in my mother's room, rank salt-bitten grass on the cliffs at Whitby, cobbled streets nearer my eye than the very lines on my palm, a smile, fugitive idly-dropped words. But I destroy what most writers keep—reviews, articles written about me, or documents to do with me. Why am I so anxious to sink without trace? Because the traces I make on the earth are not so clear as I hoped they would be?

I do keep a few papers. Among these was a bundle of letters about *No Time Like The Present*—kept, I daresay, because this book was closer to me than any novel. I had not the heart to re-read them, but as I tore them up I recognized some of the hands, Gerald Bullett, Michael Sadleir, Morley Roberts, S. K. Ratcliffe, R. H. Tawney, Sir Michael Sadler, A. R. Orage, Edward Thompson: many of them were from strangers, several had come from abroad. I dropped the fragments into a carton, and threw on top of them every letter from an exile, only keeping back—to be destroyed when the invasion started—papers about them.

In the same tallboy, in one of its two awkwardly-placed secret drawers, I came on Duckworth's reader's report on my absurd first novel, *The Pot Boils*. How the devil had I got hold of it? I must, in my innocence, have asked for it at the time (1917).

'This is a distinctly clever tract, gibing at the young intellectuals who take up social reform. It is not so much satire as irony and it is a difficult book to place. Amid much cleverness and insight, there are streaks of self-conscious smartness and labouring of the point. Still, I think it is worth some attention.

'It is loosely constructed; starts nowhere; ends nowhere; tries apparently to follow the French model [*already?*] of throwing in jabs of light on a given character from many angles. Each chapter introduces new characters, who re-appear at odd moments; and the characters are so many and so ill-defined that the reader becomes confused in sorting them out. They do not live [*not even my dear Poskett?*]; they are vehicles for the author's theories and the expounding of his theme.

'There is no plot. The book rambles round the thoughts, ideals and struggles of a group of young people from a northern university, their dissatisfaction with life as it is, their forlorn miseries over things that don't matter.

'I think it should be considered, though hardly for immediate publication. Later, the Labour question will become acute, and reconstruction will be in the air, and it might then have a chance... If it is a first book, it shows considerable promise, and the author would in any case I think be worth encouraging for his next book. There would hardly be much in this, but the man can write and is worth watching.'

Alone in my room, I laughed. Not at the awkward shabby young woman— even in her blind self-confidence and energy crazily more simple-minded than today's newest writer, the dupe of ideas, knowing too little about too much—but with her: she was irrepressible, alive with infinite hopes and childish arrogance.

In a worn-out despatch case forgotten on the top of the tallboy and thick in dust, I found the six tiny calico bags I made in 1915 when I went into my first loathed house, and labelled in marking ink: Rent and Rates; Clothes: Payments on sofa 10/-; Savings: Food: Coal Light and Gas, sharing between them each month something under ten pounds. I threw them quickly into the carton, afraid to see rising, in the wide sunlit room, a commonplace small house and the ghost of a girl lifting her heavy baby into his cot...

Instead, before I could turn away, I saw my young brother on his last leave. He was looking down at the sleeping child. 'He'll never have to fight,' he said in his young indistinct voice, '*we're* seeing to that.' He turned to me for a second the face of a boy, smooth, unformed—I saw it with shocking clarity—and asked, 'How old is he now?'

'Twenty-five.'

'I'm nineteen,' he said...

Shivering with cold, I felt an intolerable regret for my confused wasteful life.

We had a bonfire going in the kitchen garden. I emptied the carton on to it, then went back into the house and dragged from their shelves every book on economics, sociology, world politics, all Gollancz's Left Book Club works, every political pamphlet, carried them out, and flung them on the bonfire, mad with rage at the thought of the hours, days, months of my life I had wasted on them when I might have been pleasing myself, or learning to read Homer in Greek.

Watching them begin to smoulder—twice they put the fire out—I swore to myself that if I escaped the barbarians I would withdraw from the world and try to write a book, one book which recorded only the essence of my

life, the one or two ideas that were mine, not picked up from other people
or books, the one or two feelings, impulses, acts, in which my whole self
had been engaged.

It would be so difficult not to invent that I should have to write a thousand lines for ten I kept. And what a devil of a lot of paper I should waste...

## 27th of August 1964

This chimera of a book has haunted me all my life, as relentlessly and uselessly
as the impulse to withdraw from the world. Naturally I have not written
it (although each page even of these memoirs has been rewritten at least
four or five times and the waste of paper prodigious). I have continued my
improvident life and the fatal inattention to outer events which has bedevilled and bedevils it. I march with great energy—still—glancing neither to
right nor left, now and then pausing barely long enough to notice that my
garments are covered with burs, hopelessly lost. But without the lucidity,
hardness, will, to turn back...

Why write? Why write either about myself or about the ghosts who stray
into my mind—from where? Imagine that you are looking from the deck of
a ship at night at the dark limitless expanse of sea; look down at it, fix your
eye on a speck of foam sliding past, gone, lost in the black depths. Surely
the impulse to write is as absurd as if this speck wanted to explain itself, cry
out, praise or blame the sea and its works?

## CHAPTER 12

T HE CONTRAST BETWEEN Jules Romains standing up and Jules
Romains seated always surprised me, however often I saw him transformed from a Roman emperor to a short stocky peasant. I respected the
titanic energy of his ambitions as a writer: it was less easy to like the political
impulses of a French writer who was gratified when the Nazi government
turned out a guard of honour for him in Berlin at a time when liberal German
writers—these included Karl von Ossietsky, who died in Oranienburg—were
already in concentration camps.

What impersonal esteem I felt for an immensely intelligent writer died a sudden death the day I read copies of his letter to MM Bonnet and Daladier, thanking them—*vives félicitations et profonds remerciements*—for their noble conduct at Munich. 'Over the course of these tragic months,' he told Bonnet, 'I have often thanked my lucky stars for the good fortune it has been to have you in this position.'

There was no need for him to write to them. He could just as well have said his prayers to them in private. I hoped passionately that the Czech writers who had been heartened by his eloquent protestations in Prague in June 1938 would never know how warmly he had congratulated two of their murderers. They did, alas, and in December their president, Madame Tilschova, a very courageous old woman, wrote me a sorrowfully dignified letter of protest.

As soon as war broke out, he sensibly moved the Présidence Internationale to his country house at Saint-Avertin near Tours. From here he involved me in a ridiculous time-wasting tussle of wills over a 'Projet de Message' of unimpeachable patriotism, with a twist in the tail telling all writers to give unreserved support to their governments. I was in violent revolt against giving unreserved support to any politician. My idea of the writer's function in the state is that of uncynical sceptic, Socratic questioner: even if he is a soldier, and so under orders, he ought to keep his mind's eye open.

There was some malice in my feelings. For a moment the irresponsible young Eikonoklast of 1913 returned to life, delighted to mock the imposing great man under the eyes of my young dead friends. 'Let him advance himself how and when he pleases,' I said, 'but not involve us in his devotions,' and I wrote a polite letter explaining our doubts on this part of his Message, adding that democratic practice required it to be submitted to the Executive before it was sent out.

'No one,' Hermon said as he signed it, 'is so respectful of democracy as you are when it suits you—except H. G. Wells.'

The argument dragged on. In June we heard from him that he was leaving France for '*les risques, les sacrifices et les tristesses de l'exil*' in America.

'If he wants risks and sacrifices, why doesn't he come here?' Hermon grumbled.

'God forbid,' I said.

Another letter announcing his departure for Lisbon said he was moving the Présidence Internationale to New York, and taking with him all the papers to do with refugee writers in France. At this stage, unnecessary. The Czechs, Poles, Hungarians, were already making their way to England, and the Germans and Austrians were still in the internment camps where, unless they were exceptionally lucky, their Nazi compatriots caught up with them.

The relief I felt that we were not going to be ruled in London by this jesuitical figure was not unlike the childish pleasure of the old countryman confident that all would be well with us now that we had 'got rid of them foreigners'. At the same time I felt that he ought to have come to England.

On the 23rd of July we had a cable from him, from New York. It ran: 'Well. Arrived. Hurrah for England fighting for liberty. Jules Romains.'

Reading it, I burst into the jeering laughter of an ill-mannered Yorkshire schoolboy.

'What an ape!'

After a moment's rather shocked surprise, Hermon began laughing, less unkindly.

We were not left without the support of France. Denis Saurat, the director of the French Institute in London, moved quietly into the vacant place.

Saurat was one of that handful of Frenchmen who have loved England. Loved it not blindly, as many Englishmen love France, but with a clear-sighted understanding of our faults and virtues. His passionate friendship with England did him lasting harm with his countrymen.

I did not at that time suspect how many persons inhabited his skin: the ambitious administrator, the scholar, the mystical poet, the dreamer with a nostalgia for the primitive, the philosopher fascinated and a little repelled by the unconscious myth-making energies of the mind. He was not only bilingual, writing English as he wrote French, with ease, lucidity, wit, not only a scholarly critic of our literature, not only a poet in the tradition of English mystical poetry; he had an English heart living in what seemed complete amity with his mercurial French mind.

When Romains left for New York, Hermon and I invited him to lunch with us in the grill room of the Café Royal. We waited for him with a little anxiety. Since France collapsed we had not seen or heard from him, and he might—why not?—resent us.

We saw him standing in the doorway, his small frail body half hidden by the hurrying waiters. (This delicate body had a peasant toughness. During the air-raids a bomb brought his house down on him, dislocating his joints; he endured weeks of pain by coolly and subtly examining the nature of pain in a remarkable book, *Death and the Dreamer*.) He saw us and came forward, with his light dancing step, and a fine smile which, already, offered us his heart.

As he seated himself, he said, 'Well, my children, this is a writer's war, it is being fought for us.'

'So long as you don't insist on my taking an oath of loyalty to Bonnet,' I said.

He laughed gently. 'This war isn't a tragedy, it's melodrama or farce. I say that although my son is missing, perhaps dead. Individual tragedies, yes—but we are making the whole into a tragedy by thinking of it as one.'

'Has anything been heard of Giraudoux?' I asked. At that time, the two living foreign writers I cherished were Giraudoux in France and Ludwig Renn in Germany.

'No. His son is here: he got himself to Lisbon and sent telegrams to England signed, naturally, Giraudoux, asking to be picked up. They sent a plane and out stepped this young man. He can't be any use, and his father might have been.'

'Tell me something,' I said, 'there is a journalist here—Elie Bois——'

'I know him, he edited the *Petit Parisien*. I am sure he didn't sell himself, but it was a rotten paper.'

'What did he mean by a phrase he used in the *Sunday Times*—about the hold Baudouin had over Reynaud?'

'A woman,' Saurat said curtly. He added after a moment, 'More than one woman has been playing a shabby part in our politics. No, I am not going to tell you the story. Find it out for yourself. Better still, make it up.'

'I have been reading Euripides,' I said. 'He says in the *Orestes*, or he makes Apollo say, that the gods used Helen to set the Greeks and the Trojans at each other, to rid the earth of its too many inhabitants.'

'Oddly enough her name is Helen. But you must track the story down for yourself. It's not important. Novelist's nonsense... You know, there wasn't any need for France to give up, the government lost its nerve, tanks were no use except in the northern plain, it would have taken them months to get through the Central Massif. Reynaud should have said: Marseilles is now the capital of France... The truth is the rottenness spread right through the upper layer and seeped down. The Republic is finished, its only friends were decent poor men with no energy.'

'Then what's the next thing?'

'Far too early to think about that.' The ripple of gaiety spread from his eyes to his voice. 'The military imbeciles wasted our tanks by chucking them like pebbles against the German tanks instead of driving them into Germany behind the backs of the German army and creating exactly the same confusion and panic there that the German tanks were creating in France. Then we could have said: All right, you're in Rouen or Paris, what does it matter, here we are in Munich, we'll exchange capitals.'

His gaiety shrivelled abruptly. 'Let me tell you something, my friends. The English should sing small about Mers-el-Kébir. It wasn't a victory. The *Dunquerque* was the finest warship afloat, if she had fired there would have been heavy losses in your fleet. The French sailors can't have fired at all.'

Then, to comfort himself and us, he began to talk with fierce quiet devotion about de Gaulle. 'Keep your eyes on him, he isn't only one man, he is France, my France. I'll do anything on earth for him. It rather looks as though no writer has had the sense to follow him to London.'

'What do you think Gide will do?'

'Get himself shot, some *acte gratuit*! No, no—behind that ambiguous mask, he is too fond of himself. Alain is probably agreeing with Pétain, he hates war. Paul Morand will go on climbing discreetly, Mauriac—well, he is a good Catholic and a good Frenchman, he'll have to choose—Pétain, that eighty-year-old virgin, or France. As for Storm's beloved Giraudoux, he'll retire to the Limousin and write a play. Let's hope it's better than his pitiable propaganda! Romains—where is he, by the way?'

'Didn't you know?' I said. 'He's half way to New York.'

His fine smile knocked twenty years off his age. 'So it's true! I didn't think he'd go. Well, we must do without our great man.'

'Are you sorry?' I asked.

'Now, why did he go? I suppose—yes—if he had come here he'd have had to do what de Gaulle told him. He wouldn't like that, he'd rather play at *la haute politique* with the nobodies in America. Or—' his eyes sparkled—'perhaps, for once in his careful life he is backing the wrong horse.'

## CHAPTER 13

H AD I BEEN WORKING on a novel I could have gone on with it, but with invasion only a few days or weeks off, I could not begin a book which might never be finished. Hearing that the Ministry of Labour wanted volunteers, unpaid, to clear up its Special Register, I offered myself, and began work there on the 3rd of July, on a confused mass of files into which letters from writers, scholars, and other well-known or well-educated men had been thrown in no sort of order.

I made and illegally kept a copy of one of the letters I found.

'... as, however, it seems that no one over 65 (Prime Ministers excepted) is considered of any use by this Government I would be willing to push babies' perambulators for 2 hours daily for mothers employed in war work.'

It was signed by General Sir Hubert Gough, K.C.B. etc. etc.

I was involved, continually, with our refugees. The third wave of exiles had broken over us when France collapsed and the intellectuals who had fled there from Czechoslovakia and Poland had to move on if they did not want to be caught and handed over to the Gestapo. A few, very few, Germans escaped at the same time, escaping first of all from the defeated French.

Government officials, who knew something about the damage done in France by the Fifth Column, had a good excuse for exercising their habit of expecting the worst of human nature. It is true that they had less excuse than they supposed—there were no aliens in the French Fifth Column, it was a purely native industry, and included well-to-do respectable bourgeois up to the wealthiest, corrupt politicians, and a few corrupt fascist-minded soldiers. But men and women who had spent their adult lives opposing fascism in all its forms, and had already, many of them, endured the annihilating misery of concentration camps, were not tempted to betray the country they had entered in the belief that it was free and tolerant.

Very often I could only think that the jailing of these helpless refugees opened a crack into an abyss of dull meanness like the final disgusting irrelevance of Dostoevsky's cockroach.

For a bone-dry official to say that all aliens must be interned on the off chance that one of them is a spy is logical and arguable. This is not true of private individuals who suddenly discovered that their foreign, perhaps Jewish, friends were an embarrassment.

One of our interned writers had highly-placed English friends, who had known him for many years. I went to see them—after failing to get them on the telephone—to ask them to write to the Home Office about him. They were polite, friendly, evasive.

'After all,' X. said, 'think of the temptation it must be to a German, at this moment, to try to put himself right with his own government? I don't dream of blaming him. We're all capable of weakness.'

'But why suspect a man you have known for so many years of turning coward overnight?'

'My dear lady, do let us keep a sense of proportion. He may be perfectly innocent and reliable, I hope he is, it would grieve us both so much if he weren't—my wife, you know, adores him. And suppose he is, in fact, inno-cent, what a splendid chance for him to show his gratitude to this country by refusing to complain about a few months of comfortable internment! Why, I have often thought how restful a term of imprisonment would be!'

'Would you really enjoy being kept behind barbed wire for months or years? And I don't know that the camps are comfortable.'

'But no hardship for a strong healthy man!'

I tried to appeal to his wife. 'He asked me to tell you that the only book he was allowed to take with him is one you gave him.'

'Oh, the dear man,' she said tenderly. A shadow crossed her face. 'Is my name in it, I wonder?'

'I rather think so,' I said maliciously.

'You should be more careful,' X. reproved her. Turning to me, he said, 'I'm sure our friend appreciates that as a Jew he is safer where he is. I needn't tell you that I have no feelings against Jews, but there is, don't you know, a certain feeling among unthinking people that they are not, what shall I say? altogether single-minded. Both of us, I do assure you, my foolish warm-hearted wife especially, are only thinking of his comfort, physical and moral.'

There was nothing to be done with two people so convinced of the nobility of their motives for not lifting a finger to help their friend. I left, turning over in my mind phrases to soften the blow it would be to him.

Others, the obscure nobodies, were much worse off: the women who were not told that a son or a husband had been shipped off to Canada until the shipload had been sunk; the unimportant elderly professor remembering his two years in Dachau, who killed himself when the police came for him.

Rudolf Olden had been moved from his first camp to another, a disused cotton mill, bare and verminous. When I gave Ika lunch she was as composed, above a fathom of despair, as always, and her voice—delighting me by its undertone, which was the start of a single vibrating note, perhaps a low C—as warm and quiet. Kutzi was on her way to Toronto, and she was alone in the cottage, where the most innocent objects took a spiteful pleasure in reminding her of the one thing she and Rudi had refused to admit, that they were living in exile. The silence in her room was so hostile that she could not sleep.

She would not let me say that it had humiliated me to learn how callously England could behave.

'Oh, no,' she said, 'that's ridiculous. England is you and the Murrays and many others. After all—except Kutzi—we are Germans; you can't expect bureaucrats to realize that the lines dividing people now are not national, but intellectual and spiritual... What is breaking Rudi is that Gillies says he will be released if the Americans take him. He wanted desperately to share your dangers here—he was so confident, too confident, that he was useful.'

She had decided to leave the cottage—'We should have known,' she said, smiling, 'that a permanent address was one of the things we had given up...'—and move their few possessions to London, where it would be easier to work for Rudi and the others. There was only one thing I could do for her—persuade the Home Office to disgorge their documents, including Rudi's military papers; she could not take a step without papers, and every letter she had written begging for them had been ignored.

I took the list, promising recklessly that I would get them for her somehow.

When she was leaving she said lightly, 'We have been very happy here—and very lucky. In a way it is more comfortable to be like everyone else.'

*

This summer, for the first time in my life, I became aware that my body had a will and an existence of its own. Until now—I was forty-nine—we had been on the best of terms.

Here is an account of a single day, written badly in that thin canvas-backed little notebook I shall destroy (any day now), not worth calling a diary—the entries are too few, with gaps covering months or a year, and too erratic. Why, for example, did I take the trouble to record at some length the whole of this day? I have forgotten.

*July* 25 (or 29—the figure is half illegible)

Left the Ministry at 5 and went to 90 Piccadilly, Hugh Walpole's flat, to talk to him and J. B. Priestley about J.B.P.'s scheme—does he want to be our first Minister of Culture?—to force Ministries to employ writers. A room crammed with half-suffocated paintings and sculptures, jostling each other for breathing-space on the walls. I believe that Hugh, always asking himself anxiously: Am I loved?, is never entirely sure he exists; he goes on frenziedly adding possession to possession to give himself an illusion of solidity.

The view from the window, across the Green Park to Victoria's monument outside the palace—exquisite. If I lived there—and when I had cleared out nine-tenths of the paintings—I could write a masterpiece.

J.B.P.'s 'several pigeons'

I made one suggestion, brushed aside. Perhaps I had laid a finger on one of those pigeons. The list of eminent writers included two women, Rebecca West and Virginia Woolf, Clemence Dane thrown out as not in their class. Obviously I am included only as president of P.E.N., and not as writer.

Nothing will come of it. If either Hugh or J.B.P. had worked on the Special Register he would know that the last thing the authorities want to do is to employ writers: any writer they give a post to will have been commended for other qualities than his status as novelist or poet. Furious with myself for wasting time on a discussion of no interest to me. Shall I ever have the courage to say No to these music-hall turns? I haven't even any talent for literary politics, I am mortified by my incompetence, and bored, bored.

Ran almost the whole way to the New Burlington Galleries. The second of our refugee parties. Our guests this evening Czechs, Poles, French, and the three or four of our Germans who have not been interned. Standing outside the door, I thought: Is the little we can do for them any sort of weak bridge across the *abyss* dividing writers who understand treachery, cruelty, insecurity, with their living nerves and flesh from us who know them only by name? Obviously not. The signs we make to them, from behind our façade of security, must be like the twittering of birds or children.

The effort needed to go in and talk, talk, shake hands, smile, pronounce the foreign names correctly, was ridiculously heavy. Germans first. Old brave gay Dr Federn, the historian, looking more than ever like a frock-coated grasshopper—the frock-coat is getting shabby—talked to me anxiously about another German he wants us to save from internment. Listened, knew I should have to ask him about his own son, who is ill, a diabetic, and has been interned. When I did, and told him I am ashamed of the internments, he laid his skinny old hand on my arm, smiling sweetly, and said in a comforting voice, 'You are not to mind, England is still the best people in the world.'

Talked to the Czech poet, Viktor Fischl; he thanked me for writing about him to Stephen Spender and Paul Selver, but his young healthy serious face remained severe and guarded; I noticed he stood about alone the whole evening. Shy? Cautious?

Talked to dozens of people before noticing a young woman with a magnificent head, very blonde, a smiling Valkyrie. Anna Mahler, daughter of Gustav Mahler. Why, I asked one of the Germans, doesn't she join her mother in California? Would *you* want to live with Alma Mahler? he said: she is terrified of her.

The president of the Polish Centre, who has been living in Paris, is here. Maria Kuncewiczowa, a ravishing creature, clear delicate face, arched nose, small ears chiselled by a silversmith, slender hands and wrists. An elegance of the bone. Speaks halting English in the most enchanting voice. Later I heard that she was a concert singer before she became a writer, she trained in the Warsaw Conservatoire and in Paris, and has sung in Italy and Germany. Well-known in Poland: in 1937 she won the Warsaw Literary Prize given to the finest work of the year: has translated from the Russian and—this one could expect, they are birds of a feather—Giraudoux. Everything about her, voice, gestures, is charming, a controlled gaiety, Lopokhova in the Boutique Fantasque. Her parents, she told me, were exiled to Russia after the Polish insurrection of 1863, and she was born there, in Kuybishev.

'You see, I learned the habits of an exile very early, all I need is a little practice.'

Hands rising like two very young birds.

I can't imagine what it is like to be exiled not only from your country but from your language. A writer writes a little from his memory, but much more from the memories of his ancestors. These come to him stored in the words they and he have always used for the commonest things, cup, bread, sleep, grass, loyalty, treachery, kindness, death. In his turn he passes on what he has received, adding anything of value he has. I can't guess what goes on in his mind when he is suddenly and brutally cut off from both past and future, when the nerve joining him to his tongue is cut. Not more than one or two of our exiles will ever learn English well enough to write in it (the poets never)—I try and fail to imagine the force of will, the desperate courage, needed to make the effort, and the even greater courage to persist against the whole weight of the past and the protesting murmur of dead voices—all the others will be faced by every sort of barrier, the hazards of translation, reluctant publishers, lack of interest in their alien experience. How can Maria Kuncewiczowa survive when her hand, her writing hand, has been severed at the wrist?

Thanked Kingsley Martin, sincerely, for coming here, and making himself amiable to dozens of unknown foreigners. He may be an egoist, an aggressive unbeliever in the uses of tradition, but he is genuinely kind. Took the chance to ask him what he thought now about the war. He is convinced that fascism will come here, and soon—the boredom of a prolonged war, bombing, the military disasters we have to expect, will give the men who were behind Chamberlain their chance to emerge, push Churchill out, and make peace.

He said a great deal more, and I repeated part of it to dear Moura Budberg. She listened with a faintly ironic smile, and said in her marvellous voice, 'What do you make of the way the Left sees fascists under every bed? Why do they? Their own suppressed dictatorial impulses? I must tell you that H. G. believes fascism is coming here... I suppose he would go to the States.'

'Could you live in America?' I asked her.

She made a queerly evasive gesture. 'You know, I have lost all my family— my sister, my closest friend. Since they were driven from their small Baltic estate and sent to German Poland I have heard nothing, complete silence. I should hate to leave Europe without knowing whether they are dead or alive.'

Her voice moved me. I thought: In a sense you are Europe itself, in one carelessly warm body.

'Step by step you've been pushed to the edge of Europe here,' I said.

'Yes.'

She and I might be happier in French Canada than in the States, its politics wouldn't touch us closely, we could imagine we were living in the eighteenth century.

Elie Bois. Slack broad shoulders and an intelligent face, yellow, heavily lined, the face of a village mayor—good living and astute thinking together shape a face that could only be French. Questioned him about Reynaud's woman; he told me readily the whole story, and talked, with many details, about Baudouin, Mandel, Laval. I came away with a novel about France, and a play or *récit* about both wars, ours in 1914, and this, leaping together in my brain, scenes, characters, fragments of talk.

Both must be forced back, out of sight. There is no time, invasion or air-raids are too close: everything now is provisional, even or especially the things that used to demand the greatest attention.

3 a.m. Switched off the light for a minute, to look out. Low clouds have come up over what was a superbly starry sky, very clear. A fan of searchlights opened and shut, opened and shut, between two layers of cloud. A moment's quiet, long enough to give me the energy to go on typing. I have been at it since I came home—first these notes, then letters, letters, letters: to the Home Office about old Federn's friend; about Ika's documents; to Ika; to Rolly to ask her whether she has had the chocolate I sent and to reassure her about Robert; to the Home office about both of them; to Bill, who hasn't written; to Jim Putnam in New York to ask him to meet Do and the children; to Miss Hockaday about them; to poor Frau Dr H. about her crippled husband who is in Pentonville, to the Home Office about him. The words *I have, Sir, the honour to be Your obedient servant* will be found on my heart.

When I shut my eyes for a second they run against thorns and spring open.

I am ashamed of the momentary exasperation I feel, turning over Robert Neumann's already thick file. Can't he pretend to be a monk and possess his soul in patience? (These are obviously the reflections of someone who has never been shut up in prison, and is ashamed of showing emotion, even a reasonable emotion.)

Must sleep. Must turn all these poor anxious shades out of my room, I feel my last ounce of energy draining away into their fathomless anguish, I am exhausted.

## Postscript

A strange feeling of absence. The light was coming when I drew the blackout curtains, and I saw myself in the glass near my bed. But I saw a woman who had nothing to do with me, I looked at her impersonally, and made notes. In repose it is a smooth face, a little morose; a line draws down each end of the long mouth, others cross a high prominently rounded forehead above thin eyebrows; the eyes are large, long-sighted, an opaque grey-blue—colour of the North Sea on a day in late summer... A bird woke in the garden, two runs of a triple note. The face in the glass changed at once, and became young and gay, the face of a girl who had been little encouraged to exist in her own right, at her rightful time, and seized every chance to snatch another look at the world before being shown out of it for good.

## CHAPTER 14

A LL THROUGH JULY I chased the formalities needed to get my young sister and her children to the States. In these days when jealousy of America's wealth and power makes us seize every chance to damn Americans as materialists, violent, shallow, crude, we lack the grace to remember that in 1940 they behaved to us with a generosity it would be impudent to praise. No doubt they are crude, violent and the rest of it, with a leaven of civilization no larger than ours. And they give way to a generous impulse as foolishly and simply as if they did not know the value of money. Women who knew nothing about me, friends of friends, who heard I needed a sponsor for my sister, wrote and cabled that they would be financially responsible for her and hers. The offer we accepted came from Texas, from a Miss Hockaday, founder and head of a girls' school in Dallas. Not that my sister had the slightest intention of staying over there; all she wanted was to find suitable foster-parents for Nick and Judy and hurry back. An official in the American consulate warned her, 'You may find you can't get back.'

Her eyes started at him. 'What nonsense! I'd like to see anyone forbid me to come home.'

They left the house on the evening of the 1st of August, to catch the night train to Liverpool, the two-year-old girl in a rage at being wakened after a short sleep, Nicholas, as always, lively and sweet-tempered.

This was the first and only time I caught a glimpse of the agonized struggle that had been going on in my sister, in her slender body as cruelly as in her mind, for weeks. Except her husband, the two children were her dearest possessions, and she was as fiercely possessive as all the women of our family. She had to make the decision. She would not have allowed anyone to make it for her. No doubt, alone with her husband, she thought aloud, and cried, but with me she was always laconic and off-hand.

Only at the very last, before she turned to get into the car, she clung to me, her face that of a child trying not to cry. (Exactly like the very early morning when I came away, leaving her in her Swiss school: she had seemed not to care, but at the last minute, lying in bed, she locked her arms round my neck like an iron hoop.)

'Daisy, don't try to keep me in America,' she said hurriedly. 'They don't need me as much as *he* does.'

A letter from Ika that Rudi had been released. He wanted to see me. He was in a wretched state and could not leave the flat.

Taking with me an enormous parcel of German books and an old typewriter promised to one of our Germans, I went up to London. The door of the flat in a narrow Mayfair street was open. Ika, at the telephone in the hall, tears running down her face—our composed quiet Ika!—was turning the pages of the directory with one hand. 'Rudi is really ill, and I can't find the doctor's number.' I found it for her. She went back into the bedroom, and after a minute called me to come. My savage dislike of illness seized me, I went dragging my feet. He was lying on his side, his face grey under its thick film of sweat; he tried to take my hand, and stammered an apology for asking me to come, then suddenly broke down, convulsed. I fled.

When Ika came into the sitting-room, perfectly calm now, I asked, 'What did they do to him in that camp?'

'He isn't strong. It was one of the bad camps. But—no, that's nothing. It is really his disappointment that we can't stay in England. After six years. Gillies is still trying to persuade the Home Office, but... You know that Columbia University has offered him a professorship? It's very kind, and of course we shall go unless the Home Office relents. The difficulty at the moment is that we have to leave this flat tomorrow, sooner than I expected, and I can't leave him alone to go and look at two places I've been told about.'

I went off to look at them for her. It was very warm, no direct sun, a colourless leaden sky pouring down a blistering heat. Waiting in Park Lane for a taxi to come by, I felt giddy: the railings and the fronts of the houses rippled in my sight like a snake, bulging in one place and flattening out in another.

Neither of the furnished rooms I saw was tolerable for an invalid. I dropped my burdens at the agreed place, and telephoned Ika that I would go on looking, but, praise be, she was able now to go herself, and I galloped off through the furnace to meet Hermon.

We went slowly through the piles of letters and documents about the internments. The weight of so many nagging insoluble problems pressed on me until I became a fly crawling over the floor. Hermon had lost his voice.

'My God, you look frightful,' I said.

'Have you seen yourself lately?' he croaked, smiling.

We had arranged to dine at Chez Fillier, early, before going to a meeting of the Polish P.E.N., at 55 Prince's Gate. Too exhausted to eat, I drank lime juice and ate a zabaglione.

The young Pole who gave a long almost ironical account of the state of German-occupied Poland spoke with the greatest calm about the new Dark Age: the deliberate policy of the Germans to wipe out all intellectual life, by destroying the cultured and professional classes; scholars and the staffs of universities are killed off in the concentration camps and their libraries destroyed; nothing except time-tables, cookery-books, and writing paper may be printed; museums and galleries are being stripped: the German scientist who had been a guest of Cracow University, and knew where the gramme of radium was kept, wasted no time in collecting it. 'If any of us supposed that the German was *bon enfant*, he has been cured by this trick of stealing from your host. Obviously, too, there is a metaphysical side to their cruelty, it is an idea, a *volupté*, as well as a policy.' He made one or two good jokes, of the Peter Fleming type, but, alas, I forgot to write them down.

I talked to the Foreign Minister, Zaleski; he seemed tired, old, and without confidence. His young compatriot, who had fought in France, was infinitely gay and calm, but that is a Polish trick.

Almost until the last minute, Rudolf Olden hoped for a reprieve—until the moment when he looked at the Travelling Paper he had been given, in which the clause allowing him to return had been crossed through again and again, in red ink. This emphasis offended him, as though he were being not shown out but kicked out.

'Please, do not forget our little family,' Ika wrote, an hour or two before they sailed. He, too. 'Do not forget me. I hope for a better revoir. I regret to leave this country in this moment. But no choice was left to me. Please do not forget our unhappy comrades in the camps—when there will be more calm than it is now. For instance, a man as Burschell should not remain in internment...'

How many days before I stood still in a London street to read, cold with horror, that the *City of Benares*, full of children on their way to America, had been torpedoed and sunk? The vision of a terrified child in the instant of drowning in those black depths stopped my heart. The sea is every man's enemy, and to sink an unarmed ship is naked treachery. And children... My eye caught Ika's name. She hadn't, it was forbidden, told me the name of their ship. They were both lost. An English officer tried to force Ika into a boat, but she would not go without Rudi, too ill to move. I am sure she refused calmly, disengaging herself with young dignity.

My dear Ika, my poor stubborn quiet Ika.

A few lines I wrote about her in the *Manchester Guardian* drew a letter from one of our interned writers, the account of 'a Commemorating Gathering in this Internment Camp to honour the memory of Rudolf Olden, his wife, and the poor children who died with them. Our great old actor Emil Rameau recited from Goethe's *Faust*, the famous pianist Robert Friedmann played Beethoven's Death March, Ernst Urbach sang from Schumann...'

There were moments this autumn when it seemed that the whole of our civilization was living only in the internment camps where they played Beethoven and in the minds of a few hundred exhausted young airmen, boys of twenty-three who looked forty. These last not only saved England from the fate of Poland, Norway, Denmark, France, but (though they did not know it) repeated in their own way the very words of Homer's Achilles—

> 'Yet even I have also my death and my strong destiny
> and there shall be a dawn or an afternoon or a noontime
> when some man in the fighting will take the life from me
> also...'

A narrow seamless strip of time joins both fighters, both generations of young men, in the same elegance of spirit, the same hard gaiety, the same unspoken belief in human superiority to the forces crushing it. And finds room in the margin for a shabby handful of exiles listening to Beethoven in an internment camp.

## CHAPTER 15

IN SEPTEMBER the weather broke, suddenly an icy vein, the chill of autumn, and a yellow leaf, for no reason, not a breath of wind, letting itself flutter to the ground.

We were still waiting to be invaded, but with growing disbelief: only every now and then a nerve, somewhere in the ear, touched lightly, gave off a faint sound.

This month the P.E.N., was appointed by the Home Office to advise it on the standing, past life, and claims of every refugee writer who had been or might be interned, and on all appeals from 'men of letters' for release. The Royal Academy and the R.I.B.A. were advising on artists and architects, and there were committees for musicians and lawyers. No doubt these bodies had staffs to do the donkey work. Hermon and I laboured alone, to exhaustion, knowing that to make only one mistake would compromise every refugee.

This, and the house, and a report for the Ministry of Supply on women in arms factories, which involved me in a great many long train journeys, left me no time for writing. The faceless ghost of the play about both wars clung to the back of my mind, and I made a few notes for it at night. But suddenly I thought that I must re-read the whole of Chaucer, from the beginning. It was the one thing I wanted to do now. No reason, except the impulse to go back to one of those April mornings of first youth, the air cool and clear, the sharp colouring of the first spring flowers, the first stirring of sap in the trees, the first thrush, the early morning smell of the wet grass.

At this time I was ignoring a recurrent pain in my body.

Blackout curtains turned my room into a comfortable cell. It was simple to go on reading through the noise made by a German bomber, lost or delayed on its way home...

> My lord, ye woot that, in my fadres place,
> Ye dede me strepe out of my povre wede,
> And richeley me cladden, of your grace.
> To yow broghte I noghte elles, out of drede,
> But feyth and nakedness and maydenhede...

But I can't bear to sleep in a cell, and no sooner was I in bed, windows open, the darkness outside and inside the room split open at regular intervals by the finger of the searchlight nearest my bed, than the sound changed its accent. The first bomb sent an electric current to the very tips of my fingers, but only the first. In place of the excitement and suppressed panic of nights spent in London during raids, there was this acuity of separate sensations, very odd indeed, less disturbing, but infinitely more poignant: one had time to pay attention to it.

There was an extraordinary irrelevance about these bombs dropped casually in open country, due, I think, to the certainty that corn will go on ripening, gulls open their cruelly strong wings over the ploughed fields, whatever the destruction. When my father wrote that Whitby had been bombed, it seemed as foolish an irrelevance: but the bombs dropping in the field below the ruins of the Abbey and close to the place where my mother was lying uncomforted sent a shudder to the root of my life and disturbed the child sleeping in the dark quiet of a small old sea-port.

In this new war, the indecent gap between civilian and soldier closed. We were back in the time of Froissart: there is no difference between a city bloodily sacked by fourteenth century mercenaries and a modern city after an air-raid: the dead children look as dead and small.

No one, I thought, will ever again be deceived about the nature of war, as civilians were deceived when the slaughtering was done out of their sight.

This was an illusion.

Talking, in 1963, to an intelligent young man of twenty, I discovered that both wars have become as insubstantial as Troy. I wanted to pass on to him my recurrent image of one bombed house among many, nothing left except the wall at one side and, clinging to it, part of a landing and half of what had been a handsome Queen Anne staircase: when I saw it, the bottom of the flight went down into a pool of water covered thickly by a film of white grit and blackened fragments of paper: I stood close to it in the May sunlight and watched two people move across the polished floor of a room not there, out into the vanished hall, to the staircase. Nothing, I thought, is lost, nothing ends, every trivial mortal thing lasts exactly as long as the cradling mind.

I sympathized with his boredom. It was exactly mine before the excavations at Glanum. A searing Provençal sun beat down on the crumbling fragments, the white broken columns of Greek temple and market-place, the ground plan, empty sunken walls, of two streets of Gallo-Roman houses with traces of mosaic in the dry earth, the whole place very small and, to me, meaningless.

I stared at it and thought: Is this all it was?

It never crossed my young sister's mind that she could stay in America. Between the anguish of leaving her children and the indecency of abandoning her husband and country, just when it was going to be invaded and perhaps defeated, there was no choice. Told, in Dallas, that there were no passages from New York or anywhere in the States, she went to Canada and took ship there.

Early in November we had a cable that she was on her way to Montreal. Delivered by post, it had been five days coming and there were reports in *The Times* that day that a German pocket battleship had attacked a convoy 'half way between Ireland and Newfoundland', and next day a report that 'losses in the convoy are likely to be heavy'. The Canadian Pacific office in London could only tell us that, so far as they knew, their ships did not sail in convoy.

Not able to wait at home another day, her husband went off to Liverpool to wait there. He was anxious, but young enough to feel certain she was alive.

At that time I got up at six, so that Guy could take an early train to London, to his publishing office. In November it was still pitch at that hour; I dressed in the dark to avoid shutting windows and adjusting black-out: also I was half-asleep and the electric light jarred. That morning I heard wild geese, and saw them, a line of long winged arrows, flying very fast, black against a dark sky mottled by darker grey clouds. In the east a thin pencil of very clear pale yellow made it any one of predawn skies I had seen at home, but there it is drawn above moors. The familiar longing to go back seized me—why am I forty-nine, not four or fourteen? Then I remembered that the wild geese hunt dead souls, and I had a fearful vision of Do's thin body sinking in icy Atlantic waters.

The next day, the 11th, I read in *The Times* that a boat, the *Empress of India*, had been bombed and disabled four hundred miles west of Ireland; a Japanese ship had picked up the S.O.S.

I rang up Guy in London at once to tell him to talk to the Canadian Pacific people, and while I waited I ran about the house, cleaning, dusting, so that she would be pleased when she came. I remembered the Two Minutes Silence in time to stand for two minutes, thinking about my brother. But it seemed infinitely distant, as if it were part of my childhood, as if he had been killed then. He, my mother, that life, the I who lived it, were all dead.

All, suddenly, was well. The shipping office said that the *Empress of India* was no longer in their service, and that Dorothy, if she had left Montreal on the third, would be on a smaller boat which was now docking in Liverpool. Thank God, thank God...

The house, as soon as she was back, seemed to come to life after fifteen weeks of suspended animation. None of us realized then that the heart had gone out of it with the children.

Invasion or no invasion, I had to do something with my new freedom and I began planning the war play. Perhaps because it was written entirely in dialogue, and only later turned into a short novel, all the characters in *The Fort*, French, English, German, are over-articulate. The time, June 1940, the setting, the cellars of a farm near the village of Beaucourt-sur-Ancre in northern France in the path of the advancing Germans, made violence natural and inevitable, but my real interest was in the thoughts, obsessions, memories, of all these men, most of all in the older half-crippled English officer, in whose mind the images of both wars cross each other, until, at the very last moment, he is seized by a single dominant image.

The pain I had been trying to ignore, hoping it would cure itself, became acute, and very reluctantly I took myself to a doctor. It turned out to be nothing worse than a duodenal ulcer, and I was told to live on milk for six weeks.

I finished the play version of *The Fort* on the 13th of January. The moon woke me that morning, shining full on my face, at five o'clock. 'This is a little exaggerated,' I said. I turned over and lay for an hour, looking at the garden. There was nothing gentle about the light, it was ambiguous, very bright, threatening, and the trees were remote and in some way bestial. Their unkind insistence puzzled me. There was something behind it, but what?

I put *The Fort* away to revise later, when it had settled.

During the past months I had been questioning Frenchmen and reading everything I could lay hands on that might help me to live in the France that had capitulated. There were few days, even at my most preoccupied, when I did not live in it part of the time, and I was becoming a great deal too familiar with the old and young men and women, how many old, how many young, soldiers, politicians, officials, priests, peasants, workers, schoolmasters, journalists, police, who pressed on me from all sides, begging me for the life I owed them. I made careful notes of things heard or overheard, snatches of dialogue, stories of courage, treachery, intrigue, political illusions, and of scenes, the blond Loire under a cloudless May sky, the light, like no other in France, of that wide valley, the bridge at Saumur, a village—Montreuil-Bellay?—a woman dying at the side of a road choked with refugees...

The first deep crack had opened in our lives. Since July or August of last year Guy had been desperately trying to get back into the army, ostensibly because of 'the usual bloody Boches' and because he was exasperated by the idea that they were planting their hard bottoms on café chairs in France and looking round with the half-indulgent, half-brutal gaze of conquerors. In fact, because, for all its vile cruelty and filth, he remembered the years of the first war as a time when he had been acutely alive and happy. In November 1918 a life which used up the energy of every nerve in his mind and body and gave him in return friendship, and an inescapable purpose, ended.

Without knowing it, he was longing to return to that. And to his youth.

Not for a single moment did it cross his mind that he was acting with the greatest imprudence and want of foresight. What any sensible man of his age would do now was so clear that only an incorrigible un-worldling could miss it: he should stay with the publishing firm where he had been working for four years as editor, and where he was needed, and become, in due course, a director. Instead, as his exasperated employer pointed out, he 'deserted to the army', throwing away his chance of a solid future.

Neither did it cross my mind that he was behaving idiotically.

Neither of us thought or think in these terms. From a worldly point of view, we have less than half a wit between us. Sad, sad.

On reflection, I cannot explain my own lack of sense. Guy's is easily explicable; he was never, as child or young man, given any notion that his future depended on his own cunning and persistence. But I knew better: I had had to claw my way out of a narrow insecure world, I had been ambitious, possessive, shrewd.

After failing again and again to get himself taken back any other way, he was invited into the Army Education Corps, and went off, gaily, in the middle of January.

Just then, new rumours of invasion made me think I had better revise *The Fort* at once. I did this quickly, turning it into a very short novel. A pity. In spite of two or three excellent scenes, it is a respectable skeleton.

For several weeks after I had finished it, I worked on the French book, driving the characters back, keeping them firmly at arm's length. This was a sound instinct. A novel should be years in the cask. No other method gives the writer time to eat away all that is obscure or trivial in his ideas and impressions, and uncover as many as possible of the relations between feelings, events, people.

This (or any) year's crop of novels is the proof. The new X, the new Y, the new Storm Jameson, appearing duly every spring or autumn, ought to have been kept back at least six years, to mature, if capable of maturing, and its author subsidized or given honest employment...

One day in mid-April the idea for a short novel rose to the surface of my mind with the agility of a young trout. I had been wakened, very early, by the sirens, and was lying in the half-darkness listening drowsily to a succession of sounds, first that half-perceptible shudder in the air, then the planes, the first cock-crow, taken up by every cock for miles round, distant bombs, silence, an owl, another five or six bombs, the sound, dying away, of the retreating aeroplanes; last of all, a magpie calling out sharply in the garden.

I closed my eyes against a broad streak of moonlight, and in that instant the theme of the novel moved behind them. Suppose a German scientist had discovered a means, some quite simple interference with the brain, of turning the men and women of an occupied country into obedient docile animals, with healthy bodies, and neither individuality, in the human sense, nor will. Would anything, any memory, survive or revive in the nation so treated?

I began *Then We Shall Hear Singing* at once, and put it aside twice, to write an essay and a long very difficult pamphlet.

Milk is no diet for a writer, and I was often maddeningly exhausted. I could not always control my mind. Occasionally, when I was drawing the blackout, I caught it thinking: I may be killed before morning and not see this again. Then I looked long and intently at the crimson gash below a dark dove-grey cloud mass, traces of a rosy fleece in the pale zenith, bare trees, the bird in the long grass.

All this time, too, I was struggling to justify to myself my desertion, as in the first war, of my pacifist friends. I tried to dodge the knot by writing (for *The Times Literary Supplement*) an eloquent essay on the not very original theme that the crisis in our civilization is first and last a crisis of the spirit, semantic in so far as words no longer have even approximately the same meaning for two men of equal intelligence in different nations, of different political faiths, moral in that the enormous intellectual effort of the last fifty years has landed us in a situation the intellect cannot control. Rhetoric? Of course—but also the unravelling of something I believe deeply: that human nerves and sense need more time to adapt themselves than they are being given (no one has told us at what speed of change the mind ceases to think sanely; it may be quite low, the speed, say, of a man on horseback); that science has been in some way disgraced by the cruelty of its applications (this feeling is much derided); that, this time, we may well have been too clever and created a world in which our instincts cannot live. If what we think of as our civilization collapses, another may, in time, a long time, take its place, but it will not be the heir to our Christian-Graeco-Roman world. It may be Mongolian… I ended, for the gallery and for my own amusement, by comparing lengthily the virtues of France, Germany, England. Very poetic.

After this I decided, with fearful reluctance, that I ought to give a truthful account of my change of mind about this war, since, after all, I might have misled other people. To go on dodging it was a little too cowardly.

*The End of This War* did not run to more than twelve thousand words, but it cost me three months' hard work. Easy enough to stress that during the last quarter-century Europe has become a continent in which atrocious cruelties are practised on more and more people. That if man is a spirit he cannot be less in danger as a spirit than as a creature enjoying the sun, wine, books, dog-racing. That the cruelties the Nazis practise on Poles, Czechs, Jews, in the name of racial purity and on their own countrymen in the name of order may inflict a mortal injury on the human mind and spirit. Humanity, if this creed triumphed, might be reduced to the level of the mindless Nazi slave, or the still lower level of the Nazi master. There are things, precariously won human qualities, which must be saved.

But at any cost? The boy pressing his hands over a stomach ploughed by a shell, the child dying in an air-raid? They it was who had to be answered. No one else.

Of course they could not be answered. There is no answer. Answers are ruled out. Peace of mind is ruled out. For pacifist and non-pacifist alike, there is a choice between two guilts, two prices. The price of surrendering to the Nazi barbarian is Auschwitz, the camp guards pushing the living bodies of children into the gas chambers, the killing of prisoners for pleasure, the corruption, in the long run deadly, of language. The price of war is a million, ten million, broken tortured bodies, broken minds, and the destruction of long-living cities and villages.

No answer, no answer.

I turned aside to write about the absolute necessity, after so much suffering, to recast society in a form which did not, as did the one we had inherited, outrage every instinct for justice and decency in minds not deaf from birth or blind from self-abuse.

Of some hundreds of letters the pamphlet let me in for answering, I kept one, from the Archbishop of York (William Temple), for the sake of a single passage. 'We have at all costs to avoid two things: the tendency through sheer fatigue to shirk the responsibility which military success will involve, and the eagerness of the bosses to reconstitute an order which gives them power and wealth...'

During these early months of 1941 I lost control of my mind again and again, dragging it back with growing difficulty from a pit. I knew, my least nerve, the last cell of my brain, knew that war bred as much evil as it destroyed, perhaps more. Yet I could not, with the pacifists, cry: Submit, submit. The price was too high; the smell from the concentration camps, from cells where men tortured men, from trains crammed to suffocation with human cattle, choked the words back into my throat.

My despair was such that I could only let myself cry over the last war.

Now and then I had the sanity to reflect that this despair was at least partly a narrow personal grief. Again and again, trying to find my way in the darkness, I met the lighthearted girl with her child, her face turned away from home. Useless to tell her that she was making a mistake.

I was about to write that not a soul knew I was half-mad. It has just struck me, but only now, that probably one person knew—an elderly Jewish refugee. A conversation I had with him seems to belong to this time. We were standing looking at a hillside of oaks and young birches, the ground below the trees covered by a fine half-transparent cloud of bluebells, subtler than the blue of the sky, clearer than the blue of deep water, a miracle of living colour.

'You are thinking,' he said in his uncertain accent, 'that in so lovely a world the horrors are bearable.'

'No,' I said. 'I was thinking about the last man. The human race has been wiped out by a disaster which has left natural things intact——'

'Human beings are not natural?'

'They are naturally cruel. I have wiped out the animals, too. He is alone and old, this man, absolutely alone, looking for some place he remembers from the past, and can't find. He comes on this wood, and it gives him a moment of such happiness, ecstasy, that he is perfectly willing to die. Better, perhaps, an old woman. What do I know about the emotions of an old man?'

'Yes, perhaps an old woman,' he said. 'But you do know about the emotions of a man, you are of the line of old blind Tiresias.' He patted my hand with his dry fingers. 'Smile, little Tiresias, smile.'

## CHAPTER 16

T HE FIRST DAYS of spring came at the end of April, with a warm wet wind and freakish bursts of sunlight. My irrational despair began to move off. At the same time I gave up living on milk. It is mortifying to reflect that this may have had everything to do with the rise in my spirits.

Very early in May, time doubled back on itself to give me a moment of the past. A letter from Loftus Hare, living now in poverty, thanking me for my small part in the present his friends gave him on his seventy-third birthday, went on:

'I have a confession to make to you. Twenty years ago Visiak brought me a typescript on William Blake, written by a young under-graduate of Leeds University. It was too long for me to use, but I retained it, I must suppose, by some accident, and when Visiak called for it I could not be certain what had become of it. I was convinced that I had returned it to him. Now in going about I have lately found the typescript and been ashamed at my lapse. Even though twenty years late, you shall have it.'

I supposed that I had written and tried to get published an article on Blake. But what turned up at the end of the week was the bulky manuscript of the thesis for my Honours degree, written in Leeds in the stiflingly hot July and August of 1911. I had never been able to remember what had become of it.

Will anyone believe that a writer could be so indifferent to a manuscript which had involved months of hard work as not to ask for it back, and then to forget it completely?

Turning the pages gingerly—it must be unreadable—I was run through by the most acute longing for the pale smoky sunlight of the north, falling on those vast troughs of grimy streets, mills, warehouses, chapels, sluggish canals, tall factory chimneys vomiting a stream of smoke across hillsides scarred by rows of bestially ugly houses. Grey even in the light, black under icy wind-driven rain, none of them is farther than a few miles from moor roads the Roman legions took into Yorkshire a trifle of two thousand years ago.

You were a fool, I told myself, ever to leave that country of bitter winters and late heart-ravishing springs... I have always, as if by instinct, not simply disliked but hated certain things about Yorkshire people, that derisive glint at the back of the eye, their shrewd irony, their wish to jeer and deflate. But these are—surely?—outweighed by a habit of self-mockery, patience, deeply secretive kindness, and a hard incoercible temper which may yet save us from the bureaucrats.

I saw myself in the sitting-room of the house in Whitby, copying out this damnable great thesis, night after spacious September night, kept awake until daylight by the green tea I persuaded my mother to buy for me. I was as strong as a young horse. And so confident, so ignorant, so radiantly discontented, so happy, that a minute of those few years is worth at least a decade of the present.

I put the typescript away carefully. It might have a use...

The B.B.C. arranged for me to broadcast to the New York P.E.N., on the night of the 3rd of July. This meant that I should have to speak at 2.30 in the morning of the fourth. I slept a little on the floor of a friend's two-roomed flat. Wakened at a quarter to two by a call from the B.B.C., I walked to Broadcasting House through completely empty streets: it was a night of soft fine rain, the sky high and cloudy, the wind warm: the all but obliterated traffic lights down the length of Oxford Street drew it out to an infinite distance. After I had made my broadcast I walked slowly back. The rain had stopped and the wind from the south-west was stronger. The curious feeling I had of solitude and nakedness did not spring from the empty streets and the height of the faintly dappled sky, but from the sense that I had been, however lightly and briefly, in touch with a vast crowded mainland from which I had cast off suddenly. I felt the island under me lifting to the movement of the sea.

This sense of isolation persisted until I fell asleep again on the floor.

As soon as I was at home, I took the thesis on Blake from its cupboard, and destroyed it. Why keep a single useless fragment of my past?

*

Looking back today (18th of September 1964), I see that my life during the next eighteen months was quite ludicrously unnatural.

'He leads an unnatural life' is said of a person who guards himself, by rudeness if he must, from throwing away energy on social life when he has something better to do. In sober truth I had something better. For me, an unnatural life is one of dining out often, using up in amiabilities the hours, days, of silence and apparent idleness essential if one is to write anything worth the effort. To spend four or five hours talking to comparative strangers exhausts me: the amiabilities should be compressed into a few weeks a year entirely devoted to them, not allowed to gnaw the margins of every day.

I did not grudge the time spent on the exiles. Here not only conscience, that virus, but liking and fellow-feeling were involved. Time spent on merely social affairs was thrown away. Even when it fed the curiosity about human beings that my mind secretes endlessly, an unloving curiosity—I know less about the few men and women I love than about scores to whom I am totally indifferent—it was ill-spent.

One day, during a luncheon the Poles gave for a Scottish writer—there is a link between the Scots and the Poles very like the link between Scotland and France, founded, that is, on romantic misunderstanding, with a hostile side-glance at England—I caught a glimpse of the truth. The guest of honour made a long speech, larded with sharp jokes against the English. I had the Polish Ambassador on my right. 'I notice that you all laughed,' he said. 'Don't you object to his making fun of you?'

'Not in the least. The Scots do it when they get a chance, it amuses them and doesn't hurt us.'

'That is rather arrogant.'

'No, forgive me,' I said, 'you're wrong, we're very simple, and until they slap us in the face we believe that other people must like us.'

He laughed. 'That may be true. It isn't true of any other nation I know. But you have so few close neighbours. For example—you don't have to consider how to get the Russians out of your country after a war which has exhausted everyone else and left them untouched. The Germans will be defeated and, unless we are all out of our minds, not destroyed, not penalized, but kept strictly neutralized. But a strong greedy Russia—*there* is the serious problem.'

'Surely—in the end—it will depend on America?'

'Of course. But to be only a little safe we must be in East Prussia, and
do they, the Americans, even know where East Prussia is? I hope fervently
that you English will remain in Europe after the war, I hope to see many
Gibraltars in Europe, some of them on the Polish frontiers.'

I had the malice to ask him about Czechoslovakia. He said gravely,

'I like the Czechs—in spite of their bourgeois ways. In fact, because of
them. Beneš is a really great figure. He made mistakes, he relied too much
on liberal doctrine—perhaps he learned that at Geneva. You know, I was
for several years at Geneva: I went there believing that I should be able
to speak frankly. I was disappointed, and felt that I was all the time being
duped, because all the nations, especially the smaller nations, spent by far
the greater part of their energy thwarting each other. Then I began to take
a hand in it, and after a time I enjoyed the game immensely, and became
quite clever at it!'

Either because his neighbour on the other side was mute, or out of professional good manners, he went on talking throughout the meal, about Poland,
the war, politics, the politicians. I listened, I asked questions it amused him
to answer, but the better half of my mind was occupied with the atrocious
thought: *You* are beginning to enjoy this fatuous game of meeting people
you don't care tuppence for, nor they for you. What good is it? Why are
you destroying yourself?

I felt a ridiculous dismay.

I had only to withdraw from everything except the effort to help the
interned writers. Why didn't I? Out of fear. The fear of finding myself
*nothing but a writer*.

I let myself be sucked deeper into the vortex. I wasted days, weeks, on the
absurd quarrel with Jules Romains. If I had dared to be frank I would have
told the angry exiles that—in the middle of a war—the public gestures even
of a great writer are no great matter. My impulse was to leave him in peace,
to do as it pleased him. The Polish, Czech, Norwegian, Catalan, German
and Austrian writers living in London were less light-minded. They were so
angry that I did not dare let them see how indifferent I felt.

'He's in a devil of a hurry to bury us,' I said indiscreetly.

'This,' the Norwegian reproved me in his grating voice, 'is not a moment
for English sense of humour.'

Do you want my opinion of intellectuals? It is that if the next (nuclear) war leaves fifty assorted writers alive, they will have formed themselves into Academies and committees before you can say Aristotle.

I spent hours drafting eloquent letters of remonstrance to the *archifumiste* himself. Damnably long letters. When I try I can be just as boring as Cicero and as high-principled. A day when I had to write one of these rhetorical exercises was ruined for any other sort of writing.

What astounded me in him was his disregard for our vanities. Why in God's name, couldn't he use a little tact with us?

Months before this grotesque episode, we had decided to hold a Congress in London during the autumn. It was not my idea—I had lost my earlier belief that writers ought to make splendid public gestures—but I took it up with decent enthusiasm. Now, without my suggesting it, but with my approval—it would rid us of a sacred monster, and I should be spared writing him any more letters—it was decided to seize this chance to vote Romains out of office and H. G. Wells in.

All I insisted was that it ought not to be done in his absence. I wrote to him in June, begging him to come to the Congress. He refused politely—*Veuillez croire, chère Storm Jameson, à mes sentiments bien amicaux*—he was sure already that his engagements would keep him in New York right through the autumn. I tried a second time—he could come easily, since an aeroplane had been laid on to bring writers from America. I failed again. Had he come, his eloquence, eminence, energy, would almost certainly have overwhelmed his critics.

During the Congress, H. G.—as I had suspected he would—went back on his promise to take Romains's place and, without consulting anybody, invited Robert Sherwood into it. When he told me, I said, 'I hope sincerely that he will refuse.'

'And why, pray? He's a good writer and a fine man.'

'Of course. He's also too busy with official work to be anything more than a nominal president. We don't want a figurehead.'

H.G. gave me a half-malicious, half-friendly glance. 'My impression of you is that that is just what you would like.'

Luckily, Sherwood refused. We elected a presidential committee of four: Thornton Wilder, Dr Hu Shih, the Chinese Ambassador to Washington, our dear Saurat, and H. G. Wells himself.

'In my capacity as thorn in your flesh,' he said to me.

## CHAPTER 17

THE SUPREME BENEFIT to us of holding a Congress in London in 1941—other than the pleasure of bragging that London had taken the place of Paris as a cultural hive (alas, without cafés)—was that we were not embarrassed by the indifference to writers which is the mark of all English governments, from right to left. We had not to apologize to the foreigners for not entertaining them as they had been entertained in Buenos Aires, Prague, Warsaw, and elsewhere. Let them suppose that in any other year they would have been offered opera at Covent Garden, supper at the Mansion House, sherry with the Prime Minister. We offered them instead the chance of being bombed, and three days of uncensored discussion of writers' problems and duties in the post-war world, the whole world except Russia. The only Russian we were able to entice, and only to lunch, and only after he had taken a fortnight to scrutinize the list of guests, was the Ambassador, Maisky.

Two tiny incidents delighted me.

All our interned Germans had been released, and one of them, Frederick Burschell, chosen as delegate by his Centre, came to ask me, 'What must I wear, please? I have not very good clothes—' he had on a badly-worn grey flannel suit—'I have this, and also I have a black suit.'

'You should wear the grey during sessions, and the black for parties,' I said, very seriously. 'That is, if you wish to be correct.'

'I wish only to show my respect for the great, the unforgettable joy to be invited to the occasions.'

The second incident concerned the Polish woman I talked to for several minutes during the Lancaster House party. Impossible to guess her age, she had a thin sallow lined face, worn hands, and the angular body of a girl. On the lapel of a jacket shabbier than Burschell's she had pinned three or four medals. They were her war decorations, earned as a soldier in the Polish underground army during the months before she and her scholar husband escaped.

I felt the greatest respect, and told her so. Her eyes in their discoloured sockets came smilingly to life. 'But I came here to tell you that today for the first time I am not a stranger, and to thank you, you yourself, for making me know I exist.'

'Would you say that the others—I mean the other exiles—are happy?'

'They are reassured.'

If we have done nothing more, I said to myself, than reassure two exiles, a Pole and a German, that they exist, the effort was well worth it.

We had so little money, about two hundred pounds, that I decided, as any Yorkshire housewife would have done, to spend the greater part of it on a splendid luncheon, not fritter it away in small sums. Very early in our preparations, I had a sharp argument with Hermon about the need for a show of great names.

'You mean the names of great writers, E. M. Forster——'

'Nothing of the sort,' I interrupted him. 'What we need is a list of patrons so eminently respectable that the Government will be ashamed to do nothing for us—Beneš, Haakon of Norway, Jan Masaryk of course, Sikorski, a few persons like Kenneth Clark, the various ambassadors——'

'My God, why do you want ambassadors? Shall we have to stand the beasts lunch?'

'Can you think of a cheaper way of putting up a show of grandeur with nothing behind it? A line of ambassadors will take the place of Beneš's garden party and the huge official receptions and the rest.'

'It's a revolting snobbish idea.'

'Listen to me,' I said. 'We are governed by snobs, surrounded by snobs of all kinds, political, social, artistic, literary—yes, literary. They write the music. Either we play it, or we get no official help, not the very meanest, and we shall be seen—by the dear French and the others—for what we are, rogues, vagabonds, poor relations.'

He agreed, with the greatest reluctance, and our patrons numbered four heads of governments in exile, thirteen ambassadors and ministers—we did not invite the Spanish Ambassador—six High Commissioners, a round dozen eminent Englishmen, and Saurat, who was lending us the French Institute.

We were not in a position to refuse alms. The Free French, who ought to have been our guests, invited the Congress, the whole of it, to a reception in Dorchester House. For the rest, we wrung from the Government a small cocktail party in Lancaster House, for the fifty or sixty delegates only, and the use of an aeroplane to bring over two American writers.

The president of the New York Centre, Robert Nathan, excused himself in the most friendly way from sending delegates. As a neutral country, he explained, America had to move 'with Indian quiet'. I went happily behind his back to invite Thornton Wilder and John Dos Passos. Later, tongue in cheek, I apologized when he complained of my 'high-handed behaviour'.

Our two Americans were arriving at Paddington late in the evening. When Hermon and I went there to meet them, the station was in darkness and completely empty; we walked about it, losing hope, until suddenly the shadows at the far end of a platform thickened into human shape, two gay and excited shapes, our Americans. What we felt for them at that moment was love.

We had put them up at the Savoy, thinking that nothing less luxurious would be good enough. We took them there, and I said, 'My goodness, what can we do to amuse you? There's nothing.'

'S-show us the b-blackout,' Dos Passos said, stammering and smiling. 'It's the one thing we want to see.'

We walked about the unlit moonless streets, laughing, stumbling over piles of sandbags, for two hours. Then Hermon and I went back to a borrowed room to work, as we had been working for the past two weeks, until four in the morning. Afterwards, walking across Kensington Gardens, in the early light, I realized that I was not even sleepy. I was in a state of grace. When not a single cell of my mind and body is bored, I have energy for anything. Or at that time I had.

I had spent a fortnight preparing three orations, the first one to be delivered at the inaugural luncheon, before two or three hundred people (including the ambassadors). The thought of it wiped out every other fear, even the biting fear that I should not be able to find a word to say to the guest of honour, the American Ambassador, John Winant. 'He never speaks,' a member of his staff had warned me. That makes two of us, I thought gloomily, two people as mute as carps. A friendly demon put it into my head to ask him where in America he came from. He replied by two words.

'Describe it to me,' I said.

Speaking very slowly, for quite several minutes, he talked about a stretch of country, his voice suggesting by its peculiar resonance that there was an immense stretch on one side of him, and a hill on the other. When he stopped, I told him about Whitby. I cheated a little—I saw no reason to tell him how much of the simplicity and dignity it had in my childhood had been defaced by imbeciles. The place where I was born is as much part of me, and therefore still alive, as my skin and my dread of loud angry voices.

It reminded him, he said seriously, of Maine.

He talked about his own childhood. I listened attentively, and made up phrases about him: middle-aged, sensitive to a degree, nervous, humane, perpetually careful not to give himself away, detests rhetoric, a highly complex nature behind a simplicity which is only at the surface, shrewd, prosaic but with a quality not of this world, strictly speaking, unworldly.

Abruptly, because I was listening with intense concentration, I had a familiar sense of *overhearing*. I heard or rather felt for a moment a desperate effort he was making to hold together in himself the two ends of—of what?—a state of mind, a process, a thought?

To my relief, his neighbour on the other side spoke to him, and I turned to listen to Jan Masaryk.

He was in the highest good-humour. Grinning, he repeated part of a conversation he had had in the ante-room with a French journalist.

'A terrible fellow, proper——, wanted me to explain why the Czechs lost their nerve in 1938. What will Storm say to me if I kick one of her guests into the street? I said to myself, and let him off. As you know, I'm a tolerant fellow, by God I'm tolerant, but...'

'Perhaps he has a bad memory,' I said, 'or a bad conscience.'

'If you can lay hands on a French journalist with a conscience, not a dupe, not an impostor, tell me. I'll come a long way to look at him.'

His impressive public mask might have been all I saw of a great man. But the same week John Winant invited me to dinner—his other guests were R. H. Tawney and his wife. I could not dine, I had some Congress duty or other, but I went in after dinner to drink coffee with them. I found a Winant so different he might have been his own younger brother, smiling, peaceful, at ease with Tawney, who—dear Tawney—as shabby as usual, had thrust a lighted pipe into the pocket of his tweed jacket, where it had burned a large hole. Much he cared!

What surprised me was to discover that the two men were alike. Each had a dignity, a nobility, so unselfconscious that, like Tawney's shabbiness, it was part of him. I had read lately a passage from André Gide's Journal in which he orders himself 'Do not concern yourself with *appearing* to be. All that matters is *to be*.' The distance seemed to me infinite between this theatrical attitude, a man practising an expression of sincerity in front of a glass, and the innate inviolable self-possession—using the word in its literal sense—of these two men. I suppose that Harry Tawney was more casually arbitrary than the American—he had not had to school himself to patience with fools and knaves.

The fact that Winant acted a part in public—the part of the taciturn dependable envoy—is irrelevant. Almost everyone acts a part. Even a truly great man—think of Goethe—may see *the others* as spectators against whom he has to guard himself. Often he is himself one of the spectators.

Tawney never threw these spectators a glance, I doubt if he noticed they were there. He was completely, carelessly himself, in any company, and no doubt he paid a price for his indifference. With him, Winant felt safe enough to be careless, talk readily and gaily, say what jumped into his head, laugh. He had the gestures, the smiling energy, of a man at least twenty-five years younger than the man I had seen a day or two before this evening...

I have forgotten almost all the events of that week. I remember, very sharply, a few faces, Hsiao Ch'ien's fine smiling mask, Arthur Koestler's, heavy, imposing, clumsy, and—at the time this surprised me—good, Salvador de Madariaga's look of contemptuous distaste when he was quarrelling with H. G. Wells about a passage in the *Outline of History* on the behaviour of the Spaniards in South America.

They were a buffalo confronting a fiercely controlled lynx. Later in the day, the buffalo charged briefly: talking about something else, H.G. interrupted himself to say in his highest most piercing voice, 'I am not going to say very much about my nimble-minded friend, Madariaga. I have known him for a great many years and I always have a dazzled admiration and appreciation for his extraordinary nimbleness. So I, being a heavy-footed, slow-going journalist, will not attempt to do anything more than say that I hope he will continue nimble to the end of the story, and that any answer I could make today would be like trying to pick up a very nimble drop of quicksilver which had got to the bottom of a bath of hot water.'

When, shaking a little, I stood up to make my Presidential address on the responsibilities of the writer, poor driven wretch, I caught sight in the audience of the editor of *Horizon*. For some reason which had nothing to do with him, I did not know him except as a lively editor, a gust of jeering Yorkshire irony rose in me—What the devil does *he* know about life as it is?—and stiffened me to recite my long eloquent speech without much awkwardness. Afterwards, a friend who had been seated immediately behind him told me, 'Connolly said you had a pleasant voice and did it very well.'

'Damn his impudence,' I said.

I was none the less pleased.

This week was the farthest point I reached as a public figure. I was never, at any moment, tempted to go on climbing. Vanity, which has lifted so many writers of my day on to so many platforms, acts to keep me off them: I have no virtue as a speaker, and no quickness. All I can do is write, even enjoy writing, a piece of rhetoric, and deliver it as well as a not very talented actor, and that with fearful effort.

Anything more would have been teaching a bear to dance.

I have a clear memory of the furiously angry Frenchman who came up to me, when I had been making a speech about France, and accused me of sentimentality.

He may have been right. It is difficult, and in 1964 a little ironical, to recall that in 1941 not only middle-aged English writers believed passionately that they were fighting to save France.

'Sacrée Dordogne,' the Frenchman, a little man with the face of an elderly Robespierre, said violently. 'It's a river, not a reason for going into a swoon. And generous humanity! Don't you understand that we shall never forgive you because we made fools of ourselves, because we began the war with less than a dozen modern bombers, all as carefully hand-made as if they had been tooled by engravers, and because our politicians were all either fools or rascals. That's the country you've been talking about like the sentimental Englishwoman you are!'

'But not the country that will come to life after the war,' I said.

'Of course not. But don't delude yourself that the new one will be any fonder of you. On the contrary!'

'At least it will be forced to notice that we are well-meaning.'

'Error, error! It will take the first chance your politicians give it—they won't fail to find one—to notice that you are provincial and disloyal.'

The real error might only be to forget that, in one of its aspects, love is a purely selfish activity, indulged in for the pleasure of being in love. Why should the French thank us for being infatuated with the Loire, the Dordogne, the Lot?...

When I went home after the Congress week, I found that our two sixteen-year-old servants had left, to go into munitions factories. Useless to dream of finding others in the tiny village, we should have to keep the large old house in order without help. When I was ironing the sheets I had washed—I iron atrociously, I always did, from the first time I had to do it, in my very first detested house in Liverpool at the beginning of the first war—I laughed at the contrast between last week's Madame la Présidente and this week's washer-woman with the aching back. Not that I minded in the least having to take my share of cooking, scrubbing, washing linen. What I detest is being responsible for running a house.

My only other memory is of trying to take the edge off Salvador de Madariaga's just wrath. After the Congress he exchanged letters with H. G. Wells, and sent me copies. His first letter was long and courteous. The second, also very long, began, 'I must keep things on the plane of reason, much as you try to drag them down to lower levels...'

The last was short: 'My dear Wells, I can waste no more patience nor courtesy. No. You are not the man you pretend to be. The plane of reason is not accessible to you. Farewell. Salvador de Madariaga.'

I had always deferred to him. In the first place because at that time he still expected the resurrection of a Spain which would summon him to its side, and I felt sure he was going to be disappointed; even if a few persons in Spain remembered him they were already living in an age and a country he knew nothing about, which would reject him. Secondly because, in an unguarded moment, he had told me drily that certain people had dropped him now that he was no longer in a position of power...

He was, is, that noble and now mythical animal, the uncompromising European liberal. His ideas and ideals are clear, hard, precise, and would make sense to Voltaire, Herzen, even to Unamuno: in Europe now they are dry leaves rattled by the east wind.

He left the P.E.N., and the last time I saw him, in November 1959, after the meeting of exiled writers where I was the only Englishman, he reproached me for its laodicean politics.

'It is no longer my business,' I said. 'Why did you leave? You should come back and put it right.'

He gave me a hard, not unfriendly glance, and said evenly, 'I have no time for whims, irrationality, disloyal compromises, ignorance.'

## CHAPTER 18

WE HAD TO DECIDE at once whether or not to renew the lease of the house in Mortimer in the coming March. My sister hesitated. Her own much loved house in Reading would be free then, and this house, without the children, was a vast empty husk. Had I said: Let's stay, and bring the children back after the war, she might have agreed. I didn't say it. Instead, I talked of taking a flat in London.

Ever since Guy went into the army, I had had the sense of being a third beside a closely devoted pair: I missed him acutely, his lively intellect, his violent changes of mood, his spontaneity, so unlike my tortuous doubting mind. In a marriage which is an intimate friendship, what Blake called Minute Particulars count infinitely. I was bored without him. His letters from all over England, gay, lively, observant, exasperated my feeling of loss. Just at this time he was posted to the War Office. He travelled up daily by train, but the trains now were crowded, often delayed, and in winter icy.

Under cover of the truth, I am lying. A restless devil possessed me, the same restlessness and indiscipline, like the energy of an untrained retriever, that account for all my *departures*, from the first.

Then, too, like the Master sunning himself on the Janiculum in Rome on the morning of the 16th of October 1832, I had discovered—*Est-il bien possible!*—that I was fifty. The idea of writing my life did not then smile at me. If it had, I might have stayed where I was.

At the end of October, I took a small flat on the top floor of a house in Portland Place. No one wanted to live a few yards from Broadcasting House, thought a German target, and I got it on a war lease, at a fantastically low rent.

In those years London, air raids apart, was infinitely pleasanter than it has ever been since, shabby, quiet, friendly, and magnificently alive. It smelled better, too. For the first time in its long history, perhaps for the last, it was a European capital. At moments I had the sense of being in another country, all the pleasures of escape, a body suddenly younger and lighter, a mind leaving its berthing, bound away.

But, for my sins, I knew too many people.

'As I was passing, I came in...' Spoken in every variety of foreigners' English, German, Polish, Czech. Several of our exiles were working now for the B.B.C.: the coming and going was terrible.

I can write anywhere, in any discomfort, kneeling on the floor, resting my paper on the edge of a shelf, cold, tired, ill, hungry, but only if I can count on a day without a single interruption. I was deeply attached to some of the people I saw, but I should have liked to see them only in the evening, at a meal I had not had to cook...

L—— A—— might have been used by a Czech sculptor modelling the likeness of his country—quick sturdy body, thick fair hair, blue eyes with a gleam of peasant malice. She was not a peasant, but an intelligent highly cultivated young woman, the translator of T. S. Eliot into Czech and herself a poet. Her close friendship with Jan Masaryk was that of cat and dog, or foil and horsewhip. He wanted her on the State Council, and she stubbornly refused, unable to endure the intrigues and jealousies infecting every exiled government (except possibly the Norwegian—one of the unexpected benefits of a monarchy, with its immovable centre). Losing his temper, or pretending to, he shouted at her as if she were a refractory recruit: his obscenities and scurrilous irony amused her...

During the Congress I had been shocked by Arthur Koestler's description of Rose Macaulay as a charming old lady. Rose, old! In my eyes she had not altered a hair since the evening twenty years before when, timid and dazzled, I saw her for the first time. Now, listening to her rapid talk, watching the movements of her small head and abrupt flickering smile, I thought that in some persons age makes a sudden leap; overnight the flesh shrinks from the bones and hidden lines rise to the surface. But age did not account for a trace of sadness, or lassitude, given away by her voice, for all its liveliness.

Five months earlier, in May, she had lost everything she possessed when her flat was destroyed. She had written to me at the time. Her first letter was purely despairing.

'Yes, dearest Margaret, Luxborough House is no more. I wish I had been in it, I might have saved something, but I was away for the weekend and all is lost. It got first an H.E., then fire started, and wasn't put out, and everything was consumed. I can scarcely bear it—all my dear books, and everything else gone. I can't start again, I feel. I keep thinking of one thing I loved after another, with a fresh stab. I wish I could go abroad and stay there, then I shouldn't miss my things so much, but it can't be. I loved my books so much, and can never replace them. I feel I am finished, and would like to have been bombed too. Still, I suppose one gets over it in the end. I haven't a cup or plate to my name, so am stopping in a furnished room near... It is better to be alone, and to sulk by oneself...'

Written only two days later, the second was very slightly less like the movements of a numbed limb. '... my own books leave a gaping wound in my heart and mind, that is the worst part of it all—all my lovely seventeenth century books, my Aubrey, my Pliny, my Topsell, Sylvester, Drayton, all the poets—lots of lovely queer unknown writers, too—and Sir T. Browne and my Oxford Dictionary. Gradually I hope to replace some of them, but it will take years. My Animal book, that Daniel George was helping me with, sending references he found, is gone for ever; *all* my and his notes for it, and all the books I was getting the stuff out of for it. I hate that. And my partly-written new novel gone, too, but I don't mind that so much, nearly. The Animal Book was my heart's blood—it was to have been *such* a nice book! And all my seventeenth century travellers—Purchas and the rest—oh, I can't think of them, it simply doesn't do. Even Vera B. wouldn't say I was "totally unmoved" now, for my "pale sardonic eyes" keep wanting to cry, just like her pansy ones. I have been climbing about my ruins (staircase gone, but I climb precariously up charred and frail laths, up to where No. 7 was). And lo, among burnt wreckage I found my kitchen dresser, unconsumed because

sheltered by the roof that had fallen across it, and out of it I extracted (at
7.30 a.m., before anyone came to stop me) several glasses and china things
and actually a jar of marmalade and a little tea, and my old silver mug! What
a find! It's all there is—the charred fragments of my books mock me everywhere. There may somewhere be some silver buried, but the demolition men
won't go up and dig for it, they say it's not safe. But when it all comes down,
may I be there to watch, for no silver gets past the demolition men, they
say; it all goes into those much too big pockets of their dungarees—"You're
telling me," said a policeman bitterly when I said I didn't think silver was safe
with them. He says they all take what they can. He seemed really shocked
at human nature—and indeed it does seem cruel of them...'

Despite these letters, I did not believe that the change in her had much
to do with the loss of her books and manuscript. Something sharper was
biting her.

I thought: I shall never know.

One day, when she was leaving, she stood for several minutes, still talking,
on the stairs leading down to the lift. I looked at her, profiled on the wall,
narrow shoulders, delicate arched nose.

'You're very tired,' I said.

She moved down a step, paused, and looked back at me. 'Margaret, you
don't know what it's like to watch the person you love dying.'

She spoke calmly, and I felt her anguish pricking the ends of my fingers.
I supposed, for no reason, that the person was a man, perhaps already dead.
I forget my reply, but it was not a question: when a thing of this kind is said
to me I don't ask questions, I am afraid to touch the wound, and afraid that
the speaker may regret, as I should, the impulse to demand help or pity. Nor,
for fear of putting other persons on the track of a secret, did I question any
friend of hers.

Now (October 1961), I see the story told in a Sunday newspaper, for
strangers to read, with the letters she wrote a priest...

The difference between the French exiles and the others was deep. When
a German came into the room, and especially if he were a Jew, he brought
with him part of the blackness of Europe, the sense that he had his back
not to a country he had for the time being lost but to a gulf he would never
recross: the Poles had their habit of exile, which almost took the place of

a country they could not lose: the cautious watchful tough-fibred Czechs knew or thought they knew exactly how they would tidy the place up when they went back. All, in their different ways, had made themselves at home in England, much as a woman rearranges a hired room to give it an air of being lived in.

The French noticed that they were in another country only when it exasperated them or roused their derision. The rest of the time they went about their business with the self-absorption of travellers changing trains, glancing indifferently at the foreign signs and newspapers.

There were exceptions—dear Ignace Legrand, novelist, who had flung himself, at the last minute, with his wife and young daughter, on to an English cruiser leaving St Jean-de-Luz, expecting confidently to be made use of by his countrymen in London. Perhaps he was unusable. Certainly they did not want him, and he was in the depths of misery and poverty when D. L. Murray rescued him. He adored the English, forgiving them faults and weaknesses he was too intelligent not to see, for the sake of their, as he saw it, natural decency and goodwill. He was doomed: he could not become English; climate, language, food, all defeated him, and he went back to France after the war—with his utterly devoted wife, an angelic being camouflaged as a small pale gay well-bred woman—to be neglected as an alien eccentric.

At the other end of the spectrum, a man high in General de Gaulle's political service—a member now of the Conseil d'État—asked me blandly, smiling across the glass of sherry I had just handed him, 'Tell me, ought I to try to learn English? Is there anything to read?'

He was completely unconscious of the fatuity of his question, and innocent of offence.

Moving serenely between the two extremes, Denis Saurat almost brought off his attempt to be a native of both countries. How much more narrowly French he was than English I realized during an evening when he dined with us with Harold Butler (late of the I.L.O. and Warden of Nuffield), and they talked about Germany. The Englishman, loathing Hitler and his creed—it was not a creed, it was opportunism as an art—could still seem a spectator, like Dante in hell: Denis was involved as a spirit in torment.

'What,' Harold Butler asked, 'are we going to do after the war with the pure-bred Nazis, the real young thugs?'

'I don't know,' I said.

'Kill them,' Denis said quietly. He added, in a meditative voice, 'There won't be a German problem. What there will be, when the Germans are retreating, is another Night of the Long Knives. They believe they have picked up France and the other countries without paying. Every second adds to the debt.'

A vision I had of one of our Czechs, a middle-aged man with a broad good face, large hands, and small penetrating eyes, drawing his knife across the throat of one of these young thugs, wormed at heart but young, almost a boy, turned me briefly cold. I said diffidently, 'If we try to strangle Germany, the carcase will poison Europe. Think of last time.'

'One German will survive,' Harold Butler said, 'the banker Schacht. A real Prussian, brutal, sure of himself, a *large* brute. I remember an immense dinner in the Berlin Bourse, two thousand people, a river of champagne flowing from eight p.m. to five a.m. The Bourse had been closed for two days while it was prepared. Schacht was in the chair and made an arrogant speech... "In those days there were bankers in Vienna—" there were five Austrian bankers at the table—"We had to close the Bourse for this occasion, but other Bourses are closed for worse reasons, I notice that the French Bourse was closed today—" it was one of the French crises: the French Ambassador, sitting next but one to him, shouted in German, "That is an insult." Schacht didn't care. Yes, an imposing brute. I was with him and two other bankers at Basle, a meeting of the International Clearing Bank, when Hitler sent his troops into the Rhineland, the three of them were cats on hot bricks. I was sure then, as I am now, that if the French had marched, the Germans would have withdrawn and the army would have got rid of Hitler.'

'We should have had to march alone,' Denis said very drily.

Later, when Harold Butler had been saying that after the war Russian influence and prestige would be so high that the whole of Eastern and Central Europe, except just possibly Czechoslovakia, would go communist, Denis said, smiling, 'I was told last week about a Norwegian who refused to come to England from Narvik. He said he knew the Germans would go some time, but if the Russians ever got into the country there would be no getting them out again, and he must stay to see that they didn't, the English might try to help, but they always came too late and left too soon.'

'Will France go communist?' Guy asked.

'Only if we, I mean the English, make a mess of it. Throats will be cut, and there'll be a degree of civil war. The essential is for us to go in in force, every man, plane and tank we have. I want to see a company of English soldiers in every village! Unless the French *see* us defeating the Boches there'll be no union of the two countries, which is the only thing that can save civilization in Europe.'

'Union would solve one of your problems,' I said. 'In the last few minutes you have been a Frenchman talking about England, and an Englishman talking about France. Which are you?'

He laughed. 'I dream in French. In a dialect at that.'

'Well,' I said, 'don't, when you're awake, speak English the whole time. It won't do you any good with X.,' and I repeated X.'s question about the need to learn English.

'He is a rotten branch,' Denis said lightly, 'a left-over from the République des Camarades, sweating vanity and lies. He won't—believe me—last two minutes in the new France.'

My poor Denis! Was it possible to make more mistakes about the new France and your place in it than you did?

## CHAPTER 19

SOME LITTLE TIME after the United States came into the war, the head of a department in the Ministry of Information asked me if I could think of anything English writers could do to cement Anglo-American relations. Flattered as I was to be asked the question, I saw the trap open at my feet.

'Do they need cementing?' I asked.

He answered very seriously. 'You know as well as I do that there is always some degree of suspicion of us in American minds. Less at this moment than usual, but it's all the same a habit. And since no one thing is more important to us than good relations with them...'

My heart sank as I suggested that it might, perhaps, be an idea to get a score of well-known writers to make up a volume of stories, essays, poems, and sell it in America, only in America, for the benefit of the U.S.O., the body which looked after their servicemen.

He was delighted. 'Have you ever edited such a book?'

'Yes,' I said, 'once. It was hell.'

I came away from the Ministry raging against my folly and my inability to say No. But this time it was not, not only, a weak longing to be approved. I had the strongest possible sense that we were in debt to the Americans for a generosity which outweighed infinitely any suspicions they may have had that we were trying to drag them into war. The value, enormous in money, of their gifts after 1939 could not be reckoned in money.

That was one reason, the strongest, for my walking, eyes open, into the trap. The others were a wish to keep a good conceit of myself, and the absolute impossibility it is to me, in any circumstances, to say: My own writing is too important to interrupt...

As I had known it would be, the work was atrociously time-wasting. I made a list of writers, thirty-two, of every sort, from the serious to the entertaining. I wrote to G. M. Trevelyan and the Poet Laureate, wondering whether the second of these, seeing my name at the end of a letter, would remember that in her book on Modern Drama in Europe, an insolent young student had savaged joyously one of his plays. The great historian's essay was the first manuscript in my hands, John Masefield's poem not the last. I asked for and got poems from Walter de la Mare, T. S. Eliot, Edmund Blunden, Helen Waddell, Edith Sitwell, C. Day Lewis. To my friends and contemporaries who were not poets I wrote *sans façons*, prepared to bully those I could reach. It was not necessary. With one exception, the thirty-two agreed at once.

The exception was George Bernard Shaw. This singular man, in whom a poet and a fine poet lived uneasily, sharing a bed with the Fabian politician, the professional heretic, the buffoon, carried his reluctance to be duped by a generous impulse to a degree of warmth rarely seen. (I should like to be born again at the moment when Shaw the polemist and clown, so anxious to shock by his antics that he was ready to flirt with dictators, has been totally forgotten, and the author of certain scenes in *St Joan, Heartbreak House, John Bull's Other Island*, is seen for what he was, a passionate man who, for some reason known to his Maker, denied his heart oftener than he let it speak.)

His letter refusing made me grin.

'Dear Storm Jameson,

'You are most welcome to write to me at any length, at any time, on any subject.

'But I am no use in charitable matters. The work of the Red Cross should be done by the Government and paid for out of the National revenue to which everyone has to contribute. This line in preaching is not my line. I have never bought a poppy: the whole rosebud garden of girls has rattled its tins at me; but I have run the gauntlet of them all. I have never autographed a book for sale nor allowed a play of mine to be performed without payment of author's fees. Would you have me, at 85, break this glorious record to enable our warmongers to exploit your generous heart and pay their way by private cadging? Since the winter of 1939 they have had £50,000 from me.

'I tear up all MSS that I do not publish. My Irish Protestant stock revolts against relics. Anyhow my MSS are all in shorthand. The printed ones are all in the shop window. So you must write me off as N.B.G.

'Otherwise I am yours always
G. BERNARD SHAW.'

I believed I could play the ape as naturally as he did, and I spent an hour proving it, certain that I should draw a reply.

'Why, yes I would like you to go on breaking records, that is, the conventions you have made for yourself, until you are 185, and then break any convention which lays down 185 as an age to die. I can imagine no reason why you should not break any intellectual or moral record—or any physical one, either. You have taught us to look to you for it. My own hard upbringing laid it down that it is disgraceful to ask again for what has been refused once; experience, equally hard, taught me that you can avoid this disgrace and sometimes have what you want by asking in a different way. You know well that this book is not being put out to earn money for the American Red Cross. If famous and well-advertised writers run forward with saleable manuscripts in their hands it is because they hope that the Americans will say, "They must like us, they're giving us the money they have left over after they've paid their taxes. We've been mistaken, they're fine fellows and friends of ours." And perhaps the effect is not great—but I was also taught to do my best and then to do it again. You'll think: Now this ape is trying to persuade me to save the British Empire. I am not. I do not want to save what is already gone the way of other empires. What I hope for—if you can call hope what is probably only Puritan pigheadedness—is a world in which the properly English virtues can work and in which Englishmen can use their thick skulls to feel their way. Such a world will not come into being if we are on bad terms with America and the Soviets. (But let someone else ask you for a page or two to please the Soviets, I can't bother with two continents at once.) So, if I have thought of a way in which writers in this country can make modest advances to America, I am stricken in my heart by your refusal to help me.

'As a student I was one of a small society of Eikonoklasts. It was a sound instinct which drove us to demolish you with our tongues ten times for every time we attacked our other idols. We must have known that the others would end like Dagon, as stumps, but you would live on to console us, a green tree among stumps and dry wells. So it was, so it is, so it will be,

'I am always your humble servant.'

This letter was preposterously disingenuous. He had never been an idol of mine or my friends. We thought of him as a construction, something that might have been conceived in the mind of an abstract painter or sculptor, an affair of spirals and fragments of steel and wire, rather than a human being.

But he replied to it. At a tangent.

'Bless your innocence, do you suppose I have not yet expressed my sympathy with Soviet Russia? What you propose would be the most ridiculous anti-climax. From 1920, when relations between England and Russia were at their worst, and Lenin was the bogey man of the west, I sent him one of my books with a dedication that left George Washington nowhere; and lithographed facsimiles of it were still current in Russia when I was there in 1931, and was treated as if I was Karl Marx in person. Since then I have lost no opportunity of preaching friendship with Russia. I have spent years of my life preaching communism from every platform in the country.

'As to America, the newsreel which I made for them last year has had an enormous success there, and ran for many weeks in the chief New York Cinema as a star attraction.

'You will see that your notion that I could make any further impression, much less announce my much hackneyed Bolschevism as a novelty, is founded on a happy ignorance of the public antecedents of an obsolete dotard. It is 60 years since, full of Marx, I delivered my first propagandist lecture on Socialism. Your grandmother might have been present if women had been admitted to the Woolwich Radical Club, which was the scene of that obscure beginning.

'So you see it's impossible,
Always yours'

The old devil has had much the best of it, I thought, and gave up trying to trick him into making an unprofitable gesture.

It strikes me as I write that perhaps he expected me to ask permission to print his letters in *London Calling*. It never crossed my mind.

With the gift of two poems, Walter de la Mare's letter pushed me, before I could step back, face to face with an awkward girl, confident and timid, already adrift. I could do nothing for her, not even warn her.

'... How odd memory is! It slaughters so many innocents, and retains others without the least trace of any danger they may have been in of the same fate. I recall with peculiar vividness one evening when I came to the Station with you, and we shared the top of a tram. You weren't wearing a hat. But why just that? And another glimpse of when we were talking at 14...'

You thought yourself so undefeatable, so intelligent, I said coldly, and you were blinder than a bat to your blunders, your worse than blunders. I am not sorry for you.

*

Before I started on this absurd labour, I had finished *Then We Shall Hear Singing*, and returned at once, with relief—even, on days when I had nothing else to do but write it, with the liveliest pleasure—to *Cloudless May*.

*Then We Shall Hear Singing* is a curious book, curious as a proof that even a minor writer is able, now and then, to overhear the future. There are more ways of killing a cat than choking it with butter, but that serves, and it is not necessary to interfere physically with the brain to condition human beings to be apathetic or docile atomies in a dangerously overcrowded world, no nuisance to their betters...

I was working to exhaustion, trying to write as many hours a day as if I had not to keep the flat clean, shop—the burden of war-time shopping—and cook meals. Usually I sleep as soundly as a child, but I began to lie awake, wondering how, or why, I had got myself into this nightmare of wasted time and strength, hornets' nest of people, nameless boredom of what Quakers call creaturely activities.

About this time I finished my first reading of André Gide's Journal in the Pléiade edition. It had been my companion for months. I am not foolish enough to compare my mind with his, but I felt myself as I read in profound sympathy with him. (His homosexuality does not interest me, I can neither feel nor condemn it, I accept it as one of his ambiguities.) And in nothing more closely than in his recurrent laments over the way his days are broken into and his time and energy devoured by people wanting help or advice. As I have, he had a moral inability to say No. And, as I do, he longed to agree with the person he was talking to, and he listened, trying anxiously to guess what the other wanted to hear, more than he talked. And he imagined that he had made a fool of himself in company. In short, we are egoists of the same breed, if not of the same intellect.

A half-comic interlude. In March, Guy was ill, very ill, with mumps. He needed skilled nursing, and a ravishingly pretty young Swedish woman, one of Lord Horder's nurses, spent the day with us, except when she was lunching, at my charge, at the Dorchester, the only restaurant she knew. During this time I had to go down four times to Mortimer, to pack up for storing our thousands of books and other things left there. It was icy weather, I stood for hours in the overfull corridors of trains, and caught a heavy cold. One morning, luckily after the Swedish girl had left us, I fainted, a rare occurrence with me, one I enjoy—the delicious sense of escape and irresponsibility as the world fades into blackness.

Reluctantly, when the doctor came to look at Guy, I let him examine me. He talked in a portentous way about an overworked heart and an anginous precondition. I did not ask him what, if anything, these dubious terms meant. I thought him a fool and suspected him of inventing them to alarm me. I knew perfectly well that my loyal ass of a body was capable of simulating any illness to get me out of the domestic trap I was in. Twenty-eight years ago, I reminded myself, in 1914, I was making ready to move into the house in Liverpool Garden Suburb, with despair, rage, tears, *knowing* that the trap had closed on me. Since then I had torn myself out of it, again and again, with bitter guilt, and again and again been driven back... If there were anything wrong with my heart, *which I did not believe* (and I was right), it was something my body had invented, as a last effort to free me. Bless the good kind ass, but I could not take advantage of its cunning.

Because of Guy's illness we were in quarantine, and I had to warn people who were in the habit of coming to the flat. One day, I opened the door to a ring, and there stood Ernst Meyer, in his long terribly shabby overcoat. He held out a bottle of milk and four eggs.

'For you,' he said, in his gentle musical voice, smiling.

I could not refuse to take them, but I felt like tears. Gifts, and such a gift, from a refugee, hard put to it to live...

My trick, if it was one, failed. I can never keep myself in a state of exhaustion. By the end of April I was in full delirium of people again. God be thanked I have forgotten every incident of this time except two or three.

The four American writers, women, sent over to take a look at us, with one of whom, Maxine Davis, a charming vivid creature, I fell into friendship at sight (another of them, a very pretty young woman, confessed that she fled precipitately to the basement of the Ritz during alerts—'Was I yellow!' she said disarmingly).

Richard Hillary's fiercely pitiable mask...

The oranges...

Noel Streatfeild and her housekeeper were each given one orange by her greengrocer, and they decided to give them to me. No one now will be able to imagine what inconceivable generosity this was. I had not had one in my hands for at least two years. As she went off, Noel said, 'They're small and probably sour, but an orange is an orange.'

She was wrong on both counts. They were not sour, and an orange is sometimes a miracle.

## CHAPTER 20

THAT OLD CAPTAIN, my father, crosses my path again and again in the underworld, glancing at me very briefly from pale long-sighted eyes, not with reproach—he did not expect from me more than the little he got—with indifference and a faint, very faint and unwilling hope of being recognized.

It seems to me that I recognize him—a little. And a little more distinctly now than when we were children and my mother set us down to write to him to Buenos Aires or Vera Cruz or Valparaiso, and we sat frowning, gnawing the ends of wooden penholders, struggling to drag a stiff sentence or two from minds empty of any other feeling than boredom, any image of the man who would stretch out a long sun-blackened hand for the letters pushed towards him by the ship's agent in those far-off places—'Letters from home for you, Captain.' Did he, when he read the few lines, know that they had been written by heartless strangers? Probably not. Long before this, he had learned to live to himself. And with himself—with all his selves except the very last.

There were so many of them in one lean hard weathered body: the friendly almost affable man known to passengers he thought well of, full of stories you could believe or not as you liked; the man his officers respected for his toughness and magnificent seamanship, even when, as happened sometimes, they disliked him for some grudging trick he had played them; the handsome first officer a quick-tempered spirited girl fell in love with and married; the man she came for good enough reasons to detest, and at the end of her life could not endure in her sight and treated with unforgiving coldness; the thirteen-year-old child setting out in the icy darkness of a January morning to begin his life as apprentice in a sailing-ship—lucky for the child that he could not look ahead, it was a brutal life; the tall shambling old man, eighty-three when his wife died, living on alone in a house built for a large family, contented, even in his own way happy—loneliness was no new experience for him, and for the first time he was master in his house.

No one knew what went on in his mind. Would he himself have known, if it were pulled out suddenly like a dog from the burrow it had run into? This burrow was tortuous; he must have lost himself continually in blind passages, inventing triumphs, past and to come, a word, a look, a deed, forcing everyone, forcing *her*, to respect him, pursuing memories as vivid as the scream of a gull, faces, voices, cities, the changes in cities. He had been about the seas for more than sixty years; there were more harbours in his mind than feathers on the gull's wing, and he saw each of them distinctly: set him ashore in the dark on some wharf he had visited once as third mate and he could have walked without stumbling the shortest way to the agent's office.

He had become an obdurate liar. But did he know when he was lying? In the long silences, he told himself tales in which truth and lies were inextricably mixed, memory aiding and abetting. Say he recalled a street in Santiago. What easier than to imagine something happening there, and he the centre of it? Life showed itself to him with astonishing vividness, but he became uncertain where this or that belonged; he took a house from its secretive courtyard in a Spanish port and set it down in Gravesend and himself in it, carrying on a fantastic conversation with the King's surgeon whose photograph he had seen in the morning's newspaper.

At times, after he came home for good to live his stealthy isolated life in the house, unwanted, refused a trace of the respect and authority he had had in his ship, I felt a brief sympathy for him, even warmth. Some buried nerve in my mind or body knew him. Knew why he lied: knew that on his day-long solitary walks over the moors he was accompanied by a well-meaning boy no one had ever seen since the 29th of January 1868: knew why he locked up in his wardrobe a jackdaw collection, probably of rubbish: knew why, faithfully, perhaps hopefully, at Christmas, New Year, Easter, he remembered to buy and bring in some sort of gift: knew why he kept his better garments

518 JOURNEY FROM THE NORTH, VOL. 2

put away and went about shabbier than a tramp, not expecting the occasion when he might want to cut a figure, but waiting for it.

He had a virtue I respect and envy—*he did not fear ridicule*.

In the five years he lived alone, I went up to Whitby twice, and stayed the inside of a week, laying myself out to be pleasant. That was as far as my very slight feeling for him moved me.

Nothing of my mother remained in her house, which was decaying more quickly than you would expect of so solidly-built a place. He had taken possession of the whole of it, all the rooms from which, in her lifetime, he was silently excluded. He slept in the larger of her two bedrooms, in a disorder he did not notice. When a bomb blew in several windows at the back of the house, he had them boarded up, darkening the shrouded rooms. Delicate old rugs became filthy with the soil and dirt he trod into them. Clumsily, mishandling or trying to mend them, he destroyed fine old pieces of furniture, one after another. Everywhere were cobwebs, dead leaves, a dry smell of earth and dust. The elderly housekeeper who came in every day for an hour or two could not have kept so many large rooms clean, even if he had not thwarted her irresolute efforts.

I wrote to him fairly regularly. Once or twice, after I went to live in London, he sent me a shoe-box full of half-dead flowers, and once a handful of woodruff I dried and kept.

I paid him my second visit this year, in September.

The winter before, he had been ill, the first illness of his life. Looked after, in a fashion, by his housekeeper and the district nurse, he recovered quickly, but it had marked him. For the first time, he looked his age, almost eighty-eight. The skin of his face, still the colour of saddle-leather, and grained like old timber, had fallen in: it was covered by a network of dark cracks—he seldom took a bath—and hair stood out in thick quills from his long narrow head.

I asked him some indifferent questions about his illness.

'Ha, it was nothing,' he said carelessly, 'I pay no attention to such things, the sea air keeps me healthy. I never swallow medicines; a passenger we had in the *Saxon Prince*, a very clever fellow, one of the King's doctors, told me they were no good, he only ordered them for the look of it. Plenty of long walks, that's all you need. If your mother had walked more, she'd have been healthier.'

After more than twenty years, I am still trying to explain to myself a trivial incident of that visit. Bombs fell one night, about one o'clock, very near the house. Startled awake, I lay still. After a moment, the door of my father's bedroom opened softly: he came out on the landing and stood outside my door. I opened my mouth to speak to him, and felt—felt is the wrong word, but there is no other—a hand laid on it. The impulse to speak died, and I let him turn away, to pad quietly about the house in the darkness. After a few minutes he came back to his room and closed the door with the same care not to make a sound.

Why didn't you let me speak? I asked. Why did you want to deprive an old man of a companionable word at such a moment?

There had been so many nights—in fact, every night of his life after he came home for good—when he paused at the door of her room on his way to bed and said, 'Good night.' And waited for the dry answering, 'Oh, good night,' he did usually get, but not always...

An evening two months later, he wrote the daily entry in his log, in a hand little less firm than it had always been, clear, open, and sloping sharply back.

'Light NW-SW winds. Weather fine clear cold during night.

8.00 am Light SEwd. Wea. fine clear cold. Stamps-/7, papers-/7

Noon ditto. Sea strong on beach and bar, pm ditto. Cold.'

Laying the pen down, he began raking the stove before settling to his scrapbooks, or one of the newspaper competitions he was never within a universe of winning, and when the stroke fell he pitched forward, burning his hand on it. Half-conscious, he lay through the long November night until the woman came next morning.

I was in North Wales, and the war-time journey across England took eleven cold hours, until eight in the evening.

There were two women in the house when I came in: the housekeeper had moved in, and the bony loud-voiced district nurse had waited to talk to me.

'Go up and see him,' she said jauntily, 'he's expecting you.'

He was awake, and looked at me without interest. His face had become indifferent and remote, hard. I had not kissed him since I was a child, and it would be futile now.

When I went down again, the nurse said, 'The captain needs proper nursing. The nuns down the road will take him, if that's what you want.

Y'know, he's the most stoical gentleman ever was, and considerate and gentle
and tries not to give trouble—a gentleman in the thousand. I see people as
they are, y'know, and I've known few as polite and modest, yes, modest.'

You know a man none of us ever saw, I thought. Perhaps what he was
meant to be, but who knows? Is one real at the moment of death? Or is the
reality the long confused groping deluded years of living from moment to
moment? His heartless treatment of my young brother, or his courage and
seamanship and a child's endless curiosity?

The housekeeper was sleeping in my bedroom—none of the others was
habitable. I made myself up a bed on the floor of the sitting-room, and fell
instantly into a dead sleep. It was the room immediately under his, and some
time during the night I half roused to hear him call out. Less than half—my
body was a log. No, I can't help him, I thought. He called three or four times.
Then the woman went to him.

This is not my only failure to love, but I remember it whenever I catch
sight of the tall shabbily-dressed old man, coming towards me with his long
shambling rapid stride and passing me with scarcely a glance.

In the morning I let them carry him from his house to the nursing home
run by nuns, where he died the same day, easily and simply, more quietly
than a ship comes to anchor.

So they said. I was not there.

When I went to look at him, lying with closed eyes in a bed not his own,
tears rushed from me. 'He had such a hard life,' I said, excusing myself. The
nun standing beside me smiled with a serene indifference. No doubt she was
used to such useless tears, or she supposed I was crying for myself.

Do came to help me clear the house to be sold. She and I forced open the
locked drawers in the room on the top floor, and found them crammed with
the detritus of voyages, old yellowed newspapers, mildewed photographs,
fragments of exotic shells, dried flowers, manuscript books going back fifty
or more years, into which he had copied anecdotes and poems that had
caught his eye, and traced comic drawings of clowns and women in boned
stays. They filled four sacks.

But, there remained the more than forty large folio log-books, in which
every single day he recorded in close detail winds, currents, the state of sea
and sky (Midnight on the 4th of January 1908, was unusually dark, the sea

like fire and full of phosphorus intensified by the dense black sky to the NW),
minute incidents of the day's run, and the look of ports, harbours, foreign
streets, markets and the price of fruit, a view of the world as one sharp-eyed
eccentric captain knew it. After he came home, he still noted faithfully, every
day, the changes of wind, sea, sky, with a few very brief soliloquies. 'Thus
ends the year with a great feeling of something was wrong, for I don't seem
to care whether I sit or walk about, my heart is heavy although I try to shake
it off by the thought of the happy recollection this day brings forth. W.S.J.'

Millions on millions of words, his hand moving slowly across the page,
day after day, year after year.

'What,' I said, 'are we to do with these?'

'Destroy them, of course,' Do said contemptuously.

I suppose we must, I thought: I can't carry them about for the rest of
my life.

It took us several hours to destroy his life's work. I deserved the remorse I
felt when the director of the museum, to whom my father had spoken about
his diaries, asked me to let him have them.

'I destroyed them.'

'What a pity,' he said quietly, 'they would have been of great value. He
was a remarkable man.'

Not many people came to see him buried: a few cousins I did not know,
hard-eyed friendly men and women, and two or three of the old retired
captains he gossiped with when they met on the cliff-top or the pier; they
may not have liked him or believed all he said, but they were of the same
almost vanished race.

'So you h'an't laid'm wi' your mother,' one of them said.

I knew that flyting tone, half-sarcasm, half-rebuke. 'There was a place for
him with his own family,' I said, staring.

It may be only the living who recall clearly anger, resentment, enmity.
Might she have said, '*I knew you in the dark... let us sleep now...*'? I could not
have risked it, I had to arrange it as, thinking of her closed door and silences,
I supposed she would want.

Seen from up here, the coast line curves finely to the north, the estuary
widens into the outer harbour and flows silently to the foot of the perpen-
dicular wall of sea, the ancient Church crouching on the edge of the east

cliff looks stonily down at flights of worn steps and roofs half as old as itself. There is nothing more useless, more unjustifiable, than pity when it is too late. It would have mortified me to cry in front of my young sister's indifference—and for what? Because one old sea-captain had been stopped hurrying through the secretive old streets down there, making his meagre purchases, glancing from side to side as he crossed the bridge, at a sunken mooring-post, a flash of wings.

Guy met our train in London, at King's Cross. I said goodbye to my sister and her husband on the platform; they were going underground to Paddington Station, and we decided to take a bus to the hotel. We changed our minds and went back, and ran into them at a turning in the underground passage, they hurrying one way, we the other. Pleased to be going home, Do was laughing. Excitement had heightened the colour in her cheeks and darkened the clear blue of her eyes: in that place her beauty startled by its freshness. Smiling, raising her hand, she turned the corner out of sight.

## CHAPTER 21

THERE IS A MOMENT immediately before the tide turns to go back when a child standing knee-deep in the waves feels an all but imperceptible current, not yet the ebb but the turn.

I had been living in North Wales since the end of October. Guy had been posted to Harlech as commandant of the new ABCA school for officers, and as soon as I had stored books and furniture I followed him there, half reluctant to leave a flat I had made habitable, half deeply, blindly, eager to get away from London and its devouring duties and distractions. Subconsciously, I had begun to draw back, turning without noticing it towards a mole's retreat into obscurity.

Guy lived in Coleg Harlech with his staff, and batches of young officers sent to do a short course in current affairs, a project that a great man disapproved of; the Prime Minister's nose imagined a faintly subversive smell—the only current affair a soldier need have in his head was his part in the war, everything else should be left to higher authority.

I found myself two rooms in a house looking across the estuary to the hills on the other side.

Even under an overcast sky these hills were beautiful, bare, with a down of fine grass stretched across the ancient stone skeleton. The perpetual changes of light across them were as calmly sensual as the touch of a feather, and in sunlight the bay filled with light, a fleece of light in rapid ceaseless movement. Below them on the edge of the estuary, facing Harlech, distant about two miles as the gulls and cormorants flew and a great deal farther by road and bridge, was Portmeirion, the hotel-village imagined and built by Clough Williams-Ellis, landowner, architect, physically and mentally the most elegant of men, an eighteenth century wit grafted successfully on to the twentieth. A trace of the involuntary admiration one feels for a superb natural object, a mountain or a splendid tree, entered into my liking for him. My affection for his wife, sharpened by her calm insistence on using her Strachey genius exactly as she pleased, was of long growth, born at a time when her elegance, unconscious air of authority, quick racing mind, a little intimidated a badly-dressed young woman whose gauche provincialism she either did not notice or gaily ignored.

The society that had grown up round the hotel, on the edge of the park or in houses and cottages on the nearer hills, reminded me sharply of the Spanish fishing village I stayed in in 1935. Here as there a foreign body had pushed its way into old veins, with the difference that the Welsh smiled and went out of their way to be amiable where few of the Catalans, the women never, smiled or made any effort to narrow the abyss between themselves and the invaders. And, here as there, several of these were Germans and Central Europeans, writers, painters, a scholar or two, but not poor. (After a time I noticed that the friendly talkative Welsh drew a subtle distinction—an inflection of the mind, not a demonstration—between these other foreigners and the no less foreign English who, politically speaking, were the oppressor, alien in a graver sense than Germans, Austrians, Hungarians.) For all its pungent cosmopolitanism, it was a society very unlike the one I had fled from, a curiously brittle growth. I was not bored. To live in a foreign country sharpens my brain as do books, music, the theatre, and—a little less—the society of men and women more intelligent than I am, when all I need do is listen to them, as I listened to Michael Polanyi or Arthur Koestler.

I have a vivid image of Michael Polanyi walking ahead of me through
the pitch-black tunnel of a disused slate railway, towards the end of a strenuous climb across rocky hills. To lighten the way through the mud and the
fatigue of falling in and out of unseen holes and jumping the wooden blocks
between the rails, he repeated verse after verse of Verlaine, in an enchantingly
gentle voice.

An incident no less distinct and trivial taught me about Arthur Koestler
that neither his formidable intelligence nor his fits of black temper nor his
natural charm lie as near the bone as his kindness. He had George Orwell
staying with him in the farm-house he rented in the hills behind the hotel:
ill, exhausted by the journey, Orwell was sleeping heavily in the same room
as his baby son: the child woke early, and to keep him quiet, so that Orwell
could sleep on, Arthur sat beside the cot for an hour and amused him silently
by pulling faces. Nothing I know about him pleases me so much.

Living in Harlech at this time was one of those astute and intelligent
Welshmen who have no wish to separate themselves from an England
which gives their energy infinitely wider elbow room than it will find at
home—T.J. To look at—and to talk to—this elderly man, the *âme damné* of
Lloyd George and Baldwin, might have been a schoolmaster or an unfrocked
priest: short, sallow, his long large beak and narrow half-closed eyes gave
him the air of a not unfriendly cockatoo. He was as nimble-witted as the
devil, very capable of genuine idealism, blandly Welsh in his charm, shrewd,
vain, and had been so delighted to find himself, by his unusual talents and
persistence, intimate with the great, keeper of their secrets, in a position (he
imagined) to manipulate them, that for him a Ribbentrop came to have the
same weight and moral value as a Baldwin or a Lionel Curtis. I did not dare
to ask him whether he still believed that as 'a man of peace' Hitler, tactfully
handled, could have been coaxed into leaving western Europe alone. He was
anything but a fool, but it is difficult for an idealist who is also a metaphysical
politician to admit error...

I had here every condition I needed to write as well as I am capable
of writing: no responsibilities, and a room with a wide view. Each time I
glanced up from the small table where I had just room for an elbow and
the manuscript of *Cloudless May*, I saw the estuary, the opposite hills, the
light. Impossible to find words for the felicity of living at the same time

here and in the Loire valley: it is not the same light, but in both places it is incomparably spacious, suave, alive.

In writing *Cloudless May* I found, as with *Cousin Honoré*, that the initial act of transposing an unmanageably vast national theme into a narrow local one releases immense energies. The provincial Laval, the provincial Reynaud, Pétain, Mandel, Weygand and the rest, are not miniatures of the national figures: each is a person in his own right, freely available, free to manifest every passion and twisted reasoning likely to spring from his nature and situation, and to act in whatever way a human being does or may act under great stress.

This transposition avoids the basic artificiality of novels placed supposedly on a national level, with *a* Prime Minister, *a* Minister of this and that, *a* Permanent Secretary, *an* editor of *The Times*, on whom the skin hangs loosely in great wrinkled folds round a thin kernel of flesh and blood—very much as if a slender actor were impersonating Falstaff, with the garments of the real Falstaff hanging round him, three-quarters empty. Inevitably, these invented eminent persons are overshadowed and the colour and substance drained out of them by the reality hovering behind. The motives working in the *préfet* in a provincial capital may be essentially those of a Prime Minister, but their local habitation encloses them in a space which does not reduce the human being to a life-sized puppet.

This is always true. And in *Cloudless May* I was blessed by the peculiar circumstances of France in May and June 1940, when national breakdown forced a greater degree of autonomy on the province, turning it into a small State and compelling its officials to act freely, that is, to take charge of events.

It was a very difficult novel to write, and I was intensely happy.

Early in February I reached the last two or three chapters.

On the afternoon of the 10th of February, a single German aeroplane, flying at a great height, perhaps lost, perhaps avoiding a more dangerous target, dropped its bombs on Reading, a small completely undefended town, killing only civilians, among them my young sister.

After more than twenty years, I cannot write about it calmly.

The telegram from her husband was delivered to Guy at the college. When he came into my room with it, I supposed for a moment that I knew what he was going to say.

'Is it Bill?'

'No. Dorothy.'

There was no train out of Harlech for three hours. Left alone, I actually finished the sentence I had been writing when he came in: like the body of a decapitated hen, my brain went on twitching for several minutes.

You don't mind my doing this, do you? I said to her.

I reached Reading at eleven that night, without having taken in clearly what had happened. My body knew and went on shivering, not from the cold, but my mind was still stupefied by the inhuman abruptness of it.

She had been on duty, a volunteer worker, in the kitchen of the civic restaurant when the bomb crashed into it. An older woman working beside her, who was seriously hurt but not killed, told my brother-in-law that when they heard the bomb coming she had time to say very quietly, 'That's for us.'

If we had kept the children, I thought, she would not have had the time to do war work.

Since there was nothing to identify her, she was taken with others to an undertaker's house, and Robert found her only after hours of distraught search of the hospitals and casualty stations.

Early the next day, I went there with him. Disfigured but, thank God, not maimed, her young cold face, lips lightly parted, accused me of going on living. I cried difficult tears over her in that small ugly room, staring at a crack in the wall behind her, along which a small moth was fluttering as though caught in it.

My first thought was that she must come home at once: I forget how we arranged it...

Unlike every other house I have cleared up after a death, what I touched and folded and sorted in hers was the future, only the future. She had begun preparing for the children's return the very day she came home. She had very little money to spend, but each week she bought some one thing and put it away for them: there were tins of food, books, material for clothes, toys, even, dear God, the birthday cards for three more years. Such frivolities, she thought, might disappear from a straitened England.

The doll's house she was furnishing for Judy, covering chairs with scraps of silk, making and hanging curtains, lacked the final touches. For less than a minute when I was staring at it, I had the sensation of a short quick finger pointing out what remained to be done.

After so many years I still at moments have to remind myself that it is true.

Her husband had been trying to get himself into the Air Force: he had a few weeks to wait, and during this time we sold the house, and I went back to Harlech, to *Cloudless May*.

Working at it all day, I finished it by the end of the month.

For a long time I lived two distinct lives, one in which I wrote, and another at night, in the small bare icily cold bedroom, and in the daytime when I went out and walked along the coast road or into the village. Even if I had wanted to, I could not have dismissed the images, they were always close to me, waiting for me to put my pen down.

## CHAPTER 22

AFTER A WINTER and spring in Harlech, I moved to a small old hotel a few miles inland. Here the estuary narrowed to a trout stream, the valley was a desert of reeds and grass, the hills separating it from other valleys were partly covered by oak and the fine hair of pines, in the clear streams the water was soft, soft, and the air gentle. Where the hills closed in, a slate village, crushed between higher naked hills, sent rivulets of money trickling from the quarry along tributary valleys.

I had travelled farther from my own coast than if I had crossed Europe. Possibly these black-haired slender-boned men and women had been pushed to this edge of the island by my savage ancestors. I have never liked any place better, nor felt more irreconcilably an alien.

The hotel was run by a slender handsome woman, gay, friendly, sharp-tempered, at once business-like and pleasure-loving. Thus, the bath water was always hot, the food well-cooked, and the atmosphere of the place easy-going and very faintly louche. By nature and upbringing I am straitlaced, but dissolute enough in spirit to find the combination of cleanliness, order, and a not obvious licence extremely pleasant. It suited me well.

Now and then commandos from the near-by Rehabilitation Centre arrived, all young, lucidly reckless, and very imperfectly rehabilitated:

bagpipes at three in the morning disturbed less sound sleepers than I am, but complaints were not even listened to...

After weeks of planning it, and brooding—and some duty writing, a long story for the volume the Czechs put together in memory of Lidice—I began to write the partly autobiographical book I called *The Journal of Mary Hervey Russell*.

Hervey Russell is a character from *The Mirror in Darkness*, that Balzacian monster I abandoned in 1935, and my shadow. The impulse to disguise myself—not new, after all: I give way to it every time I have to talk to people I don't know—had been encouraged by reading Kierkegaard. If so scrupulous a writer could manage it, I could at least try not to lie while masking the truth.

Something happened in writing the disguised Hervey Russell's journal which may be a little like what happens in the writing of a poem. Image after image, level after level of thoughts and sensations, rose to the surface as I worked, each of them attaching itself to a great many of the others. I wrote slowly, and felt more acutely than ever the pain of writing and the intense physical pleasure of using words, and of recognizing the, so to speak, consanguinity of the images.

Somewhere, I forget where, Léautaud says that 'true literary talent lies in writing books as one writes letters: in absolute terms. Everything which fails to do so is mere pathos, posture, rhetoric, and pomposity. You must let yourself go, stop weighing your words, stop caring about "good" or "bad" style...'

If he is right I have no literary talent. But is he? I was not as I wrote conscious of cheating, but certainly I did not let myself go, and my mind was invaded by phrases like a torrent of swifts fighting for a claw-hold in the ruins of a house. (May the ghost of old Léautaud forgive the metaphor!)...

Except for the hours when I touched the icy current of my young sister's death flowing through me, I was at ease with myself...

During the whole summer I watched with amusement and misgiving the hand-over-fist climb of an ambitious young man, not in the least a jesuitical figure, a clever office-soldier with a great deal of charm and any number of personal virtues, capable in good faith of arranging to advance himself at the expense of less adroit colleagues, by any means except violent ones. He was not vain, not unscrupulous in anything except the turning-points of his career.

Since there was nothing else I could do I memorized him for possible future use...

I am not certain when I finished the *Journal*, I think at the very end of the year. Published in May 1945, it drew from R. H. Tawney a letter I read in fear and trembling, trembling with joy, fearing that I could never deserve his praise again. A miracle.

If only this one book can outlive me, I thought, if only...

(When I was asked for a manuscript to be sold for the benefit of the American War Bond Committee, I gave this, as the best I had: it is in a Pennsylvanian public library. Not to forget, I add a list of the others I gave away: the manuscript of *That Was Yesterday* to the library of St Andrews University, the three books of *A Richer Dust* to the Central Library in Leeds. Two others—*No Time Like the Present* and *The Voyage Home*—I had bound and gave to American friends for whom I could do nothing else: they in turn handed one to Wellesley College, the other to Kenyon. Odd to reflect that, after I am dust, these hundreds of pages my hand wrote with some pleasure and more labour, in every sort of place and condition, will exist.)

Some time late in 1943, Guy was dislodged from Coleg Harlech and posted to Northern Command, in York...

When I was packing my book box I came on a large folder crammed full of notes for unwritten volumes of *The Mirror in Darkness*, and began tearing them up. But mischief had been done, ghosts from the three books I had completed swarmed in my brain, demanding more life—one in particular, the tortuous uneasy figure of David Renn, to whom I was joined by more than one nerve and vein. Others leaped forward, I saw them move from the darkness into the atrociously unquiet months between May 1938 and the outbreak of war, and knew that I could not get rid of them without violence.

Almost without intending it, my hand reached for a sheet of paper and began to erect the skeleton of a novel about Renn...

With comical displeasure I realized that I had become *une machine à faire des livres*. I am without the egotist needed to dignify the role. An egotist, yes, but unable to take seriously a talent no greater than that of a score of my fellows. Such pleasure as I get out of writing is not the delight and agony of the air-borne. But—even today—if I am not writing I feel with exasperation and despair that I am failing in a task laid on me by some crackpot god. I envy, my God, the free and sane who can look at the patient face of an old woman without feeling obliged to memorize the wrinkles.

'What did you do,' the bored interrogator will ask when I present myself in the underworld, 'with the things you were given for your journey, the North Sea in summer, the great white cherry tree, the coast line, the dazzling fields of marguerites, the undersea note of the bell-buoy, and the cries of gulls?'

'I made phrases.'

'What an idiot!'

## CHAPTER 23

IN APRIL THAT YEAR, when I was in York, the weakness I had been ignoring on the theory that I was inventing it, got out of hand. I was very ill. Later, I went down to the south coast to be nursed back to strength by Leonora Eyles, wife of D. L. Murray. He was editor at that time of *The Times Literary Supplement*, an office of which he was deeply proud: his abrupt dismissal after the war mortified him deeply.

A remarkable woman, Leonora. How old was she then? Sixty? A few years younger? Her smooth unlined face, broad and flat across the cheekbones, narrowed to a small pointed chin and a firm small colourless mouth: she had pale sharp eyes and a finely arched nose—it was the face of a Flemish madonna and a benevolent spiritual bully, used to taking things and people into her hands, self-assured, a little hard, paradoxically a little voluptuous; there was even a nearly unnoticeable trace of cruelty in the short mouth, but it had been turned round to kindness. (Oddly, she and I had a trivial link she knew nothing about. In the days when I was Alfred Knopf's agent in London, Charles Evans of Heinemann told me about his vain efforts to free her from a disastrous contract with a publishing shark, and that she was desperately poor; I gave him a little money I happened to have on me, I was on my way to buy a coat I could very well do without, to give her anonymously.)

It was a strange household: David, who looked like a good-humoured priest, large, soft, delicate in mind and manner, with no vanity and not a great deal of male energy, a secretary known as Bardolph (his face 'all bubukles, and whelks, and knobs, and flames o' fire'), a one-armed woman servant, taken by Leonora out of pity, a young married daughter and her penniless husband (later, after their divorce, he became the film actor, Alexander Knox), and Charles Murray, David's father. This extraordinary man dominated the family, simply by being eighty-seven, rather deaf, rich, an ex-fencer, a dandy, and as stubborn as Leonora herself. Not that he was spared her coercive tongue, but in a curious way he imposed himself.

What at that time I saw as a Shavian comedy turned out a tragedy in the blackest manner of Strindberg. I know too little about her early life to guess why Leonora was driven by the need to punish herself—that hint of sensuality? self-destruction is *also* a pleasure. She used up her youth in calamitous efforts to save human wrecks, and then, when marriage to David could have saved her, arranged to be defeated by making herself nothing more than a household slave to Charles and the others. At my last sight of her, less than ten years after this, in a large seedy Edwardian house in London, she had become an old woman, bent almost double, moving about the vast dingy rooms in draggled clothes. David, as well-dressed and quietly genial as always, had changed little: neither had Charles: at ninety-six, he was still slim, dandified, and now stone-deaf; he was sound asleep in a small upright chair, a rather sinister figure at the back of the room. The sense of decay, deathly weariness, hatred, did not come from either of the men. But, at the end, the impulse to self-destruction overtook and trapped even David, the innocent man, the one person in the family devoid of hatred, the one in whom a delicate kindness failed only at the very last.

The preparations for the landing in France were going on round us, and I was still there when Paris was freed. David loved Italy and had little feeling for France; since he knew I had a great deal, he set me down to write his editorial about it. I had had to force back tears when the Marseillaise, violent and triumphant, sprang from the wireless, but as soon as I started my thousand words, genuine feeling withdrew, and all I wanted to do was to write as much as possible like Giraudoux at his best and least metaphysical.

If I had the patience to look it up, reprinted in *The Writer's Situation*, I should know how far I succeeded in this pious exercise.

Later that month I began to hear stories about the ugly face of Liberation. Not merely comic or ironical stories of half-innocent corruption—'*Ce qui est étonnant, ma chère Margaret, c'est la célérité de la décomposition: deux mois, et l'assiette au beurre est devenue le plat de la Résistance!*'—the subtle self-corrupting of the brave maquis fighter become a powerful official overnight, with a car, a position he is not fitted for, intellectually or socially, who succumbs almost at once to all the temptations of the abject languid Marianne of the 'thirties. But there were grim coldly detailed rumours of private and political killings done under cover of Liberation justice. I was fascinated by these. I listened avidly, trying to penetrate to the roots of the cruel tortuous acts of men who were neither monsters nor naïve scoundrels. The village Orestes, the small town Robespierre, exist in our veins, and can be understood, a little, by looking at a drop of blood under the microscope.

At the same moment I did not want to believe these stories, and sometimes shut my ears.

An item I discovered in a French news-sheet about a young Frenchwoman who had married a German officer in Normandy during the Occupation gave me the germ of a play. I felt that the young woman Vercors had imagined refusing to speak one word to the decent well-meaning German with whom she was in love was little more than a respectful gesture made towards things, not as they are, but as they would be if men were consistent: what would she have become if she had behaved as a human being rather than as a symbol?... Still too weak to write for more than a short time, I put together the skeleton of a play, acts and scenes, and wrote fragments of dialogue.

At the end of July, I insisted on leaving Leonora. She was very angry with me, but I had had as much generous bullying as I could stand.

I began writing again at once, and finished the play in November. By now, it was certain that we were in for another winter of war; I set about turning it into a short novel, and finished that in February. In its ironically emotional way, *The Other Side* is an intelligent account of a young woman, meant by her nature for happiness, who is stretched to breaking point by the tension between her feelings and her acts. There is a plot, exciting enough—but leave that. It was not the last, but one of the last of my books to be freely praised. I think it deserved it less than later novels which have been treated with cold justice.

I went back at once to David Renn, who was hunting down his friend's murderer. But this book meant as the fourth volume of *The Mirror in Darkness* multiplied in my brain until I was forced, reluctantly, to divide it into two—no publisher wanted to set eyes on a manuscript half the length of *War and Peace*. Dividing it encouraged the two parts to grow unequally, the action of *Before the Crossing* taking place immediately before the war, and of *The Black Laurel* after it, chiefly in occupied Germany. David Renn's hunt ended where in effect it began, in his own passionately ambiguous heart and mind. After the overgrown prelude, the second book became an altogether more complex affair, with a great many characters not conceived in the original series. Regarded as one work, the two form a whole I am not ashamed of, and if any soul in the future, if there is a future, is moved to turn the pages of a forgotten novelist, may his glance fall on it.

## 3rd of April 1945

The photograph in today's *Daily Mail* of a sixteen-year-old German soldier walking to his prison cage, head down in a vain effort to hide his tears, a boy's clumsy fingers twisting a handkerchief, moves me to a grief as useless as his. I have no need to look at it closely to etch his features in my memory. He is the spit image of my seventeen-year-old brother in his clumsy uniform of the R.F.C. in 1914.

On the day I finished *Before the Crossing*, in July 1945, I had the first letters, two, sent by different hands, out of Czechoslovakia. Jiřina Tůmová was alive, but her husband, the quiet seriously friendly young man I saw in Prague in 1938, had died atrociously.

'... when you will come to Czechoslovakia next time you will not find my husband... He was the sense of my living, we have gone through life nineteen years together, the last seven working illegally against the Germans. Since 1944 the danger was approaching, we got several warnings, but it was necessary to go on. At last on the 23rd of February of this year we have been caught on account of a clandestine broadcasting station. They learned nothing from him, not a name passed his tongue, neither mine. Five so-called "heavy examinations" and after these he was not any more able to speak. I saw him on the 16th of March. He was not himself any longer, he did not see me, though I stood but a few steps before him. I was held by one of the Wachtmeister and I could not speak nor move otherwise they would either have beaten me before him or him before me, it was one of their pastimes. I tried to put all my love in my eyes, but was obliged to shut them again. It was too much to stand, and we never wept before the Gestapo... The image of his face and body has not left me since that time. I dare not and cannot tell you the details. I have them in statements of his fellow prisoners and doctors who have seen him. Only this: there was not a single place on his body that was not tortured, bloodily beaten, his ribs and one leg broken, and he was left with pneumony and septic fever in his cell up to the 20th of March. Up to the 31st of March he was left in his prison. Then he was transferred to the prison hospital until the 9th of April. On that day he was brought—he could not walk—to the so-called small bathing room and strangled. I learned about his death only the 10th of May. Since the 5th when I had been set free with the other prisoners, from Pankrác, I looked for him everywhere. I could not believe that he should be dead, he who loved life so much. And then, both of us have been guilty and only he paid for it... The very sense of living is lost, the duty to live remains. Believe me, dear Margaret, you are the first person to whom I dare speak about these things. My dearest, we must not lose hope that some day people will comprehend that life was meant to be lived and not to be destroyed. It is quite unimaginable that so few understand it... My husband said: If everybody went away who will work here? I must follow his words. And I will not leave him here alone. Kind souls in the Prague crematorium have saved singly the ashes of those who have been burned. So he is home again. One Friday in February he went away, one Friday in May I brought him home. A handful of ash and it represents my earthly happiness. My beloved boy...'

She asked for a letter. I had written already, I wrote again, but what can one write to a woman whose husband has been tortured and shown to her by his jailers? Words.

I had a frightful dream. There was an insect I thought dead, but when I bent over it I saw it twitch, and someone told me that what twitched in it was the nerve of cruelty. The sky, when I looked up, was immense and full of light, and a circle of hills descended in great curves to a sea covered with tiny curled waves. I looked down again, and there was still this insect, nothing else living.

On the 6th of August, the age, or rather the interregnum which had lasted some twenty odd years, came suddenly and violently to a stop. Hiroshima marked, too, the end of the classical and Christian eras, of the Middle Ages, of the Renaissance, of the Enlightenment—in short, of civilization as historically conceived. The fact that the epoch into which we have moved may be mankind's last alters every perception, underlines with a peculiar anguish or gaiety every gesture, from that of a mother taking her new-born into her hands to that of a painter before his canvas or a writer with a blank sheet of paper in front of him.

Nothing is more ridiculous than a writer, an animal whose response to disaster is a phrase. All I could imagine doing was to write a letter to the *Manchester Guardian*, still, on the whole, a calm decent organ of liberal opinion: 'Sir, it is difficult to imagine on what grounds Mr Churchill and the leader-writers base their pious hopes that the atomic bomb will "conduce to peace among nations", or "become a perennial fountain" of anything but death. Since we have not refrained from using it to blot out a city of 300,000 inhabitants, why should we hope that the consciences of future users will be more sensitive or merciful? The example has been set.'

After I had posted it I reflected that life had become much simpler now that it was no longer a question of happiness or freedom or any other of the baits that have made the fortune of so many ambitious men, *leaders*. Now that for the first time the human species can, if it feels like it, put a bullet through its silly head and finish, we can laugh at politicians and other serious-minded buffoons mouthing 'the great questions of the day'. There is only one: Can we survive?

Before Hiroshima, a writer who feared that civilization (that is, his freedom to write) was in danger could think of finding a monastery, or could remove himself and his brain to another country, less immediately threatened by the barbarians. Now all he can do is to keep his head, listen to the warning voices from present and future, and report them accurately.

Anything more? Yes, a little.

Many people are competent to tell us what to do to survive. Only the
artist—a class of persons which includes the man who set a pot of geraniums
outside his hovel in the ruins of Warsaw—can tell us how, in what conditions,
men can survive as human beings. I mean a being who is not only human,
not an existential animal, but a creature possessed of a divine instinct to
create pleasure for himself and others. It was because he had lost his faith
in this saving instinct that H. G. Wells died in despair...

I had a feeling of exhilaration, even gaiety. Now that none of us is safe,
we can really laugh, really mock our pedantic teachers, really live.

# PART II

## The Eatage of the Fog

My life is light, waiting for the death wind,
Like a feather on the back of my hand.

T. S. ELIOT

# CHAPTER I

H AD I BEEN ASKED, that summer of 1945: What do you most want
to do? I should have answered: To get out of England.

A chance came at the end of August. The Polish Embassy in London,
not then the embassy of a wholly communist government, wanted to send
an English delegation of four or five people to Warsaw, to a 'cultural conference'. It seemed in the highest degree unlikely that such a conference
could be held there at this moment, but, I reflected, there is no accounting
for Poles.

The plane chartered by the embassy left Hendon very early in the morning, with four English passengers, the rest Poles who might or might not
want to stay in Poland. One of these was the poet Antoni Slonimski. To
distract myself as we took off, I went over the messages I had memorized
from Maria Kuncewiczowa to her sister-in-law and to various writers (if
they were alive), and from B., a poet, to his closest friend (if alive). Like all
but one or two of the exiles I knew, B. was fanatically certain that a Poland
controlled by Russia was unfit to return to. I was regretting sharply that I
had refused to take money as well as messages: we had been told that it was
strictly forbidden to take more than five pounds, and I had decided that to
be caught trying to smuggle money would compromise more than myself. It
was only when we were hurried through the controls without examination
or any but the most perfunctory questions that I realized I could have taken
as much as I liked, provided I did not declare it.

The day was marvellously clear, a sky without a cloud, and the sea as flat
and unwrinkled as a duckpond. We flew at fifteen hundred feet, staring down
at a Europe as empty as it may have been on the 9th of September 1145—
emptier. Between Hanover and Magdeburg, I counted four vehicles on the
roads. There were no trains, the junctions were a tangle of smashed lines,
there were not even ferries to take the place of the bridges sagging into the
rivers. Looking down at the bombed towns was like peering into the black
rotted centre of a decayed tooth, grim enough, but for some reason a less

disturbing sight than this collapse of Europe into mediaeval conditions of travel. The few aeroplanes hurrying officials from point to point in chaos took the place of the angels a mediaeval painter puts in the upper corners of his canvas.

As soon as we took off from Berlin, I gave Antoni my window seat, so that in the moment of crossing the frontier he could look down at Poland. To me, Brandenburg, East Prussia, and neighbouring Poland look the same, a flat country of fields, lakes, trees, but long before the navigator came in to tell us that in five minutes we should be crossing the old frontier, our Poles were tense and silent. I did not look at Antoni. I have no doubt that his calm delicate face did not change. One or two of them wept, and another, on his knees at a window, prayed.

The moment I felt like praying was when we circled Warsaw airfield, and I looked down and saw that it had been badly mauled and was as full of holes as a colander.

The young secretary from our Embassy who met us said, 'We were only told last night that you were coming. God knows where you'll sleep.'

The drive into the centre of Warsaw was disquieting, like the onset of a nightmare. The head-lights picked out shadowy figures emerging and vanishing between broken-off walls in a landscape so familiar that it was some time before I realized where I had already seen it. Like vultures, the surrealist painters had smelled it out.

The car stopped at last, in front of a whole building, the Polonia Hotel. One of only four buildings still standing in Warsaw, the Polonia housed all the legations in rooms that were bedrooms and offices in one, and every room was in use. We sat for a long time, an hour, two hours, on a first-floor landing, while W——, the gentle withdrawn Pole sent by the Foreign Office, tried weakly to find a place for us. An old man, one of the hotel staff, shuffled past at intervals, each time murmuring sorrowfully, 'Very difficult.' It was Chekhov, not Warsaw.

In the end room was made for us, and I was given an attic on the top floor, bare and very small. There was a bed, a cupboard, a chair, a wash-basin—nothing else. A naked electric bulb, black with flies. The lavatory next door was suffocatingly hot, and stank. I had not had time in London to be inoculated, and wondered whether I could escape typhoid.

By now it was going on for midnight, and we were hungry. Expecting nothing, we followed W—— to a restaurant on the ground floor and were served a superb dinner: vodka, smoked salmon, jellied eel, mounds of red and black caviar, cold meats, escalopes of veal with fried eggs, vegetables, ices—I avoided these, waiting to see whether the others were poisoned by them—real coffee, such a meal as none of us had eaten for years. A long narrow side room was crowded by dancers, girls who might be shop-girls, young men looking like clerks, all very shabby, dancing with inconceivable energy and gaiety. All round us older men and women sat eating meals as lavish as ours. But where did the food come from?

Antoni questioned the manager, and told us, 'He says that Russians eat here, and they supply the food. These other people, including the dancers, are wives and sweethearts of government officials, or are employed in Ministries; they are badly paid, but they can afford a night out now and then.' He added drily, 'No doubt they have other sources of income, this isn't London.'

Before going to bed, I walked out of the hotel and stood, a few yards from the door, breathing the coolness. At once, a man began talking in an undertone, behind my shoulder. It was too dark to see his face clearly. 'You're a visitor? English? Don't believe what they'll tell you about dead Jews. They're coming back, with their filthy tricks. Let me tell you about these——'

I walked away from him, and before I reached the doorway of the Polonia a second shadow came out from the wall and asked me whether I had pounds or dollars, he would pay four hundred to the pound: the official rate was forty-five. Afraid—he could cut my throat and vanish—I stepped back quickly into the doorway.

The bed was clean, as hard as a board, and I slept like a log.

In the morning I stared from my single pane of glass at sprawling pyramids of rubble under a hard blue sky. So far as I could see there was nothing else, only these ossuaries of fractured stone and brick. A great tangled arc of steel sprang from the collapsed skeleton of some large building to hang grotesquely in mid-air. Nothing we had seen on the way across had prepared me for a city destroyed as a human body is destroyed by a shell, a mess of torn entrails and splinters of bone.

Shaken, I went down to the first floor and found that I could get coffee in a small room set aside for chance visitors. Antoni was there, and one of the others.

There was, of course, no cultural conference. None had been planned. Smiling, lifting his thin shoulders, W—— said, 'Who knows where these ideas come from?'

Since we were here, the authorities wanted to do their best for us, and we were given zlotys, two interpreters, young women, and W—— was arranging interviews for us with Ministers. Even, unless it broke down, there would sometimes be a car we could use.

'For this morning,' he said, opening his arms widely, still smiling his patient smile, 'you are free.'

Seen at eye level, the desert of dust and bricks fell apart. In the street outside the hotel, the ruins had a solemn beauty. Hard to believe they were freshly made, they had every air—except the deep peace of age—of having decayed slowly through centuries: defaced carvings and the crumbling heads of statues clung to the façades, which might be a whole roofless front, or part of one, or only a few feet of jagged wall, or a single broken column in sunlight. The prevailing colour of the stone was a greyish rose fading to soft cindery pink or darkening to rust. Behind the disembowelled fronts, cataracts of rubble and dark dust. The wide street itself was as lively as a fair-ground. For its volume, the traffic made an incredible noise—a few lorries crammed with soldiers or workers, country carts, shabby horse cabs, a few open seatless carts plying as buses, and odd wooden contraptions pushed by a bicycle, to hold two persons.

On every side narrow lanes traced the lines of vanished streets between the scorched shells of houses, each vomiting its dust-choked torrent of rubble. With only spades and bare hands, men and a few women were working headlong to clear them. The faintly sweetish stench of the bodies rotting under the rubble still clung to it. In London all these streets would have been roped off as dangerous—as they were. But to give a thought to safety would have put the whole of Warsaw behind ropes. Small stalls backed against the collapsing ruins were selling bread, a few pounds of butter, uninviting scraps of meat, eggs, cakes, and, believe it or not, flowers. On one stall, flour in German bags, loot from the new provinces. Countrywomen with bare dusty legs squatted on the rubble behind scraps of food, and bare-footed young boys, agile dirty gutter-rats, stood about with trays of cigarettes monstrously too dear to buy—who bought them was a mystery of the same order as the channels by which they reached Warsaw.

'Poles take to smuggling as to the black market,' Antoni said, 'by a disreputable sixth sense.'

Here and there, a woman stood offering silently a single linen sheet, folded across her arm, or a curtain, or a piece of lace. A girl with a calm beautiful face held out a box of ivory chess-men. Who in this place would buy it from her?

I was ashamed to look at them.

And yet, what sprang from these stones was not sadness, not defeat. It was an inextinguishable energy. The man or woman who had cobbled together a room without light, heat or water on the upper floor of a tottering building, reached by fragments of a staircase jutting precariously from the shaky wall, would not have set a pot of geraniums on the fire-blackened sill unless he had decided fiercely not only to live, but to live gaily. And the tenant of one of the exposed cellars roofed with strips of canvas or corrugated zinc had marked the entrance to this hole in the earth by a green leafy branch.

A narrow room at street level, cleared of rubble to be used, with mad disregard of the wall about to fall and crush it, as a shop, was selling a few saucerless cups, a single pair of worn shoes—and flowers.

One part only of the ruins was without life, an emptiness—that was the vast level plain of broken brick where the ghetto had been. Here nothing existed, no single line or form, not even a seed fallen among thorns, nothing.

Warsaw was badly knocked about during the four weeks' siege in 1939, and again during the Rising. After the Rising, as a final act, the Germans destroyed, deliberately and with method, everything that was left, an act prepared long beforehand, during the Occupation, part of the plan to remodel it as a German city. Buildings were mined, staffs and demolition squads trained. During their last days they had only to blow up and burn, quarter by quarter—the libraries, the Cathedral, the Royal Castle, the baroque palaces, archives, collections of ancient documents, old churches, streets of houses, all. Warsaw when they left it was this monstrous heap of scorched refuse, covering the bodies of the killed.

When the soldiers of a mediaeval invader sacked a town they had taken, it was a cruel business—and simple. A simple pleasure in smashing, objects and bodies, an instinct any woman has seen at work in her tiny child. The destruction of Warsaw was darkened by something worse, by the perversion at source of reason itself. The Germans did not occupy Poland in the way they occupied other countries, as a military measure. In that sense it was not an occupation. It was a first stage in colonization. They were going to settle in Poland. Towards the defeated Poles they behaved with the ruthlessness of brutal colonists who have no public opinion to fear.

'Are you married?' Antoni asked one of our interpreters.

'I was,' she said quietly. 'My husband and all my family have been killed. My mother—this is really strange—was in hospital. The Germans wanted it, and to clear it quickly they killed everyone, doctors, nurses, the patients.'

The plan, insane but reasoned, to Germanize Poland involved exterminating anyone—writers, scientists, scholars—who might keep the mind of the country alive. Not allowed, even if left at large, to do their work, these died also of poverty. When the terror ended, the continuity of Polish culture had been broken. In every field, in the schools and universities, in the theatre, in music, literature, research, the older trained workers were gone, dead, part of the charred dust of Majdanek and Auschwitz, or prematurely aged, and the young not yet able to fill their place.

After a day or two in this ruined city I began to see that the pot of geraniums was saying calmly, joyously, even devoutly, 'To hell with the past.' And saying it with the energy and deep instinctive gaiety that had decided the authorities to start rebuilding a theatre; it was almost finished, a clear solid building rising from the heart of the ruins.

A pleasant young man from the Ministry of Culture took us through the National Museum. This building, modern, had not been demolished because at the end it was in use as a barracks. It was almost empty. Since 1939 it had endured all the vicissitudes of a villa in Roman Gaul during successive barbarian invasions: intelligent looting by German savants with lists made when they visited it before the war; then four or five years of carefree looting by army officers, Gestapo, and clerks of the civil administration, and the delightful habit German dignitaries formed of offering each other birthday presents, a Rembrandt, a jewelled sword, a tapestry, chosen from its collections. But it was not finished off until 1944, during the Rising, when four battalions were quartered in it. There were still some paintings and tapestries, and a great many cabinets filled with old glass and china, coins, prints, and other things—these included robes and uniforms of eight centuries. Bored, the soldiers amused themselves by dressing up in the ancient costumes before tearing them to shreds, cut up the Gobelins tapestries to use as blankets, bayonetted the Egyptian mummies, fired with bows and arrows and revolvers at paintings until they hung in ribbons, used Limoges enamels of the sixteenth century as oven dishes, used and then joyously smashed the old china and glass, pocketed the Greek, Roman, Byzantine coins, and left everywhere, between ceiling-high mounds of broken shards, splinters of old wood, torn stained manuscripts, perforated canvases, those heaps of excrement which are the characteristic German gift to houses in every country they invade. It is said that infants think of their excreta as gifts offered to a mother or a nurse so that they will be noticed and loved. How inarticulate and deep must be the German wish to give and receive affection.

'Such strange people,' Zelinsky said, smiling. 'The man, a Dr Professor Frey, who set aside the Canalettos for export to Germany, had tears in his eyes because of their beauty. And you see this—' he pointed to a damaged sixteenth century cabinet, all but three of its engraved silver plaques ripped off. 'The German expert knew at once, when he touched them, that those three are fakes, and that the others were worth a great deal. Such knowledge, such delicate fingers, and a common thief...'

At this moment, I thought of the Elgin marbles.

'And here is something so terrible I do not like showing it.'

We stared in silence at a large greyish-pink notice, carrying a list of names: one of the bi-weekly lists of men who had been rounded up in cafés and houses and shot in the street, and their bodies slung into lorries, like sides of meat. To the young Pole it meant a line of men, young, old, some of them boys, standing against a wall, naked, so that their clothes were not spoiled, their mouths perhaps filled with clay or cement to prevent their crying out. A black tablet with a cross now marked the places of execution: there were a great many of them, we had noticed one a few steps from the Polonia, the crumbling wall pitted by bullets.

Realizing that we did not see the faces, Zelinsky said lightly, 'If you hadn't seen a friend for a day or two, and you saw the notices going up, then hurrying across the street to read the names, it was like——'

He broke off, with a delicate indecipherable movement of his hands.

'Such strange people. You know, when a German officer walked past the tomb of our Unknown Soldier—it was charming, a colonnade—he always saluted it. Later, of course, they blew it up. What you call a split mind, I think?'

Perhaps...

During our interviews with Ministers I took notes in my own form of shorthand of what these overworked men told us, and typed them late at night, sitting in my small hot room next door to the stinking lavatory, typing, typing, until three and four.

I formed a curious double vision of a country stripped to the bone, without machinery, livestock, tractors, lorries—what the Germans left the Russians took—nothing left for the most elementary needs, authorities, from Warsaw to the smallest village, struggling to the point of deathly exhaustion with difficulties repeated in every single personal life: men and women without a change of clothes, workmen using their hands to clear the ruins, school-masters without books, peasants without seeds for sowing.

And a country on the edge of being swallowed by Russia: the secret police—not a new fashion on this side of Europe—were already in its efficient hands, as well as every form of propaganda. There were still four parties, only one of them communist, and non-communist politicians and Ministers—the Minister for Agriculture, a large smiling Buddha—able to joke with each other about their differences. Listening attentively at the dinner given for us by the Minister of Culture—Kowalski, a genial old boy, once a writer of peasant novels, very like R. H. Tawney to look at, which endeared him to me at sight—I could not detect any malice in the witticisms with which he peppered his colleagues.

The thousands of words I typed, and dutifully used in articles, have van-ished. What remains, what I shall carry in my skull to the last, is faces and gestures. The face of the young officer who interpreted for the Vice-Foreign Minister, a smiling mask of such fatigue that if it had been possible I would have left. The strange eyes, pale and half-mad, of the young woman, Kowalski's secretary, who told me that her husband had been tortured all day, then killed, in the living-room of their house, by Germans who were looking for her.

'The neighbours listened to it going on—and told me. They were right to tell me. Our two children ran out of the house and for a week I did not find where they were... Are you going to tell me that vengeance is mine, saith the Lord? The vengeance I want is justice... even if there is no end to it... crime, punishment, justice, vengeance for justice. Yes, yes, next time, the next war, will be the end. It doesn't matter, I tell you, I shall smile in its face!... Why did you come here, by the way?'

'A Polish friend in London——'

She interrupted me. 'Don't talk to me about the London Poles.' Her voice became a thin howl, like a dog. 'Cowards!'

I found B.'s friend in one of the Ministries, and repeated the message I had learned by heart. 'If you like,' I said, 'I'll take a letter to him.'

'Is he coming back here?'

'No.'

Turning away from me, B.'s friend said calmly, 'Then I have nothing to say to him.'

'Am I to tell him that?'

'As you please.'

The interpreter for the Minister of Culture was an aristocrat, a Radziwill. He was a very bad interpreter, stuttering, looking from one to the other of us with the sad eyes of a comedian. Five years in Buchenwald had left him very lame; he walked painfully, with a stick. Later, talking to me, he said carefully that although he was not a communist he knew that the only hope for Poland was to work peacefully and loyally with the Russians. He went over the arguments for this again and again. Clearly, he was unhappy. I wanted to tell him that I did not feel that he or any other educated man or woman ought to refuse to work for the government, at a time when two generations of administrators and teachers had been wiped out by firing-squad and concentration camp. But it would, I saw, be entirely the wrong answer. He was desperately anxious to justify his position as a *rallié*—but he had to do it as though no justification were needed. I did not think it was. But then I was not a Polish landowner who had taught himself to talk with conviction about kulaks and the need to eliminate them.

'You will explain, please, in London—you are a writer, you must know many people—that in a totally ruined country one must work with the tools at hand, whatever they are.'

'Of course,' I said.

Speaking English was an effort for him: he kept on dropping into French in the middle of sentences. 'We cannot be sorry for les possédants, ils sont les survivants *inutiles*.' He passed his hand slowly over his face. 'You know, I did not expect to return from Buchenwald. Why did I? Ah, c'est que mes enfants ont beaucoup prié pour moi.'

One afternoon a young professor, and his very young wife, came from Lódź to see us. Both had been for some time in prison camps. I took the young woman to my bedroom, to give her a spare jersey I had. Sitting on the edge of the bed, she touched it with her fingers, gently, as if it were alive. She was very shabby and very pale.

'May I ask questions?' I said.

'Please.'

'Not for myself... How difficult is it to live here?'

She shrugged her thin shoulders. 'Few of us have more than the clothes we stand up in, everything, except bread and potatoes, is very dear—no family can live on the wages or salary of any ordinary person. If there are two or three in the family able to work, or if they have something to sell, or—' she moved her fingers, a gesture of distaste or mockery—'they speculate. Others who are in government service take bribes, there are high-ups who steal boldly—do I mean boldly?'

'And the Russians?'

'They control the police. What more do they need? People disappear. Like in the sea or a nightmare... As for the rest—what could you expect, with masses of soldiers moving through the country? I can't be shocked when they mishandle Germans—the sufferings of a German seem irrelevant—but they rob and rape decent Polish women. Only this morning the shop we use was looted by Russians with guns. But why are we talking of these things? Others are more serious. It is more serious that the line between old and young scholars has been interrupted. It is serious that so many of our libraries are ash. Imagine setting fire deliberately to a great library! Has there been anything like it since the great library in Alexandria was burned? And that was an accident.' She smiled. 'What is *not* serious is to have lost everything you had. It is not a bad feeling.'

'I asked about conditions because a friend in London—Maria Kuncewiczowa——'

'I had one of her books, until I was arrested.'

'She is hoping I can advise her about coming back.'

She laughed. 'It's still true that Poland is a land for heroes or swine. Those who want to fight should come back. No one else.'

'I have messages for a writer called Nalkowska. Is she alive?'

'Very much so.' She laughed again, shortly. 'She has become a communist deputy. Don't think I disapprove of writers who work for the government. A great many do, who are not communists. She is. She is very ambitious.'

'You mean—a writer who wants to be a success and safe must be a communist?'

She smiled. 'Now I will ask a question. I have been told—is it true?—that Dresden has been destroyed. I went there with my father when I was twelve. I loved it very much.'

'Almost completely destroyed. Somewhere I read that when the Russians went in they made stacks of dead bodies in the market-place and turned flame-throwers on them.'

'I am sorry about Dresden.' She hesitated. 'But only a little sorry.'

We were invited to tea—that is, coffee, cakes, and nauseatingly sweet thick marsala—by the President. Bierut. He was excessively polite. I had seen eyes like his—quick, sly, greasy, hard—in the faces of Yorkshire business men, but his were without humour. Elongating thin lips, he said, 'Note this, my friends. I want all Poles to return. But they must be Poles who look to the new Poland.'

No, I can't advise Maria to return, I thought.

Later, talking to our Ambassador in his room in the Polonia, I said that Bierut was a thug if ever I saw one.

'I can show you someone far tougher,' he said, smiling, 'the head police-man, the Minister of Public Security, Radkiewiecz. I like these people, they are brave and in a hell of a mess and working like heroes, and I'm inclined to think that the proportion of thugs in the administration is surprisingly low.'

There is a face moulded by hard work, patience, poverty, which has always been and still in some sense is *the* human face, the one I cannot look at without a pang of grief and rage. In Poland it was the haggard unutterably patient face of the keeper in what remained of a zoo outside Cracow. He was shivering a little in his worn-out jacket. During the war, he had listened to the broadcasts from London.

'You promised to send us so many things,' he said quietly, with a poor smile, 'but nothing has come.'

He refused money, pushing the hand offering it gently away.

No doubt he had expected too much of England.

The formidable difficulties involved in transporting anything, a visitor or a truck of food, would have been farcical if it had not been so nearly a tragedy. We had not fully understood this when W—— said he had arranged for two cars to take us to Cracow, and he was disappointed that we did not recognize a miracle when we saw it. They were wretched cars, but no car would have lasted on roads as dilapidated as the road between Warsaw and Cracow.

We left shortly before twelve and reached Radom at two o'clock, to find ourselves involved in a state funeral of people killed when seven hundred 'men from the woods' attacked the little town and broke open the jail to free their friends. Every shop and eating-place was closed, but a boy led us deviously through alleys to the back door of a shuttered house: it seemed to be the local night-club, a bare room with jazz instruments leaning against a wall, and four large playing-cards as decoration. We sat here a long time, and at last were brought an admirable lunch: coarse potato soup with sprigs of fennel, escalopes, vodka.

We drove on, slowly, hour after hour, jerking violently out of deep ruts and over improvised bridges, across a country of flat planes, the lines falling over one another like folds in an endless linen sheet. Here and there in the all but treeless fields, a cluster of stone chimneys marked the place where a wooden village had been burned down by the retreating Germans: when they had time to spare for it, they killed.

Before long we became stupefied. It grew dark, and the car I was in had a burst tyre. We were starting again after the repair, when the car ahead turned back in search of us, and broke an axle in one of the prodigious ruts. Too exhausted to behave well, we abandoned it, promising to send our car back from Cracow, and went on, leaving Slonimski, the two young women, and another Pole, to be murdered by brigands.

It was ten o'clock when we reached Cracow. A deputation of writers had been waiting for us in the hotel since five, most of them had left, but a young man, a poet, called Milosz, a couple of young women, and a shabby old gentleman who had been Bernard Shaw's translator, were still there. I went to my bedroom, changed, and came down to find them still talking in the hall. At last, all went except Milosz, and we invited him to dine with us. I had found out about him from one of the young women. As they had, he had escaped from Warsaw after the defeat of the Rising: during the Occupation, when to be caught with an English book cost either a concentration camp or a quicker death in one of the bi-weekly executions, he taught himself English to be able to read our poets, and translated *The Waste Land*, finishing it, with a fine sense of justice, the day the Rising started. Young, he seemed solidly self-possessed and very attractive in spite of it, with a pale rather broad face and a mouth flattened like Pushkin's, except that his was colourless and he had an engaging smile. At the table, I was too far from him to hear what he said in his slow English. Suddenly, raising his voice, he said with calm savagery, 'No. People in Cracow have not suffered enough. Warsaw...'

At this moment, a robust middle-aged woman walked across the room from the door, with terrific energy, and seated herself in the chair next to mine.

'I expected you all hours ago,' she said. 'I am staying here, I am Nalkowska.'

I told her my name, and she professed, with a fine smile, to have read two of my novels. Then I gave her Maria's messages: she had sent a great many, more than to any other of her friends, and a question: Did Nalkowska's sister know that her husband had been shot dead on the Spanish frontier, trying to reach England?

'She doesn't know. I knew, I was told a year ago, but why tell her? She is dying herself, let her die thinking he may return tomorrow. What does it matter? She is as good as dead. Tell me, please, is Aldous Huxley alive? And Virginia Woolf?'

I answered her questions, and began talking again about Maria. She listened in silence; I got, very strongly, the impression that she was no longer Maria's friend, and reflected, for the second time, that I could not let Maria come back. Finally, tapping my hand, she said genially, 'You are tired, my dear friend. Tomorrow I have questions to ask you—not about the Poles in London, I am not going to waste this chance of talking to an English writer by discussing fools. Let me see you often, often, but for serious talk.'

I was tired to death, but I could not go to bed without knowing that Antoni and the others were safe. It was after midnight when they turned up, exhausted, and very cool about our desertion.

After Warsaw, Cracow was curiously a little unreal. Untouched, since the Russians got there in time, it was the place where the lines of past and future crossed to form a fragile present, palpitating with energy, almost violent, below a dull provincial surface. It was full of writers, painters, musicians, many of them survivors from Warsaw, working feverishly—with every material condition against them, without books, with one dress, one suit of clothes, one pair of thin shoes, living in one room—and infinitely more alive than the English writers. Are five years of a brutal Occupation less tiring than five of a grinding war? They had a raging hunger for books—'Haven't you brought anything with you? Didn't you bring even one?' I began to feel that I was denying a crust to the starving.

England has no Minister of Culture: it is in the highest degree unlikely that in a time of national breakdown its government would give a moment's thought to the lives of writers—even if half of them had been killed, and the survivors were penniless and homeless. I was astonished and humiliated to discover that a Polish writer who had written two books, or translated four, or whose work was vouched for by the Writers' Association (under its non-communist president), was being given enough to keep him alive and a roof over his head. A modest pleasant house in Cracow, the Writers' Club, housed some twenty writers, married and unmarried. After five minutes there, I knew what Captain Cook would have felt if instead of landing among savages he had found himself walking into a meeting of the French Academy, with nothing to offer it but a handful of beads.

Deprived, for six years, of even their own classics, these survivors were desperately eager to know what the scholars and writers of other countries had been about during the years when Poland was a vast concentration camp, and no voice from outside reached them—'except the wireless—not often worth what you risked on it,' Milosz said, smiling, 'your life.' Their curiosity might have been touching: in fact it was devilishly searching and informed—and a great deal wider than their questions about living writers implied. The small four-page journal they gave me—paper for printing was scarcer than gold— had translations not only from *The Waste Land* but from Crabbe and Cowper.

'Please tell me about T. S. Eliot,' Milosz said, and went on to talk himself, with cold impetuosity and vehemence, making one English word do the work of ten.

I had a fantastic sense not so much of unreality as of living in a different reality. A partly mediaeval city, a wasted country, its capital in ruins, its people awaiting the winter with dread, and I was listening to a poet talking, with intelligence and keen enjoyment, about another. It might be any moment in the past, in an interval between two barbarian invasions.

He was saying that he respected Eliot as a great poet, and the one poet of our time who fused two realities, the sensuous and the meta-physical— which may be what a modern poet must do if he is to tell even part of the truth about an age which contains Picasso, Proust, and the Auschwitz gas chambers. Not that he had any impulse to imitate Eliot. On the contrary. He believed that there is something new to be said by Polish writers—not simply because they have an immediate knowledge of hell, but because when you must, out of a past which is almost purely tragic, create a future reached across a vast graveyard, you must find a new way of saying the new thing. Or give up.

Abruptly, he said, 'Tell me—is there the slightest hope that your country and America will go on taking an interest in us?'

'I don't know. Why not?'

He smiled with extreme delicacy and extreme bitterness. 'All this fuss you are making about the Germans we have turned out of the new provinces to make room for our own peasants who have been chased out by the Russians! They have been kicked and robbed in the trains, they are going to starve in Germany. I must tell you that what looks to you like an innocent farmer looks to us like the face and hands of a murderer. You have just been trying four of my fellow-countrymen; they have been slave-workers in Germany for more than five years, and they robbed and killed a German family. Terrible. They have become beasts. And now, after six years of the life that changed them from human beings into wild animals, you are going to execute them— because they killed one or two German civilians. I don't understand your people. You have hearts, yes, but do you think with them?'

Stammering, I said, 'If there is no such thing as justice, what happened here is irrelevant.'

He smiled with the same fine bitterness.

'Since the last years I ceased to be interested in abstract justice. I can't accept as justice a verdict which kills Poles for killing Germans. That's all.'

The room was crowded, men and women, most of them young, talking with a serious gaiety—or gay seriousness. Since one cannot remember everybody I had decided to remember Milosz. But two other people forced themselves into my memory.

A young man, younger than Milosz, very lively, with the eyes of a mischievous girl. He was showing off, but it was impossible not to like him and want him to go on bounding and bouncing like a young hare.

'Why talk about what's over?' he said to me. 'All I want to know about the English is how soon they are going to stop the Russians from swallowing us. We're more than half way down their throats already.'

It was only when he flung his arms up that I saw he had no shirt under his jacket: like the others he was meticulously neat: since they were really poor, really on the edge of the abyss, they had no impulse to dress loutishly.

He laughed at my politic answer. 'You wait, Mrs Storm, we are going to fight them.'

'Don't expect us to help you,' I said.

Taken aback, he rallied at once. 'I knew you'd say that! But in the end you'll be forced to fight—you always are. When the tension between East and West splits right open...' He laughed again. 'The Russians are jealous of us and despise us—exactly what the Germans feel about the French. It's very interesting. Don't you think so? They're a dull people, any illiterate Polish peasant has more irony in his little finger than a thousand pages of Tolstoy. You wait! Nobody and nothing can regiment Poles...'

Eugenia K——, a young woman, a delicate creature, with clear fine features. She had spent five years in Ravensbrück. Like other survivors of the camps whom I met, she had curiously withdrawn eyes. How had anyone so frail been able to live? She said calmly, 'Oh, in Ravensbrück I became a Christian, because I saw that only God could help... You know, I don't like to hear people talk of punishment; what was done in Ravensbrück can't be punished, you can only forgive such cruelty.'

Thinking of Kowalski's half-mad secretary, I said, 'I know you are right, but I don't know that I could make myself feel as you do. After all, you were defenceless, you couldn't have done the Germans any harm, you weren't fighting them—any more than were the millions of helpless men, women, children, they killed as they might have killed vermin.'

'Don't ask me to defend what I feel,' she said, smiling. 'I can't, it is what I am.'

When we were leaving I looked over my shoulder at the still crowded room, seeing the lively shabby figures, movements startling in their energy, and everywhere, at the ends of eyelids, on young women's colourless lips, the print of smiles, as if from a distance. What when the Russians close in? What will happen to all this new energy?...

That evening we were taken to the ballet—the Ballet Parnella. Superb vitality, superb clowning. I was madly happy. I had not watched anything like it since Diaghilev's dancers. That was in a year when, the young dead of the first war having retreated to their place, it seemed that all of us who were left had only a future.

The first exhibition of paintings made during the war had just opened. There had been one earlier exhibition—the work of the thirty painters killed by the Germans. Among the living, one, Jonasz Stern, might have put his work in both shows. He was taken for one of the public executions, stripped, and lined up; still living, he fell under the bodies of the others, and after dark crept out, naked, and escaped. He had been dead and he lived—to paint these smiling landscapes. It seems that when you are living in hell you don't paint it: none of these paintings had a trace of the violence, the disintegration of all values, which surrounded the artists while they were working on them. Another curious thing: the experimental work was being done by the older painters, the young men and women had returned to an equilibrium, a passionate attention to sensuous forms, which might belong to a moment of ease and stability, not to the chaos they were living in.

Perhaps it was not strange. It is perhaps when you have too little other experience to set against the experience of cruelty and violence, that you keep the simplicity and humility to paint appearances. Or you paint them as a defence against one face of the reality behind them.

Looking at a plaster statue, about a foot in height, of a young woman, tears came into my eyes. The face had a purity and fineness I had begun to look for in the faces of Polish women, and, as well, a serenity the very reverse of resignation or passivity. The sculptor, Pujet, looked like a village baker, in thin worn-out clothes covered with plaster from the mould he had been working on. I asked him if I could buy his statue and send the money from

England. He asked twenty-five pounds for it, and I gave him the two I had in my pocket, all that was left of the little I had brought.

A young woman I took to be the original of my statue was standing near it. It turned out that she was a slightly older sister, and after I had talked to her for a few minutes Pujet told me a story about her. During the Occupation she had thirty children in her house, and clandestine papers passing through her hands. One evening, an unexpected raid by a German officer caught her with some of these in a bureau... 'Tell the rest yourself,' he said.

'They made a very thorough search, and when they reached my room I waited for the moment when they would find the papers, and either send me to Oświęcim or—more likely—shoot me there and then, to save themselves trouble. The walls in this room were covered by my husband's paintings, and the officer was interested by them. He examined them all carefully, one after another, then said: This place is all right, nothing here—and went out, without touching the bureau.'

'The first time your husband's paintings were worth something,' Pujet said.

The next morning, I expected Maria's sister-in-law. When I was waiting for her in the hall, an elderly woman, Julia Rylska—I can use her name, since she cannot still be alive—who had been a translator of plays, came to ask me to send her new ones from England, and burst into tears. Madame S. arrived, and I asked Rylska to forgive me. Drying her tears, she said decisively, 'I shall wait.'

I hurried Madame S. to my bedroom, less fetid than the Polonia but almost as unpleasant, and gave her Maria's messages and gifts, and a thousand of the eighteen hundred zlotys the Polish government had given each of us as pocket-money, telling her it came from Maria—as it would have done if I had been less cautious.

She was telling me, for Maria, about her life, she worked in some sort of kitchen, and about her son. Because he had been in the Home Army, he was still in some danger, but refused to leave Poland. 'He says it is everyone's duty to stay here now.'

'And Maria?' I said. 'Am I to tell her that it is her duty to return?'

'No,' she cried, 'no, no. There are too many arrests, tell her not to come now, tell her to wait——'

Someone knocked, and she looked at me in alarm, but it was only Rylska to say that she would wait in the corridor until I could see her. Vexed, I shut the door on her, but after a few minutes Madame S. had to hurry away to her kitchen, and the other woman came in, and stayed an hour, talking and crying noisily. She was the only woman I saw in tears the whole time I was in Poland, and the only one who complained. Heaven knows she had plenty to complain about and weep for, but she was a little unpleasant. She talked about the savagery of the Russians and the horror of being occupied by them—'We endured so long, we suffered so much, and now this.' And then, without a pause, she began, dry-eyed, to talk about Jews. 'We can't have them back here, you don't know them, you have never seen a child's, a Christian child's, arm covered with cuts where Jews had drawn off blood for their abominable rites...'

I can do nothing about it, I thought, it is a disease. To distract her, I made her write a list of English dramatists whose plays she wanted, and promised to send them. (I sent several but did not hear that she got them.)

When at last I was rid of her, and went downstairs, I found Milosz waiting, with a younger man, almost a boy, a journalist, shockingly thin, stick-like arms and legs, a face restless with intelligence and curiosity. I went with them to a café, where I drank three glasses of vodka quickly, to loosen my tongue. The two of them put me through a merciless examination in the English writers of the 'thirties, about whom they knew fully as much as I did.

'What happened in the last months before the war?' Milosz said. 'Did any of them become catastrophic? How did the younger writers wait for the war? Didn't they drop their emotional Leftism? I know Auden went away—was he afraid? Angry?'

Harried by questions, I disentangled for them the threads of the 'thirties, the thread of weak lamentation, the strong thread of Hopkins, the pseudo-Marxism, the surrealism. 'The Spanish war persuaded most writers that civilization can't any longer be defended in private—it cost the lives of three good English writers and spoiled tempers as well as closing the frontier between Left and Right.'

'Nothing like a war for killing off writers,' the boy said, with the sharpest of smiles. 'Now tell me the names of your new poets, all of them. I suppose they are absolutely different from pre-war.'

I could think of four names, and gave them to him. 'We, too, had a hard war,' I said, 'and two of the poets we expected most from were killed.

Something is stirring in English writing, possibly a new humanism, possibly—I don't know—a rejection of all that my generation means by humanism. It's too soon to say much.'

Scowling, Milosz said, 'But surely there is already a revolt of critics and writers against all that childish Marxism? What are the *new* writers doing? Isn't there a revolution?'

'No revolution of any sort,' I said, 'yet.'

They were disappointed. Milosz said warmly, 'Well, we shall wait a little. I hope that you in England will try to understand us, and that you won't abandon us again, as you always did in the past.'

'I forgot to tell you,' I said, 'that two or three of our young novelists were very much influenced by Kafka.'

To my great surprise, they burst out laughing. 'You don't mean it! Any Polish writer who imitated Kafka now would be *sifflé* by the public and crushed by the critics.'

Thinking about this afterwards, I supposed that the reality of terror, violence, unmotivated cruelty, had blotted out Kafka's prevision of it, or made it seem childish to these survivors...

At the theatre that evening I was reminded that the future is not always a young poet; it is sometimes the smiling worn-out face of an old professor, the single survivor of more than a hundred and thirty teachers of Cracow University arrested and sent to a concentration camp. He spoke to me after the performance.

'I shall show you my dear possession,' he said gently.

Fumbling in his pocket, he took out a membership card of the International P.E.N.

Halfway through the evening, the director made a short speech in which he said that a delegation from England was in the theatre: the audience rose, shouting and applauding, and we stood up and bowed, feeling ashamed, and forgiven for our shortcomings and our failure to send them the help they needed. This world of simply human warmth that exists, a minute kernel, inside the world of politicians, intriguers, the power-hungry, the indifferent, the cruel, is what justifies our existence on earth—if anything can.

I was fascinated by a Russian officer sitting in the row in front of ours—a Georgian, someone said. He was young, slender, not tall, with a dark face, very narrow and pointed, and black gleaming eyes, so black, so filled by a brilliant restless light that they seemed to be enjoying a life of their own in his face. He moved brusquely and gracefully; he was like a whip, no, like a young powerful animal. I noticed his hands; they were very small, white, and quick-moving and, like his eyes, seemed alive with their own impersonal energy.

On the way home, shots were fired in the road we were about to cross. The few people near us lay down, and we stood like idiots, not knowing what to do. A Polish officer came up and helped us over some barbed wire, out of the direct line of fire. Two Russian soldiers, he said, had robbed a woman of her money and coat, and to stop them the police were shooting over their heads. We walked on, keeping to the side.

Towards midnight, over a long drawn-out dinner, Antoni Slonimski talked to me with a frankness I was not expecting. I had been half asleep, but a sense that he was unhappy and disappointed roused me to listen closely. I felt for him the kind of love one can feel for music or a landscape, an emotion between gentle pleasure in looking at him, at his clear tranquil worn-down features, and affection, none the less deep for being sexless.

'You are seeing the heroic side of this country,' he said. 'I see it, of course, but I see other things which are not heroic... The survival of anti-semitism... an elderly Jewish baker... he had returned from Germany only the night before, and he was leaving again at once. No one expected him to come back, and a Pole had taken over his house and shop. It was dark when he arrived. He knocked, and stood knocking for a long time, an hour; at last the door opened a few inches, a hand came through it holding a knife, and was drawn back and the door bolted again. He understood what it meant... Few people's characters are improved by being forced to live for years in fear and slavery, and I'm not shocked by the demoralization—remnants of the parti-san army hanging out in the woods and robbing peasants, decent men and women living by what they call speculation, young thugs going through the train-loads of Germans robbing and raping. One day killing, lying, stealing, is heroic, the next it is crime... the human tragedy of boys who have lived a hunted underground life as animals so long that they can't grow into men, not even into speculators... The new government is doing many good things. In spite of the censorship and the Russian secret police, and raping and looting by Russian soldiers—who will leave when they don't need to keep a line of communication with Germany... I am sorry, a little, for the old ladies living in one room full of the furniture they managed to save when they were turned out of their estates, but they have outstayed their welcome in history...'

He hesitated, looking at me with a smile of grief, and said, 'I should have known what to expect.'

'You won't stay here,' I said.

'No.' He added after a moment, 'Not yet.'

When he did come back to live, years later, it was at a time of less freedom and greater danger for writers than in the undisciplined Poland of 1945. He behaved then with a calm courage which, a young Polish writer told me in France in 1959, 'was to all of us young an immovable rock and a, what do you say? a trumpet-call.'

Anything less like a trumpet than my dear Antoni's voice...

Writing this reminds me that after less than four hours' sleep that night I woke up and heard, very faintly, the *hejnal*, the trumpet-call from the tower of the thirteenth century church in the market-place, broken off before the last note—it commemorates some heroic act, I forget what. For a few moments I did not realize where I was, and I was swept back across Europe and the North Sea, and half a lifetime, to hear, as faintly, the distant bugle that ravished my soul every July morning in my ninth year, the year when a brigade of soldiers was encamped outside Whitby...

A handful of young men and women were trying to rebuild the film world from nothing, with almost no equipment. In a bare room they showed us an almost unendurable film of Auschwitz and Majdanek, composed from photographs: the monstrous piles of shoes, spectacles, false teeth, clothes, women's flimsy shoes, children's, even baby shoes, stripped from their wearers before they were suffocated, methodically sorted, and stacked: a dead baby lying on the edge of a pile of adult bodies, four children folded together still feebly alive and another tottering past without glancing at them. Least bearable of all, the twin children walking away, helped by a nurse: these were kept for a time when the others were gassed, because one of the pair can be used as a control in experiments carried out on the other.

At the end, as it might have been the moment when, turning his back on hell, Dante saw the stars, they showed an exquisite short picture of children's living hands.

Was it here or in Warsaw that I looked, forcing myself to look, at photographs the Germans themselves had taken? A street execution: the first line of naked dead lying against the wall, the second standing in front of it, a terrified boy, his face contorted with grief and fear, hands knotted together on his breast, an older man holding both hands queerly and stiffly away from him, as if to keep the bullets from entering his poor body, three younger men, expressionless. In another of these photographs a boy, his face beaten black, was surrounded by smiling young German soldiers, delighted with their false negro. A young woman being searched in the street, a soldier stretching the elastic of her knickers to look down them.

The passion of the Germans for recording their ugliest gestures is extraordinary: it foreshadows the impulse of a few writers of the 'sixties to write wilfully disgusting novels in which normal human acts are made filthy by language and tone. They appeal to readers who are amused by midgets and foetuses in bottles.

It is a sort of blasphemy, a religious spitting on the human body and mind—and as deadly dull as any other monomania...

If all I saw of Poland at that time had been the musicians' house in Cracow, it would have been worth the voyage. The only guests, we sat in an upper room and heard a famous singer, Aniela Szleminska, old now, but an exquisitely clear true voice, too strong for the small room, and then a violinist, Uminska, of unforced charm and power. To see Uminska standing at the end of a bare room, in her thin shabby dress and poor shoes, playing without a score, behind her the frightful nothing, the crack in the ground which had swallowed up friends, possessions, the past of her own life, convinced me that short of a nuclear war Europe cannot die; or, if it dies, will have seeded into the future too richly to be lost.

They talked with the energy, simplicity, gaiety, we now expected of these survivors.

'When I got out of Warsaw I was quite naked under this suit. I lost all my music, all. I can practise now, but without music it is a little difficult...' 'Forgive me, this is my only dress. I lost everything in Warsaw...' 'You know that all but a little of our music was burned. We've begun printing again—so far, just six scores. But look, don't you think they're well done? Of course, the paper isn't good...'

'My husband and two of my sons were shot. The third—since 1940 I don't know...'

'They weren't all brutes. I have a friend who was living, with her children, in a village, there had been trouble with partisans, and the Germans began murdering everyone: an officer came into the house and she opened the door of the living-room, pulling it on herself—that, you know, was always the thing to do, in case they came in firing. He was a middle-aged man, and seemed decent, and she begged him to stop the murders. He asked: Who is doing it? S.S. or Wehrmacht? She told him: Wehrmacht. He passed his hand over his face, and said: We used to be civilized...'

'This week I had the most superb luck. I made an expedition to look at a cottage my family had near Zakopane, it had been looted, of course, but they'd overlooked one box, I opened it and it was full of linen sheets. Five! Think of it! I spent yesterday selling them...'

Despair is not decent. Like the novel of disgust, it is the twitch of a weak nerve.

A people which has the energy to turn from the agony of its past, to accept that it has lost everything, and to look with interest at the future, makes despair irrelevant...

We were leaving Cracow after an early breakfast, and at two in the morning I was still packing, in a stupor of fatigue. There had been an official dinner-party, I remember nothing about it except a fierce argument afterwards with Milosz and a young officer.

'What the English don't understand is the anger we feel when you talk about saving Germany for Europe. Why are you saving them? So that they can start again? What use is it for us to build up our houses and our writing if every ten or twenty years they are to be destroyed?'

'I dislike Russians,' the soldier said quietly, 'but I don't hate them as I hate Germans, with my bones and nerves.'

'Why should you think I don't understand it?' I said. 'And why can't you understand that Europe must be pacified? It's the house we all have to live in.'

'Yes,' he retorted, 'and you English have the most comfortable room in it, while we live in an abominably draughty corridor.'

'The *va-et-vient* in our corridor is terrible,' Milosz said drily. 'You English can afford to make the most terrible mistakes, Singapore, Tobruk, Munich and the rest, and survive, but we have only to make one, like the Rising, and we pay terribly, all.' He smiled. 'And for your mistakes, too!'

'Was the Rising a mistake?' I asked.

'An abysmal idiocy,' the young officer said contemptuously, 'a crime. To fight in an overcrowded city, with a large German army concentrated on it. The Russians, who are not fools, let the Rising destroy itself—and three hundred thousand civilians. To play politics with people's lives!'

What else are they played with—at any time?...

Pujet had promised to deliver his statue at the hotel; he turned up with it as we were leaving: it was not packed and I realized that I should have to nurse it from now on, until I got it to England.

Since then I have wondered with a little anxiety whether he ever got the rest of the money I sent from London, entrusting it to a Pole who was going back...

Half way between Cracow and Warsaw, our car broke down completely. After we had been sitting by the side of the road for two hours, a lorry stopped: it was carrying a few Russian soldiers in dirty shabby uniforms and two officers: Antoni, who spoke Russian, talked to them, and they roped the car to the lorry and towed us into Radom, and there piled us and our baggage into the lorry, the men outside in the open, and me in the closed cab, wedged between the Soviet captain, who was driving, and the major. They were both extremely hard-bodied and very broad, and smelled strongly of a stable: I might have been sharing a stall with two powerful good-tempered horses, jostled first by one, then by the other. Neither of them could keep still, and after a time I felt I was sitting too near a menacing current of energy, dangerous if it got loose, and not likely to respond to any rational appeal. A few miles out of Radom a wheel collapsed, and the soldiers and the captain jumped down to change it: the first spare wheel they tried gave them trouble, they threw it into the middle of the road, and the officer and two men stamped on it, shouting with laughter, until they had reduced it to scrap iron and shreds of rubber. It struck me that they would kill a man or woman with the same childish impatience; they might have been a separate species of human being with its own impulses and habits.

It was ten o'clock when we reached Warsaw, and midnight before a room was found for me. I spent the time writing down the heads of a broadcast for next day, and got up early to finish it.

In the newly-built transmitting station, Polish and Russian technicians were working together with noticeable ease, like friendly schoolboys. A world run by technicians, in love with their complicated machines, might be less human and more peaceful than the one statesmen cannot keep going without killing off every year, by war, hunger, political murders, an undue proportion of its inhabitants.

The Pole in charge of my broadcast was very young, with a calm handsome face, and completely bald. Caught after two years of underground work, and sent to Auschwitz, he came out barely alive—'and like this,' he said, smiling, touching his smooth crane. 'Curious, don't you think?'

He was friendly, very gay, and moved about the room as though sitting still were too boring an effort.

'You liked Cracow? Of course—it is full of nice people with nothing to do but write. The future is being put together here, by those of us who live with it. It's difficult, of course, the days are too short, but, believe me, we're not wasting our time... The worst of the Occupation wasn't the deaths or the arrests, it was the sense of time wasted—and the fear, the sitting drinking beer in a room and hearing that a round-up is going on in another street, and the waiting, the fear and the fear and the fear.'

He was touching one shoulder against the wall behind him: suddenly he leaned against it like a man on the point of fainting; the gaiety and energy of his face were wiped off it, he closed his eyes; for a second his face was as coldly empty as if he were dead. He came to life again at once, and looked at me with the same smiling vigour.

'We are all obsessed, imprisoned in the house of our memories. When you have blown out a man's brains, even an S.S., and when you have learned to lie, rob, kill, as a terrorist kills, how do you stop? Where is the frontier? Many of my friends have remained bandits even though they are living normally.'

He smiled again, politely. 'As a writer you must find us—what shall I say?—strange animals.'

At this moment it struck me that perhaps the only habit we need to acquire, and teach our children, is the habit of loss. Then, if civilization collapses, the survivors may be able to begin again without resentment or self-pity.

To my surprise, I was being paid a fee for my broadcast, I forget how much: I gave him the address in Cracow of Maria's sister-in-law, and he promised to send it to her. I ought to have sent it to Pujet, but pounds would mean more to him.

Driving back to the Polonia after dark, the lights of the car stroking the ruins, I had a moment of giddiness: starting here, the tangle of snapped threads stretched across Europe—women from murdered villages searching for the child last seen stumbling off in the screaming darkness, wives who had given up expecting a letter from the husband in a foreign army, or his return from a camp. In 1945, Europe was a hell of memory.

I had over forty letters in my bag, addressed to men who might be alive, but certainly were not living at the address on the envelope—care of a regiment which no longer existed. I was clumsy enough to tell our Ambassador I had them. His seemingly effortless friendliness and ease of the highly trained diplomat became very slightly mocking.

'Don't,' he said, smiling, 'tell me about them. If they get you into trouble we'll do anything we can, but it's on your head.'

At the airfield, no one took any interest in my suitcase, or in my statue.

It was an uncomfortable flight. I tried to clear my mind of its illusion that it could read the future. Unless I had seen and listened to them, I could not have conceived that men and women who had suffered atrociously could do better than exist. These people were not simply existing, hanging on blindly, they were living, on the other side of despair, with passion, some at least of them with joy. In totally ruined Warsaw, the sense of life and light was infinitely sharper than in London.

The joke about human beings is that they can survive anything except the thermo-nuclear death of the planet—that is, anything except their own intellect and curiosity. Their resilience is such that they can even endure what they do to each other.

For a few minutes I felt sure of it, as I am sure of nothing else...

It was too late when we left Warsaw to reach London the same day. When we landed at Berlin the airfield commandant groaned, and said, 'Oh, my God, I was praying there wouldn't be a woman on board.'

The sheets on the bed he found for me were very dirty, and the bed itself harder than the one in the Polonia, but I slept soundly.

## CHAPTER 2

I HAD NO WISH to revisit a Prague last seen in June 1938, in its triumphant self-confidence before Munich, and I dreaded the meeting with Jiřina Tůmová and did not want to see the marks made on her by her husband's atrocious death. But I could not decently refuse to go.

Staring, from the embankment, at the massive self-assurance of Hradčany stretched out on its hill-top in the November sunlight, and at the river running full and very fast below undamaged bridges, I thought that the invader had left no marks on the city. Here, if nowhere else on this side of Europe, the roots were unharmed.

It did not seem possible.

P——, the amiable young Foreign Office clerk who met me at the airfield, said, 'Mrs Tůmová met all three planes last week. Today we didn't dare tell her you were expected.'

'I came in the first possible plane—last week's were full.'

'I know. We manage things badly.'

Not badly. With strict care for justice. In Czechoslovakia the privileged persons were a thin layer of Ministers and officials; everywhere outside and below it, an equality of discomfort and scarcity. My room at the Alcron was luxurious, and I ate atrociously, meagre unappetizing dinners, and at breakfast a cup of ersatz coffee, bitter and nauseating, without milk or sugar, and two slices of hard dry black bread. At the next table an American sergeant unwrapped package after package containing everything he needed to endure life: two eggs, slices of white bread, a tin of real coffee, butter, ham. The Czechs drinking a thin sour liquid and chewing their dry bread at the other tables eyed him without surprise, even with irony. To be eating only what they ate gave me a good conceit of myself.

At first glance I thought, scurvily thankful, that Jiřina had not altered: her profile had kept its strict purity, and her slight body, slighter than ever, its latent energy of a cord. After a few minutes, I saw the changes, a deep fold at the ends of her eyes, and a strangely fixed serenity drawn over them like a bandage. When she closed them her face had a deathly immobility and absence.

She had made a long list of people and things I ought to see—it did not include the one thing I knew I must look at, the internment camps into which German civilians had been pushed until they could be tried and deported—and left no time for the pleasure of being alone in the foreign streets. Also I felt that she might be making a duty of me, and this disturbed me.

It was not true.

'I'm not going to squander this miracle by talking about the past,' she said calmly. 'First because in Prague we are only thinking about the future. And my own past is entirely in a little dust, which I won't show you—not because I want to shut you out, my darling, but it is too narrow, too cold, without room for friendship and the perfect happiness I feel today. I have been praying for this since June. When I heard you had gone to Poland I was very angry.' She lifted small worn hands. 'You see these? I beat on the Minister's table with them. Poor man, I alarmed him, and it was not his fault.'

In the first four or five days I saw more than a score of her closest friends, older writers, actresses (she had been an actress), the young doctor who went into Terezín some hours before the German guards left, overworked professors at the university, women working for the government and in industry. I made, at once, a mortifying discovery. In seven years the shock of Munich had lost none of its bitterness. All these friendly serious men and women, only one of them a communist, admired England, read English books, spoke English, and trusted us as little as they trusted any other rotten plank. As most Poles did, they knew they had to be on terms with the Russians: unlike the Poles, they spoke of their 'Slav brothers'—who had not betrayed them and never would.

They could not help their mistrust of us; it broke through a warmth and politeness which were quite genuine—at arm's length.

It was the more mortifying that I felt deeply at ease with these energetic unsentimental warm-blooded Czech women, Jiřina's friends. They lacked the quickness and grace of Polish women, so that it was some time before I admitted to myself that they sprang from the same tough root thrust deeply into ground soaked in violence: they were hard in the same way, without a trace of aggressiveness; the lines under their eyes conveyed, with less lightness, the same intention to live without pitying themselves. The vivid intelligent creature designing fabrics for export, Josef Capek's widow searching for her husband's paintings, singers rehearsing in icy rooms, young students making up for the lost years, old tired illfed writers, all talked continually about the future.

That, when it came, it was not the one they expected, bred stoicism, not indifference—and no kindness for stragglers.

When I think about the Resistance in the occupied countries, I wonder uneasily whether I should have had the courage to take part. Here as in France the temptation not to resist had been very strong—less, I think, out of fear or cupidity than from a Czech habit of accepting what is inevitable *for the time being*, and making shrewd use of it. They are an eminently reasonable people, and don't lightly throw away a happiness at hand. I was told, and believed, that women kept themselves more aloof from the occupiers, more intractable, than men, who were after all responsible for the day-to-day running of the country.

It is a question less of dialectics than of habit and very long usage.

If some catastrophe should overtake Russia, leaving it without the means to force other peoples to be happy according to rules laid down in Moscow, I would not give much for the myth of Slav brotherhood.

When I had been less than a week in Prague I was faced with one of those problems in which two and two do not make four. The government, then turning its benevolent face to intellectuals, had handed over a castle, Dobříš, to the Writers' Syndicate. After I had accepted their invitation to lunch I was told, privately, that Dobříš had belonged to one of the Czech-Austrian aristocratic families; its expropriated owner was in an internment camp, accused of collaborating. The accusation might not be true—remembering squalid stories of denunciations in France, I felt uncertain—and John Lehmann, staying in Prague with a friend, had refused, on principle, to go to Dobříš.

He was certainly right, yet I could not convince myself that even the most honourable scruples made it right to deprive half-fed Czech writers of what a foreign guest meant to them: a tolerable meal and permission to buy wine and slivovitz for his entertainment. They called for me at the Alcron, eight young men and women, none of them known to me, huddled at one end of a large bus: it was a bitter day, with an air out of Siberia, the bus had no springs and as many icy draughts as the cave of the winds; we shivered and rattled out of the city, stopping at a wine store to present our licence and buy: they were all as shabby as their bus, and vigorously gracelessly gay. No one except a caretaker could inhabit Dobřiš in winter, it could not be heated, but a decent lunch had been prepared, wine and slivovitz loosened all tongues, even mine to make the obligatory speech, and I reflected that the noblest sentiments, untempered by mercy, rarely add to the sum of human pleasure.

I still had to see an internment camp. When I spoke about it to my bear-leader he said easily, 'Of course. Why not? You will have to spend a night out of Prague to see one. I'll arrange it for you.'

That afternoon a Dr Bruegel—he and his wife are dead now—a close friend of one of our Austrian exiles, came to the Alcron and took me to an apartment across the river, in one of the old streets. He was a civil servant, with inward-looking eyes in a thin vigilant face. Over cups of the detestable coffee substitute, he gave me a corrosive analysis of the situation. I made no notes, and what I recall is chiefly his conviction—at the time I put much of it down to his scepticism and dry cold intellect—that in a year or two the country would be entirely and savagely communist.

'Czechs enjoy being bureaucrats, and they feel that nationalizing everything means that everyone will be a state servant, and perpetually safe.' Here he smiled sharply, a bitter smile with a trace of self-complacency in it. 'Very many high-ranking civil servants have served loyally Beneš, Hacha, Hitler, and now Beneš again. But the old fellow is going to find himself out of step and the music being played a great deal too fast for him. They'll push him aside ruthlessly.'

I felt no doubt he was honest—and unable not to use his mind to destroy. When I stood up to leave, I told him I was going out to the country to an internment camp.

He stared at me. 'Why go out of Prague to see an internment camp? There's one here.'

'In Prague?'

He was silent. A very curious expression, half reluctance, half an ironical complicity, twisted his dark face. At last he said, 'Ask them to let you see Hagibor.'

'Is it in Prague?'

'Yes, yes. They won't be eager to show it, you'll have to insist—that is, if you really want to know what goes on... if you're not too polite—' he meant cowardly—'to insist.'

From the hotel I telephoned to the Foreign Office and told P—— that I wanted to see Hagibor.

'If you like,' he said, 'but it's practically empty now.'

'I'd still like to see it.'

'I've made arrangements to take you to a camp very near here, twenty minutes by car.'

Only the memory of Bruegel's ironical guess at my timidity made me say calmly, 'I'll see that, too, but I really should like to go to Hagibor.'

'May I ring you up tomorrow?...'

At an Embassy dinner-party I had on my left a politician, named Fierlinger, about whom I knew only what my host told me hurriedly before we sat down, that he was the Vice-Premier, the leader of the Social Democratic party, and had spent time in Moscow. Facing me across the table, his back to a wide mirror, was Jan Masaryk. As the dinner went on, with well-cooked food and excellent wines, he became more and more wittily scurrilous and indiscreet, jeering at Czech politics and politicians with all the mimic simplicity and impudence of a satirical clown. Listening to him, I tried to guess, as often before, what you would come on if you were able to peel off the several bare-faced personae, the natural comedian (he played only real parts), the gourmand, the ribald buffoon who enjoyed using a coarse salty tongue in solemn company, the resolute patriot, the hard liver, the son of his father, with all this implied of effort to fill out the name Masaryk: his reckless tongue was one of the ambiguous signs he made that formidable shade.

But the melancholy, the quivering sensibility I had once or twice caught sight of—where did they come from?

Neither were visible this evening. He amused himself by mocking Fierlinger and the other Minister at the table, and said he was going to form a fifth party which would have nothing to do with the 'rotten policies' of the others. Brilliant fooling and highly indecorous and absurd.

Suddenly my eye was caught by the reflection of Fierlinger's face in the glass behind Jan: he was smiling slightly, not an unfriendly smile, neutral, and oddly feline.

This smile was the first thing I remembered when I heard that Jan had thrown himself from his room on the fourth floor of the Czernin Palace, less than three years after this evening. No death of a person I liked without knowing very well so shocked me as did his—a splash of blood across the false peace in Europe. It was surely the final moment of a pause which had lasted since the end of the war in 1945 and now was over, and I thought with dread of the future. Hard to believe that his lively dangerous mind and tongue had been so easily silenced. Staring at the rather haggard photograph in a newspaper, I saw him, on the evening of the 29th of June 1938, in the Czernin garden—the fountains, the exquisite seventeenth century colonnade, the half-darkness, wine, strawberries—and heard his mocking voice—'Wells says you're not going to fight, but who knows? There are decent Englishmen. There are even Englishmen as honest as Czechs. I am not by God particularly intolerant. You can see that!'

He didn't kill himself, I thought. The certainty that he had been murdered took complete possession of me. No one who so enjoyed eating, drinking, swearing, mocking, who had so much warmth and sensibility and unused energy, would kill himself.

And then the way he died: to get rid of inconvenient opponents by throwing them out of a window is a Czech habit...

The day after the Embassy dinner-party, Jiřina asked me if I would like to see the prison where she spent several months.

'I go there every week,' she said, with her fine smile, 'and take a little bread—only a little, because it is forbidden—to a prisoner, a woman. One of our guards, who was rather kind to us. Now she is as hungry as we were.' She smiled again, this time as if she were laughing at herself. 'I shall have no trouble in getting used to myself as a skeleton. When our men broke into Pankrác and freed us, I weighed thirty-two kilos.'

In the broad corridors of the prison, the young Czech guard had none of the habits of a warder, he laughed, swung his arms, talked. We waited at the foot of a staircase for the German woman; she padded down the stairs, blowsy, untidy, her hair in grey wisps over her cheeks. As soon as she saw Jiřina she began to cry, wringing her hands, groaning.

'What will they do to me? Tell me, please. What's going to happen to me?'

'Nothing,' Jiřina said soothingly. 'We are all speaking for you, all your prisoners. We shall get you off.'

She took the bread from her handbag, the guard turning away his eyes, and gave it into a hand that clutched and pushed it out of sight inside a gaping bodice. She was still crying and snuffling. Jiřina put an arm round her and kissed her lightly: the German woman clung to her slender shoulders, sobbing like a trombone, and smiling a little. Then shuffled back up the stairs, pressing the slice of bread to the body of a fat sluttish housewife.

'*We* did not cry,' Jiřina said quietly.

In a reflective voice she added, 'She was kind, she did little things for us, but you should have seen the chief woman guard, she was the mistress of the prison governor, they were in bed together. She was consumptive. She was a born killer, she strangled women herself—when you looked in her eyes you saw death. One day about five o'clock they went to Terezín and killed some people, and came back and were merry together. The Germans always showed this hygienic prison to the Red Cross, these tall innocent Swedish gentlemen praised it, all smiles, they couldn't know what went on in these hygienic cells, the poor blood spilt everywhere held its tongue.'

By now we were two floors underground, in another of the broad passages. The guard unlocked a door.

'This is the small bathroom,' Jiřina said.

A dingy little room, like the bathroom in a cheap hotel, cracked washbasin, lavatory seat, and a single naked electric bulb. Pointing to the pipe of the cistern, Jiřina said calmly, 'They hanged prisoners from it with wire.'

The next room we went into was large, hung on all sides with heavy multifold midnight-blue curtains, the whole so like a set in some early German film of suspense that it was ludicrous, bestially ludicrous—the German imagination is club-footed. Apart from the curtains, the only furniture was a large desk, standing with its back to the farther wall.

I noticed that Jiřina's slender body had begun trembling, her fingers curved stiffly like small claws. For the first time she spoke in a voice harsh with contempt.

'They brought one of our men in here and pretended to judge him, but all they did was glance at him from behind the desk and say: You have not been granted mercy. There were four S.S. guards in the room, three of them took him through the curtains——'

Smiling, the Czech guard tugged at the black folds hiding the wall behind the desk. There was no wall. The other half of the room was in violent contrast with this: white-tiled walls like an operating theatre, concrete floor, and in the centre the guillotine. A thin hose for washing down afterwards was coiled beside it. To be used when the judges preferred it, there were steel girders grooved for the easy running of hooks like those in a butcher's store-room.

'—and drew them close again. But, of course, the judges and the next prisoner who is being told: You have not been reprieved, can hear all that goes on.'

I said nothing. I had brought down inside my skull the shutter cutting off an emotion. The young guard had been fiddling with the guillotine. Friendly, only anxious that I should not miss anything of interest, he said, 'You would like to see how it worked.'

The steel blade fell like a stone, with a loud dull sound.

Back in my room at the Akron, I made notes of all I had seen, and only when I had written the last words did I realize that I was almost too weak, my joints turned to water, to stand up. Better than I did, my body knew what it was thinking...

For days now I had been groping my way through a fog of delays and excuses about Hagibor. For all his youthfully smooth face and pleasant smile P—— was turning into one of Kafka's ambiguous officials... The day after I had been to the prison, he came to take me to Hradčany: I had been asked to tea. I had the impression that he was surprised by a civility I had expected.

'I think,' he said, 'you have been invited alone—yes?'

'Why not?'

'It is not usual.'

Guessing that he felt uncertain about me for the moment, I reminded him that I was still waiting to see Hagibor.

'I shall have news for you tomorrow,' he answered.

In the failing light, Hradčany was even vaster, more impressive, more like an enormous crouching animal, than ever. Leaving P—— —'I wait for you,' he said kindly—and climbing the staircase, I felt a familiar anxiety. Should I find a word to say to them? I need not have been anxious. True, there were no other guests, but wherever Hana Beneš was, a silent warmth and safety spread from her, the overflow of her absorbed gentleness and passion to serve her husband, and he made it unnecessary for me to talk by talking, in the voice of a man speaking to himself, almost without a pause, for two hours.

At the time I was not in the least astonished that he took the trouble
to give me, an unimportant English friend—I had, he knew, no power to
harm, and could not be useful—a long lucid account of the situation in
Czechoslovakia since he came home, and of his policy. Today, I cannot for
my life understand it. Why the devil did he do it? Not, certainly, out of a
wish to impress himself on an obscure person. That I did, this afternoon, see
in him a human being—in many ways unlike the man I had admired across
a distance—is irrelevant.

The answer may be that he was so wholly without a trace of the snob that
he could talk as easily to me as to H. G. Wells, Churchill, Jules Romains.
His politeness was a vocation.

In familiar talk, there is no faking the quality of simplicity: either the
speaker has it, deeply, or the fraud is obvious. Edvard Beneš, the man of
reason, the adroit diplomat, had it.

Even certain friends said of him: Beneš? Too clever by half, believes—
when he has talked his way through a problem—that he has solved it...
Listening to him, I became convinced that this was both true and stupid.
And not the truth. The truth about this subtle clever reasonable man is
simpler. Below every other quality, he had an intelligent peasant's belief in
the virtues of hard bargaining, and in the wisdom of keeping a bargain, once
made. What sort of a world would it be, if, after long cunning argument, after
you have got the fellow down to his lowest price, and after striking hands,
you went back deliberately on the whole thing?

There were other men in him. There was the self-cultivated intellectual,
the sensible patient teacher who believed that reason and logic can be taught,
the felicitous politician who enjoyed politics as a connoisseur. Obviously, he
had enjoyed the difficulties of the first months, enjoyed balancing between
extremes, enjoyed his own deftness in moving to the left without sacrificing
his sober vision, laid up in the bosom of St Thomas Masaryk, of the ideal
democracy (Czech water-mark).

Sipping his tea, he developed this part of his theme—to his class of
one—for twenty minutes. His wife—who knew more about silence than
anyone, and was aware of him to the ends of her fingers—moved towards
me the single plate of small round cakes, but I was too self-conscious to eat
in class. His voice changed suddenly, becoming oddly younger.

'I discussed everything with Stalin, freely and frankly. I told him what Czechs would and would not accept, I told him they would not adopt Russian methods. And he accepted completely.'

He looked at us with a slight smile. 'You know, I had far more trouble with our Czech communists than with Stalin. But I've brought them, too, to see reason: in speech after speech I've led them always a little further from the idea of an unparliamentary régime.' His smile spread to the lines round his eyes. 'You know, I can turn their own talk about democracy against them. Now I can say that a revolution has been carried out without a single shot. People were astonished at first that I talked so much about the need to go ahead in a *Czech* way, they were ready for anything, anything, if only they got rid of the Germans. But week by week they became a little stiffer, a little more stable and balanced.'

'You are clever,' I said diffidently.

He considered this for a moment, lifting a blunt thin finger.

'No. It is not cleverness. It is... to take everything into account, to take care not to be surprised... to speak to the back of the mind. So with the Slovaks—they came to me when I was in Moscow, and I said: My dear brothers, I will give you everything you want... They were startled, they suspected a trick. I said: It is not tactics, you can have everything you want, but you must pay for it yourself.'

I laughed. He looked at me with entire seriousness. 'And so their demands gradually dropped—and by the time I came back here the position was what it ought to have been before the war, they have their autonomy, and Slovakia is not one of my problems... You were in Poland in September?'

'Yes, I——'

He cut me gently short. 'Six months before Hitler attacked Russia, I asked Sikorski to come and see me—to put an end to the quarrels... I liked him, I could talk to him... And we were in complete accord, complete, until I said: We can do it only if both of us are allied to Russia. In any case, I said, I shall make a pact with Stalin... And Sikorski, even Sikorski, started back... I said: I know what you think, my friend, you think it will be like last time, Germany will defeat Russia and then be defeated by England and America. That would be a miracle, and miracles do not happen twice... He was not convinced, nor were the other Poles.'

He allowed himself a moment, no more, of ironic triumph. It pleased him that he had been so much more alert, far-seeing, sensible, than the Poles. They had not known—had they ever?—what was possible, they had not *le tact des choses possibles*, the one thing a statesman (and a peasant) must have.

'You see what happened, you see the state Poland is in now, no freedom, half the country wanting a rigid imitation of Russian methods, the other half impatient to fight both Russia and their own Left. What stability can there be in a country so torn and unbalanced?... I knew. I knew all along that we should have to come to terms with Stalin, quickly. I told Churchill so in 1941 and in 1942, I told Eden, and in the end I went alone to Moscow and had my friendly talks.'

The same flickering half-triumphant smile. 'You see the result. We keep our independent way of life. And there will be no second Munich. *Which could not be risked...* The fact that we are a small country, no prestige to consider, makes it easier for us. And we are Slavs. But—attention—we are also Western, our writers, painters, professors, look west. Always will. Believe me, the country will be kept open...'

Earlier that day I had watched the Russian troops marching out of Prague between lines of smiling hand-waving Czechs, radiant with a host's friendly pleasure in seeing the back of his guests. I said so.

Beneš laughed. 'I had to help them a little to go,' he said slyly. 'They said: We go when the Americans go. And the Americans said they would go when the Russians went. In the end I cabled to Truman, and it was arranged.'

Then—when I was not expecting it—I felt under my hand the roughness, the scar, of Munich. I had asked him awkwardly whether he thought Europe could be saved.

'Yes. Certainly. There will be years of trouble—Poland, Roumania, Hungary, Austria, Italy, will swing violently from side to side, but we shall go straight forward—' he held his hand out in front of him: he had a strong small hand—'like this, on our steady middle course. We shall be a *rock* in the confusion.' He paused. I could not read his expression—anger? grief? both? 'France... At the time of Munich I begged, yes, begged their statesmen not to do what would kill France. You are betraying France, I told them. And that is what Munich did, and what is wrong with France now. It will take them fifteen years to recover. Yet Europe cannot live without France.'

'Or England,' his wife said softly. 'Yes, or England. You are on the highest level of civilization of all peoples. Of all. And yet—' his voice picked up a thread of bitterness—'I don't understand, I shall never understand the folly, yes, folly of your ruling class, which could not see what it was doing in letting Hitler grow to his strength.'

'They were blinded by their fear of social revolution,' I said.

(We go on repeating this excuse, but is it the real one?)

'But they should have known there would be war—and that modern wars are followed by social revolution—and made their plans in advance to see that it was orderly.'

He did not say: As I have done. His eyelids lowered on lively guarded eyes said it for him.

'The English are not logical,' I said.

'Another thing... You knew perfectly well that since 1933 the Sudeten Germans were plotting to destroy us. You knew it even without Frank's cynical revelations. Yet you are shocked, you protest, when we insist on getting rid of these treacherous neighbours.' He went on coldly, 'Even after Munich—for six months—I tried to see in the future a Czech-German state. Then it became unthinkable. It is unthinkable for our people to settle down with them again now. They know themselves that they must go. I know, of course I know, what an ugly affair it is, hard, bitter... For us, too, the loss of three million people—a million workers—is serious. But—' he made so few gestures that the sound of his hand striking the edge of the tea-table shocked me—'for the sake of the future...'

When I was hesitating between two replies, both futile, Hana Beneš said in a low voice, 'We need all our friends. Tell me, please, about Mr H. G. Wells. We heard he is very ill.'

'He is dying,' I said. 'His last book was one of despair, black despair. Now he is dying.'

She murmured a sorrowful phrase.

Beneš moved his shoulders like a man shifting a weight. 'So—he has let his own death make him despair of the future.'

When I left, they stood side by side, closely, to shake hands with me, he short, stiff as a wooden post, collected in himself, she all outgoing goodness and smiling blonde serenity. I thanked her for inviting me.

'You are the friend of Czechoslovakia, and our friend,' she said.

'And you didn't want anything,' Beneš said, with a smile.

'Not everyone does,' I said.

'Of course not.'

Hana Beneš laid her hand on my wrist. 'Next time you come it will be still better...'

P—— was sunk in himself, half-asleep. It was seven o'clock.

Looking at me inquisitively, he said,

'Two hours. And he received you alone. This does not happen.'

'I knew them in London,' I said shortly.

When we stepped into the forecourt, the cold drove a knife into my chest. Plunging downhill, from the Middle Ages to the seventeenth century, we were in Apollinaire's Prague, the oppressive and menacing city of his tormented passer-by. A feeling of grief—grief or fear?—seized me. As soon as we had crossed the bridge into the modern city, I made P—— stop the car, pretending I needed to walk.

Nothing could be more absurd. I had just left a man tranquilly sure of himself and the future, reasonable, obstinate, quick-witted and endlessly patient and resourceful, and a woman in whom devotion and courage were an instinct. Then why this grief? Why, in a commonplace well-lit street, the continuing weight on me of the darkness, the raw cold, the history-soaked night of Prague?

I had to leave the hotel again at once, to spend the evening at the National Theatre, with Jiřina, listening to *Libuše*. This opera goes on for ever, relentlessly melodic, high-minded, patriotic. Towards the end I slept with my eyes open. Afterwards I sat up in my bedroom until three o'clock, writing notes of all Beneš had said.

There is no point in recording here all the words, the life-sustaining illusions, of a statesman whom even his enemies have forgotten.

I am ashamed not to record what I believe. Politically I am naive, and not much interested, but because I distrust people I know them.

About Edvard Beneš I know that, until it happened to him for the second time, he did not for a moment expect that men with whom he had talked 'frankly and freely' would, for reasons of their own, go back on their bargain. Under his adroitness, his casuistical intellect, his obsession with the idea he had formed of the future—expecting that what he had sowed prudently he would reap—he had this simplicity. In 1945 he was sure—oh, clever clearsighted wily Czech—that he had saved the country, by making terms willingly and in good time, from any second attempt on its freedom.

A press photograph of March 1948 showed him aged by twenty years, the short strong body stooped, his face creased and haggard. What the agony of Munich could not do was done in a few weeks by his countrymen...

In the morning, telephoning to P——, I found that the reasons why it was no use my going to Hagibor had sunk without trace.

'I shall take you today to Modeřany camp and then, since you wish, to Hagibor—yes?'

I thanked him.

In my heart, I shrank from knowing how men and women lived in internment; I was forcing myself to feel curiosity. Getting out of the car at the entrance to Modeřany, I felt ashamed, almost degraded.

P—— showed our permit and we walked through the barbed wire into the compound. It was near the river, and there may once have been grass round the huts, now there was only a stretch of mud, and children running about in it, madly, as though just let out. Inside, rooms like sheds or large mangers opened on both sides of the central corridor: groups of women and very young children turned their heads to us with the avid fawning movement of a dog who thinks he has at last found his master again. An old woman pushed herself to the front. When she opened her mouth I saw that she was completely toothless. A twist of white hair hung over the dark wrinkled skin of her neck. She talked, quavering, in Czech, tears pouring down her cheeks, looking so closely into my face that I could not avoid her breath, which was foul.

P—— translated.

'She wants to go home, she's done nothing wrong, and they need her at home to cook for them—she doesn't know who can be doing it now.'

He spoke to her indulgently, patting her shoulder. Turning to me, 'Don't fuss yourself, I've told her, the neighbours come in every day and do the cooking for them—' he grinned—'whoever *they* are.'

'Why is she here?' I asked. 'What has she done?'

He spoke to her again. She lifted shaking hands and let loose another torrent of tears and gabbled sounds. He listened smiling.

'She doesn't know.' He shrugged. 'She must have done something—perhaps she gave someone away to the Germans, out of fear or spite. Or said something she shouldn't. Or one of her neighbours had a grudge against her and denounced her. It will come out when she's examined, and they'll probably send her home—at her age.'

'When will she be examined?'

'Oh, I daresay in a month—or six months. So many of our judges were killed by the Germans, and the rest have too much to do. Come, please.'

He tried to move forward, but the women came round us like shades pressing themselves against a living visitor. They held out babies to me. Two of these looked strong enough, the face of another was a minute wizened root, two inches long, the fourth—opening the rags covering it, its mother showed me a skeletal body covered from head to feet in sores like puddles. The smell was horrible.

'Has a doctor seen it?' I asked.

P—— spoke briefly to the Czech guard. The man went away and came back with the elderly interned German who was the camp doctor. Glancing at the child, he said with contempt, 'She's dirty, a peasant, she doesn't keep it clean.'

It might be true. But the woman was crying bitterly.

P—— forced a way through for us. I slunk after him—to inspect kitchens, a separate kitchen for the children's food, separate washing huts with basins.

'You see,' P—— said, smiling at me, 'it is not so bad, is it? It is very cold, yes, but many of us are cold.'

The doctor was following us, and P—— asked him to show me the hospital. He opened the door of a narrow little room, empty except for three beds and one patient. A very young girl, perhaps fifteen or sixteen, turned her head with an embarrassed smile: she was a beautiful creature, dark eyes under long arched eyebrows, straight nose, fine lightly curved mouth. Lifting the hair from her damp forehead, the doctor said gently, 'You're stronger again today, my child. In a few weeks, in no time at all, we'll have you up... She's been in here and other camps since May: she and her parents and two sisters ran away from the Russians, the others were killed, she's quite alone... But you're not afraid now, are you?' he said to her.

In a low voice, she said, 'No—but if only I knew what they are going to do with me.'

She was looking at me. I did not answer. Could I have told her that her likeliest future was the clearing-house near the Lehrter Station in Berlin, the stinking rags of her fellow-travellers and her own, the coldness, the distaste, of the German nurses when they had to touch her?

Outside the camp, P—— said, 'Perhaps now you do not care to see Hagibor?'

If he had spoken with less assurance, or looked—at that moment—less damnably like a Yorkshireman, I might have seized the excuse.

'No, I'll see it,' I said.

Dusk, the cold raw November dusk, thickened by fog, was coming down when we reached the place. It was much larger than Modeřany, half a dozen long huts set close together in the compound, and a shabby brick building. The guard, brisk, smiling, with enormous hands—he kept them cupped as if trying to catch trout in a pool—led us directly to the nearest large hut. We stepped into the narrow ante-room. A group of women holding tin mugs stood listlessly before the official who had brought them the last meal of the day: pieces of dark bread, one for each man, woman, child, the guard said, with his amiable smile, and pails full of the thin 'coffee'—I knew how bitter it tasted. A few heads turned towards us with less than curiosity.

'Speak to them,' the guard said in German, 'we're not jailers, they're free to speak.'

Awkwardly—it seemed as senseless and derisive to speak to these women as to caged animals—I glanced at the one nearest me, then at the bread she was clutching, and asked, 'Is this your supper?'

This brought down on me a loud shrill clatter of Czech and German, all of them speaking together; skinny arms thrust the hunks of bread and the tins in my face. A voice, piercingly harsh and jeering, belled above the others, speaking a precise pure English.

'Yes, and our breakfast, too. And at midday, we get watery soup and no bread. And that's all we have—nothing else, nothing, nothing. We're hungry!'

I looked at the speaker. A long dark face, with the large gauche eyes of an old horse; their gentleness and the violent contempt in her voice disconcerted me. At least they're not afraid to complain, I thought. I glanced at the guard, who shrugged his shoulders.

'They don't get much,' he muttered, 'and neither do we Czechs.'

He moved forward. Rank-smelling bodies flattened themselves against the wall to make room: as I passed her, the woman who had shouted at me leaned forward and stared into my face with an air of defiance and mockery: her lips were trembling.

Inside the long room, rows of triple-tiered bunks filled every foot of space except a narrow passage down the centre. In here it was nearly dark, and in the first moments I had the sense that I was pushing through a liquefying heap of bodies, here and there in it a livid face turned upwards, the eyes staring like open wounds. The stench was suffocating. Men, women, children, stood or squatted, alone or in small groups, pressed against each other and against the bunks. A few older children were amusing themselves by rolling in and out of the upper bunks, other children sat in them doing nothing, or crawled about between the adults' legs.

The warder took seriously his duties as guide. 'Whole families,' he said importantly, 'are living here, waiting to be deported. A good few of the women are Czechs who married Germans. Some of the Germans were born in the country.'

'Then why must they leave?'

I knew the answer.

'Why? They're Germans, aren't they? Do you suppose we want them here, with their murderer's hands?'

Incautiously I stood still. Instantly women pressed round me: a young woman unwrapped the strip of worn blanket round her baby and said quietly, 'Look—it's all he has. He's not warm enough. And what am I to do when he's older?'

'Mine—look at mine. He has nothing under what you see. He's two now, he's grown out of what he had when we came, and he has no shoes——'

The guard interrupted.

'We have shoes for some of them,' he said softly. 'But not the smallest sizes.'

I tried to turn back. The women stood in my way with their children, imploring me. I thought that each of these hoarse voices had been climbing through centuries to reach me, the cries uttered by any mother in any war, any sacked town.

'My children are hungry, I tell you. A few drops of milk for the little girl, for the boy, because he's six, no milk at all—only the soup and bread...'

'Feel his hands—he's always as cold...'

'Why are we here? How much longer?...'

'Please—help me...'

'Do something for us...'

Flailing with his arms, the guard forced a way through, and P—— and I followed him. A woman holding her child in one arm seized my hand, and kissed it. Another woman, younger, who was pregnant, caught hold of my arm, smiling and crying, stammering a phrase I did not understand.

'Do you want to go into the others?' the guard said, when we were outside the hut.

I shook my head.

'Well, see the hospital,' he urged. 'We have a hospital.'

This was the brick building, from the outside a rambling dilapidated house of two stories, dankly cold, with bare stained walls inside. The whole place, the guard said in an apologetic voice, had once been a Jewish stadium; the Germans had turned it into an internment camp for Jews and Russians, these had left it falling down and infested with lice: it was now just habitable.

He had sent for the doctors. There were two, a haggard young man and a woman in middle age, with a broad good face. She reminded me of Joan Malleson, the same smiling directness, the same warmth. Both were Germans interned in the camp. Hesitantly, uncertain that I was doing the right thing, I shook hands with them. The young man did not speak, the woman smiled warmly and took my hand in a strong clasp.

'You want to see the hospital?' she said, in English, in a quiet deep voice. 'A pity to visit hell without seeing every circle.' She glanced at her colleague. 'No need for you to come with us, Joachim.'

He did not answer, staring in front of him, blankly, as though he had ceased completely to attend to what went on round him. Clumsily, I offered him a packet of the cigarettes I carried to give away. He took them in silence, with the same indifference, and turned his back.

Touching my arm, the woman doctor led me up the stairs to the upper floor. P—— and the guard came with us.

This place—in comparison with the overcrowded stinking huts—was bearable, unspeakably depressing, dark, squalid, but bearable. On the landing she hesitated outside an open door, then said, 'You would give me great pleasure if you would speak to some colleagues of mine. Being men, they suffer more than I do from their... humiliation.'

In the small room, their beds touching each other and the wall at each end, were four men who might be any age from eighty to a hundred: too little flesh remained on their skulls to tell. The doctor introduced each of them formally, by name and profession. 'X., the distinguished brain surgeon... Y., the well-known heart specialist...' They lay rigidly still; each appeared to be intent on keeping alive a different part of himself, eyelids, an index finger, a tongue, a vein in the temple—concentrating in it a last charge of energy. The one whose tongue was still alive said with weak bitterness, 'A nice way for people like us to die—of hunger.'

'Nonsense,' the doctor said, smiling at him, 'you'll live to operate on a great many more brains.'

A faint contortion passed itself off as an answering smile on the old gentleman's face.

'Next time,' he murmured, 'I shall remove the whole brain, it's nothing but a nuisance.'

When we left the room, the doctor said calmly, 'They really were well-known, and they really are dying of hunger. They can't swallow the dry bread, and there's nothing else for them. And no drugs. It's the same with these.'

In a larger room eight or nine old women were lying in narrow beds, in strange attitudes of abandon—not as a child abandons itself in sleep, but like rags thrown down. None of them spoke, but one discovered in herself a flicker of coquetry and withdrew under the blanket a disagreeably fleshless arm.

A door at the end of the landing, wide open like the others, led to a passage. The doctor seemed to hesitate, turned to P—— and the guard, and said pleasantly, 'I shall shut the door to these rooms. And you will stay outside it. None of these women can run away.'

P—— stepped back. Looking at her with a curious expression of embarrassment and irony, the guard nodded.

This unlit passage was an image of the passage leading from one wing to the other in my first shabby old-fashioned school, and it should open into a room with a twisted old crab-apple below the window and a glimpse of the upper harbour: I felt a sudden stinging joy, cut off when I stepped into the room, windowless and no bigger than a cupboard—it may have been one. The young woman lying curled up in the camp bed—it was too short for her—had her few days' old baby in the fold of her left arm. She looked like a peasant. Turning her head, she stared at me with sudden eagerness, her grey eyes as clear, as without self-consciousness as a child's. The doctor bent over her.

'Yes, now is your chance,' she said.

With the swiftest of movements, the girl thrust her free hand under the pillow and drew out an envelope addressed, in pencil, in an unformed sprawling hand.

'It's a letter she has written her husband to tell him about the birth of their child. The address, the only one she has, is the village in Bavaria where he was stationed with his company when she last heard from him, eight months ago. He's a German, in the German army. Read the letter, and if you find it all right, post it when you leave the country. Will you?'

I put it in my handbag. The face of the young woman in the bed became radiant; a smile of ecstasy crossed her full colourless lips. Outside the room, the doctor murmured, 'Of course, he's not there, probably she'll never see him again, but you've made her happy. It is worth it.'

She walked past the next door. 'I won't take you into this room, the women in there had their babies only a few hours ago. For a week or two they'll be almost content. After that—well, you understand—their milk will dry up, they have the same food as everyone else, and their babies will begin crying from hunger, the few spoonfuls of milk I'm allowed to give them are nothing... You're cold.'

The whole place was glacial, but these rooms seemed degrees colder than anywhere else. Trying to control the helpless shivering of my whole body in its warm clothes, I felt in my handbag for the two bottles of haliverol capsules I had brought from England; they were for Jiřina, but I had forgotten to give them to her. I held them out.

'What are these?'

I told her. Smiling slightly, she said, 'Perhaps it isn't kind—but I'll make use of them.'

I saw, thankfully, that there were only two more rooms. The first of these held half a dozen beds, but their occupants were too far gone to notice a visitor. Lifting a young woman's arm to show me that it was only bone, the skin a grey membrane stuck to the wrists and the phalanges of the hand, she said again, 'No, it's not kind.'

The young woman sighed, opened her eyes, saw me for a moment. 'Help us, please,' she whispered, the animal speaking.

The last room—the last circle of this infernal place—was badly lit by a single weak electric bulb. Six cots, two of them empty. From the nearest rose a thin crying, only just audible, just not an absence of sound, and continuous. Two of the other babies were lying quiet, their tiny livid faces barely visible on the mattress.

'They're nearly gone, thank God,' the doctor said under her breath. 'There's nothing the matter—a teething-rash—babies born here have no resistance, they die of a scratch. This other one may live—I don't know yet.'

This other—the fourth—had been propped up in his cot against a folded blanket. He was older than the rest, perhaps a year old. He had four playing cards he was looking at without interest, one of them dropped from his hand and lay face down in the scrap of blanket across him: he let it lie.

'Couldn't someone sit with them?' I stammered.

The doctor looked at me, smiling a slow reflective smile, indulgent. 'Why? They don't know when they die.'

I bent over one of the cots: the tiny face dissolved and for less than a breath I saw through its soft skull the guillotine in Pankrác, the walls of the little bathroom, the terror of a boy in the instant before he is killed, the decent bodies of women heaped, naked as maggots, in Terezín and Auschwitz—the spume of agony flowing back and forth across Europe.

Then I saw only the dying baby.

After dinner in the Alcron that evening, the usual wretched meal, I told Jiřina about this one room. She listened, her glance absent, almost, I thought, with a gleam of irony in it. In a dry voice she said she would do what she could about it, speak to a Minister—Clementis.

Later, she broke off what she was telling me about the younger writers, to say abruptly, 'You are disappointed, my darling, not to find the young

Prague of 1938, the Sokol children walking about the streets like dancers, and that confidence and gaiety and courage we felt then. I am sorry.'

'No,' I said, 'I didn't expect it.'

'We still, you know, have confidence in ourselves, we still think of the future.'

I hesitated. 'Suppose that Russia tried to take you over? How would you feel, what would you do about it?'

She lifted her thin small hands. 'What could we do? We couldn't fight them—what other friends have we? We could only say: Do not do us any harm, we are your brothers.'

And wait, I said to myself, with your habitual shrewdness and obedience, for the moment to shake off another servitude—and in the meantime build up a weight, a fearful weight, of resentment and anger which you could only work off on each other.

'Don't be afraid,' Jiřina exclaimed, 'it won't happen.'

'If I became afraid for this country, I should only have to think of you—you are courage, honesty, endurance, grace itself.'

'Oh, no, my dearest,' she said sadly, 'I am a fool. What to do with such a thing as a heart? Perhaps a clear mind would be some use, but after these seven years mine isn't even clear. Do you know that sometimes I am longing for Pankrác, where I had so much time to think? I used to have marvellous dreams. Once I dreamed about the destruction that was going on in Europe, and it seemed necessary, and still more destructions, if the new world was to be built. Each of us, I thought, will begin again, from the beginning, to reconstruct in himself the man, the human creature. I felt madly happy. Now... My darling, fortunately we are not only our minds.'

I spent three feverish nights, neither sleeping nor fully awake. Images of Hagibor pressed against the inner walls of my skull, a frantic pressure that distended the blood in my veins until I felt that I was being squeezed out of myself, like paint out of a tube, a horrible sensation.

When I had time during the days, I wrote a long report on Hagibor, cold, factual, ending with the room of the dying babies, to be handed to Clementis...

I was seeing too many people, and whenever I was in the house of a Czech friend allowed, for official reasons, to buy liqueur, drinking too much, to endure the cold and my growing impatience. At moments, Prague itself, with its superb palaces, its flights of baroque angels and monks, its secretive alleys and wide grey solid streets, started in me a fear of—what shall I say?—of something not so much evil as sly, and slyly cruel, like Fierlinger's smile.

Time you went home! I said to myself. That the happiness of living in a foreign city had failed me—for the first time in my life—was a little humiliating. I blamed myself for it, not Prague.

It was not easy to get away. The weather was atrocious, on some days the plane expected from London did not come, and after two or three such delays the returning plane was overfilled. I hid my impatience from Jiřina.

During these weeks I heard six operas—I adore opera, but Smetana folkishness, lively and often amusing, quickly bores me, and even Dvořák... for an hour the long liquid translucent phrases of *Rusalka* enchanted me, then I caught myself stifling a yawn.

Nothing I heard, not even the music party His Magnificence the Rector of the University gave in a baroque palace, had the poignance of Uminska playing, without a score, in an almost empty room...

Jiřina's friends were of all ages and kinds. An evening I spent with her and two young men gave me a singular pleasure; both were intelligent, quick-witted, quick-tongued, and their affection for each other was open and curiously touching. One of them, F——, small, dark, lively, a Slovak, worked in the Foreign Office; the other was a dancer and choreographer who had worked in London with Ninette de Valois, and had served with the Czech brigade. Never were two gayer, more passionately hard-working, more sanguine young men, so confident that the country was on the verge of a renaissance in all the arts that for three hours I believed them.

In May 1952, I heard that F——, implicated vaguely in one of the 'conspiracies' of that time, had died in prison. Not allowed to go on working, his friend killed himself. What a waste of two minds and bodies made to give pleasure...

I got away at last, at the very end of November, after waiting on the airfield for three freezing hours, until the pilot decided to risk the trip: it was a day of driving snow and wind.

My last sight of Jiřina was of a dark thin almost transparent figure, a leaf blown against a snowy pane, dwindling.

The aeroplane, a converted Dakota, was, of course, unheated. Huddled in my seat, I made an effort to clear out of my mind its sense of a subterranean violence, in ambush below the friendliness, the hard confidence, the energy. The impression that undamaged Prague was actually worse, because invisibly, damaged than Warsaw, persisted. In Poland the destruction could be seen and touched, here only felt. Both countries were facing the same problems of reconstruction, infinitely less acute in Prague, both turned the same glance, trusting or fearful, on Russia. But, if both were forced to turn religiously towards the east, the Poles might, it was conceivable, ride lighter, with a margin of ironic reserve...

The cold crept from my limbs to my mind: I was becoming unconscious. Closing my eyes, I drifted into a nightmare, and after a time opened them to see the co-pilot standing looking down at me. He went away, and came back with a flying-jacket he laid across me. But for the slight warmth it started, I should have lost consciousness completely.

It was dark before we reached London, and I was stone deaf. I recovered my hearing, painfully, only when I was walking about my room in the King's Cross hotel in a trance of fatigue, preparing for bed.

I was catching the morning train to Yorkshire, and fell asleep thinking, with some primitive root of my brain: There you will begin a new life, sane, settled, not writing too much, not spending too much money, not knowing too many people: learn to say No! No! and No! to the people and occasions that are only an irreparable waste of time and strength. Already the total of wasted days in your life is appalling. How, when you are dying, you will regret it. Remember...

# CHAPTER 3

IN THE MORNING, things looked different...
Is the excessive order in which I live, everything round me, on my writing-table, in my rooms, neat, dusted, or scrubbed, and in its right place, a cover-up for the profound spiritual disorder of my life itself?

Guy had been appointed to the Chair of Modern History in Leeds University; he was also head of the department. The small hotel in Ilkley, at the foot of the moor, was to be our temporary lodging until I found us a house. I succeeded—with twinges of guilt and a stubbornness of the devil—in

living there for six years, in complete freedom, six of the pleasantest years
of my writing life. Now and then, driven to it by my conscience, or by some
kind meddling body, I looked at a house or flat, and found incontrovertible
reasons for not taking it.

Guy had a working room and library of his own in the university or I
could not have held out so long.

My days were monastically ordered and delicious: I wrote through the
morning, then walked for an hour across the moor, not a North Riding
Moor, not the moor above Sleights or Aisalby, but fine enough in its harsh
way—ling, bracken, grey rocks, magnificent horizon, and a thin sharp
northern air—and came home to write until dinner.

In May I went to Stockholm for the first P.E.N. Congress since the war.
I remember little about the proceedings beyond the fact that the French
and the Centres in other countries occupied by the Germans had drawn up
a black-list of writers who had collaborated, even a little.

Only an eccentric like Paul Léautaud, or a wilfully obtuse 'liberal', could
fail to understand their bitterness. None the less, Hermon Ould and I gave
ourselves a great deal of trouble to stop any action being taken. It did not,
and does not, seem to me decent for writers to proscribe each other. Leave
that gesture to politicians. A writer has other, sharper, ways of expressing
his detestation of his fellow-writers' wickedness than by black-listing them.

What I remember above all is the charm of a city into which the sea enters
and gives the light its reverberating brightness and clarity. This light is the
one I was born into on the north-east coast of England; it is the one, if there
were another world, I would pray to find myself in after death. No other,
not even the subtle light of the Loire valley, nor the hard smooth brilliance
of Provence or Greece, would content me.

In Uppsala, seen at four in the morning, the lilacs were magnificent. It
vexes me that I cannot describe them without looking round for metaphors.
And what use is a phrase to eyes which did not see them in that light, at that
hour, on that day, the 9th of June 1946?

My other distinct memories are, as always, of people. (I noticed, by the
way, that the Swede you have listened to in the morning when he is stone
cold sober and the same man after he has drunk enough are two different
individuals: the first is more confident of his cleverness and wisdom than

the second, who has doubts, and is capable of humility and poetry.) When I could do it without being seen, I stared at a middle-aged Swedish poet—I have no idea whether he was a good poet or only mediocre. He had the face of a mediaeval devil or saint in a Gothic cathedral, or the stone effigy of a crusader: it was long and lean, with a very long, very narrow arched nose, pale eyes set so deeply in his skull that they disappeared easily, and down each cheek a groove like a wound. There was something infinitely attractive and absurd about a tortured mediaeval head set on an elongated body in striped trousers and a dark jacket and carrying an umbrella.

I made notes of this face and used it for a character in *The Black Laurel*.

At one of the sessions an old Finnish professor, Yrgö Hirn, delivered in English a speech on humanism and its future: he had been preparing it since 1939, writing and rewriting it throughout the war. In a gentle voice he told his audience of writers from some twenty-five nations that we cannot rebuild the world we have destroyed without first restoring respect for the life and happiness of the individual. The true humanist cannot give up the detachment which is his way of life, but neither can he disregard his fellows, and must take the risks involved in social intervention. Today man is cruel and violent because he is bored and profoundly afraid of the technical monsters he himself has made. In the horrors of war he has forgotten the humanist philosophy, but the moral force in men, and in the power of sacrifice, will revive it...

His hands trembled violently, rattling the sheets of paper covered by the finest of fine writing. Immediately in front of him a female writer, English, took out lipstick, powder, an eyebrow brush and hand-glass, and touched up her face. Others of his hearers went out or sat yawning. He did not notice. For seven years he had seen and heard himself giving this speech, and the effort of giving it demanded the whole of his weak energy.

'... that past-master in revaluations, death. Now that the great buildings have collapsed, it is easier to notice the flowers among the ruins,' he said quietly and, gathering up his papers, stood a moment, waiting, then walked slowly off the platform to his seat in the audience.

There were no comments, and neither of his neighbours glanced at him.

At the end of the session, I congratulated him warmly on making the most important speech of the Congress, the one none of us would forget.

After this he came up to me whenever he caught sight of me, and talked and talked, until I took basely to avoiding him.

Among human beings I prefer the very old and the very young. I listen to the old with respect, even when they talk nonsense. They are so near death! Perhaps it has always been my own old age I see in them. And the very young? Ah, think of all they risk, the disappointments, the mistakes, the useless tears. No doubt it is still myself I see and hear.

This Congress had a strange flavour, sharp, delicate, a little bitter. There were no German writers, except the exiles—it was too soon to have sorted out the sheep from the goats, or to ask, say, a Dutch or Polish writer if he cared to risk shaking a hand which might have touched hands responsible in some degree for the extermination camps. There was this black-list, and there were joyous moments when someone caught sight of a friend from the other side of Europe whom he had supposed dead—'*Ah, cher ami, c'est vous! Enfin!*'

One of the two Polish delegates was a writer I had tried vainly to see in Poland—Jan Parandowski, president of the Polish Centre since its foundation. I was told he was alive, but in the incredible difficulties of moving between Warsaw and Cracow I missed him. Now here he was, with his wife and three children, and at first sight of him I understood the stupefaction of the French writer who exclaimed, 'Parandowski alive? Oh, impossible! A puff of wind would have killed him.'

He looked as fragile as a splinter of glass, stooped, sallow, with pale eyes under a magnificently arched forehead, and thin bones. Rather quickly I realized that his was the fragility of a steel watch-spring. A scholar, learned in three languages, a writer of exquisite sensibility, incapable of a clumsy phrase, and so fixed on his one aim in life—to become more learned, to write with yet greater simplicity and elegance, to enjoy a more acute aesthetic pleasure in books, in sculpture, in music, in landscape—that he was invulnerable. The frightful hardship and dangers of the Occupation in Poland, worse than in any other country, fined him down to the bone, but did not kill him—I really think because his self-centredness made him transparent. A monument of delicacy, integrity, egotism.

A year or two after the worst of the Stalin decade, a young writer told me, 'Parandowski—yes, yes, a saint who shuts his eyes. But I respect the old boy—oh, not for anything he did, he did nothing, for being unchangeable. If it was a mask it was a good mask.'

He adored his three handsome children, and I suppose would not have hesitated to sacrifice his life for them—and possibly his work.

In Stockholm, I felt so fiercely that he and his family ought to have more than ten days' ease before going back to Poland that I persuaded the Swedish publisher of one of my novels to hand over to him a meagre sum of royalties owing to me. This accident began a friendship as formal as a minuet, friendship in the, so to speak, pure state, metaphysical and fragile, as might be the friendship between a human being and a bird. The distance between us is at least as wide as that between two species.

At one moment when he was thinking about writing his life, Stendhal reflected that, supposing there is another world, he would certainly go and see Montesquieu and ask him: Had I real talent as a writer?

Quite certainly he would do nothing of the sort, he knew perfectly well that he had a unique talent and what it was. I, on the other hand, who am not even remotely interested in placing myself, would dearly like to ask some female writer I respect what mental wear and tear, short of the death or illness of the human being nearest to her, was able to distract her except momently from the book she happened to be writing. The months after I came back from Stockholm were beyond words racked and torn by anxieties, but I got *The Black Laurel* finished—on the 12th of April 1947, a year and a half after starting to write it, many years after I caught sight of it for the first time.

The last chapter was written in North Wales, in the hotel where I had lived for a few months during the war. Towards the end I was working on it at night. I wrote the last sentence about one in the morning, slept for a few hours, and woke early, to a soft warm cloudy day. Lying in bed in a narrow room, its window facing the valley and, across a trout stream, the hill, I heard the first cuckoo. It is a sound that lays the heart open, disturbing in their sleep the remote past, youth, childhood, all that it is dangerous to remember.

The child moved in bed in the next room, and I went in. Wide awake, he looked at me with bright dark eyes, lively with intelligence and mischief. Far too intelligent and articulate for his age—five years—he was what the old women call a very noticing child; he noticed with his senses as well as his mind, everything set them instantly alight, a bus ride to Portmadoc, a line of nonsense verse, *Façade* played on the gramophone; he was ceaselessly active, impatient, but never bored. When he was younger, not three, his fits of rage had disturbed me until I realized that what started them was only a lack of words, he raged because he could not explain himself. I was more disturbed by a completely silent agony of grief over a broken toy. To be capable, at that age, of such despair...

At this time he reminded me a little of the central figure in Maurice Baring's finest novel, *C*, and since it was one of his initials, I thought of him as C.

I helped him to dress, and he came into my room and fingered the manuscript on the table.

'Is it finished?'

'Yes. I'm going to send it to the publisher.'

'Will he like it?'

'I hope so.'

'Never mind if he doesn't, we'll soon write another, I'll help you.'

His eyes sparkled. 'I wrote a book once. Do you remember?'

'You began one,' I said.

'No, no, it was finished.'

I turned up in a notebook, and showed him, the half sheet of paper on which I had scribbled his 'book' at the time, a year earlier. (He had come into my room waving a scrap of paper covered closely with pencil strokes. 'Now just you stop working and listen to this. I've written a book and this is the first chapter.' A lively mime of reading the strokes. 'Once there was an aeroplane and it landed in a field, and there were wild bulls. The ambassador said—' I interrupted him. 'Who was this ambassador?'—'He was in the aeroplane. So they killed the bulls and they roasted them——'—'Who killed them?'—'The ambassador did and the other people. And what they couldn't eat themselves they gave to the farmer's wife.' He went off into a peal of laughter. 'Do you like it?')

I read it over to him. 'You see? It's only one chapter.'

'It's quite long enough.' He looked at me through his lashes. 'Probably yours is too long.'

'Very probably.'

'Never mind that, either,' he said gaily. 'We have plenty of time. How old will you be when I'm a hundred?'

'Dead a long time.'

'How I shall miss you,' he said under his breath, 'my *best* grandmother.' Smiling, he added, 'I forget about you when I'm at home, that makes me very melancholy.'

'What you've forgotten can't make you melancholy,' I said.

He laughed. 'Oh, yes, it can! Suppose you forgot where you lived. You would be melancholy in all the streets, until you came to the place.'

Delighted to have silenced me, he rolled under the bed, and came out on the other side, growling.

*The Black Laurel* is a very good novel, one of the few really good and sound books I have written. Its two central characters, David Renn and William Gary, came from *The Mirror in Darkness* series: when I dropped it in 1935, they refused stubbornly to leave my mind. I discarded a dozen narratives until, in one of the fragments I was tearing up, notes about the tragicomic life of an imagined obscure German-Jewish refugee, I stumbled over the theme that bound together Renn, Gary, and a score of men and women, English, German, Czech, Polish—one of the oldest and darkest themes in the world, the problem of justice versus expedience. The action had to unfold where the problem itself had been opened to the quick, in Berlin and Eastern Europe, but it is neither gloomy nor political: there was room for the absurd and for gaiety and motiveless kindness as well as for cruelty, violence, ambition, failure, death. In spite of the circumstances in which, much of the time, it was written, I wrote it with the sort of confidence and humility which comes of writing about what you really know and care about intensely.

'If you think that what you have written is good, it is certainly very bad.'

This is a terribly silly axiom. No writer, unless he is very young, very green, or a hopeless amateur, fails to know the difference between a book which is competent, worth reading once, and another which has a germ of life. He knows it by the pricking of his writer's thumbs.

Published in 1948, *The Black Laurel* was all but done to death in England—the review in *The Times Literary Supplement* was a curiously cold assassination. With one exception, even the few kindly notices were stupid.

I do not know why I was not more dejected or anxious about the future. For a time I felt isolated—the isolation of being damned or praised for a novel which was not the one I had written. But, strangely, not much cast down, and not afraid. You had to write this book, I told myself; you enjoyed writing it, and it is just possible that in the year 2048 a reader will come on the one remaining copy and say: So this is what it was like to be living in Europe in 1945.

One of my least scrupulous critics, finding himself at my elbow in an over-crowded room, said, 'It would have given me so much pleasure to say nice things about your book.'

'I'm sure it would,' I said warmly.

'Yes.' He passed a handkerchief over his forehead. 'To be unkind hurts me. I'm unhappy for hours after I've written a bad notice.'

A gap opening in the crowd, he bolted through it before I could beg him, for his own sake, to take up a less self-mortifying profession.

# CHAPTER 4

A BOUT THIS TIME I went into the black market for the first and only time in my life. Not many people in England knew that one existed. It happened because Paul Tabori was asking writers to send clothes to writers in Hungary. Since I knew no Hungarians except a man who was almost certainly dead, I asked him to give me a woman writer no one else wanted. The one he gave me was called Renée Erdos, I knew nothing about her except that Paul said she had been a good writer, a friend of the older Hungarian writers and artists, and was old, poor, sick. My troubles began when I got her measurements and a poor snapshot. She was not only very broad and heavy, but very tall: nothing I or any friend of mine had would come near fitting her, and I had no clothing coupons left. There was nothing for it but to buy coupons, and I did, from a Polish émigré who would have been astonished and derisive if he had known that my crime terrified me. When I handed them across the counter in exchange for out-size underclothes, it struck me suddenly that they might be forged. They were not.

Written in eccentric English, Renée Erdos's letters were a low voice out of the darkness and the past of Europe.

'... I am ill, my heart says to me: You were always a bad compagnon to me, now I have enough from you, I am tired and repose. The magnifie shoes and clothes I received from you, and I reproached myself for making you so much trouble. But I did not think you would send me so splendid things. It is over my desire. I don't find words to thank you. Excuse me my writing, I can hardly move my hands. With the same post I send for you a small plaquette as remembrance of me when I must go away. Please behold it of my memory...'

The figure of an old woman living precariously in the misery of Budapest that winter was barely distinguishable in the shadowy multitude stretching back to the Trojan women and behind them into a darkness without a voice. She had been well-off... 'Oh, I am become a coward and a wheeping old woman, I can't wear my sort with dignity and resignation. I am full of rebellion and cannot find to join that new world round me. I have lost myself. When it was all in order and I lived at my house, when winter came I made always a journey vers Sud. In Italia or Sicily or to Grecia, to my beloved Dodekanesos and my adored Rhodos. I could not bear cold and I never wrote a book in winter. Is it not right that such an idle creature shall die of the cold and hunger in this epoch of existentialism? It is quite right, but not very easy. Not easy to be a *class-foreigner* (a new expression). My books are dead, and when my friends ask me why do you not write I am responding: I am not so full of vanity...'

She had two daughters, an invalid who lived with her, and another she called 'the talented little one', a doctor, for whom she was always afraid, since the young woman was a passionate communist—'and in those circles who is safe?' Her second husband, her junior by ten years, had left her to live with a peasant woman, and she was anxious to excuse him... 'he needs much a young woman who attends him, he has enough from the past of prince consort and now he is adored from her and that pleases him, I cannot be angry. He was here yesterday and told me he has married one day ago. He was sorrowful, I was obliged to console him and I did with tranquillity telling him: I hope she will be good for you and forget that you are old and she is young. But you must not forget it!'

Over the months her letters became more agitated and ambiguous. I pored over them, straining to see through the muddy water. In my replies I

tried to comfort her for what she had not complained of; I was groping in
the dark to touch a hand I knew was there, needing to be taken and held,
but I could not reach it. Then, in 1949, she stopped writing.

The silence lasted for thirteen months, and was ended by a letter posted
on the 19th of April 1950, the handwriting almost illegible.

'My dear friend, I could not write to you for a long time—I am coming
back from a pass where I walked between the abimes of death and madness.
On the 8 February died my younger daughter Veronica in her 31th year with
an unnatural death. I cannot tell you more about it. I am a little alive—I
have yet another daughter, and my dearest friend Irene, and your mighty
spirit is beside me. Renée.'

I never heard again. For some time I wrote short careful letters. In the
end, partly out of fear for her, partly because this year was one of great personal trouble, I stopped, and let her slip back, poor woman-ghost, into the
indifferent darkness.


## CHAPTER 5

Z URICH IS AS CHARMING in its clean elegance as any city in the
world. I would live there with pleasure. The old quarter, above the
swiftly-running Limmat, is delicious, dignified and unassuming, like the last
sober descendants of an aristocratic family, and the newer town is solidly
discreet and makes no demands.

I saw it for the first time in June 1947 when I went to the second post-war
Congress of P.E.N. This time there were Germans other than refugees. They
had come to ask leave to refound the German Centre, dissolved in 1934 at
Dubrovnik, after the Burning of the Books, against which the Centre had
not wanted or not dared to protest.

In the heat of an abnormally hot summer, the delegates of the once
occupied countries lost their tempers, not so much with the Germans as
with the lukewarm English, who felt that since sooner or later we should
have to accept the German writers we might as well make a coldly polite
gesture now, when they were still meek. It mattered very little to me whether
or not they were treated generously at this moment. Rationally, I believed

that they ought to be scrutinized and admitted. So far as my instincts were concerned they could wait on the doorstep for another year or two. I did not feel kindly towards them; their chief spokesman, Ernst Wiechert, who had spent a short time in a concentration camp before the war, annoyed me by his emotional speeches. Berthold Brecht, leaning against a wall, his thin lips tightly shut, was equally exasperated.

It cost me an effort to argue against the French. True, they were our friends in a strictly impersonal sense, and tolerated us only when they thought it discreet or useful. Their arrogant certainty (an illusion) that they alone possess what the Master called *la lo-gique*, and their distrust of the English, are an old habit. The ghost of 'perfide Albion' starts up behind our most innocent gestures. Nothing can be done about this. It is visceral. But I was unhappy. I recovered my equanimity when a Belgian writer, sweat pouring down his neck, attacked me with a virulence I listened to with the greatest pleasure, since he could not know that Hermon and I were holding our tongues about the letters we had been sent by two of his absent countrymen, denouncing him as a collaborator, with supporting evidence.

There was a second pleasant moment when Thomas Mann came to the microphone and made an impassioned speech on behalf of the handful of Germans who were being offered to us as pure in heart and soul. In a moved voice he said, 'I am ready to put my hand in the fire for these men.'

Immediately behind me, one of our German exiles muttered, 'If there is a fire, you can be sure that Thomas Mann's hand will be a thousand miles from it.'

From where I was sitting I had Mann and the French writer Vercors in profile, one appearing over the other's shoulder, the German heavy, square-shouldered, stiff, the other slender and nervously energetic. It is never going to be possible to reconcile them, I thought. And if they do come to terms, they will probably turn on us together...

A Swiss industrialist—he was also one of the directors of a bank with its own international intelligence service—invited me to lunch. Over a superb meal in a panelled room looking over the flying Limmat, he began by giving me a lecture on Russia.

'In London,' he said, 'it is not clearly understood that although Soviet industry and the army would be satisfied with a good strategic position, Stalin himself is set on world communism, and distrusts both the industrialists and the soldiers as the cadres of a new *haute bourgeoisie*. If he lives, expect terrible purges in both, as well as a cruelly intensified dictatorship in Poland and Czechoslovakia. The information we get here is fuller and sounder than anywhere in Europe. In New York, of course, they understand nothing, even their bankers are sentimentalists.'

'Sentimental?' I said.

'I mean that they can be swayed, in financial affairs, by emotion.'

'Surely the English, too——?'

'Oh, no, no. You are experienced and reasonable.' He went on in a very friendly voice, 'Such a pity that England is so far on its way to becoming a third-rate power. Even without the second war it would have been inevitable—in a much longer time. As it is...' He smiled gently. 'We shall take your place in world affairs, we shall export our brains to every country.'

I hoped he was premature, or a little drunk—I remembered the unintended pathos of the elderly Swiss lady, a warm-hearted very cultivated woman, who said to me about her countrymen, 'They become a little merry when drunk.' But, no, he was sober.

Moreover, there was nothing insolent or unpleasant about his self-confidence. It was purely a question of arithmetic, almost a moral question, in which neither sentiment nor effrontery had any place.

On our last evening, at the closing banquet, one of our exiles, an Austrian, came up to me. He was stammering with exasperation.

'There were only Swiss at my table. I *hate* the Swiss. I hate them because they're not real, they have no reality, no real sufferings, no real thoughts. They're *outside* history, they look on, they're sterile, they reproduce themselves in precision instruments and bank loans. And they are so pleased with themselves, and tidy and comfortable—if they'd been in a war they wouldn't be so filthily comfortable. And they're not even ashamed of it!'

'Why should they be?'

'Even the Swedes are.'

'Only in the evening,' I said, 'only after a very good dinner... I like the Swiss, and I find their freedom from guilt restful. And their confidence and self-satisfaction and cleanness. I should hate anything to happen to this country to spoil it. For heaven's sake, let's have one peaceful solid comfortable people in the middle of Europe, if only as an example to the rest of us.'

He was disgusted with me, and went off. It had been a fine dinner, and the Swiss had put gifts beside our plates, and were now going round offering us more of their admirable light wine, not a headache in a barrel.

I caught sight of Edwin Muir. Like the rest of us, he was pleasantly a little drunk, and looked extraordinarily young and sweet-natured—a bemused young angel. And happy—as I was myself.

The day after I got home I began a novel on a double theme, the struggles of an old writer to retrieve the memoirs he had sold unwisely, and the effects, whatever these might turn out to be, on a younger man, of running away from danger. I worked on it for as long as three months, and wrote several chapters, with a growing sense that it was no good. It was on two levels of reality, and one of them, the story of the old writer, was faked—that is, I was exploiting, not re-living, the unhappy intrigues round Chateaubriand's memoirs—and the other, the deeper theme, was too intangible to be told in this way.

After a sleepless night, I made myself destroy the manuscript on the 23rd of September.

That was the day I heard from the young Polish woman in Warsaw who had translated *The Other Side* that it had earned fifty thousand zlotys. Without having the faintest idea what the money was worth, I asked her to give it to the fund opened in Warsaw for rebuilding the city. A month later the President of the city sent me a handsome certificate made out to Pani Margaret Storm Jameson.

'When the communists take us over,' a friend said, 'you will be spared, when the rest of us are lined up and shot.'

I began again, a much less ambitious story about people who run away from their moment and place. I ought to have waited and meditated, but, as always, I needed money.

To avoid boredom, I wrote it in the form of a play.

This summer was like the summer of 1940, week after week of a hot sun, splendid cloudless skies, the trees heavy with fruit, no rain, and wide clear warm nights. And, as in 1940, we were in a poor way, an economic crisis, strikes, a dollar famine, and the threat that we might even run short of food.

But, this time, there was no exhilaration, only a feeling of bewilderment and the demoralizing sense that no one knew what to do, least of all the government.

I had nearer, sharper griefs. Used to running madly between high and low water, I could pour out money and promises, but I could not come between a high-spirited child and the weight of violent un-happiness and resentments lived under his eyes. Nor take lightly the loss of his off-hand affection and trust.

I had moments of pure happiness. The first of these came when my son wrote about the small yacht I had helped him to buy. He was living in it, alone, between flights to South America or Singapore or Africa, very pleased with it, and contented. I felt all the gaiety, the absurd pride that used to fill me, a young woman, when I had given a child something he coveted and I could not afford.

After his second marriage, when I saw him recovering what he had almost lost, confidence, youth, gaiety, I felt happiness of another sort, a divine lightness of heart, the assurance that now nothing I did or failed to do for him mattered at all. He had everything he needed for a lifetime.

I should like to think that the rather gaunt nobility of the head Anna Mahler, daughter of Gustav Mahler and the formidable Alma, made of me in January 1948 is a likeness. But since she left out both the jeering northerner and the clown, I don't dare.

I finished *The Moment of Truth*, in its form as a three-act play, on the 24th of February 1948, and began to turn it into a nouvelle. This was finished on Easter Sunday, and in the evening we drank the last of six bottles of Tokayer Szamorodner 1901, bought in Vienna in 1930 from Franz Josef's cellars below the Hofburg. It was stronger than its taste of raisins suggested. On the wireless someone was reading from Gibbon a passage about the dilemma of early Christians in a pagan empire, unable, because of the reverence shown to false gods, to share in the ordinary ceremonies of everyday life, funerals, weddings, games. Through a light fog of Tokay I puzzled over the trouble human beings—*the only animal who knows he is to die*—give themselves to avoid simple pleasures. Old Captain James, methodically eating his Christmas cake during a typhoon, to save it from being wasted if his ship foundered, seems to me the model of a wise civilized self-respecting man.

This same Captain James was remembered in Whitby in my childhood for the moment when his modest elderly wife, standing on the wharf to watch him move his ship out of dock, tripped and fell. Leaning from the bridge, he shouted, 'H'Ann, H'Ann, if tha's hurt thi bottom, say so, and I'll put t'ship back.'

What a pity that when I am dead no one will remember him.

## CHAPTER 6

EARLY THAT YEAR, Guy was offered the chance to change places with a professor of Pittsburgh University for a year. At first pleased and excited, we began to be plagued by doubts. To abandon his pupils, set aside the book he was working on—a book, not a novel—was it worth it? The salary offered was miserable, and with the Treasury forbidding me to spend my dollars, we should be pinched, and—after all—why waste time on America with more than half France still to be visited?

With a book just finished, I was riding light, and seemed, even to myself, to be disinterested. On the one hand, I should see my middle sister, whom I had not seen since she emigrated to New York at the end of the war, and my young sister's two children, living with their father and his second wife, in Kansas City: on the other I had half-formed fears that I might be too slow-witted for America: not fear of anything I could grasp, but of the amorphous monster that, when I said *America*, I saw.

'Very well,' Guy said at last, 'we'll refuse.'

Without warning, I was invaded by a storm of disappointment and grief. It rushed on me from some dark recess, nothing to do with my rational mind or my will. Until this instant, I had had no idea how savagely I wanted to go.

'We should be saved a great deal of trouble if you took a little more care to know your own mind.'

No doubt, no doubt.

I agreed readily to teach what the professor of English in Pittsburgh called Creative Writing. I took it to be an inflated term for English Literature, and felt sure I could rake together enough for a year's lectures. Had I known the goose chase I was in for, I should still have agreed, but less lightheartedly.

The evening before we left Ilkley I turned the wireless, casually, to a programme called: Women in Green: the informal story of the Women's Voluntary Service, told by W.V.S. members. It turned out to be W.V.S. women talking about their work during the war: one of them began a list of those killed in what had seemed safe jobs—three or four names, then, preceded by the split second of foreknowing, my young sister's: *Dorothy Pateman, killed while on duty at the People's Pantry in Reading.*

An absurd thought jumped into my mind: How pleased she would be if she had heard it... She had very little vanity. Hearing her name on the wireless, she would have laughed, pretending to mock herself, but with a secret warmth at her young heart.

On the day we sailed (the 27th of July), the papers were bristling with some crisis or other—Stalin, I suppose—and I reflected that we might soon be back. I have no wish to see a war through anywhere but in England.

Looking back at a year when every sensation, from happiness to moments of atrocious boredom, was sharpened to a pitch seldom reached in England, I find it difficult to say why this was so, why events, ordinary in themselves, carried a charge of excitement which was cut off, abruptly, when we left America. There is something exhilarating and reckless in American everyday life which, in England, rises to the surface only in time of danger, and only then if the danger is actual, as during the months of air-raids. The unmanageable size of America—a continent pretending to be a country—must have something to do with it, or the alarming violence of the climate.

This skulking violence seems to be reflected in the minds themselves of Americans: more than once, at innocent private gatherings, the sense of a repressed violence in the handful of people in the room became as clear as a knife opened in the hand.

An ignorant spectator, I caught myself wondering whether this pervasive violence, material and moral, was not part of an answer to the question: Why is it that, now, the big flawed novels—as well as the most crushingly bad, boring, hysterical—are being written in America while our own serious writers content themselves with an inbred spruceness? No American novelist is so urbane as Mr Anthony Powell, so careful as Mr Angus Wilson to weight his phrases with the precisely controlled charge of meaning, well this side of enthusiasm or vehemence, or so redolent of camphor.

There are exceptions in England—one every ten or twenty years.

Our Dutch boat (I have never been able to shake off a prejudice rooted in me by that old sea-captain, William Storm Jameson: he believed unshakably that only the English and the Scandinavians can be trusted at sea: none of the others can build a sound ship or navigate one safely if by some chance it turns out to be seaworthy) arrived too late to dock, and we spent the night off Staten Island, a night without a breath of air, without stars, on one side a shadowy hump of land, on the other an unbroken rippling chain of lights. It was some time before—coming from a country where shortage of petrol had cut the use of cars to a blessed minimum—I realized that it was made up of headlights.

In the early morning a sky of white-hot metal dwarfed the buildings sitting back on their haunches behind the water-line.

There is a very short time, to be measured in days or hours, after one sets foot in a country or a city never before visited, when, if not the truth about it, *a* truth, and important, is thrown between one's teeth. That first taste of America was sharper than any since. It was the salt taste of power—power, wealth, energy, restlessness.

This country, I told myself, shocked, doesn't want to conquer the world, but it will submerge us by sheer weight and impetus. Unless we repair our sea-walls quickly, the wave is bound to sweep in. And... *Je regrette l'Europe aux anciens parapets...* What's more, I thought, it is an alien country.

Upon my word, I had not expected to feel more of an alien here than I would feel in any small Czech village.

I stress this feeling of strangeness, of alienation, because, after a few weeks, overlaid by the friendliness, the astonishing warmth, of ninety-nine out of a hundred Americans, it withdrew. But it had existed; it is what I felt in the first moment, before instinct began to be adulterated by reason, emotion, memories.

No one, no European, who has not lived in America can imagine it—the awful sense of power and size is unimaginable. So is a curious emptiness, rather, an absence of meaning, which comes across the scene at moments, perhaps in a train crossing the Middle West, where for hour after hour the same field, the same town—called Warsaw or Troy or Macon—is repeated and repeated, an endless stuttering of the same unintelligible phrase.

Have the Russian steppes this non-human quality, this really appalling monotony? It would not be the only likeness between two peoples in whom everything, their natural spontaneity, inventiveness, distaste for compromise, shrewdness in bargaining, all the way to a certain childish pleasure in destruction, seems designed to make them friends for life. Let us hope for it. And that they will be content to let the rest of us, harmless dwarfs, run about freely between their legs.

I spent ten days in New York, long enough to blur but not erase that first image. I came from a country still enduring, and with that surly pleasure the English take in being uncomfortable, almost cherishing scarcity of everything. But even before the war no London shop gave this impression of bottomless wealth, wealth poured out in a torrent, given off by Fifth Avenue. That and the waste—the first time I saw a waiter scooping butter off the edge of a plate to throw it away I exclaimed in horror—would have been unbearable but for the friendliness.

In any European town or city, the inconceivable happiness I feel when I dawdle through it for the first time is given me by the place itself. I scarcely notice the people. So far as I am concerned, they are supernumeraries, actors employed by the municipality to give an air of realism or gaiety to a scene before the appearance of the principal characters—for me, the streets themselves, the café I am sitting in, the dusty square lined with plane-trees, the river. In New York, for the first time in my life I was in a place where the streets and cafés were nothing much and the people everything. I don't mean that New York is not impressive, handsome, at moments even beautiful. Only that it is infinitely less interesting, less real, than its inhabitants.

In the blinding heat, I hung about street-corners and shabby side-streets, only to catch the tones, harsh or warm, but always vibrant with undertones, of the voices. A narrow shop off Sixth, as hot as an oven, crammed with cheap untrimmed hats. The elderly shapeless woman tried on her twentieth. 'You know what,' the exhausted assistant told her, 'that does something for you. Me, I'd push it back, but you do as you please.' What can it possibly matter to her whether this fat old woman gets a hat that suits her or not? In a London shop, no one would take the faintest trouble with her. The vivacity, the incredible energy, of ordinary New Yorkers, and their lack of even the most harmless forms of vanity, left me speechless with pleasure.

One morning I got into a cab driven by an unshaven bandit with a magnificent Greek name. A fag-end between his blackened lips, he told me,

'Listen. I been up with my wife till *four*. She's in *hospital*, with a baby, and her doctor told me: Bring her a few flowers. For a bouquet I need *money*, I've been driving round since four and I haven't made it yet.' The pantomime, both hands off the wheel, head turned over his shoulder, eyes rolling, paralysed me. 'She's English—like yourself, doesn't drink, doesn't smoke, and when I come home she brings me my slippers in the English way.'

I admired his invention, but I did not give him money for flowers. Not that I have serious objections to a liar, but he was too like the luckless loose-minded Elpenor.


New York is not as I had imagined it. I expected something harsh and a little intimidating, not to say exaggerated. It is exaggerated, yes, but I had not been told that it is gay, with an exciting delicacy in the outlines of buildings otherwise remarkable only for their height.

On second thoughts, exaggeration is not the right word for a touch of excess—in elegance and squalor. The saturated squalor of Harlem is excessive, the fantastic beauty of a line of lighted skyscrapers at night is excessive, and not easy to describe, since the more overwhelming a sight the less there is to say about it. In the same way, the fashionable restaurants—all that a good Paris restaurant still is, discreet in their luxury, the food admirable—at some point exceed their model. The vice of perfection, perhaps? When everything has had to be created from scratch, and with that violent continent at your elbow, how can you be certain that enough is enough?

I believe that this subtle excess creates the feeling of unreality I had even at high noon, when the light picked out every crack, every stone, every angle in the great buildings. And had again and again—on the edge of a forest in Pennsylvania, flying between Chicago and Dallas, in Connecticut driving for hours under autumn trees, stunned by so many splendid monotonous miles.

And—no getting away from it—the country is oppressively large. In a war—that is, in the comparatively human wars we have lived through so far—an English or a French conscript is able to tell himself that he is fighting to keep inviolate something small enough to hold in a corner of his skull, the slope of an absurdly narrow field, an ugly village street, even, my God, the whole of England as a seagull might see it, crossing the country from the North Sea to the Channel. But how do you fit a continent into your skull?

On the credit side, a continent cannot be spoiled as atrociously as England is already spoiled, its high-hedged lanes flattened into motor roads, its trees and rich fields obliterated by mile on mile of faceless houses. Impossible to turn the coast line of America into a middle-class slum like the one that stretches from Kent to Dorset and beyond. There will always in America be untouched areas—anything but cosy or charming, but unmauled. With the worst will in the world you cannot—except with thermo-nuclear bombs—murder a continent.

Late one afternoon, I was in the Park Avenue apartment of my friends, Toni and Gustav Stolper. After they left Berlin in 1933, I had seen them once, in London, and I was prepared to find that America had changed them. I should have known better.

How easy to sit silent in this room, and allow a still living past to grow without shock into the present. The habit of reasoning without emotion, the instinctive tolerance, the politeness in debate, the lack of emphasis, the completely natural sophistication of a highly-cultivated and intellectually alert Austrian-Jewish household, closed round me. This room was Europe. I was no longer an outsider, an alien.

Another guest, a German, who had been back to his country, was talking about it. '... I knew before I went that it would be impossible to live there again, among people who allowed the gas chambers. But—I am forced to say this—I believe that a great many people did not know about them, at the time.'

'You believe that?'

He smiled. 'Let's put it that I believe that the one talent even stupid men and women have consummately is for avoiding unpleasant knowledge. They did not—all—know... I found—what shall I say?—no repentance. Sullenness, apathy. If souls can be indifferent, theirs are indifferent.'

Toni Stolper's voice, slow, clear. 'The only important thing is to remember how the murders came about, the mistakes, the fears, the dishonesty.'

When I came out into Park Avenue the daylight was going. This above any other is the moment and the place to look at New York. A violet haze fills the distance, buildings lose their substance and lighted windows their depths; the city becomes a living body, and the people for a few minutes unimportant.

I am told that Park Avenue has been rebuilt and vulgarized (like too much of London). A pity. But New York does not depend for its charm on its buildings, as Paris or Prague or Vienna depend. It exists by its rich physical life, its superb energy.

No doubt during my ten days I saw too much and formed too many rash opinions. Happiness makes me rash. But at the same time I could not understand why my sister preferred to live here—working hard at a dull ill-paid job—rather than come home. I understood it confusedly when I reflected that New York is the farthest she could get from Whitby. When I think of our birthplace, and the birthplace of our hard-minded sharp-tongued ancestors, it is with regret, with love for something irretrievably spoiled and lost. For her it is a memory of efforts to escape. She would go back there only as a last resort. That much I understand.

On the same basis, I understand our famous exiles—that they wanted to evade England or Europe. I cannot conceive any other reason why an English writer should choose to live in America.

I respect my sister's courage—and in a colder, the coldest possible sense, theirs. I myself would not have the courage to become an expatriate; I should have to be forced into exile. And America demands a singleness of purpose I lack. A writer, without money of my own, I should have to keep steadily in mind that the most important thing is to succeed and be seen succeeding, seen living with what my grandmother called an elegant sufficiency. I like elegance, I should enjoy living a polite much-travelled life, but that is not the only thing I want—and it is only by wanting nothing else so much that one becomes, by one's own efforts, rich.

In France, an ambitious writer devotes to becoming an academician as much energy and talent as would make him a saint if he were inclined that way. In America, after one very successful book, he lives in terror of failing.

We English writers have both diseases, vanity and ambition, but in a milder, almost benign form.

The touch of excess in America, like the excesses of Elizabethan England, may at any moment throw up a great writer as well as giving lesser ones their energy.

The train journey from New York to Kansas City gave me my first taste of the dread this continent can start in a foreigner—and for all I know in Americans. It is the sensation one has in certain nightmares, that something, some pressure, both inside and outside the mind, is increasing at hideous speed, dangerous and all but unbearable. Hour after hour, the same cornfield running out of sight to the horizon, the same white clapboard houses and wide streets lined with trees. I suppose that at night, when you can hear the trees, these towns must be friendly, like a mountain hut when darkness hides the abyss on all sides of it.

In the early morning—it might have been eight o'clock, but the way time shifts about in America confused me—the train stopped at Elkhart, a small town of frame houses, like all the others. In large letters on a shop window I read: Mothers of World War z. Unit No 9—and made a note of it for the benefit of Giraudoux in the underworld.

(I do not want to die before those mothers whose sons were killed have died: on that day, a great step will have been made toward joy on earth— *Siegfried et le Limousin*.)

We reached Kansas City at night. The family was there to meet us, my brother-in-law, his second wife, my sister's two children. The boy Nicholas was as I remembered him when they left England in 1940, the spit image of his father, but my first glance at Judy sent a shock of blood to my heart. At two, she had been any infant of my family: now she was at once my sister as a child and not her: her eyes, a greenish-grey in place of the cold pale blue of her young mother's, were shaped like wide short almonds, and her face, in every line my sister's, was curiously flattened over the cheekbones as if a hand had been pressed down on them: her neck and the line of her jaw were fuller than Dorothy's.

I took care not to show any feeling except pleasure. My brother-in-law had, I knew, been afraid that I should talk about Dorothy and perhaps start a flaw in the intimacy between both children and their kind warm loyal Texan stepmother. I was never tempted. They were American children, both of them, even the little girl.

The heat was brutal. In the streets the sunlight seared my eyelids as though they were being sand-papered. The walls, the pavements, sent out waves of heat from an open furnace. I imagined that now I knew the worst about the centre of America. This was an illusion. We had not yet seen the Ozarks.

In the kindness of his heart my brother-in-law had arranged for me to have the children to myself for two weeks, in a place in Missouri. It turned out to be a clutter of wooden houses beside a lake, miles of warm muddy lifeless water surrounded by trees and ugly hills. The hotel, thrown together out of some dark timber, consisted of a dining-room—the food fell between indifferent and terrible—a second vast room with pin-tables and a juke-box grinding out tunes of revolting sentimentality, and a great many separate cabins, each with its hard narrow bed and shower. The whole village stank of petrol, rancid fat, and a heat that clung like oil in the nostrils and round the eyelids. It was not a savage place, it was the quintessence of barbarism, graceless, tawdry, repellent, without a redeeming touch.

Yes, one. Wait.

We were no more aliens here than a New Yorker or a Bostonian would have been. The children rode the ponies I hired for them, and swam in the horrible dead lake. I kept the promise I had made, not to speak to them about their own mother, but I asked one or two not entirely innocent questions, trying deviously to find out whether one or other of them had kept an image of her, even indistinct.

'Where,' I asked Judy, 'did you get your doll's house and its pretty furniture?'

Looking down, she said absently, 'I don't know. For Christmas, I think.'

I saw my young sister's short deft fingers working on curtains for its windows and covers for the tiny chairs and beds she meant to surprise the child with when at the end of the war the children came home.

My poor girl, I thought, now you are really dead.

One day Guy complained of pain in his left ear. During the night, the pain became so severe that he did not sleep, and in the morning he was clearly very ill. In an agony of remorse—it was I who had dragged him to America to die of a mastoid in this uncouth hell—I began planning to fly him to New York. We asked if the village had a doctor. Yes—one. The door of his small comfortless shack, like every other, was ajar; we knocked, a voice said violently, 'Come in, folks,' and there he was in shirt-sleeves, standing in the middle of the room sewing a fly-button on his cotton trousers. While we stood waiting for him to finish, my heart sank and sank. I expected him to apply leeches to the ear, now insupportably painful.

Talking amiably, he peered at it and said, 'Well, I'll fill you up with penicillin.' He opened a small corner cupboard: the upper shelf held a few instruments and drugs, the lower only whiskey bottles. 'Ever had penicillin?'

'No.'

'Good. Virgin soil.'

'We'll give it until morning,' I said when we were walking away. 'If it's no better, we leave.'

In the morning, the ear was noticeably less inflamed. During the next few days Guy had heaven knows how much penicillin pumped into him with the same off-hand energy, and although he had to be doctored in Pittsburgh—with all the apparatus of sterilized tools and X-rays—this genial brigand had saved him.

There may be village doctors in England willing to act with as much lighthearted boldness, but I doubt it.

For hours during the interminable bus journey to Kansas we drove through a Judgement Day thunder-storm, the whole night sky in eruption: at one instant I saw at a great distance a hawk suspended against a hill the colour of steel, pinned there by the flash. We reached Kansas city about midnight and left again four hours later. Some time that day we spent several hours in St Louis, where in the merciless heat we could do nothing but sit in a hotel watching respectable middle-aged gentlemen playing the pin-tables as if their lives depended on it.

The next day we reached Pittsburgh. I was exhausted, and when I set eyes on the apartment the university had arranged for us to rent—on the eighth floor of a large block, two and a half rooms, shabby, airless, a grey film of dust on everything—I fell into one of the pits of rage and misery, bottomless and black as hell, scattered through my life. I can make shift to deal with a major misfortune; every now and then a minor one puts me out of my mind, blind and deaf to reason. The reporters arrived from the Pittsburgh Press, and I had to smooth my face to talk to them.

For days, locked inside my ridiculous despair, I was certain that the place was unendurable. The real root of my spleen was that I realized I had let myself in for something I was too stupid to manage. The thought of the fool I was going to make of myself, trying to teach anyone to write, I who begin each book in fear and trembling, sank me. Vanity?—yes. But rage, too, that—not for the first time—I had made a blunder. To spend nine months here, in these sordid rooms, doing badly what no person in his senses would even try to do—no, no, it was impossible.

Never make promises, my grandfather used to say drily. Implying: You may have to keep them.

My boredom and despair were atrocious and shameful. Pittsburgh is a splendid city. Built, like Rome, on hills, with two magnificent rivers, the Monongahela—five liquid syllables—and the Allegheny, meeting in the city to become the Ohio, it has a strange, awful, and at times overwhelming beauty. At night, looking down on the glittering bridges of the Monongahela from the heights at the back, it was Budapest, but the wide valley of the river, mile after mile after mile of steel mills, filling the dusk with bronze smoke, turning it brighter than noon in the minutes when a Bessemer converter flamed to heaven, was one of the faces, an inhuman one, of power.

The power hub of the world, I thought coldly: and they can keep it.

And it was another America. Another splendid fragment of a country which does not exist. Not as a country.

Even Americans had made derisive comments when I said I was going to Pittsburgh, and even in my first unreason I knew they were wrong; it is one of the finest cities in the world, the fable of the present as the Parthenon was the fable of Greece.

Also it is, or was in 1948, the city which has not yet completely resolved—dissolved—its European elements. It has more 'nations' than mediaeval Paris. This—I once heard it called *this infection of Europe*—may be a source of its magnificent energy. Czechs, Poles, Hungarians, Syrians, Greeks, Jugoslavs, heaven knows what more, formed resistant knots in the pattern. By now this rich pattern may be fading, but in my day there were students in the university who, at home, never heard a word of English.

And there were Irish. The once or twice in America when I met hostility, it came from that quarter. One day as I left a street-car after listening to the account of England, pitched to be heard the length of the car, that an Irishman was giving his friend, I turned and said loudly, 'I hope none of you believes a word he says. It is all lies and nonsense.'

Trembling with anger, I hurried off before he could deal with me. I have a horror of scenes, and he had the face of a stoat and a complacent old woman.

There were a great many Catholics, but the city's ruling caste was Presbyterian, and very much in earnest. The atmosphere was Victorian, of the simplest and finest period, and so familiar—I was brought up in the shadow of that tradition living on in a small northern English port—that I scarcely noticed it until the wife of a banker who had moved to Pittsburgh from New York spoke to me about it. She found the church-going habits of her new friends dowdy and ridiculous.

'How many better ways do you know of mitigating the inhuman size of this country?' I asked her.

'What do you mean?'

'If I were you I wouldn't pull down a single absurd out-of-date stockade. You may need them.'

'You're joking, of course.'

'No, I assure you. This country isn't humanized yet.'

One of Guy's graduate students, married, lived twenty or thirty miles out of Pittsburgh in a house he had built himself out of his own timber on the edge of a great forest above the valley of the Allegheny. We had spent two nights there, surrounded by huge lion-coloured trees. At night deer came out of the forest into the field round the house. It was superb country—I am working the adjective to death, but it would be affected not to use it—and its vast emptiness appalled me. A few human beings had made no mark on it at all. And what lay close to the surface was neither gentle nor, humanly speaking, manageable.

Or is it only eyes used to the tiny intimacies of English woods and pastures that find it alarming?

*

The university in Pittsburgh is like no other I have seen. Imagine the masons of a Gothic cathedral deciding to do without statues and, to make amends, elongating the tower to an enormous height. There are I forget how many floors—forty, forty-two? It ought to be absurd, as absurd as the mono-lithic limestone columns of the Mellon Institute near by, and is in fact very impressive, at night even charming. To look down into the great hall called the Commons Room when it is filled with students sitting about reading, arguing, drinking coffee, is to be reminded—distantly, but without any sense of incongruity—of a mediaeval refectory or chapter-house.

I faced my own students for the first time in a lecture-room on one of the upper floors. They sat on tiered benches and looked at me with polite curiosity: four 'veterans'—the eldest twenty-seven, the youngest (he must have been drafted at the end of the war) about eighteen—two very young girls, and three women of my own age, friends of the Chancellor.

Even if I had had anything to say, I could not have handled them as a class. In an agony of dismay, scarcely able to fit one idea to another, I said that if no one had an objection I would give each of them a tutoring hour every week; they could choose their own times, and fetch me anything they were working on. In the meantime, had anyone a question to ask?

After a silence, one of the ladies, a warmly beautiful creature, asked me if I had read *The Naked and the Dead*. No, I said, but if she thought I ought to read it, I would, at once.

'What I think,' she retorted, 'is that the habit of using obscene words in these war novels is unnecessary and inexcusable, and I hope you agree with me.'

Disconcerted, I did not give myself time to reflect. 'Well, you know, war is rather a bloody business,' I said.

The veteran in the front row looked at me with a blank face. Weeks later, I heard that he had enlivened a number of social gatherings with his mimicry of my, as it struck him, genteel English voice saying: 'War, you know, is rather a bloody business.' By this time, he and I were close friends.

I am an intolerant disbeliever in the practice of teaching Creative Writing (save the mark) in universities—or anywhere else. It is infinitely worse than useless. What can adolescents be taught about imaginative writing beyond a few tricks, of no value?

And why, in God's name, encourage them to think of becoming writers at all? It is a profession which should be risked only by the few for whom not to write would be physical or mental torment. Or only with the backing of another profession, or a private income.

With horror I discovered that every year an emissary from one of the New York publishing houses visited the university in search of 'talent'. The individuals who make a living by encouraging young women to go on the streets do less harm.

I don't think I harmed my students, since I did nothing for them—except read through and argue about the short stories, essays, chapters of a novel, they were writing to please themselves or a genuine professor of writing. I never had time to find out how these last went about their grisly business. The most intelligent of my veterans made a mock of what he was being taught, but for one wary soul there must—it is an enormous industry—be thousands of young men and women wasting three or four years learning nothing of moment. The few who go on to write seriously can only have learned what they had better forget quickly—if they are writers and not hacks or charlatans.

For my so-called tutoring, I was given a room, on the third floor, which had been fitted up as an early American kitchen, with small leaded windows, low ceiling, beams, a vast open fireplace in which an iron pan swung from a hook over fake logs; at the touch of a switch smoke rose from them, and there were bellows, cooking ladles, bunches of Indian corn, real, a besom, a wooden scrubbing-board, a plastic candle stuck in the neck of a bottle and dripping plastic tallow, old lanterns round the electric light bulbs, a sampler, a rocking-chair, an old settle with genuine worm-holes, and a single short book-shelf. With my student of the hour I sat at a long table, he on a narrow backless bench, I on a chair so low I had to sit on the only two books in the room. There was also a narrow panel concealing stairs to the secret room used to hide from Indians: sometimes during a tutoring hour I was disturbed, not by Indians, by a conducted party of tourists.

I may have been lucky in my ex-soldiers, but I was never bored. Nor conscious of the gap between their age and mine, their attitude to life and mine. There were moments when, glancing up as the door of the colonial kitchen opened, I should not have been startled to see any one of the young men my friends in 1914. These young Americans had a natural self-possession, a lack of pretensions, a liveliness, that made it easy for them to be friendly: it did not occur to them to think of themselves as *the young*, that ghastly invention of twentieth century psychology (or pathology): even the youngest was a self-sited individual, and felt no need to put me in my (obsolete) place.

This escape from diffidence and boredom (the mortal boredom that seizes me when I try loyally to read the novels of the young English generation) is, of all the pleasures of my American year, the most exhilarating, the one I miss.

I had a second appointment, in a woman's college, to teach fourteen girls of seventeen and eighteen: I fell back on tutoring hours here, too. This place fascinated me. Perhaps it resembled the senior form in an expensive English finishing school—I am no judge—but I doubt it: it had nothing of the gynaeceum. My pupils ranged from the children of the very rich, preparing themselves to talk entertainingly about Sartre and O'Neill, to the anxious hardworking daughter of a senior clerk. This child explained to me that she must, since she was in her last year, think about making money; she must 'write for a market', now, at once.

'But why?'

'Unless I begin to sell now I've failed!'

'At eighteen?'

Her blue eyes shifted a point. 'I see you don't understand. What does my age matter if I'm not getting a foothold? I shall have to be a secretary in some factory or other.'

'Well?'

'My parents will be disappointed. Besides, I *want* to write.'

No, that's not what you want, I thought. But her anxiety was so real, so without vanity or the wish to impress, that it impressed me. This, I told myself easily, is the trouble with America—such good people, and all of them worshippers of the bitch goddess...

I had been in America seven weeks, I had seen New York, Kansas City, the Ozarks, Pittsburgh—an infinitesimal fraction of the continent—but I knew what was wrong! God forgive me, in time I learned a little better.

Twenty-two tutoring hours a week, scripts to read and annotate, a certain amount of housework, a great deal of society, forced me to work as hard as ever in my life. The horrible apartment was cleaned for me, in a fashion, in twenty minutes, by a yellow-haired brass-throated German, a ferocious creature—it was like harbouring a wild animal. But she chose to be friendly.

'Ha-a-ahn!'—a rasping yell—'For you I wash up. Not for other women. For you. You *work*.'

I worked, yes, but not for myself. I had brought to Pittsburgh the bloodless ghost of a novel, at its centre one of those aristocratic radicals our society throws up as naturally as an oak develops galls. I had no time to consider it. Figures which clearly belonged to it stalked at the back of my skull, and if one of them had the imprudence to step forward I pushed it roughly back.

This, though I did not know it then, was one certain way of nourishing the book, probably the only certain way. How many clever novels of our day begin with a company parade of lively characters, confidently brushed in, who after a chapter or two turn out to be hollow, a series of half-seen impressions or a screen play of naïve sensations, and cease to exist. Naïve because their authors are so engrossed by the functions of human beings that they have forgotten that the heart and the other organs are not interesting as organs: what is interesting is the double activity, seen and unseen, fed by these nerves and cells.

It is the fault of the incontinence, the myopia, the frivolity, which drives us to turn out our novel a year like articulate robots, to be praised or damned by critics as unfit as ourselves to talk about novels.

If only I could begin again!

Some time during the autumn I spent a weekend in Connecticut.

Here, and later in Vermont and Massachusetts, I had for long moments a tantalizing sense of *déjà vu*. Was it nothing more than the reflection, in this handsome glass, of books read and re-read in childhood, so sharply remembered that I caught myself looking for the spider-flowers, johnny-jumpers and buttonwood trees of *Ellen Montgomery's Bookshelf*? (I have it still, loose from its spine, the brittle foxed leaves crumbling at the edges. Absurd to care what happens to it when I die! But I hope it will not be simply thrown out.)

All that can be said about a New England autumn has been said already, by writers with an interest in scenery. The scene is, in any event, indescribable. Only in dreams do such trees exist, a broad river running out of sight to the horizon, its ripples gold, black-bronze, scarlet, lunar yellow. The exquisite small towns, half-village, half-park, their white houses, white wooden churches, lawns of coarse shorn grass open to the street, have the same dream-like unreality—no, that is not strictly accurate, it is not reality they lack; in some indefinable way, they give back a hollow sound, like an empty vase or the wings of a theatre. The vase, the body, is beautiful, still apparently intact, but the soul has dwindled to a thread. During the dream, a change has taken place. Or, perhaps, the dreamer is losing his hold on it, on the unrepeatable dream that was New England, with its harsh undertones, its strength, its toughness, its narrowness, its fortitude, its innocence—if there is such a thing in the world—its candour, its spring-like delicacy.

Probably I am wrong, deaf, like all foreigners, to words I did not learn in childhood.

I came back to Pittsburgh with reluctance—and found that I was in love with it. Even Americans have mocked my infatuation with this place. What, they say, Pittsburgh? You must be mad... And like all love-affairs, this one had little to do with merit. Not that the city is less than very handsome, with an air of space, of elbow-room for large gestures, born, possibly, of the nearness of virgin forest and the immense skies of the West. But I recall with love streets which have nothing to commend them except a view across the Monongahela to the labyrinth of lights covering the flank of a hill, below an iron sky; I remember the Point, the tongue of land where the two rivers flow into the Ohio, in my day a place of derelict railway lines and stunted bushes, its one obvious charm the small dark block-house built in 1754 by the English, captured by the French, recaptured by General Forbes; I remember the rivers in winter sunlight, the many bridges, the tracery of tall buildings, spectral factory chimneys in snow, the fantastic colours of smoke from the steel mills, plumes and drifting clouds of rust-red, tawny, green, grey-blue, white. I even think with affection of the amiable store where I spent two-thirds of my salary on sending packages of food to England.

What else? The very young negress in the street-car, slowly walking its full length, her back as straight as a rod, swaying a little, with the nonchalance of a wild creature, and chewing. She was wearing a grey coat and a high-crowned fur hat on her black hair, smooth with oil. There was something insolent, almost dangerous, in her vitality and feral movements, but also something candid, free from the corruption of society.

This was my Pittsburgh, a city like no other. It has perhaps vanished. No city now knows enough to leave well alone—think of the mutilation of London since the last war.

Stranger than anything else—for the only time in my life since I left Whitby (where I had been living for at least five hundred years, so that whether I chose to be or not I was *of the family*), I was a member of a community. It was not homogeneous, except in so far as it kept traces of the New England theocracy carried south and west by earlier generations. The fierce Calvinism—Calvin rather than Luther—of the theocrats had crumbled, but something of their evangelical habit of mind remained. Apart from this, and a half-conscious pride in belonging to a province—when provincial stands for a certain freedom of spirit, a taste for experiment, a spontaneity—which marked even Pittsburghers who had come to the city from New York, it was a community of interlocking worlds: directors of steel companies and banks, professors, musicians, a well-known judge, an editor, business men, lawyers, politicians, a writer or two, all of them citizens in a sense we have almost lost, taking an active part in the day-to-day life of their city, from its splendid orchestra to its hospitals and universities and institutes.

Why am I not a member of a community in England? Oh, a dozen reasons—the exigencies of a writer's life, which demands the greatest concentration possible or endurable; laziness; my inborn fear of committing myself to live with other people. But here, thousands of miles from England, not only had I forgotten my first awful sense of being an alien, but I was at home as I have rarely been in any place for the past thirty years.

Credit where credit is due. Only a boor, a heartless idiot, would have rejected a warmth as natural as the generosity with which it was offered.

I was happy to be living with fifteen or twenty intimate friends I had known only for a month, intelligent men and women, alert, unaffected, without the vanities and jealousies of a closed society; happy to be overworked, not a moment to think of writing. Perhaps, ironically enough, this was a reason for my happiness. For the first time for years I could push aside the idea of a novel without the guilty sense of wasting time. Except in name, I was no longer a writer. I was playing a role, yes, but the role suited me.

No doubt I should not have been happy in a small town, or in a purely academic society. And no doubt I should have reached a point when the uneasiness of not writing stifled the pleasure of living a continuously active gay life. I did not stay long enough for that.

The evenings I spent in the houses and apartments of married professors might give out echoes, broken syllables, of Berlin or some other European capital—oftenest a German syllable: the United States is littered with the grandchildren of Germans—but the final word was American, Pittsburgh-American, mark 1948. Not only did our temporary colleagues take endless trouble to be friendly, but not once did I come across the vanity which uses friendship for its own gratification. Vanity is the only human habit, except cruelty, which wrecks me: I begin to be uneasy, to tell lies, to cajole it, and finally take to my heels, ashamed of myself. In this community I had not chosen, I was perfectly at ease, perfectly light-hearted.

One evening I had the illusion of seeing over my shoulder a Germany which no longer exists: it had had its throat cut soon after my first and last glimpse of it in 1932. A shabby comfortable room, dinner, cooked by the professor's wife, for eight guests: wearing her apron, she helped them to help themselves, then went into her bedroom to practise the sonata she was going to play with three of them.

It had been written by one of the guests, an old composer: it was in four difficult movements, to my refractory ear dry and discordant, inspired, he told me simply, by Dante.

When an American tells me that in his country materialism and a cancerous boredom have taken the place of the vision—what vision?—I only half believe him. The mere notion of adding snobbery, greed, vulgarity, to that room with its piano and the clumsy bunches of white lilac brought in as an afterthought is ridiculous.

Not that I did not come across snobbery, greed, vulgarity. Why not? Pittsburgh has everything.

The day before Truman won the Presidential election I was invited to lunch by six Republican ladies, all but one of them widows, immensely rich. The sum of wealth in the hands of ageing American women whose husbands died getting it must be enormous. In the kindest most friendly way in the world they told me what Dewey would do to the greedy American working-man and the Bolshevik-minded English.

'My dear Miss Jameson, tell me why, why, we should give you money to spend on socialistic experiments and social services—if that is really what you call them—for your lazy workers.'

The English worker has always been, not lazy, but taking his time—except when bullied, or in war-time, but I denied it. They smiled.

'My dear, every working-class is lazy—yours is not an exception. But why should *we* be taxed to support them?'

'I don't know,' I said. 'I was against Marshall Aid. It would have been infinitely better to be poor and independent. Better for you, too, since no one loves a benefactor.'

'You were against Marshall Aid!'

'Certainly.'

'Well—' she did not believe me—'with Dewey in the White House...'

'You are sure he will be elected?'

'Why, of course! No question.'

'The English,' I said, 'always vote Democratic in an American election. Did you know that?'

'Ah, yes—Roosevelt, that rascal, that lying twisting slimy monster, that socialist, that...'

All I could think of to say, at the end of the commination service, was, 'Forgive me, but no one in England, not his bitterest enemy, would abuse Churchill as you abuse Roosevelt. It always astonishes me.'

They were too kind and well-intentioned to do more than smile at my obtuseness. But I wondered whether the excessive rancour with which these dead hands are still raised against Roosevelt and all his works is due to fear—that they are defeated.

Not that I had any great inclination to defend him: his ignorance of Europe did us enormous harm.

'Pittsburgh,' a New York journalist told me, 'is full of Babbitts, you won't stay a month.'

He was wrong on both counts; the only two people I knew who might have deserved his contemptuous epithet were also amiable and energetic. They were a professor and his wife, both Republicans, which was unusual enough: all the others were Democrats to a man. They expected little good of an Englishman, but they had determined to be kind and Mrs B. took me with her to a woman's meeting in the Stephen Foster Memorial building on the campus. It was the week after Dewey's defeat. On the way in she said, 'I'm ashamed of America—the most terrible disaster! You, of course, being English, admired Roosevelt. People of our sort, the intelligentsia, hated him. He got his support from the mob.' She flung up plump arms, entangled in a fur. 'There now, I don't mean you're not intelligentsia, and my Johnny said I mustn't talk politics to you. Let's look at the shrine. See? These are bars of Foster's music. The only time music was ever carved in stone!'

The lecturer, a Valkyrie from the electricity company, talked about deep freezers with the cunning fervour of a revivalist. 'Oh, my stars is that good!' she cried, holding up a turkey frozen harder than Stephen Foster's semi-quavers. 'No, it's divine!' I sat in a trance of contempt as cakes, pies, loaves, were taken from the machine. Why freeze bread? Even the abominable American bread?

'Science,' Mrs B. said to me as we left, 'is what will save us—in spite of Truman. If it weren't for science, we should still all be Catholics. Oh, my, you're not one of them, are you? What would my Johnny say to me? Oh, fine. You must come to us on Good Friday, I always serve ham, our own—delicious!'

England is full of Babbitts, with less energy, less simplicity of heart, less kindness, and even more irrational. But they are rarely members of the professional caste, in which, with us, bigotry and unreason take drier forms.

One dark October afternoon, I answered the telephone in the apartment, and listened to a woman's voice, I thought a young woman, reading a cable from my son about the birth of his first daughter.

'Do you mind repeating it?' I said.

'I will.' She read it through again, adding, 'That's splendid news. I sure am pleased about it.'

'Thank you.'

'You're welcome,' she said, quickly, warmly.

Maxine Davis invited us to spend Thanksgiving in Washington. She had married since the last time I saw her in London, a Colonel of Marines who knew China intimately in the way certain English soldiers, during the heyday of the British Empire, learned to know and cherish the remote country they served in. Courage, a biting intellect and expert knowledge, in one person, might have been intimidating. That I was not intimidated by Jimmy McHugh is due to a hospitality at once formal and highly personal, a *Mozartian* hospitality. Perhaps it was Chinese. As in Pittsburgh, I forgot to guard myself and was continually happy and amused.

Washington is one of the loveliest cities in the world, and civilized to a fault. The part of it in which we lived for three days, Georgetown, is so nearly perfect that I should have been delighted to come on a flaw: perfection has one drawback—nothing holds up the glance passed over it, so that one has trouble in recalling details. I have never been back to Washington, and do not know whether the light is always that of a fine September day in Paris, clear, faintly golden, faintly vibrant. Probably not. It was probably, during those three days, in a state of grace. As I was myself.

The McHughs had a great many friends, people like themselves, intelligent, uncommonly well-informed, liberal—writers, politicians, financiers, journalists. Having written that, I realize that the whole of society in Washington is to some degree political. It is like no other capital city known to me, in that political thinking, the whole business, technical and personal, of politics, is not diluted by an equal interest in art, industry, amusement, anything you like. I don't mean that these are non-existent in Washington—only that they are subdued to the ruling passion. English political society in its upper reaches is less concentrated.

This was the most sophisticated of the several Americas I touched. No doubt the charm and elegance of this house was a personal achievement, but it did not, as anywhere else it might have done, startle. Living in it, listening to the talk at the dinner-table, I reflected that if Europe dies of its political incompetence, of the different idiocies of ourselves and General de Gaulle, its culture might, for a Byzantine century, be preserved here.

But perhaps these people were a little too intelligent, too liberal, too disinterested. And they were not—though they knew everything about them—the people who make the decisions. An intimate knowledge of China was enough to ensure that its possessor was never in a position where he would embarrass the China lobby by his knowledge. (In any event, who does make the decisions in Washington? The tug-of-war between a President and Congress never ceases to astonish and baffle an Englishman.)

On our second evening we dined in a club—very stately; it might have been the Athenaeum without its discreet discomforts and with the benefit of marvellous food. Among the six other guests were two people I had been hoping to see ever since we landed: Czeslaw Milosz and his wife. Since Cracow in 1945, I had seen them once, when they passed through London on their way to America: like other young Polish intellectuals at that time he had been drawn into government service, and from his letters since he became cultural attaché in Washington I had the impression that he was living uneasily in two worlds, Poland and an America he could not yet accept. To a survivor of occupied Poland the wealth of this country could seem an insult to so much death, cruelty, destruction, or a mockery of a Europe whose greatest thinkers have never given to happiness or success so high a value as to poverty, solitude and the tragic sense of life. The revulsion I had felt in the moment of landing in New York was instinctive—and I was not burdened by the ghosts of friends, parents, lovers, done to death in Auschwitz or in Warsaw itself. Nor am I a poet, with that heightened capacity for being flayed by my senses.

He looked much as when I saw him in Cracow, a little more solid. His young wife was unchanged, pale, blonde, quietly resolute; neither America nor the birth of a son had altered by a line the clear delicacy of her face.

One of the other guests was an international editor with the genial arrogance of his position, and after dinner, perhaps intending it, perhaps not, he provoked Milosz into an argument. When Czeslaw was in a rage he opened his eyes widely, and I had the sensation of looking through them into an endless cold empty plain. Without moving my head I could see four of the faces turned to him. That of the editor's plump good-humoured Russian wife was the most extraordinary; behind an air of simple curiosity there was a pitiless directness: her husband's face showed little but disbelief in so much passion and imprudence. Listening politely, Jimmy McHugh had all at once the look of a scholarly monk, impassive, possessed by a wryly ironical spirit. Maxine's face wore the expression of quizzical amusement she uses to hide a coolly critical mind; I was surprised to catch a trace, hidden normally by her warmth, her gaiety, of a certain ruthlessness, a masculine quality.

When I had the Miloszes alone for a moment, I asked Janka, 'Are you happy in Washington?'

She smiled very slightly. 'Yes.'

'Are you going to stay?'

Czeslaw answered for her. 'How do I know? How do I know anything which can happen to me? How do I know even what I wish to happen?...'

Blanche Knopf was staying in Washington, and next day I lunched with her. During the years, my affection for her had become a serene habit. She was now physically brittle, and so thin that I doubt she weighed five stone. Her elegance was of the bone, and her face had the purity of an abstract drawing.

'I'll tell you something that will amuse you,' she said, smiling. 'Mrs Eugene Meyer—you haven't met her yet but you will, she's immensely distinguished—I called her up this morning and asked her to dine with me. She said she couldn't because she'd been invited with the McHughs to meet a completely unknown English writer. She couldn't remember even this unknown writer's name, and asked her secretary. It was Storm Jameson... By now she will have had her secretary look you up and brief her. She's a very very fine person.'

Agnes Meyer was an elderly woman, immense rather than fat; her eyes, small and sagacious, were not unkind. When I was presented to her she smiled warmly and said, 'How wonderful. I've wanted to meet you ever since reading your *Cousin Honoré*. A remarkable book.'

I thanked her. The liking I felt for her was entirely genuine. Compliments which may possibly be sincere embarrass me terribly, but courteous kindly insincerity is the simplest thing in the world to accept.

In England at this time (November 1948) the butter ration was down to six ounces a fortnight, and eggs were almost non-existent. I discovered that I could send over by air boxes of twelve dozen eggs, and I sent one of them to F. R. Leavis's wife, Queenie Leavis, in Cambridge, a woman I respected infinitely for her own work and for an uncompromising devotion to her husband and his career, to which she subordinated her own without, so far as I ever heard, a sigh. By a stroke of luck for me, I sent them at the right moment.

'... we had a ghastly summer culminating in my going into the operation theatre on the 1st of September under suspicion of cancer and having a horrible operation which confirmed it... the whole business is working out very badly—the professionals do not conceal from me that they take a poor view of a woman who develops a cancer at the age of thirty-eight. This is of course very disturbing when one has a young family and no relatives. However, in view of the likelihood of an atomic war it seems ridiculous to worry about a little thing like this, and I try not to do so. My husband's, or I should say our book on the English novel [this was *The Great Tradition*] is at last out... It is being published in USA, too, but Frank is sending you a copy from this side in case the Am. publisher can't be trusted. I wrote a good deal of it myself, perhaps you can identify some. The children were quite overwhelmed at the sight of so many eggs and all boiling ones, and think the millennium must have come when they can have a boiled egg at breakfast, egg and cress sandwiches at tea, and apple sponge at dinner. I have already felt the benefit myself, because the op. and the radio-therapy treatment had reduced me to living on soda-water and oranges (when available) and there seemed nothing in our rationed state that I could take. One has been giving the children all the eggs, bacon, chocolate, milk, etc. for so long that when one gets ill and can't take starch there seems nothing else to eat. Egg custards and an egg for dinner have given me quite a lift. One feels ashamed when one thinks of Europe, though. Frank has had an awful time sustaining the house with one hand and the university English teaching with the other, and with the worry as well looks like a skeleton. It doesn't help that he is so sought-after that all his supervisions have had to be turned into large seminars and that his lecture-theatres are crowded to Black-hole conditions. I wish we could go visiting professorially to USA but he hasn't had a sabbatical year yet in an academic life of twenty-five years. I should like to go to California some day—we could put Kate in the swell girls' school where Auden teaches English, Ralph could study under Schönberg and Hindemith, and I should be able to enjoy little Robin before he gets too big to be nursed...'

I imagined I had only to tell the right people that F. R. Leavis might be willing to come to an American university for offers to rain on him, and I seized chances I was given at Kenyon and Columbia. In both places the answer I got was, in effect: Of course, we'd all like to have him, but my belief is he won't come; he'll never leave his position in Cambridge undefended for a year, long enough for enemies to do him a mischief...

I have no idea how just this was, or whether offers were made to him, but his wife did not get her Californian year, a misfortune which still vexes me.

I suppose there is no English university—I know nothing about other countries—where social tact (that is, a reasonable hypocrisy), smooth manners, discretion in every field, prudent scholarship, a habit of well-turned phrases, are not more useful to their possessor than all the originality and critical passion in the world.

Even before coming I had noticed that the American traveller, not rich and not a journalist, who knows Europe or a country of Europe as I know France—by heart—is rarely sentimental about it. His affection has a quality I came to recognize as peculiarly American, loyal, unpatronizing, but informed and very shrewd.

I had the luck to meet one of these uninfatuated lovers in my first week in Pittsburgh. Gay, tolerant by instinct, Ruth Crawford Mitchell knew Europe first at one of those moments when—for a moment—it seems possible that generosity, reason, and faith in the future, are stronger than injustice and old hatreds. In 1919, as a young relief worker in Czechoslovakia, she became director of the Social Survey of Prague sponsored by Alice Masaryk and an intimate friend of the family. Thus she knew about Europe not only its habit of suicidal wars, but its other habit of giving birth to great men in order to have something worth betraying.

I am an unreconstructed provincial, happy to have been born in a part of England which, in my childhood, still tasted only of itself. Paradoxically, this is what makes me an internationalist, in the sense that when I meet a man or woman of another race, it is with the greatest difficulty that I reflect: This is a foreigner, a Jew, a Frenchman, a Turk. So far as I am concerned, he is a man from another province, and if he has customs and habits very unlike mine, why, so had old Mrs Wear of Whitby, a Congregationalist, so prudish that she kept a doily at hand to throw over her husband's face when the servant came into their bedroom with morning tea.

Nationalism will keep its venom until we succeed in creating an image of the nations of the whole world as so many provinces.

This image exists in Pittsburgh, in the Nationality Rooms of the university, a series of twenty-seven rooms on the ground floor, each decorated and furnished by a National Committee in what it considered its country's finest and most characteristic manner. Thus Chinese elegance completes and contrasts with French, Swedish clarity of form with Czech or Greek.

To this splendid stroke of sanity and imagination, Ruth Crawford Mitchell devoted an energy, an inventive passion, a loyalty, justified by the result, which is worth a thousand treatises on world government. Conceived between the wars, perhaps as a gesture towards the vision, already dimmed, of a new Europe, it grew quickly: one of the last rooms to be finished before the second war was the Czech, dedicated by Jan Masaryk a few months before Hitler occupied Prague.

In 1948 the room set aside for England was still bare. I have not seen the finished room, made up of wood and stone salvaged from the House of Commons after the air-raid, with carved stone bosses round linenfold panelling, and a bomb-splintered overmantel from the Aye lobby. There may be a grim tightness in the idea. Even an Englishman who did not feel that these fragments represent the finest period of English taste need not be displeased that they survive in Pittsburgh—together with the small dark blockhouse near the river. It will be a bad day when either country forgets that it shares a nerve with the other.

I was fortunate in my year. On the evening of the 11th of December, twenty years after the first ceremony, the National Committee, meeting in the great hall of the university, were handed copies of a book of water-colour paintings and an account of the rooms, to be sent, even the Russian copy, to the great university of each country. (In 1962 no way had yet been found of presenting copies to Jugoslavia, Poland, Hungary, Czechoslovakia, Roumania.)

As each chairman went up to accept his copy, his voice evoked a double image, of his past and of a country he thought of with grief, as for a dead child, or with the respect due to an ancestor, even, in the rather brash voices of the Irishman and the Scot, with a hint of defiance. Stumbling over the unfamiliar words, the Lithuanian explained that he had taught himself to read, but read English with difficulty.

'At home,' he said slowly, 'I wanted always to go to school. The priest would not let me, he said my brother was going to a school, and that was enough for one family, I must work in the fields. I thought: I will go to school in America. But I am here a baker, I could not even go to night school.'

Taking the large handsome book in his hands of a peasant turned baker of bread, he looked at it with surprise and smiling respect. In the long pauses between his words, a country of fields, forests, rivers, had its moment of freedom between invasions. But when he looked at us from his small pale eyes, full of a shrewd goodness, I supposed there were other images, less reassuring, at the back of his cropped skull.

After the speeches, people stood about in the great warm hall and—this was presbyterian Pittsburgh—drank an innocent fruit punch. There was an untidy fire of logs, a green tree, a choir singing old carols, a flag: the simplicity of a village harvest festival, and, distilled from it, and from sources as far apart as Athens under a blistering sun, Cracow, Delhi, a Balkan capital, the rue St Jacques, a spirit of extraordinary strength and purity.

'This,' I said, 'is your triumph, dear Ruth.'

Eyes and smile brilliant with fatigue, she shook her head. 'No, not mine. What you are seeing this evening is America.'

A charming myth and the truth. Every reproach laid against America, of materialism, idol-worship, can be true without destroying its real grandeur. Soberly I thought that I really had been given a glimpse of that grandeur, which may be distorted, lost, betrayed from within, but, if it survives, might do as much for the world as Greece did for Europe.

As so often happens to me when I have been excited and moved on a deep level of my mind, my dreams that night were of the past. I was with my young sister; she was helping me with something, as so often, and we were both laughing. Afterwards, neither asleep nor awake, I felt a terrible longing and grief. Ah, if she would come only for a minute, a single minute, so that I could tell her... what?

It occurs to me now that the impulse I had felt to indulge her, as a girl and a young married woman—inexplicable by anything in her character, gaily self-reliant and intractable—might be explained by the savage notion that her early violent death threw its shadow backwards over her, unseen but felt.

This speculation is idiotic—but not more insane than the custom of sending young men to murder people in small open towns from the air. We spent Christmas in Rye, with the Henry Steele Commagers.

That house was a living spring of warmth, generosity, wit, gaiety, intelligence, all the active graces of living. At its still centre, Evan Commager, a creature as purely good as salted country butter. Seeming to do little except talk in a slow warm voice, she was the point from which the wit and gaiety rose and to which it returned.

I doubt that Henry Commager slept more than four hours a night; the rest of the twenty-four was spent writing, reading, lecturing—at this time, when his children were young, he wrote through any disturbance, stopping only to take part in their violent games or to argue with friends.

I wrote a little in this house, an article ordered by Lester Markell of the *New York Times*. When I went to see him in New York he told me that the paper never paid higher than a hundred and fifty dollars for an article. This was four times more than I should be paid in London, by *The Times Literary Supplement*, for a comparable piece of work, but before I could stop him my grandfather had said, 'That's very poor pay.'

Mr Markell looked at me with extreme sharpness. 'Do you think so?'

'I do indeed,' I said warmly. Not only had I liked him at sight, but America, there is no doubt about it, had given me, an, alas, passing trace of its *je m'enfoutisme*.

'We might go to two hundred.'

When I sent it to him from Rye he rang me up and told me that it was not what he had expected. I was dismayed, but I hate talking on the telephone, it stupefies me and I forget to be either prudent or tactful. Besides, it gives me more pleasure to throw away an article than to write one.

'What,' I asked, 'is wrong with it?'

'It doesn't fit the title.'

'Why not change the title?'

A silence. 'You may have something there.'

'It seems to me much less trouble than changing the article.'

'I'll think about it,' he said drily.

The thought of rewriting bored me, and I resigned myself to losing my two hundred dollars. I heard no more, and the article appeared as I had written it. I have not the faintest memory what it was about.

An off-Broadway theatre was playing Giraudoux's *La Folle de Chaillot*. I went to see it, not only because of my affection for his writing, not yet spent, but out of curiosity, to see whether in a city of hard outlines and parrot-shrill light anything could survive of a poet who saw the world in oblique images. That an astonishing number of these images are of treachery, despair, injustice, death, is overlooked by readers now, who find him affected, a maker of bric-à-brac. If a habit of turning reality slightly awry, to show its absurd, ironical, ambiguous sides is an affectation, they are right. But I would throw away the whole output of the last decade of novelists—except one—to discover an unpublished Giraudoux of his dexterous maturity.

*La Folle de Chaillot*, alas, belongs to a period when he was already tired, less able to keep cruelty and bad faith at a distance by mocking them. It was not the fault of New York, nor of translation into a hostile idiom, that the centre of the play was empty. A void. Jouvet could have filled it with his magnificent voice, deep, staccato, vibrant, and his controlled passion: brilliantly as she tried, Martita Hunt could not.

Each time I came back to Pittsburgh from New York or the half familiar charm of New England, I felt thankful that we had been sent there and not to Columbia, or to a place where the university dominates. True, my knowledge of Pittsburgh had narrow limits. I knew that Wylie Avenue existed and that if I walked up it at ten o'clock on any warm Saturday night I should hear real jive and see negroes jitterbug in the foetid air until their eyes rolled white and their pores spouted sweat, but I was not silly enough to go: it was no *Nigger Heaven* for curious visitors. And I was taken to look at a vast housing project for which the upper half of a hill had been sliced off as neatly as the top of a boiled egg: nothing in its vacant stare to tell me whether its tenants, moved here from the old quarter of foreign steel workers three hundred feet lower down in a pit black with its own smoke, had brought their brutal memories with them.

In the nature of things, I was not likely to get smell or hide of these, nor of the squally Pittsburgh of union organizers, coal miners, truckers, railroad flunkeys, bartenders, whores, derelicts of every tongue.

But even the bourgeois Pittsburgh I lived in was penetrated by currents of excitement which drew some of its virtue from these circles, and from being an inland continental city as well as an immense industrial nexus. There could be nothing precious, and not much that was ingrown, about a society boiling over with power like a Bessemer converter, and with two great nerves of river joining it to the endless stretches of country arched by enormous skies and licked by a searing light.

My memories of the months between February and June are confused—not because I have forgotten them, but because one memory pushes aside all the others.

Towards the end of March I flew to Texas, to Dallas, to see the two people who in 1940 took in my young sister's children and kept them until after the end of the war. A lack of courage has kept me from writing of this sooner—it should have been put first.

In the summer of 1940, when she came to Dallas, she was the guest of a Miss Hockaday, the head of a girls' school, who had been her guarantor when she applied for the visa to take her children to the States. The school was more luxurious than an English school of its kind, and she could have stayed there, teaching or helping in some way, and kept her four-year-old son and two years younger daughter with her. This was not her idea. She was determined to get back—the thought of being out of England during a war, safe when her husband and her friends were in danger, was intolerable. With that generosity as natural to Americans as breathing, several foster-parents offered themselves to her. She chose the Leakes, Sam and Betty, because they were moderately well-off but not rich—reflecting with good sense that it would not do to give two English children a sort of life they would later miss—and (this was important) because they were young, her own age: their kindness, their warmth of heart, was a young kindness, a young gentleness, a young warmth. She trusted her two to them with the confidence born of recognizing goodness at its clearest and simplest.

I left a Pittsburgh scoured by an icy wind and flurries of snow. In Dallas, less than seven hours away, the air was warmer than an English June, the sky flawlessly blue and wide, wide, with magnificent sunsets, and streets and gardens were vivid with tulips, wisteria, red-bud, azaleas.

At first sight of the Leakes on the airfield, or at first sound of Betty's low voice, I knew they were what my sister had said they were: the best people in the world. In a clear spirit one reads the first lines first and quickly.

That evening when I came down the stairs from my bedorom, calling some phrase over my shoulder, I found their black cook leaning against the wall in the living-room, her hands pressed to her throat. Staring at me wildly, pupils rolling from side to side, she said,

'Oh, Miz Daisy, you startled me near my death. I thought you were Miz Dorothy speaking.'

This was one of the few moments when I came across a trace of my young sister in this town where, for a few weeks, she was safe.

Dallas had more obvious graces and moved at a slower pace than any northern city. I met a great many people, and now and then I caught myself wondering what would happen to this friendly hospitable society when the last of the old negro servants died. I lunched in the splendid new building of the *Dallas News*, seated at one end of a long table, facing Miss Dorothy Parker, as terrible as an army with banners, in a Tyrolean hat, at the other. One evening in a restaurant I argued with a rich lawyer who *knew* that in England in 1949 we had a Communist government. I tried to convince him that all but one or two of our Labour leaders hold their noses when they pass a communist, but he knew better. Since he knew also that Roosevelt had been in the pay of the Russians, I had to abandon argument. He smiled kindly, stretching a thin-lipped mouth in the face of an elderly well-nourished baby.

'Don't try to mislead me. And as soon as they start shooting people, come back here. We'll look after you.'

I thanked him. You never know.

Another evening, as we sat listening to the wireless, Sam Leake suddenly jumped to his feet and switched it off.

'I can't stand that damn Yankee voice any longer,' he said.

No Englishman ever grasps the question of 'state rights' and their deep roots. He expects the United States to be a single-stemmed power, and is disconcerted when one of these buried roots begins to twitch in the ground.

I imagine that, even talking incontrovertible good sense—perhaps more easily then—a damn Yankee voice disturbs dust that the northerner has forgotten exists.

The whole time I was in Dallas I had one overwhelming idea, which I pursued, as reticently as possible, everywhere. I hoped, expected, that at some turn, in some word, some casual memory started up by my passing, I should catch up with my young sister. On earth as new to her as this, her light steps ought not to be confused and obliterated, as in England they were by the many times she had crossed and recrossed the same paths.

To Betty Leake I could talk freely. I told her—I had told no one else—that Dorothy's youngest child did not even know whose fingers had made the furniture for her doll's house.

'I think she does,' Betty said quietly. 'I think they both have memories they hide. As children do.'

I should have remembered this from my own secretive childhood. It might well be true.

Betty had a box filled with letters from my sister to the children, which she was keeping with the idea that she might give it to them when they grew up. I doubt she ever did this, or even whether it would be right. What could the pages of letters written by a young English woman, dead these many years, mean to two young Americans? Nothing.

Nothing.

When my sister left Dallas, she asked Miss Hockaday to let her leave a large suitcase at the school, telling her it held things that would be useless in England in wartime, she would take it when she came back for the children. Betty and I opened it together. There were clothes I had given her for America—*to mense herself*, as we say in Yorkshire—the blue taffeta evening dress, the black dinner-dress, the quilted dressing-gown (never worn), and some knitting wool, a pair of light shoes from Nieman-Marcus, and three steel pans.

Holding the shoes, I remembered that she had told me about them. 'They are beautiful shoes, too good to wear now; it will be nice to have them after the war.' She smiled, half at herself, at her habit, like my father's, of hoarding new clothes, half in pleasure at the thought of these fine shoes waiting in Dallas for her.

Oh, poor child.

'There's one person you've not seen yet, and you must,' Betty said. 'Dr Perkins is the best children's doctor we have, and he refused to charge for treating two English children.'

When I saw him, alone, I knew that any kindness he did would be the gesture of a naturally Christian soul—for all I know he was an atheist. He had a glance that raked your mind, but gently, and a singularly quiet voice. Afterwards I wrote down what he said.

'For me, your sister was England. Just before she left, she came to see me, bringing the little girl—who was, I think, just two years and five months. Since I was going to keep an eye on the two of them, she had come to tell me how she wanted them brought up—above all, to be self-reliant. At that time, you know, we all here feared and expected that England would go down. I and other people had done our utmost to persuade her to stay in Dallas, but she was absolutely insistent on going home. Looking at me, scowling at me, in fact, she said: "What I think is that Nick and Judy, and the other English children in America, will grow up and come back to England *and get it back*" I have never forgotten the tone in which she spoke the last three words, almost spitting them at the Germans—and at me if I had any doubts... The other thing I haven't forgotten is that when she dropped her handkerchief, instead of stooping for it herself, she told the child to pick it up... I have the greatest respect for your sister. As I said, for me she is England.'

*No*, I thought... She was a young English woman, the daughter of Hannah Margaret Jameson and grand-daughter of George Gallilee, that's all, that's all.

Several people spoke to me about her 'amazing composure'. I did not tell them—why should I?—that it was not, in their sense of the word, composure; it was the same impulse that makes me refuse to be seen suffering. Only to be told about this 'amazing composure' let me see the bitter scalding tears she wept when she was alone.

An older woman told me, 'I was with Betty and Sam the evening your sister left. She put the children to bed—I remember that it was Sunday—then came down and went off on the six o'clock train to Chicago on her way to Montreal, to the boat. All of us there cried, but not she. She smiled.'

The other memories of that time are less distinct. I worked harder than ever. I was inveigled into lecturing and making speeches, things I detest doing. I made the speech at the Thomas Masaryk Memorial meeting—for how much longer will that be a saint's day of the Czech colony in Pittsburgh?—preparing it with enormous care. An accident—I scribbled notes on it about the spare beauty of a Pittsburgh hillside under snow, white-roofed shacks, the spectres of steel mills—has saved the last page.

The sardonic gleam in Jan Masaryk's eye forces me to skip a lyrical passage. It ends:

'... Europe will survive, will emerge from the chaos it has fallen into, and begin again that effort towards freedom and unity it has made again and again through the centuries. In this effort Czechoslovakia will be involved both by the character of its people and the need that any future, any imaginable future, will have of them. The two Masaryks, father and son, belong to the future, not to the past. To say that Thomas Masaryk's work for his country must be done over again is a half-truth. The truth is that it was done once for all time. The country he created cannot die. The spirit cannot die, and Masaryk's Czechoslovakia is idea and spirit. In violent death once, in life always, the name Masaryk is simply another name for Europe, for the idea and everlasting life of Europe.'

If, but for an accident, I should have forgotten my words completely, I am not so likely to forget a conversation I had afterwards with an elderly Czech. He had a brown blunt face, long nose, deeply furrowed cheeks, thick coarse hair like colourless wool, a clown's mouth, from which came a voice of astonishing force. His English was uncertain.

'So, in 1945, you talked to Beneš?'

'Yes.'

'And he said that the future of Czechoslovakia was to be a rock between East and West. But his Czechoslovakia has no future!'

'How can you be sure?'

'Do you, you, believe that anything of Masaryk has a future?'

'Sometimes a man doesn't die at the time of his death. Do you think that Jan Masaryk died forever on March the tenth, 1948? I don't.'

'All that is literature!' he said, with a controlled violence.

Since I said nothing—I detest my habit of turning emotions into phrases— he smiled and went on, 'Talk of something else. Do you know that not one of my son's children speaks a word of our language? And you imagine that we here, in Pittsburgh, will keep the idea of Masaryk's Czechoslovakia alive? You are crazy. No, no, the fight is lost.' Stretching out splayed knotted fingers, he took a boy by the ear and said something to him in, I suppose, Czech. The boy grinned at him and escaped. 'You see?' he grumbled. 'My grandson, and he thinks I am an old buffoon and savage. He is an American, he knows less than my—' he slapped his lean buttocks—'about Czechoslovakia, and cares nothing.'

Another occasion when I gave a lecture prolonged itself for more than forty hours. One of my friendly adult 'pupils' and her husband drove us some eighty miles north-east of Pittsburgh to a small town with a college where, after the canonical lunch of chicken salad and ice cream, I depressed two hundred women by talking about Sartre, Malraux, and the future of Europe. It was a very worthy lecture, and could not have been less suited to its audience. Afterwards we drove to the university town of Oberlin: it was dark when we reached it, and I recall only tree-lined streets and a hotel where we could not get a bottle of wine because it was a dry town.

The next day, we drove a great many more miles west and south across Ohio to lunch with Louis Bromfield.

Not satisfied to be a successful novelist, this remarkable man was running a large farm on a method he spent time, health, a religious passion, to persuade other farmers to try. Had he any other religion? From the astonishment with which Blanche and Alfred Knopf, staying in the house, greeted us, I think we were not expected. It mattered very little: no one, not even Mrs Bromfield, knew how many guests to prepare for. In the end, after a formidable tour of the estate in a jeep Alfred and I shared with four or five enormous dogs, lunch was served to some fifteen people. Louis Bromfield questioned me about the post-war English novelists: ashamed to say I had not read them, I began improvising. He looked at me shrewdly and said, 'Don't bother, I was being polite.' He had a bottle of seaweed tablets in front of his plate, and swallowed nine. 'To give me energy,' he said.

Some time that evening we reached Kenyon. I have never seen a more charming university, and I thanked God for Pittsburgh. Cloistered in this park, what on earth should I have learned about America except that it is vast and has magnificent trees and friendly learned people?

The drive home went on for hour after hour, until two in the morning. At night, even more overpoweringly than in the daytime, the country has no beginning and no end, it stretches beyond belief, a distance without imaginable limits. It will look no different, I thought, the day after all human and animal life has been obliterated.

I have never had so strongly the sense that this can easily happen, that we are on this planet on sufferance.

At long intervals we drove through or round the threadbare edge of towns which might have been abandoned except by the couple blotted against a tree or the groups of two or three young negroes turning to the car faces made phosphorescent by the lighting. Lines of street-lamps lit up trees, shadowy white houses, the ragged ends of lawns, and stopped abruptly, on the edge of nothing. One of these towns was called Warsaw. There are forbidding enough tracts in Poland, but they are less irreducible by the mind, less inhuman, than parts of America. The continent has not been gentled yet. With its brutal extremes of heat, cold, wind, light, its grass oceans, immense rivers, wild, untamed, and to eyes used to Thames and Tweed, monotonous, I doubt it can be.

At some point in the night journey, we crossed the same river five or six times. Impossible to imagine why, in this featureless plain, it should have turned on itself so often—unless for a joke.

We left Pittsburgh in June. The train journey to New York takes eight hours—by air we could have been there in one, but it is a horrible flight, over forests that suck the air into great precipices, and with too many chances of a thunderstorm: during storms I prefer to have sea or earth under me— and I had all the time in the world to think of what I was losing: friends I was obliged to for their incomparable *bonté*—I cannot find a more exact word—and the happiness of being part of a lively idiosyncratic society. I had gained—it has not, of course, lasted—a certain insouciance towards other people's opinions; I could talk to an acquaintance without the anxious sense that I must say what I know is in his own mind. No doubt this was because, for nearly a year, I had been liked, by a number of men and women who wanted from me only my company, and with whom I had no feeling of being surrounded, as in intellectual circles in London, by vanities it is only too easy, by a clumsy gesture, to offend.

None the less it was time I left.

During the last eleven months, as if part of my life had been amputated, I had written nothing except the odd article. All writers are more or less insane and lead an unnatural life. I had had a lucid interval.

Some time during the night, a yellow-haired woman in the seat behind spoke to me.

'You are English, yes?'

'I am.'

'I was in England, once. I am German. Not a refugee—a true German. England is a kind, beautiful country, and do you know why? Because for hundreds of years its people have loved it.'

'That could be one reason,' I said. 'Parts of it are no longer beautiful. I suppose that means——'

Offended by my manner, she interrupted me. 'I meant only to say what I feel.'

'Yes,' I said. 'Thank you.'

No one had asked her, true German that she was, to have an opinion on England.

And my own opinions on America? Were they any less uncalled-for, less ignorant? I realized that I had none, I had only a great many confused notions. Without trying, I had lost almost completely the sense of being in a country more alien than no matter what primitive corner of a Europe where the dust is half human. The nightmare of a submerged Europe that seized me on landing had been transformed into a conviction which seemed splendidly rational and was in fact no better than an emotion. Lying at the side of a lake in upper New York State, I made a note on the fly-leaf of a copy of the *Mémoires d'un touriste* that I had brought with me. Having made it, I thought myself dispensed from thinking of the question again. (This saved me a great deal of mental wear and tear during arguments about the Common Market in the months before General de Gaulle's egoism turned out to be more brutal than ours.)

### 3rd of July 1949, Lake Minnewaska

A nation can only grow by engaging in an enterprise which calls on all its energies, forces it to believe in itself, make demands on itself, discipline itself. The nations of Europe can go no farther as separate entities, they will become demoralized and run down, get used to living at a lower and lower intensity. The single enterprise which can summon all their energies, rouse, excite, is to construct a *European* nation. This alone can give us a new strong pulse of life. It only can match the discipline and force of Communism by holding up to be realized a gigantic human image. Oppose, to the new Russia, a new Europe, a new intellectual inspiration, a new plan of living—voilà tout ce qu'il faut...

How positive and clearsighted one becomes, on hot afternoons, with nothing to do but stare at an immense cloudless sky, listen to the croaking of frogs in a weedy lake, turn the pages of a book read many times already, and think over a problem at the greatest possible distance from its centre!

I could not live in America—I have Europe in my bones, and I should lose my memory if I left it for good—but I cannot think without envy of the benefits to a writer of being born into this exciting, dangerous, not yet fully humanized country. Its violence may crush him but, given that he is not morally impotent, is surely as likely to give him what the habit of the sea gave Joseph Conrad, infinite patience, infinite trust in fidelity to experience, a little arrogance, a sharp eye for the visible world, and the confidence of controlled power.

At the very least, it must save him from the literary inbreeding among English novelists, unavoidable in so overcrowded a *panier à crabes*.

## CHAPTER 7

LANDING IN ENGLAND was a rapid descent into a familiar valley; I was content to be living there again, but the air, no mistake about it, was noticeably less exhilarating.

As soon as we were settled again in the Ilkley hotel I let the characters of *The Green Man* take possession of me. They did so with ferocious energy. What had begun in my mind as the portrait of a scholarly Christian gentleman and radical eccentric, not unlike R. H. Tawney, became a society, the established society of the 'thirties and 'forties reflected in the lives of two brothers, their children and their friends and associates; more than a score of men and women of many conditions and ages; social and political intrigues and jealousies; young men at Oxford, in love, marrying, divorcing, climbing, failing to climb; the war; the shifting moral currents. A single character, the Jewish newspaper proprietor, Cohen, survived from the world of *The Mirror in Darkness*; the many others had pushed themselves forward during the year in America when I was not able to write.

'What are you working on?'

'A novel,' I said, biting back the answer: My finest novel.

In the end it brought me one of my sharpest disappointments...

I did not begin writing at once; for the first time in my life I was afraid of the first step. I spent weeks meditating and planning, and in September I went to Venice for a week, to the P.E.N. Congress.

Short of writing a book in which every narrow blackish-green canal, walled garden, vast empty square of shuttered houses and dilapidated church, every dark alley, museum, neglected palace, and artisan's workshop, is set faithfully in its place round the cathedral and the Riva degli Schiavoni—still, in the teeth of tourists, alive with Goldoni's characters, passing and repassing—what can anyone say about Venice except that it would be a marvellous place in which to learn to trust in Providence. Preferably in a room looking over one of the more luminous canals.

The Congress—unless I have forgotten too much—was peaceful except for the moment when an excited Italian rushed on to the platform and challenged Ignazio Silone to a duel on the ground that Signora Silone had, the day before, spoken of his friend, a woman of untarnished virtue, as having been Mussolini's mistress. 'And she was!' an Italian yelled in the audience, so enraging the virtuous woman's defender that the speakers' table collapsed under his fists. The delegate from Scotland, Douglas Young, immensely tall, wearing, I think, a kilt, led him gently from the platform. The duel did not take place, but the incident made everyone happy and interrupted the flood of Italian eloquence sounding, because of the merciless repetition of the name Croce, like a chorus in *The Frogs*...

I came back to some of the blackest days of my life—to one day in particular when a relationship I had built up over the months, at infinite cost, was pulled down on my head in a few hours of violent fury.

Much later, I thought that there had been one moment when, if I had been truly a loving person, I could have found words to stop the destruction. So that in effect it was another failure of warmth. This, which did not occur to me for several weeks, may be true and yet it may have been impossible *not* to fail...

I write that without believing it. A failure is always a failure. The respectable reasons for it, and the excuses, are irrelevant.

I sunk myself in work. One day, at the end of November, I told myself: Tomorrow you can start writing... That night I had a curiously lucid dream. Guy and I, dead, were going up to be judged. There was a curtain over a doorway. Pulling his arm, I said: Look, there is something inside. We went in, I had a paper in my hand and laid it in a shallow box. Someone indistinct, a woman, asked me: What have you to confess? Almost crying, I said: All the meannesses. We went farther into the room; there were papers to be filled up, some sort of examination, and a friend who had died lately was beside me... I woke thinking: But you have been much worse than mean. I thought of the things I wished I had not done. No use.

After breakfast, pleasantly a little cold with dread, I began writing.

The discipline I had taught myself, and the innate egotism of the writer, his belief that what he has begun has a necessity of its own, kept me at work eight and ten hours a day, month after month, against the drag of acute anxiety.

I had not tried to discourage my son's plan to sail his 21-ton ketch to Australia, taking his wife and their baby; I had even, since he had set his heart and will on it, helped as well as I could, but during the months when he was getting the boat ready for the long dangerous voyage I lived with all the minute particulars of grief and panic.

I worked in this way at *The Green Man* through the first eight months of 1950, not letting a chapter or paragraph go until there was nothing more I could do to it. Half way through August, I put the manuscript in a drawer and we went down to a hotel on the south coast, a few miles from the yacht, for the last two or three weeks before they sailed. Longer would have been too long; I should have been in the way.

Bill had taken on a 'crew', a middle-aged ex-petty officer he had known for some time and trusted completely. He was a small man, weathered and agile, and in the instant of setting eyes on him I felt a pang of doubt, the briefest possible. It disappeared at once, and when my son asked, 'Well, what do you think of J——?' I said easily, 'Oh, he's splendid, just the man you need.'

Afterwards I thought that the old captain, my father, had jogged my elbow for a second; he had only to glance at a seaman to know whether the fellow were any good.

There was little I could do to help except look after Frances. Not two years old yet, she was an enchantingly gay sweet-tempered baby; she never cried and was never bored. (There was a moment during the first fortnight after they left when the sea came aboard: at the first moment she could leave the deck her mother ran below and found Frances sitting up in her bunk, laughing, drenched, salt water streaming off her. 'Yaining,' she said gaily.) She was ceaselessly active, and at the end of the day I was usually tired enough to be able to ignore a raging fear.

Her young mother, one of the bravest of women and very gay, had her own fears. For the first time, too late, I realized that she had been only half willing to risk the voyage. She was not afraid for herself.

One night of full moon I left the boat about eleven o'clock and stood for a minute to look at a pale sky plumed here and there with white clouds; a few barely visible stars withstood the deceptive light. The tide was out, and the mud flats had the fine seaweedy smell of the harbour at Whitby, the very same. It laid my life open—down to its earliest memory. A frightful cold lucidity seized me. Could I have stopped this mad scheme if—a thing I had never done—I had outfaced Bill's wish instead of helping it? Oughtn't I at least to have tried? And what else but my failure to bring him up carefully and wisely is responsible for his stubbornness, his reckless determination to prove himself at any cost?

I thought coldly: We do as we can... But I could not give myself absolution, and I did not know who could...

The evening before they left, we had Bill to dinner alone, and afterwards, standing on the jetty, talked for a moment about nothing.

'Off to Australia with you,' I said.

He smiled and went away.

During the thirty-nine days before I heard anything, I could not write... I sat holding my pen, to look as though I were working, and so avoid questions. A great deal of the time I was thinking about a lively well-tempered child. It was she I thought of first when the B.B.C. announcer began his account of the gale blowing in the Channel, with gusts of up to ninety miles

an hour, and small boats forced to run for shelter. One day, in London for
the week, I walked past Brompton Oratory, and turned back to go in and
kneel awkwardly behind another woman who may have known better than
I did how to pray to Our Lady. All I did was ask her that I, and not anyone
else, not my son, not his brave high-spirited wife, not his child, might be
punished for my failure.

During this time I had a letter from Maria Kuncewiczowa—I still have
it—so purely warm and good, a luminous goodness, that if I could have
taken it truly to heart I should be a humbler and better person. 'My dearest
friend,' it began, 'I know you are frightened and I know you are blaming
yourself for anything bad that is or may be happening to Bill. I know it from
my experience...'

The first word came from them early in October, a letter written in Brest.

'We must return, I am afraid. We were not beaten by the sea though it was
moderately rough or by the weather which was mostly foul and half a gale.
It was J—— who let us down, so badly I can't quite understand it. We spent
a day or two down the Chichester Channel and finally sailed out against a
fresh S.W. wind and beat against it all that night and next day, sailing 100
miles but only making 20 miles down Channel. So we ran into Yarmouth and
waited nearly a week for a more favourable slant to the wind. It was here that
J—— began to show his colours. He adopted a completely defeatist attitude
and sat round glowering all day. Finally we got away and had a magnificent
sail down to Falmouth in quite a hard wind, putting in there because it was
freshening for the S.W. again. J—— did only his bare duty and spent all his
standby periods lying on his back. Consequently Patchen and I had to do
most of the work.

'We left Falmouth against a freshening wind from the west. It was hard
going but not impossible. A certain amount of water came aboard, and
everything got wet below. Frances behaved magnificently. J—— complained
of the hard work and said of course we would be putting into Brest, wouldn't
we. I, knowing the Ushant approach and the risks of being caught in the Bay
of Biscay by a gale before we got into really deep water, drove the ship as hard
as I dared to get over the 100 fathom line and into deep water. We managed
to work her against a moderately westerly gale 90 miles south of Ushant
10–20 miles into deep water and with about 200 miles to the Spanish coast.

'It was here that J—— with a long face announced that he thought he had dislocated his back. It was obvious he wasn't going to be any more use and that Patchen and I couldn't carry on alone for another day, so we ran for Brest, at night. Most unpleasant. The mainsail began to give trouble and J—— started panicking about flares and rockets. He couldn't or wouldn't keep the ship on course, so I had to take him off the tiller, and Pat and I did it all.

'Just as we were entering Brest harbour a final squall blew out the mainsail, split it from leech to luff. That would not have been so bad out at sea or where it actually happened, but it would have been very very awkward if it had gone off Ushant where we had no sea room.

'It was now that we were really shocked by J——. He grinned all over his face, said wasn't it a good thing we were in port again, hoisted Frances on his shoulders, swung himself up and down the rigging, and generally behaved like a two-year-old. I was speechless with rage. I had put my ship in hazard because I thought he was injured, and it was now obvious that he had decided he couldn't take it and would use any lie to get into port... We shall return when we get reasonable weather. Patchen is desperately keen to do the trip. We have proved to our satisfaction that we can stand it, that the ship can stand it, and most important of all that little Frances can stand it. Damn J——.

'Expect us when you see us. It depends on the weather, because I don't consider that messing round with Ushant in anything but moderate weather is a justifiable risk, not now.'

The wretched J—— jumped ship at Falmouth on the way home. A few days after the return, Bill began flying again, this time for one of the independent airlines. I suspected that the voyage, or one like it, was only put off to a better day, but I took care not to ask, and went back to my novel.

By now I knew most of the characters as I knew myself, and I took immense pains to mistrust each of them as thoroughly as I mistrust myself, disbelieving my first impressions of them, spying on them, doing all I could to penetrate their perfectly natural hypocrisy. In solitary walks across the moor, I pored over this and that act which I had accepted at its face value until I thought I had the truth.

About this time, too, in October, I was delighted, for a reason of my own, to hear that I had been sentenced by the Soviet 'peace fighters', with much more vehemence than in the Nazi Black Book of (I think) 1940. Harrison

Salisbury, the correspondent in Moscow for the *New York Times*, sent me his article about the proposed 'Book of Death'—proposed by the Literary Gazette—containing 'the names of all those monsters and cannibals who openly preach destruction of millions of human lives and of the greatest values of world culture.' What delighted me was to find my name in a list which included one of the great novelists of our age, perhaps the greatest, André Malraux.

## CHAPTER 8

THAT YEAR WINTER began early and stayed late, weeks of freezing rain followed in the north by three months of thick snow. The surface froze and walking between the banked-up walls of snow was difficult, I fell every time I went out, but I have kept from my childhood a trick of falling light. Electricity was rationed, and between half-past eight in the morning until four there was no heat in the hotel; wrapping myself in a quilt off the bed, I sat writing in an icy room; my fingers stiffened, my brains luckily did not.

By April the last traces of the snow had gone, but the ground was water-logged and still frozen to a depth, so that the farmers could not start sowing and the lambs born earlier died. I saw the first leaf buds on the chestnut opposite my window when the trees and stunted bushes on the moor higher up were still bare and black, as though sculptured. Spring came in a head-long rush, at the very end of May, all the trees breaking into flower at once, heavy-tasselled lilacs, gross waxen chestnut candles, spume of hawthorn and wild cherry. The laburnums were magnificent, great fountains of yellow fire.

This month, June, the last visible thread holding me to Whitby was snipped by the death of my mother's sister, the last of George Gallilee's many daughters. As thin as a bone, lively, drolly kind to stray animals, detesting children as cruel noisy conscienceless little brutes, completely fearless—I am certain she never told a lie, not the whitest, in all her eighty-odd years—an unshakably firm and simple Christian, of Cromwell's sect, she had been living on in the house my grandfather bought for his children when he made his disastrous second marriage, alone except for a servant as old as herself, who had long given up expecting to be paid her wages. My aunt's income, shrinking in value all the time, was less than two hundred a year. The house, in a terrace of houses built without bathrooms, decayed, its one remaining grace a view across roofs and beyond the harbour to the ancient Parish Church and ruined Abbey on the opposite cliff. As the old servant grew older and frailer, my aunt's rooms on one of the upper floors were rarely cleaned, dust and cobwebs thickened in corners, leather-bound copies of the classics fell apart, and silk rotted: below, in the basement where old Catherine lived and slept, the walls mildewed, and larders and cupboards, alive with generations of mice, held little else except broken crockery, old yellowed papers, filthy rags.

I had never seen anyone so dead as my Aunt Jennie, so *gone*. The shrunken hawked face and thin tiny body made less mark in the bed than an infant.

When I was not struggling to clear up the disorder, I walked about the narrow streets on both sides of the harbour, talking to myself in silence. I climbed the one hundred and ninety-nine steps to look at my brother's memorial in the old church. I followed my mother's steps, at first impatient and light, then slow, in the streets, lanes, and moor roads where she wore her life away, beginning with old shabby streets she knew as a young married woman and ending in the fields behind her last house. For the last time, my very dear, I told her, for the last time.

I could not live in Whitby again, but in a sense I live nowhere else, since only there and nowhere else except on the lowest level of my being, do I touch and draw energy from a few key images, sea, distant lights, the pure line of a coast, first images and last, source of such strength as I have. Source, too, of my talent for happiness...

I wrote the last pages of *The Green Man* in June. It had occupied two years of intensely hard work, with several serious interruptions, the worst that of Bill's aborted voyage. None of them were of the kind that ruins me as a writer—no domestic drudgery, no responsibility for looking after a house. This was the last time I was able to write a whole book in freedom, at the full stretch of my—limited—powers. Since then I have contrived only weeks or a few months of that most acute of all mental pleasures. Uncovenanted mercies. Like February days when the wind is warm from the south-west and streams overrun their banks, days of false spring, no stir at the buried roots.

For what I have received may the Lord make me truly thankful. And more truly for what I have not received...

I had promised to write a long preface to the English edition of Anne Frank's diary, and began it at once.

A few days ago a friend spoke slightingly of this little book. 'Far too much fuss has been made about a thoroughly trivial book.'

'You are wrong.'

'Why? You know yourself it is trivial.'

I am not sure of that. I could argue, with Léautaud, that the finest because purest form of literature is written as easily and naturally as one writes a letter: anything else is pose, worked-up emotion, rhetoric. The fourteen-year-old child trying to hide from her butchers wrote as naturally as birds sing, as Léautaud himself. In the likeness which emerges from her diary there is nothing self-conscious, no trace, not the faintest, of showing-off, of acting a part, even before herself; she is even able to recognize the temptation to be a little sorry for herself and reject it, even comes to realize that to use a little hypocrisy would make her life in this over-crowded hiding-place easier, but does not come to using it; instead she breaks through to something like calm, to a half-tender, half-indifferent and unchildlike patience—almost to detachment; she has no vanity; she is candour, innocence, sanity, gaiety itself.

I don't rest on this miracle of simplicity my belief that her diary deserves to be remembered. Nor on the stupefying fact that to a number of her fellow human beings it seemed proper and necessary to send this charming intelligent good child to die, as people died in Belsen, of hunger, cold, weakness.

The mind cannot form any image of mass murder, and to say that the Nazis killed six million Jews evokes only an image of darkness, a shadowy river flowing sluggishly across Europe. But if, in that black stream, a face is suddenly turned to you, the face of a clear-eyed smiling child, you feel the horror in your veins, in the marrow of your mind.

Poor child. She did not ask to become a symbol. But, since she has become one, let us agree that a trivial story, a child's naïve observations and heart-searchings, are worth more to the world than all my industrious labours as a novelist.

*

'Possibly I would not ask you to do this,' Maria Kuncewiczowa wrote, 'if you were not yourself an exile in a cold tough world. I ought in honesty and love to add: One day, when you'll be in need of help, your insane generosity, on which we count, may not be reciprocated. This sounds bitter, and is only meant to be sober.'

She had founded a P.E.N. Centre for Exiled Writers. It included Poles, Czechs, Slovaks, Estonians, Catalans, Castilians, Hungarians, Russians, Jugoslavs, the definition of a writer-in-exile being: One who, were he to return to his country, would be in grave danger of denial of his human rights... Let it go as a definition.

'They are second and third rate writers,' Maria went on, 'or too young to be classed yet, but should they not be allowed their chance to write and to publish, since there is such a thing as a second and third rate public?'

Let that go, too. Any writer who is able to write against the crushing pressure of exile (cut off from his roots, his tongue removed) has something to say worth listening to. And any attempt an exile makes to break through his solitude, his alienation, implies a measure of courage, or defiance, I find moving and admirable, to be respected.

The new Centre needed money for its basic needs, paper, stamps, English lessons for those young enough to profit by them, cost of translating a few manuscripts worth the risk. Growling under my breath, I agreed to write begging letters to English writers. Since it would be no use sending out a circular letter, and I had to write them all separately myself, it took me into August to finish.

Years ago, in 1939, when I was begging for our desperately poor refugees, I had discovered that it is never the rich who give generously to causes or persons *of no importance*; it is the modestly well-off, the Olaf Stapledons, the E. M. Forsters, the Walter de la Mares. So it was now.

Next year I wrote to Walter de la Mare again, another begging letter. Jan Parandowski had taken it into his head to form a library of English books for the use of his students in Warsaw University. He wrote telling me I must ask English writers, at once, to send him—also at once—one or more of their books. 'You may ask any writer you please, with disregard of politics. Regard only his merits as a writer...' Notwithstanding this assurance that there was still, in Poland, a margin of freedom—or was Parandowski being treated as a cultural unicorn?—I chose my writers discreetly. Only one of them refused, and every book sent reached Parandowski in Warsaw.

In the letter Walter de la Mare wrote telling me which of his books he had sent, he went on, 'Do please be sure to let me know of any opportunity when you are in London to come to pay a visit to this old creature at Twickenham. He will show you a tree. When ever your name echoes in memory, for some reason it brings back to me an evening when I was escorting you to the Crystal Palace station; there was no room inside the tram, it was windy on top, you wore no hat—so I luxuriated in your hair!'

This was not the first or the second time he had reminded me about an evening when he went out of his way to persuade the youngest and certainly the most timid and least articulate of his visitors that she was no less important to him than the rest. For a moment, holding the page with its fine writing, I was filled with the secret confidence, the happiness, the insane hopes, of that time...

I went to Twickenham. It was a long time since I had seen him, and essentially he had not changed. The fragility of old age had effaced every uncertain line and colour, leaving a creature of such lightness, such transparent liveliness and gaiety, a human elemental, that he might have belonged to another kind of being, nearer the race of birds.

He had always been unlike any other person in the world—a difference hard to pin down without making him seem not altogether human. In a way—a way which did not preclude warmth, kindness, mischief, parental pride, and a quick direct heart—he was not. Not altogether.

## CHAPTER 9

THE REST OF THAT YEAR, after I had finished my begging letters, slipped through my fingers.

When Hermon Ould died, it was the quiet guttering out of a wick burned down to the last thread. During the thirty years he worked, for the wage of a clerk, as its International Secretary, P.E.N. had eaten first his talents as poet and dramatist, in which no one for years had believed, except, with less and less conviction, a few of his friends, and then his whole personal life.

He became nothing but this detached overworked apparently serene figure who—with reserved irony—kept writers of forty-odd nations more or less at peace with each other, held his tongue about all he knew of their vanity, egoism, intrigues and jealousies, befriended exiles, talked to governments on their behalf. Now, having devoured everything else in him, his—call it what you like—his devotion, obsession, inner flame—started on his flesh.

I have never been certain whether or not he guessed that he was dying of an inoperable cancer. His loyal friend, David Carver, had made up his mind to tell him the truth if he asked. He never asked. But that might have been out of politeness of heart, or his habit of detachment from himself. Or it might have been a refusal to play the part of a dying man—he had no liking for playing a part, no talent for it, and no vanity... There is a lot to be said for dying in your own home, surrounded by the things you have taken the trouble to keep near you—a hospital is already an alienation. And even more to be said for having in your life one person, one is enough, to whom, without awkwardness, you can start a sentence with the words: You might, by the way, when I'm dead, write to... tear up the letters in... sacrifice a cock to... Everything his friends said to him during his weeks in hospital was falsified and emptied of meaning by what they knew and he did not.

Coming away from one of these unreal talks, I was struck by the newly youthful look of London. Buildings that had been drab and war-stained so long were being painted in light colours: one in particular, Hawkes of Savile Row, stood out with extreme clarity, and in another Mayfair street a small public-house had set two tables on the narrow pavement. The air was warm and soft. Again and again, in a walk that took me from Bond Street to Westminster Bridge and back by way of Pall Mall and St James's Street to the Green Park, I caught sight of the exquisite ghost of the old confident friendly London, stepping forward in a clear light in one of the last moments before the rebuilders laid their filthy paws on her.

Towards the end of the year, my six years of guilty delicious freedom came to an end when I agreed to rent an unfurnished flat in Leeds. It was an ugly flat in an ugly solid building and, as everywhere in Leeds, the building itself, and the unhappy trees and shrubs of the garden, were blackened by soot. In the days, or rather, the nights before we moved in I went through innumerable—I should be ashamed to try to number them—crises of infantile despair, anger, frustration, resentment, and again despair, alternating with resolves to honour the conviction bred in me by generations of iron-souled Yorkshirewomen, that it is a woman's bounden duty to provide a home for her family.

To be a little just to myself, I should add that these crises took place for the most part out of sight. The tip of the wild beast's tongue came round the door, but not the animal. Not even Guy, with whom I am least guarded, had any notion of the black suffocating wave of nausea, revulsion and all but ungovernable terror that submerged me, again and again, night after night, like a piece of driftwood tossing in the North Sea.

Time and again in my life since a girl went weeping and raging into her first house, I have broken loose, pushing roughly or cunningly past everyone in my way, and lived in precarious freedom for a few months, even, once, for a few years. Always in the end to be driven back inside, stifling insane panic. Like any other living organism which is being suffocated, I struggle and knock my head on the walls. I do it figuratively now, in secrecy and mental darkness; when I was young I did it in sober fact. *Let me out, there's no air here...*

The frightful tension of keeping the two halves of myself, the violent conscienceless rebel and the good child, from flying apart might have sent me mad if I were not—as I am—very solid, very strong, rather well-meaning.

I am a disciplined madman—the very sanest of madmen...

Without Guy my life would lack its salt and honey, but our two needs pull diametrically opposite ways. Yet surely I could have managed better, even for myself?...

I had been commissioned to write a play for the B.B.C., and I spent my last free fortnight writing it, a sad little comedy drawn, at a great distance, from Bataille's *Poliche.*

Our furniture and books had been stored in Ilkley; we moved them to Leeds on a cold overcast day in December. It was impossible to get help and—any Yorkshirewoman will bear me out—this corner of the West Riding is as black as the Styx. I polished chairs and silver, scrubbed, dusted. I cannot endure slovenly ways and rooms, cracked imperfect objects, ugly furniture. I am a fine self-taught cook, it rests with me to rise into the class of minor chefs, but I cannot understand why the soufflés and *boeuf en daube*

I prepare for my guests do not poison them. I detest the heat of an oven, it makes me swear like a third mate, and I touch greasy pans as I would a viper, with loathing.

I darn beautifully—sometimes, when I watch it darning, my hand is my father's long-fingered hand (he darned his own socks, like any sailor): I have all his physical patience, and a metaphysical impatience of the devil.

At the day's end I was exhausted. This was the first time I noticed a real estrangement between my body and me. The beast was beginning to flag. But it was a good beast still, and needed little more than to be shown the whip—even although, under the pressure of rage and boredom, my immense energy can mimic total exhaustion to the life.

I began to understand what Dante intended by immersing sinners guilty of accidie—vulgarly called sloth—in the filthy Styx. Accidie is the wilful refusal of happiness, and a form of despair, which is the sin against the Holy Ghost. And against the spirit of a phrase I tried repeating to myself at moments: *In returning and rest shall ye be saved and in confidence shall be your strength*... But returning where?

In the end, that is, in four or five weeks, my resilience was too much for my ill-will—also, I was genuinely heartened whenever I caught sight of Guy's pleasure in working at his own desk in an incredible disorder of books, notes, unanswered letters, scraps of paper, odds and ends of every kind, the working tools of the scholar-bachelor he is at heart—and I began a novel on a political theme, laid in a South American state. Finished at the end of May, it dissatisfied me profoundly. It had a plot, an admirable one, but no theme, and my mind only exerts itself to its limit when it is given a bone to gnaw. I sent it to both my agents, A. D. Peters in London and Carl Brandt in New York, telling them I feared it was superficial.

Both agreed with me, and I told them to destroy the scripts.

'You are a good trooper,' Carl wrote, 'the only author without any vanity I have ever known.'

He was mistaken. What I lack is not vanity, but confidence. I cannot take myself as seriously, not to say solemnly, as do all, or almost all my nimble-witted contemporaries. This is a frightful drawback.

At the same time, I do know when I have written well, and then, if no animal understands me, I am vexed...

There was one marvellous break in this Stygian spring. In March, my fare paid by Unesco, I spent four days in Paris, at a meeting of the International Executive of P.E.N. I did little enough for the P.E.N. now, becoming active only at moments, like an amiable volcano. Like a torpid snake, my friend Robert Neumann said... It is possible. How do I know? One sees oneself in such a dim light.

We stayed, Veronica Wedgwood, David Carver, now in Hermon's chair, I in my ridiculous role of elder statesman, at a hotel on the Quai des Augustins, and in the morning I had the acute pleasure of watching the sun rise behind Péguy's Notre Dame, a ship moored in mid-stream, half hidden in the Seine mists.

The evening we arrived, Czeslaw Milosz came to the hotel and hurried me, in pouring rain, to a restaurant in the Place de l'Odéon. Looking at him as he talked, at a face smoothly youthful, younger than his thirty-odd years, it was hard to believe that the ironical despair and anger of what he was saying were more than a gesture. And indeed either word reflects only one facet of a mind as complicated as any poet's. Any genuine poet.

His uneasy situation at this time was even half accidental. Or rather, it had come about because he was not calculating, not adroit, not prudent, not in any sense of the word a politician. Eighteen months earlier, in October 1950, he had been posted to Paris as cultural attaché. Leaving his young wife in Washington, expecting a child, he went to Paris, then to Warsaw, where he was told suavely that his duty as a Polish poet was to live and write in Poland; he would be given a comfortable apartment, and probably a professorship. Until now, if he had thought of breaking away, he had reminded himself that 'twenty-four million Poles cannot emigrate.' But faced with the necessity of becoming part of a highly efficient intellectual machine, he felt a violent repugnance. He left Warsaw and went back to Paris, where he had friends.

From now on, he was in trouble both as man and poet. A poet's whole reason for existence, like his only valid autobiography, is in his poetry, and he had cut himself off from his audience, a form of suicide. Moreover, he was far too intelligent to accept the myth of a world eternally divided between an enlightened West and a barbaric anti-intellectual East: he could neither throw himself into the arms of exiles clinging with blind rage to the ghost of a dead Poland, nor lop his imagination to work inside a dialectic which none the less he recognized to be a powerful intellectual structure, the scaffolding of a deformed reality. The illusion outraged his intelligence by its futility, the dialectic offended his emotional and intellectual need, as a poet, to be free.

And, final irony, the American authorities were hesitating over his visa. He was sometimes half mad with anger, doubts, anxiety about Janka and his children in America. Over and above all this, he was bitterly humiliated.

It is conceivable that the émigrés in London would have embraced a repentant sinner, but what had he to repent? That he had lived through the Occupation, the Rising, and served loyally a ruined Poland they knew nothing about, where one educated survivor counted for a hundred? He had survived and he was arrogant—the arrogance of a writer who reserves humility for his work.

I had already written heaven knows how many long careful letters to anyone who might be able to move the State Department out of its paralysis—the most famous American writers, the more aggressive liberals, Felix Frankfurter, Eleanor Roosevelt—'She cannot be so good woman as you say,' Milosz said, smiling, 'she talks too much about human rights.'

What stupefied me at the time—less today—was the reluctance of certain people, too powerful to be in any danger, to lift a finger, and the shamefaced advice of others.

'Tell him to be patient, to wait. Sooner or later the political atmosphere will change of itself.'

Nothing, in our day, can be more banal than this story. It starts a question in my mind: How long, or rather how short a time will it take, in certain circumstances, for the so-called civilized countries to start burning heretics and breaking traitors on the wheel? The story ended—after some years—reasonably happily. That evening in the modest friendly café Voltaire, I could only watch the play of irony, despair, humour, across his face, and wonder how much irreparable damage was being done to one of the subtlest minds I have known...

In the morning, under a gentle light, Paris with its cathedral and palaces had the silvered delicacy of an old engraving, every stroke clear and unbroken, and a little remote.

We had reckoned on a difficult committee; it was no better and no worse than we expected. There were moments of intense happiness. Supper in a restaurant called La Grenouille, an infernally hot narrow room, the loudest French voices I ever heard, rough wine and good rough food, and the sense that not a soul in the place, man or woman, cared about making an impression of any sort, they were going straight for the essentials of a sane life. And, the next evening, a concert of Italian music of the eighteenth century, so clear, so ravishingly fresh and lively, that I had tears in my eyes.

At the end, the Orchestra Alessandro Scarlatti, of Naples, played the overture to *Il matrimonio segreto*. I listened to it for Stendhal. He was seventeen, in Italy for the first time, when he heard it, sung by a third-rate company in Novara or Ivrea: it gave him *un bonheur divin*, and from now on he knew that what he wanted most in the world was to live in Italy and hear such music every night.

The secretary of the French Centre, Henri Membré, was one of a sort of Frenchman nearly unintelligible to the English, whom he distrusted with all the force of his shrewd logical half-peasant soul. When, immediately after the liberation of France, he came to England, Hermon and I had welcomed him with open arms, laying ourselves out and emptying our thin purses to entertain him. In vain. He was still nursing his anger and resentment that we had got rid of Jules Romains as International President in 1941, at a time, he said bitterly, when no French voice could be heard.

'You don't count Denis Saurat's voice as French?' I asked.

'No.'

No explanation we offered shook his conviction that there had been a vile English conspiracy against one of the noblest of Frenchmen.

He was a good man as well as a calculating Norman and a minor writer: in 1940, harassed by anxiety about his son, who was with the army in Belgium and either a prisoner or dead, he went on steadily with his efforts to save interned foreign writers, 'trying,' Arthur Koestler said, 'to pick needles out of a burning haystack.'

I thought myself still unforgiven. On our last day in Paris, after he had given us glasses of his own *marc*, he took us out of the city to the Château de Champs. The sun was miraculously warm, and the trees a light wash of green, transparent and exciting. This chateau—built in the first years of the eighteenth century by a former valet who enjoyed it for ten years until the Regent confiscated it—is charming in a way the great châteaux of the Loire miss; they overwhelm with their splendour, one or two are even boring, but the Château de Champs is not only enchantingly simple and graceful, it can be loved.

I was standing alone in a window. Membré, who was walking up and down with the air of a peasant proprietor, stopped beside me and said, 'Do you not like this?'

'If you had been able to take us anywhere in the world,' I said, 'you couldn't have chosen a finer place.'

He was pleased. 'If you really mean that...'

'Oh, I've reached an age when I needn't make excuses for liking the architecture of the past better than the present. It's strange that we were once capable, easily, of miracles like this, and now only of a monumental dullness.'

'Yes, it is a miracle,' he said seriously, 'a French miracle.'

'Well—I'm happier in France than anywhere else—with and without miracles.'

'You are always polite.'

'But I don't always tell the truth,' I said. 'I'm being truthful now.'

He barely smiled. 'I think so... Shall I also be frank? I always believed that it was you who overturned Jules Romains. Our friend Hermon would not have had the—' he hesitated—'the arrogance.'

I seized the chance I had not expected. 'If Jules Romains had come to London in 1940, he would be International President at this moment. The people who had a right to speak for Europe were in London—or in occupied France and Holland and Norway. Not in America.'

He did not answer, but I had the clearest possible sense that—in spite of his anxious devotion to the great man—I had my finger on one pulse of his mind. And I knew what to say next.

'Listen. When our two Centres act together, we control P.E.N.—which is not a bad thing. If, when you're annoyed with us, you'll write to me—to me, frankly—I'll do everything I can.'

'You're being very clever,' he said, eyeing me, 'but—I think—you are sincere.'

'I ask you very humbly to believe that I'm sincere. And that I have never wanted to make use of P.E.N. for some personal reason. Why should I? I don't want to go about making speeches, and I have my work to do.'

He looked, at this moment, so like a middle-aged second mate of my father's, who used to let me plague him with questions when I was five or six, that I could have embraced him.

'From now on, we act together,' he said.

I liked him very much, I was glad I had convinced him, and I felt a familiar jeering laughter, in the pit of my stomach, at the pair we made, shaking hands solemnly, in this splendid room.

As soon as I went back to England, he wrote me a long letter which began *Chère Amie*, setting out all the reasons why, after so many years, he felt he could trust me. Too late. He died six weeks later, suddenly—*il ne s'est pas vu mourir*, Jean Schlumberger told me—and my interest in Anglo-French co-operation in P.E.N. disappeared with him. After that day, I never lifted a finger to try to change what has always been the attitude towards the English of the French Centre—friendliness broken by outbreaks of suspicion and irritation, not to say enmity.

## CHAPTER 10

THE FINGERS OF ONE HAND would be too many to count the times when I have looked forward to the publication of a novel. I am too wary to let myself hope, and too sceptical, seeing too clearly the width of the gap between it and the great novels. Besides, by the time a novel is published, I am already—or in those years I was—in some fashion involved in the next. But—partly because it had taken me so long to write, and partly that a very severe critic, my friend and agent A. D. Peters, had praised it when he read the manuscript—I hoped much from *The Green Man*. Hence my mortal disappointment when, a few weeks, I think three, before it was due to appear, I discovered that its publisher had so little faith in its merits, or its prospects, that he had printed less than a third of the number of copies earlier novels had sold.

It was a bad moment.

Anger restored me. It seemed to me that I ought to have been told what the firm thought about it. I more than suspected that it was not one of their own readers—publishers' readers always make me think of the old honourable profession of *castrati*—who had damned the manuscript; I forgave the assassin, but not the deception.

With the greatest politeness—after all, praising one's own wares is an awkward business—I protested, A. D. Peters protested, and Mr Daniel Macmillan who, until this moment, had not looked at the book, listened kindly, read it, and doubled the printing order, but it was too late, the leeway couldn't be made up.

Worse than my disappointment was the fact that I had no money left, or only enough to last me, with the greatest care, for another month or so. It was three years since I had published a novel, and for the past twelve months I had been living on money borrowed, on the strength of *The Green Man*, from the publisher.

Obviously, I must begin another book at once. A familiar devil seized me by the elbow. What you need, he said, to give you fresh heart, is *to get away*.

To get away. Find money somewhere. Put off starting the book for a month, a fortnight. The world might come to an end in a month. Only let me escape from these walls built round me, before I knock my brains out on them…

Incautiously, I said, 'We'll go to France in July, the minute term ends.'

Guy frowned. 'You told me yesterday that you had no money left.'

'That's no reason,' I said gaily. 'I can always find money somewhere.'

This latest evidence of my impossible character drove him to exasperation and rage. 'I can't stand this—you overwork madly, you write book after book and throw the money away. When you're not giving it away—how many hundreds of pounds have you handed out this year?—you're spending it recklessly on things we could do without. I never knew anyone so totally indifferent to money, and so careless. Why? Why?'

Resentment—against everything that forced me to live in one place and prevented me from running about the world with a pen and a ream of paper—washed across my mind in a black flood. Surely he could see that I *must* go—that by keeping me back he was destroying me and everything in me that was still confident and alive?

'I don't know,' I said. 'I'm made like that.'

Deliberately I used the voice, hard, harsh, and contemptuous, which is less mine than a voice out of the ground, out of any one of a hundred obscure northern graves, long since overgrown. I am not surprised that Guy would like to strangle it. My improvidence was inexcusable, I knew it, but I did not give in. It was he who, in the end, said, 'I'm sorry.'

This was an overwhelming relief. I would never have said it. He is my closest friend, my marriage rests on a rock of confidence and gentleness, given and taken, but I need that hand held out to break my way out of a coldness not mine.

'We'll go to France next summer,' he said, to console me.

'Very well.'

Silently, I was determined to do this.

I had been disturbed too deeply to sleep; images from the past, from my first years, trivial things, swarmed in my mind, a wordless delirium. I could not control them; choking, I tried to tear them out and could not. Again and again I begged: Let me sleep. At last I did sleep, and, as so often when my mind has been turned inside out, I dreamed of my young sister, a long dream, still sharply clear in my mind when I woke. Much of it was fantastic, and had to do with the birth of a child, but towards the end she and I walked along a wide road, between shadowy walls, and here, abruptly, I remembered that she was dead, and said to her: You won't forget me, will you? We'll meet in our next lives, and I'll try to do better, I've been so weak... Before this, it had been a very happy dream.

There was no uncertainty or fading; I woke suddenly, while it was all still vivid. The recollection that she was dead had been as it were the sign that the dream was coming to an end, but the end came in an instant, like a shutter falling.

I lay awake, thinking: I can never be reconciled to her death.

One of the ghosts at the back of my mind had been standing there patiently for several years. Each time I glanced at it the face changed slightly, acquired a line or a shadow round the eyes, but the thought behind them was always the same. Only—I did not know how to translate it into action. Briefly, it was the figure of a man trying to decide whether or not to take on himself *to do justice*, as Orestes did justice on his mother. The man or woman he might have to execute did not, in the beginning, interest me. All I wanted to know was: What goes on in the mind of a man who, with the strongest motives in the world, acts as executioner in his own family?

As soon as I began consciously to attend to the shadowy figure, a whole web of motive and intrigue rose to the surface and I had only to examine it. It was a question of treachery. In a country which has been invaded and occupied, treachery is inevitable, and involves, inevitably, actions we are in the habit of pretending do not now occur in civilized countries. Also, private vengeance or justice is likely to be more nakedly ruthless than in countries which have not been torn open to the roots of fear and hatred. (Or only a little!) Hence, I saw Orestes as a Frenchman, and with fearful anxiety laid the story in France, in a part I knew best at that time, the Loire valley. I saw it, too, as a play, not as a novel, and began to construct it as a play, with characters who seemed to take as sharp pleasure in giving themselves away as I in watching them at it. Either they had been long waiting behind my Orestes, or I know more about treachery than about any other human habit. But, in fact, the theme of treachery was subordinate to the other—to the question of what it costs a man to inflict justice on another who is wholly in his hands.

By the middle of July, I had blocked out acts and scenes, and even written down a few lines of dialogue...

We went to France then, for a fortnight. I forget where the money came from. From the B.B.C. play? I could look it up in the enormous account book in which, since 1928, I have kept a record, more or less complete, of my rake's progress. I pay my bills the moment I receive them, and add up the amounts. This gives an air of prudence and sanity to my worst extravagances.

On the way we stayed a night with the Liddell Harts. Like every place lived in by Kathleen and Basil Liddell Hart this large pleasant house was a cell of almost Chinese serenity, kindness, and intellectual excitement. I know only one other house where I am as happy, and for the same reason. I think myself supremely lucky to have been admitted as a friend into two houses where kindness, intelligence, good-humour and politeness rule. And there is only one other woman I admire as I admire Kathleen Liddell Hart, for the warmth and grace of the life she makes for her husband and their friends: she will die smiling, because her mouth curves up at the ends like a young child's, even in repose. (Look at the mouth of every woman you see during one day: over the age of fifteen, all have begun to turn down.) As for her husband, the more I admire his intelligence, his fastidious senses, calm irascibility, and uncompromising rationality, the more I love his kindness.

They had staying with them a French diplomat. He told a story which, since he is not a writer, he may never record. A pity. In a few words it concentrates a whole epoch. Two years before the war he was a young third secretary in the French embassy in Russia. The Front Populaire was at its height, every other week French socialists turned up *en pèlerinage*, and among them that autumn was the Minister of Education, Jean Zay, with his wife. The Russian in charge of the visitors was a man called Bubonov: in official circles it was known that he was already done for, but during these few days he and Madame Bubonova entertained the Zays and became very friendly with them. One day, the young Frenchman, in the Finland Station to see off a guest, noticed the Bubonovs seeing their fifteen-year-old daughter off to some safer place. 'They knew they would never see her again.' A few days later he was there to see off the Zays. The Bubonovs arrived, friendly and smiling. Leaning from the train, Zay cried, 'We'll see you in Paris very soon, you must come to the Exhibition and see us.'—'Yes, yes, we'll come very soon,' Bubonov said. Three days later he was arrested and executed: his wife, sent to some camp, was never heard of again. Shortly, a package arrived at the French embassy from the Zays, with a letter asking the young secretary to deliver it to Madame Bubonova. He opened it. It was a bottle of scent called *Moment Suprème*... A novelist would be ashamed to employ an irony so banal.

(Three years later Zay himself was dead, murdered by three of Darnand's men who took him out of one of the Vichy government's prisons on a faked order.)...

We spent our first night in France at Verneuil, in a small hotel facing the unpaved square of dusty iron-hard earth. To our great surprise—Verneuil is nothing, a dull little town of narrow streets and rather haggard buildings—the hotel was full, and we were given the last tiny attic bedroom. After dinner, sitting at one of the iron tables on the pavement, I picked up a local newspaper left lying, and read the account of a tribunal. It had just sentenced Mme veuve D—— to pay 900.000 francs to the mother of a young man who had been denounced to the Gestapo by Mme veuve D——'s daughter, Andrée, and died in a concentration camp. Andrée, a seventeen-year-old *dràlesse*,

now in prison, had been the mistress (*concubine*) of a Gestapo agent, and
her mother's guilt was that she had failed to bring her up to be incapable of
such debauchery. 'She,' said the young man's mother, 'has paid penalty; it is
up to you, Madame, who neglected your maternal duty, to pay in the civil
court for the grief I have suffered.'

Let us be honest: there is nothing surprising or disgraceful in trying to
poultice your grief with 900.000 francs. The dead boy himself would have
been the first to approve his mother's eye to the main chance. What shocked
me was the profoundly malicious satisfaction shown by the comments,
printed in the newspaper, of Madame veuve D——'s friends or neighbours.
It was even oddly impersonal, a so to say metaphysical satisfaction and cruelty. A little as though, looking into a clear river, one saw a thread of foully
black slime flowing through it. But why expect anything else? Would it have
been different in England if we had spent four years rubbing shoulders with
an occupying army, even if only one in ten thousand of the occupiers were
anything but a decent enough young fellow with no wish to be where he
was? Shouldn't we, too, have felt less loathing for the enemy than for those
of our own people who, for whatever reason, softened towards him? There
is a certain satisfaction in tormenting an enemy, but it is nothing like the
pleasure to be got out of cruelty to one's nearest. And when it can be enjoyed
as a form of justice...

In the morning we were wakened at four o'clock by the noise outside.
To see through the single pane of glass I had to kneel, almost lie, on the
floor, and squint through it. The square was already half filled by stalls and
booths and more were going up, men, women, and half-naked children running about in the first light with wooden planks, hammers, bolts of cloth,
huge live rabbits, open boxes of fruit, hardware, bread. Never since I was a
child and watched the last launching in a small shipyard have I seen people
work with so reckless an energy and gaiety; it flew out of their bodies and
voices like sparks from a bonfire. What the night before had been a place
of shabby secretive houses was more candid and alive than a healthy child.
Even Madame veuve D———supposing that yellow haggard face poked out
between the shutters of the house opposite were hers—must feel a quick-
ening in her veins. Later, in blistering sunlight, when I was pushing my way
between the stalls of the market, buying bread, cheese, peaches, and a bottle

of wine, for our lunch, I felt that there are only a few griefs I could not cure by sitting at one of the café tables in this graceless foreign street, listening to the foreign voices, smelling the foreign smells of new bread, ripe fruit and cheese, and, yes, drains. To be happy—as happy as I have been thousands of times in my life—I don't need handsome buildings, lawns, great art, sublime music. I enjoy these, they may give me the greatest pleasure, but so, and more easily because it reaches down to some secret and purely personal feeling, can an hour spent in a place as ordinary, even ugly, as the market square in Verneuil, where, at nine in the morning, the light, the noise, the voices, the toothless old hag wearing an air of sanctity to go with the religious medals she is selling, the colour of a young woman's dress, give me an exquisite happiness, the most poignant I know.

We drove south, towards the Loire. The road ran dead straight, mile after white-hot mile, between poplars, acacias, tall pines, walnuts, all old trees, and so well cared-for that they had an astonishing air of youth and gentleness, very reassuring.

The light of the Loire valley is like no other in the world, clear without a thread of stridency, inconceivably clear and suave. It changes continually, of course, but never loses this double virtue of freshness and strength, a young virtue. The river was at its lowest, narrow grey-green channels between blond sandbanks. Later in the evening, between nine and ten, the motionless water was doubled by a bronzed smoky reflection from the west, lying below the surface, and the arches of the bridge were completed, exactly, as if by an engraver's tool, by their pitch-black shadows. Standing at the end of the bridge, I watched a panel of clear bronze water, framed in the double arch, fading to grey. Bats flitted between the arches. There was a crescent moon, and two or three weak stars.

What disappointments can cancel such a moment?

Certainly not the one that caught up with me a week later, in Nancy, sharp as it was. *The Green Man*, published just before we left England, had been kindly treated by the *Spectator* and *The Times*, so, when I caught sight of a *Literary Supplement* of two days before in a *tabac*, I picked it up with confident excitement. A prudent instinct drove me to glance at the review of my novel before spending francs on it. It was brief and very contemptuous. Horribly taken aback, I did not buy the paper. I give you my word that, at

four o'clock on the afternoon of the 3rd of August 1952, in my humiliated
state of mind, the marvellous Stanislas square was the ugliest place in the
world. The White Queen's advice to Alice floated across my mind. 'Consider
what a great girl you are. Consider what a long way you have come. Consider
what o'clock it is. Consider anything, only don't cry!'

No doubt that, for an instant, only for an instant, my face gave me away.
Then I considered where I was, in the delicious town of Nancy, and what a
long way I had come from my mother's house, and—not for the first time
at such a moment—a wild gaiety filled me. This exhilaration, the peculiar
exhilaration of disaster, is like being splendidly drunk, an incomparable
lightness of head and heart. With luck, it will be my last sensation...

In Alsace, I was enchanted to discover that I had not distorted it when
I was writing *Cousin Honoré*. But the town I had been longing to see,
Ammerschwihr, and had promised myself an intense happiness from my first
sight of the cobbled market square with its sculptured fountain and splendid
sixteenth century houses and the charming double staircase leading up to
and away from the front door of the old Hôtel du Commerce, was a heap
of ruins, not a house standing. A woman in a shabby cotton dress, the only
creature there, was standing staring at the rubble of what may have been her
own house. I did not dare to speak to her, but she spoke to me. Looking at
me with frank hatred, she said, 'D'you know who did this? The Americans!'

I have never heard in a human voice anything like the bitterness compressed into the last nasal trumpet-note of—*cains*. It curdled my blood.


### CHAPTER II

'WHY,' T. S. ELIOT ASKED, 'out of all that we have heard, seen,
felt... do certain images recur, charged with emotion, rather than
others? The song of one bird, the leap of one fish, at a particular place and
time, the scent of one flower...'

Surely he knew? Any image so charged, overcharged, with emotion that
there are no words fit to describe it, or to convey the emotion, is the moment's
face of an image so old we have to grope for it in the darkness of infancy.
It is the young glance, telling the onlooker nothing, which starts suddenly

from the half-extinct eyes of an old woman. In Venice that autumn, twice I stumbled over one of these moments when past and present become one, in the body's memory rather than in the mind, moments worth a long lifetime.

Reaching the Lido after dark, I could see nothing from the window of my room except the darkness of a cloudy night. But when I woke, early, I saw wet empty sands, and sea, the steel-blue Adriatic, its horizon an edge of blindingly white light reflected from the risen sun, itself hidden behind heavy clouds. Looking back over my shoulder, I saw all my life to the mornings when, travelling to school along the twenty miles of coast from Whitby to Scarborough, I had seen the sea joined to the sky by this same gleaming half-hoop let down from the invisible sun, swallowed by a cloud-bank as it rose. And as the North Sea rose in my mind, overflowing the Adriatic, an excitement from the past filled me to an almost unbearable pitch.

And there was one evening, the evening of the 26th of September 1952, the time was between half-past eight and nine, on the Piazzetta in front of the Doge's Palace: the pinkish grey and white marble above was the colour of sea-corroded brick, and in the cloister below the gallery were a few benches against the wall, and worn stone paving: it was almost dark, and the crowd standing or walking about, between the old street-lamps, to hear the Banda C. Monteverdi play an air of Rossini, shivered a little in the wind from the lagoon. The musicians wore white uniforms. At the far side of the square, under rounded arches, the lit windows of small shops and cafés, and globes of white light at the end of the Piazza below the Clock Tower. In an interval of the music, the clock struck, with a deep note like that sent out by the Whitby bell-buoy. So there I was again in the Saloon (since miscalled the Spa), sharing with my mother a wooden bench against the wall, a seat chosen for the shelter it gave us from the sea-wind, and, in front of us, standing or sauntering in the gathering darkness round the band-stand with its uniformed musicians, a crowd of hardy ghosts, old and young: the air is, of course, Rossini's, and in the interval the tolling of sea and bell rises between the voices and the knocking of feet on old worn stone.

The passionate intensity of such moments is incommunicable. I am certain they will be the last part of me to give itself up...

As soon as I got back to England, we took C. to a hotel in the New Forest for a fortnight. I had not seen him for three years, since the troubles. As we neared the house—later than we had said we would come: we had driven a long way and lost ourselves in unfamiliar suburban streets—I saw this tall slender boy, as neat as a new pin, striding up and down outside it, with a curiously set face. Had he been afraid we would not come?

The fortnight was almost a success—that is, I succeeded partly in bridging the gap between the child and the handsome ten-year-old, half graceful intelligent boy, with an impenetrable glance, full of reserves, half young barbarian. An old German professor of history staying in the hotel got it into his Hegelian head that I did not appreciate the boy, and told me, in solemn rebuke, twice, 'But he is remarkable, he is even more than intelligent, I have never known a child so quickly to see into and through what I tell him and he is also smiling—you have here a miracle.'

At last I said coldly, 'Why should you think I don't know it?'

Miracle or not, I had one fear, that he was already hiding as many anxieties and mistrusts as I at that age, and one stubborn hope—to be allowed to give him, without expecting any return, all I could give, an education he would be able to use.

In November I took up the skeleton of *The Hidden River* again, and wrote the first scenes. Everything I had learned in France in July helped to quicken it. What can you learn in a fortnight? But it was a fortnight lived on the surface of a country where I lived the rest of the time like a mole, reading little except French, sifting my memories again and again, living in France by faith when I could not live there with all my senses. What mistakes I made were less the mistakes of ignorance than of an excessive fondness.

I spent two months writing it as a play, and another two to turn it into a short novel, in a version I like better, immeasurably better, than the one in which it was published. In this first version there was only the simplest and briefest love affair—not an affair at all, a mere hint of feelings given little chance to become articulate. I was at first pleased with it. But it had been written against the boredom, fatigue, and occasional despair I felt in the Leeds flat, and after a time, when I was copying my manuscript on the typewriter—at breakneck speed because I had promised to take Frances for a month when her mother had her second child—I began to think that very probably I had only made a hash of another theme.

By now, I and my body were entirely separate. It had become something I took about with me. When necessary, I kicked it into obedience—a Caliban—and it obeyed. For how much longer it would obey instantly I neither knew nor cared.

This was the third time I had had Frances staying with me. A much-loved child, who lived happily in the narrow spaces of a small ketch, familiar with sea-birds, tides, mud-flats, the clatter of waves against the wall of her bunk, she made herself at home anywhere. A child who by instinct noted the shape of moving objects, changes of sky, all the physical details of existence, and slept through the loudest thunderstorms. A child naturally gay, who chattered with rage when she fell on her face and I was so foolish as to offer to comfort her.

She stayed six weeks. After I had taken her home, I set to work—cursing my folly—on the manuscript sent me by one of the exiles. It had been written heroically in English, a fantastic English, and since it was intelligent I had not the heart to say to the author: Take your deformed infant away.

Long before I finished it my energy was out of sight; it came scurrying back when I wanted to fly to Dublin for the P.E.N. Congress.

I had discovered that Charles Morgan was prepared to succeed Benedetto Croce as International President.

I was comically astonished. When it had been laid on me to ask him, I felt certain he would reject it as an intolerable burden.

'I shouldn't care to stand unless I can be sure of election.'

'Of course not,' I said. 'But no one will oppose you.'

I was a great deal less confident than I sounded, and the thought of his being mortified irked me.

In Dublin I found that the French had their own candidate, André Chamson. And the Germans and Austrians were going to propose Thomas Mann. Mann was no danger—in 1953 it was still too early to put up a German, even one so eminent and politically impeccable. The Austrian president, a lovable spluttering old fellow, said to me,

'If we had known you had someone in mind... Of course we shall withdraw our candidate.'

It did not enter my head that there was anything absurd or unreasonable in pushing aside Thomas Mann to make room for an English writer, any English writer.

André Chamson was an animal of another species. I liked him extremely. His narrow head and lean prematurely haggard face, the bones scarcely covered, an almost lipless mouth that, in age, would close like a trap—it did now when he was meditating a stroke—were as attractively austere as his part of France, the Cévennes, a region of Protestants, probably, if one followed the roots underground, of Cathars; I would swear there are living roots of that severely logical faith, burned out by the Catholic church, in those hills... His early novels, laid in this region, were marvellously evocative and spontaneous, without pretensions. If he were English, I thought, he would go on writing them, to a chorus of respectful praise, and keep himself and his family alive by reviewing or writing art criticism: in France, far grander and more strenuous ways are open to him... Looking at the lines of his jaw, I felt sure he had read his maps.

He was standing beside me when the Austrian apologized for his tactlessness. His fine mouth was crossed by a brief smile of speculation and contempt. Too adroit not to know that if I were going to make the effort I could easily rally enough Centres to defeat him, he was sensitive enough to guess that the last thing I wanted was a contest, I wanted Charles to be chosen without one.

What he did not guess was that I had been seized by an overwhelming reluctance to go on with this farcical diplomacy. Never again, I said to myself.

I wrote a long memorandum about the unseemliness of a tug of war between French and English, offering, if the French would support Charles, to use any influence I might still have at the end of his term of office to secure André Chamson's election then, and arranged for this document to fall under his eye.

The next morning he came up to me outside the conference room with a friendly smile, as delicate as it was, perhaps, sincere.

'I have seen your letter to Denis Saurat.'

'Yes?'

'You know, he is not a good Frenchman, Saurat. He is—what shall I say?—denatured, he has been living out of France too long.'

Not wanting to annoy him, I did not say: What you mean is that he has lost that total ignorance of other countries which is a caste mark of so many French intellectuals.

'I am sure,' he said, 'that there are no serious differences between us.'

'None,' I said warmly.

He pricked me lightly with one of his rooted phrases. 'Il faut dire les choses *comme ils sont*.'

I forget which foreign delegate was given the duty of proposing to the Executive that Charles should be elected, but the proposal was supported, warmly, with faultless grace, by André Chamson.

The whole Congress spent a day—made violently uneasy by the tension between the two Irish nations—in Belfast. We left at midnight, in a special train. Exhausted, clutching politely the anti-Republican leaflets handed them in the station by a dozen fierce young Ulstermen, most of the two or three hundred writers slept in their seats. Pushing my way through the crowded coaches, I came to one where a bottle of Irish whiskey was keeping a score of them noisily awake. Among them was the East German delegate, a personage waiting to be born into a novel by Günter Grass: sprawling back, he was singing in German and beating time with his shapeless arms, pitifully grotesque and happy. When he saw me he stopped singing and gave me a sheepish smile. I blew him a kiss. He tried to get to his feet, collapsed, and began to sing again weakly, tears trickling over the wastes of his face.

The violent quarrel between the two Germanies had become bitter, and his position was excessively uneasy. I felt a perverse affection for him, and went out of my way to be kind. He was grateful, and frothed over with explanations. 'Believe me, Miss Storm Jameson, I should say Madam Vice-President, it is my regard for truth that forces me to take this stand, only my regard for truth. Believe me, I don't want to annoy you, but I must speak the truth.'

With the greatest difficulty we patched together a compromise which no one expected to last. Nor did it. The moment he got back to Germany it was repudiated.

Years later I made good use of him in a novel.

With some twenty other writers, I lunched at Maynooth. By this time, almost the end of the Congress, I was so tired—I had chaired both business sessions and the not at all placid Executive, and sat up at night until all hours, talking—that the faces on either side of the table became a Masque of angels and devils like the chorus in a mediaeval play: a mouth, thin and tightly shut, turned up in a sardonic V; the lame delicate Count de Morra was sporting a saintly smile, Ignazio Silone's dark heavy face scowled; Franz de Backer was as white as a sheet, a skull rather than a head; the lines running from Chamson's bony nose to his jaw had been cut into the wooden flesh with a knife; a bearded Peter Ustinov had by accident or design the air of an eminent ecclesiastic, affable and a little womanish, or, paradoxically, a little like an intelligent bull. The lunch had been a long one, with exquisite wines, which the President of the College and his priests poured out freely but did not drink. I drank a great deal, without any effect.

At the closing banquet that evening, a spectral face came towards me in a corridor, startling me until I realized that it was my own reflection.

Forty-eight hours after I got back to Leeds, I had recovered completely. Why? Because we were leaving Leeds, and this particular trap. Energy and an air as keen as salt poured into me from the door standing open at the end of the month. Guy was about to retire, and had compounded his tiny pension from the university for a sum he proposed to spend on six months in France, longer if by living moderately hard we could stretch it. We were allowed to take the money abroad only because he was writing a history of the Third Republic—scholarship still has its uses.

This is the place to remark that he has no clearer sense of reality than I have. I am recklessly improvident by nature—whose nature? what flaw in the line of sensible hard-mouthed Yorkshiremen? Guy is not reckless, not, as I am, wasteful, but he is equally devoid of any solid sense. He should have married what in Whitby they call 'a warm body, a good manager.'

I refused to look farther ahead than the coming months. Without a pang, I prepared to send our possessions and books into store again. Three weeks in Brittany with C. and then away, away. The sea-gull screech of Whitby fisher children, calling each other in the streets outside the first house I remember, echoed between the bones of my skull—*Ah-wa-a-ah!*

Every few years I am seized by a hatred of possessions. Since I cannot destroy all our books and furniture, I destroy letters and documents. The previous bonfire had been in 1940, when I burned every paper I thought might incriminate other people if we were invaded and occupied, and a great many I need not have destroyed. Now I set to emptying my files again. I came on a letter, dated the 26th of July 1946, from Leonora Eyles, David Murray's wife, enclosing the one R. D. Charques had written David saying that he (R.D.C.) had been given 'the rather grisly task of writing a stock obituary of Storm Jameson' for *The Times*, and asking David for details of my early life and career. What David, who was not only indolent, but knew very little about me, wanted—in effect—was that I should write my own obituary and send it to him to give to Gharques. The mere thought of writing it filled me with the same vexed boredom I feel when I am asked, by some publisher or some editor preparing a book of reference, to answer questions about myself and my books. This has nothing whatever to do with reserve or diffidence—it is purely sloth.

I sent Leonora a few dates and left it at that...

Re-reading her letter before tearing it up, I was hooked by the phrase 'a stock obituary'. It struck me as mean and silly, and I began to make notes for the obit I would have written myself.

'Storm Jameson, born at Whitby on the 8th of January 1891, died yesterday, in obscure circumstances, at ——. From her father, a master mariner, she inherited patience and physical strength, and from her mother, who was the daughter of a shipowner, a restless boredom which bedevilled her life. The ambition, a blind hunger to become a figure, and to use her brain and exceptional energy, which drove her to write and brought her a measure of success, was undermined by certain weaknesses of character and by a paradoxical lack of respect for money and honours, and her hatred of a settled life. In her late middle years, the impulse to turn her back on the world was strong enough to defeat her contrary effort to cut a figure in it.

'From 1933 onwards her novels were increasingly concerned with the state of the world, the mystery of cruelty, treachery etc. etc., but in daily life she showed an almost total lack of seriousness and a frivolous indifference to her own interests. Where money was concerned she was incontinent. This and her ineptitude (due largely to boredom) in practical matters, drove her to write too many books. A few of these—notably *That Was Yesterday*, *A Day Off*, *Cousin Honoré*, *Cloudless May*, *The Journal of Mary Hervey Russell*, *Before the Crossing* and *The Black Laurel* (a single novel in two volumes), *The Green Man*—were worth writing.

'When not harassed by responsibilities which bored her to death, she was naturally gay. She adored amusements, and if able to please herself would have gone to the theatre, or an opera, or the ballet, or a foreign film, every evening.

'The great passion of her life, too little indulged, was for travel. No other sensual or intellectual pleasure gave her a fraction of the acute happiness it gave her to see a foreign city or country. No other assuaged the restlessness which, more than any other of her failings, laid her waste.

'During the early part of her life she was domineering and timid, unfeeling and betrayed by her strong feelings, mistrustful and involuntarily reckless, malicious and soft-hearted, kind out of a nervous inability to stand the sight of suffering. As she aged, she ceased to be domineering. Not because she was at last ready to admit that it is spiritually and emotionally unprofitable, but because she was bored by most people. The instinct for flattery of which some persons, even some friends, accused her sprang less from a wish to be liked and approved than from the wish to reassure. For example, sitting opposite a plain elderly woman dressed carefully and very unwisely in pale pink, she had to stifle her impulse to lean forward and say: How beautifully you are dressed today.

'The least gesture of kindness from a person who had injured her, even severely, wiped out the injury. One of the signs of a weak character.

'At one period of her life she had hundreds of friends, of several nations.

'Apart from her family, she loved deeply, to the end of her days, eight people: of these, two were friends made late in life and four were her first friends.'

## CHAPTER 12

B Y ONE MEANS AND ANOTHER, without too much austerity and with only a feather of illegality, we contrived to live in France for ten blessed months. When we left, without a franc, at the end of May 1954, the French official in Boulogne who reproached us for overstaying our *permis de séjour* did so with smiling indulgence: either he was in a good humour or he pitied us sincerely for having to leave his country.

The sentimental situation of France among the nations is curious. No country, not even Italy, not Greece, has had more foreign lovers. And no country with pretensions to being a great power rouses more exasperation and abuse. In the love there has always been a tinge of unreason, a nervous anxiety to find excuses for failings—which is a profound insult. The abuse, the mockery, conceal a sour grain of envy. And none of these sentiments has any but the most superficial relevance to the real France; they exist almost wholly in our minds.

Is it true that France today is not, as in 1953 it was, a country of extreme contradictions: stretched irritated nerves and peasant stoicism, intellectual seriousness and political frivolity and corruption, insolent wealth and downright misery: a country radically stable, resting on the habits of greed and thrift which the sons of peasants take with them when they move into trades and professions, and little moved by giddy changes of government? Is it true that in the space of a few years General de Gaulle has changed all that?

Though I scarcely believe it, it is possible. The country may only have been waiting for a more adroit showman and despot than Napoleon.

Or—at least as possible—it may be that all but a few Frenchmen care very little who gives the orders. The only emotion common to every soul I talked to during our ten months was an instinctive contempt for politics and politicians—apart from the respect felt for a few, a very few, individuals. No one tried to discount the extent of political corruption. Nor was it anything new. What seemed new was the indifference to it, the total lack of heat in talking about it. The very man who had just been spitting his fury that Wall Street had forced his country to prolong the war in Indo-China ('fighting Communism with *our* bodies') became calmly cynically amused when all he wanted to say was that such and such an editor or deputy who supported the war had been paid to do it by French colonial interests. A well-documented exposure of financial thuggery, involving deputies and ministers, excited no one except, professionally, the journalists. From the man in the street, the shops, the offices, a shrug of the shoulder, a fine smile, resignation.

I came to believe that, just as the French are immune to bad drains, so they are at least partly immunized against political corruption and inefficiency—except when this last leaves them, as in 1939, almost naked before an enemy.

'In France, when all seems lost, a miracle happens.'

The pleasant fellow who repeated this facile saying went on, 'And invariably it takes the form of a man, not of a government. Let me give you an instance—every winter in Paris, walking home after dark, you might have to step over the body of a homeless man or woman trying to find traces of warmth near a ventilator of the Metro or the wall of a kitchen, and every winter a number of poor devils or their babies froze to death in the horrible shacks on the edge of the city. It was considered a sad state of affairs, and nothing was done. Until, last winter, suddenly, a man said: No, it's too much. In a few days the Abbé Pierre achieved more than any government would have done in years. It's always the same with us.'

'But the miracle isn't always on time!'

He shrugged. 'Perhaps not. But I expect it.'

With millions of others, less intelligent, he still regards de Gaulle as the just and necessary dictator. Not because he is a fascist at heart. But because, provided he is not too heavily taxed, one form of State is as good as the next; the things he considers essential to his happiness are all outside politics. A few citizens of the Fifth Republic are annoyed by its disciplines as sharply as they were by the corruption and fidgets of the Third. There are not enough of them to carry through a revolution.

Anything might follow the latest Napoleon. Even a democracy on the old model...

Our journey did not begin, properly speaking, until I had taken C. back to England and returned in the next boat to Dieppe. Except that it still has graces lacking to England—the servants in small hotels who without a breath of servility or self-consciousness give the impression that they enjoy working like slaves for sixteen hours a day, mechanics eager to flatter a sick car into health—the edge of Brittany in summer is as little France as possible. There is always the sense that the English coast is craning its neck to see across. I understand the disillusion of one of General de Gaulle's Free Frenchmen who took himself to Dover for the weekend, to be able to stare towards his country, and came back to London filled with bitterness.

'Not only was there a thick mist, but every time I made some pathetic or friendly remark to the Channel, the brute replied in English.'

'What did you expect?' I said. 'It is English.'

Guy had brought the car to the boat. I stepped in, and off we went, under a sky as flawlessly clean and new as the rebuilt towns and villages of these parts. The rebuilding has been done with intelligence (even affection): I felt a little sorry for the women still living in dilapidated unbombed cottages on the edge of one of these handsome new villages—until I remembered the weight of memory, of old beds and chairs, lace curtains, hideous photographs of weddings, christening robes, casseroles, that vanished in dust and terror.

The next morning, in Senlis, I bought our first *ficelle* of French bread, our first bottle of cheap wine and half-pound of local cheese, to be eaten by the roadside. The first moment of perfect happiness. Ridiculous—but, when I am living the sort of life which suits me, the only sort, a thread is enough to lift me to the heights.

Moving south, we sifted the familiar places through our fingers. We were making for Bordeaux, but before that, for the pure joy of it, we circled east and south, staying a night, two nights, a week—Montbard, Bourg-en-Bresse, Grenoble, Gap, Digne, Riez, Salernes, Draguignan, Grasse, Cagnes, Aix, Arles, Albi, Cahors. Living is simple and delicious when the heaviest problem of the day is a choice between two bakers, or two small shops both selling cheese, pâtés, wine. Then away, slowly, trusting in heaven that the unpromising cobbled street ahead will in a few minutes become the road south. Day after day of the solid secure warmth of the French summer, villages which seem empty, a countryside at once wide and intimate, the straight narrow streets of small towns, squeezed between the leprous walls of a sixteenth century mansion and the stunted arcade with its two small cafés side by side, strong shabby houses, a dusty square with its half-ruined fountain, the medlars, yews, and box-hedges of a walled garden, a mile-long avenue of great plane-trees, hedges covered with white dust, vineyards, deep valleys, farms, dry river-beds, olives. And we can go where we like, take any unmade road in search of a little-known church or walled mediaeval village. We are free.

The hotel in Bourg-en-Bresse, with its faded ease and dusty smell of polish and old wood, could only be French. If, when I have been buried for a century or two, I am resurrected there, I shall know at once where I am. In more than twenty years, nothing has changed: the dining-room, as bare as that in my first school, is still serving the same splendid food to the successors of the commercial travellers, the notary, the senior clerks of before the war, and the decrepit cages lining the seedy glassed-in landing we cross to reach our bedroom house the descendants, sulky and moulting, of the birds here then.

'Surely there used to be a small monkey?'

'Dead. He is dead.' A pause and a quick brilliant smile. 'We are all mortal.'

*

Grenoble. With the best will in the world to flatter him, I cannot see it through Stendhal's eyes as 'the very incarnation of bourgeois life and literally of nausea': it is an inoffensive city, not handsome but decent, and resonant of mountains.

What, to be able to love it, I look for in a landscape is a bare hard line—no doubt the line, scored across the brain at the back of my eyes, of a short stretch of the North Sea coast. This hill country of Provence fills me with a contentment which must be exactly that of an infant set to the breast, as vacantly sensual. I draw in mindlessly the naked sides of hills, grey and bone-white, covered by a cindery dust of brittle grass and shrubs, villages clinging like wasps' nests to their crests above a few roughly walled terraces of vines and olives, the livid bristling rocks, a few poplars and cypresses, the road turning on itself endlessly between eroded hillside and precipice, the hissing sound given off by scorched thistles and rosemary, the grey fields of lavender, sparse wind-stunted trees, spruce, oak, rowan, and ahead the Alp-fanged horizon. It is a landscape without a trace of sentiment.

Even before we reached Aix, the sun was beginning to press its thumb against the back of the skull. In Aix itself, it drew from the gutters and old handsome buildings a pervasive smell of decay, the August stench of a town in the Midi. Why, I wondered, have the French never managed to achieve either an efficient drainage system or an efficient system of government? The answer must be the same for both. They don't care. Charming dilapidated streets and small squares stank of a sour dust, like ancient ovens, and in the magnificent Cours Mirabeau the trees gave shade without freshness, their depths sucked dry and empty by the violent light. Giraudoux set the opening scenes of *Pour Lucrèce* in one of the unpretentious cafés facing them: the elegance, if it ever existed, has evaporated, but to sit there gave me a gentle pleasure, like fingering dried woodruff.

We stayed three days before going on to Arles. The heat now was all but unbearable, a molten torrent pouring from a sky of white-hot metal. Pulverized by the searing light, trees, the walls of houses, the road itself, flickered across the eyeballs as in a bad early film. I was rash enough to walk, in this murderous sun, the length of the Aliscamps. It was nakedly horrible.

Nothing of the poetry Rilke found there clings round the double line of sarcophagi foundering in the thick dust, or in the small empty Romanesque church, its crypt filled with a sickening breath of decay and corruption. Down here, for the first and only time in my life, I felt death as an immediate reality, filling my nostrils, eyes, mouth. I could have spat it out, and I felt ill—no, not ill, I felt that I was disintegrating, the flesh parting from my bones, an extraordinary sense of uncertainty and dissolution. Either I am going mad or I have a fever, I thought. I managed to hide my vexing state, and carefully did not take my temperature; in the morning fever and uncertainty had gone, both of them, and I felt ready for anything. Except, ever again, the dust and tombs of that abominable avenue.

Bare as it is, the bones showing through the thin skin, there is nothing arid about the country near Albi, a landscape of smoothly sculptured hills, grey-green, white, ivory, yellow, deadleaf brown, wide planes of extreme delicacy: the scattered farms of pink brick or sun-yellowed plaster, red-tiled, have an air of candour and almost of ease. Albi itself is not candid. How could it be, in the shadow of that superbly menacing cathedral, more fortress than church? Inside, an inconceivable turbulence of colour and statues, the work of sculptors whose heads were full of any but religious ideas: he was no pious fellow who modelled the fifteenth century Judith in the ambulatory, with heavy sensual lids falling over her slanting eyes, delicate nose, and fine greedy mouth and chin, long-fingered hands gathering up the folds of an opulent dress.

A slit window on the staircase of the Bishop's Palace, itself once a fortress, now a museum of Toulouse-Lautrec's profane art, looks over the old city. That day, under an unclouded September sky, the river Tarn was running clay-red under red bridges, between the faded red fleece of roofs and the massive dark red Cathedral; it was singularly disturbing, as though a vein had opened in Albi's bloody heretic-burning past.

In the bakery next morning, a middle-aged woman, tall, lean, beaked, in grey alpaca with an aggressive toque, spoke to me in a sudden harsh voice.

'Are you German?'

'No. English.'

'Ah—' an ill-humoured sound—'I was told there was a German woman here.'

Why should she have given it a second thought? France was full of Germans, in sturdy Volkswagens and immense self-confident Mercedes, more Germans than English, and with more money to spend.

Our last night before Bordeaux was spent outside Cahors, in the Château de Mercués. My room looked down a great way to the Lot, and across the valley of unhedged fields to the hills; in the clear light the reflections of trees in the water were sharp and unmoving, as sharp as their long shadows across the earth. I thought: I could stand here forever, looking.

I had twenty minutes of pure happiness—really without any reason. Charming as it is at this point, the Lot is no more beautiful than other French rivers I know. At another moment, in another light, I might have looked, and looked away.

There is no accounting for these invasions—the correct word—of an overwhelming force of happiness, irrational and piercing. Entirely unlike the pleasure one takes in a fine day, a meeting with a friend, warmth after cold, the taste of new bread, it is not dependent on anything I may be looking at or touching. No doubt it depends on what the scene itself stands for, the surfacing of a deep primitive image—in my life, the sea, distant points of light, the tolling of the Whitby bell-buoy, the burning purity of a field of dog-daisies, the line, hard, severe, living, of the Whitby coast seen from the cliffs.

To our astonishment, Bordeaux, on the 19th of September, was crowded, not a bed to be had. It was international football or a Congress—I forget. After a long search, we got a room, a very small dark room, airless and evil-smelling. At the time I did not know it, but it was the hotel in which our ambassador and members of his staff lived for a short time in June 1940—they were there when the Germans entered Paris. No doubt their rooms were more elegant than ours, but they felt the same need to console themselves by eating in the Chapon Fin, across the narrow road from the hotel.

My love for Bordeaux is a little more than the pleasure it gives me to be in any foreign city; it is twisted round my young mother's memories of its streets and harbour, and although I had given up looking for her, as on earlier visits I looked, trying to come up with her in this busy street, this narrow dark glove shop, *this* garden with its iron chairs and magnolia trees, something of that obsession remains, like the all but effaced outlines of an old photograph. It is a handsome city, not in the least gracious—*une ville de cadavres*, a young woman said bitterly, when I was speaking about it with affection.

I don't ask a foreign town to be sympathetic; all I ask of it is to be immovably *itself*, reserved, coldly oppressive, friendly, as it pleases, but itself.

After five nights in the hotel, we moved to rooms in a large solidly dignified house some twenty minutes walk from the centre. It belonged to the young-middle-aged widow of a civil servant, who ran it as a pension for American students. Since the university term did not begin for another four or five weeks we could have two rooms and a bathroom, at a cost less than the cheapest hotel possible. Obviously, the rooms would be cold—but we had to economize, and I liked Madame B. She had a quick dark-eyed vivacity and, for all that she had never expected to keep herself and her four children by turning her house into a boarding-house, no trace of resentment. She was a good manager, a little too good. The meals, except on rare days when *mon père* came from his estate near Agen for the night, bringing game, fruit, pâtés, and bottles of his own wine, were extremely meagre: a huge dish of beans, with a few slivers of stringy meat lost in it, appeared again and again during the week. At the end of a month I had lost a stone in weight. It was worth it to live in Bordeaux.

*Mon père* was intelligent and a sceptic. One day when he saw me reading a Paris newspaper he remarked drily that if he wanted news of what was going on up there he had only to read any pre-war journal *lining* a shelf in his loft. The same tricks, the same corruption, even the same names.

'D'you expect me to take an interest in these broken-winded old horses as they tumble round the ring? Some of them can't even tumble, they're stuffed with sawdust.'

I had brought with me to France the typescript of *The Hidden River*. Six months ago, when I posted it to New York, to Carl Brandt, I supposed I had done with it, but he persuaded an editor of the *Saturday Evening Post* that it only needed a few changes to be worth thirty thousand dollars, and—to make certain that I did not, out of impatience and boredom, throw away this (to me) unheard-of sum—he covered three folio sheets in his fine angular writing, telling me precisely what to do. None of the changes he suggested touched the theme of the book, it was the plot, only the plot, that needed more flesh on its classical bones, and if this could be done by involving the one English character in an emotional affair, why not? I regretted the blurring of a clear hard outline, but—more even than the money—I wanted Carl to approve of me. Most of all, I was ashamed—as I am always—to seem by refusing to put too high a value on my work.

As soon as we were settled in Madame B.'s house, I laid out Carl's pages on the table in my cold bedroom, and set to work.

Guy was working in the library of the university, and we met every day between half-past five and six in a dark worn little café on the Cours Clemenceau. I walked there, a long walk through grey sombre streets, becoming crowded and lively as they neared the centre. Very often it rained, and the cobblestones were unpleasantly greasy. I was always hungry, and our choice lay between the Café Cardinal and hot chocolate and brioches in a pâtisserie: once or twice I weakened, not many times. Not only was it cheaper to drink, but the waiter who served us was an amiable old fellow and treated us with great gentleness, as though we were friends recovering from an illness. One day when I arrived, wet and shivering with cold, he bent over me and said softly, 'Not an *amer picon* this evening. A grog!'

Heaven knows what, besides rum, was in his grog; it sent the blood swirling through my body to the ends of my fingers. After this I drank it on every cold rainy evening...

It was not always raining. Some days were fine and warm, with a light as smooth as honey, the light, exquisite, of the Dordogne in autumn. On one such day at the end of October, we drove the twenty miles to Saint-Emilion.

Anyone who wishes to see France in a day should ask to be set down in Saint-Emilion. It is a town of less than four thousand inhabitants, gripping the edge of a rocky slope above the valley of the Dordogne, in the heart of the great vineyards. The earliest houses were built by Gauls across the marks left by prehistoric man: Roman colonists added their splendid villas—did one of these belong to Ausonius?—and planted vineyards which produced a wine well thought of in Rome itself. The first barbarians to turn up sacked the villas, settled down, and let the place civilize them. Then came the Saracens; then, at the end of the ninth century, Normans who did not entirely destroy the great church dug out of the rocky cliff itself. In the twelfth,

Saint-Emilion—now a strong walled town of churches, monasteries, great houses—was confirmed in its civic rights by King John of England.

This was before the *English* were chased out of France, a disaster for both countries, which has not yet been righted.

In the following century, a French king seized the place. We retook it and, except for brief intervals, held on to it until 1453. Savaged with equal energy by both sides in the Wars of Religion, it became what it is now, a little town of steep narrow twisted streets, the fragments of great buildings woven into a living pattern: a vineyard stretches across a mediæval cemetery, wine is bottled and stored below the cloistered ruins of a thirteenth century monastery. The past is not dead here, it is in use.

It was too late in the year for tourists. We were alone in the great Collegiate Church. Its very small Chapel of the Dead had (I hope has) the most extraordinary of tombs. It was not beautiful—a mound of dry earth in the centre of the floor, the size and shape of a child's grave. Small fragments of stone had been stuck in the soil to mark out a cross, as children stick pebbles in a sandcastle. At the head of the narrow little mound, a small upright cross formed from two pieces of wood no thicker than a wrist, the bark still on them; a poilu's steel helmet rested on this cross, and a small card, pinned to the wood, read: *Les Enfants de St Emilion*. What this grave said was very severe and very simple. To hide my tears, I stared at the list of names on the wall, a long list for the war of 1914–18, a very much shorter one, fourteen names, for 1939–45, and a third list of *victimes civiles*, six men and four women. Two families, the Dubois and the Jardilliers, lost between them four men and two women.

The old chairwoman, a huddle of bones and black dusty garments, the skin of her face and neck riddled with cracks, was waiting to take us round the cloisters. I asked a timid question about the civilian dead. She made a curious gesture, as though brushing a hair from her face. 'Oh, not many, not many,' she said almost inaudibly, and began to talk about the Germans. 'Some of their soldiers came to the church. Why not? They were Catholics, after all. Everyone left them to sit alone.'

One day a German colonel came to look round the church, and asked her about a fourteenth century wooden statue against the wall.

'I told him it was English. He said it reminded him of the Baron de Rothschild. I asked him: Do you know the Baron? He said: Oh, yes, very well. Then he asked me what the English were doing here with their statue. I told him: They were occupying the place, like you.' She opened a black toothless mouth in a wavering smile. To excuse herself for her rashness, she added, 'After all, at my age—eighty-seven—can it matter what happens?'

She stood with us on the steps of the porch, the sunlight covering her wrinkled skin with a fine varnish. Her smile became ironical.

'I knew they would go in the end. Just as you went.'

Her certainty that France will always civilize or reject an invader was lightly reassuring.

Early in November we moved south to St Jean de Luz.

I am devoted to the Basque country, and I like and respect the Basques. Whatever part of Europe or Asia these people came from, they brought with them every virtue of the north except its jeering bitter humour; they are hard, direct, and seem to have no defensive vanity, either of the Southern French kind or any other. As for the coast, in certain lights it is like enough my own to bring a knot of grief and loss into my throat—and, at least once in the day, a few minutes of happiness without thought, the happiness of a child.

I wrote at a table set in the window of my bedroom. The days were warm, with only a little rain, and when I looked up from my manuscript I saw the wide bay under a sky of extraordinary gentleness and purity, even gentler after rain and when a wind from the southwest blew white flakes of cloud above the horizon as lightly as a girl lifts her long hair on the back of her hand. Towards dusk, the fishing boats, about forty of them, worked their way in. They carried one riding light, reflected in the wrinkled grey water. At the farther side of the bay, the hill was the colour of a pigeon's breast: a single red light flashed on the cliff, and another, white, sparked in and out at the end of the long jetty. There were the lights of houses, not many, along the side of the hill, above the harbour, sweeping me back every evening to my mother's childhood. Behind the low hill another, higher, darker, more blue than grey, rose brusquely at the other side of the Spanish frontier. The boats came in between the jetty and a long stone barrier, under a sky darkening to the colour of the hill, with a single very bright star.

We stayed here a full month and left reluctantly, to make our way east, very slowly, sleeping a night in Toulouse, Béziers, Aix, to Vence.

From Vence we walked about the naked stony country behind, pastures of thin turf, gnawed to the bone by the cold wind, rising, slowly at first, then steeply, towards the circle of hills, dry, flayed; a few leafless iron trees and stunted shrubs; a few villages, their outer walls so near in colour to the greyish-ochre soil that they seemed part of the rocky slope behind them, as ancient and unfriendly. A few terraces of vines and olives were scrawled with rough patience immediately below the crumbling walls. In the distance the amphitheatre of foothills hiding the real mountains, between each crest a sharp void, no softening mists.

Walking along the cobbled street of one of these villages, between squat shabby secretive houses, the only inhabitants we saw might be two or three old men with bodies like withered vine-roots, the flesh dried from the bones, sitting or standing immobile in their stained threadbare garments. They glanced at us, once, out of colourless eyes hidden instantly behind dark wrinkled lids. These men, Denis Saurat told us later, were all well-off; many of them owned property in Vence or in Nice itself. Their wealth was land, sheep, cattle. You could take away all their money, and not one of them would live any differently: they did not live on their money. The state in France has far less call on the real wealth of its members than it has in England. Hence the indifference of so many of them to its goings-on. Why should they care?

In December we moved down to the coast, to Nice, the Nice of the now unfashionable winter, belonging only to its citizens, very pleasant, and took rooms in a pension in the high Cimiez quarter. It was up here that Queen Victoria used to stay, in a vast hotel named for her, the Hotel Regina, now a great haggard block of flats, with a superb view above the town to the sea. The pension, run by a Madame P., a shuffling active old body, the veins of her neck and legs in relief, was warm and shabby. My room had its own bath-room, which stank so foully that I had to be careful to keep the door tightly shut. When I complained, mildly, of the smell, Madame P. said anxiously that something, the root of a palm-tree in the neglected garden, was chok-ing the drain. Nothing worse. One could not, surely I would agree, receive any harm from the root of a palm. I accepted the explanation, and indeed received no harm during the three months I worked and slept in the room.

Madame P. was so desperately anxious to please, and so friendly that I became fond of her, and could smile with a pretence of delight when for the fourth time in a week, '*pour changer les idées*,' she gave us fennel root, that most loathsome of vegetables. Another thing she served freely was *loup*, a fish with the texture of old flannel.

Everywhere in our zig-zag journey through France we had come on plaques and single stones carrying the names of men and women shot, hanged, or tortured to death during the Occupation. Entering the main square of Nice, we passed two of these memorials. If we had come this way on the 7th of July 1944, we should have had to pass the bodies of two young men, Ange Grassi and Seraphim Torrin, hanged and exposed in this place. The same phrase was repeated on both plaques: *Passant, incline-toi, souviens-toi.*

What, I wondered, did the French passer-by remember? True, the resisters were a handful of Frenchmen; true, the girding anxiety of most people in those years was to get hold of enough food to keep a child from becoming tuberculous; true, many men and women could say what a Parisian woman staying in the pension said to me: 'The Germans? Oh, they gave no one any trouble. Unless you were silly enough to get mixed up in something.' All true. But the discomfort, the hardships, the despair of a few, the deportations, the executions, must—surely?—have left a mark on the country. Only, perhaps, as an adult may be scarred, lightly, by an act of cruelty he heard tell of as a child. Perhaps not even that? My peacock-voiced Parisian? Madame P.'s youngest grandson, a handsome demon of four?

A village I saw later, five months later, Frayssinet-le-Gélat, on the road between Beynac and Cahors, has one of the most terrible of these monuments. Darkness was falling when we drove into the place, which seemed to be empty. I caught sight as we passed it of a large block of stone, and stopped the car to look at it. (It always seemed impolite not to stop.) There was the usual inscription—*Aux Martyrs de la barbarie Allemande*—and below the fifteen names the date, 21 Mai 1944, and the usual two words. *Souvenez-vous.*

A door opened in one of the grey houses, a woman profiled on the weak light looked at us for a moment, and closed the door again quietly. Even if she had stepped outside, I should not have dared question her. Something—the darkness, the heaviness of the stone, the dark church behind it, the silence, even the unprepossessing look of the village—started up a feeling of anguish so acute that later I wrote to the Archivist of the department (of the Lot) to ask him what had happened on the 21st of May 1944 in Frayssinet-le-Gélat. He told me. That day a German division on its way to Normandy was passing through, a shot was fired, coming, the Germans thought, from a cottage where three old women were living; the soldiers dragged the old creatures out and hanged them outside the little church, summoning the rest of the village to watch. Then they picked out ten villagers to be shot, among them a schoolboy from the philosophy class in Cahors whose parents had brought him here for safety. The father asked to be shot in his place, and the German officer added him to the rest.

That accounts for fourteen of the names. But there are fifteen, eleven men and four women. Who is the fourth woman? I feel something like remorse that I don't know how she offended or how she died, whether she was one of the two Lugan sisters, or Agathe Paille, or Yvonne Vidilles.

After a time I noticed that the apathy of many people to the political harlequinade broke, when it did break, precisely over the question of Germany. Possibly the break marked a still suppurating wound in the country's instinctive energy. No foreigner could have probed it without running the risk of an atrocious blunder. Suppose I had been unlucky enough to speak about Nazi brutality to the charming intelligent woman we met here whose husband and son had both been arrested and shot, as resisters, by the *French* police?

That happened before the Liberation. After the Liberation, thousands of innocent persons, no one knows how many, died, murdered by patriots acting on lying denunciations, or by communists getting rid at this convenient moment of political opponents, or—perhaps less often—by persons seizing their chance to lay hands on a coveted field, or to pay off old scores or to cancel a debt by abolishing the creditor. One evening at the end of September 1944, when Agen and the whole region had long been free of Germans, four officers of the local Resistance forces turned up at the farm of a family which had taken a serious and costly part in the Resistance; they walked in unhindered, and killed the twenty-year-old son of the house, his mother, and another young man, a friend. A girl, in the house by chance, was taken outside and machine-gunned, but survived. After nine years, the case came before the tribunal in Bordeaux: friends and relatives of the murdered family at last felt safe enough to tell the truth. That the *execution*—what is

JOURNEY FROM THE NORTH, VOL. 2

language for but to ennoble our actions?—had been a personal vengeance: the dead boy was believed to have in his possession a document compromising to his comrades in the Resistance.

A young man, the eldest son of a Catholic family, was denounced as a collaborator by his fellow-resisters, good Party members, and shot 'legally.' The denunciators were saving themselves the trouble of an *execution*.

The newspapers I read that December in Nice were filled with details, only now, nine years after the event, being dragged into the light, of the summary executions in the Limousin, Giraudoux's Limousin, in July 1944. During that month (two months after the Frayssinet affair), the greater number of the non-communist resisters of the region were shot and their bodies hurriedly pushed into the ground, in fields and woods, by their ex-comrades of the maquis, acting under the orders of their chief, the Liberation mayor of Limoges and a member of the Party.

'What d'you expect?' a Frenchman said—with an extraordinary air of reserve and contempt. 'That a few months or years in the Resistance would turn a loyal communist into a loyal human being?'

No person whose country has never been occupied has the right to comment. But if I were the leader of a partisan revolt or revolution, of any colour, I should be less afraid of my opponents than of the impatience of my followers. After three or four years of heroic killings what, I ask you, could be more natural than to see murder as a handy way of getting rid of an embarrassment? To think anything else about these—these exercises, is hypocrisy or moonshine.

I worked at *The Hidden River* all day. The new version was going very slowly because of my extreme boredom when I have to describe a love scene. This boredom had been growing in me for some years and had reached a point when I could write about the emotions of a pair of lovers—not to speak of their acts—only by a torturing and tortuous effort of memory. It began—my boredom—on the day when I became sensible and ceased to fall in love for a few hours with the head or profile of some total stranger.

Some time towards the end of the year I read, I think in *Figaro Littéraire*, that *Scrutiny* was going to stop, and wrote to ask F. R. Leavis if this bad news were true.

'... *Scrutiny* has stopped,' he answered, 'because I am beaten... The immediate cause of death is the impossibility of holding anything like an adequate collaborating team in the *Held*. But the radical cause is my utter defeat at Cambridge. To run a review and a one-man "English School" (the two going essentially together) in ostracism—no, it couldn't be done forever. People flatter me about my "influence", but it has *failed to get* me a *glimmer* of recognition at the place where above all it matters. How could *Scrutiny* be made a permanency, except from a continuing centre of intellectual life at an ancient university? Actually, the result of running *Scrutiny* (the reward) is that I am more isolated than ever. The fact intimately associated with the death of *Scrutiny* is that my *Education and the University* has never been recognized to exist, even to disagree with, at Cambridge. What it did was to confirm my life-long exclusion from any say in the English School. When I am retired (on the pension of one who wrested a part-time lectureship from the Faculty at forty-two, and a full-time lectureship at fifty-two) all that I have worked for at Cambridge peters out.

'I *am* sad about it. Without a focus, a source of impulsion, at an ancient university, I don't believe that much can be done in the provincial universities, or the schools or anywhere (I mean, of course, what I—am I egotistic?— have fought for)... No one is without vanity, but I think I care as little about mere kudos as anyone. But the lack of recognition in any form that could compel corresponding recognition at Cambridge has been fatal. That's why the boycott mattered... What is so depressing is the evidence—of which I'm now getting so much—of a potentially formidable public opinion, and the complete absence of any bringing to bear... And what a loss!—how irreplaceable *Scrutiny* is!—that's the chorus now...'

In this letter, and in one he wrote a month later, he spoke of his wife's bitter sense that both their lives had been sacrificed 'for nothing'.

I understood that. I know the frightful recoil of the heart in the moment of defeat. I understood with the marrow of my bones that a lifetime of exhausting work, devotion, laying aside of personal ambition, slow loss of hope, must, at this moment, turn to a nearly inconceivable bitterness and anger. She had never compromised, never sacrificed a living soul to her own ambitions, needs, hungers. Her single-mindedness and honesty were as absolute as her husband's.

The contrast between their integrity and my bad faith in altering *The Hidden River* was bitter in my belly. For a short time I wrestled with the impulse to cable to New York that I could not finish the revision.

I lacked the courage. I could not face the loss of thirty—thirty!—thousand dollars, and Carl Brandt's anger. And, too, I lacked confidence, arrogance, call it what you like. Pushed to the wall, I could not believe that anything I had written, anything I could ever write, was so good, so important that I had a duty to turn away money I needed.

I wrote a careful letter to *Time and Tide* about the death of *Scrutiny*, and went back to my task...

We had friends living ten minutes walk from Madame P.'s, in a flat in the Hôtel Regina, below the flat where Matisse was living. Denis Saurat and his wife. They came here to live when he retired from his university chair in London, after his abrupt dismissal, on General de Gaulle's orders, from the French Institute. His crime: that he loved England a great deal better than he loved the General. Yet he began, in 1940, by a passion of devotion and gratitude to the man he came later to see as a potential dictator. In 1942, disillusioned, he asked me for an introduction to a visiting American journalist, Maxine Davis; he wanted her to warn her countrymen that whether they admired or distrusted the General it was for the wrong reasons. I arranged for him to see her.

'Can I believe him?' she asked me.

'Anything he tells you will be true,' I said. 'You have only to remember that it is the truth seen by a metaphysical poet, a descendant of Cathars, an intellectual, and a shrewd administrator.'

When I left her, I caught sight of him in the crowded entrance hall of Claridge's, waiting to be summoned to her room, a frail tiny figure of a would-be giant killer.

His punishment at the end of the war came swiftly—the General is not magnanimous. And his bad reputation as a lover of the English followed him to Nice. The official of Aix University—on which the University Centre of Nice depended—detested him as an 'English interloper', and saw to it that he was never made use of by the Centre. Theirs the loss—of a lucid inquisitive mind, a scholarly gadfly, a wit.

No saint, and not without self-esteem, he resented his exclusion. But he was not unhappy, perched, a brilliant bird, in a room high above the mists of the lower town. Bird or dancer? His mind had the disciplined lightness and precision of a highly-trained ballet dancer. He talked superbly. He was never able to resist a verbal pirouette, but he pirouetted on a base of knowledge and speculation in his fields.

Listening to him here, I thought that living on the edge of an old myth-soaked Europe, under a hot sun, had brought nearer the surface the fantastic side of his intelligence— a bit of a sorcerer, a bit of a miracle worker in his native mountains, André Chamson said in a brief obituary. (How the French love a Tombeau de..., and how well, how adroitly, they write it!) The scholar drew back a little behind the wide-awake dreamer of *La Mort et le Rêveur*, the mystical poet of *Le Soldat Romain*. He amused his leisure with myths, half-believer, half-sceptic. A root of his mind was Manichean, that logical ambiguous faith. And why not? He came from a part of France where it died hardest—if it is dead.

During this winter we saw him four or five times a week. Either he lunched with us in our pension, eating slice after slice of the pale tasteless veal Madame P. provided when she knew he was coming, or we went to his flat in the afternoon. He had a great many friends—among them a retired professor of history who was unable to believe that Germans and Americans were not one and the same barbarian on the frontier.

'They come here, your Americans, like a successful man coming back to his village and finding his old cousins still living their lives by a tradition he can't feel, which makes no sense to him. And no one can convince him that civilization and power are not the same thing. Let me tell you what I would tell Americans who are not bankers like Foster Dulles or amateur politicians like Eisenhower—if I could get at them. I would say: You are handing back to the Germans the arms millions of men and women died to take from them—you hope they will glut themselves by turning east. But why, to satisfy your bankers, should we loose these brutes on Poles, Czechs, Russians, whom we have no wish to injure, nor they us? Why for the love of God should we help you to set fire to Europe? Tell me that!'

'The Americans won't start a war——'

'Then why are they *taking such* pains to provoke Russia? Oh, I know as well as you that your American market gardener and the rest is as much a victim as if he were only a poor French market gardener. It makes no difference.

Yes, there is a difference. More of them will survive another war. But they won't, for that, constitute a civilization. A French government with the moral courage of any poor devil of a second lieutenant would order America to withdraw its occupying troops and invite the rest of western Europe to join us in a neutrality pact that would satisfy the Russians they had nothing to fear in Europe. If Mr Dulles felt compelled to go on issuing his challenges it would be his funeral, not ours. No sort of obligation compels us French to join him in his bloody adventure. We should be rebuilding France, planting vines, breeding children. God send us an intelligent dictator!'

'It will serve you right if He does,' Denis said with a purely malicious smile. 'A people that can't run its affairs without one deserves nothing better.'

He had a weakness, dear Denis, for well-born women. One afternoon there were two drinking tea in his living-room: Madame de Broglie, and Madame de Clermont-Tonnerre, the first a short energetic old lady, the second holding together with difficulty a long ruined body and long yellow equine face across which an amiable smile came and went, never able to lodge itself in any of the folds of ill-fitting skin. They had brought with them a strong handsome Flemish mare of a young woman, a Comtesse de —— what? I have forgotten. A passionate argument broke out between the young woman and Madame de Broglie about loving God.

Speaking with the utmost respect, the young woman said, 'But, Madame la Duchesse, I must, I simply must believe that we can love God even though we haven't seen him. All the saints——'

Madame de Broglie had rolled a newspaper into a baton. Brandishing it, she cut the young woman short with arrogant familiarity, as though she were a tiresome child. 'My good girl, you are talking the most complete rubbish. Why bring in the saints? I behave as I was brought up to behave. How can I be asked to love any person, however exalted, whom I have never met? It's ridiculous. And perfectly unreasonable.'

Blushing a little, the young woman insisted. 'Excuse me, Madame la Duchesse, if I say that I myself——'

'No, no, no,' Madame de Broglie interrupted again, 'I could never do it. Respect, obedience, belief, anything you like, but not love. What do you want me to do about it? I'm made like that!' She turned to her old friend.

'And you, my dear? Do you love God? You know the difference between love and respect, I hope. Your husband should have taught you that.'

Her affable smile wavered across Madame de Clermont-Tonnerre's eyes, leaving them vacant and childlike.

'Yes, yes, you are right,' she said in a hoarse voice, 'between love and respect there is an impassable gulf.'

'I don't understand either of you,' exclaimed the young woman.

'Perhaps when you are older, my child, and have been married for longer than a year...'

How I regret that, a little over four years later, Denis Saurat died. We have a surfeit of visionaries without intelligence and scholars without gaiety. When he died, a little of its salt and honey vanished from this lower world. I could better spare a number of judicious intellectual heavyweights with both feet planted immovably and solemnly on the ground.

A village a few miles south of the road from Cagnes to Grasse, reached by an execrable road, is more familiar to me than the university city I am living in at this moment. There is no explaining these quirks of the mind: if I tried to say why, for several hours, I was perfectly happy and at home in a small lost Provençal village, without any obvious charm, I should write nonsense or literature.

We went there first in the middle of January, with Maria Kuncewiczowa and her husband; they knew it because they had lived in the village for several weeks, in one of the old houses of blackish stone which looked to be on the point of crumbling into rubble—if it had had a thousand francs worth of repairs done on it in three hundred years that was all, and it was good for another four or five centuries. A village of dark lanes climbing steeply, step by shallow uneven step of cobblestones and dry earth, smelling of garlic and urine, and two narrow streets of taller houses, a few of them empty, all strong and shabby, here and there doors framed in blocks of old sculptured stone. No lane or so-called street had been made; all were stony and deeply rutted, thick in dust in summer, in mud the rest of the year. Both streets cut across the side of the hill, so that houses with a single storey on one side of the upper street had three or even four on the parallel street lower down. The upper street dropped sharply, between dark shuttered houses, from the

large uncouth square, a stretch of bare earth, on the edge of the village, and
came to a stop in a narrow stony place and a shabby bistro: a few yards of
low wall outside the bistro overhung the hillside scored across and across by
neglected rows of olives, below them a rocky precipice fell steeply, flowing
into the folds of less savage hills, coiling and uncoiling, and flattening at last
into the thin glittering knife edge of the coast.

Outside the village, at its lower end, two women and a boy were gathering olives. One of the women was old, bent into a hoop of blackened skin
and bone; the other, elderly, had the profile of a Roman matron, features
perfectly regular under thick coils of black hair, pure black, shining with
oil. I had seen others of these Roman heads in this once Greek and then
Roman countryside, but never one so superbly carved and massive. Using
a long thin stick, the boy whipped the branches, and as the ripe olives fell
on to the sheet spread below the trees, the two women sorted them deftly
into baskets.

The sun, the light wind, a sky of incomparable freshness, the movement
of the Roman woman's arms, movements she had been making for a score
of centuries, at least a score, ran together in my mind to evoke an image
which may—how do I know?—have been formed there before I was born.

Maria had several friends in the place. No one, not even an inhabitant
of these savage hills, could have refused to accept a friendliness as simple
and graceful as the gestures of her fine Polish hands. She knew everything
about the marital troubles of Madame Titine, who managed the bistro
where we ate a magnificent salad and drank a great deal of strong red wine;
she knew, about the families of a few peasants and the owners of one or
two of these forbidding frost-blackened houses, stories which form part of
an Iliad of obscure hatreds, quarrels, adulteries, marriages. How, without
asking a single question, did she discover so much? Simply by living here,
by listening, smiling.

One of her friends, the gentle dark-haired boy who knitted and drew
sketches of women's dresses, and confided in her that he wanted to become
a fashion designer, turned, a few years later, into a girl.

But for Maria we should not have come here, and I should have missed a
pleasure so exactly my size that I have been drawing on it ever since. Altered,
merged with another of these villages which, seen from above or below, look

like ossuaries, indistinguishable from the livid rocks of their hill, or identical with itself, it returned in three novels.

When, in March, to everyone's satisfaction except mine, I finished the new version of *The Hidden River*, we left Nice. Aix for two nights: Valence, where we ate the most superb dinner and were kept awake until dawn by cars and lorries clattering through the walls of the room and across the beds; Nevers. This unassuming old city climbing staidly above the Loire and the Nièvre is dear to me: I fell in love with it on my first visit, without knowing why. This time—as well as cheese and bread—I bought a copy of the *Mémoires d'un touriste*, to replace one left behind in Aix: it is the one of my travel books I carry as an act of piety.

From Nevers to Paris. We stayed four weeks, and I remember little except the cold: the leaves of plane trees and chestnuts remained folded and the river as grey as though, higher up, it were full of snow: which was impossible. We saw *Pour Lucrèce*, so finely acted and presented—except that Madeline Renaud was too old for the part; she looked middle-aged, almost haggard— that it was easy to overlook the weariness, like the turns and twists of an old acrobat, still clever but tired to death, of the writer.

My other clear memory is of a visit to the remnants, outside Paris, of Port-Royal. The guide who took us round the commemorative chapel could exist only in France. Hands in the pockets of his workman's blue overalls, he discussed, with enthusiasm and knowledge, the events of the period, the characters of Louis XIV, Pascal, Arnauld, points of doctrine. No intellectual, adept in the history of Jansenism, would have shown himself subtler and more acute. A guide in a shrine little visited and, except for the death-mask of Mère Angélique, little notable—it seems nothing much. It was everything. Outlined on the clear cold March sunlight of the Ile-de-France, a whole irreplaceable civilization…

Longing for warmth, we went south again, to Provence. Still the spring did not come.

An ice-cold knife of wind moved through St Paul de Vence, and among the monstrous remnants of Les Baux and in the steep dark street of mediaeval Vaison-la-Romaine. Snow began falling in May. We crossed the Rhône and drove through snowstorms and an icy wind as far east as Roquefort:

the only guests in a hotel filled with scaffolding, we were served a dinner Petronius would have found a little exaggerated. In the morning the cold drove us away from caves filled with cheeses.

During the four days we spent in the Château de Mercués, a slight warmth began to come into the air: at midday the sun was almost strong.

Although I had seen the cave drawings at Lascaux before this, and looked at them, as I thought, carefully, I had forgotten the one radical thing about them, their purely sensuous energy. The men crouching in these dark passages in the rocky cliff had behind their eyes an image of the animal they were drawing so shockingly clear, so detailed, that it inhibited every energetic impulse except the primitive impulse of the artist, the maker, to set it free, without distortion or interference. I don't for a moment believe that they made these drawings only because they thought that in some magical way the effort helped them to hunt down the beast they drew. But no matter. The directness of these paintings and sketches, the life captured in them, places them at the farthest possible distance from abstract art—which is a sort of rhetoric in paint. A rhetoric in flight from the naked statement. Where these first artists wanted to stalk and free the force of life behind the image, the compelling wish of an abstract painter or sculptor is to free *himself* from the coils of nature. To create a style which has no frame of reference outside himself. The price of his freedom is the isolation of his work on a mandarin level of existence.

Looking closely at a modern *construction*, in iron or glass or wire, I have the sense that its maker has tried to grasp and project some hallucinating image proffered him by the nerves behind his eyes. Even successful, the attempt excludes me. Excludes any spectator unwilling to dupe himself. I could, as writers on art do, turn his constructions into literature. That is, into a construction of my own, which, if I am honest, I know has nothing in common with his. Most criticism of abstract art is, in this sense, dishonest. Reading that such and such an abstract painting of a naked man 'reveals an imaginative energy at once abstract and sensuous,' I feel that the writer, if not consciously dishonest, does not know what certain words mean. The energy in the painting he is describing is intellectual, not imaginative, and what has been ignored (by the artist) is precisely the infinite possibilities, the magnificently subtle sensuous *organization* of the body.

Moreover, the finest constructions of this sort are extraordinarily clumsy and childish compared with the complicated and very beautiful machines and machine tools designed and perfected in a modern engineering works. In September 1940 I visited a number of armaments factories—to write a short book for the Ministry of Supply, which in the end I did not write. The machines and machine tools I saw in various heavy arms works were in a real sense the modern successors of the figures of Michelangelo. Beside them, the work of any constructivist is puerile, inept, empty, derived from the brain and nerves. These machines are made with the entrails as well as with the brain.

Oddly enough, there is one art which is able to be supremely sensuous and in the highest degree abstract—music. The phrase about an imaginative energy at once abstract and sensuous applies truthfully to Schönberg. Why? I am too ignorant to know why. Possibly the ear is the channel for a subtler, more complicated sense than the eye?

Crossing the empty country north of the Pyrenees, we passed continually from sunlight to rain, brilliant colours in the fields and hedges, then a long grey rippling curtain—a chameleon would have gone off his head. At last, in Bordeaux, spring rushed in, barely ahead of summer, bringing in everything at once, acacias, lime blossom, incandescent skies at noon, long warm unblemished evenings.

We stayed in the Chapon Fin itself. It was a delicious hotel, not many bedrooms, discreet, old-fashioned, with majestic mahogany furniture, like the bedrooms in my grandfather's house, breakfasts of strong coffee and magnificent croissants worthy of the creators of the most lovable, most finely civilized, least assuming, of great restaurants. Alas, a casualty of our insensitive heartless sinister age, it has vanished. Serve us right for surviving into a time which prefers computers and the Hilton hotels to peace of mind and body and the Chapon Fin.

Nothing, surely nothing, can mar the Dordogne valley. A short way beyond Libourne there was—I have never dared to go back to see that it is still there—an avenue of limes. In the hot sun they were alive with bees. All the summers of my childhood spilled from the continuous deep note, warmth and light turned to sound, the scent of green ling and peat on the

moors, the choking smell of meadowsweet in narrow sunken lanes, even
the tiny clatter of small waves running against the pebbles. Like an old dog,
my mind turns in narrowing circles round the same point—a few yards of
earth and coarse salt-bitten grass, a few undistinguished streets, the rotting
timbers of a wharf, a laburnum.

Time was running out. From Bordeaux to La Rochelle, from La Rochelle
to Angers. And then, for the last time, the Loire.

When we came into Saumur at six in the evening, the light was a thin,
clear, amazingly clear and watery gold. Two hours later all the clarity had
been drawn into trees and the walls of houses, in sharp relief against an
overcast sky: a strong wind from the west was blowing the river under the
arches of the bridge in a flurry of steel ripples: later still, about nine, a long
sorrowful crimson gash opened suddenly in the livid clouds, and poured out
a torrent of light the colour of tarnished bronze. Much later, glancing from
my window at the trees on the other side of the Loire, I saw a tree-trunk, in
an amphitheatre of leaves, turn to a figure of light, curiously menacing and
archaic—Apollo in a mood to punish.

One more fortnight, and it was the last day of our ten months. Walking
about Amiens, in search of a street no longer there, I comforted myself with
the certainty of being dead before this country ceases entirely to keep alive a
civilization, a way of living, of which man is the measure. A ceaseless patient
and cunning effort has humanized the earth itself of France. Nowhere, but
nowhere in the world, is the precarious truce between men and nature,
between us and our own nature, so nearly friendly, informed by so tough
and resilient a spirit. In no country is the past, the memory of human toil
and genius, so part of the living present. Blois and Amboise, Chartres and
Albi, Saint-Emilion...

It could be destroyed. Saint-Emilion could be wiped out, brutally irre-
mediably ruined. The long story of the centuries still unfolding there could
be cut short.

Something would survive. In a Provençal village the strong shabby
crumbling houses would, as now, merge imperceptibly into the naked
bones of the hill. Its peasants would work from dawn to dusk. Old women
would die, smiling toothlessly, filled by a lifetime of labour. Women with
the faces of Roman matrons would kneel in the weak January sun sorting

the olives whipped from the grey trees. The rough unmade streets would keep their secrets, some of them bitter, behind closely shuttered windows. As now.

But peasant France is not the whole. The roots might be saved, yes. But how long, how many decades, before the flower?

Fine rain, a low curdled sky, flying splinters of gold. Turning a corner, I saw the long narrow spire of the cathedral, bone white and dark steel-grey, pencilled on the misty sunlight. I stood and looked at it, with an entire happiness, for two or three minutes, until the rain quickened and it was time to turn back.

## CHAPTER 13

NEXT YEAR, in April 1955, I came near enough death to imagine that I recognized her in the person of an elderly matron of a hospital. I meant to go to Vienna, and since, as happened now and then, I had worked myself to a standstill, I agreed with my doctor that this was a good moment to spend a few days in bed. (I agreed reluctantly—I have every intention of dying like Emily Brontë, in my chair.) 'We'll get rid of that,' she said, touching a fine knot of vein, 'and you'll have a week's rest and go to Vienna refreshed,'

I did not go to Vienna, and I stayed in that London hospital for eight mortal weeks.

So much for doctors and their powers of prediction.

I took it that the pain after the operation—which became agony when I put foot to the ground—was a perfectly normal thing. After a day or two, I asked for a walking-stick, and was refused it—on the ground that there were none on this floor. So much for hospitals.

I had begun to find it difficult to breathe.

Late in the afternoon of Easter Sunday I stopped breathing. Luckily for me, a very young nurse was in the room at the time. I had an instant left in which to say to her, 'Goodness, I'm going to faint,' and hear her cry, 'Oh, *no!*' A weight of darkness dragging me backwards, then nothing, then a sort of tent over my face, a voice telling me to breathe, and I breathed.

'How long,' I asked later, 'did it take you to get that thing into my room?'

It looked like the work of a surrealist sculptor, I thought it sinister, and wanted it taken away.

'Exactly one minute.'

It was a few minutes after this that I saw the elderly black-clad woman. The door was to the right of my bed: she came in silently, and, still in silence, walked, eyeing me the whole way, along the wall facing the bed, turned at the corner, and went out again. Well, that's Death, I said to myself: who could have known she would look so expressionless and respectable.

I remembered that I had seen her before—during the night after my son was born. But that was in a half-dream.

'Who on earth was that old woman?'

The nurse almost crossed herself in surprise at my blasphemy. 'That? That was Matron herself!'

Later still, much later, my surgeon came into the room. I was surprised to see him, but even now it did not cross my mind to wonder why they had thought fit to bring him up from the country on Easter Sunday. He leaned against the wall near the door, listening to my duologue with the house doctor. I liked him: the nurses gave him a reputation for foul language when he was operating, and he was certainly something of a brute, as some surgeons are, but I prefer a controlled brutality to what used to be called a good bedside manner. My sense of smell is as acute as my hearing: the smell of very good brandy reached me across the room, and I thought: I interrupted his dinner. I intended to use his dark hooked Welsh face some time, in a novel, and I kept one eye on it when I was answering the house doctor's questions.

'Describe the pain in the chest.'

I did so.

'How long had you had it?'

'Oh, about three days.'

'Why didn't you speak about it?'

Useless to tell this severely patient man that I had been brought up not to bore people with my ailments. 'It wasn't a bad pain.' I lacked the insolence to add: Not like the other, for which I was refused a walking-stick.

'And then this afternoon it suddenly got worse,' he said.

I detest having words put in my mouth. I was delighted to be able to contradict him. 'No. No worse at all. Exactly the same.'

The lightest possible twitch of amusement—noted for use—crossed my surgeon's face, but he said nothing until the examination was over, then all he said was, 'This afternoon I had to pick up a child who fell out of an apple tree, and——'

For some reason I now felt pleasantly excited, as if I had been drinking. I interrupted him. 'And tonight you had to pick up an ageing witch who fell off her broomstick.'

He laughed.

That night turned out the most extraordinary I can remember. In the first and longer part of it I did not dream. I was asleep, but in a state of heightened consciousness, a contradiction, a paradox that I grasped clearly enough to think: So, after all, the darkness is not dark. In this marvellous lucidity I passed through sensations as if I were moving from stage to stage of consciousness. My brain was full of light, like a plain flooded by the moon. In the morning I wrote down as much as I could recall, but the words distort even that little.

I was an impulse, a sort of energy, reflected in an image of myself. This circle was broken by an image stepping out of the image. I felt I had lost something, some harmony, and I began to multiply the images in the hope of recovering it. But it was useless, I only fell farther and farther down, an immeasurable distance, until I was looking at what seemed the final image. Now I began reasoning. This creature, I reflected, is entirely irrational and on the point of dissolution: I need not wake her up unless I decide to, I can let her die here and put an end to the whole coil of waking and sleeping, changing, making, and not-changing. It means depriving her of her acute senses, but why not?

At this point I began to be afraid of the distance I still had to fall, and made an effort to wake up. I woke in the first light, with a feeling of pleasure and sadness, some hint of the ravishing lucidity still there, but only for an instant.

I fell asleep again. This time I dreamed. One of the worst dreams I ever had in my life—I think the worst I remember. My son, a baby, burrowed under, or rather into, something like a vast mattress. I called, he answered, but I was certain he must be suffocating, and I began to tear my way into the thing, tearing up cork carpet and the boards of the floor, searching frenziedly and calling, calling. He was nowhere. I found odd things, including a little clay group of three figures together, which I vaguely knew to be a votive object: one of the figures was a minute elf-like boy. By now I was in agony of mind. Do, my sister, a young Do, about fifteen, was there, and my mother, also younger, about fifty, and they helped me a little. I went on with my anguished search. My sister came to me, exclaiming that they had found a clue; she had the tiny figurine in her hand, and said smiling, 'You see, Dear Dog, it wasn't a boy at all.' With despair, I realized that I had lost him, there was nothing to be felt in the mattress, no little body. There were other rooms I went into, and other incidents, which I forgot.

I woke in the same heavy despair and grief. It was lighter in my room, but still very early. I lay thinking—for the ten thousandth time—that leaving my child and going to London at the end of 1919 was the first fatal error of my many errors, the one for which there is no forgiveness, no redemption.

Thirty-seven years. A long time. Perhaps it is because I have never suffered any of the physical or metaphysical anguish which is said to afflict ageing men and women at a certain period in their lives that these other regrets are still alive and young...

During that interminable morning, the consultant of the hospital was called in, an amiable simpering comforter. My own doctor was on holiday abroad, and no one thought fit to tell me what had happened. I waited day after day, expecting some kind of explanation—and too determined to show no concern for myself to ask for it. But apart from telling me, almost in an aside, that the deep thrombosis which in a few days followed the lung embolism had been expected, they explained nothing. The simperer overflowed with sweet oil, and evaded me when I asked, 'How long am I going to be here?'

As the weeks passed, I not only became used to my weakness, I began wearing it like an old comfortable coat. I was not bored. If a prison cell were airy, with a good bed and a window, it would suit my unsociability, my distrust of people, very well. I had as many books as I chose, and as few visitors.

The visitors I enjoyed were those who came with a story burning the ends of their tongues. They sat down, asked one or two ritual questions I could evade, then laid in front of me some tale I listened to with the delight of a child brought a new toy.

There is something strange, and a little disconcerting, about the readiness with which people confess themselves to a friend they imagine to be very ill, perhaps *dying*...

The food in that hospital was no more horrible than in any other. Why in the name of Aesculapius must patients in English hospitals choose between a fast to the death and an insult to their helpless bodies? My friend Doreen Marston twice brought smoked salmon and brown bread, and my friend A. D. Peters brought eggs from the country. In the two months I was there these were the only tolerable meals I ate. They eat a great deal worse in concentration camps. True, true, but do hospitals fall into that category?

During these lost weeks I made efforts to balance my moral account, in advance of another death. But I fell into endless reveries in which I was not thinking but drifting from scene to scene, some recalled, some, the most charming, invented. In the end, to keep my mind at heel for an hour or two, I took to writing and folded the pages into a volume of Kafka I had been yawning over—in a cell the hermetic is a bore.

Here is part of it:

I am ashamed of my growing indifference. It couldn't be said that I live as I please, but what has become of that burning political passion of the 'thirties when I wrote and signed manifestos against fascism, attended meetings called to condemn the coming war, and toiled at every sort of flimsy barricade against it? Dust in corners...

I began calling myself a socialist when I was sixteen. Mine was the simplest and most emotional of creeds, a violent anger when I thought of children growing up in cancerously mean streets. All the economic arguments in the world are irrelevant to this single injustice. That there are people not shocked by this separation of children into two categories never ceases to astonish and offend me. Moreover I detect a line running underground from this relatively innocent inhumanity to the sickening inconceivable inhumanity of the gas chambers.

I am exaggerating? Oh, if you think so. What you think is not my business...

This has nothing to do with liberty, equality, fraternity and the rest of it. Equality is an illusion—attempts to enforce it involve the death of liberty. But brotherhood—ah, that is God, the Son, and the *Holy* Ghost of my creed...

I have no energy left to do anything about it. Spurts of flame from the ash, impotent rage. Nothing more. I was never a revolutionary—an instinctive rebel, but not a believer in revolution. Too much cruelty, too many deaths, merely to replace one autocracy by another. The Labour Party, which began in the fraternity of poor men and is now another power machine, is necessary: two, three, ten power machines are more tolerable than one. But why should I feel any devotion to the politics of a machine?...

Of all my passionate concerns—in the Quaker sense—two remain.

I can give very respectable reasons for the concern I still have for those of my friends and fellow-writers who are exiles. They add a sharp taste to our dull island soup. So much new energy, so much courage, so many new minds, added to the spiritual life of this country, are pure gain. They form a new *ordo vagorum*, carrying ideas and opinions across the barbed wire that disfigures and brutalizes Europe, and remind us that our fellow-countrymen bear names like Capek, Unamuno, Freud, Einstein, Pasternak.

But they are my fellow-countrymen in a deeper, colder sense. The country they return to in sleep, filled with voices from the other side of a closed frontier, voices of estranged friends, of a dead mother, a lost child, is as much mine as theirs. And if they delude themselves that they can return in reality, that Ithaca is not lost to them forever, that, too, is one of my own delusions, not the least indestructible.

And the other concern? One I share with millions of equally helpless men and women. Between 1914 and 1918, though I subscribed with my tongue to the protests of out-and-out pacifists, in my heart I thought less well of them than of my friends who were fighting, even the conscripts, either for an idea they had of England or out of a simple wish not to be safer than the others, or with no reason at all except that they had been conscripted. In that war, the vileness of what one of its soldiers, Major-General Fuller, called its 'ritual of slaughter' could be set against the patience, courage, and decency of the young men. Even in the second war it was possible to feel that Belsen was a worse evil than bombed cities. But nothing, not even the Belsens still existing in Europe, is as evil as what is politely called megadeath. Or overkill.

My young brother, killed in 1917, was not alone in believing, with the greatest simplicity, that the war he was fighting in would be the last. Poor child. What he died for was Hiroshima. And that affair was only a rehearsal, almost gentle.

What is so hard to believe is that any creature with only as much human warmth as serves to pick up a fallen child can think of the act of using thermo-nuclear weapons as possible, let alone as one of the things he might be obliged to do. Or can dupe himself with the argument that the existence of these obscene objects makes another world war less likely because we shall fear to use them.

We no longer believe that greater knowledge will benefit us. Traditional knowledge, the experience of our ancestors, ceased to be a help to us as soon as by our inventiveness we had destroyed the kind of society they knew how to live in. It has become fashionable to mock or snub humanists who distrust 'science'. But science is as disgraced by some of its fruits as the Christian church was by the Inquisition.

Reading a cold analysis of the condition of a world which has been only partly reduced to radio-active rubble, one exclaims: No, it's not possible!

On the contrary. It is possible that man is the only creature with the ill-will to make an end of himself.

Then you would rather not be defended by thermo-nuclear weapons?
Much rather.

And the children? You would leave them defenceless?

If their temporary safety can only be bought by the agonized death, the flesh seared from their bones, of other children, yes.

I was not always without equivocation in this bloody business of war. Just as I was not always without political principles—without principles *tout court*, some of my friends would say. (Our friends are not our friends for nothing!) The last war was the turning point: up to the day it broke out I was frothing over like a mustard-pot with political commitment. At the end, nothing was left of it, nothing—except my involuntary neighbourly love for our exiles and my hatred of war...

I was writing the last words of this apologia when my friend Adela (not her name) came into the room. I was delighted to see her, because she felt no need to treat me gently, as an invalid. We argued, I forget about what, but it ended in her saying sharply, 'You are always so calm and decided. A monster of confidence! You know exactly what you want to do and how to do it. You don't know what it's like to be an ordinary woman, full of misgivings and indecision, as I am—perfectly ordinary and normal.'

When she had gone, drawing on her elegant gloves and smoothing her hair under a new hat, I wondered whether or not to congratulate myself on the air of confidence and strength of mind behind which I hide unplumbable weakness, indecision, nagging anxiety, hesitancy, uncertainty, moodiness—inherited, or made to measure.

Perhaps I had once been what she called me—a monster of confidence? Yes, of course—young, very young, I had the greatest confidence in my talents, and the energy of the devil. My dreams were all of love, glory, excitement. And then, gradually, it all ebbed. Now, I thought, I have almost none, I'm no longer able to take decisions, for myself or others—as if my will had snapped. I'm indifferent—an indifference at the roots.

Who, what, is to blame? No one, nothing. Myself. With both hands I destroyed myself, denaturing my senses, tearing out energies, desires, greeds, the innocent with the corrupt. I *tamed* myself. Why?

Even the desperate need to be right, my mother's need repeated in me—I have overcome even that... It took a long time. Not until I was at least fifty did it become even barely possible for me to admit that I am not invariably right and moved by the most irrefutable motives.

I began to laugh, and laughed quietly but uncontrollably until the pain in my body checked me...

Later, a nurse came in and switched on a lamp. When she had gone, I lay looking at the white globe, and wondering why only to hold it in my mind gave me this feeling of happiness, as fine as a fine blade, exquisite. Suddenly I knew. It had the same shape and slightly oily gleam of the huge hard ostrich eggs my father brought from Africa, on which I painted, in oils, exotic birds, copying them, feather by minute feather, from a large book.

We had a round dozen of these. Where are they now? Smashed? Given away by my mother in one of her clearing-out moods? One of them may still be lying in some room in Whitby or in a junk-shop. I should know it if I saw it.

I have a puritan horror of drugs, but always at nine o'clock I accepted thankfully the mild pain-killer they brought me. I could have had it at any time during the day, but I made a foolish point of enduring. I fell asleep at once. My mind in these weeks sent me a succession of landscape dreams, the happiest I ever have. Happiness as sharp as a knife. Nothing exists in them except a landscape—sometimes remembered from an earlier dream—of intense beauty or grandeur. Very often it is a coast, one of my five primordial images. In others I recognize the east cliff at Whitby, the harbour and the Esk valley, but only as a basis, an outline overlaid by the colours and details of the finished painting. Others may be memories of foreign cities seen in my earliest years, rising in all their freshness, as without blemish as the eye that saw them.

In these dreams I don't act. I *look*—with an ineffable happiness which, in the moment of waking, becomes a longing heavy with the loss of the heart of life, the worth, the meaning.

The pain woke me soon after midnight. Then I called round me images from my happy life, to deceive it and protect me.

The last notes of the 'Nachtmusik' in Vienna, played in the small courtyard in the Hofburg, dark except for the musicians' lights and a few windows in the Pallavicini Palace, rose, died away, swelled and became Monteverdi's *L'Incoronazione di Poppaea* heard on the 13th of September 1949, in the Palladian theatre in Vicenza: I moved my hands over the stone seat, feeling the smooth cold in my fingers, staring into the deceptive distances of the stage, drunk with the Italian voices, in which the vocal cords seem part of the whole sensual system of the singer. The double sounds moved inside my skull, coiling and uncoiling like snakes warmed by the sun.

The forms and colours of water. The sea off the island of Tjømo in the Oslo fjord in June, completely naked, a blue without flaw, the air carrying lightly its splinters of salt and the hot scent of pines: the narrow water-lanes in the centre of Amsterdam, flanked by houses too self-possessed, too charming, for their weight of secrets, some of which have been cruel: the estuary at Portmeirion, a faint bloom of mist over the hills, softening and blurring their already soft green and black-green colours, the water a glass reflecting sharply grey clouds and an acre of blue sky, the sun, withdrawn behind massed clouds above the hills nearest the open sea, its unseen rays turning their peaks to a mountain range of blinding incandescent whiteness. And very thin, and piercing the brain, the screech of gulls.

I was near the oldest images now, the seething whiteness of marguerites, the sea-bird voices of Whitby children.

On many of these nights, because it was closest to me in time, less than half a year away, I went back to Cyprus. My son was stationed there, living with his wife and two children, the younger less than a year old, in a bare white house: the street, filled with stones and deep ruts, was called Irene Street. This was before the madness began in earnest. We could climb safely in the ruins of mediaeval castles holding crazily to the steep flanks of rocky hills, and walk about these hills, between the stunted cork trees, the scented herbs crumbling to dust in the fingers, the Greek columns on a headland above a sea passing from blue to dense violet-green, the colour of a ripe fig...

Since I had a room to myself I was able sometimes to quiet the pain by a familiar thread of sound:

> There was an old woman went up in a basket
> ninety times as high as the moon...

What chaff for a grown woman to cling to! But this woman's mother had taught her tune and words; she in turn taught them to her son, who very likely did not remember them. Why should he? These memories have to end somewhere, or the world would be choked by them like a gutter by dead leaves. The almost tuneless old tunes, the lichened stones of old walls, the innocent curve of lanes, have to be effaced to make room. And if the future is less harmless? So much the worse for it...

The days became weeks, and I could get no satisfaction out of the simperer. I had better hopes of my surgeon, and when he came to take the stitches out of my wounds, which he did with sadistic speed and efficiency, watching to see me flinch—the only coquetry I have left is to do nothing of the sort—I asked him what had happened.

'The operation was a disaster,' he said coolly, 'you'll go out worse than you came in.'

I hardly believed him—but he was right. At the time his frankness stiffened me against the smiling deceit of the consultant, whom I despised for his good intentions.

At the end of eight and a half weeks I limped out of that place, to begin the long task of restoring myself to life.

## CHAPTER 14

S INCE A DEGREE of bodily pain, several degrees, is infinitely less demoralizing and destructive of my wits than domestic life, I lived happily in a country hotel in Surrey and wrote a novel, *The Intruder*. It was laid in the hard Provence of the hills behind Vence, in a village resembling the one I knew—to which I moved the remnants of a Celto-Ligurian city. These ancient cities sunk in the earth are the subconscious mind of Europe, its obsessions and its layer on layer of memories and races. The book was a study of obsessions, among them an old archaeologist's obsession with the springs of cruelty. I explored my own through his.

The village we lived in had no railway station, and was simple and empty, a green thought in a green place, not much more than the houses and cottages scattered round a large rough common, and the friendly hotel itself. The garden ran away gently into cornfields and meadows, and I looked at them—watching the colours change slowly through a dry summer and autumn—as I wrote, the sweat of pain trickling over my forehead in drops that fell on the paper.

I have never been more content.

My only distinct memory of these months is of a crisis not in my life, but in C.'s. In September, now a tall good-looking boy of thirteen, he started as a weekly boarder at Westminster. Something—perhaps the strain of living in a large exacting community after years of easy triumphs as a clever day-boy in a small school—touched off in him an uprush of anxiety so violent that if he had not had a basic strength of character—such as none of us had the right to expect in him (but I took it for granted)—he might have come to grief. And if he had not by the grace of God had a housemaster of the greatest wisdom, kindness and patience. I can well believe that in earlier generations he might have been handled in a way that would have ruined him for life. With his mother he raged like a mad creature. At school, during the week, he was dangerously controlled.

'He looks at me when I talk to him,' his housemaster told me, 'with polite cold hatred, it is like talking to a caged wild animal or a block of ice. I can't reach him.'

Had I been less sunk in my work and my racked body, I should have been more anxious. And more conscious of the risks we were running. The letter he wrote at the end of September, to tell me that I was wasting my money on sending him 'to a school full of reactionary traditionalism', was so acute in its feeling for the words that would be the most likely to shake me, so calmly intelligent, that I felt more admiration than pity for the young creature writing it, coldly, out of his irrational anguish.

By the end of the first term he was, if not yet entirely reconciled, on an even keel.

At the end of the year, *The Intruder* finished and revised, I began another novel.

It was one I ought to have tackled years before, when the doctrinal split of our time—between a militant communism and a liberalism gone in the tooth—seemed as deep and incurable as that between an uncompromising early Christian and an educated Roman outraged by a faith which seemed to involve the death of society and demand of its adherents that they hand over their conscience to a narrow merciless creed. I might have done better to obey my first impulse and lay the novel in Roman Gaul. In 1956, the split was already beginning to lose every quality of a religious war except its bad temper, and the excuses it offers for cruelty, intimate betrayals, devotion.

My mind still houses the ghosts of an abandoned task, and two of these seized on me, the children, now grown up, of Frank and Sally Rigden, humble characters in *Company Parade* and its sequels. *Pour changer les idées* (Madame P. would have said, handing the abominable fennel root), I wrote this book in the first person—the person of the Senior Tutor of an imaginary Oxford college—intending to turn it into the third when I came to write the second draft. Its title, *A Cup of Tea for Mr Thorgill*, annoyed reviewers who read enough of it to discover that Mr Thorgill was a minor character, but not enough—or they lacked the wit—to notice that he was a measuring rod for the *mauvaise foi* of the others. The book was perhaps written only to bring him in.

I wrote the first version quickly, and finished it in April. It was six months before I had time and peace of mind to take it up again and rewrite it in the third person.

During the next two or three months I had a recurring sense that I was living backwards. Many things I touched split open like husks to let fall a sharp kernel of the past. In May, when the Society of Authors was giving Osbert Sitwell a piece of glass engraved by Laurence Whistler, I was asked to make the presentation—and the speech—at a luncheon. The thought that I might not do it well enough chilled me, but I was ashamed to refuse.

It was not a large luncheon, perhaps twelve people, held in a private room at the Ritz. As if he were accustomed to doing it, the head waiter cut up his meat for Osbert, who could no longer grasp a knife. Sitting beside him, in anguish about the speech I was going to make, I was uneasily two persons, I was the schoolgirl, Daisy Jameson, listening with passionate attention to adults talking about the legendary Sitwells. Ten years and a war later, I was in Whitby with my three-year-old son, penniless, a little desperate about our future, mine and his: a General Election, the mean-souled Khaki Election, was going on, with Captain Osbert Sitwell standing as Liberal candidate for the Scarborough and Whitby division (I usually write this the other way round, incorrectly but involuntarily). Who can have asked me, an unknown young woman, to sit on one of his platforms, and what, except vanity and the wish to outrage my Tory father—my mother, a Tory from habit, was indifferent, and secretly pleased by the sly glances of her friends ('Ha, I see y'daughter's got herself into politics')—made me do it?

I did not remind him of an episode he must long have forgotten. We talked a little of his novel about Scarborough, and he asked me how often I went back to those parts.

'Very seldom,' I said. 'Whitby and Scarborough have both been vilely fingermarked—the marks show worse in Whitby because it is a *small* town. I don't want to efface a living memory by the dead graceless reality.'

'No, no, you're right, don't go back. No point in tormenting oneself. A writer has all too many reasons to be irritated and angered, he must defend himself—all the more if he refuses to join a herd.'

'How does one defend oneself?'

He moved a shaking hand in a curiously light gesture. 'One way is by arrogance. A writer must be arrogant.'

'That,' I said, 'may be natural and easy for a Sitwell. My father was a sea-captain.'

'I always supposed that sea-captains were very arbitrary individuals,' he said, smiling—a warmly gentle smile.

I thought that, unlike his formidable sister, whom I admired and had never feared, he made little use of a mask: his arrogance, his aristocratic feeling for equality, his innate kindness, did not entirely hide a certain insecurity. I did not know enough about him to be able to guess where this thread of insecurity came from, but I could not be mistaken. I knew the trait in myself. I liked him the better for it, and for his polite heart.

What did I say in my speech? I have forgotten that completely.

In the letter he wrote to thank me for it, a phrase struck me: 'Even elderly writers like myself need encouragement, and you have always been one of the people who have given it...'

A polite gesture, yes, but also, without his intending it, an admission.

Once the past has opened a breach into the present, there is no damming the icy trickle. During the splendid London Congress of P.E.N. in July, I met ghosts at every turn, once in the shape of an old Jewish refugee who said very softly, 'I think all these days of the Congress in 1941, yours and Hermon's, simple and friendly, where I am someone. Here, what am I? Nobody.'

'Ah,' I said, taking his hand, 'the past is a fine place, and you and I are together in it, two nobodies.'

This comforted him, but there was no comforting the elderly lady, a Pole or an Italian, I am not sure which, who seized my arm during the reception in the Mansion House, and spoke in a deep voice, hoarse with despair.

'*Pour moi, madame, un buffet froid, c'est une catastrophe.*'

Czeslaw Milosz had come over from Paris. When I was talking to him in the crowded hall of Bedford College, I caught sight at the other end of Antoni Slonimski. It was the first time I had seen him since he went back to Warsaw for good, and I felt a sudden warmth and lightness of heart. It struck me then that these two Polish poets had not spoken to each other for a great many years, and without giving myself time to doubt I said, 'Antoni Slonimski is over there. Will you talk to him?'

'Why not?' Czeslaw said slowly.

'Don't move from here.'

I pushed my way through the chattering groups. For a moment, in the pleasure of seeing him, I forgot my purpose: then I said, 'Czeslaw Milosz is here. Will you meet him?'

'If he wants it,' Antoni said quietly.

I hurried him the length of the hall. Czeslaw's face wore the look of simplicity with which he covered up anger or excitement. The two stood some way apart, eyeing one another.

'Who the first?' Antoni said.

Czeslaw stretched his arm out and they shook hands. It was pure Conrad. Since they were both too polite to speak Polish so long as I was with them, I went away. Glancing back once, I saw that, still a yard apart, they had begun to talk with a certain unsmiling liveliness.

On the last day, unable to face another reception, I went down to the Embankment and stood a long time looking with pleasure at the ripples curling over behind a string of barges. The evening sun poured a yellow oil over the water, it ran away in veins twisting and sliding below the surface. Every now and then a smell like the smell of an old wharf, rotting wood, seaweed, tar, wet rope, overwhelmed the stench of petrol from the road. I had a delicious sense of freedom and lightness.

If instead of standing here, I reflected, you were in that ship moving down river, you would be perfectly content.

## CHAPTER 15

IMMEDIATELY AFTER THIS, all panic stations manned, I moved into what my sick fear of being trapped saw as a black stifling tunnel.

It turned out to be less like a trap than any place of my own I ever had. In the first place, a window in the living-room, the length of the wall, looked clean over Hyde Park to south London and, on a clear day, to the edge of the Surrey hills. We had been able to rent a flat on an upper floor in the terrace of tall white houses facing the Marble Arch end of the park, so well-bred and puritanically elegant that it is surprising they have not yet been torn down; and from the day we moved in this view made the joy of my life: at any hour of the day, in any light, I had only to stand and gaze at it for my body to free itself: the paths crossing stretches of grass still, at the end of July, a vivid green, drew my glance, as smoothly as a ship is moved by its tugs, to the broad chimneys of the power station on the north bank of the Thames and beyond them into a distance I could stretch as far as I liked: the human figures sauntering across the park were dwarfed by the great trees and the spaces. This same scene in winter under an overcast sky, the black leafless trees, their trunks smeared by yellowish lichen, the dark iron-hard paths, with perhaps two figures turning away at the end of an avenue of naked branches became almost unbearably full of regret and smiling bitterness, like the lines it evoked... *Dans le vieux parc solitaire et glacé, Deux spectres ont évoqué le passé... Ton coeur bat-il toujours à mon seul nom? Toujours vois-tu mon âme en rêve?—Non...* Silhouetted on the mist, the tall buildings south of the park slowly became formless; at four o'clock, street lights came on, blue, white, orange, circling the park; an hour later the pent-houses of Grosvenor House hotel floated to the surface and hung there above a street visible only as two double lines of cars and buses, inside and outside the park, their movements too smooth to be those of wild animals, yet oddly menacing in the icy dark.

Lights sunk in the night have always, since I saw them first as a child in Whitby, given me one of my rare moments of ecstasy, immense joy rising through my veins to my throat, until I can scarcely breathe.

One day in the week before we moved in I had gone to bed in the grip of the insane panic, unmanageable and instinctive, that seizes me when I am being forced into a house. I fell asleep after a time, and seemed to be wakened by a voice, not like the voices in dreams, which are felt, not heard, a cold slow northern voice, speaking aloud, which said: My girl, you need a lesson... I knew at once that this voice came from the horse's head nailed above the doorway in the fairy-tale of the goose-girl, and, at the same time, it was my father's.

With this voice in my ears, I woke.

The lesson was not long in coming. Guy had been coughing a great deal, and now the X-rays discovered a shadow on one lung. He was to go into hospital for an operation, on a day three weeks ahead of us, at the end of August. We were preparing to go to Sweden for a month, taking C., and I decided that it would be better to go for two weeks rather than hang about in London, waiting.

We went. In that clear air, as clear as the finest glass, in the white light, among black pine-trees breathing salt and resin, spectres are easily kept at arm's length.

Two days after we got back I went with him to St Thomas's Hospital, splendid worn battered ugly pile, and left him in a room looking across the Thames to the House of Commons. At that hour the river was running fast and dark.

That night, getting ready for bed, I thought suddenly: I am an old woman walking about an empty house... The staircase in the first house I remember climbed unknown depths to reach me, and I saw myself standing with a lit candle in the doorway of my bedroom, an attic, listening to the beating of my heart and the sound, far out at sea, of a ship's whistle. I had an instant of overwhelming excitement, as though I had only to move a finger to touch the cold rim of the candlestick. Something—what?—moved in me to begin again...

'Don't,' the surgeon had said to me, 'ring up the hospital. I'll ring you.'

In the protective apathy I can—often—sink into, I waited all day, walking between the window of the living-room and the telephone, which was on a shelf in the entrance hall. The brilliant green of the grass rasped my eyelids. White smoke from the power station stood in relief on a sky of rusted steel, fading to a tarnished yellow in the west above the dying sun. There was a wind. For the first time I noticed the stone drinking-trough opposite the window, at the other side of the wide road; I watched the reflections of branches in the water: it was a long double trough, the lower part almost on a level with the pavement, within reach of any creature, however weak and small...

'Everything went off very well. You can go to bed and sleep. Everything is all right.'

'Are you sure?'

'Of course.'

I went back to the window. In my brief absence the view had changed radically; the distances had become lightly foggy, and the chimneys and domes south of the park a delicate pencil sketch in mauve behind the dark mass of the trees. I stood for an hour, two hours, watching the black gleaming road, the sheaves of light thrown down on it by moving cars, the lower branches of trees an acid green, the dark sky, the dark cliff of Park

Lane, the livid fish-belly white of faces, the livid white columns of the park gates, the single point of light on the crane, a gigantic antenna, on the roof of Grosvenor House, the sombre fermenting crowds at Speakers' Corner. Torn rags of sound, the cries of hawkers, a woman's shrill voice, and, below everything, the ceaseless rumour of traffic, thunder and clatter of the North Sea breaking on the rocks below an old pier.

At this moment I knew that the basic need of any human life worth the name is need and pity, the need to accept the death of the senses, the sinking to a little ash of sensual and primitive love, the pity born from the knowledge, taken into the mouth and chewed like a bitter root, of death. We have a minute in which to be kind, I thought. And in the end, nothing I do, nothing I could do, minor writer that I am, nothing I want, is anywhere nearly so important as this. This truth, and my knowledge of it, lie as deep in me as my hunger for freedom. But I touch it only in a moment of crisis, like this one.

I was asleep when the telephone rang in the early morning. Shaking, cold with the certainty that I was being called to the hospital, I ran to answer it, and heard Guy's voice, clear, weak. His instinctive movement when he woke had been to stretch a hand to the telephone on his bed-table, to talk to me.

The supreme warmth of my life.

Late in October, I took up *A Cup of Tea for Mr Thorgill* and rewrote it in the third person. On its level it is a good book, at times a little too violent—it should have been laid in France or some Central European country where doctrinal passions are still apt to be murderous—but worth writing.

I finished it on the 23rd of December. One of my rare, very rare, sleepless nights followed (like the old sea-captain, I can go without sleep for two nights running, and fall asleep by closing my eyes). Feeling feverish but not restless or unhappy, I lay awake and got up before daylight. The first sign of light came at seven o'clock, a sharpening of the delicate outline of the crane and the tops of buildings. The sky changed almost imperceptibly. Then came a tinge of colour in the east. Slowly, very slowly, the sky roused, with the sluggish motion of a treacherous sea. The street-lamps were still burning. The finest conceivable web of naked branches moved, with infinite gentleness, against the grey void of the park.

I shall only deform or destroy the happiness of these moments by trying to describe it.

## CHAPTER 16

GUY MADE A GOOD RECOVERY, but the London winter, fog and an acid grime in the air, was hard on his lung, and in the New Year we rented one of the Portmeirion houses for two months. The air in that corner of North Wales is soft and clear, and since the hotel was closed there were only a few people living on or near the estate; farmers and landowners: the handful of young and middle-aged intellectuals who had had the good sense or the supreme confidence in themselves to settle down here and attend to their minds and bodily needs, as in the Middle Ages they might have looked for a not too austere monastery.

The greatest of these was Bertrand Russell, a great mind and, in the proper sense of the word, a personage. His head would have made the fortune of a mediaeval stonemason at work on a Gothic cathedral: the arched forehead, powerful nose, fine sensual mouth, narrow jaw, lean sunken cheeks, and, above all, the eyes—half closed under heavy lids, with a smile of sly amused malice. How many times have I seen that smile on statues in the porches and ambulatories of the great French cathedrals? In conversation—when he was not involved in a hot argument—he was amusing, affable, friendly. I felt a cold respect for him and small liking, and this was not out of fear of a great man: for another great man, R. H. Tawney, I felt as much love as respect. His high screeching laugh rasped my ear-drums. Yet many women were drawn to him, he had had four wives: three of his marriages had broken down, the fourth was completely successful and happy. He was not a libertine; whatever his lustful or ecstatic reasons for falling in and out of love, a polite and puritanical regard for the conventions drove him into marriage.

Listening to his voice rather than to what he said, and watching with pleasure the flicker of irony across his gargoyle of a face, I thought that he might be capable, at moments when another human being ceased to be anything more than an object in his mind, of intellectual cruelty—not of physical violence, he was infinitely too fastidious—of a shocking anger, of cold metaphysical unkindness.

After a time, I realized that he was a late heir of the Enlightenment in a sense which goes some way to account not only for the impact of his powerful intelligence on two or three young generations, but for the particular affection—or hatred—in which he is held. To put it shortly, too shortly, he invests in Reason so great an imaginative passion, so furiously religious a belief, that he makes it a question of conscience. And nothing, but nothing, so claws at the innermost spirit of an irreligious age as respect for conscience: it is in the name of conscience that a radical supports the ruthlessly nationalist ambitions of an African politician, in the name of conscience that he pulls down the old shaky dykes against nihilistic drift before erecting others.

What forced my own respect, cool but boundless, for him, was much less things I had been told about him—his aristocratic sense of family duty, his generosity—than the fact that he, an old man, who could have said: What does the future matter to me? was as passionate as an adolescent. An act of injustice, the thought of nuclear war, provoked him not only to rage but to do something about it. What he did might be useless, but he had given in neither to old age nor human folly. He fought.

So much holy anger in an old man is to be respected.

> Do not go gentle into that good night
> Old age should rave and burn at close of day...

In so far as they are intellectuals, Elizabeth and Rupert Crawshay-Williams were living here on the same terms as the others. But they had made their own terms with the place—to give it more than they took. Their house was, is, a cell of friendly warmth and sanity in a shaken world, a perpetual reproach to my restlessness, as Elizabeth is an involuntary reproach to my spiritual clumsiness. She is what Rilke required the poet to be, a praiser of life. The strict truth is that she is a genius in living by virtue of the same hard work and devotion that makes another woman a great dancer: the muscles she exercises are kindness, spontaneity, scepticism, gaiety, tolerance, a mocking indifference to pretensions, and a saving salt of wit, even malice. I could say to her what the Earl of Salisbury wrote to Henry, Prince of Wales, in

December 1608—'Such is the disproportion between you and me (you the son of Jupiter and I his poor beagle)...'

The estuary at Portmeirion is more beautiful in winter than at any other time. As I wrote I saw it from the windows of the room I slept and worked in. At low tide, there were only thin channels of water between the stretches of sand. The tide came in swiftly, a grey flowing light, merging the channels into a flood the colour of the sky. Black hills overtopped the lower grey-green slopes shutting in the valley. Except the cries of cormorants and gulls, there were no sounds.

At my age no image is single, just as time is not a succession of minutes but a labyrinth where the threads of past and present cross and recross, fusing, separating, turning on themselves, without rest. The estuary at five in the afternoon, a winter sun gone, the sky above the open bay beyond the mouth grey and primrose yellow, the very colour of the half moon, the tide far out, the water in the channels yellow and slate-grey, the sand a dun grey, the hills dark heliotrope, without any substance, was also the lagoon between Torcello and Venice seen eight years earlier, a stretch of grey silk, saturated with light, and, flowing in me at a great depth, below every other image of water, the estuary of the Esk emerging between low hills into the harbour and the North Sea...

We had brought C. with us for a week. He was now, within a month of fifteen, six feet tall, handsome, with a clear narrow face, half composed young man and half intractable schoolboy. He was very impressionable, and yet controlled, for his age remarkably controlled, so that in spite of the liveliness of his mind and quick humour I had a sense of his watchfulness. It worried me a little, but he was gay, he thought clearly, and had his own ideas and views.

The day he left I started to write a novel I had been carrying about in my mind, like all my better novels, for a long time. The theme, too large for me, was exile.

Only a great writer, the poet of the *Inferno* or the creator of *War and Peace*, could find words direct enough, hard, burning to the touch, palpably real, to contain the vision of our age of exile: the unnumbered thousands of men and women trying to escape the bestialities of the totalitarian states, lucky when they were not turned back at frontiers or crowded into the rotten holds of ships without a sure harbour. I had the wit or the heart to know that an exile is a man, or a child, who suffers the human condition directly, without benefit of a cloth over his eyes, turned violently round to face the void from which the rest of us, as long as possible, look away, but not the imaginative energy to do more than say it.

The actual plot of the novel had to do with the bitter depth of the abyss dividing a man, a Pole, who had lived in Poland after the war, from his fellow-countrymen who left it in 1939 and were frozen into their memories of that now vanished country. When he talks to them they don't hear him.

'The truth is, you haven't a future. You've committed suicide. Like me, you're a Ulysses too many. Even if, in Ithaca, a few persons remember you, or only your name, the place itself rejects you. You will never reach it, never live there again. The people at home have forgotten you, they're living in another age—their own. You can't go back. The country you dream about returning to isn't there. If the young men you know nothing about are ever able to free the country, you'll have to wait on the doorstep. And, if you're let in, keep your mouth shut—like any other *revenant*, any anachronistic ghost. The very best you can hope for—if a revolt starts—is to get over the frontier and be allowed to fight in it as an obscure nameless person. Not a leader—you have no right to that, and no qualifications.'

You, too, I thought, as I wrote, you, too, and the Ithaca you think you are seeking. When in fact you expect nothing from it, and don't want to arrive. All your happiness comes from the harbours you touch at, the foreign places you see for the first time. Ithaca is for the old.

My own age—I could not remember it off-hand and had to do a sum in my head—seemed to me irrelevant. Or less important than, let's say, my long sight, acute hearing, and indifference, in the last instance, to failure.

As soon as we were back in London, in March, I had the two children, Frances and Troy, to stay in the flat. They were astonishingly unlike. Frances, self-contained and smiling, used her quick wits to get her way with as little trouble as possible. Capable of sudden brief rages, she was physically placid, and fell asleep as she stepped into bed. Troy, fine, small, stubborn, was more difficult in every sense. She slept lightly and woke at a touch.

One night she was still restlessly awake at near midnight. I lifted her out of bed and held her, rolled in the quilt, in the window of her room, to look at the fantastic view. I thought: These are the things a child remembers. I thought I might be passing on to her my own childish ecstasy of pleasure in lights seen at night. But perhaps she noticed quite other things, the three ghostly beds of daffodils (now buried under concrete) on the edge of the park opposite the house, or the gleaming piebald trunks of trees, or the young, very young, very black prostitute in a yellow coat, walking up and down, up and down, a few paces each way, twirling a small yellow umbrella.

When I felt her little body relax in my arms, I put her back into bed. 'Now go to sleep.' Closing her eyes, she said, 'No, I'm still wide awake.' A moment and she was asleep.

The only change I noticed between myself now and myself twenty years ago was that the exhaustion of looking after two young lively children was not cured by a night's rest. And yet I was tireless. I galloped to the shops and back, carrying heavy parcels, took pains to cook well, wrote, when I could, for long hours. Offered a pleasure, or a visitor, or a task there was no getting out of, I rose gaily from the dead. ('Tha's unabateable,' a servant said to me when I was four, 'but time 'ull cow thee.'—'That it won't,' I said.)

After the children left, I had to take the chair at the meeting of the International Executive Committee of P.E.N. Nothing on the agenda interested me except the suggestion to do away with the Centre for German-speaking Writers Abroad, founded in 1933. Why, merely because they preferred to live in London, should any Germans be allowed in 1957 to pose as exiles? Why indeed? I was determined—a question of sentiment—to keep the illogical indefensible Centre. During the long rather surly debate its president made two speeches, the first sensible and moving, the second clumsy. Germans always say a few words too many. But I got my way.

A Roumanian writer, president before the war of a Centre in Bucharest, had written to ask us to admit a new Roumanian Centre.

'Is it really his signature?'

'Yes, yes.'

'But is it certain,' Paul Tabori asked calmly, 'that he hasn't already been sent back to prison?'

A little irritated by this purism, André Chamson said, 'We are in a situation where arrests are too usual...'

At the other side of the table, the Belgian delegate stroked his heavy sensual jowl, a proconsul in a good temper.

'*Ils* sont dans cette situation,' he said, grinning...

What moved intelligent men, and one or two women, hardworking respectable writers, to spend their time and energy on these committee meetings? The pleasure of saying Yes or No to Roumanians or Germans? The weak impulse to escape from the isolation of a writer's life? I watched the face of the elderly delegate from Tokyo, a wrinkled simian mask stretched over a tiny skull, surely the most menacing mask ever used to hide an anxious friendliness and a child's pleasure in being accepted. The sight of his skeleton at the resurrection won't surprise him, I thought; he sees it every time he passes a looking-glass... Our exiles had at least one good reason for coming: the longing to be in touch for a moment with the young man imprisoned in an ageing thickening body and still living in a country which no longer existed except during these two or three days when they were able to talk about it... The dignified ex-ambassador who was not displeased to be addressed as Your Excellency, the Catalan professor who wanted us to protest against Franco's restrictions on his language, the once blond now greying Latvian poet who enjoyed sitting in my flat and drinking glass after glass of sherry while he read out to me the clandestine messages he had received from 'my friend who did not come with me in 1939...'

And you, why do you waste your time?

Perhaps merely in order to read a letter like the one the German-speaking Writers Abroad sent me after this meeting. 'May I in the name of Dr Hans Fleisch, our members and me too, thank you for your kind, I must even say, touching words on our behalf at the Committee meeting. I will forget these as little as I have forgotten what you have done for our comrades in 1938...'

A month later I finished the first draft of *A Ulysses Too Many*. It was reasonably complete. There would not be much new writing to do.

The first minutes after finishing a book are extraordinary. At one moment I was living with every sense but one in the sordid little bedroom above the bar of a seedy café in Nice, plagued by memories of an enemy, a friend, a mistress, and making energetic plans for my future. Future of a character who is existing in the last sentence of a novel. I dropped the pen, moved my stiffened fingers, and went over to the window. Below drifting slate-grey clouds in the east, the sky reflected the colours of the setting sun, celandine yellow, bronze, pale peacock green. The stink of anchovies, tobacco, acid urine, equally acid coffee, dust, cheap strong alcohol, from Bouttau's café, was still in my throat, and I saw a stained wall, a skylight, and a strip of worn dirty carpet, and through them the deep pink brown of houses in Park Lane, forced into relief by the level rays. Then the last images of the attic bedroom, and the images of past and future *in Nadzin's mind*, faded completely, and I saw only the first quick pointed lights at the far side of the park, and the young green, each furled leaf a thread of bright colour, of the trees immediately below the window.

I felt something very like remorse. What was to become of Nadzin and the others, men, women, children, even the two people who existed only on the last page but one, Bouttau's new baby, a scrap of yellow flesh, and its mother, smiling, showing the gaps in her teeth and a cross wedged in the fold between baggy discoloured breasts? To create and then to destroy—or create in order to destroy—what do you call such an impulse?

Creation and cruelty may, may they not?, be two sides of the same coin. And if that is true, it explains a great deal that puzzles me. The deaths of children in gas chambers...

## CHAPTER 17

DURING THE THIRTY and more years it had been there, my young brother's memorial in the Parish Church of Whitby had been eaten away by the sea air. Another few years and it would be as illegible as so many of the ancient wrinkled stones outside, leaning, sunk, in the coarse salt-bitten grass between the church and the edge of the cliff. Even if no one looked at it now, I could not let that happen. I sought and after a long time found a firm of engravers who could copy the original brass in a hard metal that salt would not corrode. The new tablet had been in place now for a year and I had not been to see it. In May, I went up to Whitby.

On a brilliantly clear morning, the sea glassy smooth, sky and gulls immaculate in sunlight, I climbed the one hundred and ninety-nine worn-down steps from the old street by the harbour. The ghost walking with me, her remote glance fixed, unseeing, on the ancient houses sunk, one above the other, in the side of the cliff, could only climb them slowly. At the top I turned aside from the stone-flagged path to find the Church Maid's house, and get a key to let us in to the gallery of the church. A small cottage, two rooms, very old, very solid, it looked down to the harbour and across it to the other, the west cliff, and the line of the coast running north. Not what you would call a civilized landscape, or even a friendly one, but *my* coast line, my place. My only place.

A friendly lively old woman, the Church Maid. The entrance to the gallery is by an outside staircase. At the top a narrow door opens on a passage that leads to the gallery, wide enough for one person to walk between the wall and the high timbered walls of the pews. A little light comes through low windows. The boards creak.

His tablet had been fixed to the wall at the height of the eyes of passers-by... To the memory of 2nd Lt. Harold Jameson, Médaille Militaire, D.C.M., M.C., Royal Flying Corps...

'It looks well,' I said.

'Eeh, you did right to change it,' the Church Maid said, smiling. 'What's the good of these things if you can't read'n?'

'Does anyone read it?'

'Oh, ay. Sometimes. Last year there was an American came and asked me to let'n see it. He said he'd read about it. Fancy! I showed it to'n, and he asked how old is this church? Eight hundred years, I told'n, and he said—nay, I forget what he said, they say owt, and half the time I don't listen.'

I walked round the gallery to my grandfather's pew, to look down from it into the body of the church, at pews like square roofless rooms set round the three-decker pulpit—lower deck, main deck, bridge.

'You won't remember my grandfather, George Gallilee, or Hannah Margaret Jameson, my mother?'

'No,' the old woman said. She smiled again, ironically. 'You can't remember everyone.'

I did not stay in Whitby overnight, for fear that the squalid changes in it since the first war became fixed in my mind. As things are, I forget them, and when, in unguarded moments or in sleep, I go back, it is to the old simple town I lived in as a child, the town my mother lived in in her childhood, and her mother, and the ancient dead. I was staying in Goathland, a moor village a few miles inland.

It is a small scattered village, naked to the sky, almost treeless, the air as thin and pure as anywhere in the island. You have only to cross the rough turf of the common and you are on the moor. I had been happy here often enough as a child, I was happy now.

The place judged me, of course, judged coldly my restlessness, my egoism, my foolish ambitions, my greeds, but in some curious way I felt, oh, not acquitted, but—for a few moments—free. As though I had been mercifully forgotten.

If you had the courage, I thought, you would stay here.

After three days I went back to London, to the second version of *A Ulysses Too Many*. I finished it, and put it away to be looked at again later, and the next day I began to think hard and patiently over another novel, and make notes. It, too, had been lying in germ a long time. Or its characters had. A man called Mott, born in Whitby in the same street of small houses where I was born, had made his way up to a position of respect and influence as a writer and Director of an Institute of Fine Arts in London, remodelling himself, with instinctive sureness and pleasure, as he went. At fifty, he was a complicated and impressive *construction*, a Christian of the Anglican persuasion, living a carefully civilized life, even to his choice of wife and friends, a sensitive kindly man, without crude vanity. Suppose that at this point he made an error, one clumsy error, social or moral—and made the further error of lying about it? What would take place in him as the truth began to eat its way into his life? (My first name for this book had been *The Man Sought by God*. Later, when I thought I knew too little to call it that, it became *The Road from the Monument?*) I found that already I knew him intimately, and a number of other men and women. Never since *The Green Man* had I had this sense of overwhelming energy, of being assailed by characters who forced themselves on me, demanding their chance to live through my nerves and blood.

In spite of this feeling of power, I could not start the book. Heaven alone knows how many times I wrote and tore up a first chapter—ten, fifteen. I lost count. After a time, driven almost out of my mind by this perversity of—of what? characters I knew as well as I knew myself? my mind?—I began to suspect that there was a piece missing. Now and then I caught sight of a figure, a man, a shadow losing itself in shadows, but never saw him distinctly. For a time I thought he might be the old sea-captain, Mott's dead father, but I was forced to drop this idea: that gaunt stooped old fellow had his part in the story of his son's discovery of himself, but it was not at the beginning.

That year June was abnormally hot, day after day of blistering oily sunlight; the nights were close and airless, dulled by an acid breath of dust, petrol, dry leaves, sweat-soaked bodies, shoe leather. I wrote and tore up, wrote and tore up, day after day, evening after evening. The nights were hallucinatory. I heard voices, and watched scenes play themselves through, but I could not write them, because I could not flush the missing creature out of its earth.

I spent hours standing in my window. In June it was still daylight at nine, but the light was filtered through a thin veil, it glowed dully, like over-heated metal. Lines and colours had an extreme sharpness and precision, as though bitten in by an acid, or as in the background of a mediaeval painting: the massive green of trees, the contours of buildings south of the park, heavy grey-white plumes above the power station, the white stems of flag-staffs, the white pillars of the park gates, a woman's red dress splashed on an asphalt path, the violent scarlet of buses. The coffee-stall at the other side of the road, near the drinking-trough, was open all night. People stood round it in groups, and sat, a long row of bodies leaning slackly against each other like cheap puppets, on the low stone coping at this side of the park fence: in the sodium light of the street-lamps their faces and bare arms looked to be in the first moments of putrescence. Only the young black prostitute, yellow handbag swinging as she walked, was impervious to its virulence—she, and a negro in overcoat and bowler hat inviting a woman to dance with him, posturing in front of her, gesticulating, smiling.

Even I could not sleep in the exhausted air. At two o'clock one morning the moon glared into my eyes, and I got up to look out.

The coffee-stall was still serving a score of people, youths in white shirts, a young negro with fluttering hands and a curious out-of-date elegance, really exquisite, four stork-legged streetwalkers in their summer uniform of full skirts, thin almost transparent blouses, and long wide scarves: one of them was laughing her head off, her mouth a black hole in the face of a corpse. Three boys with skiffle instruments started to play, jerking like marionettes, faces wooden, and a girl in the tightest of black trousers cut short at the ugly bulge of her calf swung her buttocks from side to side like captive balloons. A tramp, a heap of bones and rags the colour of dark clay, slept, arms dangling, head between his knees, on the low wall.

It was light enough in the room to write. I made notes, I knew I was not making them for myself, and I went on scribbling and staring until half-past four, by which time it was beginning to be day, the coffee-stall man was rinsing cups and plates in the trough, the last customers were drifting away, dragging their toes, and the tramp, sunk deeper into himself, still slept.

I slept a little then, until I was wakened by the thin spattering cries of birds, piercing the roar of traffic.

The summer was a hell of visitors from abroad (these included a stray professor from Zagreb, sent by the P.E.N.). I have never known how to keep what Montherlant calls *biophages* at a distance.

'But surely, as a writer, you need to meet a great many sorts of people?'

'No. No, no, no. As a writer what I need is strange countries, solitude, books, music, the theatre. Nothing else at all.'

'Then as a human being.'

'Not even as a human being. There are a few people, not all of them English, to be counted on the fingers of both hands, whom never to see would be an amputation. To be forced to meet others costs me as much moral effort as writing a book.'

'What intolerable egoism!'

One of these torrid afternoons I had a visitor who started in me a conflict of admiration, respect, and mild discomfort. A face and body burned down to the wick, black and as it were fused eyes, the look of a slightly mad mendicant friar. Except for this dissolution of his flesh in the flame of a single vision, he had changed little since my first sight of him—one day either just before the second war, or shortly after it started. I arrived at the office to find Hermon Ould involved with this curious figure.

'This is Miron Grindea. He wants to start an international literary review, and he wants us to support him, morally and with money. I've already told him that you'll give him your approval, but that what little money we have we're spending on our exiles.'

'Surely,' I said, 'this is the wrong time to start such a review?'

The glance Grindea turned on me was that of a Savonarola at the stake: anguish, a blind resolution, serenity. I thought him mad, and certain to fail. Worse, as I always am I was repelled by an implacable obsession. But at least his mania was innocent—in a decade fouled by every sort of cruelty and guilt. What I could do to help him, very little, I did.

Nothing defeated him, he started *Adam*, and kept it going, year after year, without money, with fanatical devotion. At one time or another every celebrated writer in Europe gave him a piece of writing, shamed into it by the spectacle of a total dedication. His life since the idea seized him had been that of a *monstre sacré*, prepared to sacrifice everything—and everybody—to his hunger. If the only way to bring out another issue of *Adam* had been to throw every stick of furniture, every object in the house, his wife's clothes, his child's toys, into the furnace, and himself after them, he would have done it without a tremor.

I looked at him now, three-quarters consumed, a thin flame. He had come to ask me to help him raise a ludicrously small sum of money to keep the review going. Surely I must know rich people who would give it to him?

Not only do I know very few rich people, but I felt certain he would not get even the little money he needed. He had no alloy of self-interest in him; his lack of it, and his obsessive idealism, made a great many right-minded people uneasy. He was, they felt, unmanageable. *Perfecti* of his sort can count on praise, respect, flattery even, dislike, but money—no.

After he had left, a little comforted by my promise to write to one or two people, I sent him twenty pounds I could not afford. Not out of generosity. In the same spirit as a sinner gives away alms on his deathbed, in the hope of earning divine grace.

## CHAPTER 18

G UY HAD BEEN INVITED to go to Princeton in September, to the Institute for Advanced Studies. I looked forward to it with an indescribable joy—as an escape from a state of affairs that made it impossible for me to work. I was profoundly disgusted with my life at this time, and with myself for not managing it better.

Before then, to give him the semblance of a holiday, we took C. to Switzerland for three weeks.

A Swiss writer had talked to me about the marvels of Einsiedeln, and on the way back from Lake Constance we stayed a night there. It is a place of pilgrimage, with a Benedictine monastery and a Gothic Black Virgin. Whatever the village may have been in the past, it exists now for pilgrims; the shops on both sides of the narrow street are crammed with holy images, in plaster, in sandstone, in papier-mâché, in glazed pastry. The street climbs towards an immense square, the splendidly simple façade of the monastery stretching the length of one side: in the centre, dwarfed by the space, a fountain, a squat semi-circular arcade of booths like loose-boxes for the sale of images, and a flight of wide steps becoming a stone ramp rising steeply to a narrower flight: beyond this, another clean ordered waste of cobblestones before you arrive at the portico of the monastery, flanked by towers.

Our rooms in the hotel looked out across the square to the steps, the ramp, and the great sandstone monastery. At this height you saw the hill behind it, black with firs, and a vaporous sky which gave the impression of being a superb back-drop using real trees, real clouds.

A suave authoritative manager—no doubt an actor rehearsing the part— said, 'You will want to hear the *Salve Regina*—sung at four o'clock. You have fifteen minutes.'

C. refused to go with us—his amiability drew the line at a religious service.

I was stunned by the inconceivable extravagance of the interior: a jungle of painted walls and ceilings, a swarm of saints in the likeness of fauns and over-ripe nymphs and—breaking out on all sides, springing from ledges, from brackets, from the arched vault, hanging by a wing-tip, a single foot, a finger—angels with trumpets, with out-spread wings, with scrolls, with wreaths, smiling, gesticulating, half-naked in flying garments, gilded, painted in all the colours of a shoal of tropical fish. Like the village, it stank of the profits of piety. And, as I sat listening to the singing—a choir of monks out of sight behind the high altar—an extraordinary feeling of peace took possession of me, a strange deep joy. I felt that I was dissolving into a silence created by the voices—a sense of absolute security, absolute quiet.

It was unexpected—and undeserved.

Late in the evening I was looking from my bedroom at the square—empty and, except for a circle of coldly unreal light near the steps, dark. As I watched, the first ripple of a thick black stream of men and women appeared at the far edge; it flowed sluggishly up the steps, and up the ramp, endless. Priests carrying large candles came towards it from the church and waited at the upper flight of steps. Between them and the monastery was black night. After what seemed a long time, a shadowy mob—here and there a face picked out by a candle hung in the darkness like a fish in the artificial current of a tank—had seeped up at the foot of the monastery.

When the last figure, the last candle, disappeared into the church, I went to bed.

Ever since we landed in France, I had been living again in the world of my unwritten novel. Everything I looked at was attached to it at some point by an unseen thread: walking about the enchantingly dignified and friendly library of St Gallen I caught glimpses of its characters, and overheard remarks, even whole dialogues. This novelist's trick, which is involuntary—I never heard of anyone who can induce it—has a drawback: the actual world loses substance, or, rather, since one has withdrawn part of one's attention from it, the kind of things happen that might happen to a shortsighted man who refused to wear glasses, blunders, errors, stupidity. And something else which can be humiliating or shameful. A real incident which relates itself, suddenly, to something the writer is in process of inventing (or discovering) may cease entirely to be real in itself, and become real, charged with emotion, only in the imaginary world of the novel.

This happened to me in Einsiedeln. The clatter of bells woke me before daylight. I lay still for some minutes, listening to the sound of feet striking the cobblestones. At last, driven by curiosity, I got up and went to the window. It was a little after four o'clock: a grey sky closed in the monastery, the black fleece of trees on the hill, the vast square, and the slow-moving file of pilgrims. Had they been coming up the street and across the square all night? At this hour no one met them; they went straight into the blackness of the church. I watched the last in, and was going back to bed when I caught sight of something—a large dog?—moving in the empty square.

After a moment I saw that it was a man in a dark macintosh, shuffling forward on his knees. Infinitely slowly, he moved up the first flight of steps, the ramp, the second flight, and on towards the monastery. For less than an instant, I had an impression of atrocious despair and anguish. Then I thought coldly: You must remember this for Mott, and use it.

When I was making a note on the back of an envelope in my handbag, I thought that there is something positively evil in the way a writer makes use of other people's emotions, even of agony. It was not the first time I had thought it.

It may not be only evil. Nothing is pure or single; there might be compassion in the impulse as well as coldness and inhumanity.

I finished my note and put it away carefully. The dog-man had reached the church and vanished.

We spent our last night in France, in Rheims, a sordid hotel and a sordid city, an ill setting for the smile of Rheims.

## CHAPTER 19

THE RELIEF AND JOY of getting away lapsed into the familiar excitement of landing. New York at six in the morning: in an overcast sky a magnificent arc of sunrise, fading quickly into a dull glow more like a sunset. Then a subdued daybreak, the lights on shore becoming fewer and dimmer, and the dark outlines of a tower, houses, taller buildings, cranes, leaping forward like animals—even on a grey day, the energy of America has this quality of brightness and menace.

In Princeton we lived in the Nassau Tavern, in two narrow overheated rooms looking over a garden. I was continually happy, as always when the burdens and irritations of a domestic life are lifted from me. There was an admirable small shop across the street, kept by an unlikable German, where I bought sandwiches of rye bread and bottles of thin Californian wine, very drinkable, and five evenings out of seven we dined on these in my room, in great contentment of mind and body. Guy spent his days at the Institute, and I sat in my room from breakfast until five or six, writing.

I had scarcely arranged my papers on a table set in the narrow window, the first morning, when the figure I had been groping towards for so many weeks moved into the light. He was no one I had ever known, and I knew him at once. An underpaid old schoolmaster, widely and curiously learned, a mathematician who could not pass examinations, at seventy almost penniless, wearing a threadbare, repellently stained and creased suit—a small shrivelled old-womanish old man, in no way attractive, with harsh ungracious manners and a maliciously sharp eye. I saw him with astonishing clarity, even to the well of tenderness in his ruined body.

To see Mott first through old Paul Gate's eyes was in a sense to judge him before he had spoken for himself, yet it was right, because the old man loved Mott. And he himself was better worth recording than any of the obviously important persons in the book.

The short first part of *The Road from the Monument*, thirty-seven pages, is better than anything else in a long novel. Would the book have continued on this level if I had been able to live in the Nassau Tavern until I had finished it?

I don't know. It is not important.

This was the first time since *The Green Man* that I had the acute happiness of writing in freedom. It was also the last.

In Princeton, too, we had the uncovenanted good luck to make two friends. One of the scholars working at the Institute was George Steiner, a young man overflowing with intelligence, kindness, malicious irony, incomparable energy of mind and body, erudition, gaiety. I lacked the courage to talk, but I listened to him, and watched Zara Steiner moving about the room with the tranquil dignity of a good child. She was carrying her first child at the time. I should have liked to know where this extremely intelligent young woman, an historian by training, had learned to cook like a Frenchwoman.

If I had not, in the first moment, noticed the reckless generosity and warmth behind George Steiner's subtly aggressive genius, I should have been intimidated by it...

I was in Princeton when *A Cup of Tea for Mr Thorgill* was published in England.

Can I write about the reception given to this novel without seeming to be resentful, or worse, low-spirited? What, in sober truth, I felt was stupefaction. I had written a novel round the forms a para-religious doctrine can take in the heart and mind, and among its characters were two—or is it three?—communists, and one smeller-out of heresy who boasts that she is able to detect treachery by its 'vibrations'. Several critics (they included a comically outraged woman in that most respectable of liberal papers, the *Manchester Guardian*, who thought it 'unworthy and dishonest') persuaded themselves that I had set out to expose Oxford as a 'nest of communists', or 'riddled with communism.'

I was absurdly baffled. Indiscreetly so when a journalist well-known to me by name, wrote me an angry letter about my slander on Oxford. I could not believe that an intelligent man could be so obtuse, and I took the trouble to answer truthfully that if I had not wanted to write a little about the marring of Oxford I might equally well have laid the novel in Leeds or Cambridge or anywhere. From the abusive reply I got I realized that I might as well save my breath, he was in a completely irrational state of mind.

Is it possible for educated people to be, in good faith, so fatuous? I take enormous, but enormous pains to write clearly, and with as much or as little elegance as is suitable. What happens? Through naïveté or dullness, or, perhaps, ill-will, only a few people read what is under their eyes. (In the case of professional reviewers, this may be due only to laziness or lack of time.)

It is absurd, and I should despair if I were not, in the final resort, indifferent...

In December this blest interlude came to an end. Leaving Guy to follow me in the New Year, I left in one of the small Cunarders, to prepare a family Christmas in the flat. It was a fairly rough crossing, on the second day the life-lines were run out along the decks, and on the third we spent hours hove-to in what seemed the tail of a hurricane. For most of the voyage I was alone at my table, which pleased me. I am vain of my steadiness at sea.

One evening the only other person in the small bar was an American, a staff officer serving in Europe, a charming man with a passion for German baroque churches and German poetry. One of the recurrent crises in our relations with Soviet Russia was under way, and he talked very sensibly about the suicidal results of the thermo-nuclear war.

'Not,' he said, with a reassuring smile, 'that it need—I say: need—be a totally destructive multi-megadeath affair.'

'Do you mind translating that?' I said diffidently.

'Oh, there might be as many as a hundred and eleven million killed in my country—that is, a hundred and eleven megadeaths. In a nuclear exchange between missile sites and airfields. I'm not talking about anything more than that.'

'It should be enough.'

'What one hopes, of course, is that between us—assuming that the Russians are not determined to reduce strategy to national suicide—we shall keep conventional forces large enough to provide a rational alternative to nuclear war.' His thin face of a mediaeval monk was serene; there was even a faint gaiety at the back of his deep-lidded eyes. 'We must pray it won't come to that, but—in a war against evil itself... if our choice lay between that risk and the abandonment of all spiritual values...'

When I hear military men talking about spiritual values I am outraged and contemptuous. They chose a profession which in its principles, its methods, is the negation of the spirit. I feel more respect for Napoleon's generals; most of them were uncultivated brutes, but they did not discuss spiritual values. Any such value supposes in its holder the refusal of cruelty, an absolute respect for human freedom and dignity, without exception or reservation. If, by an awful paradox, we must kill to preserve a measure of these, let us do it without cant.

These are obviously the reflections of an obtuse irrationalist. And unjust to a man who will probably die quoting Rilke.

But I shudder at the state of mind which sentences children to death, and the unborn generations who might, even under what is misnamed communism, a religion I detest, follow the pursuit of happiness. If it echoes the mental state of the American ruling classes, what hope is there that anyone will survive on this planet longer than a few more years? Paradoxically, the impulse to write is sharpened by danger. 'Depend upon it, sir, when a man is going to be hanged in a fortnight, it concentrates his mind wonderfully...'

In London I laid in vast stores of Christmas food, and a tree on which to hang the self-same glass bird, the very stars our mother had bought in Whitby market. In a few days I had dissipated the energy brought from America.

Recovered, I took out the manuscript of *A Ulysses Too Many*, revised it, polished it a little, and sent it to the publisher.

I had the weakness at this time to ask its English publisher how many copies he had sold of Mr Thorgill's book. Only a few over eight thousand.

This was no worse than, from the notices, I had expected; it dejected me only because so much depended on what my novels earned now.

One mid-January night, about eleven, I was looking at the power station south of the park, flood-lit—two great columns, with a column of white smoke blown horizontally from west to east so that it lay across them, the image of a ruined acropolis, lifted up against a restless sky, such as I love. Lights flashed along the edge of the park between an amorphous mass of buildings and the black spectral web of trees.

I thought: I no longer believe in myself. I am ready to agree wholeheartedly with any ass who thinks or writes against me. I expect nothing for the future.

In this instant I realized the exact difference between expecting and hoping. To expect nothing, or very little, does not mean to be without hope. Hope is a talent like any other. I have as stubborn a talent for hope as for going on living.

In the shock of hearing that Charles Morgan was dead, I remembered that his last letter—not his last, the last I had kept—had saddened me, for no good reason, and I looked for it and read it again.

It was not unhappy. Yet I had been right, the shadow was there. A light shadow, very light, distant.

'... I have been wandering in France becoming an Academician, wearing a beautiful frock by Lanvin, and eating and drinking and talking too much... France was very happy and triumphant. As no other English novelist except Kipling has ever had that particular honour, your young man of *My Name is Legion* is happy. But the older man is tired... And for heaven's sake let us meet when we can.'

If I had thought about it, I should not, let me be honest, have expected the sudden end of more than thirty years of cool enduring friendship to grieve me as it did. For all his singular kindness, he had not the gift of intimacy. But, once given, his friendliness was given for good, with a modesty and loyalty not to be shaken by circumstance, divergence of views, age. It was given with reserve: there was always a distance, a space of—the word coolness will not do, it carries an overtone of indifference which would be entirely unjust—of, let us say, quietness, as though his affection, its warmth, its simplicity, had to cross a space set between him and the world. It was not set by self-regard. Perhaps by his perpetual attentiveness to an inner world. Certainly by a diffidence, an instinctive delicacy, which forbade him to do more than lay the lightest possible pressure on the mind and spirit of a friend.

I had heard him accused of arrogance. And defended as seeming to be arrogant only because he was very shy. Neither word is exact. Arrogance begins in a greed for personal power—of which he was wholly free. And in a grown man shyness—I know this about myself—is usually the fear of not being taken at one's own value by the world. Charles's values were centred outside himself, in the world he entered when he sat down to write.

The same man who accused him in my hearing of arrogance went on, 'He reminds me of that detestable fellow, Chateaubriand—the same hard vanity, the same superciliousness, coldness, stiffness.'

I could only say angrily, 'You are entirely wrong,' without being able to offer proofs. One cannot *prove* that a certain image is just, a certain landscape or a certain concerto beautiful. And he had to die before I needed to think about him with an attempt at detachment.

He was not cold. He could—a few persons know this—be burned to the bone by a passion, driven to the edge of madness. And could oppose to it—nothing self-interested, nothing timid—a living idea of order.

Although he did, during the years I knew him, construct from the author of *My Name is Legion* a self already there in the seed and, touch by touch, work on it until he died, what drove him was not vanity. It was an imperative impulse towards elegance and control in word and gesture. When he had to make a speech he worked on it with the care of a great actor preparing himself to play a part. I have heard a number of eloquent speakers, usually French. None of them, not Jules Romains, nor André Chamson, is able to send a shock through the nerves of his hearers like that started by the opening phrase of Charles's speech, in 1954 in Amsterdam: *A June night and no war...* Because, as in so many of Charles's contrived strokes, his heart was involved.

Tormented by his passion for elegance, for perfection, he quite deliberately wrote at a remove from life. He was not a great novelist—these monsters devour life whole. But he was a conscious artist, and dear knows the animal is rare, all but extinct.

Dead, a new trait showed in his face, a something feminine in its strength, that is, a vein of steel. The other traits, masculine delicacy, withdrawal, reserve, were even more marked than in life, since they had to do without the flicker of gaiety, the twisted smile, the kindness. Above all, the kindness.

Thinking of his reserve, his half deliberate distance, I might have expected his death to be no more than the widening of an existing gap. Not true. I felt and still feel a new loss. It is a little more than the loss of a friend who made no demands. In a world growing daily colder and more menacing, his calm greeting, the good manners directed by a polite heart, are a continuing lack. He would not have identified good manners with morality, but he knew instinctively that to mind one's manners, in daily intercourse, in friendship, in writing, is a better road than many to a society fit to live in. So much so that, with him gone, the moral climate of our writing world has worsened a little.

Nonsense, he would say, with his curious smile, nonsense; the climate changes with every young man writing his first book, suffering his first fever of hope, disappointment, renewed hope.

Perhaps. But something strictly irreplaceable had disappeared from my life and from a world increasingly indifferent to perfection, reticence, politeness, measure.

## CHAPTER 20

I HAVE NEVER KNOWN—how should I?—why my son, whose life as an airline pilot is anything but monotonous, had this stubborn wish to cross the Atlantic in his small yacht. Perhaps the familiar reason—because the Atlantic is there; perhaps because the pilot of a jet plane sees only the wrinkled surface of the sea (if he sees that): perhaps only a habit of mind common to so many obscure men whose graves, foundering in the harsh grass of a disused churchyard, carry the words: '... master mariner of this parish, drowned at sea, March 18, 1771... died of fever in Vera Cruz, June 3, 1735... lost with his ship off Archangel in the winter of 1783...' Or perhaps an echo of my own restlessness—but then where did that come from, if not from these others?

738

JOURNEY FROM THE NORTH, VOL. 2

His defeat in 1950 when he was forced to turn back from Brest in his first ship, the ketch *Nina*, had exacerbated his obstinacy.

He and his high-hearted young wife had lived in yachts since they married. The one they owned now, *Tally Ho*, was their third. Built in 1910 by Stow, she won one of the early Fastnet races, a fine ship, with a good length of straight keel, deep bulwarks, and full-bodied hull. They had worked on her, modifying the sail plan and replacing the heavy tiller by wheel steering, and late in 1957 they began to make her ready for the voyage, working patiently through the endless list of things to be done, spares and equipment to be bought, stores, charts, radio, a trawler's emergency four-man rubber dinghy and survival pack, a pump able to shift some ten tons of salt water an hour, down-wind sails to make her self-steering in the Trade Winds: the abortive voyage of 1950 had had its life-saving lessons. The preparations went on through the winter and spring, and in April I put aside *The Road from the Monument* and went down to stay near the Hamble river. They meant to set out at the end of May or early June—this time without a crew. On this point I was corrected by Frances.

'Nana, you forget. Troy is a passenger, I am a member of the crew.'

'This time,' my son said, 'we haven't made the mistake of wasting time smartening the ship to Cowes standard, she's fairly smart, and she's completely seaworthy. She looks well, don't you think?'

'Yes.'

I thought she looked even smaller than her overall length of forty-seven feet, forty-four on the water-line: between two Atlantic rollers she would be invisible.

'You don't have to worry. I know what I'm doing.'

His likeness at this time to photographs of my father in his handsome youth and young middle-age startled me, as if the lean shambling body of the old sea-captain had split open under my eyes to set free a younger self. But at no age would my father have dreamed of crossing the Atlantic in a twenty-nine ton ship with his wife and two little lively girls.

Of the five weeks I hung about, helping where I could, I remember clearly only the last day. I knew that they did not want to be seen off, and I arranged to leave before they did. That morning I woke early, a few minutes before half-past four—half-past three by sun time. After a minute there was the first weak bird note, alone for a few seconds, then another, and a third, and in less than two minutes the chorus belling out, filling the whole air with a web of differing cries and single notes, the strong whistling of one bird piercing the rest. Now and then the prolonged cry of an owl. Then, behind the bird chorus, a distant noise of hounds, like a peal of bells flawed by a shriller cracked note, something of a pigeon's throaty groaning cry and something of a wild duck, a curtain of sound rising and falling in the grey light. And then, some long way away, the cuckoo.

Without warning I was invaded by a sadness inexplicable even by my fears, an awful swollen tide of grief in my throat. Then, very distinctly, as if I had only to reach an arm out to touch him, I saw my son as a young child, perhaps two: he was smiling, his hair a yellow cloud round his head, his eyes widely-open and brilliant.

If you cry it will be for yourself, I thought. I said, 'Forgive me.'

He had already gone. With despair, such despair, I thought: Who will forgive me?

During the week before they left, the wind blew stubbornly from the west, sometimes gale force, the worst quarter for them. It was still coming from the west when Bill rang me up to say that they must start. 'We can't wait forever.'

'When do you go off?'

'Tomorrow morning at eleven.'

'Well, the best of luck.'

'Thanks for all you've done. We're very happy.'

'That's fine.'

'Very happy. We'll write.'

'Ah, do.'

Beginning young, I have had a great deal of practice not only in hiding my feelings but in hiding from them. It embarrasses me to be pitied. A membrane in my mind closes at once over any strong emotion—anxiety, dread, hope. A membrane is not a shutter: what is behind it can be felt moving. I went on with my novel, and took care not to say that I was afraid. The truth is I was afraid the whole time, whatever I was doing. And at night.

I am not a stoic. No doubt even my fear of pity and ridicule come down to me from long-dead women who were not encouraged to make a song about what went on inside the hard bones of their skulls.

After they left Falmouth in early June, the first news came from Corcubion, a tiny dilapidated village round the corner of Finisterre. They were trapped in the little Spanish harbour, with the tunny fleet, by southerly gales. When they went ashore the first time, the village had waiting for them its one English-speaking inhabitant; they were led to the store and the children given bunches of larkspur and carnations: the difference between the two of them leaps to the eye in what they did; Frances carried hers politely and patiently all morning, young Troy, disliking the messy stems, handed hers to her mother to carry.

On the 21st of July I had a telegram to say they had reached Lisbon. The same day I finished the second draft of my novel and put it in a cupboard, to revise later.

They had a rough passage, eight days, from Lisbon to Gibraltar, and wired asking us to fly there to see them. My heart leaped crazily. It was impossible to go, I was in Portmeirion with C.—his only holiday—and I drove the thought from my mind. Suddenly, when they reached Las Palmas, it surfaced, and I dragged a reluctant Guy round the shipping quarter of east London in search of a ship with room for us. There was one sailing from Southampton in less than a week, a Spanish boat. She turned out to be an emigrant ship for Venezuela, shabby, the passageways and bare cabins filthy, every water-closet blocked most of the time and stinking to heaven. And speaking of heaven—after I had watched the Spanish crew knocking out the rotten wood in the lifeboats and patching the gaps with white deal, I decided that she was as unseaworthy as she was squalid. The captain and officers were invisible, rigorously incommunicado, but the crew were gay and friendly. Indeed, apart from the stench and discomfort, she was a sympathetic ship. The bread, baked in what no doubt were appalling conditions, was delicious.

At Corunna we took in our first emigrants—two hundred of them. Something like a fiesta raged on the wharf, a laughing yelling chanting weeping mob of friends and relatives. Women carrying children, and younger women, newly married, with gawky boyish husbands in stiff new clothes, came aboard with faces swollen to twice their size by three hours of hard crying. They settled down quickly, and took over the ship. The eight or nine so-called first-class passengers were not merely in no way privileged, they were discriminated against in a score of ways. Since I was not going to spend longer than ten days with hundreds of restless parakeet-voiced Spaniards, I liked this. I liked it still better when I thought about the clean unnatural luxury and horrible diversions of the English liner we might have been in. At the same time I decided that, should we run into weather that was too much for the ship, I would not compete for a place in one of the four lifeboats. Simpler to drown at once.

Of the two weeks of heat and smooth massive light we spent in Las Palmas, a single scene stands out with the sharpness of an illuminated initial in a half-obliterated manuscript. The afternoon when I was alone on the sands with Troy and, suddenly, she ran into the sea, which that day a hot wind had blown into great clawing breakers; the under-current sucked her little body out like a twig, in mortal fear I rushed after her and dragged her back. I scolded her furiously. Sobered by the shock of feeling herself pulled into the sea, she sat curled up in my lap in silence. I held her, and to calm myself stared at the very strange hills behind the port, bare, sculptured, changing in the light from the livid grey of dry earth to lion colour, with that velvety blackness *under* the tawny glowing skin. Gradually an extraordinary peace came from—from where? The child and I were enclosed in a bubble formed of the hard bright light and the foreign voices. I had the brief sense that I had been born only for this one action, these silent sheltering minutes.

We were returning in a Union Castle boat. When we left the hotel for the last time I gave the servant some pesetas, not many, I was saving what I had left, to give to Bill. A flame of surprise and joy ran across her sallow face, she poured out a long smiling sentence, of which I understood only the last words—*Vaya con Dios*.

The family came on board with us. Looking round the ship with a fine smile, Frances said, 'I like *Tally* millions better than this great thing—don't you, Troy?'

Troy did not answer.

I sent them away an hour before we sailed. The sister ship to ours moved out ahead of us, and ours blew long ritual farewell blasts. The deep note echoed back and back through my childhood, tears forced themselves under my eyelids: I got rid of them before they were noticed.

Later I stood staring at the long waves, leaping, slavering foam, green above black-veined troughs. Let them be safe, let them be safe. *Vaya con Dios. Vaya con Dios*. In London I took the *Monument* from its shelf and revised it very carefully. In the end, since, for once in my life, I had a year's income in hand, I decided not to publish it for another two or three years, to give myself a respite from reviewers.

(To be entirely honest, I was naively a little confident that they must and would praise this book. This was an illusion.)

Another novel—its theme as old as humanity: how much evil, how much violence to the rooted decencies of the human spirit, can you bring yourself to do for a good end?—knocked on my skull. I kept it at arm's length, to give it a little room to grow.

During the whole of this time I lived and worked in front of a vast screen stretched behind my eyes: everything I did, between waking and lying down, took place in front of it. Behind every gesture I made, every image, every event, there lay the waste of water, under a dull sky grey and menacing, in sunlight a web of glittering points running out to infinity. Nothing, not even hearing of a friend's death, blotted it out.

It invaded the Memorial Service for Rose Macaulay, blunting the strange pang I felt, less for her than for the changed figures I watched come in, changes which seemed to have been hurried into overnight—the church was full of people who had not yet learned their roles of ageing men and women—the yellow sagging jowls of a celebrated woman writer, Harold Nicolson's heavy movements, another well-known face so creased and misshapen that for a full minute I did not recognize it. The images of Rose herself were less desolate. I could look full at the slender young woman with the head of a Greek statue, and at the older woman turning on the stairs of the Portland Place flat to look back at me and say: Margaret, you don't know what it's like to watch the person you love dying. And at the skeletal Rose of the last ten years... They had left Las Palmas on the 7th of November. There was silence for thirty-three days, then the telegram from Barbados: ABILITY 33 DAYS ALL FLOURISHING LOVE.

*Ability* is the old merchant sailor's code word, standing for: Arrived all well. My father always used it, and I had taught it to Bill.

One thing in their first laconic letter—apart from the incident of the cockpit drain broken at the skin of the boat eighteen inches below the waterline and plugged, in mid-Atlantic, with a cork—that struck me was that in thirty-three days they sighted only one ship, the *Jessie Gulva*, a small Danish cargo boat, which changed course to come and look at them and wave, but did not speak to them. Another was that Frances really had the right to call herself a member of the crew; she learned to steer a compass course, and in good weather took the wheel for an hour, alone. I tried and failed to overhear the thoughts of a ten-year-old child confronting that steep immensity of sea from an eye-level not much above that of a gull's resting on the crest of a wave. Thought is a clumsy word: probably she only *saw*—light, space, glitter of water, clouds.

What was I at ten? Already anxious, ambitious, eager to please, something of a hypocrite and a mule.

I was assailed at this time by a novel I had no intention of writing. It began one night in sleep. A woman was playing hide and seek with her young child, in a large garden, like a Welsh one I knew. She was a little bored, but she went on alternately hiding and seeking, calling dutifully, 'Hello, hello,' as she sought. For a time the child answered in an excited voice. Abruptly, he stopped answering. Becoming afraid, she ran wildly from shrub to tall dark shrub, calling, looking, not finding him.

When I woke the whole novel moved in my brain. It was about a woman whose life was shaped by a conviction of sin, an unreasoned agony of guilt. Driven by her savage energy, she went out into the world, coming back at intervals to see an only child. One day she came back to be told that he had disappeared. The rest of her life became a frantic search for him, like K's search for the Castle, or his baffled efforts to find out from his accusers what crime he had done. There were moments when she caught or imagined she caught a glimpse of him, and others when it seemed that he was in some other room of the house. Her life went by. Now and then she saw a young man who resembled him, and now and then spoke to one of these, who jeered at her. When she was dying he came into her room for a few seconds, an indistinct figure, glanced at her in silence and went out.

If I were a poet I could perhaps have fused these innumerable images and sensations into a poem, without deforming them—a novel cannot do this, it operates at too slow a heat. A talented choreographer might make them into a ballet. Or a childless writer, able to keep her cool distance, pick them up without burning her hand to the bone.

She can have them.

## CHAPTER 21

I AM ALWAYS BEING REMINDED that English writers exist at several removes from reality.

Last year (June, 1964) I was reminded of it again at a P.E.N. Congress in Oslo, where the subject under discussion was semantics. On the first day it became clear that semantics is not only a mode of life, one of the most deeply-rooted, but one of the most dangerous. Words an Englishman can hold in his hand safely, play with, use for a rhetorical exercise, may kill the writer of another country who handles them. The delegates from countries where honesty or rashness or want of adroitness in touching certain words mean torture, imprisonment, death, were speaking on another wave length, and their English colleagues heard them, if at all, very indistinctly. (On this occasion, their French colleagues heard nothing except their own eloquence, and did not try to hear anything else.)

'Listen to our tears, our grief of small nations at the mercy of great ones,' the Vietnamese delegate said—explaining quietly and patiently that, in his country, the meaning of the word *freedom* was *freedom to go to prison*. 'Help us to endure, to reach a level where life will have a meaning...'

In 1959, a meeting in London of the International Executive stumbled over the same word. Several of the delegates had come determined to get rid of the Hungarian Centre, for the sound reason that Hungarian writers were being jailed as political prisoners and the Centre had made no effort to help them. I looked down the long table. There was an almost visible mark on the foreheads of delegates from the Iron Curtain countries: the East German's small lined worn-out face carried it: not in any English sense of the word free, sitting there quietly repeating his instructions, Bodo Uhse was none the less in some way more real than most of us, the dangers he was facing were real dangers.

Speaking for the Writers in Exile, Paul Tabori made an unanswerable speech, answered at once by the delegate from Prague, a charming and intelligent young woman.

'Don't forget,' she said, smiling, 'that the four Hungarian writers you are speaking about were not put in prison as writers, but because they had broken the law.'

'They were not put in prison because they had stolen or murdered,' Tabori said quietly, 'but because they had written something.'

One of the East European Centres had tabled a resolution which allowed the offending Hungarians another length of rope. The committee of the English Centre had instructed me to vote against what it considered, rightly, an indefensible compromise. Listening to the debate, I thought briefly that more than a continent separated the warm room we sat in from Tibor Déry's uncomfortable (if no worse) cell. The Chinese delegate from Taipei had just said, with a diminutive gesture of quite astonishing beauty: We shall be making history... What is coldly termed *little history*, I thought, the history of unimportant persons, that is, of ninety-nine and nine-tenths per cent of the whole. Even though the effect of any protest we make here is probably, certainly, zero, we need not think too lowly of ourselves... I reflected that, if we expelled the Hungarians, then the Czechs, the Poles, the East Germans (about these I cared little), might be forced by their masters to expel themselves, and my poor friend Parandowski would lose one of his chances of talking about Mallarmé to a French scholar. A number of weak threads—but stretching across frontiers—would be slit... The resolution was being voted on by naming Centres. Against: the exiles, the Chinese Centre at Taipei, the American, the Latvian, the Estonian, the Australian... I can be something of a Calvinist and something of a hypocrite in a good cause, but could I carry it to the extent of asking writers in Budapest to risk their own lives to save Tibor Déry's? Who am I to ask them to be heroes?... On the other hand again, I could not support the motion.

Four Centres had abstained from voting. It was my turn. My friend Tabori looked at me confidently.

'I abstain.'

I avoided Paul Tabori's eye. Not that he would reproach me. Too humanely cynical, he expected too little good faith or singleness of purpose from human nature, or from my nature.

What is more, my dear Paul, we are both right, you to be uncompromising in a matter of political and human decency, I to compromise, English fashion, to the limit of tolerance. The damage either of us, acting alone, is able to do, is halved by our co-existence...

Again and again, staring across the abyss dividing the provincial-minded English from the continentals, I realized that the last are in a situation from which there is no issue—except through the death of society. Two years later, the Hungarians were up for judgement again, with the difference that the Centre had rid itself of the police dog and elected a scholarly critic as secretary and a new president who was a professor. They came to London as delegates—or defendants—and David and I seized our chance to see them alone, before they faced the Executive. The argument ran, lap after lap, round the same track. The secretary coldly, the other with warm anxiety, reminded us that Budapest is not London... 'Déry is in prison for urging writers in the factories to come out on strike. You don't understand what that means. Here you can have strikes and nothing happens, all are calm, friendly, like lambs. In Hungary there are no political lambs, agitation is less than one step from civil war. We *can't* go through that bloody business again. Try, please, to understand us... If this new resolution of the English Centre, suspending us, is passed tomorrow, it will make a terrible impression on Hungarian writers. We are full of hope now, we have a new active Centre, we are prepared to do all we can to work with you. Don't make it impossible for us.'

For a moment, I saw what the speaker was seeing, our abysmal distance from the naked realities of power, our self-righteousness, our easy chatter about democracy, lambs frisking in the absence of wolves. If I were to say to him that pretence has its uses, that we English are right to behave *as if* freedom (the freedom to advocate what you will) is an absolute good, he would look at me with polite contempt and curiosity.

When they were leaving I told the secretary, 'I'll do what I can for you.' He thanked me drily.

I liked him. He was as hard as nails, and without vanity; it had been burned out of him by an acid stronger than that used to cure warts. My friendliness appears to him as nothing more than liberal-minded weakness, I thought, but just possibly he suspects that I know what he thinks of me.

From Brussels a year later I brought away a single document from a session at which I took the Chair. Scribbled on the back of a page of 'Resolutions proposed by the French Centre,' it runs:

3 inconnus
1 libéré
1 libéré
1 amnestié
1 libéré
1 libéré
1 libéré
1 libéré
1 libéré
1 condamné pour des meutres: ancien S.S.
1 agent
$\left.\begin{array}{l}1\\1\end{array}\right\}$ action criminelle—trahison

Voilà fifteen out of twenty-four, the others not traced yet.

As a comment on Europe in 1962 it could not be more concise.

One of our self-imposed duties is to make lists of gaoled writers in countries where imprisonment is an occupational disease of writers, and to plague authority with questions about them.

Imagine for yourself the state of mind of the secretary of, say, the Hungarian Centre, confronted by his virtuous English confrères with a dozen or so names of imprisoned writers and the demand to press his government to release them. I have my share of obtuseness, but that—I confess—goes against my grain.

That year the longest list was the East German one, and the commonest answer to letters about the East German prisoners was silence, or invective in the correct Cold War language. I was the more surprised when the East German delegate rose and began his reading of a long statement, name by name. He read it slowly and calmly, in French.

A pale slender handsome creature—thirty-five? forty?—with a fine arched predatory nose, hard very well-shaped mouth, small fine ears, rather pale eyes, bright and deeply-set, thick hair—a face at once delicate and powerful: good teeth and good strong hands. I watched him while I pencilled my notes. He was guarded, adroit, intelligent, and, I thought, a really first-class tactician.

He was heard in silence.

When I spoke to him afterwards, he smiled with the greatest sweetness and frankness—across an impassable no-man's-land. It is possible to talk as a friend with a Pole and, a little less easily, with Czechs and Hungarians, but not with an East German. I was the ambiguous liberal, to be politely or contemptuously discounted as not fit to grasp either his situation or his mental reservations.

In fact I understand our East Europeans a great deal better than they do me. And I can never shake off my sense that they—unlike us, with our lists and scandalized questions—are playing their heads. Reality in England, even in the 'sixties, is not edged.

My less reputable reason for being in Brussels this week was that—in the conditions of civilized society—no group of human beings offers so many *monstres sacrés*, displays so many naked emotions so shamelessly as a body of writers. The president of the Centre was a brilliant lawyer, a poet (praised by Cocteau), a brave citizen, a force of nature, and an orator of vehement eloquence with the voice of a cathedral organ. At the closing banquet, he recited a long roll of dead writers.

'... je pense à Piérard—mort, à H. G. Wells—mort, à Charles Morgan—mort...'

At each reverberating cry of *mort*, the chandeliers and the wine glasses rang, and an icy shiver moved down the spines of his listeners. He used his authority to persuade a Minister at the table to sign a document allowing the East Germans to stay two more days in Belgium. Turning to me, he said amiably, 'Not another country in Europe would do that.'

'Perhaps not another president of P.E.N. has so much influence with Ministers.'

He smiled. 'That also is true.'

At this moment, a card was handed to him along the table. He read it, frowning, and threw it down in front of me.

'Inconceivable! Abominable! What do you think, eh, Madame Storm Jameson.'

It was the place card of the elderly Iranian delegate, on the back of which he had scrawled: 'Cher ami, je sais qu'on dira quelque mot de moi. J'aimerais que vous disiez un mot sur mon livre *Le Prophète*. Merci.'

'Not in the least inconceivable,' I said.

He reflected for a moment. An expression of profound simplicity and guile crossed his face. 'If he asks me about it, I shall tell him that van Vriesland promised me to say some words about it in his speech...'

Forgive this long parenthesis. I am trying to soften the image of myself as a female Tartuffe.

At the dinner-party given to the 1959 Executive Committee by the English, the guest of honour was the German Ambassador—because the forthcoming Congress was being held in Frankfurt.

I found myself sitting on his right. Before we went in to dinner, an official of the Foreign Office talked to me about him: he was fifty-five—he looked twenty years younger—and had been posted to London as 'a goodwill envoy.'

'What kind of a diplomatic animal is that?' I asked.

My friend smiled slightly. 'You'll see.'

Calculating rapidly as I took my seat, I made him thirty-five in the year the war started. He was charming. He took every opening, the smallest and least promising, to convey his distaste for Hitler and the Nazi régime. It was done with fine tact, without affectation, without the use of a single clumsily assertive word. He knew what he was about. *What he did not know is that he was being listened to intently by an equally accomplished soft-speaker.* On his other side he had the president of the Dutch Centre, our dear turbulent highly cultivated Viktor van Vriesland, who had learned during the Occupation to detest Germans with such bitterness that he would not be able to bring himself to go to Frankfurt. Turning to me after he had been talking to Viktor, His Excellency said seriously, 'I have been thanking him for speaking to me, he a Dutchman, in German... I hope you are going to enjoy your week in Frankfurt.'

I did not tell him that I had no intention of going. I said I was sorry that Goethe's birthplace there had been destroyed during the war.

He smiled finely. 'Well—we started it, after all.'

He went on to tell me that Anne Frank's father had called on him. 'He thanked me for receiving him. I said, "It is for me to thank you for coming." I was having a gathering of English boys and young Germans, one of them a young von Moltke, in the afternoon, and I invited him to come to it. He came, and it was a great success, it turned out that all the German boys had read the Diary.'

The ghost of that lively intelligent child must have smiled a little.

In his speech he made the same subtly unstressed confession of regret.

Afterwards, invited by Viktor, he came to Brown's Hotel to drink coffee and brandy, and was so charming, friendly, simple, neighbourly, that I saw myself and dear Viktor as two Neanderthal ghosts. I remembered suddenly the Radziwill I met in Warsaw in 1945. Unlike this German aristocrat he was unhappy.


## CHAPTER 22

T HROUGHOUT THE FIRST MONTHS of 1959 I was at peace about the yacht. They were moving gently about the Windward and Leeward Islands, Bequia, St Lucia, Martinique, Antigua. On the 25th of April, they left Antigua and sailed north—twenty windless days to Bermuda. From there they wrote that to attempt the North Atlantic crossing before the middle of June would be suicidal folly. Good, I thought, I have four, five, even six weeks: we can safely lose ourselves in France.

I have given up trying to explain to myself why I have only to cross the Channel to reach a state close to perfect contentment. The run of the grain—my grain? Or the existence of wide, but not too wide spaces—say the Landes, all that immense area of pines, dunes, fields, charmingly plain villages and single houses, many of these very old and very dilapidated, yet keeping a touch of dignity, a little the fold of self-satisfaction in an old woman's ruined face? Or the sense of eternity in a shabby changeless town of two or three thousand inhabitants—let's say in the Dordogne?

This recurring sense of eternity, of the unimportance of time and change, may have everything to do with a happiness I can no more account for than a young man can give an account of the emotion one face among many rouses in him. He can enumerate features, a smile, a turn of the head, and I could run off a catalogue of images drawn from this six weeks alone, the green quiet of the upper Garonne, the exultant dead calm of certain ancient buildings, St Savin, St Bertrand de Comminges, St Michel de Cuxa, Conques, fields of wild flowers in the Ariège, the friendliness of a bare clean hotel in Espalion, the sun of Perpignan and Banyuls lapping bones stiffened by the northern winter. But none of it explains my love of France, my deepest sensual and mental pleasure, even to myself. Why not simply say: A love affair? And leave it at that.

In six weeks we drove slowly 3,500 miles, turning aside again and again to follow thin veins of road to some neglected church, fortified village, river valley enclosing silence. We slept in twenty-eight towns, villages, isolated small hotels, without a trace of harassment. The sense of eternity again? Or the taste of the bread.

Between Perpignan and Foix we turned off the road to look for the ruins of Montségur. In the thirteenth century, some four hundred persons, men, women, children, believing Cathars, held out in this remote fortress for ten months, from May to March, against the Crusading force. Defeated in the end by hunger, thirst, sickness, they surrendered to the besiegers—that is, to the Inquisition—on terms which issued in an immense pyre, large enough to burn two hundred persons at once, erected on the south-east face of the mountain below the castle. Sick and wounded were thrown on to the faggots, and in a few hours two hundred living bodies were a mass of raw blackened bleeding flesh, slowly burning to cinder under a thick cloud of smoke, and filling the valley with the stench of burned meat. A triumph for the true faith, and the visible end of the heresy of Catharism.

It was a hot brilliant day, a jewel of a day, the air so clear you could see a mote at the farther end of a room. The narrow road to Montségur climbs in a series of hairpin bends, steeply. Suddenly, between one breath and the next, the castle leaped into sight ahead, at a great height. More climbing, more narrow turns, and there, on the left, the high green hill, thinly wooded on its lowest slope, then short rough grass with a thin spatter of broom and yellow rattle, then naked rock, the whole tapering to the blunt point into which the castle digs its claws. Other hills, with the light mark of all but obliterated terracing, stood round, pressing closer on two sides, and mountains craning their necks behind the hills. To catch sight of the village sunk in the deep valley between Montségur and the bare nearer hills, you must walk on farther, until you can look down, over the crumbling edge of the road, on to the fleece of tiled roofs, none of them less than centuries old, in every colour of faded reds and yellows, pressed into the ground by the hills, by Montségur, by an immense sky.

That day there were no other visitors, not a soul anywhere, and no sound except the crickets. The sudden noise of blasting in a quarry sent a current of fear through me, thunder clattering from hill to hill and curling like a lash round Montségur itself. Then the silence closed in again, empty of everything except fear and the burden of the grasshopper.

Ruin that Montségur is, all other castles seem no more than its shadow. It draws up into itself the whole hill. It sends strong taproots down into the Manichean underworld of the human intellect and spirit. Catharism is surely the most logical of faiths. That may be why it laid no stress on the duty to burn your neighbour.

We stayed five days in the mountain village of Le Vernet—a village which has a charm and dignity not wholly due to its magnificent position at the heart of savagely wooded hills. It is a village with the soul of a civilized city. And it contains one thing I have seen nowhere else, a monument to the dead of 1914–18 which recognizes that France had allies in that war. Standing at the highest point of the village, in a small square, the Place Entente Cordiale, with ruthlessly cut-back acacias, it has no aesthetic worth of any sort. But at the back of the pedestal it has this plaque which recites the name of every ally, in Europe and outside, beginning with Bolivia and ending with Uruguay. Lower panels on the four sides list the battles, the fourth ending with the triumphant words: *La France sur le Rhin*. Above the wide main panel bearing the names of the dead of 1914–18, a smaller panel records those of 1939–45. A family name which appears three times in the earlier lists appears again on this. The monument itself is of two expressionless female figures seated side by side, England identified by her trident, France by a sword. Both have plump cheeks and buns of hair, good middle-class housewives transmogrified.

One afternoon when I was sitting in this minute airy Place, a very plain-faced young woman, holding the hand of her very plain dark-haired child, a little girl, walked past singing, in a low tuneless voice, to words I did not catch, a tune my young sister sang to her first child as she bathed him... Nick nack paddy whack, give a dog a bone... The thread of sound led back and back to my sister in her dark underworld: weak as it was, inconceivably weak and thin, it was strong enough to carry across almost twenty years the voice and smile of a young woman bent over the child in her hands. Everything else, the room she sat in, other faces and voices, have sunk without trace. Since I have forgotten so much, why have I kept this and a few other fragments as senseless? The word is unkind, and just.

I have remembered what I can. But she is dying, I know it, from the earth, the traces on it of her light feet, in streets and lanes, becoming fainter every day, more nearly effaced. And nothing, since I can't live forever, to be done about it.

The yacht left Bermuda on its return voyage on the 11th of June. There was no word until the 18th of July. Then I had a letter from the Azores.

At the time I read it I did not know how dangerous a passage it had been—gales, four of them of Force Eight or better, three following each other with scarcely an hour's interval. In one of these the top-mast snapped off level with the mainmast head. It took three hours to clear up the mess, with Frances steering. Cracks, which could be seen working, appeared in the rudder head, and Bill spent some hours hanging over the stern in big seas, head downwards, fixing into place a strip of brass taken from the locker and fashioned to fit the stock. It was to repair the rudder that they had to make for the Azores.

London in July was stifling. I had no help in the flat—the genteel young woman who had been coming two or three times a week had given it up. Oppressed by the hideous traffic noise and fumes, and the flow of *biophages*, Guy was raging to leave London for good. The half of my mind holding a mirage of country solitude and quiet agreed with him. The other half was in the blackest rebellion against the effort of finding a house and moving to it, and tormented by the reflection that since I finished revising *The Monument* I had written nothing. Between doubts and frustration, I drifted.

I knew indistinctly what I wanted, and that it was out of my reach. My fever, inherited, transmitted through my blood, was incurable.

Writing is only my second nature. I would infinitely rather write than cook, but I would rather run about the world, looking at it, than write. The person I have spent my life defeating, the silly sinner (the old sea-captain's word for a fool) who panics at the thought of being shut up in a house of her own, is not the writer.

After they left the Azores on the last leg of the voyage, I waited without patience, in growing fear. On the 13th of August, I wrote in the front of a book: The 21st day has come and gone.

The telephone rang less than an hour later, and my daughter-in-law's light gay voice said, 'Hello, darling, we're at Falmouth.'

It is impossible to be happier in this world.

Next day I started work on *Last Score*. I finished the first draft in September and began rewriting at once. I finished this second version late on the 26th of November, and put it away.

In the morning I woke a few minutes before seven, and saw a singularly clear last quarter of the moon on her back in a smooth darkish grey-blue sky, with one brilliant star above. Far below her, a bank of dark clouds behind the lighted buildings of Park Lane, and, south of the park, a building lit over its height and length, like a liner. I stood admiring it, and thinking—no doubt I had been thinking it as I slept—that I had wasted too much time in the past year to leave my manuscript lying in a cupboard.

I took it out again, and finished the third and final version in January.

Its theme was the one that has obsessed me all my life: Why are human beings so cruel? Life so short, and the world so beautiful, why do they give so much time and ingenuity to torturing each other? Why does cruelty give pleasure to a creature of flesh and blood and spirit? So acute a pleasure that it supports a vast intricate web of argument, sophistry, poetry, reasoned justification of a sensual act. *Last Score* was an enquiry into two aspects of the mystery. Is torture ever justified? (The other day I listened to an intelligent warm-hearted woman arguing that it is clearly right to torture one man to save the lives of, say, a hundred. I take this to be heresy, an infinitely viler heresy than that held by the thousands of Cathars burned by a Church which had no doubt that torture can be justified.) What is the effect on a deeply civilized man if he decides that, in some instance, it is right to use torture?

Not one of its English critics noticed what the book was about. The anonymous reviewer of *The Times* decided easily that it was 'an enquiry into the problem of responsibility and power', adding that C. P. Snow would have done it much better. While being very sure that anyone could do better what I had not tried to do, I was irritated by his dullness, as I am when I cannot explain myself to some wretch who is perhaps less ill-willed than vacant or pressed for time.

The failure was partly my fault. My passion for economy in writing, which had become an obsession, is hard on careless or stupid readers—but this is not a valid excuse. Had I thought over the book for another year or years, or worked it out at greater length...

## CHAPTER 23

THE YOUNG GREEK ENGINEER in Rhodes said, 'No one is too old to come to Greece for the first time.' Perhaps not. But to wait so long was a mistake.

*17th of April 1961*

We left London at night. At the air terminus an official glanced up from Guy's passport and said drily, 'I suppose you know this is out of date?'

Our luggage was already on its way to the airfield. After dismayed minutes, another official advised us to go on, and risk being sent back from Athens. 'If you had been going to France or Germany, or Spain, I'd have said no, it's no use. But Greece—well, you stand a good chance of being allowed in.'

We landed in Athens in the first calm light. I took Guy's passport and laid it, with mine, in front of the first of the three men waiting to look at them. Not knowing whether he had any English, I pointed to the date and said we would take it to the consulate and get it put right. He glanced at it with indifference and waved us on. The other two did the same.

Later in the morning we bought a street map and walked a long way, in searing heat, to the consulate. Exhausted, I thought I had been a fool to come, I should have gone to France, to the Dordogne, and slept for two days. Each step on the way back was a fresh effort.

Our hotel was on the edge of the old quarter below the Acropolis; by leaning dangerously far out over the narrow balcony I could see four or five white columns, and a thread of excitement wound itself round my throat: the window on the other side of the room looked down into the attics of a house I thought derelict until I caught sight between crumbling boards of a heap of rags which moved and became two skeletal children and an old woman with a dark wrinkled neck, her body hanging from it like a dead branch.

Watching her hands as she touched one child's face lightly and drew its rags round the other, I thought: One says, How could they find a single human being willing to push children into the gas-chambers? But is there no single thread joining that indifference to the passive discomfort with which I peer into this attic?

I lay down, and fell asleep like dropping through a black sea, and woke able to go out. In the darkness we stumbled along streets not a great deal wider than gutters, until we found a small very plain restaurant at the far side of a dusty courtyard smelling of tarred rope, where we ate a decent enough meal.

What unless it is the light sets Greece apart from all the foreign places where I have been happy, serenely happy? Not only the light, nakedly clear, but the hardness. Greece has the hardness—not of stone, which can soften— of marble. The sunlight glances off it, piercing the eyelids. Thus the Acropolis is not simply a remarkably handsome ruin—which no Englishman can look at without a feeling of shame: when are we going to have the decency to send back what we as good as stole?—it is alone, isolated in time and space by the burning whiteness of the light recoiling from it.

And then, the firmness of the lines—the cape at Sounion has no distance to go to join in my mind the line, dark, living, severe, of the coast curving north in my first memory of lines and curves. A line as pure as these gives me the same pleasure music must give anyone for whom sound is all. But only in Greece is there this double intensity, the clearest light, a light from the first day of creation, joined to the clearest line. I saw it over and over again.

I saw it at Mykonos at five in the afternoon on the 2nd of May: a pale hot sky, the sun two hours from setting, one wide segment of the sea a moving fleece of light, blinding, the water nearer the island an unwrinkled stretch of grey silk, without brilliance, but alive. The single fishing-boat leaving the harbour drew after it a tail of separate explosions of light. The nearest island a black rock: behind it a violet shadow that was Rhenea, the island to which the dying and women about to give birth were sent from ancient Delos, too sacred for these first and last convulsions. At my back the flat-topped houses of Mykonos were white against the bare hill, dark, blackish brown tinged faintly with green, verdigris on a bronze shield.

In Delos itself, apart from the small admirable museum and a shabby building or two, there are only sun-warmed ruins, and the bounding whiteness of the lions. And the quiet, like an old smile, older, far older, than the smile of Rheims, less evasive, less subtle, with a divine indifference.

And again, in the bare calcined hills of Arcadia, the lines, not only of the corroded hills themselves, but of the villages clinging under their ribbed acre of bleached tiles to the sides of cliffs, are drawn not in colour but in a light out of my past.

And at Delphi, where—all those olive-trees—we might have been in Provence, except that the cliffs at the back of the shrine were made immeasurably older than anything Provençal by the way the light, not softened even by the fine rain, worked on them, stripping them to the bone. Large eagles flew off the rim of the cliff and dived upwards into a thinner and more dazzling light. When I stooped over the spring to drink from it, the water in the palm of my hand was cold, as cold as any northern beck.

Rhodes is completely different, a different grandeur, suaver, a little corrupt. I have no idea where the suavity comes from—not from the Templars who left the city of Rhodes their street of superb houses and a few tombs in the museum, not from the reticent houses of the Turks, and certainly not from the tactless Italians. All these successive invaders made marks on the island—which is green, full of trees and flowering plants—without erasing the older marks. In some inexplicable way the acropolis at Lindos seems closer in time to the village at the foot of its headland than any of the later fragments, but this might have been because our meal of fish and white resinated wine cannot have been very different from meals eaten in the tenth century B.C. by the builders of the acropolis. Or by St Paul when he landed in the little harbour.

When we came back to Rhodes from Lindos I was rash enough to buy *The Times* of the day before, and found in it the contemptuous notice of *Last Score*. It should have warned me against buying the Sunday newspapers when they came. All three of them damned it heartily: This I thought an excess of zeal.

Somewhere—I think in *Racine et Shakespeare*—Stendhal remarks that the writer and the soldier need exactly the same kind of courage: the first must take care not to think about the journalists, and the second to forget the field hospital.

He is right, of course he is right. But there is always the first moment of disappointment, and the image of oneself as the circus clown who gets slapped. And the fear that no one will buy a novel which has been damned in four important—commercially important—newspapers.

But—according to these same papers—it was raining in England, and I was in Rhodes, in brilliant sun, eating macaroons and drinking Turkish coffee at a table facing the harbour. It would need a more serious misfortune, some personal loss—a danger threatening my family or a close friend—to get past my happiness in being in a foreign country.

If I could spend my life travelling I should escape entirely these moments of diabolical self-doubt and boredom.

Kamiros, where we went next day, made the disrespect of—the names have gone—seem only a bad habit, like nail-biting. The road turns and twists, steeply, between pines. Suddenly, at the top of the hill, there is the dead city, with the temple on the lip of the cliff; below it, far below, the splendid valley and the hills folding it in; on the right the peacock-blue sea and the three green headlands. The silence is not a dead silence; not only do the Greek inscriptions on the stones keep it alive, but there is all that soft fine hair of grass springing between them, and the small flowers, and in the clear heat a scent of herbs and pines.

And the light, passing its sharp edge over columns, stones, pines, sea, all.

I suppose that one reason for the stubborn persistence in us of Greece, a seed, a face waiting to be recognized, is that, in this light-scoured country, one is able, no, forced to impose a myth on the reality. At Mycenae the myth becomes more than the reality, even more insistent and harder than these hard fragments at the top of the dusty hill, or the great bee-hive tomb. Standing in this tomb, I did not at first know what the sound was, a ceaseless deep murmur, until when my eyes were used to the half-darkness I saw the bees moving outside the crevices in the wall. Agamemnon a black bee.

There were other people at the top of the hill, in the ruins of the palace, but the guide took them to look at some fragment or other, I forget what, down the other slope of the hill. I pretended to be too tired to go with them, and was left, alone, sitting on the dusty earth, my back against a broken wall. Where the country is concerned—I am not talking about cities—I have little liking for any but a bare landscape. This one was bare, an anatomy, and at the same time violently alive. The sky was immense and immensely blue, white wisps of cloud scrawled across and across it; the hills were dark and bony, like Provence, but the bones here are even harder; in the empty plain a few cypresses, a few olive-trees, a few narrow strips of green. The silence over it was as naked and enduring as these Cyclopean walls, what is left of them. The light wind raised the dust in tiny spirals. Some flower I didn't know the name of, a deep lilac blue, like a small periwinkle, grew close to the ground under my hand. Two swallows darted from wall to wall, so near me that I felt the air from their wings, and I watched a large black ant, Clytemnestra, suddenly attack a black bee crawling on the ground as if it were wounded, kill it and carry it off, pushing it in front of her: again and again a puff of wind blew her back, and again she set off with her prey, and disappeared behind a wall.

I recognized the desert of dryness inside my skull. Unlike this empty plain below Mycenae, it was a sort of nothing, a meaningless abyss, not even memory. It struck me that I had been running away all my life, and that I was very near the end of this flight into words. There was nothing more I wanted to say, and no more words to escape into—and I couldn't now, even if that had ever been possible, escape into some sort of action.

There was still, if I could have afforded it, one way of escape open—into the distraction of travel, into the pleasure which has never yet failed me, of looking at a fresh country. Impossible.

What I must do, I thought, is to find some other way of enduring the silence, the regret, and wait in it, as I am sitting here, in the light, perfectly content. Perhaps the escape into death is like escaping into words, a substitute life?

For the first time since I was left alone here, I heard sounds, men's voices a long way off, in the Argive plain, and a single sheep bell, also a long way off—as far as the Whitby bell-buoy ringing at sea when I was a child. However far you go, I thought, even here, under this incomparably brighter sun, the original images, the original sounds, follow you.

Now the others came back, toiling up the hill in the great heat. The charming Frenchwoman with the small black darting eyes asked me, 'What have you been doing all the time?'

'What did you expect me to do?' I said. 'I slept.'

## CHAPTER 24

THERE IS SOMETHING truly comic in the way I run head on into the same mistake, the same trap, again and again. In December 1914 I went into my first house. Today (21st of November 1960) I began living in a place I like no better—the same flat country, the same absence of a view, against which my glance hurls and hurled itself like a demented bluebottle. And the same revulsion and panic, entirely involuntary, of my whole being. The two moments confront each other inside my skull. The difference between them is not that the first house was small, mean, shoddy, where this one is spacious and uncommonly well-built, it is that in the first I was young, seething with an angelic (or devilish) energy. Today I am forced to notice, with rage and exasperation, that my once unabatable energy is flagging, I can no longer live two or three lives at once.

I might have begun the story of my life here and worked backwards to the moment almost half a century ago of despair, tears, rage. Time, for any organism, is circular, a continuous present filled with ghosts and chimeras. In the darkness of the underworld I cross and recross my tracks. I change, but only into myself, until the minute of the last irreversible change.

Nothing is harder than to collect the fragments of oneself. Even I, a comparatively immature person, have as many walking-on parts as there are leaves in a bundle of grass. Which one you are talking to depends on what you asked. In all but a very few actions of my life I have been acted—by my fears and diffidence, by greed, by a sensual obsession, by politeness, by a wish to give pleasure, by a well-meaning child still making gestures of love towards an alien adult world, by my nervous dislike of the sight of unhappiness, my skill in playing a part, my dread of boredom, and by my ancestors, silent powerful ghosts.

Time to settle the account. To arrange to make a friend of the knowledge that wherever you go in the short time left you will find yourself in the same street, the same place, landing in the same harbour.

When I was young, when my magnificent strength, given me, was at its height, I wrote book after book, always against time, when I was well, happy, tired, ill, confident, afraid. What an ape! What a fool! What an ignorant clumsy provincial fool.

Any writer who says that this—this respectable breeding and raising for market of a novel a year—is what he intended is either half-dead or a liar. Unless he was always only a clever swindler, he must once have believed that he was going to write what would change the men and women who read it. Nothing else is worth writing, and no novelist worth glancing at but knows it, even when he is busiest combing and clipping another of his marketable books.

'Il n'y a pas de pire carrière que celle d'un écrivain qui veut vivre de sa plume. Vous voilà donc astreint à produire avec les yeux sur un patron, le public, et à lui donner non pas ce que vous aimez mais ce qu'il aime, lui, et Dieu sait s'il a le goût élevé et délicat... J'ai toujours dans le mémoire les figures tragiques d'un Villiers de l'Isle Adam, d'un Verlaine, avec les restes de talent sur eux comme les derniers poils d'une vieille fourrure mangé. Il n'est pas honorable d'essayer de vivre de son âme et de le vendre au peuple.'

Claudel had taken the precaution to get himself into the French Consulate in Prague before writing this to his friend Jacques Rivière in 1910. Would to God he had written it to me a few years later. But should I have believed him? Probably not.

For one thing, although I wrote too much—I spend recklessly and needed money—I did not write to make money. The spectacle of humanity on the edge of the pit, the darkness closing round us, excited me like a fever. Any European writer, I told myself, who concerns himself with anything less than the life and probable death of Europe is a cheap-jack, even if what he peddles is amusing, charming, comforting—especially if it is comforting. I became André Malraux's humblest disciple; I admired even his faults. When he wrote that by virtue of our passionate curiosity, our rage for discovery, Europe would not only survive but 'mould a new man from the clay', I thought I had found the subtle Hermes I was seeking.

(Had he lost faith in the saving virtue of curiosity when, for whatever good reasons, he lodged himself in a wing of the French cultural establishment, and seems to be without further interest in *la mise en question de l'univers*?)

The raw nerve-ends of our time are all outside England. Problems which with us have remained embryonic, come monstrously to life in countries where a moment of disloyalty or fear could condemn a score of men and women to torture and death, and where the most commonplace, the least heroic might suddenly have to take a decision involving the life and death of wife, child, friend. With bitter dread and anger I returned again and again to ideas, events, that I had neither force of intellect nor strength of imagination to turn fully into words. They needed a Tolstoy—at the very least a Malraux. In my fascinated search for answers I laid novels in France, Poland, Norway, Czechoslovakia, risking the mistakes due to ignorance, to the impossibility of knowing what a Pole means when he says *bread* or *forest* Some few of these novels are admirable, *Cousin Honoré*, *Cloudless May*, *Black Laurel* with its prologue *Before the Crossing*, *The Green Man*, one or at most two others. The absence of my name from critical summaries is not wholly deserved.

Indelicate? 'Damn your delicacy. It is a low commercial value.' (Byron).

The irony, the side-splitting joke, is that I cared far more passionately about what goes on in the human heart. Not the soul. The heart, a less exalted organ. The world and the frightening things I knew about it distracted me and kept my eyes opened outwards when they might have been sorting the entrails. Yet what writer, having seen the room of the dying babies in an internment camp in Prague could do less or more than spell it out?

'You would have done better to write humbly what would have been, if not the truth—that chimera—your truth.'

No doubt, no doubt.

I have an inexcusable fault—what Valéry called *le mal aigu de la precision*. I hold that the writer has a duty, sink or swim, to be lucid. To be, when it is fitting, profound, subtle, allusive, sincere, startling, difficult, but to struggle with all his energy to be clear. Not concise, not correct, not simple, not single-stranded—but lucid, as lucid as possible. A lucid sentence may not convey the truth, there may, at a given point, be no expressible truth.

But incoherence, confusion, obscurity, which do not yield to hard effort to grasp what is being said, are always the work of a charlatan, a self-deceiving humbug, or a clumsy idiot. Writing—since about 1933, when I first realized my clumsiness and dishonesty—with a fanatical attention to clarity, I have deserved the epitaph on my tombstone: Here lies an accomplished writer.

I am genuinely puzzled by the indifference, even hostility, so many writers (critics and others) feel for clear writing. I am prepared to work hard and loyally to find my way in the deeper, less readily intelligible levels in a work, but only if I can believe in the writer's good faith. Only if I can believe that he at least tried to be accessible.

What makes a wilful or careless obscurity—that of a great deal of experimental writing—seem a guarantee of intellectual virtue, and the obese messy incoherence of a William Burroughs excusable or exciting? A legacy from that distrust of the rational meaning which issued in surrealism and its fragmentation of the image? The Sartrean anti-humanism reflected in a cheap cracked glass which distorts Sartre's creaking metaphysics, his agile word-spinning, into raw contempt for a culture taken to be morally bankrupt? I recorded this dialogue at the time.

'What you call the classics—in writing or music—make me vomit.'

'Can you explain to me why?'

'Easily. They're part of the dead cat's meat forced down my throat at school. Read the right books, pick up the right accent, eat the right toads—toads, turds—and you'll rise out of your uneducated family and class as from a dung-hill. You'll get the right values and with the right values you can go anywhere. Oh, can you? Try it—that's all. Try to break through the unconscious condescension, the oh so unaffected friendliness, of the pair of upper-class socialists who ask you to dinner and play you Webern on their hand-made record-player.'

'I was a scholarship brat, and so were my friends. It never occurred to us that we were inferior to anyone except a genius——'

'I never said I felt inferior! I said that Trollope and Pope and Mozart and Dante—and Eliot on Dante—nauseate me.'

Without kindness, I supposed he was afraid that if he once let in Pope and Mozart he would be asked to revere all the other idols of respectable well-heeled *salauds*. These exist to be mocked by the young, but not, my God, with this sourness.

Financiers assure us that all our troubles can be summed up in the single word: Inflation. This same mortal illness has infected language. I am prejudiced in advance against a novel I might enjoy, sensible, perceptive, a decent very drinkable little *vin du pays*, when I am told that its author is 'the English Proust'.

Reading over what I have just written, I see that I shall be thought ill-tempered. I am not, I was never gayer. I am in a passion, yes. And why not? With passions, said Stendhal, we never grow bored, and without them we are inane.

If I live much longer I shall be reduced to re-reading the nineteenth century Russians, Proust, Stendhal, and an occasional new novel by a talented eccentric. And my rather friendly young anti-classicist will tell me I am an arid snob...

Is it possible that I became a novelist from the least pure motives—to enjoy a sense of power: the child other children called a freak avenging herself? An abysmally ignorant young creature who supposed she was writing when she was simply trying to draw attention to herself and her cleverness? It is possible.

Writing was a chimney for my blazing ambitions.

Yet, yet, my passion for words was genuine. They delighted me. Like a character in my absurd first novel, I turned everything I noticed into phrases, repeating them to myself with voluptuous excitement. At the time I did not suspect the penalty for practising this trick. The very act of writing, of turning pain, grief, joy, into words, creates the Doubles of these feelings, so that innocently the writer places between himself and reality a charming or dreadful mask. Unless he fights with these masks they end by replacing him. That is not all. In a final sense, the truth is exactly that which can't be got into words. We are forced to lie, a little or, if we are inferior, much. The writer's mind is a country of words sundered from his being, alien to it, almost hostile. A cruel paradox forces him to realize his living self only in silence, when he is not making phrases—that is, when as a writer he doesn't exist.

For a time I used words without precautions. I wanted to disappear into them, I fled into the bovaryism of the writer trying to create an effect.

I feel some sympathy with young Daisy Jameson's craving to be not-there; it is even joined, somewhere in the darkness, to the child hiding in the water-closet at the end of the long passage in No. 5 Park Terrace, putting off for a few minutes the beating she is about to receive. Oh, and to the wish to be not the freak but the someone gay and free I think I was born...

I don't understand the foxy glances of my English reviewers. The strict justice I receive baffles me, since I seem to myself to be gentle and well-meaning. Nothing to be done about it. A little late in life, I realize that sympathy and aversion rarely have a logical base. Yet there are moments even now when I should be enchanted if—like F. Sarcey on some occasion—I could say to one of my young judges, '*Bah! Après moi, c'est vous qui serez la vieille bête!*'

For a long time I was madly ambitious. I dreamed about worldly success. But, alas! I also despised it.

This is too clumsy a definition of a natural process. Suppose that in 1930 someone I admired had said to me, 'My dear girl, the mistake you and people like you, who have fought their way out of nowhere, are prone to make is to believe that to be respected, reasonably well-off, etc. etc., it is enough to have a mind and teach it to write as well as possible. You imagine that because this was true *at first*—clever little Daisy Jameson could and did climb right out of the world of her childhood—you had only to go on working hard and loyally. This is an illusion two other sorts of clever persons do not fall into. First: those who realize at an early enough age that respect and success depend only half on merit; the other and equally important half demands a certain impudence, the patience to force or coax other people to notice and applaud that merit, which not enough of them will do without being persuaded. And second: people born into an already influential circle who assume as their right advantages their birth gives them, use them naturally, and are as naturally admired for their grace and self-confidence. This is not cynicism, it is the recognition of a rule so seldom broken that it is childish to overlook it.'

The advice would have been wasted. I am lazy, and solitude comes easier to me than *camaraderie*. I have never tried to attract *useful people*, never taken the trouble to secure my lines into the future. In the first moment of receiving an invitation to a party my impulse is to refuse—since it will be impossible to go disguised as the English Proust.

I am forced to agree that this lack of sense is not due either to virtue or pride. It is partly vanity—there is no merit in rejecting the world out of a fear of being unable to shine in it—but much more a deep, an unseizably deep sloth. In the last resort I can't be bothered.

Because of this ineradicable indifference and imprudence, I can blame no one for my lack of reputation except myself.

'Beware the writer who has made a career without asking anything of anyone, and who has worked fifty years without a title to show for it. He can be nothing but a lonely pessimist, and a dangerous one at that.'

Oh, my dear Léautaud, to whom is he dangerous—except, a little, to himself?

There was, after all, something I wanted more, infinitely more, than I wanted reputation. That was to look at the world. My God, to look.

I cheated the energy and restlessness of my born nature by writing books. If I could put in one scale the displeasures they have brought me and in the other the pleasure, gaiety, the thousands of moments of perfect happiness that I have had through my eyes, the second would far, far, far outweigh the first.

And now? I am very cool (it is time!) and I see distinctly what is left. Three things. Precisely this fury and cruelly fierce pleasure of looking. The fear and sharpness of love, sharper because of the fear. The sense of being almost pure memory, the coming nearer of the dead who, for a few years or many, have been content to stay quietly in their place.

Who moved, turning the head in a known gesture, at the back of this room? Oh, nearer to me than my hand.

I am thankful that I was alive during the short exquisite flowering of life in the last year or two before the first Great War. You who were not there cannot imagine what it was like for the very young. Never to have known anything about war, and so never to have been afraid. To fear nothing except that, with so many roads at our feet, we might not be able to walk on all of them. Walk? Run.

Children born during the second war seem like us—far more so than any generation in between—lively, sceptical, inquisitive. They are, I think, very fine. So were my friends.

*16th of March 1965*

This morning Gerald Bullett's last letter fell out of a volume of his poems. No, not the last. The last of the few I kept. '... your letter has raised me from the dead. You describe just the kind of poems I want to write—and imply that I have written them. That what you say is too good to be true doesn't in the least diminish my happiness in hearing it said... I won't pretend to you that I think ill of them: I allow myself to believe that the best of them are good in their way: but God forbid that I should indulge in visions of posthumous glory. That kind of daydreaming is the last refuge of frustrated vanity... What annoys me when I look back on my "career" is the thought that if only I had had more character, staying-power, perseverance and what not, I could have made at least a respectable living and have enough money now to support me (quietly) in my declining years—instead of being always nagged by anxiety about the future...'

Dear Gerald, it was not character you lacked, nor courage, nor loyal perseverance. Now that you are dead, I will tell you. Your novels were those of a poet forcing himself to use his genius and lucid senses to do well a task they were only half fitted for: you had irony, sly humour, a shrewd and thinking heart, a fastidious mind—and little or none of the born novelist's gross appetite for life. Your instinct as a writer was the poet's to fuse memory, emotion and experience in a single resonant image. And you had even less instinct for making yourself secure than I have. It was not simply that you had no gift for putting yourself in a favourable light, you did not put yourself in any light at all. You never lifted a finger to call attention to yourself by the half deliberate, half natural manoeuvres of novelists no more intelligent than you were but more adroit and more personally ambitious. Critics in a hurry, used to writers who take themselves and their talents with devastating solemnity, were able to ignore you. They knew, they knew by instinct, as a hog smells out truffles, that you neither could nor would repay them in kind for any good they did you, or any ill...

I knew him when we were both young and poor. A year or two before he died in 1958, I turned in a brightly-lit and overcrowded room and saw in the doorway the young man I used sometimes to see coming into my room in Sloane Street in the 'twenties. Even when he was standing in front of me, the change in him was slight—a look of fatigue, a certain heaviness of movement, a few, remarkably few lines. His youth had not been obliterated by time, it had stepped back a little—that was all. It may be that we are ravaged not by time, but by our lies and the compromises we make. Something recklessly truthful and uncompromising remained alive in Gerald, some reality of innocence.

I think I have had better friends than I deserve.

With any luck, I shall be outlived by the three I made first, Oswald of the flaming hair, now white, his brother Sydney, still the most unsubdued and inquisitive of scientists, Archie, whom I respect more than anyone.

One of the uncovenanted benefits of living for a long time is that, having so many more dead than living friends, death can appear as a step backwards into the joyous past, to the edge of a morning sea, for instance, or into a warm shabby room in a vanished London, with the broken-down sofa and the large creaking wicker chair.

## CHAPTER 25

*24th of March 1965*

How many times have I drawn back from an underworld darkness I fear, closing my long-sighted eyes, blocking my keen ears? Possibly the journey backwards, against the current, through the tangled roots of withdrawals, evasions, lies, was from the start no good. I may have pursued a phantom: the person I made bit by bit out of my fears and greeds—that fake, that *construction*—may have strangled whatever infant reality once existed.

When I was a child I had already cut my stick to be famous. I was born as stubborn as the hardest wood and unwilling to learn what bored me. I read for pleasure and, now and then, to astonish my teachers by seeming to know more than I did. (One day, during a visit home, I was turning the pages of an old encyclopædia my mother bought when we were children. I found words—*Good—Yes, I see—To be looked into*—pencilled in a large perfectly round hand beside the articles on Plato, Hegel, Kant, Leibnitz and some others, and remembered the afternoon when I decided to read the philosophers, all of them: filled with excitement I began by reading about them, and chased them through the eleven large volumes with baffled patience.) As I look over my shoulder, the years divide: beginning in eternity, I came early into the suburbs of time. The years from my twelfth are marked off by public examinations that fell in December and June; I went at these like a man cutting steps in a rock face—they were my road to the world. I had no guide but my devouring ambition—not a guide, a thorn in my flesh, a fever.

More than anyone I knew then, I wanted to live. My hunger was a wild animal in my senses and brain. Perhaps its violence defeated it. The savage beast was probably blind.

I am deeply convinced—so deeply that it will be no use citing against me married women who are famous scientists or architects or financiers—that a woman who wishes to be a creator of anything except children should be content to be a nun or a wanderer on the face of the earth. She cannot be writer and woman in the way a male writer can be also husband and father. The demands made on her as a woman are destructive in a peculiarly disintegrating way—if she consents to them. And if she does not consent, if she cheats... a sharp grain of guilt lodges itself in her, guilt, self-condemnation, regret, which may get smaller, but never dissolves.

Yet I could have managed my double life better than I did. A choice—in spite of the error of an early disastrous marriage—was possible. I could have chosen the monk and let the restless greedy mountebank starve. Even to refuse to choose is a choice. Say I *chose* to drift, to let the mountebank make a hare of the monk and debauch the writer, and the monk trip up the poor restless mountebank, in a perpetual bedlam. But why? Why construct round myself something more intricate than any abstract sculpture, and again and again, sitting silent and unmoving, hammer on it in impotent rage, shout unheard, weep inwardly tears as bitter as gall? Why?

'It is a strange madness,' Petrarch told his travel-worn secretary, 'to be forever sleeping in a strange bed.' The secretary, a good one, could not bear not to go away, he left and came back more than once. Petrarch himself never stayed long in one place.

Alive in me forever, ports not touched at, voyages not made.

Years ago I said Yes when I should have said No. That Yes took me out of my way. But it was I who said it. And I who, long before that moment, encouraged the birth of the smiling fake other people, beginning with my mother, drew out of me to take my place. I *am* my choice. I am what I made of my original condition.

Ah, say it, say it. You had not the courage to choose the creature you were born, avid *to get away*, to be perpetually footloose, without responsibilities, material or human. This famished *vagus*, as in-disciplined, graceless, arrogant, as his mediaeval kind, clown, spendthrift, gay, eager to be amused, has made antic hay of my life without doing himself any good. I clipped his nails. If he drove me to a series of departures, I hamstrung him by clumsy attempts to live what my forbears called a decent life, tearing pieces out of myself to make the remnant match, compromising, dancing like a bear, speaking softly. I could pretend I did it because I was ashamed to disappoint human beings who depended on me—including the one who is the salt and armature of my life. It would be only half true. The habit is only a few years younger than I am.

Robert Graves is of the poetic opinion that only the baser sort among the dead rush to drink from Lethe. Perhaps—but there may be no other way of reconciling me with myself. As the old women say: What you can't forgive, forget. The grain of guilt is still there. Look for it in my dust.

The early sun of my setting-out was a cold northern sun—sun and salt, a great deal of salt, in the air, on the lips. My confidence was limitless and absurd. It took a long time, years, to vanish out of sight, its place taken by a blind patience—promised in the persistence of a six-months-old child climbing stairs she was beaten for climbing, six attempts, six beatings, before her baffled young mother threw her into her cot to sleep it off. Today I feel my knees failing me before those stairs, but there is no escaping them. How many times, how many more times, before, unforgiven, I find my way back? I have the gross strength of my original hunger. Punished—sometimes just-ly—I get up and start again, always with less ease. I know whom I have to thank for my power of resistance, for the habit of enduring, the habit and pleasure of hiding behind lies, dissimulation, tricks.

I am writing this at a table of plain wood. Just now, when I ran my hand along the edge, a tiny splinter caught the edge of my palm. Pulling it out, I felt a wave of happiness, even gaiety. It had not come from one of those exultant moments when, dropping with sleep, alone in some cold room, I stumbled on words that I believed came from a centre of my body rather

than my brain, but it belonged to that family. Another instant and I had it...
I am in the kitchen of my mother's house, facing an iron range, the curtains
drawn across the window on my right, one weak lamp throwing its yellow
hoop on the square of cardboard under my hand. The calendar I am making
for my mother in the hope of pleasing her and being praised has the months,
days, figures, copied in red and green ink, and the wide margins filled in with
an intricate pattern of small blue flowers, each petal painted separately with
the point of the finest brush, scores of flowers, hundreds of petals. Slowly
adding flower to flower, stopping only for a second to pull out the splinter
my left hand has picked up from the rough edge of the table, I am happy,
my God how happy.

Surely, somewhere, it is still alive, the gaiety, the simple patience?

Of course. How else could you live?


## CHAPTER 26

VOICES OUT OF DARKNESS, out of sleep, enclosed in memory as
in a black bubble. Briefly, as I listen, it is myself I hear speaking in a
young barely recognizable voice.

Are these phantoms who live in me lighter than the few, very few objects
towards which I feel piety and shall carry about as long as I can—to be sold
or destroyed by my heirs?

Phantoms. In half-sleep it can seem that my mother only yesterday stepped
out of reach, and the feeling of desolation is acute. At other times I see myself
turning from her at a dip in this path between bracken and foxgloves or at
that end of a narrow steep street.

Showing a friend round Westminster Abbey, I took her into a side chapel,
the St Nicholas Chapel, and there—I did not know it existed—found the
W.V.S. book of volunteers killed in the last war. I turned the pages to the
county of Berkshire. There was only one name, my young sister's. It seemed
to belong to her less than did two words I saw afterwards cut in a wall in the
cloisters—Dear Child. No name—only Dear Child.

No one can tell the story of his life. I have tried not to lie, and doubt I
have told more lies than truth.

I could have written it in several ways, all half true, half a lie.

As the story of a young woman raising herself from obscurity to a shadowy success.

As a chain of failures. Always, under different forms, the same failure—to love enough. Only to write this makes me tremble with cold.

Why don't I forgive that restless young woman? Only a fool measures himself for a hair shirt. Very well, I am a fool.

In a world like ours, brutal, violent, menaced, is anything more important than faithfulness, than the loyalty one human being offers another? Anything? Your life, the lost years, foreign cities and harbours, the fever in a young body...

I may have been hoping that if I looked my trespasses in the face they would disappear. Idiot. Failures to love are irremediable and irredeemable. The best I can do is live with them, and make no appeal against the judgement my heart passes on them.

The hunger of the spirit for eternity—as fierce as a starving man's for bread—is much less a craving to go on living than a craving for redemption. Oh, and a protest against absurdity. Atheism is ultimately a question of will, not of intellect. Left to itself, the intellect is bound to reject the notion that human life is a scurf lying in patches on the surface of the universe, the immensity that frightened Pascal. A thinking scurf? What nonsense.

What fascinates me about life itself, what is most astonishing and unassimilable, baffling, absorbing, is its steady movement towards death. You enjoy, suffer, ask questions, work, and all the time this is what is coming. Surprise will be my last emotion, not fear. When I think of the young dead of two wars, of my young brother, my young sister, of the boys I knew in 1914, who have preceded me with their light quick bodies, how could I be afraid of the last minutes?

Yes, surprise and a light regret that I cannot go on looking.

I hope that the very last moment will be without emotion, a pure act of memory. That the images I carry in my skull, clinging to them with a passion I should be put to it to account for in rational terms—a shabbily-furnished room for four poor scholars, the vanished London of the sixpenny gallery and the Vienna Café, fields of narcissus between Espalion and Le Puy, the Loire in sunlight, a dark bookshop in Nevers, a Vienna without neon lights, the bare savage country between Vence and Manosque, broken columns asleep in the Greek light, the great curved eyelids of the gold mask in the Museum in Athens, a street in Bordeaux—will detach themselves, one after another, hesitate for less than a moment, vanish, leaving room for the few I had in my hand at the beginning, the North Sea flowing over the foreign rivers, the grand violins silenced by a boy whistling the first line of *Sir Eglamour the valiant knight* in a street of small houses.

Surely I can hope to end where I began, in a Whitby which no longer exists, small, stubbornly old, not yet spoiled? In an unchanging present, in an intense clarity, among my few indestructible images: the distant points of light, the dazzling whiteness of a field of marguerites, the pure curve of the coast, the sea-gull screech of children—*ah-wa-a-ah!*

Away!

This is sure. However sudden, the last of my departures will start from the half-darkness of the kitchen in Park Terrace, along that narrow passage with the stairs going up on the right, down that flight of stone steps into the garden with the laburnum and the lilac, down more steps to that tall iron gate, cold passing from it into my fingers, into the empty morning street and the hired cab, down the steeply-falling North Bank to the harbour—the tide out, ebbing back from the mooring-posts and the broken timbers of the shipyard—past the plain-faced houses of Windsor Terrace to the low grey squat station, through its dark entrance, and away. Away.

An old woman dies. Elsewhere the sea rolls to the foot of the cliff, the coast runs north, the fields dazzle with flowers, quiver with long grass, stir with tiny creeping insects: light breaks. 'Friends, we do not know where the darkness is, or where the dawn; where the sun that shines for mortals rises, or where it sets...'

**FORBIDDEN NOTEBOOK**
ALBA DE CÉSPEDES

**COLLECTED WORKS: A NOVEL**
LYDIA SANDGREN

**MY MEN**
VICTORIA KIELLAND

**AS RICH AS THE KING**
ABIGAIL ASSOR

**LAND OF SNOW AND ASHES**
PETRA RAUTIAINEN

**LUCKY BREAKS**
YEVGENIA BELORUSETS

**THE WOLF HUNT**
AYELET GUNDAR-GOSHEN

**MISS ICELAND**
AUDUR AVA ÓLAFSDÓTTIR

**MIRROR, SHOULDER, SIGNAL**
DORTHE NORS

**THE WONDERS**
ELENA MEDEL

**MS ICE SANDWICH**
MIEKO KAWAKAMI

**GROWN UPS**
MARIE AUBERT

**LEARNING TO TALK TO PLANTS**
MARTA ORRIOLS

**THE RABBIT BACK LITERATURE SOCIETY**
PASI ILMARI JÄÄSKELÄINEN